seventh edition
Personal Selling:
A Relationship Approach

seventh edition

Personal Selling:
A Relationship Approach

Ron Marks
University of Wisconsin–Oshkosh

Cincinnati, Ohio
www.atomicdog.com

Book Team

Vice President, Publisher Steve Scoble
Managing Editor Kendra Leonard
Director of Interactive Media and Design Joe Devine
Director of Quality Assurance Tim Bair
Production Coordinator Jana Staudt
Web Production Editor Angela Makowski
Quality Assurance Editor Dan Horton
Marketing Manager Mikka Baker
Cover Design Joe Devine

Library of Congress Control Number: 2005929457

ISBN 1-59260-228-2

Printed in the United States of America by Atomic Dog Publishing,
35 East Seventh Street, Suite 405, Cincinnati, OH 45202

10 9 8 7 6 5 4 3 2 1

Dedication

To
Nancy, Jill, Heather,
Brian, Lindsay, and Evan.
They make it all worthwhile.

Contents

Chapter 3

Toward Professionalism—The Salesperson's Legal and Ethical Responsibilities   75

Chapter 4

Buyer Behavior   99

Chapter 5

Effective Communication   133

Chapter 6

Beginning the Relationship Selling Process   163

Chapter 13

The Art of Closing 397

Chapter 14

Retail Selling—A Special Type of Selling 425

Chapter 15

Self-Management 445

Chapter 16

Sales-Force Management 473

Preface

Introduction to the Text

This text is targeted at marketing majors taking their first course in sales. Because nearly 75 percent of graduating marketing students enter their first job in sales, *Personal Selling: A Relationship Approach* was written with three important student needs in mind:

1. To assist students in making a professional career choice
2. To expose students to techniques that will prove of immediate value in their first selling position
3. To provide students with opportunities for practicing these techniques under conditions as realistic as possible

To aid students in making a career choice, *Personal Selling: A Relationship Approach* provides information on important career characteristics. The text counters negative aspects of the popular, but mistaken, stereotype of salespeople. To give students pride in a future career, selling's critical role in the efficient functioning of our economic society and its role in the marketing mix of the firm are described. I have learned through experience that many students will not seriously consider a career in sales because they believe unethical practices to be a prerequisite for success. The early chapters of the book demonstrate how this impression errs and present an accurate picture of selling. Chapter 3, which covers legal and ethical questions, has been expanded and includes references to the lapses in ethical conduct endemic to today's business. I have outlined new legislation occasioned by developments in technology, such as the National Do-Not-Call Registry and the CAN-SPAM Act. The text also describes the many different types of sales positions—another source of misimpressions for students. Job opportunities are outlined, along with current salary figures for sales personnel; a frank discussion of both the financial and non-financial advantages and disadvantages of a selling career follows. Finally, to assist students in securing their first sales position, Chapter 17 offers suggestions on the job search, resume writing, and interviewing.

A second major objective of this text is to expose students to selling techniques that they can use in their first sales position. Too often, marketing courses ignore the immediate needs of students, instead emphasizing theoretical concepts that are more properly the concern of upper management. *Personal Selling: A Relationship Approach* emphasizes skills that will help students make a success of their initial selling assignments. Field-proven methods for prospecting, approaching, questioning, presenting, and closing are explained, along with numerous examples. Both verbal and nonverbal ways of improving communication are discussed. With the latter, the importance of dress, voice intonation, facial expression, and body language to salespeople is explained. Because so much of selling is associated with understanding and developing empathy for buyers, some common buying motives are presented, but only those (such as personality styles) that are easily transferable to the job. Sales management principles and methods are also outlined. This helps students relate to superiors on their first job and prepares them for that step into sales management, which is not always the easiest transition for field sales representatives.

The third and final objective of this text is to provide students with an opportunity to apply the selling skills they have learned to a situation resembling as closely as possible a realistic sales interview. To this end, a highly structured role-playing assignment that can be videotaped is described at the end of Chapters 6 and 8 and in the *Instructor's Manual*.

Book Organization

In the early chapters, students receive current information upon which to base a career choice. Chapter 1 presents an overview of selling, including its value to economic society and its vital role in the individual firm's marketing mix. There is a discussion of the likely changes in selling's future, primarily occasioned by rapid developments in technology and the use of wireless devices like the cell phone. The diversity in sales positions is described in Chapter 2. Beginning and long-term salary information is provided, and there is a frank discussion of the advantages and disadvantages of a career in selling. Useful counsel on building a positive self-concept appears here—not just advice, but concrete behavioral steps that can lead to a more positive self-image. The new emphasis in selling on establishing long-term relationships with customers, a dominant theme of the book, is first outlined in Chapters 1 and 2, and later explained in detail in Chapter 6. Chapter 3, which outlines sales legalities and ethics, has been moved forward from previous editions to reflect its importance, especially with relationships so critical. Chapter 4 describes common consumer needs and customer personality styles with which salespeople must deal effectively. This topic, which includes information on how the impact of sales presentations and closing techniques can be dramatically improved by taking customer personality style into account, is pursued in later chapters. For those familiar with earlier editions of the book, material on organizational behavior has been moved forward to Chapter 4, a logical integration. Unique here is its treatment of tactics of selling to groups, increasingly characteristic of organizational selling.

Chapter 5 describes the communication process, including listening, speaking, proxemics, dress, pacing, and other forms of nonverbal behavior—topics that typically receive abbreviated treatment in sales texts, although experts believe that well over half of all communication is nonverbal. Chapter 6 is a pivotal chapter. It formally presents the philosophy of relationship selling, the foundation for which has been built in earlier chapters. The latter half of the chapter outlines the differences between relationship selling and transactional selling (its predecessor), relates how to create "value added," describes the variables critical to the relationship, illustrates practical selling techniques for building the relationship, and depicts successful after-marketing activities.

Chapter 7, the first chapter formally relating sales tactics, outlines methods of prospecting for customers—traditional ones as well as new techniques initiated by the Internet and contact management software. Chapter 8 sets forth a "telephone track" to secure sales appointments over the phone (either with the prospect or via voice mail), as well as attention-grabbing approaches for the first personal meeting between salesperson and customer. Chapter 9 outlines methods of questioning for discovering prospect problems, one of the most important aspects of any sales call. The so-called "lantern" process to questioning is also introduced. Chapter 10 describes proven methods for creating effective and dramatic sales presentations. A unique feature of this chapter is its emphasis on individualizing presentations for customers, depending on their personality style and their characteristic way of processing information, a new science of human behavior called neurolinguistic programming. Chapter 11 not only enumerates the standard generic methods of handling objections but it also offers advice on strategies for responding to the more common sources of objections—price, procrastination, skepticism, indifference, need for the approval of others, and overstocking. Chapter 12, which covers sales negotiation, recognizes the new competitive realities of relationship selling in the twenty-first century. To establish relationships requires extended negotiation, one that culminates in a "win–win" situation for both partners. Many buyers look for a negotiated partnership, involving not only price and quality, but a myriad of other factors that create value-added, as well. Without knowledge of negotiation techniques, the untrained salesperson will be at a great disadvantage. Although *Personal Selling: A Relationship Approach* recommends "principled" (or "win–win" negotiation), it also enumerates some of the common manipulative tactics of "win–lose" bargaining and offers ways for dealing with them. Chapter 13 presents methods for closing the sale and, unique among sales texts, relates these to the personality styles of buyers, because not all buyers will react the same way to any given close. At this juncture, students have all the information they need to participate in the videotaped role-playing experience. Chapter 14 explains the idiosyncrasies of retail selling, beginning with how the service approach (i.e., "May I help you?") is counterproductive. Alternative approaches, appropriate presentation practices unique to retail selling, and practical retail closes are illustrated.

Chapter 15 relates ideas on self-management—how salespeople can optimize their time. This is a topic of great importance; survey after survey of sales managers points to this as the prime source of salesperson failure. Again, the impact of technology is emphasized. To provide students with a better understanding of sales and a broad view of the selling profession, Chapter 16 covers sales management. The student will gain insight into the most important of sales management skills: recruitment and selection, compensation methods, and motivating and evaluating the sales force.

Chapter 17 offers advice on identifying job opportunities in selling and interviewing, including how to assess one's strengths and weaknesses, prepare a resume, behave during the interview, and secure an offer.

New to This Edition

This edition of *Personal Selling: A Relationship Approach* is fully revised and updated. Chapter 1 includes coverage of today's most cutting-edge sales techniques and uses of technology to make the job of a salesperson more productive, including the use of multimedia sales presentations, teleconferencing, and technological aids such as the PDA and sales management software. In Chapter 2, I discuss the slowly changing image of the salesperson and the types of selling that have evolved as the most efficient in our over-scheduled, time-hungry business communities. Chapter 3 deals with ethics and professionalism and includes updated information on the CAN-SPAM legislation, the National Do-Not-Call Registry, and other recent laws and movements that affect the selling profession. In Chapter 4, new research and data helps students understand the psychological types of buyers and their behavior in groups and as individuals. In Chapter 5, I discuss communication and body language, taking into account the new relaxed modes of dress and communication that salespeople may encounter in business today. This chapter includes guidelines for "business casual" dress. Chapter 6 covers the relationship selling process. I introduce students to modern methods of sales research as part of precall preparation and follow-through. Likewise, Chapter 7 explains the important role of the Internet and how to use it effectively for the best prospecting. Telesales, e-mail promotions and selling, and maintaining electronic records are all included in the discussion. In Chapter 8, the classic advice on making a successful approach is updated and refreshed with information on handling voice mail and e-mail. Chapter 9 provides up-to-date examples of problem recognition and steps salespeople can take to question prospects. In Chapter 10, I added information on the best use of multimedia in sales presentations and give examples of when it should and should not be used. Chapter 11 helps students handle objections and offers new examples salespeople are likely to hear from today's managers and buyers. Chapters 12 and 13 are refreshed to bring all of the materials on creating the personal relationship with the client and closing the deal up-to-date, and Chapter 14 discusses retail selling in all of its modern forms. Chapter 15 offers the newest and most effective tips for self-management and time-management, and Chapter 16 covers current sales-force management techniques and policies. Finally, Chapter 17 provides students with everything they need to know to land a sales job in today's marketplace.

Pedagogical Features

Hyperlinked streaming video clips in the online edition illustrate sales tactics. Mere descriptions of sales techniques can never describe them as well as seeing them in use. The video clips exhibit the nuances of nonverbal behavior, which, according to communication theorists, is the major cause of miscommunication. It has been said that the goal of salespeople should be to create an atmosphere in which an act of trust can occur (i.e., buying); much of this trust is communicated nonverbally.

Using the Print and Online Editions

To assist those who use the online and print versions together, the primary heads and subheads in each chapter are numbered the same. For example, the first primary head in Chapter 1 is labeled 1-1, the second primary head in this chapter is labeled 1-2, and so on. The subheads build from the designation of their corresponding primary head: 1-1a, 1-1b, etc. This numbering system is designed to make moving between the online and print versions as seamless as possible.

Finally, icons similar to those on the left appear throughout the print book to designate interactive figures and video samples that are available in the Online Edition of this book.

Ancillaries

Atomic Dog is pleased to offer a robust suite of supplemental materials for instructors using its textbooks. These ancillaries include a *Test Bank, PowerPoint® slides, Instructor's Manual,* and *Lecture Animations.*

- The *Test Bank* for this book includes multiple-choice questions in a wide range of difficulty levels for each chapter. The *Test Bank* offers not only the correct answer for each question, but also a rationale or explanation for the correct answer and a reference—the location in the chapter where materials addressing the question content can be found. This *Test Bank* comes with ExamView Pro software for easily creating customized or multiple versions of a test and includes the option of editing or adding to the existing question bank.
- A full set of *PowerPoint® slides* is available for this text. This is designed to provide instructors with comprehensive visual aids for each chapter in the book. These slides include outlines of each chapter, highlighting important terms, concepts, and discussion points.
- The *Instructor's Manual* for this book offers suggested syllabi for 10- and 14-week terms; lecture outlines and notes; in-class and take-home assignments; recommendations for multimedia resources such as films and websites; and long and short essay questions and their answers, appropriate for use on tests.
- *Lecture Animations* allow instructors to use the animations from our online editions in their own PowerPoint® slideshows. These include all of the animated figures from each chapter of the text in an easy-to-use format.

About the Author

Ron Marks is uniquely qualified both experientially and academically to write about sales. He began his career many years ago selling mainframe computers for Burroughs (now Unisys) and hospital supplies for Superior Surgical (examples of these experiences are replete within the text). Over the years, he has published in the *Journal of Personal Selling and Sales Management, Journal of Retailing, Journal of Health Care Marketing, Journal of the Academy of Marketing Science, Management Education,* and others. Lately, his interests have turned toward online education, which explains the presence of digitized video, both conventional and streaming. Graduating from the University of Missouri with his Ph.D. in Marketing, Marks has been at the University of Wisconsin–Oshkosh for 31 years, teaching a variety of marketing and statistics courses.

The Role of Personal Selling

Key Terms

advertising
approach
closing
customer relationship
  management (CRM)

marketing concept
marketing mix
objection
personal selling

prospecting
relationship marketing
target market

Learning Objectives

After studying Chapter 1, you will understand:

- The role of personal selling in the economy
- The importance of personal selling in the marketing mix
- One definition of personal selling
- The typical duties of salespeople
- The differences between personal selling and advertising

- The steps in the selling process
- An appreciation for the "marketing concept" and relationship selling
- Projected developments in selling in the twenty-first century
- Why it is valuable to study personal selling

Salespeople are critical elements of our society: Nothing happens until something is sold. Without salespeople, we might as well not produce anything, for who would there be to sell it? Goods would pile up in stores, and economic society would grind to a halt. Yet few professions are misunderstood more than sales. To many, salespeople are stereotyped as smooth talkers who are adept at manipulating people into buying things they don't need—they are never to be believed or trusted. But as it pertains to today's successful salespeople, this image is false. They are individuals of knowledge, motivation, dedication, and integrity, who are vital to the sale of over $11 trillion worth of goods and services each year.[1]

1-1 The Role of Selling

Personal selling is an integral part of the U.S. marketing system. Here, we define *marketing* to be the development and distribution of goods and services to satisfy the needs of consumers and industrial buyers. As part of marketing, selling performs valuable functions both for society as a whole and for the individual firm.

1-1a Selling's Importance to the Economy

If nothing were sold, goods would pile up in warehouses, and massive unemployment would soon follow. Although this has not happened *en masse,* the inability of salespeople (and marketing people, in general) to perform their jobs in the best manner has had adverse effects on the economy. A former secretary of commerce once stated that the primary economic problem in our society was not so much the actual production of goods but that their marketing—especially on a face-to-face selling basis—left a lot to be desired.

Some marketing theorists even maintain that the first step in the economic development of less developed countries is the implementation by government of a customer-oriented marketing philosophy. This contrasts with the normal practice of most less developed countries (LDCs), which first try to develop a manufacturing sector, ignoring the demand side necessary for sale of the manufactured products. A marketing orientation, instead, will lead to a free market, free enterprise, and democratic society, as the LDC responds to the pressure of a competitive arena where consumers seek the highest-quality consumer product at the lowest price. Individuals will create much of the needed institutional infrastructure as they recognize opportunities for profits and will, in turn, demand products and services with their newfound wealth. The end result will be a higher standard of living for all and the development of an entrepreneurial culture. Theorists cite Japan, Taiwan, Korea, and more recently India as examples of where this theory has been successfully implemented.[2]

In their endeavors to restructure their own less developed economies from centrally planned to a market base, Eastern Europeans are learning the importance of selling. Eastern managers say four decades of churning out products to meet centrally planned quotas led to distortion. "In the Communist economies, the emphasis wasn't to sell but to produce; in the Western markets, it's the opposite," says one manager in the Czech Republic. "Our businesses have developed in an isolated way."[3]

As part of a 2-week training seminar in Western marketing, he and other officials from Czechoslovakia made several supervised sales calls in London—one to a bank to discuss a hypothetical loan, another to an airline to discuss the hypothetical sale of an aircraft. Both visits went so well that they led to follow-up talks about a real loan and a real aircraft sale.

Many instructors and students say the biggest problems are attitudinal: Most Eastern managers are inclined to ignore their customers, who didn't matter much under the old command economies. During a training session in Romania, two executives practiced a role-playing exercise involving a sales call. The "salesman" sat behind a desk with crossed arms, while the customer entered hat in hand, humbly seeking the chance to buy the salesman's products.

Jan Kaspar, a business manager for Slezak & Spol, a Czech firm that sells painting materials, spent seven weeks at British retail giant Marks & Spencer. He was stunned by the cordial treatment afforded customers. The store even took back defective merchandise, he recalls with amazement. "In [the Czech Republic] everybody tries to protect himself, but at Marks & Spencer, they assume the truth is with the customer."[4]

In this light, what crucial societal role does personal selling play?

Personal Selling Creates Utility

Selling (and marketing in general) helps to provide the three basic utilities of time, place, and possession—utility being defined as the ability to satisfy human needs. To illustrate how important these utilities are, let's assume you have been offered a new sports car for $2,500. Interested? Here are the terms: It's sitting in a warehouse in London without the proper shipping documents and can be delivered in no sooner than six months. Still interested?

Without its being in the right place when you want to buy it and without the proper documentation, the sports car is not worth as much, is it? It is up to marketers like salespeople to add value to the product with time, place, and possession utility. In the case of the car, they must anticipate demand and have enough on hand for customers to buy; if they do not, they must arrange for prompt delivery from either the manufacturer or, in the case of an English sports car, probably a wholesale importer. Moreover, without legal title to the automobile, it is going to be rather difficult for you to get it registered.

Selling Increases Total Demand

By contributing to time, place, and possession utility, salespeople increase the demand for goods and services. This has two beneficial effects for society. First, the total number of people employed grows. If salespeople increase their sales, then more production workers, secretaries, and managers must be hired to handle the additional volume. Second, the additional demand created by sales personnel reduces

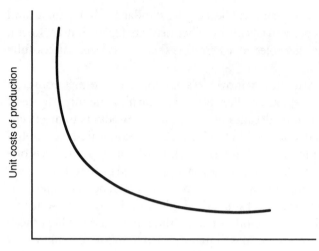

Figure 1-1
How Selling Helps to Reduce Costs

the unit cost of production, providing a cheaper product for all and making purchase possible for some who might not otherwise be able to afford it. This process is illustrated in Figure 1-1. The price of cellular phones has dropped dramatically since their introduction a few short years ago, largely because of the efforts of salespeople. When cell phones were first introduced, many consumers and businesses could not afford them. Because they were produced on a small-scale basis, prices were high, primarily because the fixed costs of overhead had to be allocated to a relatively limited number of machines. But as sales representatives persuaded more and more customers to buy cell phones, technically advanced methods of production could be used, and overhead could be apportioned in smaller amounts to increased numbers of cell phones. The lower costs, in turn, made cell phones attractive to even more businesses. Much the same occurred with fax machines a few years ago and now DVD players, DVD recorders, CD-writers, and DVD-writers on PCs. In general, the efficiency and cost savings of mass production technology require a mass market. Without the efforts of salespeople who find buyers, sell to them, and service their needs, products would be considerably more expensive.

Selling Fights Inflation

Salespeople help lower prices by increasing the number of buyers and encouraging less expensive methods of production. They also help decrease inflation in their role as disseminators of information. By focusing buyer attention on buyers' problems and presenting the product features that resolve these problems, salespeople help buyers spend their money wisely and effectively. The competition thus encouraged among manufacturers helps hold down prices for the entire economy.

An Agent of Change

Society's habits tend to change slowly, and certain members of society are responsible for changing these habits by promoting better ways of doing things. Salespeople are such individuals. Without salespeople, the rate of innovation in society would decline, resulting in a lower standard of living for all. To convince people to install telephones in their homes, Alexander Graham Bell hired salespeople to go door-to-door. Commented one Maine farmer when approached by one of Bell's sales reps and told how he could talk to people in Boston, "A-yup, that's all very well and good, but who in the name of Beelzebub needs to talk to anybody in

Boston?" The adoption of wonder drugs and the computer would have occurred more slowly, if at all, were it not for the efforts of sales personnel. Who would travel on the highways, if not for Henry Ford's selling the public on the merits of the Model T?

Thomas Edison is remembered as the quintessential American inventor, making basic advances in the stock ticker, the telegraph, the telephone, the lightbulb, the phonograph, and the motion picture, but Edison's zeal for promotion was just as important. Edison understood better than any of his peers that creating a market was as valuable as the invention itself. He doggedly whipped up enthusiasm for an invention before it had even been produced, cultivating the press and painting vivid pictures of future life transformed. At times, his predictions seemed reckless: He promised to bring electric light to Manhattan before he had finished making a durable lightbulb. Edison realized that "the race was not to the swift, but rather the man with bravado, endurance and money."[5]

Edison's meshing of invention and promotion would be well understood by his modern day counterpart, Bill Gates, whose own incessant descriptions of future, unfinished products often draw complaints, yet serve the purpose of whetting consumer appetites for even more technology. Then there is Steve Jobs, the "comeback kid" who resurrected Apple's fortunes and recently unveiled its iTunes Music Store, which has broken the logjam between record companies and online retailers, making it possible for the music industry to successfully sell tunes on the web. Jobs got the major labels to agree to an appealing, simple set of terms. All songs would sell for 99 cents, with no frustrating restrictions limiting fans' rights to burn them to CDs, load them on a portable player, or share them with a few friends—quite a selling job indeed for Jobs.[6]

In e-commerce, one example of a change agent is Jeff Bezos, the folksy CEO, founder, and chief sales representative of Amazon.com, the online retailer. He has relentlessly dropped prices on books and other products and offered free shipping on orders over $25. His newest initiative is a newly formed unit to help more retailers sell to Amazon's 33 million customers, as the likes of Target and Toys 'R' Us already do (in effect forming an online shopping mall). Says Bezos, a frequent guest on business news channels, "We know how to develop world-class technology to make the customer experience in e-commerce really good."[7]

For almost any new product that can be identified, sales representatives did much of the important pioneering work. Television, stereos, videotape recorders, instant cameras, food processors, calculators, and faxes all owe a great deal of their success to the sales forces that first presented them. Besides being remembered as the inventor of the Polaroid camera, Edwin H. Land was a master presenter. When first starting out, one of his most promising creations was a process for making polarized filters, for which he hoped to get financing from the country's largest maker of sunglasses, the American Optical Company. His sales presentation to them, which he set up in a Boston hotel room, had to be perfect. When there was a knock at the door, Land rose to open it. The three representatives of American Optical walked into a room filled with blinding sunlight. As they squinted against the intensity of light from the windows, Land pleasantly commented, "I apologize for the glare. I imagine you can't even see the fish." His visitors glared at Land. "Here, look through this." Land gave each a square of polarizer. As they faced the windows, the glare vanished. There, magically, appeared the fishbowl. "How many fish do you see?" asked Land. "Six," they replied dutifully. "This is what your new sunglasses will be made of," said Land. "It's called Polaroid."[8]

1-1b Selling's Importance to the Firm

Personal selling is vital to the economy, and it is important to the well-being of the individual firm. To appreciate this importance, it is necessary to describe the marketing activities of the firm in total, or what is known as the firm's *marketing mix*. By looking at the elements of the marketing mix—product, place, pricing, and promotion—personal selling's contribution to the success of the firm truly becomes evident.

The Marketing Mix

To maximize the impact of the marketing mix, the marketing manager must begin work before the product goes into production. There is little sense, after all, in making a product that no one wants. Millions of dollars have been spent on producing goods that failed in the marketplace when an accurate appreciation of consumer needs and reactions would have prevented this waste. The Edsel, the Newton (Apple's precursor to the Palm Pilot), Crystal Clear Pepsi, and newer Internet failures, such as Petstore.com, Pets.com, and Toysmart.com, all failed because of their inability to satisfy consumer needs. Like many e-commerce failures, these and other ventures failed to take off because they offered nothing new to the customers—neither inexpensive products nor inexpensive and reliable delivery. These companies are criticized for targeting a niche for which demand had never been—and probably, never will be—proven.[9]

To satisfy buyer needs and make a profit for their companies, marketing managers must recognize opportunities and develop marketing strategies. In this process, managers are concerned with two basic (and related) considerations:

1. The **target market**: A group of consumers with homogeneous needs to which the manager aims the mix.
2. The **marketing mix**: The variables the manager can structure to satisfy the needs of this target market.

To perform their job successfully, marketing managers must recognize a favorable opportunity—a target market whose needs are not being fulfilled with current offerings—and develop an attractive marketing mix to satisfy these needs.

Although literally hundreds of variables may be associated with a marketing decision, they can be classified into one of four basic elements:

1. Product
2. Place
3. Pricing
4. Promotion

Figure 1-2 shows these four elements of the marketing mix and their attention to the needs of a target market, which appears in the center.

Product planning involves developing the right product for the right target market. This may include decisions about package design, branding, trademarks, warranties, service, product lines, and virtually anything else associated with the product. Place strategy basically involves choosing the channels of distribution through which goods and services reach the customer. Any sequence of marketing institutions from producer to final user, including any number of intermediaries, is called a *channel of distribution*. Channels of distribution may include retailers, wholesalers, and other institutional intermediaries. Pricing strategy deals with methods of determining prices that will be both attractive to the target market and profitable for the company. Promotional strategy is concerned with personal sell-

---

target market   A group of consumers with homogeneous needs to which the manager aims the mix.

marketing mix   The marketing variables the manager can structure to satisfy the needs of the target market.

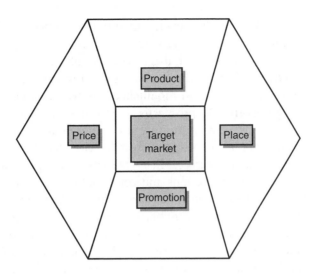

Figure 1-2
The Marketing Mix

ing, advertising, and sales promotion methods. Promotion's task is to communicate to the target market in the most effective way possible.

A strategy based on target marketing has much to do with product success. The United States Display Consortium (USDC) first developed an active-matrix flat panel display screen—in effect, the first "paper-quality" screen, with each pixel linked to its own transistor—and targeted the product at some of the world's leading air forces, a segment with a pressing need for the latest technology. Xerox used target marketing for their new digital copiers designed by its Office Document Product Group. The copiers, which have faxing, scanning, and printing capabilities when connected to the personal computers of Hewlett-Packard (H-P) customers, are targeted toward H-P and its dominance in the printer market. Amgen has pitched its new hepatitis C treatment drug, Infeger, at those customers for whom the existing treatments, such as Schering-Plough's Intron A or Roche Holdings' Roferon A, have not been successful.[10] Porsche markets only two-seaters to a target market of financially successful individuals, resisting the temptation to expand its line to four-door family models. Its customers include professional athletes, entertainers, people who own small businesses, stockbrokers, and others who have set for themselves what they perceive to be extraordinarily high personal and professional goals and who expect the same in their cars.[11] Recaro is offering a top-of-the-line child's safety seat—the Recaro-Start—that appeals to wealthier parents who place high priority on their children's safety. The company is playing heavily on its reputation for producing high-tech safety seats for Porsche and Aston Martin. MicroFridge targets its combination microwave/refrigerator/freezer at college dorm residents, who are often woefully short of space. Neiman Marcus, the exclusive specialty store, targets women over 25 years of age and with an income greater than $90,000. Ford's highly successful Focus, Chrysler's Cobalt, and General Motors' Saturn are aimed at a distinct market of younger people who despise the BMWs, Saabs, and Mercedes of their Baby Boomer parents. Product or services that feed the need of young singles to stay in touch and in control at the same time will do well. Hence, the future is bright for cell phones, answering machines, and email. These are necessities, not luxuries, for younger consumers.[12] Busy, convenience-oriented consumers are beginning to use online grocery shopping and delivery from services like Peapod, which is currently located in Chicago, Boston, Washington, DC, and other markets.[13]

In 1971, a 30-year-old entrepreneur named Len Riggio bought a floundering Manhattan bookshop called Barnes & Noble. Today, Barnes & Noble is the nation's largest bookseller, with fiscal 1999 sales of $3.3 billion. Respect for the customer has been at the heart of the company's rise. Riggio's biggest idea was that books appeal to most everyone, not just to intellectuals, writers, and students in cosmopolitan cities. Riggio listened to prospective customers who wanted bigger selections of books, more convenient locations, and less intimidating environments. He put superstores in all types of communities, from big cities like Atlanta and Chicago to smaller cities like Midland, Texas, and Reno, Nevada. His respect for the customer led him to create stores with spacious and comfortable interiors, easy chairs for relaxing with a book, and Starbucks coffee bars. To this day, he considers his best decision the installation of easy-to-find public restrooms in the stores. As he said in a recent speech, "You work so hard and invest so much to get people to visit your store, why would you want them to have to leave?" Besides the large selection of books, the stores also have an active calendar of author signings, poetry readings, children's events, and book discussion groups. Many Barnes & Noble superstores have become a social arena in which busy consumers—who normally rush in and out of other stores—linger.[14]

The ultimate in target marketing is mass customization. Today's markets are changing faster and customers are more demanding than ever. Thus, mass customization is emerging as a solution to address these new market realities, while still enabling firms to capture the efficiency advantages of mass production. Mass customization meets the requirements of increasingly heterogeneous markets by producing goods and services to match individual customer's needs with near mass production efficiency. This proposition means that individualized or personalized goods can be provided without the high cost (and associated higher price) usually connected with (craft) customization. To deliver mass customization, firms have to find new ways to interact with their customers during the process of codesigning and configuring a customer-specific solution. Companies like Procter & Gamble, Lego, Nike, Adidas, Lands' End, BMW, or Levi Strauss, among others, have started large-scale mass customization programs.[15] Perhaps, the preeminent example is Dell, where a customer may call or order online a custom PC system with interchangeable components, built exactly to fit his or her needs. Automobile manufacturers are also offering such services, although at an earlier stage of development.

Promotional Strategy

Of most concern to us is the marketing mix element of promotion. The components of the promotional mix are personal selling and nonpersonal selling (including advertising, sales promotion, and public relations). Of these, personal selling and advertising are the most significant because they usually account for the bulk of a firm's promotional expenditures.

The most crucial promotional decision facing a marketing manager is deciding the proper mix between personal selling and advertising. Here we define **personal selling** as a seller's presentation conducted on a face-to-face basis with a buyer. **Advertising** is defined as a nonpersonal sales presentation paid for by an identified sponsor, usually directed to a large number of potential customers. It involves the use of mass media such as newspapers, radio, television, magazines, and direct mail. In deciding whether to emphasize personal selling or advertising in the promotional mix, the marketing manager must consider a number of factors (see Table 1-1).

As Table 1-1 shows, personal selling is primarily emphasized in the sale of industrial goods; advertising tends to be dominant in consumer-goods marketing.

personal selling A seller's presentation conducted on a face-to-face basis with a buyer.

advertising A nonpersonal sales presentation paid for by an identified sponsor, usually directed to a large number of potential customers.

T a b l e   **1-1**   **A Comparison of Advertising and Personal Selling**

	Advertising	Personal Selling
Where predominantly used	Consumer goods	Industrial goods
Cost/Contact	Low	High
Impact	Low	High
Flexibility in tailoring message	Low	High
Flow of communication	One-way	Two-way
Complexity of message	Limited	High

The explanation for this is rather simple. The cost of a personal sales call is high—$211.50, by latest estimate[16]—and most industrial goods require a more detailed explanation than advertising can deliver. It would not make sense for Procter & Gamble to sell detergent door-to-door, given the costs of personal selling. In contrast, with the sale of a mainframe computer system worth millions of dollars, the costs of a sales call can be more easily afforded. Moreover, the sale of a large-scale computer requires the communication of extensive technical information, something virtually impossible through advertising.

Personal selling and advertising differ in their impact. It's much easier to turn away from a television advertisement than from a sales representative who is there in person. The duration of a sales interview tends to be considerably longer than an advertising message. Television advertisements, for example, last only 30 seconds. Moreover, during the course of the sales interview, the impact is increased by the ability to repeat the message a number of times. Usually, advertising repetition occurs over the course of days, weeks, and months, and there is no guarantee that the same audience is present each time.

Personal selling is more flexible in its ability to tailor a message to a specific consumer. Advertising must be written to appeal to the needs of a large group of people, while personal selling can be adjusted to the needs of one buyer. When it comes to selling a high-end digital photocopier to the Acme Construction Company, the sales representative can explain how the machine will make clear copies of blueprints, office memos, and bills, saving Acme money in the process. Designing an ad for national television specifically addressed to the needs of the Acme Company would make little sense.

Finally, the flow of communication differs between advertising and personal selling. In advertising, the communication is one-way. The viewer sees the advertisement on television or in the newspaper, and that's it. There is no opportunity for the viewer to ask questions or request additional information. With personal selling, however, buyers can check their understanding with the salesperson and seek further facts. By the same token, the salesperson can check to determine the buyer's reaction through verbal or nonverbal cues. Feedback with advertising typically requires expensive and time-consuming market research studies.

Lest the reader get an impression to the contrary, it is not necessary for marketing managers to invest all their promotional dollars in personal selling to the exclusion of advertising, or vice versa. A firm typically employs both methods simultaneously, with different dollar amounts allocated to each. A firm such as Procter & Gamble concentrates on media advertising but maintains a field sales force to follow up on the advertising. Similarly, industrial firms that concentrate on personal selling invest part of their promotional budget in advertising and other promotional methods to back up the efforts of their sales force. Don Fregelette recalls how he used to spend hours "driving around looking for smokestacks." But it wasn't to admire the architecture. As a salesperson for Micro Motion, which supplies industrial flow-measurement devices to factories, Fregelette was hunting for leads. Today most of Micro Motion's leads are generated from trade-publication advertisements, direct-mail campaigns aimed at purchasing managers, and trade shows in such target industries as chemicals, oil, and pharmaceuticals. These leads are followed up with a personalized letter from Micro Motion's director of marketing and a questionnaire asking for information on the respondent's purchasing authority, time frame, and budget. According to the vice president of sales, "Letting [people] reply themselves proves their qualifications. If [a prospect] asked for information and was sent a questionnaire, but didn't return it, why would you give that lead to a salesperson?" Upon receiving the returned questionnaires, leads are categorized by interest level. Prospective customers who are very interested in purchasing a Micro Motion product, or who request more information, are categorized as "hot." All hot leads are forwarded to the appropriate salesperson.[17]

Of course, now there is the web, a digital environment characterized by "face-to-screen" exchange relationships and electronic images and offerings. That is, in a limited sense, it possesses interactivity and the ability to buy immediately, as in personal selling. It involves two-way buyer–seller electronic communication in a computer-mediated environment in which the buyer controls the kind and amount of information received from the seller. For salespeople, the web allows contact initiated by prequalified buyers, already knowledgeable with facts from the website, a very cost-effective means of prospecting. However, the range of products that customers will buy directly over the web is limited: highly standardized products and services for which information about price is important (such as auto and home insurance); products for which prepurchase trial is not necessarily important (such as books and consumer electronics); and items that can be delivered digitally (such as travel reservations, software, brokerage services, etc.).

Most websites are promotional websites, which have a very different purpose than transactional sites. They advertise and promote a company's products and services and provide information on how items can be used and where they can be purchased. They often engage the visitor in an interactive experience involving games, contests, and quizzes with electronic coupons and other gifts as prizes. Promotional websites can also be used to support a company's traditional marketing channel and build customer relationships. This is the objective of the Clinique Division of Estée Lauder Companies, which markets cosmetics through department stores. Clinique reports that 80 percent of current customers who visit its website later purchase a Clinique product at a department store, and 37 percent of non-Clinique buyers do so.[18]

Mass media can help salespeople also, providing recognition with potential buyers. In the age of dot-coms, which increase their storage requirements five to eight times a year, the emphasis on storage is coming to the forefront more than ever. Every time somebody uses an ATM, buys an airline ticket, or logs onto Amazon.com, all of that data has to go somewhere. Not a day goes by that a consumer's life isn't in some way affected by a storage system, and it's likely that system came from EMC Corporation (EMC). The Global 2000 companies (the world's largest businesses) are doubling their need every two years—these systems are no longer peripherals—and EMC has spent years trying to elevate awareness not only of the company but of the storage category, as well. The company's old slogan, "The Enterprise Storage Company," was changed to something that's easier to relate to and better relates the company's true business, "Where Information Lives." In the United States, EMC is publicizing itself through television ads, programs, and sponsorships, including the EMC World Cup/World Championship (where Tiger Woods is expected to play this year), the Boston Symphony Orchestra, and the EMC Golf Skills Challenge.[19]

Of course, telemarketing continues to grow in promotional use as inside telephone salespeople provide precision support to face-to-face salespeople. The inside team can qualify prospects generated by advertising, get referrals, take incidental orders, follow up, and take care of paperwork that would otherwise fall on the salesperson on the road—who can now spend more of his or her time productively in front of customers. According to the American Teleservices Association, telemarketing sales currently exceed $500 billion.[20]

1-2 The Selling Process

Sales jobs are characterized by one or more of the following steps. That is, some sales positions require all; others, only a few. In later chapters, beginning with Chapter 6, we will investigate each of these steps in depth. Briefly, the steps in the selling process (see Figure 1-3) are as follows:

1. *Precall preparation.* At this beginning stage, salespeople should become intimately acquainted with their industry, their company, their product or service, their competition, and their customers. Like a student before an exam, the sales representative must not walk into an interview unprepared. Lack of preparation will result in a failing grade for either student or salesperson. The more prepared the salesperson is, the more likely it is that he or she will make a sale.

2. *Prospecting.* In many types of sales positions, sales representatives must engage in **prospecting**; that is, they must identify potential new customers for their wares and qualify them (that is, make sure they have the need, ability, and authority to buy). This may involve contact by telephone, letter, or even directly at the prospect's office. The last is known as *cold calling* or *canvassing.* Also at this stage the salesperson may decide to gather as much information as possible about a prospect before actually making a personal visit. In selling

prospecting The identification of potential new customers and their qualifications (i.e., need, ability, and authority).

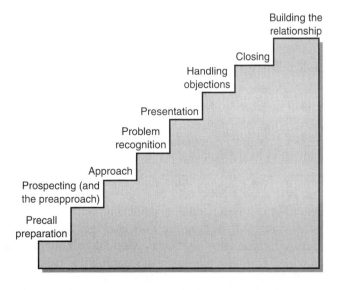

Figure 1-3
Steps in the Selling Process

Box 1-1

The Duties of Salespeople

- Dispensing knowledge to customer
- Acting as a source of intelligence
- Providing service
- Contacting buyers
- Coordinating the selling effort

---

terminology, this is known as the *preapproach,* although the point at which prospecting ends and preapproach begins is somewhat unclear.

3. *Approach.* The **approach** is where salespeople meet customers in person for the first time. During the approach (what some have called the most important 30 seconds in selling), sales representatives must capture the attention and interest of customers, or the rest of their actions may be for naught.

4. *Problem recognition.* Before making the presentation, the salesperson helps buyers recognize their needs and problems through careful questioning techniques. Otherwise, there is no guarantee that the prospect will appreciate the content of the presentation.

5. *Presentation.* Once a problem is clearly defined, the salesperson is ready to explain and dramatize relevant product features and benefits.

6. *Handling objections.* The salesperson must handle **objections,** which includes resolving any remaining doubts the customer might still have about buying.

7. *Closing.* **Closing** the sales call occurs when the salesperson secures the customer's commitment to buy.

8. *Building the relationship.* In the past, this has been construed to merely mean after-sale service. Today, it means building the relationship between buyer and seller for the long term and usually (in the business-to-business sector) the merging of systems and personnel.

approach The first face-to-face meeting between salesperson and customer, during which the sales rep must gain the potential customer's attention.

objection Concern or question raised by the buyer.

closing Securing the customer's commitment to buy.

1-3 Duties of Salespeople

While progressing through the steps in selling, salespeople perform vital duties for both their employers and their customers. These duties are listed in Box 1-1.

1-3a Dispensing Knowledge to Customers

The salesperson dispenses knowledge to buyers. Without relevant information, consumers are likely to make poor buying decisions. Computer users would not learn about new equipment and new programming techniques without the activities of data-processing sales representatives. Doctors would have difficulty finding out about new drugs and procedures if it were not for the efforts of pharmaceutical salespeople. As part of its marketing philosophy of strategic partnerships, Gerber is sharing a good deal of its information with retail accounts. Because of its extensive computerized data gathering, Gerber reps know more about a store's inventory status than even the store manager does. It's not unusual for a rep to tell a buyer, "Do you know that every Monday half of your stores are out of stock of certain Gerber products because of weekend business? You should either increase your order of these items or schedule more deliveries to the stores." Store managers find such information invaluable, because they don't want angry shoppers who can't find what they need or saw advertised. Buyers in the commercial heating and air-conditioning industry expect and prefer regular contact with sales engineers, said a recent study. Although some of the buyers polled hinted that sales calls can occasionally be pestering, 75 percent of mechanical contractors surveyed expressed their dependence on sales engineers for keeping them abreast of technological developments and indicated they are disturbed when such information is not forthcoming.

To provide buyers with useful buying information, salespeople must engage in extensive precall preparation. They must possess in-depth knowledge about their company, their product, their competition, and the industry in which they work. To use this information effectively, sales representatives must identify the buyer's problems. Whether the potential buyer is an industrial purchasing agent or an individual consumer, the creative salesperson must determine the buyer's needs and problems that relate to the product or service being sold. Once buyer needs are identified, the salesperson must come up with a creative presentation and demonstration that will show buyers how the product or service will satisfy their needs.

Michelle Race, sales rep for Pillsbury, spends about 30 hours a week working in her home office on her laptop computer. Besides her home software, she's connected to the Pillsbury data system, which allows her to access current and past client information–shipping dates, orders, promotions, etc. She's also online with the large market research firm, Nielsen, from which she receives consumer purchase data—market share, demographics, psychographics, trade promotion, etc. "The days of spreading pixie dust are gone," she explains. "Selling has to be data and information-based. The time you spend face-to-face with customers is limited. At Kroger I'm allowed 15 minutes to say what I have to say. That's all. There's the Procter & Gambles, the Krafts, and others also waiting for time. A lot of the work is preparation and research and making sure you all have the information you need to go in and sell. The more information you have, the more you help the consumer."[21]

1-3b Acting as a Source of Intelligence to Management

VIDEO

Marketing success depends on satisfying consumer need. If there is an absence of satisfaction, marketing management must be informed. If current products don't adequately fulfill consumer need, then an opportunity may exist for a new and profitable offering for a potential product. If there is a problem with an existing product—it doesn't work properly, breaks down, or requires frequent adjustment—customers must be apprised of the fact. With either potential or existing products, few are in a better position to know consumer need than the sales representative. After all, who in the company is closer to the buyer? For this reason, salespeople are asked to fill out reports indicating consumer complaints and suggesting new-product opportunities. Many new products are initiated at the suggestion of the sales force. Many existing ones are altered on the advice of salespeople.

Salespeople at Medtronic, the world leader in the heart pacemaker market, are in the operating room for more than 90 percent of the procedures performed with their product and are on call, wearing beepers, 24 hours a day. " 'It reflects the willingness to be there in every situation, just in case a problem arises—even though 9 times out of 10 the procedure goes just fine,' notes one customer."[22]

Ballard Medical Products, a small hospital supplies company, has been able to compete with vastly larger competitors, such as Baxter Health Care and Johnson & Johnson, by being more sensitive to the needs of the market and responding with faster turnaround on new products. The key to this—the sales force—is the primary source of new-product ideas and is intimately involved in product development. For example, salespeople were instrumental in designing Trach Care, Ballard's most profitable product. It allows nurses to suction excess secretions from the lungs of patients who are connected to respirators without temporarily disengaging the patients from the respirator. Salesperson Bob Myers was further instrumental in designing improvements to the product. Trying out the new product, a surgeon expressed concern that the suction catheter could accidentally slip down the patient's trachea. "How do I know that it's pulled back where it belongs?" he asked. "At a glance, you don't," Myers had to reply. Then Myers called the home office, relayed the question, and within weeks the company had printed a black line on the catheter, indicating the proper retraction position. The heir apparent to renowned president Andy Grove at Intel, Paul Otellini, is responsible for the design of their new chip for laptops, the Centrino. When he noticed that laptop owners add wi-fi cards to their machines to connect with the Internet, he asked why not build wireless connectivity into the chip itself? The result was the Centrino, which was launched in March 2003 and netted $2 billion in revenue—about a third of its quarterly total. Otellini offers an unusual perspective for his industry: that good marketing makes all the difference. "Our whole job," he says, "is to create demand."[23]

In the process of talking with contact-lens wearers, salespeople from SmithKline kept coming across the same problem: "itchy-scratchy eyes." Based on the suggestions of the sales force, the company began working on the problem, and that was the genesis of an immensely profitable product. At SmithKline, about $100 million of the company's $200 million in revenues now comes from a family of ointments aimed at helping these contact-lens wearers.

Perhaps the epitome of intelligence gathering is one institutional textile sales manager for Milliken & Company, who spent two weeks working in a major hospital as part of the housekeeping staff. He worked the second shift (3 P.M. until midnight) and actually cleaned carpeting as well as hard-surface floors. At the end of the time, he revamped his entire marketing program, and he plans to repeat the hospital experience every six months.

1-3c Providing Service

The sales representative's job does not end with the sale. A mainframe computer salesperson may be even busier once the system is installed. Operators must be trained to work with the new system. Programmers must learn new computer languages and system capabilities. Top management must learn in a general way what the computer will and will not do. This service function becomes the sales representative's primary responsibility for the next five to six years, for that's how long it takes before the next system is ordered.

Service is also the primary function for other sales personnel. Procter & Gamble sales representatives are not as involved in seeking orders as they are in advising intermediaries (middlemen) on maximum use of shelf space in the supermarket, preparation of advertising copy for the local newspaper, and optimal design for point-of-purchase displays. Sales engineers represent salespeople with service as their primary function. They must be available to tell clients about ways of maximizing performance from their machines, to answer technical questions, and to ensure that replacement parts are shipped without delay. The retail salesperson who calls a customer about a new outfit that has just arrived, gift wraps purchases, and informs customers about the layaway option also provides a vital and appreciated service function. The rewards of providing superlative service have never been more evident. A recent study of the impact of customer relationship management (CRM) on the profitability of high-technology firms provides detail and insight into the importance of customer service. The consulting firm Accenture found that excellent CRM performance could improve a company's return on sales by as much as 64 percent over merely average performance. For each billion dollars in sales, Accenture estimated impact on increased profitability as follows: customer service, $42 billion; sales and account management, $35 million; and marketing, $34 billion.[24] Although this study is for high-technology products, expectations for customer service have escalated for all products in general, much of this due to the Internet, where customers expect to find assistance "24/7." Typically, it is the salesperson who is the most prominent service representative at customer sites. One step up on this idea, Campbell Soup Company assigns a salesperson full-time to each of its 10 plants that make direct shipments. His or her job is to ensure that grocers get the products they want when they want them, even if that means disrupting production to load, ship, and bill an emergency order in one day. "Most companies have a transportation or warehousing type to handle this function," observes a Campbell executive. "But we find that keeping a salesperson at the plant makes everybody there better respond to customers." General Electric (GE) engineers are stationed full-time at Praxair, Inc., to help boost productivity at the maker of industrial gases, which uses GE-built electrical equipment. Says GE, "Customers demand a new intimacy."[25] At AMP, a producer of electrical products, salespeople had a difficult time retrieving product specifications and performance data on AMP's 70,000 products quickly and accurately. The company now records all information on CD-ROM disks that can be scanned instantly by salespeople and customers. Customer value is also created by salespeople who follow through after the sale. At Jefferson Smith Corporation, a large supplier of packaging products, one of its salespeople juggled production from three of the company's plants to satisfy an unexpected demand for boxes from General Electric. This salesperson's actions led to the company's being given GE's Distinguished Supplier Award.[26]

How about this example of customer service? A day after his 51st birthday, Marty Pay, a Farmers Insurance agent in Tehachapi, California, developed what he thought was a bad case of heartburn during a bike ride. Before taking antacid, he called his pharmacy to ask whether it would interact with his diabetes medication. The Rite Aid pharmacist, Ronde Snell, asked about the nature of the pain, whether he had had heartburn before, and about his medical history. Based on their 10-minute conversation, Snell told Pay that she thought he could be experiencing heart pains (which could be a precursor to a heart attack)—not heartburn—and that he should go to the emergency room. She said, "Even if it's not (heart pains), they will be glad you came in, so they can rule it out." A couple of hours later, Snell called the local hospital and learned that Pay hadn't been in yet. Then, she tracked him down at his office and told him again to go—immediately. The doctors confirmed Snell's suspicions: Pay had 95 percent blockage of one artery, and within days he underwent an angioplasty. "Literally, if it wasn't for her," Pay says, letting the sentence trail off. "A month later, I was back on my bike." The pharmacist–customer relationship became a core focus of Camp Hill, Pennsylvania–based Rite Aid two years ago, when the drugstore chain, looking for ways to stand out in a crowded market, learned through marketing research that customers wanted superior and personal customer service in their pharmacy, says John Learish, Rite Aid's vice president of marketing.[27]

How important service is to customers is illustrated by Snap-on Tools, an $890 million company that sells such mundane products as wrenches, screwdrivers, and other tools customers can purchase anywhere. The Snap-on sales and marketing plan is relatively simple: Rather than make the customer come to the company, the company comes to the customer. Every day, hundreds of white and red Snap-on Tools vans pull up to garages and gas stations around the country. In addition to regular weekly delivery, Snap-on also offers relatively easy credit terms. The result: Mechanics are often waiting for the van's arrival as it pulls in.

1-3d Contacting Buyers

If nothing happens until something is sold, it is also true that nothing happens until a buyer is found. Prospecting is a major, if not the preeminent, duty of many salespeople. For manufacturers that sell equipment installed for long durations, it is critical that the sales force continually identify potential new users, because reorders are long in coming. As a young mainframe computer sales representative, I first had to identify large organizations that either had a need for a mainframe computer or already had one and needed to upgrade to a more powerful one. This necessitated a great investment of time and effort

1-3e Coordinating the Selling Effort

As the number of products a company sells increases and as the diverse needs of buyers similarly expand, several salespeople and technical experts may all be calling on the same customer. For example, a selling team might consist of a salesperson, a sales engineer, a service representative, and a financial expert, each of whom would deal with a counterpart in the customer's firm. At IBM, for example, some salespeople may be responsible for selling smaller office products, others for personal computers and data-entry terminals, and yet others for large-scale computer equipment. Additional IBM personnel would be responsible for service and software support of the data-processing equipment. At a large account, all of their efforts are supervised by an account manager, whose responsibility is to coordinate their activities and centralize communication with the account. If problems arise anywhere, customer departments can contact this one account manager for remedy. In this manner, each product line is sold and serviced by well-trained specialists, and yet there is an overall manager who ensures that the equipment fits into the customer's comprehensive plan and budget. This reduces the chance that salespeople will work at cross-purposes to one another. This is a distinct possibility because all kinds of equipment, from small to large, are increasingly interconnected. Having an overall account manager also mitigates the frustration of customer personnel who must sort through the various IBM reps to determine the proper one to talk to for their individual needs or service problems. Only the account manager need be contacted.

The idea of a sales rep as a coordinator and team leader has also spread from the computer field. Other companies are finding that groups of salespeople, techies, and customers unearth problems, solutions, and sales opportunities than not one of them could alone. Procter & Gamble uses teams of marketing, sales, advertising, computer systems, and distribution personnel to work with its major retailers, such as Wal-Mart, to identify ways to develop, promote, and deliver products. Recently, George Martin, a sales veteran with IBM and AT&T, was charged as vice president of sales for Dun & Bradstreet (D&B) with changing the company's sales approach to that of a sales team composed of representatives from the company's credit, collection, and marketing business units. The mission was to call on D&B's top 50 accounts, meeting with higher-ups, isolating customer problems, and proposing solutions. Martin and a sales

Box 1-2

The Marketing Concept

- Concentrate on satisfying consumer needs and wants.

- All company activities are organized around providing a service to the public, but with a profit.

- A recent corollary is relationship marketing, which stresses that the selling firms concentrate on the relationship with buyers and suppliers throughout the life of the product or service.

---

team met with the chief financial officer of a major telecommunications company and, in an hour of discussing customer problems, identified $1.5 million in sales opportunities from what had been a $700,000 account.[28]

1-4 The Marketing Concept

In performing their duties, today's salespeople are guided by a philosophy of marketing. This marketing concept, as it has come to be known, states that management decision making should concentrate on satisfying consumer needs and wants. The marketing concept holds that all company activities should be organized. A relatively recent development, the marketing concept represents a rather dramatic change from previous marketing thought. Perhaps the best way to illustrate this is by briefly outlining the history of marketing and the philosophies that have guided marketing decisions. Of course, by doing so, changes in emphasis in personal selling are also noted. Marketing and selling are by no means a modern development. Archaeologists have found evidence of ancient peddlers in the Middle East and in advertisements written on the walls of Roman ruins. In colonial America, the arrival of the Yankee peddler was eagerly awaited in the frontier areas. However, it was not until the Industrial Revolution of the mid-1800s, with its rapid expansion of manufacturing facilities and transportation, that the salesperson became essential to business. As mass production developed, manufacturers expanded rapidly and needed to seek out new customers for their wares. This led to the rise of the traveling "drummer," the emissary of abundance.

At this stage of its evolution, marketing could be characterized by a selling philosophy. There was no attempt to find out what products the consumer really desired; there was only mass production of a uniform product. It was then up to salespeople to convince customers to buy, even when a standardized product did not perfectly match a customer's needs. As one retired computer salesperson, Bill Gardner, confessed, "I sold systems that people didn't want, didn't need, and could not afford."[29] Now, however, Gardner's statement is embarrassing to most professional salespeople, who work philosophically with the marketing concept, as described in Box 1-2.

Even today, companies fall victim to an outdated selling philosophy. Despite its reputation for technological brilliance gained with the invention of instant photography, Polaroid has paid for a myopic product and selling orientation. Polaroid's management was too inbred to notice that the world was changing, critics say. "Here's a company that had a field to itself for a long, long time. Many executives spent their entire careers on internal problems and technology. Some didn't consider it important to take a close look at the outside world," said Murray Swindell, a former marketing executive who departed in frustration. As a result, the company

marketing concept The belief that management decision making should concentrate on satisfying consumer needs and wants.

lost heavily in developing an instant movie camera, Polavision, which at $700 didn't have sound and took only two minutes of film at a time. It was no wonder that the Japanese buried it with the VCR and digital camcorders. Moreover, the development of klutz-proof 35mm, and later digital cameras, took America by storm. One-hour photo development in drugstores and mass merchandisers or downloading digital images at home made instant movie cameras moot. Polaroid has only recently emerged from bankruptcy court after purchase by private investors.[30]

By the end of World War II, the factors that spawned the selling philosophy of marketing had changed. Most products could be simply and bountifully produced, and the number of items available increased dramatically. Accordingly, competition increased at a rapid pace. Consumers had lots of money and lots of pent-up desires for goods they had not been able to buy during the war. Under these circumstances, manufacturers soon realized that marketing success depended on understanding consumer desires and then designing a product and a marketing program that fulfilled these desires. This represented a marked departure from the selling philosophy, which would have produced a product first and then sold it to consumers, regardless of whether they really liked it. The formal recognition of satisfying consumer needs is represented by the "marketing concept."

As might be expected, the goal of personal selling has changed in conjunction with the marketing concept. Here, the task of personal selling is defined as the process of analyzing potential customers' needs and wants and assisting them in discovering how such needs and wants can be best satisfied by purchase of a particular product, service, or idea. This view of personal selling emphasizes the necessity for salespeople to be communicators. They must listen closely and ask questions in order to determine customers' needs. There is no place here for a glib tongue and flashy mannerisms. Putting something over on the customer simply will not work in today's business environment. Successful salespeople are good communicators and credible sources of information. They are people whom customers trust and look to for advice.

Some excellent examples of the marketing concept are presented by Southwest Airlines, Nordstrom, and Hertz.[31] In a recent incident, a businessman purchased a "nonrefundable" and "nonchangeable" round-trip ticket on Southwest for LA–Las Vegas–LA through a travel agent. When purchasing the ticket, he did not realize that he would be able to catch an earlier return flight than the one scheduled with this particular ticket. When he arrived at the Las Vegas airport four hours before his scheduled departure, the Southwest attendant told him that his ticket technically could be used only for the later departure time. But, understanding his wish to leave earlier than scheduled (i.e., need orientation of marketing concept) and not wanting him to sit idly at the airport for four more hours, she graciously—at no additional cost to him—changed his ticket to the earlier flight.

Southwest Airlines has the goal of dignifying the customer; Nordstrom has the goal of delighting their customers. Nordstrom employees receive excellent training and are empowered to offer extra service on their own. They are shown the importance of having an unrelenting pursuit of customer service excellence. They are encouraged to use sound business judgment, are empowered to give refunds with no questions asked, and to go out of their way to please customers. They are also given instant desktop access to an up-to-date database containing customer characteristics and account history. This knowledge helps create familiarity with customer needs and requirements and conveys to customers that their expectations are understood and respected.

Asking customers what they want, and listening and responding to those requests, is one of the things that has enabled Hertz to maintain its lead in the highly competitive car-rental industry. Every time a customer returns a rental car to one of its 5,000 locations worldwide, the Hertz Corporation asks its customers a simple question: "What can we do to improve our level of service to you?" The response: "We want a clean, safe car that's easy to return at a price we can afford (no hidden costs, please)—and we want it fast!"

Recently, there has appeared a new term in the marketing literature, **relationship marketing** or "partnering," which stresses that the selling firm should concentrate on the relationship with buyers as well as suppliers throughout the life of the product or service. A recent survey of 300 senior sales executives revealed that 96 percent consider "building long-term relationships with customers" to be the most important activity affecting sales performance. Companies such as American Express, Electronic Data Systems, Motorola, and Owens-Corning have made relationship building a core focus of their sales effort.[32] Although this is really an extension of the marketing concept, it has only recently become a driving management focus. The traditional emphasis has been a transactional one, focusing on getting the sale and ignoring the period after the sale. The traditional approach of the selling organization after the sale is that the product does not break down during the warranty period. Though some after-sale communication might have occurred, it is nothing compared to what is expected in relationship management. Relationship management goes further than sellers have ever gone before to bind the buyer and seller together for the long term. In relationship management, buyer and seller are not viewed as opponents, but as partners. The payback? One study estimates that a decrease in the customer defection rate by 5 percent can boost profits by 25 percent to 95 percent.[33] At IBM, where "pushing metal" used to be the unwritten sales rep motto, there is now a more professional customer-driven approach. Robert LaBant, senior vice president, says every percentage point variation in customer satisfactions scores translates into a gain or loss of $500 million in sales over five years. What's more, he says, developing new business costs Big Blue 3 to 5 times as much as maintaining the old.[34]

Recent examples of the marketing concept, including its partnering corollary, are represented in the success of Microsoft. Microsoft has become the global leader in software not only because of its technical expertise, but also because the company has forged close partnerships with its key customers and developers. Microsoft circulates early versions of its software to solicit ideas for further product features. These ideas aren't just perfunctorily swapped; they are jointly discussed, debated, and incorporated. These software prototypes effectively become the medium for partnerships. Microsoft's own product teams don't individually shape the final product; it's the collaboration with customers and developers that jointly create the finished product. It's a virtuous cycle of creative partnerships creating innovative prototypes that foster further partnering.

Wallace, now Moore-Wallace, is an integrated supply and total print management company. The company produces and distributes business forms, labels, direct response or direct-mail pieces, commercial printing products, and office supplies. What distinguishes them from the competition is their ability for customers to outsource their entire forms management system, design to delivery, to Wallace. ShopKo, a regional mass merchandiser, for example, used to employ business form designers, use purchasing agents to bid contracts to forms vendors, and inventory forms in their own warehouses. By outsourcing solely to Wallace, ShopKo saves all of these personnel and inventory carrying costs, as they now simply order all forms from Wallace online. The forms are then delivered 48 hours later.

Relationship marketing does not eliminate the idea of discrete transactions, which typically involve limited communication over a short period of time and a

relationship marketing
The marketing principle that stresses that the selling firm should concentrate on the relationship with buyers throughout the life of the product or service with the emphasis on service and value-added activities.

Table **1-2** Relative Amount of Time Spent in Each of the Selling Steps

Traditional Selling	Selling Step	Relationship Selling
Low	Precall preparation	High
High	Prospecting	Low
High	Approach	Low
Low	Problem recognition	High
High	Presentation	High
High	Handling objections	Low
High	Closing	Low
Low	Service	High

straightforward exchange of benefits. A single sale represents a discrete transaction. For example, one might be a "one-time purchase of unbranded gasoline out-of-town at an independent station paid for with cash." However, this does not excuse selling products or services customers don't need.

There are several differences between the process used in relationship selling and the process of traditional transactional selling. Table 1-2 shows these differences in emphasis in the steps of the selling process.

As can be seen in Table 1-2, the relationship salesperson spends more time in precall preparation and problem recognition (i.e., questioning), especially the latter, which, in fact, is paramount in relationship selling.

1-5 Selling in the Twenty-first Century

1-5a More Relationship Selling

Probably nothing will change the role and activities of the salesperson more in the twenty-first century than the aforementioned concept of partnering and its mandate for relationship marketing and selling. Although the terms have been used indiscriminately to describe any number of so-called "new" marketing actions, basically relationship marketing is defined as:

> Long-term agreements between buyers and sellers that reduce conflict and promote mutually beneficial ties between two firms. Using purchasing partnerships, buyers are supposed to receive a continuous stream of quality products and services, while suppliers are assured of a significant portion of buyers orders. The relationship enables the partners to plan requirements on a mutually beneficial time schedule with mutually satisfactory pricing.[35]

Besides more relationship selling, additional changes are enumerated in Box 1-3.

Procter & Gamble (P&G), once the most resented of manufacturers by distributors, demonstrates the new partnering and relationship marketing process. Once, the only contact between P&G and its distributors was the salesperson, one of whom characterized his job as to "stack it high and price it low." "My main ammunition was a smile and a slap on the buyer's back. I just sold, and if my actions created problems (for the customer), so be it."[36] Punch and counterpunch characterized the relationship. P&G would use aggressive advertising and trade allowances to control retailers,

Box 1-3

Trends for Selling in the Twenty-first Century

- More relationship selling
- Advances in technology
- More telemarketing, teleconferencing, videoconferencing
- Productivity growth
- Higher percentage of college graduates
- Increased team selling
- Greater intelligence gathering by salespeople

- "Rehumanization"
- Shorter product life cycles
- More salespeople will sell intangibles
- Sophisticated Internet and database software
- International selling

but giants like Wal-Mart responded by overordering during promotions, either transshipping to geographic areas not covered under the promotion (diversion) or simply loading up with low-cost inventory. Upon analysis, P&G realized that this transaction-based marketing created spikes-and-valleys in ordering, delivery, inventory, and payment that were costly to both P&G and its retailers. The costs were ultimately passed on to consumers, who delayed purchasing until lower-priced promotions became available. Thus, large retailers were easily identifiable as potential partners, rather than adversaries. The new partnering approach has been extraordinarily successful in improving the relationship with distributors, and some larger retailers now trust P&G enough to allow direct access to their warehouse inventory systems. P&G prepares new orders based on movement of products in the customer's storage facilities—a process called *continuous replenishment.* The practice has lowered customer operating expenses by shortening the lead time needed in ordering and thereby reducing unnecessary inventories. It has also helped P&G by smoothing out the flow of manufacturing demands. What P&G has accomplished in establishing relationships with customers has prompted some marketing theorists to call customer-centric marketing.[37] First, whereas traditional marketing has been concerned with demand management, customer-centric marketing will lead the marketing function toward "supply management"—the ability to rapidly respond to customer requirements rather than focusing on controlling them. Second, traditional marketing practices emphasize the acquisition of customers, while customer-centric marketing emphasizes the retention of the "right" customers along with the "outsourcing" of the rest. Third, whereas traditional firms and customers are institutionally separate with little interaction, customer-centric marketing will lead to customers and firms cocreating products, pricing, and distribution. Fourth, customer-centric marketing will be characterized by more fixed costs and fewer variable costs; companies will make infrastructure investments, such as merged computer networks, as with Wal-Mart, that greatly reduce transaction costs. Finally, the vocabulary, metrics, and organizations will evolve toward a customer focus rather than product focus or segment focus. For example, Procter & Gamble renamed its channel sales organization customer business development in early 1999.

A corollary trend is that companies are reducing the number of vendors with which they do business. Xerox, for example, reduced its approved suppliers from

4,000 to about 500. "Vendors are no longer just salespeople. They are now strategic partners with their business customers," said Allen Konopacki, president of Incomm International. Michael Lavelle, an Evanston-based salesperson for Gettings-Castle, a hospital equipment company, and Michael Shanley, outside salesperson for Liebovich Bros., Inc., in Rockford, a subsidiary of Los Angeles–based Reliance Steel & Aluminum Co., can point to numerous examples of how their day-to-day work life is now different than it was before the Internet explosion. "I would go out on the street and sell a product and then let the in-house people handle the rest," said Lavelle. "Salespeople didn't use to have a lot of connection to the office. Now, with the Internet, we are connected and we can track shipping and delivery. We are more connected to the processes at the home office and we are also a partner with the customer. Sometimes, in fact, the customer may want us to tap into their computer system for tracking and follow-up." And, Shanley said the sales cycle is now shorter. "If you use the computer more effectively, you will be able to stretch yourself out more and call on more people," he said. "You can use the Internet, for example, to send clients product and market information by email. If you know the price of stainless steel is going up in the next 60 days, for instance, that is something you send your customers."[38]

Moreover, futurists have suggested that the United States is changing from an industrial-based to an information-based economy. Over the last 20 or so years, the quality movement has showed us how to make products with few defects. Service quality techniques have also taken hold in the services sector. Product/service quality is now necessary but not sufficient. Customers are looking for more, and value-added services are usually information-based. How much good does a digital camera, a smart cell phone, or a telephony-service-like number recognition system do if the customer doesn't have the information necessary to use it properly?[39]

1-5b Changes in Technology

The foremost cause of the change is the ubiquitous computer. Moreover, all salespeople will experience changes in their jobs because of developments in information-processing technology. "Just think," commented one sales manager, "what a professional salesperson can do in one day in the electronic age: call on five new prospects, not one; touch base with 10 current customers; prescreen leads by phone and personal computer; instantly close a sale . . . and improvise variations on the theme; call up data on competitors' products, and compare the data with theirs; instantly estimate production time and delivery dates; and cover his or her whole territory by scanning the computer screen for incoming messages . . . all without a gallon of gas, without jet lag."[40]

The computer frees salespeople from many of the routine aspects of their jobs, but it also adds demands. With the development of laptop computers, salespeople are able to order directly from their customers' offices or from their cars without spending time on unproductive paperwork. They also act as information brokers for their customers, accessing their company's system and finding out about the status of previous orders. Not only do they need knowledge of their own system, but they also have to know their customers' systems as orders have to be edited online to ensure that price, freight allowance, promotional allowance, and other factors are correct. Much of the tedious work of preparing bids has been automated, freeing salespeople for more personal calls. Such was the benefit realized by the microscope division of Carl Zeiss International after computerizing the quote preparation previously prepared by hand by the firm's 70 technical sales reps. Previously, when finished meeting with customers, reps had to go back to their offices to prepare microscope diagrams and bids by searching spec sheets by hand. When completed, they were forwarded to company headquarters, where they were laboriously input to computers, generated, checked over by management, and returned to the rep. Intended to take 24 hours, this was actually the exception. When revamped, the reps could generate a bid from a laptop computer within minutes at the customer's office. Not only does this speed up the order process, but it also impresses the customers at the research institutions, universities, government agencies, and manufacturers that constitute Zeiss' buyers. More than once, the immediacy of bids has won orders from slower-moving competitors.[41]

Of all salespeople, the ones most affected by the computer are those who call on retailers. The increased use of scanners in the food, drug, and hardware business (and wherever else chains predominate) allows inventory to be updated daily. Whenever supplies drop to a predetermined level, the computer issues an order, often over fiber-optic lines direct to a vendor's computer. Much routine work is no longer necessary, and the work that remains is performed increasingly by part-timers who check out shelves, bring material from the backroom, build displays—do the "grunt" work a sales rep used to do. Salespeople have evolved into small select groups of computer-oriented sales consultants, dealing primarily at the major account level. These "super-reps" do what salespeople do best—advise their clients on almost all phases of marketing strategy. Their jobs are more quantitative-oriented. If, for example, the buyer says the product is doing poorly in his or her store based on daily scanner data, and the rep knows the product is doing well in competitors' stores, the rep must know how to analyze the information and point out what the buyer's store is doing wrong. Selling, in other words, has become much more information-saturated than it is today.[42] With increasingly more sales forces restructured for additional autonomy at the regional level, territory sales representatives will have significantly more money for local advertising and promotion. They will have to know their territory intimately and look for local promotional opportunities, such as events, couponing, sampling, refunds, direct mail, product seminars, or in-store demonstrations.

1-5c More Teleconferencing

With the increased costs of making a personal call, more business in the twenty-first century will be conducted over the phone, between two people, through teleconferencing, or even videoconferencing. Almost 20 percent of domestic industrial firms now use telemarketing in some capacity. Use of this particular medium increases about 25 percent each year, resulting in about $525 billion in annual sales most recently. There are many advantages to adding telemarketing to the marketing mix. On the business-to-business side, with the cost of a field sales call rising steadily, telemarketing can be a cost-effective alternative. In some cases, it can be used to replace face-to-face selling on smaller accounts. In others, telemarketers qualify leads before handing them off to field salespeople, providing service to existing customers, managing and screening inquiries, setting appointments, announcing new products, cross-selling or upgrading existing customers, and building a database. In both business-to-business and direct-to-consumer marketing, a telephone call is more attention-getting than a direct-mail piece. Also, it provides a faster response than the mail, and it is more certain: You not only know that the call was received, but you also know *when* it was received.[43] Still other developments in communications technology, such as email, voice mail, videophones, and PCs with video capabilities, are likely to have a further impact on selling.

Videoconferencing has been around for years, but it has taken awhile for it to catch on. According to Frost & Sullivan, the previous generation of videoconferencing systems had problems associated with video quality and complex user interfaces. Newer systems have addressed these issues by providing better sound and pictures, easy-to-use capabilities, and centralized management tools. Technologies such as video streaming and web-initiated conferencing are also fueling the adoption of videoconferencing by industry.[44]

Another factor favoring videoconferencing, of course, is that more workers are engaged in "virtual" work. A survey by WorldCom found that 48 percent of workers have participated in virtual teams, and 91 percent said they enjoyed the experience. A *virtual team* is defined as employees in different locations who rely on email, conference calls, fax, the Internet, and videoconferencing, among other tools, to accomplish their goals. The same survey reported that 73 percent of respondents said they would like to engage in virtual work more frequently. With the way technology is improving, it looks as if these workers will get their wish.[45]

A salesperson can now walk into a meeting room, open up a laptop and projector, and be ready to start a presentation in seconds, not minutes. Does this sound farfetched? Sony has developed e-Conference software that allows plug-and-play connectivity from laptop to projector without wires or cables. E-Conference resides on the company intranet and allows devices to talk to each other.

1-5d Productivity Growth

Already, many salespeople work out of "virtual offices" in their homes; these offices include a telephone, personal computer, modem, printer, and fax. When they go on the road, they take with them a laptop computer, cellular phone, personal digital assistant (PDA) or BlackBerry, and portable printer, and they are accessible to their companies almost anywhere. Don King contacts clients via radio, on his Nextel phone, Nextel i95CL. The $10-a-month service connects the company's reps from Georgia to California. A continuous connection to the Internet means that emails sent to King's account in his office are uploaded onto his phone throughout the day. Most of the company's customers have similar devices, so they can radio King or one of his reps in seconds with a personal request. The phones also alert King to business changes that can affect the outcome of sales calls. Just before a recent presentation to Wal-Mart in LaGrange, Georgia, King's office tipped him off via radio that Wal-Mart's vice president of operations would be attending the presentation. "Sitting in the parking lot, we adjusted our presentation on our laptop to include a matrix that showed our service levels if we outsourced our technology," King says. The original presentation would have been too general, he adds. Because the vice president was a decision maker on the deal, this was an opportunity for King to close, rather than simply make inroads, as he'd initially thought—and close he did, on a deal worth about $1 million a year in revenue.

On July 4, Ron Romanchik had plenty to celebrate, the country's birthday being the least of it. The vice president of global sales for Ai-Logix, Inc., a telecommunications company based in Somerset, New Jersey, closed a $1 million-a-year deal while lounging on the beach. How? By conducting business through his BlackBerry 6750. The popular handheld lets Romanchik receive calls and emails simultaneously. So, while negotiating contract specifications and pricing changes with e-learning company Envision, Romanchik could talk on his BlackBerry to the four Ai-Logix employees involved in the deal at the same time that he was opening Microsoft Word attachments on the device. "If I'm on a call on my BlackBerry, I can hide the phone call and go right to an email that I've received, open up the attachment on the Black-Berry, and view it as I'm talking," Romanchik says. Without his BlackBerry,

Romanchik would have had only one phone line to use at his beach house. "I'd have had to dial into a server on my laptop to retrieve information about the deal," he says. "Then I'd have to hang up, call back my reps, and make conference calls to close the deal, which would have been impossible. I probably would have been on the phone for countless hours trying to get everything coordinated." Instead, about an hour on his BlackBerry was all Romanchik needed for Ai-Logix to seal the deal.

You could call Paul Wolbert's Cassiopeia 200 his lifeline—at least when he's in the field. The powerful PDA's biggest advantage is its ability to quickly sync with his computer in the office. With a single plug-in from his PDA to his computer, Wolbert, director of franchise development for U.S. Lawns, a landscaping company in Orlando, Florida, updates files on both devices daily, allowing him to carry only the PDA outside the office. It's the freedom the device offers that's most important, he says. Recently, U.S. Lawns bid to win a landscaping contract with Bank of America, whose property was being managed by commercial real estate firm Trammell Crow Property in Dallas. While traveling, instead of running to a Kinko's to fax or email the prospect with the latest pricing offers, Wolbert simply pulled his car off the road and renegotiated contract specifications via the device. Wolbert maintained contact with his salespeople and the client hourly via his PDA and ultimately beat out five competitors for the $4 million deal. "The whole thing about this technology is that it doesn't limit you with where you need to be," Wolbert says. "You can be anywhere and conduct business."[46] Soon to come: the "desktop sales call." Using multimedia presentations, searchable databases, customized information, and interactive on-screen demonstrations, sales forces in the next century can rely more on digital manipulation and less on physical travel. Of course, as to be expected with the rapid pace of technology, newer devices such as smart mobile phones are replacing personal digital assistants as the must-have tools of salespeople. Smart phones have many of the same features as PDAs, such as calendars and address books, plus they make calls, and many salespeople like carrying only one device.[47]

Technology can even ease the job of sales "road warriors." When Steve Saslow slips behind the wheel and heads for a client's office, he often hasn't a clue where he's going. But that hardly matters, because he's equipped with Televigation's TeleNav navigation system. The global positioning system device, about the size of a deck of cards, sits on his dashboard and plugs into his cigarette lighter, which connects to his cell phone to offer him driving directions via visual cues and voice commands. "I call on a lot of accounts that I've never been to before," says Saslow, a data consultant for the Redmond, Washington, office of Nextel. "TeleNav leads me turn by turn, and never makes a mistake," Saslow says. The result of all this technology: improved productivity.[48]

1-5e More College Graduates

The salesperson of the twenty-first century will have to be more of a professional; certainly, computer literate. Those who are not will suffer from great competitive disadvantage. College graduates will be in more demand for sales positions. From 1992 till 2002, the percentage of salespeople holding a college degree has increased appreciably (see Table 1-3), especially in the more demanding fields, such as financial and business services.[49] It obviously takes more than a smile and handshake to make it in sales. As evidence, selling has become much more sophisticated in the so-called smokestack industries. At AmCast Industrial Corporation, selling used to involve little more than what company officials referred to as "chasing smokestacks," a description for the process of driving from one customer to the next to make sales calls. But AmCast has had to change its ways. No

T a b l e **1-3** Changes in Educational Attainment

	Share of Employment in Occupational Group		Workers Age 25–34 with Bachelor's or Higher Degree		Workers Age 25–34 with Advanced Degree	
	1992	*2000*	*1992*	*2000*	*1992*	*2000*
Sales occupations	12	12	31	37	3	4
Sales representative, finance, and business services			54	60	7	6
Sales representative, mining, manufacturing, and wholesale			48	54	4	5
Sales worked, retail, and personal services			17	20	2	3

Source: "Outlook and Earnings for College Graduates, 2000–2010: College at Work," *Occupational Outlook Quarterly,* Fall 2002, p. 14.

longer are its sales representatives mere glad-handers, skilled at wining and dining purchasing agents in hopes of getting a share of an order.

Today there are college graduates with metalworking backgrounds who deal not only with buyers but also with customers' engineers, marketing specialists, and manufacturing personnel and get involved as early as possible in the business plans of potential customers. Salespeople of the twenty-first century will also have to know a great deal more about finance. As one marketing manager commented, "We want them to know about the cost of money and be able to relate that to the customer's inventory and accounts receivable situation, so that they have an idea of what financial package will swing the sale." Comments one knowledgeable consultant, "The selling function will be less pitching product and more integrating your product into the business equation of your client, understanding the business environment in which your business client operates." This will require intelligence, in-depth knowledge of the latest business practices (especially advances in computer technology), and a thorough grasp of financial strategies. As the salesperson of the future, "you have to be a financial engineer for your client. You need an understanding of how your client makes money and how your firm makes money."[50]

1-5f Team Selling

As buyers have become more proficient, salespeople will have to respond in kind. At one time many sales could be made by developing close personal friendships with underpaid purchasing people through long lunches and evening entertainment. Such is now more the exception than the rule. Buyers are well trained and better paid. Because companies now recognize that much of their profits are tied up in purchasing, buying teams are more prevalent. Hence, a salesperson may make one presentation to an engineering expert, another to a materials requirement planner, and yet another to the company president. Indeed, this may be beyond the capabilities of one salesperson; a team selling approach may be required in which each person in the selling company calls on his or her counterpart in the prospect's buying organization. In this environment, the salesperson's success will depend not only on persuasive ability but also on the ability to plan strategy and manage the activities of others. In other words, he or she will have to be a team leader. When dealing with major accounts to establish a relationship, it is necessary to send a team of logistics, marketing, accounting, and engineering people, who can help you understand what the other guy needs, how he makes money, and what extras you can sell. As a result, many qualities once prized—intense independence, self-sufficiency, a need to control, quest for high personal achievement, and a commission-driven, transaction-focused mind-set—have been replaced. The new qualities are a "we" orientation, flexibility, a commitment to sharing, and putting the group's welfare above one's own.[51]

1-5g Intelligence Gathering

Salespeople will spend more of their time in intelligence gathering, which requires a greater knowledge of market research techniques and questioning methods in general. According to Gordon Sterling, a division manager with American Cyanamid, "Ten years ago, it was sales, sales, sales. Now we tell our salesmen: 'Don't just sell—we need information.' What do our customers need? What is the competition doing?" Knowledge can make all the difference. In this weak economy where dollars are scarce and competition is fierce, an extra scrap of knowledge can mean the difference between a closed deal and a colossal mistake. Companies are increasingly turning to competitive intelligence (CI) to determine the strategies of rivals and the needs of the customer. An SMM/Equation Research survey of 291 sales managers revealed that 89 percent ask their salespeople to double as information agents. Details on the competition's price and new products are most in demand. A recent study by PricewaterhouseCoopers (PwC) found that one-third of CEOs consider CI more critical to success than a year ago; 84 percent consider it a prime driver of profit growth. "Our volatile economy has left businesses scrambling to neutralize or undermine whatever perceived advantages their competitors may have developed," says Steve Hamm, managing partner of PwC's middle market advisory services. "It's little wonder that competitive intelligence is valued more highly today—and why so many firms are focusing on ferreting out information about any new competitor initiatives."[52]

Selling skills will have to be more finely honed in the twenty-first century. Once a competitor is firmly established on a buyer's computer system, orders will automatically be forwarded to that vendor whenever supplies drop below a given level. For a new vendor to receive entry to the system, the benefits will clearly have to outweigh the costs of making the requisite computer changes. Salespeople will have to expend much effort on researching buyer needs to discover competitive advantages.

1-5h "Rehumanization"

Yet as technology creates demands in some respects, it will ease performance in others. Through computer data banks, salespeople will be better able to take account of each other's expertise. Lotus *NotesSuite* and Xerox's *Docushare* allow the creation of a database filled with new product information, sales presentations, and customer profiles that can be accessed remotely and updated continuously by members of a sales team. In a similar way, tele- and videoconferencing will make it more economical for salespeople to make contact and compare strategies and skills with one another.

At the same time that high tech proliferates and dramatically changes professional selling forever, it also creates greater demand for old-fashioned selling skills. The more high tech we see, the more "rehumanization" salespeople will be called upon to display to counterbalance its depersonalizing effects. This doesn't mean a return to 2-hour gabfests when salespeople call on accounts; busy customers no longer have the time or patience for that extravagance. But as one purchasing agent in the paper products industry so eloquently explained his feelings, "Most of the day I'm buried in computer printouts up to my shoulders. When I communicate with people, half the time it's over teletype or remote terminal. When I need an answer or some data in a hurry, I push a couple of buttons. By the time I come face-to-face with another human being, I'm hungry for a bright smile, a kind word, and companionship." A Chicago-based Internet company, BidBuyBuild.com, has certainly found that it requires a human sales force to get its e-commerce site, where builders can purchase supplies and equipment, up and running. "The human touch is needed to explain to builders how to use the site, and to verify to manufacturers that they will be dealing with legitimate builders and contractors," said Bob Stockard, president of Salience Associates, an Andover, Massachusetts, sales outsourcing firm. Indeed, Stockard says that in the world of e-commerce, he expects more companies to contract with firms like his, whereby a sales staff can temporarily boost web sales via old-fashioned human skills.[53]

1-5i Shorter Product Life Cycles

Many of the trends already cited will combine to make the job of the salesperson more demanding—and more frustrating. Technology will make the product cycle much shorter. The ever-more-rapid pace of innovation is demonstrated by personal computers. In the old days, computer life cycles took three to five years, and companies had plenty of time to recoup research and development costs. Now a product will be new only for a short period before clones or close substitutes are forthcoming. The salesperson will have a limited period in which to exploit a competitive advantage. Moreover, with more close substitutes, more sophisticated buyers, and team buying, there will probably be an elongated sales cycle. This will mean more presentations, more meetings, extended bid cycles, and ultimately more time. Exacerbating this trend will be the demand for specific, custom-made solutions instead of generic ones. Many companies today have a deep commitment to quality. Generic, mass-market solutions generally can't fit the needs of such companies, and this will also demand more of the salesperson's time and effort.

1-5j Selling Intangibles

As the economy tilts more and more toward services, more salespeople will be selling intangibles. Selling intangibles such as advice, insurance, and market forecasts is tougher because you can't come in with a prototype that everyone can look, touch, and feel. An intangible service is just something in your head in the eyes of prospects. Consequently, the process of selling intangibles is generally more elongated and difficult.[54]

1-5k International Selling

In the twenty-first century, international selling will be more critical to the success of American companies, and there will be a requisite demand for salespeople with appropriate skills. Examples of selling mistakes made by naive American salespeople in the international marketplace are legion. Accepting a Japanese executive's business card in a cursory manner, for example, and placing it with a brief glance in one's wallet will horrify the executive; the Japanese believe that a person's name, written or spoken, is something close to sacred. Similarly, presuming that all the French executives sitting in a room speak English, without first asking in French whether they do, is a tactical blunder because the French are extremely proud of the heritage and expression of their language.[55] In Germany, a salesperson should not reach across a client's desk to shake his or her hand. Business etiquette there calls for the client to walk around his or her desk and greet a visitor.

1-5l Internet and Database Software

The Internet has occasioned many tectonic changes in the global economy, marketing, and sales. The Internet has led to disloyalty and erosion of pricing power. Competitive products are only a mouse-click away. Just as visitors can find their way to a website with the click of a mouse, they can find their way out just as quickly. Switching costs are virtually zero. The Internet as a distribution channel for product sales and information has caused many consumers to change buying habits and methods. Researchers report record-low consumer loyalty in the Internet environment. Consumers are smarter and expect more. As the general population becomes better educated, consumers approach purchase decisions with greater scrutiny, and they have access to more data for comparison shopping. Now, customers can glean a clear idea of what the dealer has paid for the car on the Internet. Some people will take that figure and still haggle, even asking for a price below what they know the dealer has paid. Others will tag on a few hundred dollars, deeming that is a fair dealer profit. The salesperson is still negotiating with the customer, only now the talks are probably more specific on dealer costs. With greater scrutiny comes stronger expectations and demand for product quality and customer service. To meet these demands and emphasize differentiation and added value, companies launch loyalty marketing programs.

Price-based switching programs change expectations. Most of us have gotten a tempting offer to switch telephone service: Switch your long-distance service to the company that's calling, and it'll send you a check. Some were worth $20, some $50, and during extremely competitive periods, some companies offered as much as $100. These price- or cash-based offers have taught consumers to be on the lookout for the next best offer. But in many industries, loyalty marketing programs have helped companies establish value and create barriers to exit.[56]

Advancements in software will have a coincidental impact on the salesperson of the twenty-first century. "Relationship-oriented" salespeople must have immediate computer access to facilitate the relationship between their company and their customer. Assisting them is a new class of software known as **customer relationship management (CRM)**, which involves the use of technology—including, increasingly, the Internet—to accomplish two goals: (1) It enables companies to gather, analyze, and refine customer data with precision, segmenting customers into "markets of one" and identifying those customers with the greatest potential value. (2) It makes it possible to share that data, the database, with all departments directly involved with customers, notably sales, marketing, and customer service and support. As a result, CRM equips each of those departments to deal with customers as individuals, tailoring products and offers to their specific needs. Done right, this will strengthen relationships with customers and increase their loyalty.[57] In the future, there should be even more emphasis on this type of information-based selling. Because loyalty extends only as far as the next link, customer relationship management software aims to keep track of customers, learning about each one's likes and dislikes from various sources like transaction records, call-center logs, website clicks, sales rep's call reports, and search-engine queries. Effective CRM links data received from the different channels that companies offer to their customers. CRM applications are designed primarily to reach real-time information; to forecast effectively based on individual product, market sector, or customer groups; and to identify trends to help create targeted marketing campaigns. For the past two years, Chase Manhattan has been putting together a CRM system for its retail banking division's marketing, sales,

customer relationship management (CRM)
The marketing strategy that combines sales force automation, marketing, and customer service into a seamless provision of products, service, and customer support, typically using software that creates a customer database.

Box 1-4

Uses of Database Software

- Automate an entire sales process, from generating a lead to closing, providing easy access to customer and contact information

- Improve customer communications by automating letter-writing, faxing, emailing, and even dialing the telephone

- Rapidly generate many reports, including lead sources, close rations, geographic trends, and industry sales trends

- Easily plan trips geographically

- Share information and ideas on a real-time basis

- Mail or fax customized personal letters in bulk to specific customer groups

- Improve close ratios by focusing sales efforts on the people most likely to buy

- Keep track of customer needs and buying schedules

- Serve customers better by giving them easy access to the information they need

and service departments. It groups and analyzes the data pulled from the bank's tellers, ATM machines, website, and telephone service reps to mine information on its 3.5 million customers in a 720-branch network. With this, Chase can segment customers by current and potential value. Chase reports that the CRM program is directly responsible for a 4 percent increase in the retention of high-net-worth customers from January to June 2000 and a large increase in the amount of assets the bank manages for its most affluent customers.[58]

The combination of new technology, including the Internet and database software, have turned the traditional marketing model upside down, enabling companies of all sizes to identify and focus on the people most likely to buy. The payoff: They achieve their objectives for a fraction of what it used to cost. The technological revolution has transformed sales and marketing. The relatively low cost of Internet services and of sales and marketing automation make it possible for any company to compete by applying what is coming to be called the *New Marketing*. The result is a significant savings in time and money and a sales organization that requires fewer high-paid "closers."

Before the advent of low-cost Internet and database technology, marketers resorted to highly inefficient marketing methods that favored companies with the most money to waste. Just think of the value of database software, as enumerated in Box 1-4.

Because it was impossible to identify precisely most of the people interested in their products or services, companies generally relied on strategies that inevitably delivered a vast audience with little interest in buying. Despite the traditional media's efforts to "narrowcast" their audiences, it is generally impossible to target people searching for information on a specific topic at a specific time. In addition, the high cost of database systems has made it difficult for organizations of any size to keep track of anybody but their most serious customers. Until recently, almost none could track serious prospects. Many of the world's largest business-to-business marketers don't know the names of their prospects. Typically, they depend on their salespeople to maintain such information, a practice that can backfire when those people resign and take the prospect list with them.

With New Marketing, marketers seek to target people in a buying and planning mode and to build a relationship with potential customers over time. Although the details of a New Marketing plan depend upon the product or service and its market, the basics are the same for all companies:[59]

- Consumers and business buyers are overwhelmed with information and pay little attention to marketing messages unless they are relevant to immediate needs.
- Consumers and business buyers are much more likely to respond to a marketing initiative when they are actively searching for a product or service.
- New Marketing lowers costs in three ways: (1) It enables the organization to focus marketing resources on the people or businesses most likely to buy: people searching for information about the company's product or service; (2) It facilitates tracking the results of every sales effort, including the source of new business and the potential value of each customer or prospect; (3) It emphasizes retaining customers rather than continually spending money to replace them.
- All efforts of the organization are directed at identifying, selling to, and satisfying customers, one by one.
- Inexpensive database technology, including sales-automation software, makes it possible for companies of any size to identify the people most likely to buy and to focus their sales and marketing efforts accordingly.

Until recently, the cost of obtaining and maintaining data made it impractical for all but the largest companies to track customers and prospects, but hardware and software prices have come down to a point where almost any company can do so. Marketers with prospects numbering in the tens of thousands can make do with sales automation software that ranges from simple off-the-shelf products to customized solutions appropriate for large organizations.

Sales-automation software (i.e., CRM or a lesser version, contact management) makes it easy and inexpensive to turn your sales force into a prospect-tracking system. The key processes to be automated include keeping track of potential prospects by source, buying qualifications, and timing; communicating with potential prospects at the right time by telephone or mail; and tracking what happens to each prospect over time. With these programs, salespeople maintain prospect information on their laptop computers and regularly upload information into a central database. At any time, top management can see how many prospects the organization is working on, the quality of those prospects, and the status of each account. Michael Shanley of Leibovich Bros. Steel adds that although his business customers use the Internet to purchase, he also uses it to determine prime sales prospects. "A salesman spends a lot of time qualifying customers, or figuring out whether a business manufactures products that would entail the use of our products. We used to have to look in manufacturers' directories. Now, you can easily pull this kind of information off the Internet, and you can do it quickly."[60]

With sales increasingly involving research, analysis, and problem solving, many people who think they're not aggressive enough for sales may be missing opportunities. A librarian or an accountant could conceivably find a niche in sales, experts say. "The demand for talented salespeople has never been keener," said Harms of CareerEngine. To help their sales force become more effective in these changing times, Konopacki says industry surveys show companies are spending more each year on sales training. Although the B2B arena is where more of the higher-paying, complex sales positions are found, in many cases, selling to consumers is also evolving because of e-commerce. "I see email in my sleep," said R. J. Serpico, Internet sales manager for Arlington Heights Ford. Customers often start shopping on the web, he said, and email him to inquire about options and prices. "Many of the same processes are still involved in selling cars," said Serpico, "but they are now altered somewhat due to e-commerce." For example, salespeople and customers have long negotiated over the price of a vehicle. "The speed and pace of the economy are quickening and there is a need to manage more and more information," said Harms. "It has all changed the role of the salesperson."[61]

1-6 Why Study Selling?

So far in this chapter, we have outlined the importance of selling to the national economy as a whole and to the marketing efforts of the individual firm in particular. We have also pointed out how this role has evolved over time. At this point, the student may be inclined to comment, "This is fine, but what's in it for me?"

There are six answers to this question:

1. Everyone is involved in selling, even those who do not earn their living in professional selling. Samuel Johnson, the great English essayist, once said, "There is no man who is not in some degree a merchant; who has not something to buy or something to sell." Everything you do for the rest of your career requires selling ideas, products, concepts, people. Even in industries where marketing and selling have traditionally never been recognized, there is no appreciation for their value. Banks, for example, generally offer similar products. Bank branches and ATMs are across the street from each other. Telephone and Internet channels are built on comparable models. Superior service, then, is what can set one bank far apart from its peers. Traditionally, banks, including KeyBank, hired financial types for every job, but reflecting on bank similarity, KeyBank decided they wanted bankers who love to work with people, have outstanding communication skills, and are results-oriented. Today, 70 percent of their new hires are nonbankers with proven sales competencies. They're coming from service-oriented retailers or from pure selling roles in industries such as pharmaceuticals or technology. Proven selling skills were already in place, so they concentrated on teaching them about financial products and services.[62] A study of the selection process for public accounting firms, for example, found that personalization of service (the degree of rapport between client and CPA firm) is the most important factor influencing the selection of a firm. Recently, some law firms are asking their lawyers to participate in several day boot camps in sales skills, ranging from how to maintain eye contact with prospective clients to how to divine the legal problems of companies that didn't even know they had problems. Employees are also taught that "The client rules."[63] Unless someone works in a job that does not involve working with others, he or she must learn to get along with people. At EMC, the focus on serving customers is so ingrained into the everyday function of the company that the running joke around the office is that EMC actually stands for "Everybody Makes Customer Calls" (E and M are for founders Richard Egan and Roger Marino; the full name is "EMC Corporation"). The company newsletter, called *EMC. Now,* features stories about employees who exemplify the culture EMC aspires to, in the hope that it reinforces that kind of behavior throughout the company. (A recent issue profiled the work of the Customer Action Committee, a group that deals with resolving customer problems.)[64]

In growing numbers, people with sparse, if any, sales experience are coming to terms, one way or another, with jobs that demand a more sales-oriented approach than they once did. As mentioned earlier, in developing a buyer–seller relationship, engineers, accountants, logistics experts, and data processors are likely to be drawn into selling. The Wicker Corporation, a maker of equipment for the plastics industry, is one example. Starting last year, the Atlanta-based company instituted a program designed to motivate its engineers, researchers, and manufacturing staffers to get involved in sales. "It seemed like our salespeople were running dry as far as getting high-quality leads," says James Kurd, vice president of sales. So the company began paying others for their efforts in the sales process. They were awarded bonuses if they provided leads that turned into sales, and they began calling on customers with the salespeople. "Our new business went up 15 percent last year," Kurd says. "A big reason is because we got others in the company involved in sales. They helped provide a different voice while on sales calls, and they identified new prospects."[65]

2. The second reason for studying a course in personal selling is to allow undergraduates to discover if selling is really for them—to "test the waters," if you will—before they commit themselves to a job as a salesperson. It represents a low risk strategy for determining the direction of one's professional career.

3. The skills taught in a course in professional selling have immediate payoffs and long-term benefits in job performance. Table 1-4 shows the factors employers consider most important in selecting a hiree. Note that communication and interpersonal skills are among the most important attributes for a graduating student to possess. Bill Coplin, author of *10 Things*

T a b l e   **1-4**   Factors in Rating Student Attributes

The Rating Criteria

Recruiters in the *Wall Street Journal*/Harris Interactive survey rated each business school on these student and school attributes. Here is the percentage of recruiters who said each attribute was "very important."

Attitude	Percent Very Important
Communications and interpersonal skills	90
Ability to work well within a team	87
Analytical and problem-solving skills	85
Personal ethics and integrity	84
Quality of past hires	81
Leadership potential	75
Fit with the corporate culture	74
Strategic thinking	67
Likelihood of recruiting "stars"—that is, graduates who are very likely to be promoted within the company	64
Student "chemistry"—that is, the general like or dislike you have of the students overall	49
Willingness of students to relocate to the job location you require	47
Original and visionary thinking	47
Retention rate of past hires	37

Source: "Factors in Rating Student Attributes," *Wall Street Journal,* September 17, 2003. Copyright © 2003 by Dow Jones & Co., Inc. Reproduced with permission of Dow Jones & Co., Inc. in the format Textbook via Copyright Clearance Center. (ONLINE) From "Factors in Rating Student Attributes" which appeared in Wall Street Journal, September 17, 2003. Reprinted with permission of Wall Street Journal, Copyright © 2003 Dow Jones & Company, Inc. All Rights Reserved Worldwide.

Employers Want You to Learn in College, stresses the importance of establishing a work ethic, developing physical skills, communicating verbally, communicating in writing, working directly with people, influencing people, gathering information, asking and answering the right questions, and solving problems.[66] Moreover, sales skills taught in the course are of immediate value on the job. Most college students gripe that they can't do anything in the real world with majors like English, history, and philosophy. Dale Mizer solved that problem: He majored in sales. Now the 27-year-old University of Akron alumnus is making more than $50,000 a year as a concrete and masonry distributor.[67] "If I had just studied liberal arts, I wouldn't have a college degree right now—it wouldn't have held my attention," says Mizer. For Mizer, the son of two Northeast Ohio factory workers, majoring in sales was a crucial first step up the socioeconomic ladder. "My parents have been working in a factory for 30 years, staring at the same four walls every day," he says. "It's a warped life, and I would go crazy doing that. I need to be out in the field, in new situations, meeting new people every day. I wanted to learn to sell." All three of these skills are taught in a personal selling course. Preparing written sales proposals and making oral presentations are an integral part of the course; the latter, especially in the form of role-playing exercises, will help develop poise. Additional studies show that the biggest reason for failure—especially in the early and middle stages of a manager's career—and the most crucial flaw to recognize and remedy is deficiency in interpersonal skills.[68] "Our surveys show that executives who have advanced the fastest here have strong interpersonal skills," says Wayne Davis, corporate staffing representative at Baxter Healthcare in Deerfield, Illinois.[69] The teaching of interpersonal skills is an integral part of a good personal selling course. People must be able to sell other people on themselves and their ideas. Whenever managers are asked about skills needed for success, they invariably indicate that the ability to interact with and motivate people is a critical one. One study showed that high-achieving executives could work successfully with others; low achievers could not. Stanford Research Institute says that the money one makes in any line of endeavor is determined only 12 1/2 percent by knowledge and 87 1/2 percent by one's ability to deal with others. The Carnegie Foundation spent $1 million over a 5-year period for research that proved that only 15 percent of a person's ability to get a job, keep a job, and move ahead in that job was due to knowledge, and 85 percent was due to his or her ability to deal with people.[70]

4. To survive in the next few decades, all businesses will have to focus on understanding and fulfilling customer needs. When it comes to understanding customer thinking, no entry-level position does a better job of training than selling. In the corporate decision-making process, especially at the executive level, the opinion of the person who has sold to the customer is held in higher regard than that of the theoretician. This should bring about a swifter promotion of those with sales experience into the ranks of senior management.

5. As a consumer, you need to know about selling. Everyone deals with salespeople at one time or another. You deal with retail sales personnel each time you go to the store. Also, you might someday become a purchasing agent—perhaps even an executive—and find yourself dealing with salespeople on a day-to-day basis. The more you know about their activities, the better you will be able to interact with them and perform your own job.

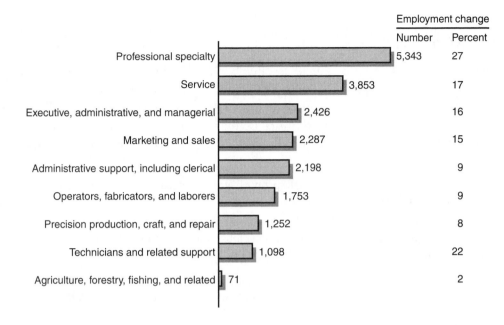

Figure 1-4
Employment Growth by Major Occupational Group, Projected 1998–2008
Source: Occupational Outlook Quarterly, Winter 1999–2000, p. 11.

6. Selling offers numerous employment opportunities at attractive salaries. Selling can be a rewarding career for college graduates who are willing to work hard. The Bureau of Labor Statistics reports that almost 16 million people work in sales in the United States.[71] Included in this figure are manufacturing sales personnel, real estate brokers, stockbrokers, and salesclerks working in retail stores. In fact, however, virtually every occupation that involves customer contact has elements of selling. Attorneys, accountants, bankers, and personnel recruiters all sell, whether they would like to admit it or not. About 20 percent of the CEOs in the 1,000 largest U.S. corporations have sales and marketing backgrounds, like Anne Mulcahy at Xerox. Although sales is the most frequent of job skills training, unfortunately only 30 percent of all firms provide sales training in any form (see Figure 1-4). This, of course, varies by the size of the firm; 58 percent of medium-sized firms offer sales training and 71 percent of large firms.[72] Because career choice is such an important topic, it will be covered in depth in Chapter 2, "A Career in Selling." The field is wide open.

Chapter Summary

This chapter presented an overview of the field of personal selling from both the standpoint of the economy as a whole and that of the individual firm. The place of personal selling in the promotional strategy of the marketing manager was indicated, along with an explanation of the differences between personal selling and advertising.

Next, the steps in the selling process were outlined: (1) precall preparation, (2) prospecting, (3) the approach, (4) the presentation, (5) handling objections, and (6) closing.

The duties of salespeople while progressing through these steps were discussed. These include dispensing knowl-edge to customers, acting as a source of intelligence to management, providing service, contacting buyers, and coordinating the selling effort. It was emphasized that the marketing concept should guide the salesperson in performing these duties. A discussion of probable changes in the salesperson's job through the twenty-first century followed. The chapter ended with six important reasons for studying selling, whether the student plans a career in sales or in another occupation.

Discussion Questions

1. What are the three basic economic utilities? With which is marketing most closely associated?

2. "Selling serves no useful purpose in our economy." Discuss.

3. "If you build a better mousetrap, the world will beat a path to your door." Discuss.

4. Explain how selling helps to lower costs.

5. What is the marketing mix? How does selling fit into it?

6. A friend of yours has just opened a retail store called The Computer Shoppe. In the store are home computers that can handle myriad tasks, from balancing a checkbook to regulating the heating system. He has asked you to recommend whether he should emphasize advertising or personal selling. What is your recommendation?

7. In what ways does personal selling differ from advertising? In what respects are they similar?

8. Cite some examples of products and companies that failed. What happened?

9. "All salespeople do is talk with customers." Discuss.

10. What are the typical duties of a salesperson?

11. What is the marketing concept? How has it evolved over the years? Do you think it needs to be updated? Why?

12. What is relationship selling? How will it affect selling in the future?

13. "Salespeople haven't changed at all over the years." Discuss.

14. What developments are likely to change the salesperson's job in the twenty-first century?

15. Define New Marketing.

16. Your roommate has just told you, "There's no reason for me to study selling. I'm going to be a CPA in an accounting firm." How would you respond?

17. Why study personal selling?

18. Explain the steps in the selling process.

Chapter Quiz

1. Selling (and marketing in general) helps to provide all of the following utilities *except*
   a. possession.
   b. time.
   c. place.
   d. title.

2. Selling benefits society in all of the following ways except that it
   a. increases total demand.
   b. helps fight inflation through increasing the number of buyers and encouraging less expensive methods of production.
   c. increases the wage rate through increased production.
   d. acts as an agent of change in society by promoting better ways of doing things.

3. In many types of sales positions, sales representatives must identify potential new customers for their wares and qualify them (that is, make sure they have the need, ability, and authority to buy). This activity is conducted during the _____ step of the selling process.
   a. precall preparation
   b. prospecting
   c. approach
   d. problem recognition

4. To provide buyers with useful buying information, salespeople must engage in extensive precall preparation, which involves the salesperson's
   a. gaining an in-depth knowledge about the buyer's company, their product, their competition, and the industry in which they work.
   b. qualifying the buyer through making sure the buyer has the need, ability, and authority to buy.
   c. capturing the attention and interest of the customer.
   d. building a relationship with the customer.

5. In the process of talking with contact-lens wearers, salespeople from SmithKline kept coming across the same problem: "itchy-scratchy eyes." Based on the suggestions of the sales force, the company began working on the problem. This illustrates the duty of salespeople to
   a. dispense knowledge to customers.
   b. provide a service.
   c. act as a source of intelligence to management.
   d. coordinate the selling effort.

6. Under the marketing concept, the task of personal selling is defined as the process
   a. of analyzing potential customers' needs and wants and assisting them in discovering how such needs and wants can be best satisfied by purchase of a particular product, service, or idea.
   b. of convincing customers to buy, even when a standardized product does not perfectly match a customer's needs.
   c. of analyzing potential customers' needs and wants and then convincing customers to buy a particular standardized product.
   d. of concentrating on developing long-lasting relationships with buyers as well as suppliers throughout the life of a product.

7. All of the following are trends for personal selling in the twenty-first century *except*
   a. more relationship selling.
   b. longer product life cycles.
   c. more team selling.
   d. more college graduates.

8. Because personal selling provides many skills needed by individuals and businesses, it is an important course for college students. According to recruiters in the *Wall Street Journal*/Harris Interactive survey, the most important attribute for a potential employee to possess is
   a. the ability to work well within a team.
   b. analytical and problem-solving skills.
   c. personal ethics and integrity.
   d. communications and interpersonal skills.

9. Of all of the various types of salespeople, the ones most affected by advances in computer technology are salespeople who
   a. work with manufacturers.
   b. call on retailers.
   c. sell high-tech types of products.
   d. are involved in team selling.

10. Because of computer technology, orders will automatically be forwarded to vendors when supplies drop low. For a company to switch to a new vendor, the benefits will clearly have to outweigh the costs of making the requisite computer changes. In this environment, to be successful salespeople will have to
   a. spend considerably more time developing relationships with buyers.
   b. utilize teleconferencing to reduce the cost of sales calls with prospects that are not likely to make the switch.
   c. form teams with computer experts in order to convince companies they have the capability to provide the product as well as make the necessary computer changes.
   d. expend much effort on researching buyer needs to discover competitive advantages.

Web Exercise

Siebel is a company specializing in products to assist with customer relations, tracking, and care. Visit their site for CRM at www.siebel.com. How does Siebel sell its products to small companies? To large ones? What features does it emphasize in its introduction to CRM software? Explore the website fully and list the features offered for various packages of software that might be used by the following Siebel clients: a small, family-owned car dealership; a large (500+ employees) restaurant supply company; and an insurance company of about 35 employees.

Notes

1. U.S. Department of Commerce, Bureau of Economic Analysis, www.bea.gov/bea/newsrel/gdpnewsrelease.htm, 2004.
2. Alan C. Reddy and David P. Campbell, *The Path to Wealth*, Westport, CT: Quorum Books, 1994.
3. Tim Carrington, " 'Know-How Funds' from West Teach Capitalist Survival to Czechoslovaks," *Wall Street Journal*, December 27, 1991, p. A12.
4. Ibid.
5. G. Pascal Zachary, "Seeing the Wizard Anew, As Marketer," *Wall Street Journal*, March 15, 1995, p. A12.
6. "The Comeback Kids," *Business Week*, September 29, 2003, pp. 116–118.
7. Ibid.
8. "Selling at the Top," *Success*, March 1988, pp. 44–47.
9. Nora Isaacs, "Crash & Burn," *Upside*, March 13, 2001, No. 3, pp. 186–192.

10. Chris Easingwood and Anthony Koustelos, "Marketing High Technology: Preparation, Targeting, Positioning, Execution," *Business Horizons,* May/June 2000, pp. 27–34.

11. Peter Schulz and Jack Cook, "Porsche on Nichemanship," *Harvard Business Review,* March–April, 1996, pp. 98–106.

12. Karen Ritchie, "Marketing to Generation X," *American Demographics,* April 1995, pp. 34–39.

13. Amber Holst, "Online Grocer Peapod Feels Chill of Its Rivals' Failures," *Wall Street Journal,* July 23, 2001, p. B6.

14. Leonard L. Berry, "The Old Pillars of New Retailing," *Harvard Business Review,* April 2001, pp. 131–137.

15. Dr. Frank T. Piller, TUM Research Center, Mass Customization & Customer Integration, www.mass-customization.de/index_english.htm, 2004.

16. "What a Sales Call Costs," *Sales & Marketing Management's 2000 Cost per Sales Call Survey.*

17. "Channels by Industry," *Sales & Marketing Management,* 1998, pp. 12–01.

18. Kerin, et al., *Marketing,* McGraw-Hill, New York, 2003, pp. 574–576.

19. Erin Strout, "Only the Strongest Survive," *Sales & Marketing Management,* November 2000.

20. American Teleservices Association, www.ataconnect.org/index.html, 2003.

21. Jan Gelman, "Something to Sink Their Teeth Into," *Selling,* September 1995, pp. 70–72.

22. "America's 25 Best Sales Forces," *Sales & Marketing Management,* July 2000, pp. 57–85.

23. Chris Taylor, "The Salesman of Silicon Valley," *Business Week,* December 22, 2003.

24. "How Much Are Customer Relationship Capabilities Worth?" www.accenture.com, 2001.

25. B. G. Tovovich, "Partnering at Its Best," *Business Marketing,* March 1992, pp. 36–37.

26. "America's 25 Best Sales Forces," *Sales & Marketing Management,* July 2000, pp. 57–85.

27. Dana James, "Lighting the Way," *Marketing News,* April 1, 2002, pp. 1, 11.

28. "Creating and Sustaining Customer Value through Cross-Functional Team Selling," *Markering Newsnet,* McGraw-Hill, 2003.

29. Jaclyn Fierman, "The Death and Rebirth of a Salesman," *Fortune,* July 25, 1994, p. 80.

30. www.biz.yahoo.com/ic/11/11198.html, 2004.

31. John E. Richardson and David L. Ralph, "The Ethical Treatment of Customers," *Annual Editions: Marketing,* McGraw-Hill/Dushkin, 2002.

32. David Cravens, "The Changing Role of the Sales Force," *Marketing Management,* Fall 1995, pp. 49–57.

33. Rahul Jacob, "Why Some Customers Are More Equal Than Others," *Fortune,* September 19, 1994, 223.

34. George Meadow, "Selling Has Changed," *Sales & Marketing Management,* July 2000, pp. 23–46.

35. Eugene H. Fram and Martin L. Presberg, "Customer Partnering—Suppliers' Attitudes and Market Realities," *Journal of Business & Industrial Marketing,* Vol. 8 (4), 1993, pp. 43–51.

36. Robert J. Berling, "The Emerging Approach to Business Strategy," *Business Horizons,* July–August 1993, p. 16.

37. Jagdish N. Sheth and Rajendra S. Sisodia, "High Performance Marketing," *Marketing Management,* September/October 2001, pp. 18–23.

38. Marilyn Kennedy Melia, "The E-Volving Salesman," *Chicago Tribune,* June 11, 2000.

39. Mary Lou Roberts, *Internet Marketing,* New York: McGraw-Hill, 2002, p. 14.

40. Mike Sweeny, "Selling in 1990," *Personal Selling Power,* October–November 1992.

41. Thayer C. Taylor, "Making More Time to Sell," *Sales & Marketing Management,* May 1994, p. 40.

42. Thayer C. Taylor, "How the Game Will Change in the 1990s," *Sales & Marketing Management,* June 1989, p. 157.

43. Rayna Skolnik, "Customer Relationship Management through Call Centers," Sales Marketing Network at info-now.com, No. 1211.

44. "New Tools for Presentations," Sales Marketing Network at info-now.com, No. 7610.

45. Ibid.

46. Betsy Cummings, "Tools of the Trade," *Sales & Marketing Management,* October 2003.

47. Micahael Kessler, "Smartphones Increasingly Leaving PDAs in the Dust," *Wall Street Journal,* February 10, p. B1.

48. Betsy Cummings, "Tools of the Trade," *Sales & Marketing Management,* October 2003.

49. "Outlook and Earnings for College Graduates, 2000–2010: College at Work," *Occupational Outlook Quarterly,* Fall 2002, p. 14.

50. Francy Blackwood, "From Salesperson to Consultant," *Selling,* July/August 1995, p. 55.

51. Mary Connors, "From 'I' and 'Me' to 'Us' and 'We': The Future Belongs to the Team," *Selling,* July/August, 1995, p. 52.

52. "Know Thy," *Sales & Marketing Management,* January 2003.

53. Marilyn Kennedy Melia, "The E-Volving Salesman," *Chicago Tribune,* June 11, 2000.

54. Suzanne Alexander, "Research Firm Taps Oceans of Data to Bail Out Clients," *Wall Street Journal,* April 3, 1990. p. B2.

55. "Helpful Hints and Faux Pas in International Sales," *InfoWorld,* September 16, 1995.

56. Bruce Bolger, "The New Marketing," Sales Marketing Network at info-now.com, No. 9105.

57. S. Tamer Cavusgil, "Extending the Reach of E-Business," *Marketing Management,* March/April 2002, pp. 24–29.

58. Bruce Bolger, ibid.

59. Bruce Bolger, ibid.

60. Marilyn Kennedy Melia, "The E-Volving Salesman," *Chicago Tribune,* June 11, 2000.

61. Jack Kopnisky, "Breaking the Mold," *Sales & Marketing Management,* January 2004.

62. Ibid.

63. Tyzoon T. Tyebjee and Albert V. Bruno, "Developing the Marketing Concept in Public Accounting Firms," *Journal of the Academy of Marketing Science,* Spring 1992, pp.165–188.

64. Erin Strout, "Only the Stongest Survive," *Sales & Marketing Management,* November 2000.

65. "Everyone's a Seller," *Sales & Marketing Management,* March 2003.

66. Margo Frey, "College Grads Need Good Skill Set to Go with Grades," *Milwaukee Journal Sentinel,* November 23, 2003.

67. Geoffrey Brewer, "Can You Teach People to Sell?" *Sales & Marketing Management,* July 1998.

68. Tony Lee, "Making an Impression," *National Business Employment Weekly,* Spring 1999, pp. 30–31.

69. Thayer C. Taylor, "How Popular Is Sales Training?" *Sales & Marketing Management,* December 1994, p. 38.

70. *Wall Street Journal,* August 22, 1992, p. 1.

71. *Occupational Outlook Quarterly,* Winter 1999–2000, p. 11.

72. "Who's the Boss," *Sales & Marketing Report,* May 2001, p. 7.

Case 1-1

Len Jones, known as "Lenny of the Valley" in his advertisements, has just contracted to buy three DVD players for his automobile dealership. When attached to a television set, they will play back up to two hours of video stored on each side. Len plans to record presentations about the cars he sells at his dealership. When a customer walks into the showroom, he or she will pick out the tape for the appropriate model and watch a taped presentation about the car. Each car will have a non-negotiable sticker price (basically, manufacturer's invoice plus $100) affixed to a side window. There will be no deviation from this price and the consumer must take the car with its options as is.

Ted, Len's accountant, has commented, "Why do we even need to keep the salespeople around? We have to pay each of them $500 per week and much of the time they're not even dealing directly with customers. Each machine will cost us $295, but that's it, except for periodic maintenance."

Len promised to think over Ted's statement. He cannot imagine there being any fun in having machines rather than sales personnel around the floor; but on the other hand, Ted's argument makes a lot of sense.

Question

1. How would you advise Len? Does he need a sales force to sell cars?

Case 1-2

For years, Stan Sibley saved money for the day when he could open his own restaurant. Finally, Stan has opened the Gourmet Sandwich Shoppe at the corner of Sixth and Jackson, just across from the University of Wisconsin. It has long been Stan's contention that "if you make a quality sandwich, the public will pay for it." At the Gourmet Sandwich Shoppe, the menu includes such delicacies as the "Alaskan Crab Delight," "American Sirloin Sandwich," and "Italian Pizza Treat," the last being made with imported Italian sausages and cheeses. Other gourmet sandwiches appear on the menu, with none of them costing less than $12.95. Side dishes are also available, including batter-fried mushrooms and cauliflower, American fried potatoes, and Caesar salad. Soft drinks are offered, as are beers such as Beck's, Guinness, and Heineken.

Stan believes that his sandwiches will appeal to the college students at the university. He insists, "After eating a steady diet of dormitory food, they should be glad to have my shop right across the street."

Questions

1. Do you think Stan is following the marketing concept or an earlier selling orientation?
2. Has Stan chosen the correct target market? If not, what is the correct market? How would you change the marketing mix for his Gourmet Sandwich Shoppe?

A Career in Selling

Key Terms

developmental selling
emotional intelligence
maintenance selling
missionary selling

new-business selling
permanence
personalization
pervasiveness

retail selling
technical selling
teleselling
trade selling

Learning Objectives

Learning Objectives

After studying Chapter 2, you will understand:

- That selling is not a mystery and that selling skills can be learned and developed
- That salespeople are made and not born
- How the popular stereotype of salespeople is incorrect
- The diversity of sales positions
- The differences between trade, missionary, technical, new-business, retail, and telephone selling
- The rewards and drawbacks of a career in sales
- What it takes to be successful
- How to build a positive self-image

Chapter 1 examined the role of the salesperson and explained how the nature of selling has changed in recent years. As a consequence, the type of individual needed for professional selling has also changed. This chapter examines a career in sales, beginning with a discussion of some mistaken but common myths about selling that keep many from choosing this rewarding profession. In fact, the entire profession suffers from a serious image problem (even calling sales a "profession" is subject to debate in some circles). Selling is constantly being disparaged, ridiculed, sneered at, mocked. A *Reader's Digest* poll conducted by Ipsos-Reid shows that pharmacists (91%), doctors (85%), and airline pilots (81%) are given top marks for "trust." This is in comparison to national politicians (9%), car salespeople (10%), and local politicians (14%), who are at the bottom of the list.[1]

2-1 Myths about Selling

Like any other profession, but more than most, selling is hindered by misconceptions. Because selling involves human interaction, people are perhaps too willing to accept ill-founded beliefs without question. Since communication between people cannot be readily reduced to a mathematical formula, myths about selling have developed that are false and counterproductive to success. Two of these myths are that selling is a mystery and that salespeople are born.

2-1a "Selling Is a Mystery"

According to this myth, selling is unknowable, and we can never hope to understand it. Even some salespeople with years of experience believe this. Unfortunately, this idea is much too pessimistic, and it discourages attempts to improve one's selling skills. Through modern behavioral research, some of the complexities of human interaction have become known. The characteristics of good communication have been identified; hence, good communicators can be trained. Salespeople who are willing to devote the effort can improve their selling and communication skills.

2-1b "Salespeople Are Born"

It is widely believed that selling success requires a person to be born with sales ability. This myth has two severe effects. First, it discourages many from entering the selling profession, although with experience and training they could develop into productive salespeople. Second, the myth of the born salesperson discourages attempts to study and learn selling skills, for what is the use of trying if success is predetermined by one's abilities at birth?

The truth is that there is no such thing as a "born salesperson." It is ridiculous to assume that someone is born ready to make sales calls, detail a product, handle objections, secure the close of a sale, and make service calls. Take Bill Gates, who many might consider to be an unlikely candidate as an example of a brilliant salesperson. Creating the technology that would change the world is one thing, but making the world believe in it took brilliant selling skills. "One of Gates' biggest strengths is his ability to invent the future," explains an entrepreneurial friend. "That takes innovative selling skills. Gates is a visionary who looked at the facts today and said, 'Out of these possibilities, what can come true tomorrow?' Once he did that, he knew how to commit himself and his company to making it happen." History proved that true. In 1975, Gates came up with the concept of "a PC on every desktop, a PC in every home." He was going out on a limb making that prediction 25 years ago. This was a time when computers were clunky game machines. Gates is only one example. Virtually every company head who has built a successful technology also boasts excellent selling skills.[2]

This is not to deny the existence of certain abilities that make it easier to become a salesperson. Some people are good speakers; others are good listeners. Some naturally present a good appearance, while others have to work at it. Some individuals are aggressive; some are rather unassuming. Still, all of these people must practice in order to become successful salespeople. Moreover, because there is more than one type of sales job, individuals with one type of personality may be better suited for some sales jobs but not for others. A wide enough variety of selling positions exists to accommodate all kinds of people, and the individual who works hard can be successful in most positions.

In fact, a review of past empirical research on the issue of requisite inherent traits reveals the following:[3]

1. No personal characteristic appears capable of explaining a very large percentage of variation in salesperson performance.
2. The studies suggest that different personal traits, aptitudes, and skills are required for success in different kinds of sales jobs.
3. On average, factors that sales managers can control or influence (e.g., role perceptions, skills, and motivation) account for the largest influence on performance.

2-2 Stereotype of the Salesperson

Unfortunately, the public at large generally has a poor image of personal selling. "Arrogant," "maladjusted," "deceitful," and similar terms are used to characterize the salesperson's image. The old-school misperception is that salespeople have to be overly aggressive, tenacious, and ready to pounce on prospects—a persona Blair Singer describes as the "Pit Bull" in his book *SalesDogs*. Singer, a Scottsdale, Arizona—based sales coach, also worked early in his career for Burroughs Corporation, where he says he was expected to be an "aggressive Pit Bull" when cold-calling, much to his embarrassment. He tried to become one through concentration, making about 60 unsolicited calls one day in attack-dog mode. "By the tenth call, I was screaming and ranting and raving, and I sold nothing that day," he says. "I didn't care what people were saying; they laughed, yelled, and swore at me. I thought, 'How much worse could it get?' "[4]

Our culture perpetuates, if not inflames, the despicable, greasy, slick, glad-handing image of salespeople.[5] Try recalling a movie or novel in which a salesperson played the hero. I bet you can't think of one. Now consider this sample of how authors, playwrights, movie producers, and TV scriptwriters have portrayed sellers: Classic fictional characters such as the tragic Willy Loman in Arthur Miller's *Death of a Salesman,* "Hickey" in Eugene O'Neill's *The Iceman Cometh,* and Harold Hill in Meredith Wilson's *Music Man* have contributed to the image. In the latter, Professor Harold Hill tries to dupe the parents of a small town into buying musical instruments for their children so the kids can start a marching band—even though none of them knows the difference between a tuba and a kazoo. In the movie *Cadillac Man,* Robin Williams plays a womanizing automobile salesperson who attempts to sell a new car to a funeral director, whose hearse has stalled and thus brought the parade to the cemetery to a halt. The salesperson leaves his business card with the bereaved widow, who has come to the front of the procession to see what's happened. In the 2000 movie *Boiler Room,* a young man has dropped out of Queens College but desperately wants to please his father, a federal judge who's harsh with his son. At his father's insistence, Seth Davis closes a casino he operates in his own house, mostly for college students. Thinking he'll please dad, he takes a job in a small brokerage house, an hour from Manhattan, where trainees make cold-calls to lists of well-paid men, and then apply high-pressure tactics to sell initial public offerings exclusive to the firm. He's terrific at sales. Once training is over, the pay is phenomenal, and Seth wonders why. Curiosity leads him to ethical dilemmas, encounters with the Feds, and new territory with his father.

Clearly, the arts have done the sales profession few favors. The stereotype and the downgrades are encouraged not just in entertainment but also in our everyday dialogues. We constantly hear of people "selling out" or being "sold a bill of goods." You don't brag to mom about being compared to a "used car salesman" or a "traveling salesman." And how many of us want to be "hustled" or "pitched" or "closed"?

Yet another major source of this dire stereotype are car dealers and insurance agents. For more than a century, some of the two have pitched consumers expensive and intimidating products with high-pressure tactics. Also, try the department stores and other retail shops where too often part-timers and high school students are selling pricey products (dishwashers, dining-room sets) without the proper qualifications. Or castigate those annoying telemarketers; they have conspired against us, picking our favorite hour—when we're trying to eat dinner—to pitch to us.

With all these negative stereotypes in literature and the movies, it is no wonder that when most people hear the word *salesperson,* honesty is one of the last things that come to mind. In addition to the poll cited earlier, when *People* magazine asked its readers to rank professions from 1 to 10 in order of trustworthiness, with "1" as the most trusted, sales representatives averaged 7.02. This rank was considerably lower than the ones for teachers (2.93) and doctors (3.48), and it was just above the rank for elected officials (7.23). A Gallup poll found that most people perceived car sales as the least ethical occupation among 26 careers considered (druggists and pharmacists finished first; the clergy, second; and dentists, third). Insurance salespeople didn't fare much better; they were voted 23rd, ahead of members of Congress but behind such folks as lawyers, labor union leaders, and even journalists.[6] The irony of this is that our own salespeople are different. Even the person who doesn't like insurance salespeople in general often has high regard for his own broker. He, of course, is different. Similarly, the fellow who sold them their last three cars isn't really a salesperson like all the rest. Of course, if this is universally true, then one wonders how the really stereotypical salespeople make a living.

The common image of the typical salesperson is not a positive one.

Still, a study of college students' attitudes about selling as a possible career uncovered the following responses:[7]

- Selling is a job, not a profession or a career.
- [Salespeople] must lie and be deceitful to succeed.
- Salesmanship brings out the worst in people.
- To be a good [salesperson], you have to be psychologically maladjusted.
- A [person] must be arrogant and overbearing to succeed in selling.
- [Salespeople] lead degrading and disgusting lives because they must be pretending all the time.
- The personal relations involved in selling are repulsive.
- Selling benefits only the seller.
- [Salespeople] are prostitutes because they sell all their values for money.
- Selling is no job for a [person] with talent or brains.

Although this study was done 30 years ago, evidently not much has not changed in the meantime. Recently, a study conducted by two professors at Texas Tech University basically duplicated this perception college students have toward the sales profession. Professors John Sparks and Mark Johlke asked 160 students in an introductory marketing class to read a series of scenarios involving salespeople and then answer questions regarding sales practices and ethics. The different scenarios featured both male and female reps, and the selling of technical and nontechnical products. According to Sparks, the collective results from the students' answers provided this conclusion: "Most college students don't have a favorable view of sales. In absolute terms, college students are not predisposed to a career in sales."[8] A recent survey conducted jointly by the University of Rhode Island and South Bank University in the United Kingdom reports that students—both here and abroad—have very low opinions of the sales profession. The study asked 544 students (about one-third each from the United States, the United Kingdom, and Thailand) to rank, in order of career preference, seven job opportunities in marketing: advertising, direct marketing, market research, product management, retailing, sales, and wholesaling. Advertising ranked first overall, and sales came in fifth, ahead of only retailing and wholesaling. In the United Kingdom and Thailand, sales ranked sixth. Although more than 72 percent of the respondents agreed with the statement that "the financial rewards from selling are excellent," 40 percent believed that a salesperson's job security was poor.[9] These attitudes toward selling exist despite their inappropriateness to a strategy based on the marketing concept. After all, salespeople who conduct themselves in a lying, deceitful manner would not remain in business long. They would always have to rely on finding new, unsuspecting customers, but even these buyers would dwindle in number as buyers heard about the salesperson's shady practices from others. The simple fact of the matter is that the stereotype is untrue. Let's examine why on a point-by-point basis:

1. "The personal relations involved in selling are repulsive." It has been said that the salesperson's job is to create an environment in which an act of faith can take place. In this light, the relationship between a buyer and seller must be based on mutual trust and honesty. This would hardly qualify as the "repulsive" relationship assumed in the stereotype.

Alfred Carl Fuller of Fuller Brush fame hardly fit the stereotype of a salesperson. He did not smoke, drink, gamble, or swear. He was a somewhat shy person who freely admitted preferring seclusion and contemplation. Intensely religious, Fuller was a warm, courteous gentleman. One writer said that Fuller gave the impression of a pleasant, undynamic farmer, who would never be able to sell a Fuller brush.

In truth, salespeople are in an enviable position. As with relatively few other professions, they are able to help people and directly observe their satisfaction with the results. This is the basis of the most rewarding relationships among people.

2. "To be a good salesperson, you have to be psychologically maladjusted." In truth, the really good salesperson has to possess a lot of maturity. Selling frequently involves rejection; not every call will be successful, and because rejection creates strain, the salesperson must be better adjusted than the average person.

3. "Salespeople must lie and be deceitful in order to succeed." This is totally in conflict with the marketing concept. The majority of corporations rely on repeat business for sales. If customers have been deceived, repeat sales will not materialize, and the company will find itself in trouble. You might fool someone in the short run, but eventually the customer is going to find out, and the long-run profitability of the company will suffer.

4. "Selling benefits only the seller." Again, this element of the salesperson's stereotype is false. According to the marketing concept, the true goal of the firm is to satisfy consumers' needs. An examination of most product failures will show that the product failed to meet such need.

5. "Selling is no job for a person with talent or brains." Successful selling requires the ability to analyze a customer's business, determine his or her needs and problems, and recommend a solution. This is not an easy process, because customers do not always have a ready picture of their problems in mind. An accurate assessment of client need requires great observational, analytical, and communication skills on the part of the salesperson. The development of these skills requires intelligence, talent, and training.

Further confirmation of the inaccuracy of the selling stereotype is offered in a survey of purchasing agents (PAs), the group most often in contact with professional salespeople. According to them, sales representatives shouldn't be pushy, arrogant, dishonest, unreliable, condescending, too talkative, or ignorant about their products. The qualities they liked best are "honesty, admits mistakes, dependable, problem-solving capabilities, adaptability, well-prepared, knows my business, and patience."[10] Similar results are evident in another recent study.[11] A survey of customers in various industries found these traits in salespeople to be most bothersome: difficult to communicate with, don't know customer's company, overaggressiveness, slow delivery, and overpromising.

2-3 Types of Sales Efforts

A fundamental source of the myths about selling and the stereotype of the salesperson is the general public's failure to recognize the wide diversity of selling jobs. The stereotype is based on an outmoded image of the "traveling salesman." The truth of the matter is that many different sorts of selling positions exist, and only a few resemble that of the old traveling drummer.

It is easy enough to say that there are many different types of sales jobs; it's considerably more difficult to come up with a classification scheme that is both descriptive and complete. For this reason, there are several ways of classifying sales positions. Some categorize jobs by the type of employer. Under this method, one might be a manufacturer's salesperson, a wholesaler's salesperson, a retail salesperson, or even a self-employed manufacturer's agent. Other methods classify positions by the type of customer: industrial (including governmental and institutional), trade (wholesale and retail), and individual consumers. Others classify sales jobs by the product itself. One might sell a tangible physical product, an intangible (such as insurance), or even a specialty or staple item. Other classification methods are based on the purposes of the buyer, the characteristics of the salesperson (part-time or full-time, etc.), the features of the sale (bid versus negotiation), or a hierarchy of sales jobs arranged in order of increasing amounts of selling creativity.

The classification method we shall examine in depth cuts across industry boundaries to a large degree and is behaviorally based. That is, it is based primarily on what the salesperson actually does on the job. It places salespeople in six categories: trade selling, missionary selling, technical selling, new-business selling, retail selling, and teleselling.[12]

2-3a Trade Selling

Trade selling predominates in the food, textile, apparel, and wholesaling industries. The primary task of trade salespeople is to build sales volume for their company through promotional assistance. If the product is well established, personal selling is less important than advertising and sales promotion efforts. Traditionally, this type of selling has tended to be low-key, and trade sales representatives aren't pressured to prospect and get orders from new customers, as are some other kinds of salespeople. For a complete description of trade selling, see Table 2-1.

Let's follow the trade salesperson on a typical sales call. A sales representative for a national food company might call on a supermarket manager about a new advertisement or coupon the company is using; the salesperson's objective is to gain additional shelf space. Trade salespeople are responsible for administering contracts for co-op advertising funds with supermarkets, and it is quite common for them to plan and lay out such advertisements before approaching customers with their recommendations. After checking existing inventory, the salesperson might discuss reasons for consumer acceptance of the product, any deals and allowances, some point-of-purchase materials the supermarket manager should display to build trade, and matters of cost, price, and profit margins. Trade salespeople have little if any contact with supermarket shoppers, the ultimate users of their products.

Trade selling has traditionally been low-key, but there are signs that it is heating up, at least for those selling to the grocery trade. Total shelf space in supermarkets for many food categories has grown less than 8 percent in recent years. With food companies introducing 20 to 30 products a week, the problem of gaining shelf space for products has been exacerbated.[13]

Valerie Foster-Starr, a salesperson for Campbell Soup Company, recently lobbied a Chicago supermarket until she was allowed to move Aunt Jemima waffles

VIDEO

trade selling
The primary task of trade selling is to build sales volume through promotional assistance.

T a b l e **2-1** Some Aspects of Trade Selling

Trade Salespeople Can Expect

- Maintenance selling
- Contacts with distributors
- Limited technical expertise
- Personal characteristics needed: Empathy, congeniality, limited assertiveness

Trade sales can involve taking stock, store visits, and securing cooperative promotions, such as local advertising.

to the back of the frozen food case and fill the hole with Campbell's breakfast sandwiches. "It's a war," explained Foster-Starr. "You have to get that space." Every two weeks, Mark Wallace, an account manager for Quaker Oats Company, visits 22 Chicago areas to defend the shelf facings of more than 100 Quaker products. Juggling 200 Quaker instant oatmeal boxes, sliding them together, and packing them in, he eked out 15 inches' room for three more rows. It was Campbell's sales force that kept its frozen vegetables in pastry alive. Initially, many stores put the vegetable pastries next to the budget-priced frozen vegetables. Campbell salespeople persuaded grocers to move them to the more expensive end of their frozen-food cases, next to the fancy vegetables, where they were more successful.[14]

The trade salesperson has become more of a marketing consultant for a product category. The salesperson has to have data, market information, and myriad things not needed in past years, when a handshake and slap on the back were sufficient. If, for instance, a particular retail customer features Brand X napkins in its advertisements for one week every month but the brand commands only a 10 percent share of the napkin market, "that's probably a misallocation of ad space," claims a vice president for consumer sales at Kimberly-Clark. If, instead, the retailer advertised the leading brand in the category, "the store could really build category profits," he says.

Trade salespeople need to have greater analytical abilities than in the past. In effect, they will have to become marketers in partnership with retailers. The retailers with single-source market research information readily available from scanners know exactly the effects of promotion on consumers. They need not rely on less reliable data, such as the sheer amount spent on promotion by the manufacturer.

With single-source data, they now know exactly what items are moving. As more retailers become sophisticated users of this information, it will be more difficult for trade salespeople to execute promotion programs not in the retailers' best interests. It will demand that the sales rep explain a well-documented mutually beneficial promotion, rather than simply giving a retailer a price discount and hoping for the best.[15]

Because trade salespeople see their customers regularly, it is important for them to develop friendly relationships. Empathy, maturity, and customer knowledge are important traits; assertiveness, product knowledge, and persuasiveness are not, although competition may be intensifying in gaining shelf space. Technical knowledge of the product is less important than expertise in merchandising techniques, and merchandising's primacy is growing.

2-3b Missionary Selling

The primary responsibility of **missionary selling** is to provide the firm's direct customers (wholesalers and retailers) with personal selling assistance. This is done by providing product information to indirect customers and persuading them to buy from the firm's direct customers. For example, a brewer's sales rep might call on bar owners and attempt to persuade them to order the company's brand from its local distributor. Thus, a missionary sales force sells *for* its direct customers, whereas trade salespeople sell *through* them. Another example of missionary salespeople is those who work for Ansul, a manufacturer of high-quality fire extinguishers and other fire-protection equipment. The primary job of Ansul salespeople is to recruit new distributors and to assist both new and old distributors by working with their sales and service people, helping to sell and train product end-users municipal fire departments and manufacturers with potential fire hazards. Ansul salespeople spend their time making joint calls with distributor sales reps, training them on new products, riding service trucks to see how Ansul users and equipment are being cared for, and training user personnel in the proper use of fire-fighting equipment. For a complete description of missionary selling, see Table 2-2.

The archetypal example of missionary selling is represented by pharmaceutical "detail reps." Their objective is to call on doctors and persuade them to recommend or prescribe the product for the ultimate user, the patient. In the pharmaceutical industry, where reps often have nothing to distinguish themselves from their competition except their entertainment budgets, doctors are increasingly choosing to work with those who use such consultative approaches. Many of them, says Lisa Lane, a Clarksburg, New Jersey–based pharmaceutical sales consultant and trainer, are coming to expect more than mere bribery in return for their attention. What they want is a newspaper clipping, a journal article, something that establishes the rep's knowledge and background, something that makes a sales pitch worth the doctors' five free minutes in an afternoon. And

VIDEO

missionary selling
The primary responsibility of missionary selling is to provide the firm's direct customers (wholesalers and retailers) with personal selling assistance. This is done by providing product information to indirect customers and persuading them to buy from the firm's direct customers.

Table **2-2** **Some Aspects of Missionary Selling**

Missionary Salespeople Can Expect

- Maintenance selling
- Contacts with users to stimulate demand for distributors
- Considerable technical expertise (e.g., medical detail reps)
- Personal characteristics needed: Energy, verbal skills, persuasiveness

for many clients a free lunch doesn't carry that weight. Most pharmaceutical companies now put their salespeople through extensive training programs, so that those who don't have a background in science—although many of them do—are thoroughly educated. "You want to get in and you want to be aggressive, but you can't just have a direct approach with it," Lane says, "You're trying to build a relationship."[16] They don't actually "close" or take orders from physicians; they hope that "detailing" (explaining) the product to physicians will ultimately result in sales for pharmacies, their direct customers. Pharmaceutical salespeople visit physicians in their offices on a regular basis and provide up-to-date information on pharmaceutical products. They typically focus their efforts on new products, but describing new applications for existing ones is also common. To support their claims, detailers usually make available drug samples, product literature, and reprints of medical journal articles. In many companies, they are also given responsibility for calling on druggists to check their inventories, take care of returns, answer questions, and assist the druggist in ordering from the manufacturer, the detailer's employer. Pharmaceutical reps usually have less than five minutes once a month to make their points to doctors—and there may be as many as five competing salespeople a day pleading benefits and leaving free samples.[17]

New challenges are arising in the detail rep's environment. Historically, reps have only had to communicate technical information; with changes in the health care industry, however, economic justification is becoming more of a factor. Traditionally, the physician has been the sole decision maker for prescription items, but that is changing. The physician is no longer necessarily in private practice. Often, he or she is involved with health maintenance organizations or with other third-party payers, and they are demanding economic justification for a prescription decision. Managed-care networks must document the benefit and outcome of every treatment, which means that the detail reps have to do the same for their products. Pharmaceutical selling, then, is more sophisticated and demanding than in the past.

Pharmaceutical selling requires a great deal of technical knowledge. Merck uses an exemplary training program to turn new hires into the kind of salespeople who uphold the drug company's number one rating for service to pharmacists and doctors. Aspirants first study basic medical subjects including anatomy, physiology, and disease for 10 weeks, and they must score 90 percent or better on a weekly test to stay in the program. In phase two, they spend three weeks learning how to discuss and present Merck's products; then, they go on a trial basis for six months, making presentations in the field alongside their district managers. Phase three is another three weeks at headquarters, brushing up on presentation skills. Even after completing more than 11 months of training, salespeople must regularly attend "primary didactics," medical classes conducted at Harvard, Johns Hopkins, and other universities. "Training is our obsession," says Jerry Keller, a vice president at Merck.[18] On their own, pharmaceutical reps should keep current by reading company training bulletins and medical journals. They should be well versed in technical and laboratory specifications, and contraindications (that is, conditions under which drugs should not be used).

Missionary selling is low-key, as is trade selling. Missionary salespeople need to be energetic and articulate. They must make enough calls to ensure adequate coverage of the market, and they must be able to make a persuasive, but succinct, presentation of product features and benefits. They need not be particularly aggressive, because the people they call on don't order directly from them.

Missionary salespeople, often called "detail reps," explain new drugs to doctors and leave samples, hoping that patient trials will lead to formal prescriptions.

2-3c Technical Selling

Many products and services, especially those purchased by large companies and institutions, are highly complex. The primary responsibility of **technical selling** is to increase the company's volume of sales to existing customers by providing them with technical advice and assistance. In addition to maintaining current clients, technical salespeople help clients work out any problems that arise when the product is installed and may continue to serve as a liaison between the client and their company. In addition, due to their familiarity with the client's needs, sales engineers may help identify and develop potential new products.

This type of salesperson is well represented in the chemical, machinery, and heavy equipment industries. Technical reps often work with the customer and the production, engineering, or research and development departments of their company or of independent firms to determine how products and services could be designed or modified to best suit the customer's needs. They also may advise the customer on how to best utilize the products or services being provided. For a complete portrayal of technical selling see Table 2-3.

As an example of technical selling, consider the salespeople who work for the Tiffen Company, based in Hauppauge, New York, who have supplied photo optics to Hollywood for the past six decades. When the company manufactures photo optics, they guarantee them to be repeatable—that is, that the quality of the lens is consistent from one product to another. When film producers use three cameras on a shot, it's got to stay consistent when they cut from one to the other. The technical sales staff of 22 reps calls on cable TV stations and production companies. Their job is simply to listen and hear what the customers want. This is a technical

technical selling
The primary responsibility of technical selling is to increase the company's volume of sales to existing customers by providing them with technical advice and assistance.

Table **2-3** **Some Aspects of Technical Selling**

Technical Salespeople Can Expect

- Maintenance selling
- Contacts with industrial buyers
- Considerable technical expertise
- Personal characteristics needed: Analytical skills, interpersonal skills

market; "It's not a situation where we develop something and then try to shove it down their throats," remarks Steven Tiffen, CEO. Although Hollywood likes to do a lot of high-dollar marketing to consumers, selling to the industry itself is completely different. It's the product itself over anything, so the sales staff tries to listen to what kinds of shoots they want to do on a regular basis, and find out where the market is going.[19] Aircraft salespeople represent another example of primarily technical selling. Most have engineering degrees, and experience in aerospace manufacturing is a common route into sales. Airline experience is prized because a salesperson must navigate the airlines' bureaucracy and be fluent in the arcane language of load factors, spill, and gross takeoff weight. Selling transpires over long periods and involves in-depth analysis. Each airline sales rep becomes an expert on the airline for which he or she is responsible, determining where the airline wants to grow, when it wants to replace planes, and its financial requirements. It is typical to simulate through computers the customers' (and competitors') routes, cost per seat, and other components to demonstrate how their offering is superior.[20]

Compared with their trade and missionary counterparts, technical salespeople need analytical skills and technical expertise that helps them identify customer problems and recommend solutions. They must possess persuasive skills but not be so aggressive as to raise questions in customers' minds about their objectivity. They do not have to close (that is, get an order signed) very often, and when they do, they must act subtly; too much pressure can alienate customers for the long term. Finally, they must be able to interact amicably with many sorts of customer personnel: purchasing people, production controllers, engineers, high-level executives, and so on. Hence, important characteristics to have are education and product knowledge; traits of less importance are empathy, persuasiveness, and aggressiveness.

2-3d New-Business Selling

new-business selling
The primary responsibility of new-business selling is to seek and persuade new customers to buy from the firm for the first time.

This kind of selling is typified by canvassing, prospecting, bird-dogging, and cold-calling. The primary responsibility of **new-business selling** is to seek and persuade new customers to buy from the firm for the first time. This type of selling is represented in the sale of office copiers, data-processing equipment, and other business machines. Persuasiveness, persistence, and aggressiveness are prerequisites for the job. Strong closing skills are needed, and the new-business salesperson must be hardened to the rejection prevalent in the job. The greatest difficulty in new-business selling is the frequent rejection and deflation of one's ego. Challenge and independence are attractive job characteristics, and new-business salespeople are well paid for their efforts, since considerable selling skills are mandatory. A thorough depiction of new-business selling appears in Table 2-4.

T a b l e **2-4**   **Some Aspects of New-Business Selling**

New-business Salespeople Can Expect

- Developmental selling: Prospecting and closing critical
- Contacts usually with industrial buyers
- Considerable technical expertise
- Personal characteristics needed: Assertiveness, ego strength, persuasiveness

2-3e   Retail Selling

The characteristic that distinguishes **retail selling** from other types is that the customer comes to the salesperson. Whether selling shoes, computer equipment, or automobiles, retail salespeople assist customers in finding what they are looking for and try to interest them in buying the merchandise. They describe a product's features, demonstrate its use, or show various models and colors. For some sales jobs, particularly those involving expensive and complex items, retail salespeople need special knowledge or skills. For example, salespeople who sell automobiles must be able to explain to customers the features of various models, warranty information, the meaning of manufacturers' specifications, and the types of options and financing available.

Consumers spend millions of dollars every day on merchandise and often form their impressions of a store by evaluating its sales force. Therefore, retailers stress the importance of providing courteous and efficient service in order to remain competitive. When a customer wants an item that is not on the sales floor, for example, the salesperson may check the stockroom, place a special order, or call another store to locate the item. Salespeople also may handle returns and exchanges of merchandise, wrap gifts, and keep their work areas neat. In addition, they may help stock shelves or racks, arrange for mailing or delivery of purchases, mark price tags, take inventory, and prepare displays. Frequently, salespeople must be aware of special sales and promotions.[21]

The retail salesperson can also exercise creativity by suggesting and selling related items. The television buyer might also be sold a set of video games or a DVD player. The teenager who comes into a store to buy a dress or pair of slacks for Saturday's football game might also be sold a matching sweater and jacket. Knowledge of the items in stock, prices, and materials is critical to the success of the retail salesperson. Through suggestion selling, product expertise, and dedication to satisfying the customer, retail salespeople can do quite well. Graduation from a 4-year college typically qualifies one for management training with a retailer. Once initial training is completed, the graduate usually works as an assistant department manager, one of whose major responsibilities is to supervise and evaluate the department sales staff. Obviously, a thorough knowledge of selling techniques is needed for such a job.

Although retailing has traditionally had an image as an unsatisfactory profession for college graduates, this image is erroneous, given the career opportunities offered by contemporary retailers. As a result of discounters and explosive growth, thousands of managers must be hired or promoted each year to run new superstores for Wal-Mart, Home Depot, Target, Circuit City, Phar-Mor, and Computer City. Such positions offer quick advancement and pay that can run well into six figures. Starting pay is good; in Wal-Mart's training program. Twelve weeks out of school, they can have 20 employees working for them and responsibility for an

retail selling
The characteristic that distinguishes retail selling from other types is that the customer comes to the salesperson.

$8 million department. They can become managers of small stores in as little as three years, at an annual salary of $50,000 plus bonuses. Larger units, such as combination grocery and general merchandise stores, pay a base salary of more than $100,000 plus bonuses of as much as $40,000.[22]

teleselling
Salespeople who work in making telephone contact, inbound and outbound, with customers and prospects.

2-3f Teleselling

Teleselling involves salespeople who work in making telephone contact, inbound and outbound, with customers and prospects. U.S. companies spend $525 billion annually on telemarketing, and 2002 employment was 428,000.[23] The latter number is expected to decline in the near future, as the Do-Not-Call List, which provides a government registry for consumers who want to block sales calls, goes into effect.[24] However, more than 55 percent of telemarketing is business-to-business, and that percentage is growing. We are assuming here that business-to-business teleselling is the career path for college graduates. Because of rapidly changing technology, the call center is becoming an integral part of a company's customer relationship management strategy. Working with customers and prospects one-on-one, the call center can be as important as the direct sales force in gathering data, providing personalized attention, and creating customers for life.

As companies strive to differentiate themselves from their competition and build long-term relationships with loyal customers, they use every available marketing tool. Because of rapidly advancing technologies, the telephone is becoming one of the most potent tools in the kit. It can be integrated with other interactive media, such as direct mail, email, faxes, and the Internet, all of which can be used to create a dialogue with customers and prospects. For example, Internet shoppers can view a product and then click to talk with an operator who will answer a question or take an order. Nonetheless, the telephone is the only one of these channels that permits direct vocal contact. Consequently, its potential for making or breaking a customer relationship is greater than that of any of the other channels.

The evolution from call center to customer interaction center (CIC) is the result of changes in both managerial attitudes and telephone technology. Companies are realizing that the features and benefits of their product or service are no longer enough to attract and retain customers. To be a market leader, a company must offer superior service, and must do so in the course of each and every customer contact. As companies search for ways to strengthen service, they are rediscovering the call center, recognizing that it can be one of the most productive grounds for nurturing customer relationships. They also realize that a poorly managed call center, or one that is treated as an afterthought, can quickly destroy customer relationships.

As for technology, a steady stream of faster, "smarter" equipment continues to increase call-customization and customer-interaction capabilities. When technology provides a telephone services representative (TSR) with current, detailed data, the customer does not need to repeat information, thus removing a source of irritation for the customer and saving time for both parties. The customer feels important, even appreciated, and the TSR can comfortably assume responsibilities well beyond those of a conventional telemarketer. Today's TSR has immediate access to such information as product preferences, purchasing patterns, service history, and credit history, all of which can be used to cross-sell, sell a higher-price alternative, or make a special offer.[25]

The sort of individual required for telemarketing varies, depending on the breadth of the job. In some telemarketing jobs, repetition and structure are typical, with personnel expected to make calls and sell from a prepared script. It should be noted, however, that account management, which is the most advanced form of

Telesales, organization-to-organization selling, is a rapidly growing segment of the sales industry, as it is very cost-effective.

business-to-business telemarketing, requires many of the same creative problem-solving skills expected from the field rep. As the costs of field calls increase and as videoconferencing becomes more widespread, the latter will become more prevalent. Fidelity Investments, the largest seller of mutual funds in the world, for example, employs more than 2,000 telereps to answer investor calls. These telereps, who are all college graduates, have to pass intensive exams on investments to earn a license to provide information on mutual funds, stocks, and bonds. Moreover, they must pass Fidelity's own 14-week sales training program. When asked what he likes best about his job, Fidelity telephone representative James Marcus tells the story of a call from a woman who was recently widowed. "She was nervous and had no idea what to do about her finances," he recalls. "I reassured her that we would do our best to help, and then we went over her investments. By the time we finished, she felt comfortable. I like it when I help someone."[26]

Some types of teleselling are clearly more aggressive. Maria Bartolome is a master teleseller. She has never met a customer, never wined and dined a big account, and never made a face-to-face call, yet she has racked millions of dollars of sales for IBM. "What does it take," according to Bartolome? "You have to be on all the time," she says. "Telesales reps are constantly selling. They have to stay energetic and upbeat for hours on end. Tone of voice and attitude are critical. If you're not enthusiastic, it will show in your voice." Though telesellers have to be personable, they rely more on product expertise than charm. "Buyers," asserts Bartolome, "are interested in talking with someone who knows what they're talking about and can provide information quickly. And, they have to be able to close swiftly in a quick transaction." As might be expected from the latter, some have described teleselling as traditional selling played on fast forward.[27]

2-3g Putting It Together

By this time, readers may recognize the wide diversity of sales positions, but they may not yet have had a chance to review and assimilate this information. Table 2-5 integrates the discussion of selling tasks into one comprehensive form. It examines trade, missionary, retail, technical, new-business, and telemarketing selling with regard to several factors: maintenance selling versus developmental selling, contacts, technical expertise, and important personal characteristics. **Maintenance selling** typically involves (1) servicing existing accounts, (2) securing promotional cooperation, whether in the form of media advertising or point-of-purchase displays, (3) counting inventory and taking replenishment orders, (4) developing and perpetuating personal relationships with potential decision makers, and (5) delivering the product. In contrast, **developmental selling** is characterized by (1) locating and qualifying potential buyers, (2) securing specification and approval for purchases, and (3) closing sales (that is, actually getting the order). With maintenance selling, there is either an absence of dealing with orders (as in missionary selling) or, if there is order taking, it tends to be perfunctory. The customer takes the initiative in ordering, primarily from habit or from the influence of merchandising methods (for example, advertising, couponing, and so on). In contrast, order getting is characteristic of developmental selling. Here the salesperson must seek out potential buyers (who are not using the product or who are using a competitor's or a substitute product) and gain their order.

Within this framework, trade selling would be considered maintenance selling. Trade salespeople deal with existing customers, assisting them with merchandising and taking their orders for stock replenishment. Trade sales reps' contacts are with distributors and not the ultimate users of their products. Technical expertise, at least with respect to the product itself, does not have to be great, but knowledge of advertising, optimal store layout, credit policies, display methods, and pricing should be extensive to assist distributors in moving their goods. Trade sales reps should be mature and empathetic with their customers because they see them on a recurring basis. Outright aggressiveness is not appropriate, because trade reps service accounts over the long term; in the grocery trade, however, they must be assertive in securing shelf space for their product, often at the expense of competitors.

maintenance selling
Typically involves (1) servicing existing accounts, (2) securing promotional cooperation, whether in the form of media advertising or point-of-purchase displays, (3) counting inventory and taking replenishment orders, (4) developing and perpetuating personal relationships with potential decision makers, and (5) delivering the product.

developmental selling
Characterized by (1) locating and qualifying potential buyers, (2) securing specifications and approval for purchases, and (3) closing sales (that is, actually getting the order).

Table **2-5** A Classification of Sales Tasks

	Selling Type					
Task	*Trade*	*Missionary*	*Retail*	*Technical*	*New-Business*	*Teleselling*
Maintenance selling or developmental selling	Maintenance	Maintenance	Both	Maintenance	Developmental	Both
Contacts	Distributors, not the ultimate consumer	Users, to stimulate demand for distributors	Ultimate consumers	Typically, industrial buyers	Typically, industrial buyers (but may be individuals, as with insurance sales)	Business buyers, mostly
Technical expertise (with respect to the product)	Limited	May be considerable, as with medical detail rep	Limited	Considerable	Considerable	Moderate (but considerable in high-tech areas like computers)
Personal characteristics	Empathy, maturity, congeniality; assertiveness is of increased import in some fields (e.g., grocery trade)	Energy, verbal skills, persuasiveness	Congeniality	Analytical skills, interpersonal skills	Aggressiveness, ego, strength, persuasiveness	Pleasant voice, congeniality, energy, and aggressiveness in some fields

New-business salespeople engage in extensive developmental selling. They must continually prospect for new customers and get their orders for the product, which usually involves a dramatic change in customers' ways of conducting business. Since their contacts usually are industrial buyers, new-business reps must possess considerable technical expertise. New-business salespeople must be self-starters since they must continually seek out new customers with little direct supervision, and they must be assertive enough to close orders. They must possess considerable ego strength to withstand the rejection that goes along with new-business selling.

2-4 Rewards of a Sales Career

2-4a Monetary Rewards

The monetary rewards of a career in sales are illustrated in Table 2-6. Total compensation for executives rose about 6 percent in 2003 to $144,653, compared with 2002, with both bonuses and commissions rising 7 percent. Total compensation for sales staffs has also increased. The average total compensation rose 15 percent to $111,135, with top performers handsomely rewarded for good results; their total compensation rose 10 percent to $153,417. It is vital to reward the top performers because they bring in the most business.[28] And despite what you may believe, few salespeople are paid on a straight commission basis (though this figure was derived from a survey weighted toward manufacturers rather than services and high technology). Salary plus bonus (44%) is the most common form of sales compensation.[29] Reflecting the significance of relationship marketing, companies providing team performance reward increased in numbers from 5 percent to 13 percent in 2001.

Although beginning salaries for sales and marketing positions are somewhat less than those in technical fields such as accounting and engineering, the gap narrows after five years. After 10 years, salaries in sales and marketing are often higher than those in general business and engineering.

Companies are increasingly tapping the sales and marketing ranks for their top jobs.[30] Executives with backgrounds in sales and marketing are taking over. The reasons for the shifting hiring tendencies are numerous—the need for strong leaders, the increasing importance of profitable revenue at companies, a renewed focus on branding, and the important role a CEO plays in attracting and retaining top salespeople. However, one factor is critical: a strong focus on the customer. In recent years, companies have placed a higher importance on customer relationships. They've changed their sales strategies to emphasize building long-term partnerships with customers. And they're building profitable businesses on the notion that it's far cheaper to sell to current customers than it is to acquire new ones. Sales and marketing executives are the ones who

Table **2-6** Monetary Rewards

	Average Salary for Sales Staffers in 2003		
	Total Compensation	Base Salary	Bonus Plus Commissions
Executive	$144,653	$95,170	$49,483
Top performer	153,417	87,342	66,075
Mid-level performer	92,337	58,546	33,791
Low-level performer	63,775	44,289	19,486
Average of all reps	111,135	70,588	40,547

Source: "The 2004 Compensation Survey," by Christine Galea, *Sales & Marketing Management,* May 2004. © 2004 VNU Business Media, Inc. Used with permission from Sales and Marketing Management.

have this knowledge, this background with customers, this understanding of how nothing is more important than customer satisfaction. And it's no surprise that they're the ones being tapped to lead companies. "I think we are seeing more CEOs from sales and marketing because they have highly developed communication and persuasion skills," says Al Lewis, assistant dean and director of the Center for Entrepreneurial Management at the A. Gary Anderson School of Management at the University of California, Riverside. "And they have a high level of awareness about the importance of a customer." Take Jeffrey Immelt, for example. After 20 years of holding various sales and marketing positions at General Electric, Immelt took over Jack Welch's CEO office in September 2001. Although his pizzazz, charisma, and gregarious nature obviously helped get him the top spot, it is Immelt's sales and marketing experience and long history with customers that sealed the deal. "There's no doubt that Jeff has a track record of close relationships with customers," says Bill Fiala, an analyst who covers GE for Edward Jones. "He's already brought that sales and marketing experience to the CEO job. GE is so large and so many of its relationships are with some of the biggest companies in the world, solidifying those relationships is what Jeff's doing now."

Lisa Cash started out in sales in the mid-1980s at the Club Corporation of America, based in Dallas, Texas, working her way up to regional sales and marketing manager. In 1992 she joined Bell Atlantic (now Verizon), where she managed two separate, $100 million divisions. Intrigued by the fast-growing tech sector, Cash took a step back in her career to become part of a software company. She was hired as east coast sales manager of Princeton Softech in 1997. "I found myself bored after a few months, because I overestimated how difficult it would be to understand the business," she says. "So I started taking on all sorts of additional projects that utilized my experiences." One of those was to implement a telesales channel for the company. Cash says she's always felt that if something needs to be done she just does it, rather than leave it for someone else. That attitude—and her impressive résumé—earned her the adulation of Princeton Softech's vice president of sales. "I began getting more responsibilities that weren't typical of my job," she says. "By the end of 1999, I was operating more as a COO, dealing with departments not usually associated with sales." When the vice president of sales left, Cash got her job. And when the company's CEO (also one of its seven founders) decided to leave, it was Cash he recommended to replace him. Ann Mulcahy, the 24-year veteran of Xerox who worked up the ranks of the sales force and the human resources department until she was named COO and president in May 2000, is the real engine behind the company's recent turnaround, much of which was due to her reorganizing and reenergizing the sales force.[31]

Besides being well compensated, skilled salespeople can count on job security. If salespeople produce a profit for their company, it is unlikely that they will be laid off; the same cannot be said for many in middle-management positions, especially those in a staff capacity. Moreover, experienced salespeople are always going to be in demand by competitors and other companies in similar lines of business. When the securities firm of Drexel Burnham Lambert filed for bankruptcy, three-quarters of the sales force, the biggest producers, immediately found work at other securities firms.[32] To completely assess the nonfinancial rewards of a sales career, see Table 2-7.

2-4b Psychological Rewards

According to a survey given by industrial psychologists to 500,000 employees, the happiest workers are salespeople.[33] Although monetary remuneration is important, it is not the sole source of job satisfaction; the psychic rewards—the enjoyment one receives from performing the job itself—are equally important, and some would say

T a b l e **2-7**   **The Nonfinancial Rewards of a Sales Career**

- Monetary
- High rate of worker satisfaction
- Independence
- Direct relationship between efforts and results
- Psychological
- Enthusiasm and positive attitude carry over into personal life
- Intellectually challenging
- Satisfaction of helping people
- Variety

even more important. Certainly, selling has a number of attractions apart from money alone. First, there is the independence enjoyed by the salesperson. Once training is completed, many salespeople are relatively on their own. There's no one looking over their shoulders as there is in an office environment. Salespeople are free to set their own schedules and determine how much time and effort they will allocate to their customers. In many sales jobs, salespeople have complete control in deciding when they will work, where they will work, how long they will work, whom they will call on, and what they will do. Of course, they should not abuse this freedom.

The second psychological reward is that salespeople are often alone (or charged with responsibility in a team environment) in their territories; hence, they have the satisfaction of seeing a direct relationship between their efforts and what they achieve, something lacking in many other professions. After switching to a sales career path, Allison Farber described her prior desk job with Time, Inc. "At Time, politics played a big part in climbing the corporate ladder. Also, they made a lot of promises they never kept. Here [in sales], you prove yourself and your paycheck increases automatically. There's a lot I can do to make it myself. I can develop what I do into a whole department and go out and hire four people to sell under me. As I see it, in selling, whatever you put into it is what you get out of it."[34] Commented one sales rep, who had originally been a grocery buyer, "It would be extremely difficult for me to go back to the other side. I think I'd find it a little boring and a lot less fulfilling. There's a feeling you get when you land a major account that people who haven't experienced it can't know. It's similar to winning a football game. These have been the most rewarding years of my life."[35] More than most jobs in business, selling is a true meritocracy; its rewards are usually tied to one's real performance.

Third, the practices of professional selling carry over into a person's everyday life. The enthusiasm and positive attitude that characterize successful salespeople usually lead to active participation in community life. Salespeople are valued members of social, religious, and service clubs, as well as professional organizations.

The fourth psychological reward is that selling is intellectually challenging. In fact, it reminds one of a good detective story. Instead of whodunit, the mystery is: What needs to be done? Like a detective, the sales rep must sift through the clues, investigating even the smallest pieces of evidence, to build the overall picture that makes sense of the jigsaw. Most of the time this requires a number of calls and careful ongoing analysis. Oftentimes, winning the order is only a bonus; the real reward is the challenge.[36]

Yet another reward, perhaps the greatest, is the satisfaction of helping people. In few professions is it possible to see a direct relationship between one's actions and the satisfaction of others. Like doctors, professional salespeople diagnose problems and prescribe solutions. True, need satisfaction is the rationale for the existence of all business organizations, but sitting at a desk amongst coworkers makes it difficult to see the smile on the customer's face. Many salespeople are intimate friends of their customers, interacting socially or working together on community affairs.

Finally, no job in business provides the variety of sales. Where else does one get to meet so many new people, solve so many new problems, find oneself in so many different situations, and have an opportunity to learn so much? All too many jobs are repetitive, but not sales; diversity is the rule.

2-4c Some Drawbacks

No job is free of disadvantages. A career in selling also has some undesirable characteristics. Among these are long working days, the self-discipline needed for success, job pressures, travel, and the problems of handling dissatisfied customers.

Sometimes salespeople find it necessary to work beyond the normal 9-to-5 routine. Some appointments may have to be scheduled for early-morning breakfasts or late-evening meals, and paperwork sometimes requires late work. Although the independence of a selling career is attractive, it also represents a risk. It is all too easy to use one's time inefficiently. Sales managers universally agree that the primary reasons salespeople fail are a lack of initiative along with poor planning and a poor use of time.

In today's restructured and increasingly technical business environment, additional drawbacks have arisen.[37] Problems can exist with sales support staff. Complaints about employees paid to fill the orders, check the credit, and answer customer queries are common. High turnover and limited compensation are problematic here. Another contemporary complaint is that salespeople are ignored when it comes to the introduction of new products, although salespeople have the most intimate contact with customers and are often the best judges of which products will fail or succeed. Email is another common complaint; the sheer volume of messages is sometimes daunting. Salespeople also suffer from the disease of the information age: overload. Many reps are overwhelmed by the information sent to them by their companies—new products, new policies, new prospects, and so forth. One high-tech rep read 28 magazines a week and still found herself falling behind the technology. Online services that allow the rep to call up the latest company or industry news are a big help here.

Every profession has its drawbacks, such as those indicated in Table 2-8. Doctors are always on call. Business executives face pressure to meet deadlines and performance objectives. Accountants work long hours during tax seasons. Professional athletes are always on the road, living out of suitcases and making mistakes in front of crowds of thousands. On balance, personal selling is preferable to many alternative careers. In few other jobs can one see such a direct relationship between effort and reward. In many careers, especially those of the office variety, it is difficult to evaluate individual accomplishment. This is not the case with selling. What salespeople achieve is largely the result of their own efforts. At the end of the day, they can proudly point to customer problems solved, new accounts opened, and sales made.

T a b l e **2-8** **Some Drawbacks to Selling**

• Long working days	• Travel
• Mandatory self-discipline	• Handling dissatisfied customers
• Job pressures (e.g., meeting quotas and bonus)	

2-5 What It Takes

Despite years of research, no one has discovered a set of personality traits that is absolutely necessary for success in selling. Research has yet to find the profile of a "born salesperson." In other words, a mature individual who is willing to work hard and has good communication skills could develop equal proficiency as a trade, missionary, technical, or new-business salesperson. In this respect, the process of becoming a good salesperson is dynamic, and individuals should never stop trying to improve their skills.

Although no ideal set of characteristics has been found to guarantee success, a number of factors are strongly related to performance: hard work, working smart, the ability to set goals, emotional intelligence, a good appearance, communicative ability, dependability, honesty, and integrity. In some instances, the individuals may possess these traits instinctively, but in all cases, these characteristics can be developed through thought and careful practice. In the process of looking inward, however, one should be careful. It has been said that "perhaps no other occupation has been subjected to quite so much amateur analysis and pseudo-psychology as personal selling, without moving one step closer to an understanding of the problems and influences involved."[38] Still, a careful review of the characteristics enumerated in Table 2-9, in conjunction with a detailed analysis of personal strengths and weaknesses, can be a valuable exercise.

2-5a Hard Work

Salespeople who work hard are described as "motivated" and "self-starting" or are said to have "drive." These terms all mean the same thing: The people have initiative, persistence, and the ability to manage their own efforts. This is what recent college graduates notice first about sales. Brian Noyes, a new hire with Camadon, a marketer of photocopiers and fax machines in the Midwest, says "I remember how tired I was at first. Coming right out of college, I was used to going to a couple of classes a day and having a day off sometimes. Suddenly, in the workplace you're out there from seven in the morning to six o'clock at night, day after day, constantly going."[39] Because sales personnel usually work without immediate supervision, they must have enough initiative to make sales calls on their own. When 7 A.M. Monday arrives, it's easy to roll over and sleep a while longer. After all, who's going to know what time you start work? It's easy to rationalize and postpone the call. "Business is bad," "This guy doesn't like me," or "I'll see them next week" are typical excuses. Many salespeople take Friday afternoon off, saying that their customers aren't interested in seeing anyone at that time. But in truth, Friday afternoon is as good as any other time, maybe better. After a long, hard week of work, many customers see the salesperson's visit as a welcome diversion.

Making an extra call every day helped Shelby H. Carter's career. When he started selling typewriters right after college, he was living in Baltimore, but he had to cover the Annapolis territory as well. That meant a 40-mile drive to work every

T a b l e **2-9**   **What It Takes for Success**

• Hard work	• Emotional intelligence
• Smart work	• A positive self-concept
• Goals and plans	

day. So he kept a big jug of lemonade in his car to save the time he would lose having lunch. He figured if he could make one more call a day, that would be five a week and 20 a month, a total of 240 for the year. All those extra calls and not too many years later, Carter's system seems to have worked pretty well. He became a vice president with Xerox.

Hard work on the part of the salesperson also involves persistence. Frequently, a client is not sold on the first call or even the second or third. Selling computers is an example. The average mainframe computer system has a replacement cycle of five to six years. But salespeople must be on hand during that entire period to sell the product continually, regardless of whether their company already has the account or whether the customer is seeking to replace the system with a different one. "Never give up" is the rule. In a study of industrial salespeople, as indicated in Figure 2-1, it was found that 80 percent of the orders were written during or after the fifth call. The study also found that only 10 percent of the salespeople had the persistence to call back often enough to secure the order.[40] This does not mean that each contact must necessarily be face-to-face. It may be in low-cost, non-personal ways, such as letters, phone calls, faxes, or email.

Of course, there is a fine line between being persistent and being pushy. Persistence is necessary in salespeople, because it is important to success, as we have seen. Buyers actually admire persistence, and they usually appreciate help in making up their minds. Unfortunately, too many salespeople are reluctant to press for decisions for fear the buyer will feel uncomfortable. When the choice is sale or no sale, however, professionals take the risk. Usually the difference between being considered persistent and being called pushy is the manner in which the salesperson presses. The use of questions is one great tool that can make the difference. Instead of telling the prospect, "You really ought to buy this—you need it," ask a question that will lead the prospect to make his or her own decision, such as "How do you feel about the time wasted by your employees when your current copier breaks down so often?" Instead of saying, "But, Mr. Foster, you're losing a lot of money by not taking my suggestion," which is a pressure statement, say, "We've determined that you can save at least 53 hours a week with this change. How much would that amount to in operator wages?" That's persistence with a softer touch. Moreover, being aggressive means failing to listen, using a demanding tone of voice, continuing when it is obvious the customer is annoyed,

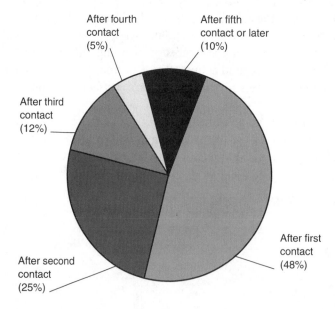

Figure 2-1
When Do Salespeople Quit Selling

Source: Adapted from Dartnell Corporation.

and using words that insist (e.g., "This is the way. . . .") Assertive means listening, having a reasonable conversational tone of voice, and not overstaying one's welcome.

You have probably heard that "there's no substitute for hard work." This is doubly true in selling. The plain fact is that the most competent and successful salespeople are also the hardest workers. As one successful salesperson commented, "The harder I work, the luckier I get."

2-5b Smart Work

There is no denying that hard work is a prerequisite, but working smarter is at least as important, perhaps more important, according to one authority.[41] Working smarter is defined as tailoring presentations to match the individual needs of customers, making prudent decisions on how to spend time, and investing time in new skills. How does one orient himself or herself to working smarter? First, is your attitude toward lost sales attributed to poor strategies or insufficient effort? The former leads the sales rep to use different approaches with customers as well as varying methods across customers. An attribution to insufficient effort, however, leads the sales rep to push himself more in the same direction, doing the same thing over and over again. Another important discriminator is whether the sale rep has a performance orientation or a learning orientation. Salespeople with a performance orientation tend to focus on winning other people's approval. They assume that their skills and abilities cannot be changed and an increase in effort is the answer to better performance. In contrast, learning-oriented salespeople are motivated to improve skills and abilities. They consciously seek out complex social interactions to improve their skills, and they change in response to feedback. Moreover, performance-oriented salespeople are more likely than learning-oriented ones to give up. When their increased efforts don't improve success, they make personal, permanent, and pervasive attributions for failure. For example, they might say to themselves, I am no good in selling to financial-oriented customers. I just cannot understand their thinking. Such self-induced despondence can be overwhelming.

2-5c Goals and Plans

Initiative and persistence will be for naught if salespeople do not learn how to manage their efforts properly. Haphazard effort, no matter how great, is likely to be ineffectual. Work must be carefully planned and organized. We all work harder when we have established our goals and the methods by which we expect to meet these goals. Salespeople must set goals and, from them, plan the number of calls to be made, which customers to visit, how often, and what they plan to accomplish on each call.

IN LIFE, MOST PEOPLE AIM AT NOTHING AND ACHIEVE IT WITH AMAZING ACCURACY.

Suppose you are a personal computer salesperson who wants to earn $90,000 for the ensuing year. At a normal commission of $300 per PC sold, this translates into 300 unit sales per year or an average of 25 per month. This in turn means that you have to sell one PC per working day to meet your goal. If you are able to make one sale for every three presentations made, then three qualified prospects are needed every day. If five phone calls yield one appointment, then 15 calls per day are required. In sum, 15 calls every day will produce at least three appointments and one sale each day, 25 per month, and 300 per year, for a total of $90,000 in commissions. When I started my career in sales many years ago, I was taught, "Plan your work and work your plan."

Planning each sales call is critical. Because it's estimated that only 4 percent of all sales calls end in a sale, it is good idea to set multiple objectives for a call. On an initial call, for example, the minimum objective might be to get acquainted with the prospect, to establish needs, and set a date for a future meeting. Such multiple objectives take away the fear of failure that salespeople often feel; they should be able to meet one objective, and this gives a feeling of making progress.[42] Each word of the sales call does not have to be written down and memorized; in fact, rehearsing the presentation in one's mind is probably a better idea anyway. If there's one thing a salesperson must be, it's prepared, say sales managers.[43] A salesperson's failure to do his or her homework can not only lead to lost sales and a poor reputation, but a lot of embarrassment for the rep and company alike. Michael Friedman, sales account manager for Pepperidge Farm in Wisconsin, says he has had to deal with salespeople who've gone into stores completely unprepared. "I try to encourage them to have a working outline of what they want to say to their clients about new products, test marketing, promotions, and price discounts," says Friedman. "Salespeople have to learn that they just can't go in there [to see their prospect] cold and dance their way through the sale," says Gary Slavin, president of Multimedia Marketing, Inc., in Florida. "They really have to learn as much as possible about the client beforehand. They need to get annual reports, 10K reports, the works." Pretty basic stuff, right? "That's exactly what it is," adds Slavin. "But it's the basic skills that, for some reason, salespeople never seem to implement."

2-5d Emotional Intelligence

emotional intelligence
Has five dimensions: (1) self-motivation skills; (2) self-awareness, (3) the ability to manage one's emotions and impulses; (4) empathy, or the ability to sense how others are feeling; and (5) social skills, or the ability to handle the emotions of other people.

A person's success at work depends on many talents, including intelligence and technical skills. Recent research indicates that an individual's emotional intelligence is also important, if not more important for salespeople. **Emotional intelligence** has five dimensions: (1) self-motivation skills; (2) self-awareness, (3) the ability to manage one's emotions and impulses; (4) empathy, or the ability to sense how others are feeling; and (5) social skills, or the ability to handle the emotions of other people. Salespeople must demonstrate great emotional intelligence in spite of the rejection they often face. It takes emotional stability not to withdraw, become defensive, or react aggressively in the face of rejection. Yet successful salespeople learn to accept a "no" gracefully and continue with their job. Sooner or later a "yes" will be forthcoming.[44]

It turns out that psychologists can see the future by watching 4-year-olds interact with a marshmallow. The researcher invites the children individually into a plain room and begins the gentle anguish. You can have this marshmallow right now, he says, but if you wait while I run an errand, you can have two marshmallows when I get back, and then he leaves. Some children grab for the treat the minute he's out the door. Some last a few minutes before they give in, but others are determined to wait. They cover their eyes; they put their heads down; they sing to themselves; they try to play games or even fall asleep. When the researcher returns, he gives these children their hard-earned marshmallows. By the time the children reach high school, the test results are still remarkably accurate. A survey of the children's parents and teachers found that those who as 4-year-olds had the fortitude to hold out for the second marshmallow generally grew up to be better adjusted, more popular, adventurous, confident, and dependable teenagers. The children who gave in to temptation early on were more likely to be lonely, easily frustrated, and stubborn. They buckled under stress and shied away from challenges. And when some of the students in the two groups took the Scholastic Aptitude Test, the kids who had held out longer scored an average of 210 points higher.

If there is a cornerstone to emotional intelligence on which other emotional skills depend, it is a sense of self-awareness, of being smart about what we feel. A person whose day starts badly at home may be irritable all day at work without quite knowing why. Anxiety is an emotion difficult to control. Worrying is a rehearsal for danger; the act of fretting focuses the mind on a problem so it can search efficiently for solutions. The danger comes when worrying blocks thinking, becoming an end in itself or a path to resignation instead of perseverance. Being worried about failing increases the likelihood of failure; a salesperson so concerned about his falling sales that he can't bring himself to pick up the phone guarantees that his sales will fall even further. The idea of being able to predict which salespeople are most likely to prosper was not an abstraction for Metropolitan Life, which in the mid-'80s was hiring 5,000 salespeople a year and training them at a cost of more than $30,000 each. Half quit the first year, and four out of five quit within four years. The reason: Selling life insurance involves having the door slammed in your face over and over again. Was it possible to identify which people would be better at handling frustration and take each refusal as a challenge rather than a setback? Why are some people better able to "snap out of it" and get on with the task at hand? Again, given sufficient self-awareness, people develop coping mechanisms. Sadness and discouragement, for instance, are "low arousal" states, and the dispirited salesperson who goes out for a run is triggering a high arousal state that is incompatible with staying blue. Relaxation works better for high-energy moods like anger or anxiety. Either way, the idea is to shift to a state of arousal that breaks the destructive cycle of the dominant mood. The head of the company approached psychologist Martin Seligman at the University of Pennsylvania and invited him to test some of his theories about the importance of optimism in people's success. When optimists fail, he has found, they attribute the failure to something they can change, not some innate weakness that they are helpless to overcome. And that confidence in their power to effect change is self-reinforcing. Seligman tracked 15,000 new workers who had taken two tests. One was the company's regular screening exam; the other was Seligman's test measuring their levels of optimism. Among the new hires was a group who flunked the screening test but scored as "superoptimists" on Seligman's exam. Sure enough, they did the best of all; they outsold the pessimists in the regular group by 21 percent in the first year and 57 percent in the second. For years after that, passing Seligman's test was one way to get hired as a MetLife salesperson.[45]

One practical conclusion from this research: Don't be afraid to fail. Baseball immortal Babe Ruth is not remembered for the number of times he struck out: 1,330; he is famous for the number of home runs he hit: 714. The same is true with selling. The heavy hitters are the ones who also strike out a lot. The most successful people in life are those who not only do not fear failure but also fail repeatedly before achieving their goals. R. H. Macy failed seven times before his store in New York finally caught on. The famous inventor Thomas Edison had his share of failures. Among them were a perpetual cigar, a kite airplane, and cement furniture. What causes most of us to fail is that, after just one failure, we quit trying. There are over 17.5 million businesses in the United States. If you moved extremely fast and called on a 100 businesses a day, it would take you 850 years to call on each business once. If it took you five calls to close a sale, you would be able to sell your product or service to every U.S. business in less than 4,250 years. So don't quit trying; obviously, there's always another prospect over the horizon.

In fact, pursue failure! Try to get all the rejections you can, because you are also bound to have your share of successes. If a salesperson makes one sale for every five calls, at the end of a week of 20 rejections he or she will have made four sales. It is a matter of simple arithmetic; the more rejections you get, the more successes you will have. Like Babe Ruth, you will be remembered only for the successes. Successful people make things happen; the unsuccessful may sit for a lifetime waiting for success to come to them.[46]

Unfortunately, most of us grow up equating our self-worth with our performance. In other words, we tell ourselves, "If I don't perform (or make a sale), I'm not worth much. I'm a failure." The irony of such thinking is that it makes failing that much more likely. If you need the sale to prove your self-worth, you end up trying too hard. You will be too intense, even pushy, on calls, and when you are rejected depression may follow, making the next call that much more agonizing. It is better to approach each customer with this attitude: "If I make the sale, that's terrific; if I don't, that's fine, too. I like you and maybe we'll do business some other time." In selling, your focus should be on enjoying what you are doing for its own sake. Successful salespeople have this attitude.

Top-performing managers have their own way of preparing to handle failure that salespeople might be well advised to emulate. A study of outstanding managers found that they prepared "catastrophic expectations reports" either in their minds or in writing before taking a major risk. They set out the worst that could possibly happen and decided whether they could live with it. If so, they moved ahead confidently. Others failed to go through such a process, and their actions were hampered by a sense of impending doom.

2-5e A Positive Self-Concept

"Love thy neighbor" is one of the world's great human relations principles, yet most people forget that the statement ends with "as thyself." In fact, before one is able to interact amicably with others, one must first "love thyself," or have a positive self-image. As the famous psychologist Alfred Adler noted, "Everything begins with self-esteem." If your self-esteem is positive, you will be able to learn and grow and go on to ever more achievements. On the other hand, if you have a negative self-concept and have learned to expect failure, then failure indeed is what you will live down to. This reflects a self-fulfilling prophecy. No matter how hard you work for success, if your subconscious thoughts are saturated with fear of failure, it will kill your efforts, neutralize your endeavors, and make success impossible. As the renowned salesperson and motivational speaker Earl Nightingale exclaims, "You become what you think about."

One salesperson, the well-known author and speaker Zig Ziglar, tells his own story of reprogramming his self-image in his book *See You at the Top*. Early in his career as a sales representative, Zig attended a sales training session conducted by a top-performing salesperson, P. C. Merrill. After the training session, Merrill took Zig aside and told him: "You know, Zig, I've been watching you for 2½ years and I've never seen such a waste. You have a lot of ability. You could be a great salesman and maybe even the best in the nation. There is no doubt in my mind that if you really went to work and started believing in yourself, you could go all the way to the top."[47] Zig so admired Merrill that he began to believe him and started seeing himself as a top salesperson. He began to think, act, and perform like one. Within a year, Zig ranked number two among 7,000 salespeople. By the following year, he was one of the highest-paid salespeople in the country, and later became the youngest division manager in the company.

As with Zig, changing your self-concept can release and utilize all of your innate talents—that which is within you. You can change the course of your life, even without your own Merrill. Here is a list to follow in building your own self-concept and releasing all of your innate talents and capabilities:

1. *Learn to accept imperfections in yourself.* None of us is perfect. All of us make mistakes. After all, it is only human to err. Demanding perfection of yourself and inevitably failing leads to dissatisfaction and a negative self-image. Even

worse, it makes one intolerant of others' mistakes, a fatal trait for salespeople. It is far better to set one's expectations realistically and look upon mistakes as learning opportunities.

2. *Appreciate and respect yourself.* Clarify your values and live according to these standards. If you continually violate your personal standards for conducting your life, you are not going to have much respect for yourself.

3. *Make decisions.* In their studies, psychologists have found that children who are taught to make their own decisions early in life grow up to be more confident adults and to have stronger self-images. Making decisions can help develop your own concept of yourself. If you hesitate, continually putting off decisions, you cannot help but feel bad about yourself. Gather all relevant facts, analyze them, talk with knowledgeable others, and make the decision. Even if the consequences are not necessarily favorable, at least you will respect yourself for making the decision.

4. *Hate the activity, not yourself.* If you do things you do not like, then hate the activity, not yourself. Otherwise every occurrence will cause you to say, "I hate myself for doing that." Such an attitude is guaranteed not to build a positive self-image. Spend your time on changing a bad habit or trait, not on admonishing yourself for it. One method for accomplishing this is to take out a sheet of paper after a sales call or at the end of the day and divide it into two equal parts with one vertical line down the middle. Write your critical thoughts about yourself on the left side. Once completed, appraise each item on the left side and write down on the right a more rational response. At a minimum, this will let you see how really hard you are being on yourself.[48]

5. *Act "as if."* We now know that the mere act of smiling (even by trained actors) produces a flood of brain chemicals that starts one on the road to feeling good. We also know that our thoughts, positive and negative, have a powerful impact on our body's immune system.[49] Even if your knees are shaking and your hands are sweating, act as if you are confident on that first sales call and you will be surprised how well you do. Acting "as if" allows you to practice the behavior before it becomes a natural part of you. If you want to be confident, sensitive, calmer, or whatever else, conduct yourself accordingly, even if somewhat self-consciously. Before long, you will incorporate the desired trait into your self-concept.

6. *Spend time on your physical appearance.* Dress according to the image you wish to project. Have you noticed how much more professional and business-like you feel when you wear a suit or dress rather than jeans and a sweatshirt? You will feel more confident on sales calls if you are confident about your appearance. Moreover, how you dress affects the way you are received by customers. Dress greatly influences salespeople's credibility, the extent to which buyers believe and trust them. It pays for a salesperson to be careful with suit or skirt, shirt or blouse, tie, stockings, and shoes. Length of hair is important, too.

7. *Use reinforcement techniques.* Compliment yourself whenever you behave as you wish. Following a successful sales call, tell yourself, "That was a great presentation." Closely watch and spend time with others who have good self-images. Collect quotations or brief passages that portray the qualities you would like to develop.

8. *Develop expertise in some area.* Perhaps you have special abilities in math or writing or some other area. In sales, you can develop special talents in selling to certain customer types: financial institutions, for example. Being

recognized as an expert in some area will help build your self-concept. Identify an ability that you can develop into real expertise and do it. Moreover, the more you know about it and how it benefits prospects, the more enthusiastic you will be. Be on the lookout for miracles among your own customers. Not only will it also build enthusiasm, but you will also have valuable testimonials at hand.[50]

9. *Dedicate yourself to learning throughout life.* Continual self-improvement, whether in a formal or informal educational environment, builds one's self-concept. Professional selling people never stop developing their selling skills. They enroll in the many selling seminars available from universities and private organizations. They purchase and listen to tapes on selling, often in their cars between calls. Professional selling people might even pull out a textbook like this and read it every so often.[51]

10. *Maintain an optimistic outlook.* Based on his research into emotional intelligence, psychologist Seligman has created an optimism training program for Metropolitan Life and written a groundbreaking book, *Learned Optimism,* in which he shows how a simple technique, borrowed from cognitive psychotherapy, can turn a quitter into a successful sales rep. The key to this process is changing your explanatory style—your way of explaining life events to yourself.[52] You should write down each pessimistic thought and categorize it as **pervasiveness**, **personalization**, or **permanence**, the classic pessimistic fallacies, as explained in Table 2-10. Then you challenge each thought with an appropriate argument. Suppose the salesperson has started prospecting a new territory. On the first call, a woman keeps you on the phone for 10 minutes, chatting about her husband and children. Finally, she decides to mention that they already have life insurance (See Table 2-10 for explanations).

pervasiveness Universalizing one bad experience.

personalization Blaming yourself for a bad sales experience, rather than externalizing the problem.

permanence Telling oneself that a sales experience will last indefinitely.

2-5f Communicative Ability

The ability to communicate is necessary in all fields of selling. In few other occupations is this ability as critical for success. Salespeople should possess an adequate vocabulary and be able to express themselves intelligibly. Not only that, but because their credibility is greatly affected by the quality of their voices, care must be exercised in developing speech habits.

Although the ability to express oneself is important to salespeople, perhaps the ability to listen and accurately analyze what others are saying is even more important.

T a b l e **2-10**   **Explanatory Thoughts That Lead to Pessimism**

Pervasiveness: "What a day!" you think. "How can I stand eight more hours of this?" Universalizing one bad experience is illogical and the surest route to hopelessness. It's ridiculous to let one call pervade your whole day. Challenge this pessimistic thought with this one: "I've made one phone call and wasted 10 minutes. So what? I have 90 calls ahead of me and a potential sale on every call!"

Personalization: You say to yourself, "How could I have been so stupid? I should have had that blabbermouth pegged in the first 10 seconds." Challenge this thought by externalizing the problem. Blame the real culprit. That woman knew you were a salesperson. If she wasn't interested, it was inconsiderate of her to distract you with social chitchat.

Permanence: You think, "That *always* happens to me! I never get good prospects." Recognize that words like *always* and *never* are rarely accurate and usually lead to despair. Instead, challenge these thoughts by emphasizing the temporariness of the situation: "Most days I make lots of sales. In fact, this is the first time I can remember ever wasting 10 full minutes on a no-go."[53]

This was borne out in a survey by Communispond, a New York consulting firm. When 432 corporate buyers were asked to identify the number one problem of salespeople, nearly 50 percent said salespeople were "too talky." Approximately 85 percent said most salespeople don't know how to ask the right questions about their companies' needs, and 95 percent said they prefer the soft sell to the hard-driving sales pitch. When asked the biggest reason for switching vendors, they cited an out-of-touch sales rep.[54]

If sales representatives are to be problem solvers, they must first determine consumer problems, which presumes interpersonal skills, primarily the abilities to listen and analyze. One study found that one of the primary differences between superachievers and average performers was their exceptional social skills. The fullest development of these skills is the ability to empathize with the customer. Empathy is the ability to feel as another individual does, to put oneself in the other's position to fully appreciate his or her situation. "Empathy identifies similarities in value systems," writes Billy Skinner, author of *The Soul of Selling*. "Bonding with people through similarities inspires the behavioral adjustments required to complete the sale." What Skinner is saying is that if you demonstrate empathy, customers will recognize this, and it will, almost subconsciously, reinforce their buying decisions.[55] Likability and empathy are important factors in building trust, a critical factor in sales success. Salespeople with poor empathy aim at the target as best they can and proceed along their usual sales track; but if the target (the customer) fails to perform as predicted, the sale is missed. Salespeople with good empathy, in contrast, sense the reactions of the customer and are able to adjust to these reactions. They aren't bound by a prepared sales track but can function in terms of the real interaction between themselves and the customer. Sensing what the customer is feeling, they are able to change pace, double back on their track, and make whatever creative modifications might be necessary to zero in on the target and close the sale. Some people are naturally high in empathy and others must work at it, but it is a skill that can be developed with practice.

2-5g Dependability, Honesty, and Integrity

The development of credibility with customers greatly depends on their being able to rely on salespeople. If sales representatives say that a piece of equipment will perform in a certain manner, they had better make sure that it will. If salespeople set up an appointment for a certain date, they had better be there on time. Arriving late signifies to customers that they aren't important enough to matter. Always make it a point to be on time, or better, early.

Sales representatives must never consciously mislead or deceive customers. In the long run, the results will be disastrous. Salespeople should take care to avoid making exaggerated claims, to use facts and figures to back up their points, to demonstrate product features and benefits whenever possible, to use solid testimonials that can be followed up, to promise only what can be delivered, and to put promises in writing. In total, they should put customers' concerns ahead of their own.

In its study of sales competency, Forum Corporation ascertained that "high performing salespeople take a two-way advocacy, representing the interest of their company and of their clients with equal dignity and skill. They . . . enthusiastically take the initiative in doing what is in the best interest of the client."[56] In studying its agents, Sentry Insurance of Stevens Point, Wisconsin, found that the best ones were high in candor.[57] Another confirmation of the importance of honesty and integrity is the result of a survey of customers who were asked to choose between two salespeople. Salesperson A was asked by a customer to deliver an order two weeks early to ease a crisis the customer had encountered suddenly. The salesperson pulled some strings and the delivery was made. Salesperson B was asked if a certain product was capable of meeting the customer's next level of technological sophistication, to which the salesperson replied he was not sure. Customers overwhelmingly chose salesperson B, explaining that although they value a salesperson who is quick to act in a crisis, more important is the one who refuses to make promises he or she may not be able to keep.[58] If one needs final confirmation, the Harvard Business School studied the common characteristics of top salespeople and found that they were impeccably honest with themselves and their customers.[59] No matter the temptation to fudge, they resisted and gained the ongoing trust of their customers. Of such importance are honesty and integrity; this is the subject of Chapter 3, "Toward Professionalism—The Salesperson's Legal and Ethical Responsibilities."

Chapter Summary

Chapter 2 began with a discussion of two common myths about selling: selling is a mystery and salespeople are born. Both myths were proven false. Selling has been studied intensively with modern behavioral research methods; consequently, selling skills can be taught and learned. The belief that salespeople must be born with their talent appears to be false, because years of research have yet to discover the profile of a born salesperson. Moreover, it appears that with practice and training, many types of individuals can develop into successful salespeople, especially given the different types of selling positions available.

The stereotype of the salesperson was studied. Elements in the stereotype were reviewed, including beliefs that:

The personal relations involved in selling are repulsive.

To be a good salesperson, one has to be psychologically maladjusted.

Salespeople must lie and be deceitful in order to succeed.

Selling benefits only the seller.

Selling is no job for a person with talent or brains.

Each of these points was shown to be without substance. It was concluded that many of these elements in the stereotype were based on business practices discarded long ago.

Next, the various types of sales positions were explained. The wide diversity of sales jobs and resulting difficulties in categorizing them were pointed out. Two methods of classifying sales positions were offered. In one scheme, sales positions were categorized by the creativity required. In the second, positions were categorized by on-the-job activities, resulting in a classification into trade, missionary, technical sales, new-business, retail, and teleselling positions. Each of these six categories was discussed in depth, and job descriptions were provided.

The rewards of a career in personal selling were described in terms of financial and psychological rewards. Figures showed that salespeople are well compensated for their efforts in comparison with other fields. Also discussed were the nonfinancial rewards of the job: the independence, the direct relationship between effort and achievement, and the enthusiasm that carries over into everyday life. Some drawbacks of the job were also mentioned: the long days, the travel, the pressure, and the problems with disgruntled customers.

The requirements for success in selling constituted a significant portion of discussion in the chapter. Although no characteristics have been discovered that predetermine success, a number of factors strongly relate to performance: hard work, goals and a plan, maturity, a positive self-concept, communicative ability, dependability, and honesty and integrity.

Discussion Questions

1. What are some myths associated with selling? Explain why they are untrue.

2. If selling is so important, why are salespeople so often held in low repute?

3. What is the stereotype of a salesperson? Where does it come from? Is it accurate?

4. What are the differences in selling for IBM, Procter & Gamble, and Sears? What are the similarities?

5. "Salespeople all do the same thing." Discuss.

6. A friend of yours has told you, "I wouldn't be good at selling. I'm not much of a talker." How would you respond?

7. What are the rewards of a career in selling? What are the disadvantages?

8. "Salespeople are born, not made." Do you agree?

9. Sit down and analyze yourself. Do you think you could be successful in selling?

10. Think of some people you know in selling. Why are they successful? Or are they?

11. Think of the last time you had occasion to deal with a salesperson. Would you say that he or she was good at selling? Why?

12. You have gone to a party. In the course of the evening, you mention that you plan to enter selling after graduation. Someone comments, "I couldn't be a salesperson. I wouldn't be able to make people buy things they didn't need." What would you say?

13. Explain how trade, missionary, technical, new-business, retail, and teleselling differ. Are the personal characteristics required for success in each different?

14. What leads to success in selling?

15. How does one handle rejection in selling?

16. What practices help one build a positive self-concept?

17. Glance through the want ads in your local newspaper, cut out 10 ads for salespeople, and classify them as being for trade, missionary, technical, new-business, retail, or telemarketing salespeople. Or do the same on the Internet from your local newspaper or a job site such as Monster.com

18. Which type of selling would you prefer? Why?

19. Interview two salespeople with different assignments (for example, trade, missionary, technical, new-business, retail, and telemarketing). Point out the similarities and the dissimilarities of their jobs.

20. What is emotional intelligence?

21. How does one build a positive self-concept?

Chapter Quiz

1. Past empirical research on inherent traits in salespeople has found that the largest influence on salespeople's performance is
   a. internal factors that a person is born with.
   b. aptitude and skills inherent within a person.
   c. factors that sales managers can control or influence, such as role perceptions, skills, and motivation.
   d. understanding the sales process.

2. A stereotypical statement about salespeople is that they "must lie and be deceitful in order to succeed." This is totally in conflict with the marketing concept because
   a. to succeed salespeople must understand the needs of customers.
   b. the majority of corporations rely on repeat business for sales and if customers have been deceived, repeat sales will not materialize.
   c. the goal of selling is to satisfy the needs and wants of customers.
   d. such an approach would not be self-satisfying for the salesperson.

3. The primary task of _____ salespeople is to build sales volume for their company through promotional assistance.
   a. technical
   b. retail
   c. missionary
   d. trade

4. The primary responsibility of the _____ salesperson is to provide the firm's direct customers (wholesalers and retailers) with personal selling assistance. This is done by providing product information to indirect customers and persuading them to buy from the firm's direct customers.
   a. technical
   b. retail
   c. missionary
   d. trade

5. _____ is typified by canvassing, prospecting, bird-dogging, and cold-calling.
   a. New-business selling
   b. Teleselling
   c. Retail selling
   d. Technical selling

6. The most common type of sales compensation is
   a. straight salary.
   b. straight commission.
   c. salary plus commission.
   d. salary plus bonus.

7. Common psychological rewards enjoyed by salespeople include all of the following *except*

   a. satisfaction of seeing a direct relationship between their efforts and what they achieve.

   b. greater pay and greater career advancement opportunities.

   c. freedom to work independently without supervisors peering over their shoulders.

   d. practices of professional selling carry over into a person's everyday life.

8. All of the following are typical drawbacks to selling *except*

   a. long workdays.

   b. travel.

   c. low pay and few rewards.

   d. handling dissatisfied customers.

9. There is no denying that hard work is a prerequisite, but working smarter is at least as important, perhaps more important. Working smarter is defined as all of the following *except*

   a. developing better communication and presentation skills.

   b. tailoring presentations to match the individual needs of customers.

   c. making prudent decisions on how to spend time.

   d. investing time in new skills.

10. Approximately ____ percent of all sales calls end in a sale.

   a. 4

   b. 7

   c. 10

   d. 13

Web Exercise

Want to test out your own EQ? Go to www.queendom.com/tests/iq/emotional_iq_r2_access.html and give it a try. What do the results tell you about your own personality?

The Emotional Intelligence Consortium at Rutgers University looks for ways to implement EQ information in orga-nizational settings: www.eiconsortium.org. Download some of their reports on uses of EQ to evaluate and improve business–customer relations. How can these be applied to sales situations?

Notes

1. "So, Whom Do We Trust? *Reader's Digest* Trust Survey," *Ipsos-Reid Public Affairs,* January 22, 2004.
2. Bob Weinstein, "You'd Better Believe Bill Gates Can Sell!" *ITworld.com,* May 3, 2001.
3. Gilbert Churchill, Neil Ford, Orville Walker, Mark Johnston, and John F. Tanner, *Sales Force Management,* New York: McGraw-Hill Higher Education, 2000.
4. Julia Chang, "Born to Sell," *Sales & Marketing Management,* July 2003.
5. Charles Butler, "Why the Bad Rap," *Sales & Marketing Management,* June 1, 1996.
6. Ibid.
7. Donald L. Thompson, "Stereotype of the Salesman," *Harvard Business Review,* January–February 1972.
8. "Sales Strikes Out on Campus," *Sales & Marketing Management,* November 1997.
9. Charles Butler, "Why the Bad Rap," *Sales & Marketing Management,* June 1, 1996.
10. "PAs Examine the People Who Sell to Them," *Sales & Marketing Management,* November 11, 1995, p. 38.
11. "Quick Hits," *Performance,* November 1994.
12. Derek A. Newton, "Get the Most Out of Your Sales Force," *Harvard Business Review,* 47, September–October 1969, pp. 130, 143.
13. Robert Johnson and Betsy Morris, "Food Companies Fight to Display More Products on Less Shelf Space," *Wall Street Journal,* April 10, 1996, p. 27.
14. Ibid.
15. Michael Weinreb, "A Fine Line," *Sales & Marketing Management,* October 2002.
16. "Doctoring Sales," *Sales & Marketing Management,* May 2001.
17. "Eli Lilly Lauded for Its Bedside Manner," *Sales & Marketing Management,* September 1991, p. 56.
18. Bro Uttal, "Companies That Serve You Best," *Fortune,* December 7, 1997, pp. 98–116.
19. "A Clear Vision for Growth," *Sales & Marketing Management,* March 2001.
20. Shane Tritsch, "Waiting Out the Turbulence," *Selling,* September 1993, p. 24.
21. "Retail Salespersons," *Occupational Outlook Handbook,* 2002–2003 Edition, U.S. Department of Labor, BLS, Bulletin 2540.
22. Kevin Helliker, "Retailing Chains Offer a Lot of Opportunity, Young Managers Find," *Wall Street Journal,* August 25, 1995, p. A1.
23. Rayna Skolnik, "Call Center Overview," Sales Marketing Network at info-now.com, No. 1210, 1998.
24. "Do Not Call Is Constitutional," *Sales & Marketing Management,* February 18, 2004.
25. Rayna Skolnik, "Customer Relationship Management through Call Centers," Sales Marketing Network at info-now.com, No. 1211, September 28, 2004.
26. "What Salespeople Are Paid" *Sales & Marketing Management,* February 1995, p. 30.

27. Bill Kelley, "Is There Anything That Can't Be Sold by Phone?" *Sales & Marketing Management,* April 1999.

28. Christine Galea, "The 2004 Compensation Survey," *Sales & Marketing Management,* May 2004.

29. *2002 National Occupational Employment and Wage Estimates, Sales and Related Occupations,* U.S. Department of Labor, Bureau of Labor Statistics, February 27, 2004.

30. Eileen Zimmerman, "So You Wanna Be a CEO," *Sales & Marketing Management,* January 2002.

31. Kathleen Cholewka, "Xerox's Savior," *Sales & Marketing Management,* April 2001.

32. Michael Siconolfi and William Power, "Only 20 Percent of Ex-Drexel Workers Find Security in Their Industry," *Wall Street Journal,* April 11, 1990, p. Cl.

33. "The Most Satisfied Worker?" *Wall Street Journal,* December 30, 1995.

34. Arthur Bragg, "Shell-Shocked on the Battlefield of Selling," *Sales & Marketing Management,* July 1990, p. 54.

35. David Mercer, *High-Level Selling,* Houston: Gulf Publishing, 1990, p. 123.

36. Ibid.

37. Weld F. Royal, "Pleading Their Case," *Sales & Marketing Management,* February 1995, p. 50.

38. V. R. Buzzotta, R. E. Lefton, and Manuel Sherberg, *Effective Selling through Psychology,* New York: Wiley Interscience, 1972, p. 46.

39. Arthur Bragg, "Shell-Shocked on the Battlefield of Selling," *Sales & Marketing Management,* July 1990, p. 54.

40. "Winning through Persistence," *Sales Force,* June 1995, p. 3.

41. Robert Sharoff, "Acquiring a Taste for Selling," *Selling,* July/August 1994, p. 72.

42. Malcolm Fleschner, "Work Hard, Work Smart," *Personal Selling Power,* May/June 1995, p. 40.

43. "What Common Mistakes Do Your Salespeople Make?" *Sales & Marketing Management,* May 1993.

44. Daniel Goleman, *Emotional Intelligence: Why It Can Matter More Than IQ,* Bantam, September 1, 1995.

45. Martin Seligman, *Learned Optimism: How to Change Your Mind and Your Life,* Free Press, March 1, 1998.

46. Lew Riley, "The Babe Ruth Theory of Success," *Creative Living,* Winter 1981, pp. 25–27.

47. Zig Ziglar, *See You at the Top,* Gretna, LA: Pelican Publishing, 1975, p. 99.

48. Ibid.

49. David Burns and Gerhard Gschwandtner, "How to Overcome the Fear of Disapproval," *Personal Selling Power,* April 1994, p. 78.

50. Eric Olsen, "Beyond Positive Thinking," *Success,* December 1988, pp. 31–38.

51. Barry L. Reece and Rhonda Brandt, *Effective Human Relations in Business,* Boston: Houghton Mifflin, 1991, pp. 90–92.

52. Martin Seligman, *Learned Optimism: How to Change Your Mind and Your Life,* Free Press, March 1, 1998.

53. "Talk, Talk, Talk, Talk: Try a Little Listening," *Wall Street Journal,* March 22, 1990, p. B1.

54. Gerhard Gschwandtner, "How Superachievers Win," *Personal Selling Power,* May/June 1995, p. 27.

55. Billy L. Skinner, *The Soul of Selling: How to Focus Your Energy to Achieve a Successful and Happy Sales Career,* Amacom Books, November 1, 1994.

56. Pat Raffee, " 'Yes' Power," *Sales & Marketing Management,* April 1, 1985, p. 13.

57. "The Keys to Good Selling," *Sales & Marketing Management,* January 1990, p. 32.

58. "Mean It When You Say Yes," *Sales & Marketing Management,* June 1989, p. 23.

59. "What Are the Shared Qualities of Top Sellers?" *The Selling Advantage,* June 1995, p. 2.

Case 2-1

John Hintz is a first-semester junior in the College of Business at the University of New Mexico. After this semester, he will have completed most of his general business requirements and will have to declare a major. He is confused, however, about exactly what type of career he wants.

John has a 3.0 grade point average and is active in the business fraternity at school. He is president of his social fraternity and on the student senate. He is active in most sports and takes pride in the fact that he is a fourth-seeded player on the university tennis team.

John spends several hours each week working in a big brother program. He takes his "little brother," Buddy, out to play tennis and softball and to see university football games. John is especially proud of the fact that since Buddy joined the big brother program, his grades have improved and he gets into less trouble.

Several options are open to John. He can major in marketing, accounting, management, or finance. He wants a job that will be challenging and exciting but also secure. He would like to think that he can help people in his career, but he also recognizes the importance of a good salary to his own welfare.

Questions

1. Would you recommend that John choose a career in selling? If so, what type of selling?
2. What points would you bring to his attention before he makes his decision?

Case 2-2

Shirley Spale recently graduated from Washington State University. She has sold business forms for Standard Register for a year, and now she is receiving her first performance appraisal since training from her boss, Bob Niendorf. Comments Bob:

Shirley, I see a great deal of variation in your number of daily sales calls. Some days, I see only two or three calls; other days, I see five or six. Besides this being under our average of seven calls, it appears that you seldom make calls until 9:30 or 10:00 A.M. Moreover, it seems as though you don't stick with prospects long enough; at most, I see just two or three calls per prospect. As you might expect, your sales volume could be better.

Shirley, with her head turned downward and failing to make eye contact, replies:

Selling is so hectic. I have difficulty deciding what to do first. Also, it seems as if by the time I go through my mail, review my to-dos, and sort through my prospect records, I can't get out of the office until at least 9 or 10 P.M. As to closing, once I get a "no" from a prospect, I tend to leave them alone. I guess the rejection just gets to me. I never seem to get good prospects. Also, my first call of the day pervades the rest of the day. If it goes badly, I have trouble from there on. I have trouble maintaining my confidence, and I'm sure prospects can tell.

Question

1. How would you advise Shirley to change for the better?

Toward Professionalism—The Salesperson's Legal and Ethical Responsibilities

Key Terms

CAN-SPAM Act	monopsony	requirements contracts
ethics	National Do-Not-Call Registry	sales puff
exclusive dealing	price discrimination	slander
libel	product disparagement	tying arrangement
misrepresentation and breach of warranty	reciprocity	unfair competition
	refusal to deal	

Learning Objectives

Learning Objectives

After studying Chapter 3, you will understand:

- The importance of ethical conduct in successful selling
- That honesty and high ethical standards are good business
- Major legislation that affects personal selling

- Situations in which salespeople may have to make difficult ethical choices in dealing with customers, competitors, and even employers

As a theoretical subject, ethics is difficult to discuss; it is even more difficult to draw conclusions about the ethical nature of our daily conduct. How often do we find ourselves in conflict over what we feel to be right and what we feel pressured to do? How often have you told a "white lie," for example? Is it always to protect a friend from harm? Or is it sometimes just expedient, or, in truth, merely meant to protect ourselves? Business and selling are no different from everyday life. Although some acts are clearly unethical or even illegal, others are less clear; they present a dilemma for the individual. Unfortunately, this dilemma is exacerbated for the salesperson because of popularly held views of selling and marketing in general. Many salespeople believe in their heart of hearts that they are behaving unethically, when there is no reason whatsoever for them to think that way. Solving customer problems and providing needed products and services should not cause professional salespeople shame, nor should it place them in ethical dilemmas. But it is often difficult to avoid feeling so, when prejudice against marketing and selling is so widespread.

The issue of business ethics has been exacerbated by the scandals of the past few years: WorldCom, Enron, and myriad financial firms. Unfortunately, their actions have eroded trust in the marketplace and trust is the cornerstone of business. Market participants must trust—and be able to verify—that the goods offered are what they are supposed to be; that their product or service is being considered without prejudice; that their orders are being processed fairly; and that the market isn't rigged to their disadvantage.[1] In the absence of such trust, the entire system is at risk; sellers will be afraid to sell; buyers will be afraid to buy; and the entire economy stagnates in a pool of mistrust, anger, and resentment. Though critical, laws alone will not eliminate the problem without internalization of ethical behavior on the part of participants; if every transaction ultimately ends up in court, the system will be clogged and come to a standstill. Moreover, with unethical behavior at the top, there is a "trickle-down" effect to the rest of society. In Fort Wayne, Indiana, before her conviction, 7 of 10 brides used to ask for a "Martha Stewart look" for their flower arrangements at Lopshire Flower Shop, according to the owner. Other local businesspeople say the scandals have impacted the way they deal with colleagues, employees, and loved ones. They worry when their children seem nonchalant about all the greed and cheating in the news.[2]

3-1 The Importance of Ethical Conduct

According to the marketing concept, the crux of marketing success is satisfying customer need. It is hard to imagine doing so while deliberately setting out to deceive customers. Admittedly, it might happen in the short run, but any salesperson and company should not expect long-run success, or even continued existence, with such a policy. That is, unethical activity might succeed in a single transaction, but the development of a true relationship demands complete honesty and integrity. The best policy for salespeople—and the most profitable—is to be honest and forthright with customers. The ones buyers continue to do business with are the ones they trust. Good ethics are good business! Contrast these two examples. Executives of 3M phased out production of a chemical that the company had manufactured for 40 years, used in products ranging from pet food bags, candy wrappers, carpeting, and 3M's popular Scotchguard fabric protector, upon discovering that the chemical appeared in miniscule amounts in humans and animals around the world and accumulated in tissue. Believing that the substance could be harmful in large doses, 3M voluntarily stopped production, though acknowledging a potential loss of $500 million in annual sales.[3] Contrast 3M's practice to that of Bridgestone/Firestone, faced with questions about the safety of selected Firestone-brand tires that had been linked to crashes that killed 174 people and injured more than 700. In 2000, the company recalled 6.5 million tires under government pressure. After the recall, Firestone tires fell by nearly one-half. Ford Motor Company, a large buyer of Firestone tires, ended its exclusive contract with the tire producer.[4]

Until this point, ethics has been discussed without a formal definition. Here, **ethics** is defined as moral principles and values that govern the actions and decisions of an individual or group. They serve as guidelines on how to act rightly and justly when faced with moral dilemmas. According to one ethicist, "A genuine consideration of others is essential to an ethical life."[5] Of course, perceptions of right and wrong vary considerably from one person to the next. So, generally, an ethical standard is considered operative if it is accepted by the majority of people to whom it applies. It may be codified into law so that violation of the standard will result in punishment. However, an ethical standard does not necessarily have to be a legal standard of conduct. Not kissing on the first date is an ethical standard for some people but not a legal one. Violation of this ethical standard carries no penalties, at least from legal authorities. But violating any of the many federal, state, and local laws affecting business does carry penalties.

ethics
Moral principles and values that govern the actions and decisions of an individual or group.

3-2 The Law and Selling

One study reports on the results of an inquiry into the extent to which industrial sales representatives correctly perceive the legality of various selling practices. The legality of just over half of the practices was reported correctly by the overall sample. The percentage was even less for smaller than for large companies.[6] Yet, the consequences of this ignorance can be staggering. In one case, one insurance salesman lost his $1.1 million insurance sales position for misrepresentation to customers.[7]

3-2a Misrepresentation and Breach of Warranty

By using certain statements, salespeople can embroil themselves and their companies in lawsuits. When a customer relies on a salesperson's statements, purchases the product or service, and then finds that it fails to perform as promised, the customer can sue for **misrepresentation and breach of warranty**. Generally, salespeople can get into trouble when they make statements of a factual nature that turn out to be untrue. In one recent case, the state of Massachusetts is seeking to recover as much as $146 million from contractors responsible for the downtown Boston highway project (popularly known as the "Big Dig"). The suit says the contractors concealed

misrepresentation and breach of warranty
When a salesperson begins to make statements of fact regarding product capabilities, the law treats these as statements of actuality and warranty. When a customer relies on a salesperson's statements, purchases the product or service, and then finds that it fails to perform as promised, the customer can sue.

true cost estimates from state officials and "as a result of the breach of their contractual and fiduciary, the defendants have been unjustly enriched . . . the plaintiffs seek judicial determination that the defendants be required to disgorge all or some of their profits and fees."[8]

sales puff
Opinions, not fact (e.g., "it's the best around" or "our service can't be beat").

Salespeople must first be able to distinguish between **sales puff** (or opinions) and statements of fact plus the legal ramifications of both. When salespeople loosely describe their product or service (e.g., "It's the best around" or "Our service can't be beat"), such statements are viewed as "opinions" and cannot be relied on by customers. Thus, whenever companies are sued for misrepresentation and breach of warranty (which for our purposes will be treated the same, although legally there is a difference), the standard defense is that the purchaser cannot rely on the salesperson's puffery because it's unreasonable to take these statements at face value.

When the salesperson begins to make statements of a factual nature regarding the product's capabilities (e.g., results, profits or savings, what it will do for the customer, how it will perform, etc.), however, the law treats these as statements of fact and warranty. There is no particular set of words that is damaging; each case is decided individually on its own merits. Generally the less knowledgeable the customer (often the case with high-tech products), the greater the chances the court will interpret a statement as actionable. In one suit settled for the unknowledgeable plaintiff, the salesperson said the proposed construction machinery would "keep up with any other machine then being used and that it would work well in cooperation with the company's other machines and equipment." The court ruled that these statements were factual and were "predictions" of how the equipment would perform, making them more than just sales puff.

In one case, Metropolitan Life was penalized by the state of Florida for misrepresenting insurance policies. The state ruled that it was unacceptable for agents to call themselves *nursing representatives* because it was a made-up title; that *deposit* was a misleading substitute for *premium;* that *retirement saving plan* was an unauthorized term; and that insurance could not be referred to as an *investment.*[9] As history repeats itself, in a more recent case, another insurance company's sales practices are being investigated, as some policyholders have complained they were misled to believe that they were buying primarily a retirement investment vehicle, not insurance. One buyer complained his policy was pitched as a "tax-free" or "tax-deferred" investment, but discovered in truth that any withdrawals would count as loans, incurring interest.[10] Similarly, the Federal Trade Commission (FTC) announced it had filed a complaint in a federal court in Maryland against AmeriDebt. The agency alleged the firm misrepresented that it charges no upfront fee for services. Consumers are urged to make an enrollment payment that AmeriDebt keeps as a fee instead of disbursing to creditors, the FTC alleges. "This case is about deceiving the public," said the director of the FTC's consumer-protection bureau. "We're alleging AmeriDebt misled consumers about what it is, what services it provides and what it charges." The FTC accused AmeriDebt of misrepresenting that it operates as a non-profit organization. The FTC alleges the firm doesn't operate for charitable purposes but instead to make money for affiliated for-profit companies. The complaint also alleges that AmeriDebt doesn't teach consumers about their finances.[11]

How should salespeople act? They must realize that there are differences between puffery and statements of a factual nature. The following have been treated as statements of fact by salespeople and are, hence, legally actionable:

- This refrigerator will preserve foods in the warmest weather.
- This tractor has live-power take-off features.

Box 3-1

Selling Guidelines for Avoiding Misrepresentation

- Be sure all specific product claims (technical characteristics, useful life, performance capabilities) can be accomplished.

- Be certain all specific positive statements about offerings can be verified. If not, be very general (e.g., "high quality" or "great value").

- Customers should be reminded to read warnings, particularly if they seem to be ignoring them.

- Immediately warn customers considering improper use of equipment.

- Warnings should be very specific and related to each customer's product usage situation.

- Judge each customer's level of sophistication—the more unsophisticated, the more careful the salesperson should be.

- Be able to verify all negative statements about competitors' products, business conduct, and financial condition.

Source: Selling Guidelines for Avoiding Misrepresentation from "Legal Dimensions of Salespersons' Statements: A Review and Managerial Implications" by Karl A. Boedecker, Fred W. Morgan and Jeffrey J. Stoltman, *Journal of Marketing,* January 1991, pp. 70–80. Reprinted by permission.

- Feel free to prescribe this drug to your patients, Doctor. It's nonaddicting.
- This mace pen is capable of instantaneous incapacitation for a period of 15 to 20 minutes.
- This is a safe, dependable helicopter.

Unless there is firm evidence, salespeople should avoid making statements such as "this will reduce your inventory by 40 percent." This is especially the case when the salesperson's company has a reputation of technical expertise in a field and/or its products or services are sold in highly specialized areas to unsophisticated buyers who must rely entirely on the expertise of the sales representative. When dealing with a customer experienced in trade, however, the courts have ruled that knowledgeable buyers have a duty to look beyond the assertions of a salesperson and investigate the product on their own.[12] To avoid misrepresention when selling, see Box 3-1.

3-2b Sherman, Clayton, Federal Trade Commission, and Robinson–Patman Acts

Federal laws regulating business have been passed with two main intentions: (1) to prevent the formation of monopolistic concentrations of economic power and (2) to prevent unfair and deceptive practices in the course of business. Although it is beyond the scope of this text to cover these laws in detail, we can allude to the sections that deal most directly with sales and marketing in general.

Individuals, including sales managers, field salespeople, and company officers, may be personally liable for failing to act within the law. Penalties can be severe. Fines of up to $350,000 for individuals and $10 million for companies can be imposed. This is in addition to criminal sanctions (up to three years in jail) for violations of the Sherman Act and the Clayton Act. Moreover, in formulating a defense to charges, there usually are substantial lawyers' fees. It is also true that under the Federal Trade Commission Act, the FTC can issue "cease and desist" orders for which failure to comply can result in fines of $10,000 per day.[13]

Some areas where the law is directly applicable to salespeople and their managers follow:

Business Defamation

The following forms of wrong fall within this general heading of defamation.

slander
When an unfair or untrue oral statement is made about a competitor to a third party (e.g., a customer) and can be construed as damaging that competitor's business reputation or the personal reputation of an individual with that company.

libel
Unfair and untrue statements in writing communicated to customers.

product disparagement
False or deceptive comparisons or distorted claims concerning a competitor's product, services, or property.

unfair competition
Statements made by the salesperson that reflect upon his or her own product and misrepresent its characteristics or qualities.

1. Business **slander**: This arises when an unfair or untrue oral statement is made about a competitor to a third party (e.g., a customer) and can be construed as damaging that competitor's business reputation or the personal reputation of an individual with that company.
2. Business **libel**: This is constituted by unfair and untrue statements in writing, communicated to customers. These statements can be contained in letters, sales literature, advertisements, or company brochures.
3. **Product disparagement**: This is represented by false or deceptive comparisons or distorted claims concerning a competitor's product, services, or property.
4. **Unfair competition**: These are statements made by the salesperson that reflect upon his or her own product and misrepresent its characteristics or qualities.

All of these methods of business defamation fall under "unfair and deceptive acts and practices" in the Federal Trade Commission Act.

In the following actual instances, sales talk has gotten a company into trouble:

- Accusing competitors of engaging in illegal or unfair business practices
- Saying that a competitor fails to live up to its contractual obligations and responsibilities (e.g., ships defective goods and is always being sued) when the allegation is untrue
- Making untrue statements about a competitor's financial condition
- Making false statements that a principal executive of the competition was incompetent, of immoral character, unreliable, and dishonest

In one example of a suit for slander, SCO Group, Inc., has filed a slander suit against Novell, Inc., saying the Provo-based firm has hurt the Lindon-based company's business by falsely claiming it owns the copyrights to the Unix computer operating system and UnixWare.[14] It contends that Novell's claims that it owns Unix and UnixWare copyrights have harmed SCO's copyrights, its business, and its reputation. "SCO takes this action today given Novell's recent and repeated announcements regarding their claimed ownership of the Unix and UnixWare copyrights," SCO attorney Mark Heise said.

The best way of avoiding this type of suit is to have statistical evidence collected by an independent testing company (e.g., Underwriters Laboratories). This information should be depended on to prove a product is safer, more cost-efficient, and so on.[15]

Unfair Methods of Competition Respecting Orders, Goods, and Terms of Sale

It is unfair for company salespeople to substitute goods different from those ordered, misrepresent a delivery date, fail to fill an order, or not fill an order within a reasonable time following acceptance. Also illegal is sending unordered goods or larger amounts than ordered hoping the buyer will pay anyway. It is unfair to represent terms and conditions of sale by falsely stating important terms: warranties or guarantees, ability to cancel a contract and receive a refund, or concealment of important facts in credit and financing.

Among the specific acts ruled "unfair or deceptive" under this section of the Federal Trade Commission Act are these:

- Statements that a product is custom-made when this is untrue
- Statements that a product was "proved" when there is a dearth of scientific and empirical evidence substantiating this
- False statements that a product is fireproof and flame-resistant
- Passing off certain company personnel as experts when they are not
- Awarding a dealer's sales staff for product sales of a salesperson's company without the consent of the dealer[16]

Resale Restrictions

The Sherman Act states that someone who purchases a product has the right to do with it what he or she wishes, without restriction by the seller. Therefore, it is not legal to restrict a retailer to sell only within a specified market or geographic area. When it comes to pricing, court rulings have tended to make matters murky. Vertical price-fixing—an agreement between a supplier and a dealer that fixes the minimum resale price of a product—is a clear-cut antitrust violation. It also is illegal for a manufacturer and retailer to agree on a minimum resale price. The antitrust laws, however, give a manufacturer latitude to adopt a policy regarding a desired level of resale prices and to deal only with retailers who independently decide to follow that policy. A manufacturer also is permitted to stop dealing with a retailer who breaches the manufacturer's resale price maintenance policy. That is, the manufacturer can adopt the policy on a "take it or leave it" basis. Agreements on maximum resale prices are evaluated under the "rule of reason" standard because in some situations these agreements can benefit consumers by preventing dealers from charging a noncompetitive price.[17] For the most part, however, it is legal to (1) assign a distributor an area of primary responsibility for selling a product or service or (2) not appoint any other distributor in a distributor's exclusive territory. The Sherman Antitrust Act does not restrict the right of businesspeople to select customers. **Refusal to deal** is the right of businesspeople to select customers, *provided they have a good business reason for doing so that can be proven.* The following have been upheld as rationale for doing such:

- The distributor does not sell enough or cooperate in the seller's prices and programs.
- The dealer fails to purchase an adequate volume of product or fails to promote and advertise the line adequately.
- The dealer does not adequately support the manufacturer's image (e.g., inadequate or sloppy display).
- The dealer is responsible for excessive cancellation, or "cherry-picking" the line (i.e., selectively distributing only the best selling or most profitable items). **Exclusive dealing** arrangements, however, such as forbidding a distributor to handle competitive products, are usually vulnerable under the antitrust laws.

Tying Arrangements and Requirements Contracts

A **tying arrangement** requires that in order to receive a desired product in a manufacturer's line, the distributor must buy a substantial or even full line of offerings. A salesperson, in other words, might say to a distributor, "Look, I know you only want our B-10 model, but if you want it, you'll have to purchase six B-14's also. Otherwise, no deal." This constitutes a direct violation of Section 3 of the Clayton Act.

refusal to deal
The right of businesspeople to select customers. Generally, they can cut off business or refuse to deal with someone, *provided they have a good business reason for doing so that can be proven.*

exclusive dealing
Forbidding a distributor to handle competitive products, usually vulnerable under antitrust laws.

tying arrangement
Requirement that in order to receive a desired product in a manufacturer's line, the distributor must buy a substantial or even full line of offerings.

requirements contracts
Contracts in which purchasers
are required to buy or lease a
specified percentage of their
requirements for a product
from a vendor, typically within
a specified lapse of time.

A recent example: The FTC charged a pharmaceutical manufacturer with tying the sale of clozapine, an antipsychotic drug, to a blood testing and monitoring service.

Another practice closely scrutinized by both the Justice Department and the FTC is the offering of **requirements contracts**, in which purchasers are required to buy or lease a specified percentage of their requirements for a product from a vendor, typically within a specified lapse of time. A salesperson might state, "If you want to buy our product, you must buy X amount or else no deal." Usually this is illegal, because it forecloses competition among a significant number of vendors.[18]

Price Discrimination

Both the Clayton Act and Robinson–Patman Act are intended to ensure the existence of equality of opportunity for dealers and distributors. In effect, unless similar buyers are treated equally in price and promotional opportunities, criminal penalties may be imposed—on both the manufacturer and any participating dealers cognizant of their special treatment.

Price discrimination generally occurs in two ways: through arrangements with competitors (generally covered in the Sherman Act and the Clayton Act) or relations with distributors (explained in the Robinson–Patman Act).

Relations with Competitors

It is unlawful to make arrangements with competitors: "To agree to fix prices, stabilize prices, agree to a formula to determine price, or enter into any agreement which may even have a remote or indirect effect on prices." Examples include agreements to

- Divide or allocate markets, territories, or customers
- Rig bids or submit bids knowing they will be unacceptable
- Charge a maximum price
- Limit production, set quotas, or discontinue a product
- Boycott third parties
- Depress the prices of raw materials with other raw materials purchasers
- Establish a system for determining delivered prices or a specific method of quoting prices

These have been taken from actual cases where they were ruled *per se* violations (i.e., cannot be defended or justified in any way whatsoever). The penalties for doing so may be considerable. In a recent case, two former Honda executives were sentenced to prison for their role in receiving $15 million in kickbacks from dealers and competitors. The former assistant advertising manager was sentenced to two years in prison and fined $67,000. Another sales manager was sentenced to 20 months in jail and fined $10,000.[19]

Recent cases involved a group of physicians charged with using a boycott to prevent a managed-care organization from establishing a competing health care facility in Virginia and retailers who used a boycott to force manufacturers to limit sales through a competing catalog vendor. At issue in one recent case was an agreement between cable television companies not to enter each other's territory. Restrictions on price advertising can be illegal if they deprive consumers of important information. The FTC recently charged a group of auto dealers with restricting comparative and discount advertising to the detriment of consumers. A professional code of ethics may be unlawful if it unreasonably restricts the ways professionals may compete. Several years ago, for example, the FTC ruled that certain provisions of the American Medical Association's code of ethics restricted doctors from participating in alternative forms of health care delivery, such as managed health care programs, in violation of the antitrust laws. The case opened the door for greater competition in health care.[20]

The courts decided many years ago that certain practices, such as price-fixing, are so inherently harmful to consumers that a detailed examination isn't necessary to determine whether they are reasonable. The law presumes that they are violations (antitrust lawyers call these *per se* violations) and condemns them almost automatically. Other practices, such as monopoly, unfair methods of competition, and mergers and acquisition, demand closer scrutiny based on principles that the courts and antitrust agencies have developed. These cases are examined under a "rule of reason" analysis. A practice is illegal if it restricts competition in some significant way and has no overriding business justification. Practices that meet both characteristics are likely to harm consumers—by increasing prices, reducing availability of goods or services, lowering quality or service, or significantly stifling innovation.[21]

Although already covered by antitrust laws, a relatively new issue is that of **monopsony**, which arises as more markets are dominated by a few big buyers. It is similar to a monopoly, but where a large buyer (not seller) controls a large proportion of the market and drives the prices down; this is sometimes referred to as buyer's monopoly. International Paper, for example, faces a lawsuit that it conspired with its timber buyers to depress softwood prices in several states. Insurance companies have been targeted for imposing contracts forcing down fees charged by hospitals and doctors. According to the Justice Department, "price-fixing and other forms of collusion are just as unlawful when the victims are sellers rather than buyers."[22] In some respects, such behavior represents the "dark side" of relationship marketing. As more and more companies buy through sole or a limited number of suppliers, especially through coordinated computer systems, the opportunity for such behavior increases.

monopsony
Similar to a monopoly, but where a large buyer (not seller) controls a large proportion of the market and drives the prices down; sometimes referred to as *buyer's monopoly.*

Relations with Customers and Distributors

Violations here are concerned with the Robinson–Patman Act. Passed during the Depression of the 1930s, the Robinson–Patman Act represented the lobbying efforts of small retailers seeking to protect themselves from the competition of large chains. The wording of the act is somewhat confusing, making illegal any **price discrimination** between different purchasers of goods of "like grade and quality" that may tend to "injure, destroy, or prevent competition." In effect, the law rules that manufacturers could not grant discriminatory price breaks to large chains without granting them to smaller distributors as well. The Robinson–Patman Act also regulated against discriminatory practices in granting advertising allowances that were not available to all customers on "proportionately equal terms." For example, under the current guidelines, if the seller's basic plan offers to pay, say, 50 percent of the cost of newspaper advertising up to 15 percent per unit purchased, he or she must offer an alternate program for stores that can't afford newspapers. This must be on terms identical to the main plan but must embrace less expensive media, such as handbills or in-store displays. As a result of an FTC investigation, Gillette modified one program, requiring that a store print only 2,500 handbills to qualify for co-op funds instead of the previous stipulation of 5,000.

price discrimination
Prices charged different purchasers of goods of "like grade and quality" that may tend to "injure, destroy, or prevent competition."

Another vexing problem that has recently arisen is the so-called slotting allowance, which, besides an outright fee charged by retailers for stocking new products, may include local media advertising and promotion, and even changes in pricing policy. Commented one antitrust lawyer, "I don't know for sure that every manufacturer who's offering [a payment] is offering it to every one of its competing grocers in the same market. The FTC says it is studying the issue of slotting allowances."[23]

Because of the Robinson–Patman Act, salespeople must be careful not to favor some customers over others. If they grant price breaks or extra cooperative advertising expenditures to one customer, they must offer the same programs to all others, with two exceptions. First, if differences in costs of doing business can be demonstrated, some price discrimination is allowable. For example, if a seller sends a few packages parcel post to a small retailer and sends a full truckload to a large discount store, all or part of the cost savings may be passed on. Second, a seller may discriminate in price between customers if a price is lowered at one in order to meet the equally low price of a competitor. As you can imagine from the preceding discussion, the Robinson–Patman Act tends to be a confusing piece of legislation. Because of the original intent of the act and its vague wording, some marketing theorists have argued that its net effect has been to reduce competition. Whether this is true or false, salespeople must be careful in their treatment of customers, making sure to treat them equally, except under the two circumstances outlined here.

3-3 Privacy Laws

3-3a National Do-Not-Call Registry

National Do-Not-Call Registry
The registry is nationwide in scope, and commercial telemarketers are not allowed to call consumers if their number is on the registry.

Recently, pursuant to its broad authority under the Telephone Consumer Protection Act (TCPA), the FCC established a **National Do-Not-Call Registry**. The registry is nationwide in scope, applies to all telemarketers (with the exception of certain nonprofit organizations), and covers both interstate and intrastate telemarketing calls. Commercial telemarketers are not allowed to call you if your number is on the registry. As a result, consumers can, if they choose, reduce the number of unwanted phone calls to their homes. Placing one's number on the National Do-Not-Call Registry will stop most telemarketing calls, but not all. Because of limitations in the jurisdiction of the FTC and FCC, calls from or on behalf of political organizations, charities, and telephone surveyors would still be permitted, as would calls from companies with which you have an existing business relationship, or those to whom you've provided express agreement in writing to receive their calls.[24]

3-3b The "CAN-SPAM" Act

CAN-SPAM Act
Law requiring that "from" lines identify the email message initiator. The Act makes it clear that the initiator will almost always be the advertiser or marketer. Under most circumstances, it will not be a party who merely transmits the message, such as an email service provider.

High on the radar screen of most marketers today is the **CAN-SPAM Act**. Congress passed the CAN-SPAM Act in December 2003 as a result of great public outcry at the amount of unsolicited commercial email filling people's in-boxes on a daily basis. The Act applies to any marketer using email as a marketing medium, so long as the "primary purpose" of an email is the advertisement or promotion of product or service. "Transactional" messages, such as emails sent to complete a sale of merchandise or to confirm shipping information, are excluded from most requirements.

Amongst the provisions of the law, it requires that "from" lines identify the message initiator. The Act, by way of a series of definitions, makes it clear that the initiator will almost always be the advertiser or marketer. Under most circumstances, it will not be a party that merely transmits the message, such as an email service provider.

The CAN-SPAM Act prohibits false or misleading subject lines. Mandatory opt-out is central to the Act. Each commercial email message must include an opt-out link or valid return email address by which the recipient can request to be removed from future emails. It can also include an opt-out list or menu, which allows the recipients to opt out of only those categories of emails that the recipient selects. Importantly, if you choose to offer such a menu, it must include an option to opt out from all future emails.

Commercial email messages must also include a valid physical postal address for the sender. There has been a fair amount of debate regarding whether a post office box will meet this requirement. The general consensus, however, is that the legislative intent was that the word *physical* requires an actual address for the sender's place of business.

Finally, if an email is unsolicited, meaning that the recipient never gave express consent to receive message in response to "a clear and conspicuous request for such consent or at recipient's own initiative," then the email must be identified as an advertisement somewhere in the email. The law does not specify where this must appear, and placement at the bottom of the message is acceptable.

As for the consequences of violations, CAN-SPAM provides for civil penalties of $250 per violation (each noncompliant email is a violation) with a cap on damages at $2 million. These damages can be tripled for knowing and willful violations or if the violations include dictionary attacks, address harvesting, or other "aggravating" circumstances.[25]

3-3c Unwanted Faxes

A telephone facsimile (or "fax") machine is able to send and receive data (text or images) over a telephone line. The Telephone Consumer Protection Act of 1991 (TCPA) and Federal Communications Commission (FCC) rules prohibit sending unsolicited advertisements, also known as *junk faxes,* to a fax machine, tying up the machine for more useful purposes. This prohibition applies to fax machines at both businesses and residences. Recently, the Federal Communications Commission imposed the largest fine ever against Fax.Com for sending out so-called junk faxes. The agency said Fax.Com broke FCC rules 489 times, each instance carrying an $11,000 fine.[26]

3-3d Internet Privacy

The United States has a general preference for industry self-regulation in the field of privacy, in general, and the Internet, in particular. The FTC has defined acceptable practices for development and posting of privacy policies, although there is no law that requires a privacy policy or mandates the content of one. What businesses must remember is that, once a privacy policy is posted, the enterprise is responsible for abiding by the policies they have announced. The three areas in which explicit federal legislation has been passed in the United States are children, financial services, and health. As to the first issue, parental notice, parental consent, parental access to the information collected by the child, allowing parents to prevent further use of information, limits on incentives, and security of information collected are limited. The Gramm–Leach–Bliley Act requires explicit notification to consumers of the data practices and policies of financial services institutions. The Health Insurance Portability and Accountability Act covers several areas of concern about health insurance. It requires stringent controls over the disclosure of medical records in ways that affect even the ability of health care–related firms to rent mailing lists with providing assurances that patients have exercised the required control and given the required permission for release of any information.[27]

3-4 Ethical Responsibilities

Ethical standards may extend beyond what is codified into law. Because enforcement is difficult and because salespeople frequently find themselves in a position where knowledge of legal requirements would be of limited immediate value, they must often set the standards for their own conduct. Under these circumstances, it is a temptation to do the expedient thing and rationalize later. Yet if selling and salespeople are ever to achieve the respect due them, they must act in a manner deemed ethical by the public. Other professions in this country owe much of their public regard to standards of conduct established by their professional organizations. Reflecting this, the American Marketing Association has adopted a code of ethics, which appears in Box 3-2 and, more specifically for the Internet, Box 3-3.

Ethics is a difficult subject in the best of circumstances. It should not be surprising, then, that it is difficult to arrive at a universally applicable rule for the conduct of salespeople. Maybe the only reasonable suggestion (made earlier) is a variation of the Golden Rule. In a situation where questions of ethics arise, salespeople can tell themselves, "A genuine consideration of others is essential to an ethical life." The same holds true in handling the competition. Another pithy question for salespeople to ask themselves when presented with ethical dilemmas: "Would I be willing to explain my decision on network television?" Yet, even with a general standard of conduct, it is difficult to determine proper reactions in specific circumstances.

Although it is true that many unethical or illegal actions simply arise out of salesperson ignorance of the law and company codes of conduct (implying more training), it is also true that many abuses arise out of.[28]

- A "win-at-any-cost" attitude by management
- No clear understanding by salespeople of expectations
- Communication breakdown (i.e., subordinates have to feel comfortable speaking frankly with superiors)
- Rules that are dictated from the top down without input from salespeople
- A feeling that they (the salespeople) are only "cogs-in-the-wheel," with management making money at their expense, engendering a mind-set of getting even
- Increasingly competitive market conditions
- Overly aggressive compensation plans overemphasizing commissions for short-term gains
- An environment in which employees don't have a clear understanding of what is expected of them

The ideal approach is for an organization to have a written code of conduct that everyone receives and reads. It doesn't have to be formal; expectations regarding ethical conduct can be effectively communicated in meetings, orientation, bulletins, and email. A communication breakdown can exacerbate the situation. Employees need to feel comfortable talking to supervisors. Otherwise, they will be less inclined to report ethics violations. Rules dictated from the top down are especially damaging. Smart employers bring their people together to talk about common issues such as gifts and entertainment, and the use of email and other company resources. The most effective rules result from employee input and feedback. A win-at-any-price attitude from management may be the worst detriment to ethics. Management leads by example, and if executives send signals that grabbing short-term profits is desirable regardless of the consequences, workers throughout the organization will reflect that attitude in their behavior. This may manifest itself in a commission-centric environment. Commissions can be tricky and run the risk of distorting judgment, especially when they put salespeople's personal interests at odds with those of the customer or client.[29] Some software companies built their reputation on cutthroat

Box 3-2

American Marketing Association Code of Ethics

Members of the American Marketing Association are committed to ethical professional conduct. They have joined together in subscribing to this Code of Ethics embracing the following topics:

Responsibilities of the Marketer

Marketers must accept responsibility for the consequences of their activities and make every effort to ensure that their decisions, recommendations, and actions function to identify, serve and satisfy all relevant publics: customers, organizations and society.

Marketers' Professional Conduct must be guided by

1. The basic rule of professional ethics: not knowingly to do harm;

2. The adherence to all applicable laws and regulations;

3. The accurate representation of their education, training, and experience; and

4. The active support, practice, and promotion of this Code of Ethics.

Honesty and Fairness

Marketers shall uphold and advance the integrity, honor, and dignity of the marketing profession by

1. Being honest in serving consumers, clients, employees, suppliers, distributors, and the public;

2. Not knowingly participating in conflict of interest without prior notice to all parties involved; and

3. Establishing equitable fee schedules including the payment or receipt of usual, customary, and/or legal compensation for marketing exchanges.

Rights and Duties of Parties in the Marketing Exchange Process

Participants in the marketing exchange process should be able to expect that

1. Products and services offered are safe and fit for their intended uses;

2. Communications about offered products and services are not deceptive;

3. All parties intend to discharge their obligations, financial and otherwise, in good faith; and

4. Appropriate internal methods exist for equitable adjustment and/or redress of grievances concerning purchases.

It is understood that the above would include, but is not limited to, the following responsibilities of the marketer:

In the Area of Product Development and Management:

- Disclosure of all substantial risks associated with product or service usage;

- Identification of any product component substitution that might materially change the product or impact on the buyer's purchase decision; and

- Identification of extra cost-added features.

In the Area of Promotions:

- Avoidance of false and misleading advertising;

- Rejection of high-pressure manipulations, or misleading sales tactics; and

- Avoidance of sales promotions that use deception or manipulation.

In the Area of Distribution:

- Not manipulating the availability of a product for the purpose of exploitation;

- Not using coercion in the marketing channel; and

- Not exerting undue influence over the reseller's choice to handle a product.

In the Area of Pricing:

- Not engaging in price fixing;

- Not practicing predatory pricing; and

- Disclosing the full price associated with any purchase.

In the Area of Marketing Research:

- Prohibiting selling or fundraising under the guise of conducting research;

- Maintaining research integrity by avoiding misrepresentation and omission of pertinent research data; and

- Treating outside clients and suppliers fairly.

Organizational Relationships

Marketers should be aware of how their behavior may influence or impact the behavior of others in organizational relationships. They should not demand, encourage, or apply coercion to obtain unethical behavior in their relationships with others, such as employees, suppliers, or customers.

1. Apply confidentiality and anonymity in professional relationships with regard to privileged information;

2. Meet their obligations and responsibilities in contracts and mutual agreements in a timely manner;

3. Avoid taking the work of others, in whole, or in part, and representing this work as their own or directly benefiting from it without compensation or consent of the originator or owner; and

4. Avoid manipulation to take advantage of situations to maximize personal welfare in a way that unfairly deprives or damages the organization of others.

Any AMA member found to be in violation of any provision of this Code of Ethics may have his or her Association membership suspended or revoked.

3-4a Dealing with Competitors

Some competitive practices are clearly unethical. Boeing learned a hard lesson about business ethics: The aircraft manufacturer lost more than $1 billion in Air Force contracts to rival Lockheed Martin after former employees were accused of stealing Lockheed documents. As a result, all employees of the involved Boeing unit underwent a mandatory, 4-hour ethics training session.[31] Another unfortunate but common situation arises in stocking the shelves of retailers, especially supermarkets. Sales are greatly affected by the amount of shelf space available and the shelf position of the product. One beer sales rep I know would take competitors' 6-packs of beer from the middle of the cooler and place them at the bottom, filling the vacated space with his own brand. Spying a new stand-up rack stacked with a competitor's wares, sales representatives have been known to remove the top few rows of merchandise and replace them with their own. Or they might perform a similar stunt with a jumble display (a bin full of a competitor's product at the end of an aisle), spreading their own wares over the top of the bin. In the grocery business, milk salespeople have also been known to employ unethical tricks. Typically, when driver salespeople deliver fresh milk in the morning, they put yesterday's leftovers up front so that they will sell before turning bad. By placing these cartons in the back again, competitive salespeople may cause sour milk to be sold to their rivals' customers. Such activities are decidedly unethical and should never be practiced, because, if for no other reason, they can easily backfire on the salespeople involved. If the supermarket discovers such tricks, the salespeople may be dismissed from the account with a warning never to return. Sabotage carried out on a large scale can also result in governmental prosecution, involving both the company and its salespeople.

Apart from such clearly unacceptable practices, there are questions of competitive responses that are not as easily answered. For example, in the course of making calls, salespeople often must answer questions about the competition. It is a great temptation to belittle them, picturing their products as inferior or even shoddy and worthless. But before doing so, sales representatives should put themselves in the customer's position. In the computer business, for example, when increased use demands an upgrade of equipment, it is a real temptation to knock the competition. However, when an H-P salesperson belittles Dell PCs to a customer who has had Dell computers for years, he or she is also discrediting the customer's judgment. The same is true of new purchases. If a customer is already leaning in one direction, the disparaging remarks of a competitive salesperson will meet with little favor.

It is doubtful that customer relations can be developed in the long run by shortsighted reactions to competitors' efforts. A salesperson's maintenance of customers' goodwill requires open and honest relationships. Misrepresentation of competitors' offerings is likely to create an image of an untrustworthy salesperson. It is preferable that sales representatives provide an objective description of their products in relation to the competition. IBM has begun to compensate their salespeople on the basis of customer satisfaction. If this means recommending competitive equipment on occasion, then the rep is empowered to do so.

3-4b Dealing with the Salesperson's Employer

A number of difficult ethical questions arise in dealing with the salesperson's employer. It is understandable how an attitude that justifies ripping off the company might develop. Disagreements over commission payment, expenses, and credit approval may encourage unethical conduct toward the salesperson's employer. Such perceived mistreatment can result in irresponsible behavior in some of the following situations.

Expense Accounts

She didn't mean to spy on her marketing team, but during a quiet moment on an otherwise regular day, Susan Marshall couldn't help but overhear the conversation outside of her office. A veteran employee at the small marketing firm in the Midwest was coaching a rookie on the finer points of the "10 percent rule."[32] It was that day more than a year ago that Marshall, a former marketing executive at the company, learned it was common practice for her employees to add 10 percent to every expense report they filed. They attached a few dollars to tips, bumped up mileage, or upped their gas on trips—always accounting for more than they actually spent. They were so subtle that neither managers nor accountants ever realized that thousands of dollars were being lost each year. And the "10 percent rule" was being passed from generation to generation of the firm's employees.

Depending on the particular method of handling expenses, salespeople may see an opportunity to pick up some extra income furtively. Outright falsification of expense records is not a good idea, because discovery can lead to dismissal and consequent difficulties in getting another job. Still, there is a gray area in which salespeople can engage in "creative" deception, especially if they feel that company policies are unfair. If the company only allows $30 per day for a motel room, salespeople can add extra mileage to their expense reports, making up for the costs of a more expensive room. It is easy enough to rationalize such practices. After all, the company *is* being unrealistic. The problem is when to stop. In one company I know, sales managers encouraged salespeople to cheat on their expense reports to get extra income. Perhaps they should not have been surprised when half the sales force had to be fired for arranging kickback schemes with customers to win trips and merchandise in a sales contest. It is also true that widespread cheating on expense reports can lead to higher costs of doing business and higher prices, possibly putting the company at a competitive disadvantage. In addition, the problem may expand. The risks for executives will also mount if dishonesty becomes an organizational problem. They will pay in public perception problems, lawsuits, reduced sales, and decreased market share.

Misuse of Company Time and Resources

Because the salesperson is usually in the field with little day-to-day supervision, it is not difficult to misuse company time. It is easy to sit in a restaurant, avoiding calls and telling yourself you need a break. Of course, this hurts your own productivity, not to mention doing a disservice to the company that is paying your salary. Misuse of company time can also involve holding more than one job. Some salespeople have been known to work another job in the evening or have a business of their own on the side. As a rule, this is frowned upon by companies, because it usually involves less than a complete commitment of time and effort to selling. Managing your own clothing store is unlikely to leave enough energy and enthusiasm for selling.

When it comes to contests, salespeople have ample opportunity to place their own interests ahead of those of their company and customers. For example, is it ethical to withhold customer orders for weeks until the start of a sales contest? After all, there is a trip to Hawaii at stake. It is easy enough to blame late delivery on the company, or the railroads, or trucks. Or is it ethical to sell customers unneeded products or overstock them with needed ones to win a prize? Here again, it is easy to rationalize. After all, isn't it the company that is encouraging these practices by sponsoring the contest?

3-4c Responsibility to Customers

In the old days of the so-called nineteenth-century "drummer" or conman who sold to unsophisticated customers and was rarely in town long enough to incur their wrath when dissatisfaction arose, unethical tactics might have worked. Even then, however, it is doubtful if they worked with all customers, or even most of them.

Customers are sophisticated in today's business environment, so fraud and deception are unlikely to be successful except in the very short run. Nor is the lesser offense of misrepresentation likely to succeed in the long run. Dissatisfied consumers are not going to become repeat buyers, and they certainly are not going to trust the salespeople the next time around. Furthermore, if they feel they have been substantially harmed, contemporary consumers can seek restitution through an increasing number of government agencies.

Aside from any adverse consequences of unethical behavior, a salesperson who acts ethically and professionally will find a receptive group of customers. Studies of the attitudes of buyers and purchasing agents reveal that they are heavily critical of a salesperson's lack of product knowledge, failure to follow up, general unreliability, slavish adherence to "canned presentations," blatant use of flattery, bad manners, and commercial dishonesty. Sales representatives who conduct themselves in a professional manner, contrary to these tactics, are likely to gain the trust of their customers and, in the long run, be successful in terms of both sales and their own self-esteem. The establishment of a relationship demands no less.

Still, deciding what is ethical is not always easy. Some situations force the salesperson to make difficult choices. Most of these situations originate from competitive demands or pressures from the salesperson's own company. An unfortunate example is that of a young broker involved in mutual fund sales for Morgan Stanley. Anthoney DiMeo joined Morgan Stanley the day after college graduation in 2000 and began training as a stockbroker. He says he soon realized his career depended on selling Morgan's in-house investment products, even if non-Morgan products were better for customers. "There was tremendous pressure, constant pressure to sell the in-house funds," according to Anthoney, who has since left the firm. He said his bosses "would come down on us pretty hard," if brokers directed clients into non-Morgan funds. "They forced us to justify why we wanted to do business with a non-Morgan product." The pressure was especially high for new hires, for whom compliance could become an issue deciding whether they kept their jobs. The result: As part of a settlement, Morgan Stanley agreed to pay $50 million and make a number of changes to its business practices.[33] Among other areas for potential conflict are bribes, gifts, entertainment, and reciprocity.

Bribes

Unfortunately, some companies feel compelled to offer bribes. In turn, this puts pressure on competitors to respond with bribes of their own. For salespeople who see potential sales going to the competition, there is great temptation to encourage their company to pay off customers. Or they can act on their own, falsifying breakage and damage allowances to induce customers to buy.

Dangers are present, however, for companies and salespeople offering bribes. Salespeople acting on their own can be dismissed. Companies that engage in systematic bribery may find themselves running afoul of the law. A number of U.S.

companies (Rockwell International, United Brands, Lockheed, and Gulf, among others) were prosecuted and fined for making illegal payments to foreign customers. Many of the individuals actually involved in the bribery were forced to resign. Even if they believed they were acting with company approval, they were dismissed with minimal prospects for getting another job.

As an example, two top executives at United Gunite Corporation, a national firm with offices in Irvington, New Jersey, that sells concrete products, pleaded guilty in federal court to offering graft to city officials throughout New Jersey for contract work worth millions of dollars. The company's president, W. Steven Carroll, and its top marketing executive, Gerald Free, claim they were strong-armed by municipal leaders into buying furniture, designer suits, trips to Rio—and in one case, a custom-designed waterfall for one city official's backyard pool—in exchange for their influence in getting lucrative contracts. "These men were told by their clients they had to pay to play," says Carroll's attorney. "They were under tremendous pressure." Such pressure was apparently what prompted Free to also hand out $100 bills, along with a business card, at a trade show for municipal leaders in Atlantic City in 1996, as recorded by a *60 Minutes* cameraman. Carroll and Free face up to five years in prison, although they may get substantially less time by cooperating with federal officials in the probe. In the meetings industry, a sales consultant and professional speaker based in Scottsdale, Arizona, says that he routinely gets requests from meeting planners who book him to speak at their engagements to elevate his fee to their clients by 25 percent—with the implication that the additional fee will be kicked back to them as a personal thank-you for the booking. In the same industry, hotel executives report that meeting planners sometimes ask them to tack on a few extra dollars to attendee room rates and give them the extra money as an under-the-table payment.[34]

Aside from legal considerations, bribes can escalate to a point where it is no longer profitable to "buy" sales. So most companies categorically refuse to give bribes or "rewards" to customers. From a societal standpoint, bribes are to be discouraged. Instead of the most efficient manufacturer receiving the order, the one with the greatest slush fund may get it. Society as a whole is the loser because efficiency is not promoted. Moreover, a customer who demands a payoff is not likely to be a loyal one.

Gifts

Gifts can easily begin to resemble bribes. At one time, gift giving had gotten completely out of hand. Companies found themselves competing with one another to give their customers better and better gifts. Although these were not outright bribes, they came close to being so. When the government passed the Revenue Act of 1962, which limited tax-deductible gifts to $25 to any one individual in a year, many companies were happy to see the escalation in gift giving stopped.

This is not to say, however, that all gifts are categorically unethical. If the intent of the gift is to express the regard of salespeople and their company for a friend, who also happens to be a buyer, it is difficult to fault the gift as unethical. At Christmastime, there would seem to be nothing wrong with the practice. If gift giving involves items such as calendars and pens carrying the names of the company and salesperson as reminders, then it is also difficult to criticize the gift. But when gifts become a means of buying business, they are to be frowned upon. Salespeople may come to feel more like delivery people than competent professional sales representatives.

Understandably, some companies have instituted a "no-gifts" policy. However, as one sales vice president expressed it, "The flip side of companies not giving gifts is the incredible emphasis everyone is putting on partnerships and building relationships today." Giving a gift is a way to demonstrate visually to your customers that you appreciate their business. You still need to show you care.[35] In fact, the executive's company ran an experiment in which they established two different sample groups consisting of 5,000 customers each and for two years sent chocolates to one but not the other. The increase in business was greater from those who received chocolates than from those who didn't.

So what is the individual salesperson to do? If company policy prohibits gift giving, then there's not a problem—don't do it. If the company itself sends out gifts, again, no problem. However, if gift giving is left to the individual salesperson's discretion, then a few guidelines are appropriate: Keep the dollar value within reason (otherwise, it looks like a bribe); restrict gift giving to important dates (e.g., birthdays, anniversaries of contract signings, or the birth of a child); take careful note of holidays (e.g., a Christmas gift to a Jewish customer may not be appreciated); attend carefully to packaging and the enclosure card (often the sentiment expressed in the latter is the most important element); and don't give alcohol (even if the client drinks). A pretty good rule of thumb: Anything more than $100 is most likely questionable.

Entertainment

For several reasons, most companies place restrictions on the amount of entertaining they will allow. First, it can get too expensive. Second, salespeople may come to feel that entertaining can substitute for effective selling skills, even though entertaining can never replace good products and service. Finally, entertainment can backfire, because customers may resent attempts to buy them with expensive lunches and dinners.

Nevertheless, reasonable entertaining by the salesperson can be a useful tactic. It helps the salesperson get to know the customer on a more intimate basis. The customer may be more attentive in the relaxed atmosphere of a business lunch or dinner than at the office with its numerous distractions. And entertainment at lunch or dinner gives the sales representative a welcome break from the normal workday routine, improving his or her presentation.

Reciprocity

Often, in industry, a firm is both buyer and seller in its relations with other firms. **Reciprocity** involves firms arranging to buy goods or services from one another to the exclusion of competitors. Some companies even have rules that, all else being equal, their customers should receive preferential treatment. Still, the practice can get out of hand. It is not unknown for a sales rep to hint, "If you don't buy from me, I won't buy as much from you." This is a form of commercial blackmail and will be treated as such by many buyers; hence, it can backfire for the salesperson. Even if it is widespread in an industry, the salesperson may rely on reciprocity too much, failing to provide good selling and service, and lose the account, reciprocity notwithstanding.

Finally, when reciprocity gets out of hand, the Federal Trade Commission has been known to issue cease and desist orders to stop the practice. If competition is seriously lessened, the offending firms may be prosecuted under the Clayton Act.

reciprocity
Firms arranging to buy goods or services from one another to the exclusion of competitors.

Chapter Summary

The general topics of this chapter are ethical standards and how they affect the performance of the salesperson's job. Ethics were defined as standards of right and wrong. The difference between ethical standards and laws is that laws are ethical standards that have been codified by society so that violation may result in prosecution and punishment.

Major topics of legislation regulating selling were discussed. These included misrepresentation and breach of warranty; unfair methods of competition respecting orders, goods, and terms of sale; refusal to deal; and price discrimination.

Sometimes salespeople have to make difficult ethical choices. These occasions may involve dealing with customers, competitors, or employers. Subjects of concern include use of expense accounts, company time and resources, bribes, gifts, and entertainment.

The long-term development of a business relationship with a customer requires that the salesperson be trustworthy. Acts of deceit and misrepresentation are unlikely to contribute to this needed credibility. Consequently, maintenance of high ethical standards is simply good business. This is especially true given the influence of the consumer movement. Contemporary buyers are demanding and receiving increased value and satisfaction for their money; if they do not receive it, they are quite willing to demand assistance from their government.

Discussion Questions

1. Your roommate notices you reading this chapter and comments, "Why does your book have a chapter on ethics? It wouldn't seem like ethics had a place in selling." What would you say?

2. Why are ethical standards necessary in selling?

3. How would you define ethics?

4. Why have laws been enacted to regulate the actions of salespeople and marketers in general?

5. Just before making a sales call, your sales manager tells you, "Ray over at Northside Liquor has been buying Rio Grande Beer from us, but we want him to buy all our products. So tell him he only gets Rio Grande if he agrees to buy our malt liquor and our premium brands of beer, too." What do you say?

6. What is exclusive dealing? Describe tying contracts.

7. When are salespeople guilty of misrepresentation and breach of warranty? How do these crimes differ from "puffery"? In what sort of situations has the court tended to rule in favor of the buyer?

8. Would you agree with the statement that salespeople have nothing to fear regarding the law—only their superiors do?

9. What is business defamation? Slander? Business libel? Product disparagement? Unfair competition?

10. What are unfair methods of competition respecting orders, goods, and terms of sale?

11. Are marketers at risk for refusal to deal?

12. What is the best method of defending oneself against charges of unfair competition?

13. What is price discrimination?

14. What is prohibited by the Robinson–Patman Act?

15. How are relations with competitors restricted?

16. You are in sales training with a company. The vice president of sales calls you in and says, "Here's your price book. It's for our regular customers. Of course, we have some special customers who get 5 percent off any price in the book, so be careful about what prices you quote." Is this ethical? Is it legal?

17. How should salespeople conduct themselves with regard to competitors?

18. At your first sales meeting, another salesperson tells you, "Your expense report is worth at least another $25 a week. See me later, and I'll tell you how." What would you say? What would you do when it comes time to fill out the report?

19. If your company allows only 15 cents per mile, what is wrong with reporting extra miles when you know mileage costs more than that? What about exaggerating your expenses for lunches and motel bills?

20. Your boss tells you, "Take this package and give it to Ted Johnson at ABC Distributors. He's expecting a delivery." On the way over, the string breaks, and you see that there is a bundle of money inside. What do you do?

21. If bribes are a common way of doing business in an industry, what is an individual salesperson to do?

22. Is there anything wrong with taking customers to lunch? Is there anything good about it?

23. What is reciprocity? Should the salesperson use it to make a sale?

24. Interview a salesperson and ask about any ethical dilemmas he or she faces on the job. Be sure to indicate that he or she will remain anonymous.

Chapter Quiz

1. _____ is defined as the moral principles and values that govern the actions and decisions of an individual or group.
   a. Ethics
   b. Morals
   c. Common law
   d. Culture

2. When a customer relies on a salesperson's statements, purchases the product or service, and then finds that it fails to perform as promised, the customer can sue
   a. under the provisions of the Clayton Act.
   b. for product disparagement.
   c. for misrepresentation and breach of warranty.
   d. for slander.

3. _____ is constituted by unfair and untrue statements in writing communicated to customers.
   a. Business slander
   b. Business libel
   c. Product disparagement
   d. Unfair competition

4. Because of limitations in the jurisdiction of the FTC and FCC, the National Do-Not-Call Registry permits calls from or on behalf of all of the following *except*
   a. political organizations.
   b. charities.
   c. companies that contacted you prior to registering on the National Do-Not-Call Registry.
   d. companies with which you have an existing business relationship.

5. All of the following statements about the CAN-SPAM Act of December of 2003 are true *except*
   a. the CAN-SPAM Act prohibits false or misleading subject lines.
   b. the act applies to any marketer using email as a marketing medium, so long as the "primary purpose" of an email is the advertisement or promotion of a good or service.
   c. each commercial email message must include an opt-out link or valid return email address by which the recipient can request to be removed from future emails.
   d. The email must be identified as an advertisement somewhere in the email, regardless if the email was solicited or unsolicited by the recipient.

6. Unwanted advertisements, or junk faxes, are prohibited by the
   a. CAN-SPAM Act of December 2003.
   b. Telephone Consumer Protection Act of 1991 (TCPA) and Federal Communications Commission (FCC) rules.
   c. Robinson–Patman Act.
   d. Gramm–Leach–Bliley Act.

7. In terms of privacy, the United States has a general preference for industry self-regulation except for explicit federal legislation that has been passed protecting the privacy of all of the following *except*
   a. children.
   b. financial services.
   c. charitable donations.
   d. health records.

8. In the course of making sales calls, salespeople often must answer questions about the competition. Misrepresentation of competitors' offerings is likely to create an image of
   a. an untrustworthy salesperson.
   b. a hard-nosed, uncompromising salesperson.
   c. a shrewd salesperson.
   d. an aggressive "always win" salesperson.

9. In terms of unethical conduct towards one's employer, a potential tactic used by salespeople to enhance their sales for a sales contest is to
   a. inflate sales figures during the contest.
   b. add additional expenses to their expense account to convey the concept that they are working hard.
   c. ask customers to wait until the sales contest to place an order.
   d. withhold customer orders until the beginning of a sales contest.

10. The practice of reciprocity can become unethical when salespeople state or imply
   a. that if you don't buy from me, I won't buy as much from you.
   b. that all else being equivalent, customers should receive preferential treatment.
   c. that the customer's boss expects reciprocity.
   d. that reciprocity is against the company's rules.

Web Exercise

Go to the following corporate sites and examine their ethics policies. How are they similar? How do they differ? If you were a sales representative for these companies, would your behavior differ between them? Which ethics policy do you admire the most? Which need changes or improvements?

Merck: www.merck.com/about/cr/policies_performance/social/ethicalpractices.html

Mattel: www.mattel.com/about_us/Corp_Governance/ethics.asp

General Electric: www.ge.com/en/commitment/social/integrity/index.html

Time Warner: www.timewarner.com/corp/corp_governance/governance_conduct.html

Notes

1. Arthur Levitt, Jr., and Richard C. Breeden, "Our Ethical Erosion," *Wall Street Journal,* December 3, 2003.
2. Jeffrey Zaslow, "Feeling the Shivers of Faraway Scandals in Fort Wayne, Indiana," *Wall Street Journal,* February 6, 2004.
3. "3M's Big Cleanup," *Businessweek,* June 5, 2000, pp. 96–98.
4. "Anatomy of a Recall," *Time,* September 11, 2000, pp. 29–32.
5. Richard C. Chewney, *Business Ethics and Changing Culture,* Reston, VA: Reston Publishing, 1984.
6. David L. Kurtz, "An Examination of Industrial Sales Representative Accuracy in Discriminating Selected Legal and Illegal Actions," *Journal of Personal Selling & Sales Management,* Spring 1994, pp. 67–72.
7. Weld F. Royal, "Scapegoat or Scoundrel," *Sales & Marketing Management,* January 1995, pp. 63–69.
8. "Massachusetts Lawsuit Seeks to Recover $146M from 'Big Dig' Companies," *Wall Street Journal,* March 18, 2004.
9. Greg Steinmetz, "Former Agents Draw a Picture of Met Life's Sales Practices," *Wall Street Journal,* October 8, 1993, p. B1.
10. Theo Francis, "Northwest Mutual Faces Investigation," *Wall Street Journal,* February 14, 2004, p. C2.
11. "FTC Sues AmeriDebt for Misrepresentation," *Wall Street Journal,* November 20, 2003, p. 6.
12. Steven Mitchell Sack, "Truth or Consequences," *Sales & Marketing Management,* October 1986, pp. 59–60.
13. "Price-Fixing Plays a More Visible Hand," *Sales & Marketing Management,* December 1995.
14. "SCO Group Sues Novell, Alleges Slander," The Associated Press, January 21, 2004.
15. Steven Mitchell Sack, "Watch the Words," *Sales & Marketing Management,* July 1, 1985, pp. 56–58.
16. Steven Mitchell Sack, "The High Risk of Dirty Tricks," *Sales & Marketing Management,* November 11, 1985, pp. 56–59.
17. "Illegal Business Practices," *Promoting Competition, Protecting Consumers: A Plain English Guide to Antitrust Laws,* www.ftc.gov/bc/compguide/index.htm.
18. Steven Mitchell Sack, "Treat the Customer Right—Or Else," *Sales & Marketing Management,* January 13, 1986, pp. 63–64.
19. "Newsmakers," *Sales & Marketing Management,* October 1995, p. 23.
20. "An Antitrust Primer," *Promoting Competition, Protecting Consumers: A Plain English Guide to Antitrust Laws,* www.ftc.gov/bc/compguide/index.htm.
21. "Illegal Business Practices," *Promoting Competition, Protecting Consumers: A Plain English Guide to Antitrust Laws,* www.ftc.gov/bc/compguide/index.htm.
22. John R. Wilke, "How Driving Prices Lower Can Violate Antitrust Statues," *Wall Street Journal,* January 27, 2004.
23. Steven Mitchell Sack, "Price Advice: Keep It Fair," *Sales & Marketing Management,* May 1986, pp. 53–55.
24. "National Do-Not-Call Registry," Federal Communications Commission, www.fcc.gov/cgb/donotcall.
25. Dan Goldstein, "Overview of Data Privacy," *2004 MarketingPower, Inc.,* The American Marketing Association.
26. "FCC Fines Marketer for Faxing Unsolicited Ads," *Wall Street Journal,* January 6, 2004, p. D1.
27. Mary Lou Roberts, *Internet Marketing,* New York: McGraw-Hill, 2003.
28. Gilbert, Jennifer, "A Matter of Trust," *Sales & Marketing Management,* March 2003, pp. 30–35.
29. Michael Weinreb, "A Fine Line," *Sales & Marketing Management,* October 2002.
30. Ibid.
31. "Codes of Conduct," *Sales & Marketing Management,* November 2003.
32. Erin Strout, "Are Your Salespeople Ripping You Off?" *Sales & Marketing Management,* February 2001.
33. Tom Lauricella, "The Constant Pressure to Sell," *Wall Street Journal,* March 27, 2004.
34. Melinda Ligos, "Gimme, Gimme, Gimme," *Sales & Marketing Management,* March 2002.
35. Anne M. Phaneuf, "Is It Really Better to Give?" *Sales & Marketing Management,* September 1995, pp. 95–104.

Case 3-1

Dean Haase is a sales representative for the Twin City Liquor Company, one of the largest firms in the industry. Dean has just joined Twin City and is proud and excited that his first job is with such a prestigious company.

Dean's salary is based on a program of commissions on top of a modest fixed salary. He has just made his first sale to a local distributor and is already planning how to spend the commission he will receive.

At the office, Dean's sales manager has congratulated him and told him it is a policy of the company to send a gift of one case of Scotch to customers who purchase in quantities of $500 or more. Dean questions this policy, but is informed that he may think of the gift as a free sample if he so desires.

Questions

1. Is this gift ethical?
2. What would you do if you were in Dean's place?

Case 3-2

Denise Peckham is an agent of the MLM insurance company, which offers several types of insurance, including auto, home, health, and life. Denise is proud to be an employee of MLM and has a distinguished sales record. In the past, she has enjoyed representing MLM because she thought the coverage they offered clients was among the best in the industry. Recently, however, MLM raised its premiums for coverage, making them among the most expensive in the business.

Denise's salary is based on a rather modest guarantee and a program of generous commissions and bonuses. Since the rise in rates for life insurance, the commission for writing both whole life and term policies has increased dramatically.

In addition, her new sales manager, Barry Bickel, has been hassling her to increase her sales of life policies. At the monthly sales meeting Denise was cautioned by Mr. Bickel that her guarantee might be cut if she did not perform.

This afternoon Denise received three inquiries for quotes for life policies. The first was from her best friend, who also has policies with Denise for her house and car. The second was from an established client who had purchased auto, home, and business insurance from her in the past. The last call was from a complete stranger with whom Denise had never had any contact prior to the phone call.

Denise dutifully quoted what she knew were outrageous rates to all three prospects. Her best friend told her to write up the policy because after all, they were friends, and if your best friend would not look out for your interests, who would? The established client also told her to write up the policy, as did the first-time caller.

Questions

1. What would you do if you were in Denise's position?
2. What is the ethical thing to do?

Case 3-3

The elderly woman greets the insurance agent meekly as she ushers him into the parlor of her home. The room is filled with furniture in various states of disrepair, while the rug has frayed ends and a surface covered with stains of various hues.

One by one, the insurance agent goes through the policies the woman has to supplement her Medicare coverage. He criticizes each one, saying, "We can do better than this for you," and "Our coverage is more complete in this area." Despite his best efforts, however, the woman proves tougher than he imagined and refuses to sign a policy. Finally, he gets aggressive. "What if you

should have a heart attack today?" he shouts, pounding the table. "Our policy will be in effect the moment you give me your check." In submission, she signs the policy and makes out a check.

Questions

1. Do you believe the salesperson's actions constitute unethical behavior?
2. Do you feel that legislation needs to be drawn up to regulate such practices? If so, how should it be written?

Buyer Behavior

Key Terms

amiables
analyticals
assertiveness
buyclass
buyers
decider (or economic buying
  influence)
drivers
esteem needs

expressives
gatekeepers
influencers
modified rebuy
motives
need
new task
personality
physiological needs

problem
responsiveness
safety needs
self-actualization needs
social needs
straight rebuy
user buying influences

Learning Objectives

After studying Chapter 4, you will understand:

- Why it is important for salespeople to understand consumer buying behavior
- The steps in the consumer and organizational buying process
- The hierarchy of motives that influence both individual and organizational behavior
- How to make use of the hierarchy of motives in selling
- How to interact as a salesperson with the four major consumer

- personality types: analytical, driver, amiable, and expressive
- Differences between individual and organizational buying
- The organization decision-making process
- Who is involved in the organizational buying process
- Motives of industrial buyers
- Selling to groups

Bob Harris is a life insurance sales representative. Before he calls on prospects, he tries to find out their age, occupation, number of children, and the amount of life insurance they carry. Through experience, Bob has learned that people don't buy life insurance for its own sake. They buy the benefits that it provides them, and these benefits may vary considerably from one buyer to the next. By gathering information beforehand, Bob hopes to determine his client's insurance needs and structure his presentation accordingly.

If product knowledge was all that was needed to make a sale, a buyer could merely read descriptive literature without any help from a salesperson. The fact of the matter is that people don't buy product features. They buy the benefits those product features provide them. When people consider buying a product, they ask themselves, "What will this do for me?" It is up to salespeople to communicate how the product will satisfy a person's needs. Before each call, salespeople should ask themselves, "Which needs will my customer satisfy by purchasing my product?" The more that salespeople understand what motivates buyers, the more sales they will make.

Skilled salespeople know that they must attune their discussion to the motives of the buyer. If the prospect's motive is primarily economic, then Bob Harris must relate how his insurance plan will provide the most protection for the least expenditure. If the customer is motivated primarily by status needs, then Bob might emphasize that clients of the same age and occupation are buying insurance plans of similar amounts. Bob will adjust his presentation to conform to the buyers' various needs, such as security, investment, or reputation.

4-1 Individual Determinants of Buying Behavior

Although demographic characteristics will answer questions such as "Who buys?" "What do they buy?" and "When do people buy?" they provide only a minimal understanding of "Why do people buy?" An example may illustrate this point. You have probably heard the saying, "If you build a better mousetrap, the world will beat a path to your door." Years ago, a company tried to do just that. They built a better mousetrap, one that allowed fewer mice to escape, but few of these new mousetraps were sold. Later analysis revealed the reason. Although the trap was more efficient, it required the user to remove the dead mouse from the trap. Because the trap was more expensive, the user could not simply throw the trap and mouse away, as with cheaper models.[1] As you might imagine, people were less than enthusiastic about pulling dead mice from the trap. No amount of demographic analysis concerning income, age, and geographic distribution would have revealed this phenomenon. Accordingly, it is necessary to examine consumer behavior at a deeper level. Full understanding requires an examination of psychological characteristics such as motives, attitudes, perceptions, and personality. If you don't think emotions can make a difference, imagine two young men standing on the side of a highway, backpacks resting on the ground, hoping to hitch a ride. One holds a sign that says, "Akron." The other's sign reads, "To Mom's for Xmas." Which do you think is more likely to make the sale?[2]

4-1a The Buying Process

Because it is impossible to physically open up the minds of consumers and become privy to the processes by which they arrive at a purchasing decision, it is necessary to hypothesize about what goes on. The hypothetical model that appears in Figure 4-1 helps to explain the actions of ultimate consumers like you and me, not the concerted actions of corporations and other organizations. The model outlines the steps that may be present in a consumer buying decision. First-time purchases probably include all the steps and require a great expenditure of time, while recurring ones—buying your favorite soft drink—require little time and include only the first and last steps.[3]

As depicted in the figure, motives trigger the buying process. Here we define **motives** to be the "drives, urges, wishes, or desires that initiate the sequence of events known as behavior."[4] Motives serve both to lead off and to direct behavior toward a desired outcome. Although salespeople can exert great influence over the buying process, most of their persuasive efforts should be directed at later stages of the process. Changing motives is almost impossible; it is better that salespeople determine operative motives and work with them as given.

Once a motive is aroused, either because of an internal imbalance (e.g., hunger) or because of external stimuli (e.g., a salesperson), problem recognition occurs. When there is a difference between an ideal state of affairs and the current state, then a **problem** is said to exist. For example, if a person becomes hungry while doing homework, he or she is motivated to look in the refrigerator. If nothing is there, then a problem exists; there is a serious difference between the actual state of affairs (an empty stomach with nothing immediately available to fill it) and the ideal (a full stomach). Similarly, a tax accountant may become aware of the immense amount of time spent researching cases in the law library, when that same time could be spent more profitably with clients. Here, too, there is a difference between an actual state of affairs and the ideal state, a problem the accountant recognizes.

At the problem-recognition stage, salespeople can exercise influence in two important ways. By questioning potential customers carefully, they can make them aware that a problem exists. Although motives are relatively unchangeable, they must be activated for behavior to occur, and the salesperson's questioning serves this purpose. Further, by underscoring the inadequacy of the current state of affairs and pointing to the desirability of the ideal state, salespeople can hasten the advent of ensuing steps in the buying process.

Once a problem is recognized, consumers begin to search for information regarding a solution. The search may be internal—reviewing prior knowledge in one's mind—or external—attending to media or seeking the advice of friends. Our

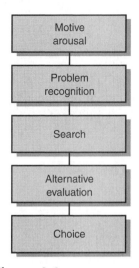

Figure 4-1
The Buying Process

motives
Drives, urges, wishes, or desires that initiate the sequence of events known as behavior.

problem
Difference between an ideal state of affairs and the current state.

hungry consumer will try to recall where there might be food besides the refrigerator—a cupboard with a bag of potato chips, for instance. Or failing this, she or he might consult the phone book for the number of a restaurant that delivers pizza. Similarly, our accountant will review what she or he already knows about time-saving methods. If this information is limited, the accountant will seek advice from other accountants, look through professional journals, or consult with salespeople offering computer time-sharing services.

Once consumers feel that they possess enough information, they will compare purchase alternatives using criteria they deem important. These criteria can be objective (e.g., price and service) or subjective (e.g., an automobile's image). Our hungry consumer will choose a restaurant to deliver the pizza on the basis of price, variety, reputation, and speed of delivery. Our accountant might decide to hire a junior associate to research cases at the law library or to contract with a computerized time-sharing service that has legal cases stored in its computer data bank. The alternative selected will depend on which is less expensive, requires less time, and does the best job of selecting relevant cases. At this stage of the purchasing process, salespeople can be influential by introducing additional criteria and by relating how their products or services satisfy important buying themes.

At the last step of the purchasing process, consumers make a final buying decision. By using their persuasive skills, salespeople can often prompt consumers to select a model and a supplier, and ultimately to go ahead and expend the money.

Throughout this description of the buying process, we have emphasized that salespeople are well advised to work with consumers' existing buying motives. Although salespeople can introduce additional criteria of which consumers might not have been aware, the underlying motives making these criteria important must be present. This places a premium on the ability of salespeople to know the typical buying motives of their customers and to recognize which are preeminent with any individual buyer.

4-1b Needs

Because we cannot directly see a need, we must infer its existence from the behavior we observe. If we see a man get up from his favorite chair, drive to the store, and buy a 6-pack of his favorite beer, we might assume that he was motivated by thirst. Similarly, we might infer that the purchase of Michelob rather than a cheaper beer was motivated by a desire for status.

Some analysts theorize that salespeople do not actually sell, in the traditional sense of the word, as much as activate needs that already exist within consumers and motivate them to make the final purchase decision. This implies that salespeople should be "applied" psychologists, at least in the sense of being intimately acquainted with the needs of their buyers. The good ones are—at least within the narrow realm of their own specialty. In writing a textbook, however, it is difficult to include the entirety of diverse human needs that predominate in each narrow selling specialty. Psychologists themselves have enough trouble coming up with exhaustive lists of human needs; certainly, it is beyond the scope of this text to cover them all. However, a useful and fairly comprehensive theory of needs is presented in the work of A. H. Maslow, who conceptualized a hierarchy of five basic needs.[5]

Needs talk to us as feelings. Maslow says a **need** is a "feeling, which, if left unsatisfied, produces anxiety or tension . . . yet if satisfied, imparts a sensation of well-

need
A "feeling, which, if left unsatisfied, produces anxiety or tension . . . yet if satisfied, imparts a sensation of well-being."

being." This sounds very similar to the definition of *motives* that we saw earlier. Indeed, needs and motives are words that are used interchangeably. Typically, we act when problem recognition occurs, when an existing situation in which we find ourselves appears less favorable in satisfying our needs than another situation we have in mind. It is the contrast between what we want (or are afraid of losing) and what we've got that motivates action. The greater the contrast, the more the need is felt and the greater the tendency to move toward resolution of the problem. Quite often, salespeople need only point out this contrast in order to "sell."

According to Maslow, needs work in a hierarchical order; each higher level of need will not be activated until the preceding need has been satisfied. A hungry person, for example, is unlikely to be interested in Guess jeans until his or her hunger is abated. An industrial buyer whose organization borders on bankruptcy is unlikely to be interested in decorative, status-oriented office furniture. In actuality, it is probably true that needs at each level are never totally satisfied, and they may act as an impetus to buying behavior at any moment. Maslow's five levels of need are as follows.

Physiological needs: This group of needs includes basic necessities such as shelter, clothing, food, water, sex, and sleep. In Western culture, most of these are fairly well satisfied. However, people can readily adjust their needs upward; in an organizational setting, these new needs are realized in terms of pleasant working conditions, more leisure time, avoidance of physical strain or discomfort, and increased salary as a means of better providing for one's creature comforts. A Burger King ad featuring a juicy double cheeseburger seeks to activate the need for food.

physiological needs
Group of needs that includes basic necessities such as shelter, clothing, food, water, sex, and sleep.

Safety needs: These needs are associated with the desire to avoid physical harm, the need for economic safety and security, and a preference for the familiar rather than the unexpected. Life and health insurance, stocks and bonds, real estate, radial tires, burglar and smoke alarms, and travelers' checks all represent purchases motivated by the desire for safety and security. Education, vocational training, and membership in the local health club are services for which safety and security are important motives. On the job, safety and security needs are reflected in a preoccupation with fringe benefits such as hospitalization, retirement provisions, pension plans, workers' compensation, safe working conditions, seniority protections, and clear and consistent performance standards. Smoke detector and burglar alarm manufacturers also focus on these needs.

safety needs
Needs associated with the desire to avoid physical harm, the need for economic safety and security, and a preference for the familiar rather than the unexpected.

The desire for the familiar rather than the unknown represents one of the more exasperating obstacles for the salesperson. We have all met people who feel safe only when doing what they already know, who are extremely reluctant to change to the new and different. Only when such people view something new as less threatening—when the old way or doing nothing seems a greater gamble—are they motivated to change.

Although safety and security are undoubtedly important motives, the salesperson must be judicious in using them. Results have been contradictory in studies on the effects of fear appeals in marketing.[6] A strong appeal to protect one's safety may cause the buyer to repress the need ("This can't happen to me"). For example, a life insurance salesperson could remind a buyer of the chances of dying from cancer at any moment, only to be escorted out the door shortly thereafter.

Box 4-1

Determining Your Predominant Need in Maslow's Hierarchy

To determine your predominant motive in Maslow's hierarchy, complete the form below. In answering this questionnaire, you will be asked to rank groups of five statements. There are no "right" or "wrong" rankings. The best responses are those that reflect your feelings. The more open you are, the more possible it will be for you to gain insights into your real preferences.

In ranking, it is often easier to pick your top choice first, then your last choice, then your choice next to the top, then your choice next to the lowest. The remaining choice becomes your middle choice. By each of the statements, place a number that indicates its importance to you within the group of five statements. Use "5" to indicate your highest ranking, then "4," "3," "2," and "1" to indicate you lowest ranking. (For now, disregard the letters by each question.)

1. Rank these factors as to their importance to you in a job ("5" is high, "1" is low).

   L. _____ Being given recognition and attention for achievement

   V. _____ Working for a strong, stable organization

   Q. _____ Opportunity to belong to a good group

   D. _____ Developing your abilities to their full potential

   G. _____ Opportunity for independent thought and action

2. Rank these factors as to how concerned you would be with them on the job ("5" is high, "1" is low).

   H. _____ Able to accomplish the job on your own

   R. _____ Development of close friendships on the job

   W. _____ Good benefits and job security

   M. _____ A source of pride when you accomplish something

   E. _____ Real achievement and personal growth required

3. Rank the most important factors to you in going to a new job ("5" is high, "1" is low).

   A. _____ The learning and growth you would obtain from the experience

   K. _____ Prestige and respect from others because of the job

   F. _____ Freedom to operate on your own

   P. _____ Friendliness of coworkers

   U. _____ Assurance that you would maintain job security

4. Rank the factors in the order you would like them most in a job ("5" is high, "1" is low).

   T. _____ Congenial working relations

   I. _____ Able to set own directions and make own decisions

   B. _____ Interesting and meaningful work

   X. _____ Few changes so that you knew where you stood

   N. _____ The job being seen by others as important

5. Rank these factors as to the need for them to be present for you to work your hardest ("5" is high, "1" is low).

   Y. _____ Stable and orderly job to be done

   C. _____ Meaningful work and growth opportunities

   O. _____ Full credit for accomplishments

   J. _____ Freedom and independence to get the job done

   S. _____ A real feeling of belonging to a team

Now list and total the point ranking assigned to these letters:

I	II	III	IV	V
A. _____	F. _____	K. _____	P. _____	U. _____
B. _____	G. _____	L. _____	Q. _____	V. _____
C. _____	H. _____	M. _____	R. _____	W. _____
D. _____	I. _____	N. _____	S. _____	X. _____
E. _____	J. _____	O. _____	T. _____	Y. _____
Totals: _____	_____	_____	_____	_____

(*Note*: If you score highest in I, then you are motivated most by self-actualization; II in independence, which is also included in some conceptualizations of the hierarchy; III, esteem; IV, social; and V, safety.)

Social needs: At this stage of the hierarchy, individuals begin to experience their need for love, affection, and belonging. They desire the presence of friends, a mate, children, and a place in a group. Physical and psychological isolation is one of the most feared human punishments. Many have been able to survive long terms of ordinary imprisonment without drastic personality deterioration, but few can long endure the agony of solitary confinement without profound personality changes.

Any evening's viewing of television will demonstrate that marketers have seized upon social needs for emphasis. Advertisements for clothing, soap, perfume, deodorant, mouthwash, and toothpaste are filled with appeals to the desire to belong and be loved. Though these appeals are sometimes repetitious, there is no doubting the importance of social needs.

Esteem needs: These reflect an individual's desire to feel a sense of respect from others. This group of needs may also include desires for (and actions to avoid loss of) strength, achievement, adequacy, independence, and self-confidence. Esteem needs are closely related to social needs, but the individual desires not just acceptance but also to stand out and be recognized. Many products are purchased with esteem as the primary motive—conspicuous homes, club memberships, clothes, restaurants, and cars. If one trades in a Ford Focus for a Mercedes-Benz, a feeling of self-worth and prestige is gained. The American Express Gold Card and Brooks Brother Clothiers appeal to these needs. Of course, status symbols vary considerably from one person to the next. An 18-year-old may consider a beat-up Volkswagen van a status symbol; a 65-year-old might feel a retirement home in Arizona serves the same purpose.

Self-actualization needs: These needs represent the desire to grow, to fulfill one's capabilities, to become everything that one is capable of becoming. Maslow suggests that even when needs lower in the hierarchy are satisfied, we may expect "that a new discontent and restlessness will soon develop. That is, it will appear unless the individual is doing what he's fitted for, what his talents allow him to do. A musician must make music, an artist must paint, a poet must write, if he is to be ultimately happy. What a man can be, he must be." In other words, self-actualization simply reflects individuals' desires to become the best they possibly can at whatever they choose. It is the desire for self-actualization that has prompted many individuals to seek second and even third careers. A long-running U.S. Army recruiting program invites enlistees to "Be all you can be."

Using the Hierarchy of Needs

The salesperson can make use of the hierarchy of needs in developing a number of buying appeals for a product. If a woman has made up her mind to buy a fur coat, but is undecided about style and prestige, it would be unwise to emphasize benefits such as warmth and comfort. Instead, emphasize a name designer, a unique style, or an elegant look. An automobile salesperson questions customers about requirements. If they imply the need for image and status, he emphasizes "esteem" needs—the deep rich color, the metallic paint, the alloy wheels. If they, instead, want safety, he links it to "security." If they prefer a light color, he says, "It may not be fashionable, but it's safe." He follows with other safety features—the structure, the airbag, and so forth. Let us take the example of a salesperson selling a personal improvement course, such as the Dale Carnegie program. The sales representative

social needs
At this stage of the hierarchy, individuals begin to experience their need for love, affection, and belonging.

esteem needs
Needs that reflect an individual's desire to feel a sense of respect from others.

self-actualization needs
Needs that represent the desire to grow, to fulfill one's capabilities, to become everything that one is capable of becoming.

Box 3-3

American Marketing Association Code of Ethics for Marketing on the Internet

Preamble

The Internet, including online computer communications, has become increasingly important to marketers' activities, as they provide exchanges and access to markets worldwide. The ability to interact with stakeholders has created new marketing opportunities and risks that are not currently specifically addressed in the American Marketing Association Code of Ethics. The American Marketing Association Code of Ethics for Internet marketing provides additional guidance and direction for ethical responsibility in this dynamic area of marketing. The American Marketing Association is committed to ethical professional conduct and has adopted these principles for using the Internet, including online marketing activities utilizing network computers.

General Responsibilities

Internet marketers must assess the risks and take responsibility for the consequences of their activities. Internet marketers' professional conduct must be guided by

1. Support of professional ethics to avoid harm by protecting the rights of privacy, ownership, and access.

2. Adherence to all applicable laws and regulations with no use of Internet marketing that would be illegal, if conducted by mail, telephone, fax, or other media.

3. Awareness of changes in regulations related to Internet marketing.

4. Effective communication to organizational members on risks and policies related to Internet marketing, when appropriate.

5. Organizational commitment to ethical Internet practices communicated to employees, customers, and relevant stakeholders.

Privacy

Information collected from customers should be confidential and used only for expressed purposes. All data, especially confidential customer data, should be safeguarded against unauthorized access. The expressed wishes of others should be respected with regard to the receipt of unsolicited email messages.

Ownership

Information obtained from the Internet sources should be properly authorized and documented. Information ownership should be safeguarded and respected. Marketers should respect the integrity and ownership of computer and network systems.

Access

Marketers should treat access to accounts, passwords, and other information as confidential, and only examine or disclose content when authorized by a responsible party. The integrity of others' information systems should be respected with regard to placement of information, advertising, or messages.

---

techniques and on motivating salespeople through fear and the promise of a huge commission. At its most bloodthirsty, Oracle had its salespeople sign "commits'" to bring in a certain amount of business; had Brink's truck drivers deliver gold coins to the desks of the best salespeople; and had singled out the worst of them in regular emails. Weighed down by that pressure, Oracle salespeople reportedly danced around their clients' concerns through half-truths and hard-sell tactics, and, according to one lawsuit filed by a rare-coin broker, allegedly sold an e-commerce software program by touting functions that didn't exist.[30] The cog-in-the-wheel trap works against ethical behavior. If employees are proud of their organization and feel a sense of loyalty, their conduct is far more likely to be ethical. But if they feel management is making profits at their expense, there could be a mind-set of getting even.

might appeal to prospective buyers' physiological and safety needs by explaining how the course will increase their incomes and make them more valued employees to their companies. The salesperson can speak to the prospects' social needs by mentioning how the course will teach techniques for getting along with people and winning their approval. Esteem needs can be addressed by telling how the course will make individuals more successful, winning them promotions and the admiration of their colleagues. And finally, there is an appeal to the self-actualization need by emphasizing that the course's ultimate objective is to develop people into the sort of individuals they want to be.

Even with industrial buyers, the influence of personal motives should not be dismissed. Performance-related buying criteria are predominant, but personal motives unique to the buyer as an individual are not to be ignored. No matter how straightforward it might appear that one vendor has the edge in product quality and price, hierarchical needs can still change the outcome. The buyer may have a great incentive to "play it safe" and purchase from the market leader, the supplier with the recognized name in the field. Or if something should go wrong, the individual buyer reasons, he or she might be better off with the well-known firm than the lesser-known one. In the former situation, there would be less of a tendency by upper management to second-guess the individual's decision. Similarly, salespeople should understand that any buying decision that brings profits or cuts costs for the company also brings recognition (and perhaps a promotion) to the individual decision maker. This personal motive can be subtly incorporated into the sales presentation by the skillful salesperson. Moreover, arguably the motivation to avoid pain, loss, or ridicule (i.e., security in the hierarchy of needs) is stronger than the motivation to gain pleasure, profit, or pride. Prospects might be more motivated by a presentation focused on avoiding losses rather than gains. If you really want a customer's attention, talk trouble—lost sales, wasted time, excessive turnover, customer complaints. In other words, get them dissatisfied and insecure. However, as mentioned earlier, it is important not to severely frighten the buyer, as this can easily backfire.

As Figure 4-2 demonstrates, there is a parallel to Maslow's hierarchy of the individual to the customer–supplier relationship. When organizational customers are looking to purchase goods or services from a particular supplier, they operate on a similar hierarchy of needs, called the *Stages of Organization Need.*[7] Organizational customers possess a priority of needs and a level of satisfaction with their current supplier, based on how well the supplier meets those needs. This analogous hierarchy portrays the relationship a buyer desires, all the way up to a partnership with suppliers.

The lowest individual need is physiological. Business firms need, for survival, at least three resources: money, employees, and raw materials and equipment. Moreover, organizations need essential products or services that work. Most likely, businesses at this stage are commodity purchasers, looking primarily for low price and acceptable performance. The next highest human need is safety—security, protection, reliability, and freedom from anxiety. At the corporate level, this translates into essential services associated with the product, such as timely delivery, absence of damage, and insurance against loss of property and assets. These services also guard against liabilities that may arise in various business transactions. In a service business, the equivalent is accessibility, timely hours of operation, or local service access. The third basic individual need, social (or belongingness), can be equated with an organization's need for an accessible, two-way relationship. A sup-

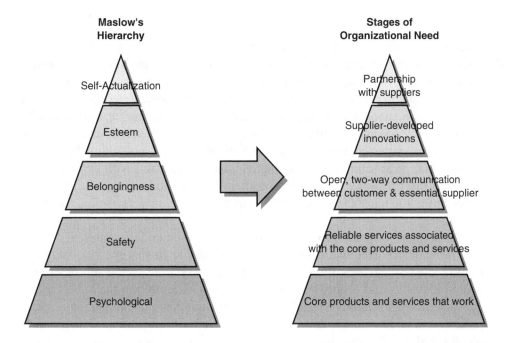

Maslow's Hierarchy

- Self-Actualization
- Esteem
- Belongingness
- Safety
- Psychological

Stages of Organizational Need

- Partnership with suppliers
- Supplier-developed innovations
- Open, two-way communication between customer & essential supplier
- Reliable services associated with the core products and services
- Core products and services that work

Figure 4-2
Maslow's Hierarchy of Consumer Needs and Corollary for Organizational Needs
Source: Adapted from Stanley Brown, "This Is No Psych Job," *Sales & Marketing Management,* March 1995, p. 32.

plier's employees must listen to and communicate with organizational customer workers at all levels to understand unique expectations and resolve problems. It might also translate into the need for recognition by peer organizations; being listed in the *Fortune* 500 or on the New York Stock Exchange; and receiving ISO qualification or the Malcolm Baldrige award for quality. These would also help fulfill esteem, the next need in the hierarchy. The fourth need in Maslow's hierarchy is esteem, the need for acknowledgement, or having a favorable reputation, prestige, or expertise. In business, suppliers grant the customer prestige and stature by committing resources to understanding and anticipating changes that affect him, and then developing new products and services that accommodate those changes. Such suppliers must be proactive and informed about market conditions, and who operate as an extension of the customer's sales force. High Point Chemicals, for example, sells specialty chemicals to the textile industry. The marketplace for its customers is highly volatile, because fashion trends are so short (two years, on average). Hence, it's in the best interest of High Point and its key customers to cooperate so they can develop the next generation of dyes and finishing chemicals in advance of fashion changes. The highest human need is for self-actualization, or mastery. Analogously, at the highest level of organizational need, the supplier's mastery of the customer's business drives the relationship. The self-actualized customer relationship is a true partnership, one in which the supplier is a full participant in the long-term conduct of the customer's business. Bandag, which sells truck-tire retreads to more than 5,009 dealer-installers, offers extra services. For example, it assists dealers in filing and collecting on warranty claims from manufacturers and now offers comprehensive fleet-management services to its largest accounts. Bandag plans to embed computer chips in the rubber of newly retreaded tires to gauge each tire's pressure and temperature and to count its revolutions. That information will enable the company not only to tell each customer the optimal time to retread each tire (thus reducing downtime caused by blowouts) but also help it improve its fleet's operations.

4-1c Personality

If needs have a marked impact on consumer buying, it's also true that buyers' personalities exert a great influence on what they buy, why they buy, and how they interact with salespeople. By **personality**, we mean an individual's characteristic way of reacting to situations. If we observe people who never drive above 55 miles per hour, who check over each answer before handing in their exams, and who spend hours, days, even months before making a buying decision, we say they are cautious. Any experienced salesperson will tell you that understanding buyer personality is critical to sales success. A tactic that is successful with one customer may have just the opposite effect on another. Witness the following exchange between buyer and seller as testimony to the importance of understanding customer personality.

A salesperson strides into a buyer's office, warmly extends his hand, and greets the client, "Hi, Dale, how are you? Nice enough day to be playing golf, don't you think?" The buyer reluctantly extends his hand in response (while still remaining behind his desk) and immediately sits back down. After asking the buyer several questions about his family and talking about the weather, the salesperson begins a presentation addressing general features and benefits of his product. The prospect remains quiet and stone-faced for the most part, occasionally asking for detailed technical explanations, to which the salesperson responds with his own opinions and personal reassurances. The interview ends without a sale—not even a date for a further call. Later at his office, the salesperson comments on how picky and aloof the buyer was; at the same moment, the buyer is thinking how uncertain the salesperson was about his facts and how intrusive he was regarding matters unrelated to business.

What happened? What occurred was that two individuals of different personality styles failed to communicate with one another because of their fundamentally divergent ways of reacting to people and their environment. The basic reality is that businesses do not buy products and services—people do, on behalf of businesses. Salespeople, then, will find it easier to get along with some of their buyers than with others. Because they are typically in the position of seeking the buyer's approval, salespeople must adjust their own style to that of the buyer. This requires that they first know their own personality style, its strengths and weaknesses, and how they are likely to be received by buyers of different styles. Take a moment and complete your own personality inventory in Box 4-2 and plot your personality style.

The application of the concept of social style to the art of selling and the inventory was developed by David Merrill and Roger Reid, who discovered patterns of communication that people use when interacting with one another.[8]

Are you a Driver, an Analytical, an Amiable, or an Expressive? To define these four styles, it is first necessary to describe the scales by which they are defined. **Responsiveness** refers to the readiness with which a person outwardly shows emotions or feelings and develops relationships. **Assertiveness** refers to the amount of control and forcefulness a person attempts to exercise over other people and over situations.[9]

Using the two traits of responsiveness and assertiveness, Figure 4-3 illustrates four possible personality styles. Although most people have characteristics of all four styles in various degrees, typically they have one dominant style. There is no one best style for salespeople; each has its own unique strengths, and successful interaction with buyers depends greatly on the buyers' particular style.

Analyticals are technicians; they are persistent, systematic, problem solvers. Details of performance are their forte; they gather all the facts and attempt to

personality
An individual's characteristic way of reacting to a situation.

responsiveness
Readiness with which a person outwardly shows emotions or feelings and develops relationships.

assertiveness
Refers to the amount of control and forcefulness a person attempts to exercise over other people and situations.

analyticals
Technicians who are persistent, systematic, problem solvers. Details of performance are their forte; they gather all the facts and attempt to make decisions free of personal and emotional considerations.

Low Responsiveness
Rational, disciplined, task-oriented,
formal, independent, businesslike

**Low
Assertive**
Cooperative,
slower acting,
avoids risk,
go-along person,
nondirective

**High
Assertive**
Competitive,
faster acting,
risk-taker,
take charge
person,
directive

D	C		B	A
1		Analyticals		1
			Drivers	
2				2

		Amiables		
3				3
			Expressives	
4	D	C	B	A	4

High Responsiveness
Friendly, informal, open, emotional,
undisciplined, relationship-oriented

Figure 4-3
Your Personality Style

make decisions free of personal and emotional considerations. Because they are so preoccupied with the task at hand, Analyticals are often described as quiet and aloof. Analyticals prefer written proposals and agreements that nail down as many details as possible and expect to have time to weigh the buying decision carefully. Overall, their actions and decisions tend to be extremely cautious and slow. When analyticals raise objections, they expect salespeople to back up what they say with facts, and they are willing to wait for those facts. Price, as measured against durability and dependability, is an important buying motive for Analyticals. When at last ready to buy, Analyticals expect a direct but low-pressure request from the sales representative.

Drivers are task-oriented; "efficient" is a common description for them. They like to take control of people and situations. Drivers find it difficult to communicate a warm, caring attitude; they often seem insensitive to the feelings of others, evoking adjectives such as *cold, dominating,* and *pushy.* Like Analyticals, Drivers prefer facts but of a different sort. Drivers are bottom-line oriented; rather than being interested in the technical performance aspect of the product, they are interested in what the product will do to lower costs, raise income, streamline production schedules, and achieve a quick return on their investment. Because they like independence, Drivers are attracted by things that give them greater independent control over their departments. Drivers are upwardly mobile and, if products help build their track record in the corporation, so much the better.

In dealing with Drivers, salespeople should be organized and to the point; Drivers are very time-disciplined. Small talk is of limited value. Attempts by salespeople to dominate Drivers are destined to backfire. When Drivers raise objections, they expect quick answers, since they expect to make quick decisions; "impatient" is another description of them. When asked for the order, Drivers expect a direct, businesslike approach and a rapid follow-up.

Expressives are animated, intuitive, and lively. They thrive on involvement with others. They like informality and prefer to deal with people on a first-name basis.

drivers
Individuals who are task- and bottom-line oriented, high in assertiveness, and low in responsiveness.

expressives
Individuals who are lively, animated, and intuitive; high in responsiveness; and high in assertiveness.

Box 4-2

Personality Profile

The following sets of adjectives can be used by others to describe you or be used by you to describe others. You must choose those words or statements that best describe how others might see you. Circle the number 1, 2, 3, 4, or 5 based on the nearer the number is to a word, the stronger you feel that the word describes you. Do not circle the number 3 unless you are very uncertain which word best describes you. Please be as candid as possible in filling out this questionnaire. There are absolutely no good or bad connotations associated with any of the words or statements on this form. Apply each of the descriptive words to the statement, "I am most often seen by others as one who is . . ."

1. Prefers to deal with facts	5 4 3 2 1	1. Prefers to deal with opinions
2. Disciplined about time	5 4 3 2 1	2. Undisciplined about time
3. Friendly	1 2 3 4 5	3. Businesslike
4. Fun loving	1 2 3 4 5	4. No-nonsense
5. Animated facial expressions	1 2 3 4 5	5. Few facial expressions
6. Cautious and careful	5 4 3 2 1	6. Open and careful
7. Likes people-involving tasks	1 2 3 4 5	7. Prefers problem-solving tasks
8. Pushes for facts and details	5 4 3 2 1	8. Little interest in facts and details
9. Easy to get to know	1 2 3 4 5	9. Hard to get to know
10. Uses infrequent eye contact	5 4 3 2 1	10. Uses frequent eye contact
11. Critical	5 4 3 2 1	11. Permissive
12. Imprecise and general	1 2 3 4 5	12. Precise and specific
13. Uses hands infrequently in conversation	5 4 3 2 1	13. Frequently uses hands in conversation
14. Shares personal feelings in conversation	1 2 3 4 5	14. Limits sharing of personal feelings in conversation
15. Seeks close relationships	1 2 3 4 5	15. Keeps a distance
16. Formal	5 4 3 2 1	16. Informal

Total 1–16 _____Responsiveness

17. Active	5 4 3 2 1	17. Reserved
18. Cooperative	1 2 3 4 5	18. Competitive
19. Quiet	1 2 3 4 5	19. Talkative
20. Fast actions	5 4 3 2 1	20. Slow actions
21. Uses voice intonation	5 4 3 2 1	21. Little use of voice intonation to emphasize points
22. Easy going	1 2 3 4 5	22. Aggressive
23. Fast-paced speech	5 4 3 2 1	23. Slow-paced speech
24. Takes risks	5 4 3 2 1	24. Avoids risks
25. Passive	1 2 3 4 5	25. Active
26. Thoughtful	1 2 3 4 5	26. Makes quick decisions

Soon after meeting you, they are ready to begin sharing personal points of view. Unlike their opposites, Analyticals, they are not interested in equipment for its own sake but rather as a means to achieve status and recognition for themselves. A Mercedes-Benz for Expressives is less a means of transportation than a way of showing that they have "made it." Expressives will tune out technical explanations; they prefer dramatic sales presentations with creative graphics, showmanship, and a mention of

27. Makes statements	5 4 3 2 1	27. Asks questions
28. Vague and general	1 2 3 4 5	28. Organized and specific
29. Tends to use power	5 4 3 2 1	29. Avoids use of power
30. Strong opinions	5 4 3 2 1	30. Moderate opinions
31. Supportive	1 2 3 4 5	31. Challenging
32. Go along	1 2 3 4 5	32. Take charge

Total 17–32 _____ Assertiveness

Plot Your Personality Style

Mark your total responsiveness score vertically and your assertiveness score horizontally.

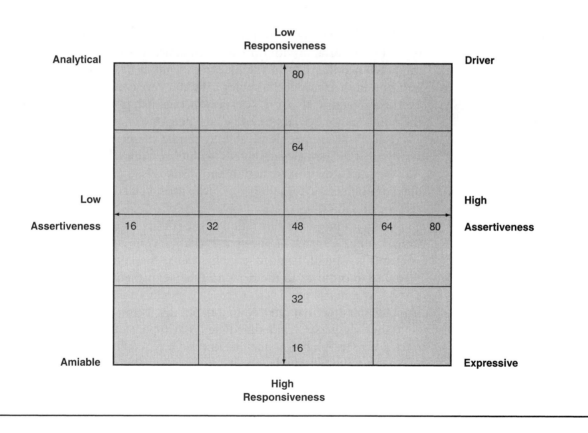

companies already using the equipment—the greater the stature of these companies, the better. If Hewlett-Packard laser printers are what the "winners" have, then those are what Expressives want, too. They expect immediate responses to their objections—ones that speak to their dreams, their opinions, and their personal stake in the buying decision. Expressives generally prefer an informal, relaxed request for the order, but one that appeals to their need to stand out can also be effective.

T a b l e **4-1** Interactions with Different Buyer Types

	Buyer's Social Style			
Preference	*Driver*	*Expressive*	*Amiable*	*Analytical*
Sales interview environment	Professional	Informal, relaxed	Open, honest	Professional
Salesperson's use of time	Effective, efficient	To develop relationship	Slow to develop relationship	Thorough, accurate
Pace	Rapid	Rapid	Purposeful	Purposeful
Information provided by salesperson	Salesperson's qualifications; value of products	What salesperson thinks; whom s/he knows	Evidence that salesperson is trustworthy, friendly	Salesperson's technical expertise
Winning customer acceptance	Documented evidence, stress	Recognition and approval	Personal attention and interest	Evidence with technical details
Presentation of benefits	What product can do	Who has used the product	Why product is best to solve problem	How the product can solve the problem
Assistance to aid decision making	Explanation of options and probabilities	Testimonials	Guarantees and assurances	Evidence and offers of service

amiables
Individuals who are high in responsiveness and low in assertiveness. They value highly personal relationships, dislike risk, and are slow to act.

Amiables are highly responsive, unassertive, and supportive. Most people feel very comfortable with Amiables. Amiables dislike conflict so much that they might tell people what they think others want to hear rather than what is really going on in their minds. In buying, Amiables are concerned with the human aspect; they require that the salesperson establish a personal relationship with them first, and they want to know how new equipment will affect their employees (e.g., "Will my people be able to handle the new system?"). Moving along slowly with personal guarantees of performance is a good idea. Because Amiables are slow to take action and dislike risk, getting the order from them may be problematic for salespeople, who must be patient and must minimize the risk for Amiables.

A rather innovative illustration of the effective use of personality style is illustrated by the campaign of one pharmaceutical company. In an effort to secure appointments with difficult-to-see physicians, the company customized its sales literature to conform to the personality style of the individual physician. Receptionists of Amiable physicians were left a product folder with a handwritten note from the sales rep that referred to a recent discussion. For down-to-business Drivers, the salesperson underlined new or important information on a quick-reference page. Analytical doctors received a typewritten note, a copy of a recent research article, and a folder opened to the page showing charts and graphs. Within six months, many of the previously unapproachable physicians were accepting appointments with the company's sales personnel.[10] Salespeople should adjust their interactions with buyers according to the buyer's style and preferred way of doing business. Table 4-1 provides suggestions.

4-1d Identifying Styles

Although you can easily understand the importance of recognizing the buyer's personality style, the $64,000 question is, "Of what use is this knowledge if I can't identify my customer's particular style?" After all, it is difficult to come right out and ask, "Could you take out a pencil and complete this personality inventory so I can decide how to deal with you?" The answer to the problem, described in Table 4-2, is to first note the buyer's surroundings and then his or her actions, both verbal and nonver-

T a b l e **4-2** Ways of Identifying Personality Styles

	Expressive	Driver	Amiable	Analytical
Behavior	Extroverted	Forceful	Relaxed	Direct/To the point
Surroundings	Disorganized/Personal things	Plaques/Signs of achievement	Cherished memories of personal effects	Organized/Diagrams
Business style	Sociable/A people person	Outcome driven/Bottom line	System orientation	Hard data/Facts
Temperament	Amiable	Fidgety	Evenly paced	Standoffish
Attentiveness	Wandering	Restless	Accepting	Listens critically
Talks about	People and events	Accomplishments	Processes/Systems	The "Company"
Approach	Empathy/Caring	Takes charge	Goes along	Evaluates others
Decisions made	By how they'll look to others	Fast/Realistic	Over time and after deliberation	Only if all the "data" is in
Time usage	Often wasted/Behind schedule	Always pressed	Respects it/Not pressed	Uses it well/Precisely scheduled
Body language	Animated	Restless	Precise/Deliberate	Reserved/Controlled
Attire	Contemporary	Impeccable/Well tailored	Conforming	Conservative/Subdued
Needs	Visibility	Achievement	Others' approval	To be right
Monitors progress by	Recognition	Measured results	How others feel about them	Self-satisfaction
Responses to pressure	Battles with emotion	Battles with reasons	Complies	Escapes with logic

bal. When first entering the client's office, do you see diplomas, awards, and other signs of achievement affixed to the walls? If so, you may be dealing with a Driver. Or are there family pictures on the desk and walls? If this is the case, then you may be selling to an Amiable. Is the office neatly arranged, or are papers strewn all over at random? Is there a simple, functional chair across the desk from the buyer? Or two overstuffed leather armchairs and a small table by the side of the desk for intimate conversation? The former could suggest an Analytical; the latter, an Expressive. What about the buyer's actions? Is the handshake firm or weak? How does the buyer's voice sound? Is it hearty and dominating or subdued? In identifying personality styles, experts recommend that one first determine the buyer's responsiveness because it is more easily recognized than assertiveness, which can be kept in check. Does the buyer have animated facial expressions, much hand and body movement, a flexible orientation toward time, a preference for anecdotes rather than facts, a tendency to share personal feelings, and immediate nonverbal feedback? If so, he or she is probably an Expressive because responsiveness is high. Is the handshake firm, the eye contact steady, the communication emphatic, the vocal volume high, the voice speed rapid, and the questions challenging? Then assertiveness is high and, in combination with high responsiveness, this alerts the salesperson that the buyer is definitely Expressive. These cues and others for spotting personality style are presented in Table 4-2. Another fruitful way of gathering information on buyers' personality styles is to ask questions of their secretaries. Here are some sample questions:[11]

Is Mr. Johnson easy to get to know, or does it take him a while to become comfortable with others?

Does he speak exclusively about business and work or does he like to discuss his family, outside life, and thoughts and feelings with others?

In a meeting, does Mr. Johnson readily voice his opinions, or is he more of a listener?

Table **4-3** Behavior Modifications for Salespeople

To Increase Responsiveness:

- Share your feelings; let your emotions show.
- Respond to the expression of others' feelings.
- Pay personal compliments.
- Take time to develop the relationship.
- Use friendly language.
- Communicate more; loosen up; stand or sit closer.
- Use a few more "easy" gestures like leaning forward, smiling, or gently patting the other person on the back or shoulder (be careful of personal space, however).
- Be willing to digress from the agenda; go with the flow.

To Decrease Responsiveness:

- Get right to the task, the bottom line, the business at hand.
- Maintain more of a logical, factual orientation.
- Keep to the agenda.
- Leave when the work is done; don't waste time.
- Do not initiate physical contact.
- Downplay enthusiasm and body language.
- Use businesslike language.

To Increase Assertiveness:

- Speak and move at a faster pace.
- Initiate conversation.
- Initiate decisions.
- Recommend; don't ask for opinions.
- Be direct rather than circumspect.
- Use a strong, confident voice.
- Challenge and disagree, but tactfully.
- Face conflict openly, but don't argue.
- Increase eye contact.

To Decrease Assertiveness:

- Move more slowly in all ways.
- Seek out others' opinions.
- Share decision making with others.
- Let others assume leadership.
- Restrain your energy; "mellow out."
- Don't interrupt.
- Pause when speaking to allow others a chance to respond.
- Don't criticize.
- Choose words carefully so as not to offend.
- Use less eye contact.

Does Mr. Johnson make decisions quickly, or does he prefer to mull them over for a long time?

Is Ms. Schuldt a bubbly person or does she hold in her enthusiasm and act all business?

Does she control her time rigidly or flexibly?

Does she like working with others, or is she happier working by herself?

Is Ms. Hart a detail-oriented person or does she look at the big picture?

4-1e How to Modify Your Style to That of the Buyer

Because you will be dealing with all four types of personality styles in selling, it is important that you be able to adjust your behavior to that of the buyer. To do so, it is helpful to a look at what you can do to modify your responsiveness and assertiveness. Study the information in Table 4-3.

4-2 Organizational Selling

One good way of understanding the industrial market is to compare it with the consumer market. Several major differences exist between these two markets. At this point, a brief description of these differences will help the reader gain a feeling for the complexity and sophistication of the industrial market.

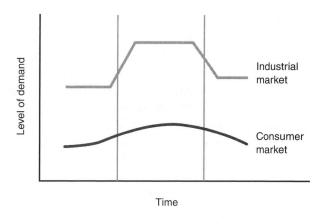

Figure 4-4
Changes in Consumer
Demand are Magnified
in the Industrial Sector.

4-2a Differences between Individual and Organizational Buying Behavior

Derived Demand

One major source of difference is that the demand for industrial goods is derived from the demand for consumer goods. The demand for lumber is derived from the demand for houses; the demand for plastic is derived from the demand for trash containers; the demand for rubber is derived from the demand for tires. Figure 4-4 illustrates the concept of derived demand.

Derived demand is characterized by great volatility, or fluctuations, in sales. Imagine a manufacturer of sinks used in the kitchens of recreational vehicles (RVs). If RV sales drop by 20 percent, then we would also expect a 20 percent drop in the production of sinks. Right? Unlikely. The RV manufacturer buys sinks for storage in inventory, so they will be available for installation as RVs roll off the production line. This magnifies fluctuation in the demand for sinks, since, as RV sales decline, the RV manufacturer will use up the inventory of sinks before buying any more. The classic example of this occurred during the Great Depression, when the production of consumer goods dropped 20 points, from an index of 100 to 80. At the same time, industrial spending dropped 65 points, from 100 to 35. It is easy to understand from this example why industrial firms are so careful in their production and inventory planning. Accordingly, industrial salespeople must know a great deal about the industry and firms to which they sell. An impulse purchase in the industrial market is a rare occurrence.

Concentration of Buyers

Another important difference between the industrial and consumer markets is the concentration of the industrial market with regard to both size and geography. Less than 2 percent of all industrial firms (those employing 500 workers or more) account for 50 percent of all manufactured goods and 42 percent of all the people employed in manufacturing. Four companies produce more than two-thirds of all tires. B. F. Goodrich, for example, sells its original equipment tires to fewer than 10 car manufacturers. The four largest companies in the tin-can industry account for 80 percent of total output. One computer company controls 70 percent of the mainframe computer industry.

Of the nation's approximately 3,000 counties, 294 are considered manufacturing centers. It is estimated that these 294 counties account for about 80 percent of all industrial buying power. New England, the Midwest, and Great Lakes represent almost 50 percent of total U.S. shipments of manufactured goods. Another 20 percent is in the Southeast, and 11 percent in the Far West. The buyers for some of these large manufacturers are often even further concentrated in home offices, often in large metropolitan areas. U.S. Gypsum, one of the largest buildings materials manufacturers, does most of its buying for over 50 plants out of its Chicago offices. Additionally, there are 1.6 million retailers and 521,000 wholesalers in the United States. There are also about 88,000 government units who buy goods and services.[12]

With the intense concentration of the industrial market, industrial sales representatives cannot afford indifferent preparation and sloppy selling tactics. A mistake can cost their company thousands or even millions of dollars.

Multiple Buying Influences

The typical industrial buying decision involves more than one individual. Although the number may vary considerably by industry, the average number of buying influences in manufacturing is five people. The choice of a vendor for industrial drill presses, for example, may be made jointly by the production, engineering, and maintenance departments, as well as the purchasing agent. Each of these departments will have a different viewpoint that must be reconciled before an order is placed. This, of course, makes the job of the industrial salesperson that much more difficult.

Size and Frequency of Orders

The size of orders placed by industrial buyers is considerably larger than those in the consumer market. For example, Motorola was awarded a $63 million contract to install a cellular phone system in Brazil.[13] An industrial order may involve millions of dollars' worth of goods and services, though typically the period of time between orders is longer. A company may order a computer system and not change it for five to six years. Even so, service requirements will continue during that time, and the salesperson will have to be available for that moment when another order is placed.

Derived demand, the size of the purchase order, and the number of potential buyers will all contribute to the success of the new A380 superjumbo jet (seating 500 to 800 passengers) being developed by Europe's Airbus Industrie.[14]

Sophisticated Buyers

Buyers in the industrial market are considerably more sophisticated than buyers in the consumer market. Economic rather than emotional motives predominate. The technical requirements of items purchased are such that trained professional buyers are employed. Although the characteristics of individual buyers are important, generally the requirements of the organization are more critical in vendor selection.

Shorter Channels of Distribution

Channels of distribution in the industrial market are generally shorter and more direct. In most instances, few if any intermediaries are involved. Because of the increased size of orders and fewer customers, the use of personal selling becomes much more feasible. With the average industrial sales call costing more than $200, it is difficult to justify using salespeople when the order size is small, but for a sale of thousands or even millions of dollars, it is another matter.

4-2b Understanding Industrial Buying Behavior

The industrial salesperson must understand both the organizational buying process and the motivation of those participating in it. In the sale of a large computer, it is not enough to know that the purchasing director, data-processing manager, controller, and chief financial officer must all approve the purchase. The motives of each of these individuals must be understood so that the salesperson can formulate a sales presentation that satisfies each of them. Speaking to the CFO about the internal speed of the machine will not improve the sales representative's chances of making a sale if the controller is interested only in the return on investment. Similarly, a presentation on available programming software is unlikely to please the purchasing agent.

The Organization Decision-Making Process

As Figure 4-5 indicates, the buying process may be divided into three buyclasses, which are categorized according to the newness of the buying problem (new task, modified rebuy, and straight rebuy) and hence involve extensive problem solving, limited problem solving, and routine response, respectively. A **new task** situation refers to circumstances never before considered by buyers, which accordingly demands much learning and deliberation on their part. For a new task buy, customers are likely to seek out salespeople and welcome their advice. The buyer in **modified rebuy** buying seeks to make modifications in product specifications, delivery schedules, prices, or suppliers. For instance, when energy prices started increasing, firms in the construction industry started shifting from ordinary flat glass to insulating glass. Although modified rebuy buying is less complex than a new task buy, it still may involve multiple buying influences. Alternative suppliers who better fit buyer needs may find opportunities to take business away from current vendors. A **straight rebuy** refers to the perfunctory purchase of a standard item from the same supplier on a routine basis. Typically, a straight rebuy is triggered by low inventory level, which initiates a purchase order being issued electronically to an approved vendor. Wal-Mart and Kmart have such a relationship with Procter & Gamble for ordering and replenishing P&G's products in their stores. By using computerized cash register scanning equipment and direct online connections to P&G, these retailers can tell P&G what merchandise is needed, along with how much, when, and to which store to deliver it on a daily basis. Clearly, this tends to lock in organizations to their current suppliers. Though advantageous for the "in" vendor, "outs" have difficulty breaking in. Buyers may feel that they already know all there is to know about the product in question, and they may be unwilling to listen to alternatives. In fact, salespeople may have difficulty just getting an appointment. To crack such accounts, they must begin by patiently examining buyers' needs in depth and then pointing out how their product will do a better job. Of course there is always the possibility that the in-vendor will make a critical mistake. This happened in one instance, when a forms supplier provided labels to a catalogue company at a good price only to have the labels fall off the shipping packages; another vendor was immediately contacted.

new task
A buying circumstance never before considered by buyers, which accordingly demands much learning and deliberation on their part.

modified rebuy
Buying that seeks to make modifications in product specifications, delivery schedules, prices, or suppliers.

straight rebuy
Perfunctory purchase of a standard item from the same supplier on a routine basis.

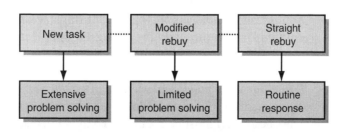

Figure 4-5
Three Types of Industrial Buyclasses

Buyphases

Some of the eight buyphases in the procurement process may occur simultaneously, but generally the eight phases take place in the following order:

1. *Anticipation or recognition of a problem (need) and a general solution.* Nothing fruitful can occur until a problem or need is recognized. This may be initiated by an organization member—anyone from factory worker to president. Often it is an outsider, such as the salesperson, who first points out a problem. At this stage, there is also likely to be the recognition that a solution to the problem lies in making a purchase.

2. *Determination of the characteristics and quantity of the needed item.* This step may be perfunctory in the case of a routine item. Once inventory of a commonly used item drops too low, the computer flags it, and a purchasing agent (or the computer itself) issues a standard purchase requisition. If the item is new, however, the using department probably will have to determine the characteristics.

3. *Outline of the description (specifications) of the purchase.* It is not enough that desired characteristics be identified. They must be specified objectively so that a buyer can work with them. A clear and comprehensive list is essential for subsequent stages of the procurement process.

    In phases 2 and 3, great opportunities are available to diligent salespeople. If they know of a corporate need, they can begin to work with the initiating department, assisting in drawing up specifications for the needed item. Prospects are usually only too happy to have this offer of help. Producing the specification is often a real pain for a prospect, because he or she simply does not know enough about the product. Of course, by offering assistance, the salesperson hopes to obtain specifications that favor his or her product. This must be done subtly, however, and must be backed by a firmly reasoned justification; the overall specification has to be sound and obviously in the prospect's best interests. Still, the competent salesperson should be able to do that and still write specs that favor his or her product. Preemption always beats competition. Salespeople coming into the picture after specifications have already been set are likely to find themselves hopelessly disadvantaged. As the buying process unfolds, there occurs a "creeping commitment" on the part of the buyer, which gradually narrows the field of potential suppliers. As decisions are made at each step, the range of alternatives narrows; the customer becomes more and more committed to a specific course of action and even a specific vendor. After all, with a new buy, it is the supplier who likely possesses the most technical knowledge.

4. *Search for and qualification of potential sources.* Once the characteristics of the item are identified and clearly described, a search for qualified vendors begins. If the item is simple or if the purchase is routine, a vendor that the company has long employed may be sought out immediately. If the purchase is a new one, the search may be extensive.

5. *Acquisition and analysis of proposals.* At this stage, proposals from alternative vendors are scrutinized. In the case of the simple item, this phase may consist of nothing more than consulting a catalog. If the article is complex or new, then proposals are likely to be lengthy and detailed.

6. *Evaluation of proposals and selection of supplier(s).* In this phase, the affected departments in the organization study the proposals and make a decision. The salesperson must be cognizant of the information flow between

departments, which is often difficult and frustrating work. After selections are made, negotiations may continue regarding such matters as price, terms, and delivery schedules.

7. *Selection of an order routine.* During this stage, the buyer places an order with the vendor. The order is processed, shipped out, received, and inspected. Then payment is made.

8. *Performance feedback and evaluation.* The performance of the product and vendor are analyzed. The system may be formal or informal, but the salesperson should closely monitor the feedback to ensure favorable evaluation.

Figure 4-6 illustrates how the **buyclass**—new task, modified rebuy, and straight rebuy—affects the buyphases for an industrial drill. Note that the new task situation is marked by more buying influences, more suppliers, and a lengthier decision period. In fact, with the straight rebuy, many of the phases are so perfunctory as to border on the nonexistent.

Whether a firm is "on" the list of suppliers or even the sole supplier or "off" the list of suppliers will obviously affect marketing strategies. The latter will have to exert much greater effort to get an order, especially in a straight rebuy situation. A summary of how selling strategies will vary for "in" and "out" firms by buyphase is presented in Table 4-4.

Determining who is involved in the buying process and their position in the organizational hierarchy is critical to the success of the industrial salesperson. The participants and their positions may vary widely from company to company, but some generalizations can be made.

In the big or complex sale, sales managers are apt to tell their salespeople to contact "my old friend Bob Thompson" or the head of a certain department at the buying organization. They rely on "friends," people who have been important in the past, or the heads of departments whose titles sound as if they would logically be involved in a buying decision.

buyclass
One of three types of organizational buying situations: new task, modified rebuy, or straight rebuy.

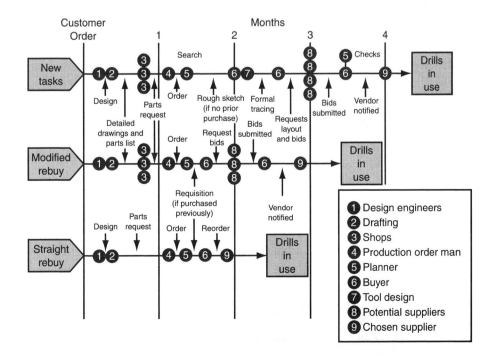

Figure 4-6
How the Decision-Making Process Varies with Each Buyclass

T a b l e **4-4** **Strategies for Vendors**

Strategies for "In" and "Out" Vendors

Buyphase	In Supplier	Out Supplier
New task	Monitor changes in needs; respond quickly; participate in early phases	Search for leads; suggest new approaches; supply technical advice
Modified rebuy	Act immediately; reexamine needs	Respond more quickly; sell on alternative competitive advantages
Straight rebuy	Exceed expectations; reinforce relationships	Sell superior benefits; seek "foot-in-door" orders

4-2c Who Is Involved in the Organizational Buying Process?

There is, however, another approach.[15] Here, salespeople are told to look for certain key buying roles that are common to all organizations involved in the complex sale, as shown in Figure 4-7. Although personalities and titles might change, these roles remain constant, and salespeople should identify the role players before embarking upon the selling process. In every complex sale, there are thought to exist five critical buying roles. The number of people involved in the buying decision might be one or 100, but they can usually be identified as playing one of these five roles.

decider (or economic buying influence)
Role in buying center with the formal power to select or approve the supplier that receives the contract.

Decider (or economic buying influence): Although many individuals or committees may be involved in the overall buying decision, ultimately there is only one person who can give the final approval to buy. The Economic Buyer can say "yes" when everyone else has said "no," and vice versa. His or her focus will be the bottom line and the impact of the sale on the organization and its goals. Failing to identify the Economic Buyer early in the selling process has ended many "a sure thing," when someone hitherto unidentified puts everything on hold. If possible, the Economic Buyer should be contacted first.

The individual who is the Economic Buyer can change from sale to sale, and depends on a number of factors, but almost by definition you won't find people who can give final approval far down on the corporate ladder. For example, the chief financial officer at a hospital may make the final decision on a purchase because of payment terms, but leave the purchasing details to the purchasing agent. In small organizations, the Economic Buyer is typically the owner or CEO. Beyond this, the person who plays the role of the Economic Buyer depends on a number of factors. If Southwest Airlines decides to buy a new fleet of jet airliners, the CEO will make the decision. The greater the dollar amount of the sale, the higher up in the organization the Economic Buyer is likely to be. Every company has "cutoffs" at which approval for a purchase goes

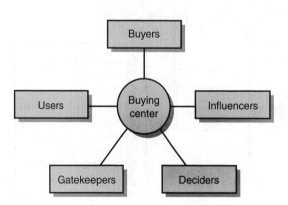

Figure 4-7
Who Is Involved in the Organizational Buying Process?

either up or down the ladder. These points relate to the dollar amount of the sale relative to the size of the buying company. In the small organization, the CEO may get involved in any decision over $10,000; for the large organization, the comparable figure may be $100,000. It is also true that business conditions can alter the identity of the Economic Buyer. In recessions, many salespeople are surprised to find the CEOs of even *Fortune* 500 companies signing off on every purchase over $5,000. It is also typical that the less experience the organization has had with the salesperson, his or her company, and the product or service, the higher up in the organization the Economic Buyer will be. Finally, because the Economic Buyer's focus is on long-term stability and growth, buying decisions that radically affect these areas will involve a higher-placed person playing that role. It is important to remember that there is no one individual who is the Economic Buyer in all instances; it varies from sale to sale, depending on the previously mentioned factors.

If the Economic Buyer is the CEO or chair of the board (or at a similarly high level), it may be difficult to get to that individual, especially if your access is blocked at a lower level. One practical approach to use in reaching these individuals is to use your own management. It is quite reasonable to say that your manager would like to come and meet the prospect; and, as a matter of courtesy, he or she would naturally expect to meet your contact's manager. This is a very difficult ploy for the contact to avoid, since protocol demands that he or she agree. Another possibility is to use a reference to provide you with an introduction to a higher level. Your own directors often will have contacts in common with your prospect; the old-boy network can be very useful.

User buying influences: The role of User Buyers is to make judgments about the potential impact of the product or service on their job performance. For example, drill press operators at Southwest Airlines might request that the purchasing agent buy drill bits from a particular supplier because they stay sharp longer and reduce downtime in maintenance. Quite often, users initiate the purchase process. User Buyers are concerned primarily with how the sale is going to affect everyday performance in their own areas or departments; their focus is thus much narrower than that of the Economic Buyer. People acting as User Buyers will ask about factors associated with immediate day-to-day operations: product reliability, service record, retraining required, downtime record, ease of operation, maintenance, safety, and potential impact on morale. Because their personal success may depend on the successful performance of the product or service, User Buyers may make subjective decisions. The User Buyer cannot be ignored by the salesperson in the long run, because the way they use the product directly affects how that product is viewed by everyone else in the organization. Even if the salesperson manages to get around the User Buyer's initial "no," the chances for follow-up sales may be stonewalled by the resentment and lack of cooperation of User Buyers.

user buying influences
Buyers who make judgments about the potential impact of the product or service on their job performance.

Influencers: These would be individuals who influence, while not actually having formal decision-making power, such as Research and Development (R&D) people who help write specifications or supply information for evaluating alternatives. They exercise great power in some decisions or they may simply provide information. In a hospital laboratory, for example, technical people may be critical in specifying one product or vendor over another. At Southwest Airlines, for example, flight engineers and pilots often influence purchase decisions based on their experience with various vendor options.

influencers
Individuals who influence, while not actually having formal decision-making power.

gatekeepers
Their role is to screen out possible suppliers. Their focus is on the product or service itself, and they make recommendations based on how well the product or service meets a variety of objective specifications.

Gatekeepers: The role of the Gatekeeper is to screen out possible suppliers. Their focus is on the product or service itself, and they make recommendations based on how well the product or service meets a variety of objective specifications. As one disgruntled salesperson put it, these are "people who can't say 'yes,' only 'no'—and usually do." Their job is to act as gatekeepers, to screen out potential vendors. Quite often, purchasing agents act as gatekeepers, screening out vendors based on price, delivery time, failure to meet quality-control specifications, logistics, and even references.

Gatekeepers control the kind and amount of information to other people involved in the purchasing process. A Gatekeeper may control information going to the organization's purchasing agents, the suppliers' salespeople, and others on the selling and buying teams. Information technology (IT) people are often Gatekeepers because they frequently hold the information that is key to decision making. There are two types of Gatekeepers: *screeners* (like secretaries at Southwest Airlines, who decide whose phone call is put through to the executive or purchasing agent) and *filters* (like the Southwest Airlines purchasing agent who gathers proposals from three companies and decides what to tell others in the buying center about each company). The purchasing agent filters information, choosing to pass along some but not all of it to influence the decision.

buyers
People who actually contact the selling organization and place the order.

Buyers are the people who actually contact the selling organization and place the order. In most organizations, Buyers have the authority to negotiate purchases. In some cases, they are given wide discretion. In others, they are constrained by technical specifications and other contract requirements determined by technical experts and top administrators. At Southwest Airlines, the level of authority to buy is determined by the size and type of purchase involved. In many organizations, the decision may be referred to a buying committee, which may either vote or reach a consensus on which vendor to buy from or which product to buy. Purchasing agents (individually or in committees with other executives) often perform the role of Buyers.

Different members of the buying center may participate—and exert different amounts of influence—at different stages in the decision process. At Southwest Airlines, people from engineering, quality control, and R&D often exert the greatest influence on the development of specifications and criteria that a new product must meet; the purchasing manager often has more influence when choosing among alternative suppliers. The makeup and size of the buying center varies with the amount of risk the firm perceives when buying a particular product. The buying center tends to be smaller—and the relative influence of the purchasing manager greater—when reordering products the firm has purchased in the past than when buying something for the first time or buying something that is seen as risky.

4-2d Motives of Industrial Buyers

Industrial buyers are motivated by both economic and noneconomic (or personal) motives. With industrial buying, economic factors predominate, but noneconomic considerations, especially those personal to the individual buyer, should not be ignored. Often the buyer may not even be consciously aware of these factors. It is, in fact, quite likely that the salesperson will have to recognize the influence of these personal considerations, even if the buyer does not.

Economic Motives

It would be impossible to list every economic buying motive, but some of the more important ones follow. Seven of the most commonly used criteria are (1) price, (2) ability to meet the quality specifications required for the item, (3) ability to meet delivery schedules, (4) technical capability, (5) warranties and claim policies in the event of poor performance, (6) past performance on previous contracts, and (7) production facilities and capacity.[16] It is important for the industrial salesperson to recognize which of these motives are most critical to the specific organization being approached. It is also important to realize that different buying centers may be interested in different combinations of buying motives.

Personal Motives

Because industrial buyers are also people, they are motivated by personal considerations. Many of the motives discussed earlier affect buyers within the context of the organization. Safety, one of the five motives in Maslow's hierarchy of needs, has an important influence on organizational buyers' decision making. Should they make a bad decision, not only may the organization suffer but so may their reputation; it is conceivable that even their job security may be jeopardized. To minimize this risk in decision making, buyers often rely on the size and reputation of the supplier. A salesperson from a company without a reputation may face a skeptical buyer.

The salesperson may take several measures on his or her own to reduce the risk a buyer sees in a purchase decision. The salesperson should make sure to present a credible image. Proper dress and attention to nonverbal behavior will help when first approaching the buyer. Thoroughly researching the buyer's problems and making a good presentation will further reduce perceived risk. Testimonials from satisfied customers are valuable, as are warranties that guarantee performance. Visits and reassurances from executives in the sales representative's company also are effective. Free samples or trials may eventually clinch the sale, but they cannot be used with all products, especially expensive items.

Corporate Culture

Salespeople also should be sensitive to the idiosyncrasies of the companies with which they deal. Some of this is due to the preponderance of personality styles that some industries seem to attract. As noted in Figure 4-8, the percentage of Drivers, Analyticals, Expressives, and Amiables varies widely among selected industries.[17] This alone will dramatically affect the personal motives that characterize buyers.

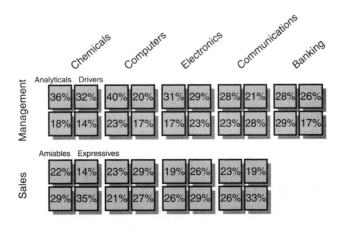

Figure 4-8
Personality Style Distribution in Selected Industries
Source: Adapted from Wilson Learning Corporation, Eden Prairie, MN.

Box 4-3

Sample Recommendations for the Salesperson

Structure Presentations to Airlines in the Following Way:	Structure Presentations to Banks as Follows:
• Stress new developments and new or improved features of products or services.	• Stress one's credibility by emphasizing experience and a tradition of success.
• Make the presentation with a fairly fast delivery—about 200 words per minute.	• Compose one's appeal with an average or slightly slower-than-average rate of delivery.
• Allow one's voice to sound enthusiastic and very upbeat.	• Make one's voice sound contained and reserved.
• Keep language simple, using one- and two-syllable words along with a sprinkling of insider jargon.	• Use more-refined language, employing occasional multisyllabic terms to elevate the perception of the vendor as a fitting and proper firm with which to do business.

Moreover, companies themselves have their own corporate cultures. It's 11 A.M. on a fall Thursday in Silicon Valley, and Sergey Brin, the 28-year-old cofounder and president of Google.com, isn't exactly tearing up the streets on his morning commute—via Rollerblades. Not that he cares; there's no official starting time at Google—or ending time for that matter. It's not about rules here. Workers at the fifth most popular website in America set their own hours, get backrubs from a company masseuse, and even bake bread from scratch if the mood strikes them. When he does arrive, Brin skates into the Googleplex, as headquarters are called—past the red, blue, and yellow lava lamps, the crimson couch, and the self-playing ebony grand piano with Muppet-theme sheet music. He's just missed one employee's two children throwing gigantic rubber balls at each other. This is typical as are the three employees suited up for a 50-mile, mid-morning bike ride. At any moment, Yoshka, a 100-plus pound Leonberger, might come trotting around the corner with his owner.[18]

In contrast, EMC Corporation is a company that's been leading the competition within the enterprise storage industry. Everything about EMC is fast, yet disciplined. CEO Mike Ruettgers is a no-nonsense leader who demands absolute dedication from each employee to help grow the business and stay ahead of the industry. "The first sales manual we had was written by a guy named Charles Darwin, and we've reprinted that about a dozen times," he says with a laugh. "We are very results-oriented, we have a very high sense of urgency. The motto of this company—instilled from day one of training, when new hires are asked to run across hot coals as an initiation into EMC—is 'only the strongest survive'. 'There's no whining, which sounds silly . . . we won't tolerate folks who see the obstacles," he says. "Because of that, it remains an upbeat place to be. We hire people for their attitude and train them for everything else. For example, we just hired a lot of Marines—they aren't experienced in customer service, but because we are a place that has established missions, they will succeed. It's all about attitude."[19]

Taking into account the culture of the industry to which they are selling, salespeople should change the words and tone of their presentations. When they speak to two contrasting industries as outlined in Box 4-3, airlines and banks, they must change their approach. When they talk with executives in the airlines, they find people who sound "well informed," and are somewhat "trendy," "energetic," and "harried" by their struggle to keep up with a deregulated, hectic, and constantly changing environment. At the same time, bankers are much more "calm" and "collected," and their speech reflects their "self-confidence" and the relatively "stable" nature of their field.

4-3 Selling to Groups

Quite often, perhaps most of the time, industrial salespeople must deal directly with groups of individuals in the buying organization; that is, they must make their presentation to an assembled group of executives from the prospect's company. The dynamics of communicating directly with groups are much more complex than when communicating with individuals.[20]

4-3a Special Problems of Dealing with Groups

Salespeople face unique problems when selling to groups:

1. As the number of people in a group increases, the sales representative's ability to monitor the reactions of any one member decreases. Additionally, the quality of feedback declines. To a substantial degree, as one group member speaks, the salesperson must analyze the nonverbal reactions of the other group participants—and analyzing nonverbal behavior is far from a science.
2. It is virtually impossible for the salesperson to personalize the presentation for each group member as would be the case when seeing each individually.
3. The dynamics of group interaction are such that knowledge of these dynamics is more important than knowledge of each individual's separate psychological makeup. That is, the role of an individual in the group is more predictive of buying behavior than that individual's own unique personality traits.
4. As the number of participants increases, the likelihood of noise (misunderstandings, distortion, and misinformation about the salesperson's message) increases.

4-3b Why Selling to Groups Is Important

Selling to groups is critically important because

1. Research seems to indicate that in industrial selling, the salesperson must influence three or more individuals to close a sale.
2. A salesperson can deliver a presentation to many, thus economizing on his or her use of time.
3. In a group setting, the pecking order of authority often becomes apparent, with some members of the group deferring to those with authority. The latter, once identified, can be visited individually later.
4. Often, those opposed to the salesperson's proposal may be convinced by other, more favorably inclined group members, something the salesperson might not be able to do on his or her own.

4-3c Dealing with Groups of Two

It is useful to make a distinction between buyer groups of two and groups of three or more. In a sales call on two buyers, the salesperson should first determine the relative positions of the buyers in the organization. If one is the superior and the other a subordinate, the salesperson can concentrate on the former, while making sure to be polite to the subordinate. The superior should be allowed to set the tempo for the meeting. If the two are of equal rank, the salesperson must treat each equally. The salesperson must not ignore one party enough for that person to lose interest. If the two parties are interested in different purchase criteria (e.g., a research engineer and a purchasing agent), the salesperson should concentrate on common points of interest to both and leave their unique interests for subsequent personal meetings with each person.

4-3d Dealing with Groups of Three or More

Analysis of the problem of handling more than three people indicates there are several actions that can be taken to simplify the salesperson's task and to increase the odds of success.

1. Try to reduce the number of people in the group. Of course, the salesperson should take care not to offend those ignored. To avoid this problem, at the start of the meeting, the salesperson can ask for the group members to identify themselves and their reason for attending the meeting. Some may be there as observers for their superiors, and the salesperson can largely leave them out of the discussion because their role is mostly passive. The salesperson should be alert to those whom the group regard as dominant; if one person is clearly dominant, the salesperson can work largely with him or her. Until the spokesperson emerges, however, the salesperson may want to treat all group members as equals.

2. Establish an agenda. It is critical that the salesperson keep the number of topics discussed to a minimum. Otherwise, the group's attention may wane, and their minds may wander. Accordingly, conversation must be kept to the essentials of the salesperson's proposal. The easiest way of doing this is with the assistance of handouts, flipcharts, or a chalkboard on which points are enumerated. With these before the group, the salesperson can tactfully restrict the discussion until all points are covered. This has the added advantage of letting participants know how the discussion is progressing and how long the meeting will last. People are more relaxed and cooperative when they are familiar with the environment than when they are uncertain about what is going to transpire.

3. Draw conclusions from the discussion rather than leaving this to each group member individually. In an interview with one prospect, this is easy for the salesperson to do with appropriate questioning, but polling each individual is impossible with a large group. The salesperson therefore should summarize the discussion on each topic on the agenda and state the conclusion reached so the group can respond to it. If the group does not accept the conclusion drawn by the salesperson, discussion of the topic must be reopened until there is agreement. This technique of frequent summarization makes it more likely for group members to leave the meeting basically in agreement with the salesperson's proposal.

4. Bring up and concede weaknesses voluntarily rather than defend them after someone in the group has cited them as reasons for not buying. This is especially true of early meetings when the salesperson knows competitors will be following his or her visit. By anticipating the points that the competition will raise and responding to them, the salesperson minimizes their effect.

4-3e Maximizing Participation

It is essential that group members participate in the discussion; a lecture by the salesperson is guaranteed to fall flat. Yet, to do so is not easy; groups tend to intimidate many people. Here are some suggestions for maximizing participation:

1. The salesperson should indicate that he or she desires participation and act accordingly.

2. Unless already deeply involved in discussion, the salesperson should address questions to specific individuals rather than the group in general. Especially early on, addressing questions to the group as a whole is not likely to meet with success.

3. Develop interaction among group members. When one person has finished speaking, the salesperson can address another: "Why do you agree [disagree] with that view?"

4. Avoid calling on shy individuals in the early phases of a meeting. Not only are they embarrassed, but others also tend to resent the salesperson for putting the shy individuals on the spot.

5. Open up the discussion with questions about facts, not opinions. In the early stages of the meeting, people are loathe to express opinions:

6. Explain that participants will profit from the meeting in direct proportion to their participation. By stating their ideas, they can receive immediate criticism and new information and clarify their thoughts.

7. Use challenging and controversial statements to stimulate discussion early on. One college teacher I know begins his discussion on criminology by stating that crime is hereditary and worse in the South because Georgia originated as a penal colony. He never has any problem getting discussion started.

8. The salesperson should be tolerant of poorly developed ideas or opposing points of view.

9. Restrict individuals who try to monopolize the conversation.

Chapter Summary

Chapter 4 emphasized how important it is for salespeople to have an intimate understanding of the buying behavior of their customers. The chapter began by outlining the steps through which consumers typically progress when making a purchasing decision: motive arousal, problem recognition, search, alternative evaluation, and choice. Motives are drives or urges that initiate behavior, and until a motive is aroused, buying behavior will not occur. Once activated, a motive will lead the consumer to recognize the existence of a problem. Here the consumer realizes the difference between an actual state of affairs and an ideal state, a situation that will likely impel the consumer to search for information, either internally or externally. With the possession of enough information, the consumer will assess purchase alternatives, given his or her set of alternative criteria. The final step in the process is the decision to buy, along with the selection of an appropriate manufacturer and model. Throughout this process, it was emphasized that salespeople must recognize relevant consumer buying motives before making a presentation, because motives tend to remain relatively unchangeable.

Much of Chapter 4 concentrated on the individual factors that influence consumer behavior—motives and personality styles. Needs are impelling urges that drive people to satisfy certain goals. According to Maslow, needs can be classified into physiological, safety, social, esteem, and self-actualizing needs. As one level of needs is satisfied, the next becomes the dominating force. Personality is defined as the generalized ways people react to situations. Four different personality styles can be identified: Driver, Analytical, Amiable, and Expressive.

The second part of this chapter discussed the behavior of the organizational buyer, starting with an examination of the differences between the industrial and consumer markets. Distinguishing characteristics of the industrial market include derived demand, concentrated buying power, multiple buying influences, larger and less frequent ordering, buyer sophistication, and shorter channels of distribution.

The organizational decision-making process includes three buyclasses and eight buyphases. The buyclasses are the new task, the modified rebuy, and the straight rebuy. A new task situation refers to circumstances never before considered by buyers and therefore demanding much deliberation. A modified rebuy occurs when a buyer decides to change suppliers, product specifications, prices, etc., for a product previously purchased. A straight rebuy refers to the perfunctory purchase of a standard item from the same supplier on a routine basis.

The number of people involved in the buying decision might be one or 100, but they can usually be identified as playing one of five roles. Although many individuals or committees may be involved in the overall buying decision, ultimately there is only one person who can give the final approval to buy, and this is the Economic Buyer. The role of User Buyers is to make judgments about the potential impact of the product or service on their job performance. Influencers would be individuals who influence, while not actually having formal decision-making power, such as research and development (R&D) people who help write specifications or supply information for evaluating alternatives. Gatekeepers screen out possible suppliers. Their focus is on the product or service itself, and they make recommendations based on how well the product or service meets a variety of objective specifications. Buyers are the people who actually contact the selling organization and place the order. In most organizations, buyers have the authority to negotiate purchases.

After a discussion of the economic and personal buying motives of industrial organizations (often a reflection of corporate culture), the chapter ended with a discussion of proper selling tactics for the salesperson making a presentation to groups of buyers, including the importance of selling to groups, common roles of group members, and how to deal with groups of two and three or more.

Discussion Questions

1. "Salespeople don't have to know anything about buying. All they have to know about is selling." Discuss.

2. Why must salespeople understand consumer-buying behavior?

3. What are the steps in the selling process? Briefly explain each step. How might the salesperson be influential at each stage?

4. Use "Ways of Identifying Personality Styles," Table 4-1, to identify the personality styles of your professors.

5. How can Maslow's hierarchy be applied to the customer–supplier relationship?

6. Explain the process by which someone decides to buy a new automobile. How might the salesperson be influential in this process?

7. What are needs? Name a few. Which motives are likely to influence the purchase of an automobile?

8. What is Maslow's hierarchy? Do you believe that the hierarchy accurately describes how motives affect behavior?

9. Is a purchasing agent for U.S. Steel likely to be influenced by Maslow's hierarchy in his or her buying habits?

10. What is personality? Name the four general types of personality. How do they affect the salesperson?

11. "A good salesperson can sell to any type of buyer." Do you agree?

12. A salesperson is preparing to deliver a presentation to a buyer identified as an Amiable. What suggestions can you make to improve the effectiveness of the sales call?

13. Given your own personality style, how would you plan making a sales presentation to an Amiable? Driver? Expressive? Analytical?

14. What clues can help identify the personality style of buyers? Cite buying behavior you have recently witnessed—in yourself or others—that was motivated by physiological, safety, social, esteem, and self-actualization needs. Do the same for purchases that can be explained by personality style.

15. How would you define organizational selling?

16. "Selling is all the same, whether it is to consumers or industrial organizations." Do you agree or disagree?

17. What are the major differences between consumer and industrial markets?

18. A marketing manager for a manufacturer selling transmission parts to the automobile industry is debating whether to lower prices. Automobile sales have been sluggish recently, and, in fact, several companies have laid off workers. How would you advise the marketing manager?

19. What are the three buyclasses? Name the eight buyphases. How do they affect the salesperson's job?

20. How does selling in a straight rebuy situation differ from selling in a new task situation or a modified rebuy situation?

21. What are buying roles? Identify the four buying roles.

22. Explain the role of the Decider, the User, the Buyer, the Influencer, and the Gatekeeper.

23. What are multiple buying influences? What are their implications for the industrial salesperson's job?

24. Talk with an industrial salesperson you know about a recent sale. Try to apply the industrial buying model to explain what happened.

25. What are some common economic motives of industrial buyers?

26. Can the personal motives of industrial buyers affect their overall decision? What can the salesperson do about this?

27. Select a local company of consequence. Does the decision-making process change depending on the type of product and whether it is a new task buy,

modified rebuy, or straight rebuy? Who are the major decision makers, and what differential buying criteria are most important to each?

28. Why is the ability to sell to groups so important for industrial salespeople?

29. How should the salesperson conduct himself or herself with two buyers?

30. How should salespeople conduct themselves with groups of three or more?

31. What are some roles that are often found among group members?

32. How can the salesperson maximize group participation?

Chapter Quiz

1. During the _____ stage of the buying process, salespeople can influence customers by asking questions that will activate the customer's motives and make them aware a problem exists.
   a. problem-recognition
   b. information search
   c. alternative evaluation
   d. purchase decision

2. Many products, such as conspicuous homes, club memberships, clothes, restaurants, and cars, are purchased to fulfill _____, which includes the need to stand out and be recognized.
   a. safety needs
   b. social needs
   c. esteem needs
   d. self-actualization needs

3. According to Maslow, the lowest individual need is physiological. For business firms, survival needs are
   a. essential services associated with the product, such as timely delivery, and absence of damage and insurance against loss of property and assets.
   b. resources such as money, employees, raw materials, and equipment.
   c. profits earned on the company's products and services.
   d. sufficient financial resources to pay bills.

4. In terms of types of personalities, _____ are animated, intuitive, and lively. They thrive on involvement with others. They like informality and prefer to deal with people on a first-name basis.
   a. Drivers
   b. Expressives
   c. Analyticals
   d. Amiables

5. To win customer acceptance when the buyer's social type is Amiable requires from the salesperson
   a. documented evidence.
   b. recognition and approval.
   c. personal attention and interest.
   d. evidence with technical details.

6. If the salesperson wants to increase his or her assertiveness to fit the buyer's social type, the salesperson can do all of the following *except*
   a. speak and move at a faster pace.
   b. recommend, don't ask for opinions.
   c. increase eye contact.
   d. pause when speaking to allow others a chance to respond.

7. In terms of the buying center, the role of the _____ is to screen out possible suppliers. Their focus is on the product or service itself, and they make recommendations based on how well the product or service meets a variety of objective specifications.
   a. User
   b. Gatekeeper
   c. Buyer
   d. Influencer

8. The buyer in _____ buying seeks to make modifications in product specifications, delivery schedules, prices, or suppliers.
   a. new task
   b. evaluation
   c. straight rebuy
   d. modified rebuy

9. The best strategies for firms that are "out" suppliers in modified rebuy situations are
  a. respond more quickly; sell on alternative competitive advantages.
  b. sell superior benefits; seek "foot-in-door" orders.
  c. search for leads; suggest new approaches; supply technical advice.
  d. act immediately; reexamine needs.

10. In dealing with groups of three or more buyers, to maximize his or her effectiveness a salesperson can take all of the following actions *except*
  a. call on individuals who are silent or seem to take a back seat to the others.
  b. try to reduce the number of people in the group who must be dealt with.
  c. draw conclusions from the discussion rather than leaving this to each group member individually.
  d. bring up and concede weaknesses voluntarily rather than defend them after someone in the group has cited them as reasons for not purchasing.

Web Exercise

There are lots of ways of analyzing personality types. Take these online tests and see where you fit. Do you agree or disagree with the results? How can you use this knowledge about yourself to improve your selling skills?

www.personalitytype.com/quiz.asp
www.humanmetrics.com/cgi-win/JTypes1.htm

Notes

1. Leon G. Shiffman and Leslie Lazar Kanuk, *Consumer Behavior*, 7th Edition, Englewood Cliffs, NJ: Prentice Hall, 1999.
2. John O' Toole, "Logic of the Emotional Sell," *Selling*, September 1994, p. 87.
3. James F. Engel, Roger D. Blackwell, and David T. Kollat, *Consumer Behavior*, 9th Edition, Cincinnati: Thomson Learning, August 2000.
4. Toger A. Kerin, Eric C. Berkowitz, Steven W. Hartley, and William Rudelius, *Marketing*, New York: McGraw-Hill, 2003.
5. A. H. Maslow, *Motivation and Personality*, New York: Harper & Row, 1970.
6. Leon G. Shiffman and Leslie Lazar Kanuk, *Consumer Behavior*, 7th Edition, Englewood Cliffs, NJ: Prentice Hall, 1999.
7. Stanley Brown, "This Is No Psych Job," *Sales & Marketing Management*, March 1995, p. 32.
8. David Merrill and Roger Reid, *Personal Styles and Effective Performance*, Radnor, PA: Chilton, 1981.
9. *Social Styles and Sales Strategies*, Eden Prairie, MN: Wilson Learning Corporation, 1977.
10. Jack R. Snader, "Amiable, Analytical, Driving, or Expressive? Base Marketing Style on Prospect's Behavior," *Marketing News*, March 16, 1984, p. 3.
11. Tony Allesandra, Phil Wexler, and Rick Barrera, *Nonmanipulative Selling*, New York: Prentice Hall, 1987, p. 243.
12. *Statistical Abstract of the United States: 2000*, 120th Edition, Washington, DC: Census Bureau, 2000.
13. "Latin Trade Connection," *Latin Trade*, June 1997, p. 72.
14. "Rumble over Tokyo," *Business Week*, April 2, 2001, pp. 80–82.
15. Jerome Katrichis, "Exploring Departmental Interactions in Organizational Purchasing Decisions," *Industrial Marketing Management*, 27, March 1998, pp. 135–147; Philip Dawes, "Information Control and Influence in Emergent Buying Centers," *Journal of Marketing*, 62, July 1998, pp. 55–69.
16. "What Buyers Look For," *Sales & Marketing Management*, August 1995, p. 31.
17. Hugh J. Ingrasci, "How to Reach Buyers in Their Psychological 'Comfort Zones,' " *Industrial Marketing*, July 1991, pp. 59–64.
18. Betsy Cummings, "Beating the Odds," *Sales & Marketing Management*, March 2002.
19. Erin Strout, "Only the Stongest Survive," *Sales & Marketing Management*, November 2000.
20. Gary M. Grikscheit, Harold C. Cash, and Clifford E. Young, *The Handbook of Selling: Psychological, Managerial, and Marketing Dynamics*, 2nd Edition, March 1993.

Case 4-1

A salesperson responsible for selling sales training programs has an appointment with a bank president to talk over the possibility of enrolling the bank's tellers and trust people in a sales training session. On entering the president's office, the sales representative notices the decorations on the walls: a picture of the new bank on which construction is to begin shortly, several graphs of interest rates and money supply from the Federal Reserve Bank, and a diploma from the American Institute of Banking. The salesperson is motioned to sit down in a comfortable but functional chair directly across from the president's desk, on which there appears nothing but a blotter. Before taking a seat, the salesperson extends his hand warmly.

Salesperson: Good morning, Ted. How are you today? Sure is nice weather we're having.

President *(a little hesitant, at first, to extend his hand):* Yes, it certainly is. I have about five minutes to talk with you. I'm running on a tight schedule today. Now tell me something about your program *(sits down to listen expressionlessly).*

Salesperson: Well, let me tell you how I got around to calling you. I was talking to Bob Johnson over at Century Realty. We just completed a sales training program over there for his real estate agents. Do you know Bob?

President: Yes, I do. He does business here at the bank.

Salesperson: A great guy. He and I play golf all the time. He's a scratch golfer, but every once in a while I take some money from him. Do you play golf?

President: No, I don't *(looking at his watch).*

Salesperson: Well, anyway, out at the course—make that the clubhouse—Bob and I got to talking and he mentioned that you were getting interested in marketing your bank more seriously. I'd just like to say that's a great idea. More bank presidents should think like you.

President: Yes, we hope to increase our competitive market share vis-a-vis the other banks in town by at least 5 percent. We feel that's realistic, given the experience of other banks that have become marketing-oriented. Now, tell me something about what your program can do for us at First Federal.

Salesperson: We can do some great things for you. After completing our training program, I can guarantee your tellers and trust people will be real go-getters, the kind of salespeople any company would be proud to have.

President: I'm sure. What sorts of sales skills does your program cover?

Salesperson: Why, we teach every selling skill the successful salesperson needs to know. Bob Johnson really found our program helpful to his people. Business doubled shortly thereafter, and he credited it to us.

President: Doubled?

Salesperson: At least. No question about it.

President: I wonder if you could be a little more specific about exactly what you propose for training our people?

Salesperson: We use a number of different methods: role-playing, lectures, transparencies, and slides. We've got the best program around. Just listen to some of the companies we've worked with . . .

President: Excuse me for interrupting, but I see that our time is up and I have a meeting coming up shortly. Why don't you leave some information listing the details of your program.

Salesperson: Fine. Here we are. Listen, maybe we can make an appointment to meet out at the club for lunch.

President: I usually go over to the YMCA to run at noontime.

Salesperson: That's great! I bet you're in great shape. Well, I guess I can get in touch with you for another appointment.

President: Contact my secretary. She keeps tight control over my schedule.

Questions

1. What happened? In terms of personality style, how would you describe buyer and seller?
2. If you had been in the salesperson's position, what would you have done differently?

Case 4-2

Robert Boyd, salesperson for NRC Corporation, has just received a bid request from the city of Akron, Ohio, for a new computer system. The following conversation occurs when Robert visits the city's data-processing manager:

Robert: Good morning, Mr. Thomas. My name is Robert Boyd. I'm with NRC and I'm here to talk with you about the bid request I just received in the mail.

Data-Processing Manager: Good. What can I tell you?

Robert: Well, first let me say that I'm glad to see the city is going to buy a new system. NRC will do everything possible to comply with your bid request. I must admit, however, that I'm disturbed to see the way the specifications for the system have been established.

DP Manager: What do you mean, Robert?

Robert: It seems to me that the specifications heavily favor BMI. Now, I believe our system is better than theirs, but I don't think your specifications necessarily provide a fair comparison.

DP Manager: Robert, I really don't know what I can do for you.

Robert: Is there a possibility for changing some of the specifications?

DP Manager: I'll be perfectly honest with you, Bob. Our hands are tied on this matter. The data-processing department simply doesn't have the authority to change specifications. By the time we received authorization for a new system, we had to write specifications that fulfilled basic guidelines established elsewhere. The county board and our accounting department had a lot to say about guidelines, especially Art Bigelow, who heads up accounting. You know Art worked with a BMI system for years before he came with us.

Robert: Well, all right, Mr. Thomas. I guess I'll have to work with what I've got.

Questions

1. Explain what happened to Robert.
2. What should Robert have been doing prior to the call? Whom should he have called upon?
3. Do you believe he has a chance of changing the specifications now?

Effective Communication

Key Terms

decode	message	pacing
encode	noise	proxemics
feedback	nonverbal communication	source

Learning Objectives

Learning Objectives

After studying Chapter 5, you will understand:

- The elements of the communication process
- The importance of two-way communication to successful selling
- How dress affects the credibility of salespeople
- The importance of listening to successful selling
- The major elements of nonverbal communication

Several times, we have emphasized that building a relationship with a customer is critical to long-term sales. If so, the cornerstone of this relationship is mutual trust. Continuing sales depends on how well or how poorly the relationship is managed by the seller, with future marketing success contingent upon the development of an in-depth account relationship based upon mutual trust. Research has demonstrated that trust in the buyer–seller relationship depends on five selling behaviors:[1]

1. Candor (truth of words)
2. Dependability (predictability of actions)
3. Competence (ability/knowledge/resources)
4. Intent (or empathy; placing the customer's interests on par with the seller's; a commitment to be there, be responsive, etc.)
5. Likability (though emotional and difficult to clearly define, a perception of commonality by both parties)

Examined in detail, these five aspects of trust all involve communication, verbal and nonverbal. As already indicated, candor is established with words (and follow-up actions). Dependability means fulfilling prior verbal promises. To establish competence, the salesperson must demonstrate his or her technical command of products and applications (i.e., accurate, complete, and objective). Intent, or empathy, means that the salesperson understands buyer needs and equates them with his or her own. Likability is validated with courtesy and politeness, commonality of interest, and positive emotional feelings.

Unless salespeople can communicate the superiority of their product or service to potential buyers, the product will remain unsold. To persuade prospective customers of this superiority, salespeople must be able to identify accurately the needs and wants of customers. Salespeople must listen closely to what customers have to say, analyze their spoken words, and be attentive to their nonverbal behavior. Customers' eyes, gestures, vocal intonations, and overall appearance will reveal much about their thoughts. Salespeople must take their impressions of these verbal and nonverbal expressions and structure communication that relates the critical product features that satisfy customer desires. In short, salespeople must be effective communicators. They must be able to formulate their thoughts and ideas so that others can understand them. Moreover, they must be adept at analyzing and understanding what customers are saying to them, as well as their own communication, verbal and nonverbal.

5-1 The Communication Process

The development of communication skills requires, first, that one have an understanding of how communication takes place. Figure 5-1 diagrams the communication process.

As depicted, communication begins with a **source** or initiator. For our purposes, the source will be a salesperson, but it could just as well be the announcer in a television commercial. The source has certain thoughts and ideas in mind to communicate to the receiver. To accomplish this, the message (sales presentation) must first be **encoded** into a form that can be transmitted to the receiver. This involves transplanting ideas into symbols—words, pictures, and numbers—that represent the ideas. In this book, for example, I have used words and figures to transmit my ideas to you, the receiver. It is important that the source use words and symbols that have the same meaning to the receiver. This notion goes beyond mere semantics. Think of the computer salesperson who says to the prospect, "You should install our new zip drive with its 29-millisecond seek time, 100 megabyte storage and removable disk, which will reduce total system overhead devoted to backing up the hard drive." You must use words and symbols that the consumer will be familiar with and understand. You may impress people with a big word, but you will seldom sell them anything.

Besides avoiding big, confusing words, salespeople also should avoid the use of abstract rather than concrete words. For example, it is much more clear if the sales representative says, "This unit copies 100 documents per minute," rather than "This unit copies fast." It also is a good idea to describe things in the active voice instead of the passive voice. "She bought that car without driving it" sounds much stronger than "That car was bought by someone who had not driven it." One final and important point to remember is that seemingly synonymous words evoke far different emotional reactions. In the minds of buyers, there is a vast difference between *boat* and *yacht*. In real estate, salespeople sell *homes*, not *houses*. The former brings to mind images of the family sitting around the fireplace; the latter does not. Similarly, *cellar* is out and *basement* is in; *basement* suggests a paneled family room, while *cellar* is where vegetables are kept. Good salespeople don't use the term *development*, preferring *area of new homes*. And when discussing financing, *initial investment* is substituted for *down payment*.

Once ideas are encoded into words, the **message** is transmitted to the receiver. This may occur by voice waves carried through the air, by various forms of writing, or by electronic media such as television, radio, or Internet. The importance of nonverbal communication, however, must not be overlooked. Such forms of expression as dress, body movement, voice intonations, and sounds of laughter or surprise all enter into the communication process.

source
The initiator of communication who has certain thoughts and ideas in mind to communicate.

encode
Translating ideas into symbols—words, pictures, and numbers—that represent the ideas to a receiver.

message
Communication, both verbal and nonverbal, that is transmitted from source to receiver.

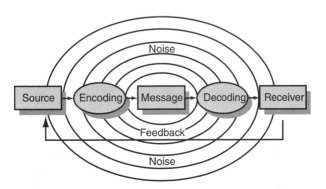

Figure 5-1
The Communication Process

noise
Any unneeded factor that interferes with transmission and reception of a message.

The accuracy of communication is affected greatly by the amount of noise that occurs during transmission of the message. **Noise** refers to any unneeded factor that interferes with transmission and reception of the message. In personal selling, noise can consist of interference from ringing telephones and clattering printers or interruptions by secretaries, subordinates, and other workers. These are all physical distractions. Mental distractions are mental side trips, preoccupations, and fantasies. Factual distractions occur when one gets so preoccupied with individual facts that they miss the main point. Semantic distractions occur when we overrespond to an emotional-laden word or concept. Just think, for example, of the distinction between *welfare* and *aid to dependent children.* For which are you in favor of cutting government expenditures? Then, there are factors within ourselves that interfere with effective listening—self-focus, defensiveness, experiential superiority, and egocentricism. Self-focus is a preoccupation with thoughts about ourselves; more positive feelings about oneself and others are required for effective listening. Defensiveness usually results from one's feeling threatened, generally because of negative feedback. People who have lived through a variety of experiences manifest experiential superiority over those with less, failing to listen to the latter. Egocentricism is self-focus carried to an extreme; it is the tendency to view the self as the center of every activity.

decode
To translate a message from source to receiver in ideas.

For effective communication, the content of the message as **decoded** by the receiver must be identical to that transmitted by the source. This does not always occur. The receiver may have difficulty comprehending the message because of noise or because of preoccupation with other matters. The receiver may also engage in selective perception. This phenomenon has been extensively researched in the social sciences. Basically, it means that people will pay more attention to a message with which they agree than to one with which they disagree. Also, people will tend to interpret a message in keeping with their own beliefs, attitudes, and past experiences. What implications does this have for salespeople?

The salesperson must always be sensitive to selective perception. People not only interpret things in terms of their existing attitudes but they also sometimes fail to notice information in opposition to their existing beliefs. Although salespeople may think they have given a good presentation of a superior product, they may ultimately lose the sale. Selective perception may have influenced the outcome in two ways. First, prospects may have tuned out relevant portions of the presentation because they disagreed with them. Second, prospects may reinterpret the presentation to conform to their own beliefs. For example, when a salesperson says, "This Savin is the finest copier money can buy," a prospect favoring Xerox machines may take this to mean that the Savin is expensive, maybe too expensive.

feedback
Communication to determine if the receiver understands the message as sent by the source.

The last element of the communication process is **feedback**. It is vital that the source know if the receiver is getting the message. As we have seen, there is no guarantee that the message sent is identical to the message received. A question from the receiver, a frown, or even no reaction at all may indicate that the source should modify the message and try again. With feedback, understanding is more likely to occur; without it, there may be no understanding at all. In other words, communication is a two-way process.

5-1a Sending Messages Effectively

1. *Clearly "own" your messages by using first-person singular pronouns ("I," "my").* Personal ownership includes clearly taking responsibility for the ideas and feelings that one expresses. People disown their messages when they use phrases such as "most people," "some of our friends," and "our group." Such

language makes it difficult for listeners to tell whether the individuals really think and feel what they are saying or whether they are repeating the thoughts and feelings of others.

2. *Make your messages complete and specific.* Include clear statements of all necessary information the receiver needs to comprehend the message. Being complete and specific seems too obvious, but often people do not communicate the frame of reference they are using, the assumptions they are making, the intentions they have in communicating, or the leaps in thinking they are making. If you are selling digital cameras, should you assume that the customers know what *megapixels* are? Do they understand why they need more? Do they know the difference between *optical zoom* and *digital zoom*? Don't make untested assumptions about the sophistication of the customer.

3. *Make your verbal and nonverbal messages congruent.* Every face-to-face communication involves both verbal and nonverbal messages. Usually these messages are congruent: The person who is saying that he appreciates your help is smiling and expressing warmth in other nonverbal ways. Communication problems arise when a person's verbal and nonverbal messages are contradictory. If a person says, "Here is some information that may be of help to you" with a sneer on her face and a mocking tone of voice, the meaning you receive is confused by the two different messages being sent.

4. *Be redundant.* Sending the same message more than once and using more than one channel of communication (such as pictures and written messages as well as verbal and nonverbal cues) will help the receiver understand your messages. However, while keeping the message the same, change the context. The Miller Lite commercials are a good example; "Tastes Great, Less Filling" is always the message, but the environment (e.g., beach or home party) of the ad changes. In this manner, one does not offend the receiver.

5. *Ask for feedback concerning the way your messages are being received.* To communicate effectively, you must be aware of how the receiver is interpreting and processing your messages. The only way to be sure is to continually seek feedback as to what meanings the receiver is attaching to your messages. For example, periodically ask, "Am I making sense?"

6. *Make the message appropriate to the receiver's frame of reference.* Explain the same information differently to an expert in the field and to a novice, to a child and to an adult, to your boss and to a coworker.

7. *Describe your feelings by name, action, or figure of speech.* When communicating your feelings, it is especially important to be descriptive. You may describe your feelings by name ("I feel sad"), by actions ("I feel like crying"), or by figures of speech ("I feel down in the dumps"). Description will help communicate your feelings clearly and unambiguously.

8. *Describe others' behavior without evaluating or interpreting it.* When reacting to the behavior of others, be sure to describe their behavior ("You keep interrupting me") rather than evaluating it ("You're a rotten, self-centered egotist who won't listen to anyone else's ideas").[2]

5-1b Two-Way Communication

A little story might help make the point here: Imagine you sell photocopiers and that the secretary of a prospect calls saying her boss needs to buy a copier and wants to see one that afternoon. You skip lunch, load your top-of-the-line model into your car, and drive 50 miles to make the presentation. You arrive early to ensure you have plenty of time to set up because your product does everything—runs colors, collates thousands of pages, handles two-sided copies with ease and speed. You're confident the prospect will be wowed. So far, so good. However, the prospect walks in, takes one look at the machine, and says he doesn't need such an advanced model. "We never do colors and we don't have any use for collating," the prospect tells the rep. "What I want is a machine that will give me top-quality prints of single pages and spit them out in a hurry." And that was that. The rep never even got a chance to give his presentation. The salesperson said he could be back the next morning with the right machine, but the prospect said he was going out of town that night and suggested the rep call the following week to set up an appointment. When the rep did so, he learned the prospect had bought a competitor's inferior product for a higher price than the top-of-the-line model he'd just rejected—all because the rep failed to ask a few basic questions before hitting the road to give his presentation.[3]

Some theories of selling and many practicing salespeople, as well, put great emphasis on dominating the prospective customer. Their idea of selling stresses one-way communication—from the sales representative to the prospect, with little or no feedback. The objective of one-way communication is to dominate prospects verbally so that they are compelled to buy the product by the overwhelming weight of the salesperson's argument. One-way communication views customers as passive, unthinking, and easily manipulated by salespeople. Some companies have adopted this theory of selling, even going to the point of having their sales representatives memorize a canned sales talk that every customer receives regardless of the individual situation. They believe that certain key words and phrases will compel the prospect to buy; accordingly, the entire sales force commits the words to memory.

The fact of the matter, as we saw, is that effective communication involves two-way interaction. Without feedback from the receiver, one cannot even be sure that the message received is the same as the one transmitted. Moreover, according to the marketing concept, the goal of marketing is to satisfy consumer needs and wants. Without two-way communication, it is doubtful whether these needs and wants can be identified. Two-way communication provides the opportunity for continuous feedback, allowing salespeople to determine their progress and to identify those points in the presentation that require further emphasis or explanation. Communication is more accurate because the sender can better determine if the message is getting across to the receiver.

Two-way communication is advantageous from another standpoint. We know that we seldom enjoy being talked to without a chance to answer. How do you feel when someone attempts to control the conversation, jumping into the middle of your sentences without regard to what you are trying to say? One-way communication is anything but ego-gratifying to the customer. The fact of the matter is that the more people participate in a discussion, the more likely they are to convince themselves. If the salesperson asks the right questions and allows customer participation, many times customers sell themselves on the product.

5-1c The Importance of Active Listening

The popular stereotype of the salesperson is that of the glib talker. Certainly many salespeople seem susceptible to the disease of talking too much. Someone once commented that salespeople seem to have been vaccinated with a phonograph needle.

Whether or not this is true, the drive and ego strength that impel one to make sales calls also tend to make salespeople talk at length about their product and company. To perform effectively, however, salespeople must obtain information from their customers about their specific situations. Does the customer have a need for the product or service? If so, will alterations have to be made? Can they afford it? The easiest way of gathering these facts is by listening closely to what the customer has to say. Yet, as Figure 5-2 indicates, both salespeople and buyers alike believe sales reps talk too much. Although the figure dates from 1994, recent material supports the same tendencies.[4]

Despite its importance, most individuals, including salespeople, are inefficient listeners. Tests have shown that immediately after listening to a 10-minute oral presentation, the average listener has heard, understood, properly evaluated, and retained approximately half of what was said. Within 48 hours, that drops off another 50 percent to a final 25 percent level of effectiveness. To summarize, we comprehend and retain only one-fourth of what is said.[5] This is in spite of the fact that of all our communicative skills, listening is used the most—more than speaking, reading, and writing. How good are you? In the "Web Exercise" section at the end of this chapter, you'll find an exercise that helps you assess your own communication skills.

Perhaps the major reason we are such poor listeners is the prevailing attitude that listening is passive—that persuasion requires forceful speaking. We seem to believe that speaking is power; that is, our speaking has the ability to persuade the other to our point of view without question. Whenever we describe someone who ought to take sales as a career, we say they have the "gift of gab." In fact, the listener has more power, for he or she understands not only what they know, but also what the speaker knows. Watch what happens if one party to a conversation continues to speak; eventually, the speaker is the one who becomes uncomfortable, because what he or she knows of the other party is necessarily limited. Moreover, listening conveys a powerful message to the speaker: "I'm interested in what you say and in you as a person. I think you're worth listening to. I may not always agree with you, but I respect your right to express your views."

How does one become an active listener? By careful practice, as with all other sales skills. One must conscientiously apply oneself to listen to what others have to say. Research has shown that effective listening is hard work. Increased heart action, faster circulation of blood, and even a slightly increased body temperature are characteristics of active listening. Salespeople must make a commitment to practice this skill. Table 5-1 shows a few other suggestions on how to become an active listener.

VIDEO

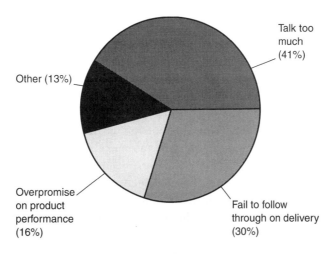

Figure 5-2
The Number One Problem of Salespeople
Source: Adapted from "Seventh Annual Communication Survey," Communispond, Inc., 1994.

Talk too much (41%)

Other (13%)

Overpromise on product performance (16%)

Fail to follow through on delivery (30%)

T a b l e **5-1** Suggestions for Active Listening

Watch for nonverbal behavior.	Do not listen to only the words themselves; also watch carefully for cues about the speaker's real intentions. Buyers may say "no!" but if they are smiling, sitting with a relaxed body posture and open hands, or if they continue to study and look at the salesperson's samples, the contrary may well be true.
Reject the attitude that speech equals power.	Our mental ability creates another major problem with listening. It is known as the *interaction rate*. Consider the following: • We can speak at the rate of 125 to 150 words per minute. • We can listen at between 275 and 300 words per minute. • We can think at more than 3,000 words per minute. These figures show that we can listen at three times the rate most people can speak, and we process words at almost 20 times the rate most can speak. Therefore, your mind can race ahead and wander while someone else speaks. We can plan our day and contemplate what we will do after work and still get the gist of what someone is saying. But while our minds wander, we miss much of what we are capable of capturing.
Be sensitive to personal pronouns (e.g., "I," "we").	Practice being interested in what others have to say. You are not always the most interesting one around. Become sensitive to the prospect's use of personal pronouns, such as *I, we, you, us,* and *our.* These are cues to things that really interest the prospective customer.
Invite amplification (e.g., "Did anything else happen?").	Invite additional comments. Phrases like "Go on," "What else?," "How do you feel about that?," and "Did anything else occur?" encourage the speaker to say more and to continue to share ideas and information (not to mention thinking positively of the questioner).[6]
Establish eye contact.	Establish eye contact with the customer quickly. The ears tend to follow where the eyes go. Maintaining eye contact also makes it more difficult to feign attention. Moreover, it will help you spot changes in the buyer's facial expressions or body movements.
Ask clarifying questions (e.g., "So what you're saying is . . .").	Ask clarifying questions to test your understanding of a message. Ask, "Did I understand you to say . . .," "It sounds like you're saying . . .," "It seems as if you feel. . . ." As the last question implies, it is important to verify not only facts but also feelings—often they are much more important. Not only do such questions act to clarify but they also demonstrate caring. There is an old saying in selling: "Your customers don't care how much you know until they know how much you care." Feeding back what they are saying (both content and feeling) demonstrates caring. Rephrasing is one of the most powerful listening techniques available to you, and one of the easiest to learn.[7] Simply think carefully about what you just heard, put it in your own words, and say it back to them in the form of a question. For example, when someone indicates to you they are concerned about getting new service to their facilities under construction, your rephrase and their response might sound like the following: "I can certainly appreciate why having the service ready when you are has to be important to you!" Rephrasing shows the other person that their situation sunk in with you and you really understand it. It also gives the person a chance to reiterate and expand upon their concern, which makes them feel better about it and gives you the chance to identify something you can do to make a difference. Some good ways to begin rephrase questions are the following: • "As I understand it . . ." • "Do you mean . . ."

5-2 Nonverbal Communication

nonverbal communication
Actions, gestures, facial expressions, and other nonspoken forms of expression that reveal underlying thoughts and emotions.

Nonverbal communication refers to actions, gestures, facial expressions, and other nonspoken forms of expression that reveal underlying thoughts and emotions. It may or may not occur simultaneously with verbal communication. Attention to nonverbal cues from customers can tell much about their thoughts, particularly those they might not wish to disclose in spoken form. Nonverbal communication represents a substantial proportion of the communication process. According to an expert in the area, Albert Mehrabian, 55 percent of our communication is through posture, gestures, and facial expressions; 38 percent through our tone of voice; and only 7 percent through words themselves.[12]

Mehrabian indicates that nonverbal communication, as indicated in Table 5-2, indicates the degree of liking, status, and sheer responsiveness:[13]

One step up from reflecting on the implication is responding to the feeling, or empathizing with another person. It means putting yourself in their shoes and really feeling how they must feel. To respond to the feeling, all you have to do is put some version of the word *feel* in your response. That includes the forms of *found* and *felt*. Examples of this technique in response to a customer who tells you about being billed incorrectly are as follows:

"You must feel frustrated having to correct this situation."[14]

"We at XXXXX feel frustrated as well."

Don't interrupt.	Above all, when customers want to talk, shut up and listen. Never be so involved in what you are going to say next that you cut them off, jumping into the middle of a sentence. How do you feel when someone interrupts you? Don't you feel like saying, "Please, let me finish!" As a professional salesperson, you should never have occasion to hear this.[8, 9]
Suspend judgment.	Although it is important to determine the speaker's main points and paraphrase them in your own mind, it is absolutely critical to suspend judgment. The latter will prevent understanding and color one's further effectiveness as a listener.
Demonstrate attention through nonverbal behavior (nodding head, etc.).	Some theorists argue that the majority of active listening is demonstrated by nonverbal behavior. Some suggestions: demonstrate positive bodily responsiveness (i.e., don't shake your head in disbelief); lean forward; directly face the speaker, don't angle away; use relaxed, but alert posture (e.g., don't slouch, but don't be tense); establish an open body position; nod your head in agreement and smile; be aware of proper proxemics (distance); and use vocal responsiveness (i.e., change pitch, rate, inflection, and volume periodically).[10]
Look for commonality of interests and experiences.	Identify areas of agreement or common experience. Briefly relate similar past experiences, or explain a similar point of view. This demonstrates understanding.
Listen for ideas, not just facts.	Salespeople should listen for ideas, not just facts. A study conducted a number of years ago at a midwestern university determined the differences between the best and worst listeners. The poor listeners expend too much effort on trying to remember all the facts. The good listeners spend their time evaluating central ideas. For example, when a speaker starts enumerating a list of seven points, poor listeners try to remember it in detail. Meanwhile, the speaker has progressed to point two, as the listener tries to catch up, only to discover that point three is now being discussed, and on it goes. The poor listener has retained only disassociated fragments, rather than trying to understand what the facts add up to by relating them to each other and seeing what key ideas bind them together.[11]
Encourage communication through responses that let the speaker know you are paying attention.	Periodic responses such as "uh-huh," "yes," and "I see" encourage the speaker. Avoid complete silence. The lack of any response whatsoever implies you are not listening. It may result in defensiveness or anger on the part of the speaker.

1. *Liking* is often expressed by leaning forward, a direct body orientation (e.g., standing face-to-face), close proximity, touching, relaxed posture, open arms and body, positive facial expression, and direct eye contact. Observe, for example, males watching sports on television and drinking beer.

2. *Status,* especially high status, is communicated nonverbally by bigger gestures, relaxed posture, and less eye contact. Male executives will talk to subordinates (or professors to students) while leaning back in their desk chair with their hands behind their head and their elbows out (very relaxed), but the subordinate (or student) seldom behaves the same way.

3. *Responsiveness* nonverbally is exhibited by moving toward the other person, by spontaneous gestures, shifting posture and position, and by facial expressiveness. These are all positive examples of responsiveness.

T a b l e **5-2** Nonverbal Communication

Liking is expressed by	Leaning forward
	Direct body orientation
	Close proximity
	Open arms and legs
Status is expressed by	Bigger, more expansive gestures
	Relaxed posture
	Less eye contact
	Leaning back in chair with hands behind head
Responsiveness is expressed by	Moving toward the other person
	Spontaneous gestures
	Facial expressiveness

5-2a Pacing

The importance of effective listening and questioning in fostering two-way communication should be obvious by now. Some recent research in social behavior also has implications for selling.[14] This research indicates that one of the most powerful ways of gaining rapport with people is by first pacing (or "tracking") them, that is, aligning oneself as closely as possible with the other in mood, attitude, and verbal and nonverbal behavior. **Pacing** involves presenting to another person those aspects of yourself that are most nearly like those of the other. The principle is that likes attract, and once someone likes you, he or she will want to agree with you. Thus, the salesperson should first pace and then lead. An expressive salesperson dealing with an analytic-type buyer, for example, should tone down his or her approach to secure rapport.

pacing
Aligning oneself as closely as possible with another in mood, attitude, and verbal and nonverbal behavior.

Pacing may be thought of as holding a mirror up to people so that what they see, hear, or feel is consistent with their experience of themselves and their reality. Pacing involves getting into agreement or alignment with, or bearing a likeness to other people in a way that communicates, "You can trust me. I'm on your side. I'm like you." The salesperson should attempt to match the posture, facial expression, gestures, and breathing of the client. People tend to like people like themselves and will want to agree with people they like; pacing is critical to this process.

Pacing calls for the salesperson to match the client's verbal behavior. Imagine a sales representative from New York trying to do business with someone from Alabama. As the New Yorker talks ever more rapidly and frenetically, the relaxed Southerner responds more slowly, wondering what in the world is motivating this animated creature. It also makes sense for the salesperson to incorporate client words and phrases into his or her own speech. The idea here is for the client to think, "I like this person—he [or she] speaks my language."[15]

Pacing extends to nonverbal behavior, too. Consider this quote from a study published in the *Harvard Business Review:* "In moments of great rapport, a remarkable pattern of nonverbal communication can develop. Two people will mirror each other's movements—dropping a hand, shifting their body at exactly the same time. This happens so quickly that without videotape or film replay one is unlikely to notice the mirroring. But managers can learn to watch for disruptions in this mirroring because they are dramatically obvious when they occur. . . . Instead of smooth mirroring, there will be a burst of movement, almost as if both are losing balance."[16]

By implication, salespeople should do the same. The more that the salesperson and client share movements or posture, the greater their feelings of acceptance, belonging, and well-being.

Evidently, pacing is innate and something we often do instinctually. At the Child Development Unit of the Boston University Medical Center, Condon and Sander studied films that showed the "correspondence between analysis of the soundtrack of [an] adult's speech and body movements of [an] infant."[17] In some cases, the infant was barely 12 hours old. Other researchers have found that newborn babies orient themselves to sound, preferring the sound of the human voice, especially a woman's voice. They prefer to gaze at faces rather than at objects; their eyes follow a turning human face, and they may imitate certain facial gestures. In *Beyond Culture,* Edward T. Hall cites studies in which movies "taken in a variety of settings and circumstances reveal that when two people talk to each other their movements are synchronized."[18] This synchronization, Hall instructs, occurs in barely discernable ways: an eyelid blinks or a finger curls in synchrony with a particular word sound or voice stress. In other circumstances, two bodies may move entirely in synchrony with one another, "as though the two were under the control of a master choreographer." Furthermore, observes Hall, "Viewing movies in very slow motion, looking for synchrony, one realizes that what we know as dance is really a slowed-down, stylized version of what human beings do whenever they interact."[19]

Some people are surprised to learn that successful salespeople even pace the negative body language of their listeners. By temporarily adopting the customer's body language, salespeople initially establish agreement on a nonverbal level. Simultaneously, they pace the prospect verbally and in mood. The latter may seem especially strange, but think back to the last time you were in a bad mood. Suppose you were having a bad day and someone were to comment, "You know, I'm not myself today. I don't know why, so I'm just taking it as it comes. But I can still find a few things to enjoy. Like talking to a friend or going out for a walk." Once the prospect feels the sales rep is in step and understands, he or she can begin leading toward the positive.[20]

If the general idea is for the salesperson to pace and then lead, what happens if the client fails to respond? The answer is simple: resume pacing. When rapport is fully developed, then try leading again.

5-2b Source Credibility

Nonverbal communication is especially important in establishing the credibility of the salesperson. A prospective buyer's response to communication is heavily influenced by his or her attitude toward the source of the communication. If the source is viewed as believable, the message is more likely to be influential. For example, an article concerning business's future role in society would be more persuasive if it appeared in the *Wall Street Journal* rather than in *Penthouse.*

Several factors influence source credibility. In the initial meeting, the salesperson's company identification is likely to carry much weight with the prospective customer. A data-processing salesperson from IBM will have a much easier time gaining the confidence of a U.S. prospect than would a sales representative for Bull (a French computer manufacturer). The perceived expertise of salespeople also affects their credibility with the customer. It is important for the receiver to feel that the sender of the message is knowledgeable about the product or service.

The external characteristics of salespeople are of great importance in conveying an image of credibility. Gestures, appearance, dress, and language all provide cues to source credibility. The critical aspect of nonverbal behavior to the salesperson is that if a discrepancy exists between verbal and nonverbal behavior, the latter will be believed. If the salesperson expounds eloquently on the virtues of his or her product, but fails to make eye contact, crosses his or her legs, or fidgets nervously, the verbal will all be for naught.

5-2c Body Language

Body language is regarded by many as the most important element of nonverbal communication. It is critical for salespeople to recognize the messages present in clients' body language, because these messages reveal much about their thinking. Salespeople should also recognize the ability of their own bodies to communicate. Salespeople can increase tension and decrease trust by projecting negative body language, or they can evoke contrasting effects through positive body language. Knowing how to use body language is an added dimension toward understanding both oneself and others. Recent research by Professor Goldin-Meadow in her book, *Hearing Gesture: How Our Hands Help Us Think,* concludes that gesture "plays an active role . . . in the thoughts we think."[21] Gesturing seems to decrease "cognitive load," the amount of mental effort needed to perform some task. Gesturing is a way to take your thoughts and put them out there for you and others to see. It may help you examine your thoughts, even if not consciously. So, the smart sales rep will pay more attention, the more the client gestures.

Individual gestures are similar to individual words in a sentence. By themselves, they mean little, if anything. Just as many words can be put together to form a sentence, gestures can be put together to compose a complete picture. Yet one must be cautious in interpretation; body language is an inexact science. At times, a gesture has meaning, while at other times, it is simply a more comfortable position for the individual.

Some of the basic elements of body language are the eyes, face (especially the lips), hands, arms, legs, body posture, and walk. In combination, these elements can communicate just as effectively as words. For example, can you interpret what message the customer in the photograph is conveying? If you were a salesperson who had completed a presentation to her, how well would you say you had done?

The customer in the photograph has adopted a defensive posture. His body is rigid, his arms are tightly crossed, his lips are pursed, and his left fist probably clenched. This crossed-arm position is common in everyday life and seems to be used universally throughout the world to communicate defensiveness. Teachers use it, especially when questioned too closely by students. The very young will cross their arms when defying their parents. The very old will use it when defending their right to be heard. The position acts as a guard against anticipated attack or as a fixed position from which the individual prefers not to move.

When confronted by a buyer in a defensive posture, salespeople may respond in several ways. After brief pacing, they might seek to convey their own sincerity and openness through appropriate body language. By opening their hands, moving closer to the client, unbuttoning or removing a coat, or sitting at the edge of a chair, salespeople may reduce the client's defensiveness. They might hand the prospect a sales brochure or proceed to demonstrate some feature of the product. They might also ask carefully worded questions to draw out the source of the client's resistance.

The same tactics are appropriate when the prospect signals outright rejection by touching or rubbing the nose, crossing the arms and legs, throat clearing, hand rubbing or ear tugging, and glancing sideways. Here it is particularly critical that salespeople ask questions to draw out the problem: "I think there's something here that doesn't sit quite right with you. I wonder if you could tell me what it is?"

A classic defensive gesture

In contrast, the salesperson may hope for a favorable evaluation from the prospect pictured. This prospect has adopted the classic body language for evaluation. She is leaning toward the person who is speaking, is making eye contact, and looks friendly, inviting conversation.

This body language so characteristic of evaluation was first pointed out by Charles Darwin in his early studies. He also observed that both human beings and animals tend to cock their heads slightly whenever they hear something that interests them. Stroking the chin also tends to be a universal gesture.[22] Many Western movies include a scene where the deputy strokes his chin and says, "I don't know, Sheriff, if that's the best way to catch that outlaw gang." In the musical *Fiddler on the Roof,* whenever Tevye, the lead character, has to think things over, he invariably strokes his beard.

Outright acceptance on the part of the prospect is indicated by leaning forward (if in a chair), with a relaxed body posture, open hands and uncrossed legs, and a lively and well-modulated voice. If this is the case, the salesperson should cease further presentation and seek to secure an order. Continuing when the customer is ready to buy may lead to boredom and eventual loss of the sale.

It is especially important for the salesperson to watch for conflicts between verbal and nonverbal behavior. If prospects state emphatically that they aren't interested in a product and simultaneously lean forward and stroke their chins, their gestures indicate a true interest. In such a situation, the salesperson should attempt to open up the prospect with careful questioning.

There is not space here for an exhaustive discussion of body language, but some of the more important gestures are explained in Table 5-3.

After studying Table 5-3, see if you can identify the emotions portrayed in the photo. Now that you are becoming an expert, remember one thing: Sometimes a gesture is a gesture and nothing more. The client with whom you seem to be failing miserably might just have the flu!

Starting from the left corner of the photo, can you associate the gestures on the right with their emotions? Your choices are boredom, defensiveness, rejection, openness, nervousness, confidence, frustration, and evaluation.

(Answers: 1. rejection, 2. openness, 3. nervousness, 4. evaluation, 5. defensiveness, 6. confidence, 7. frustration, 8. boredom)

While the salesperson is busy observing the prospect, the prospect is busy observing the salesperson's nonverbal behavior. A blank face and an uninterested air with limited body movement are likely to create little enthusiasm in the customer. Smiling and nodding one's head represent marked improvements. According to a Johns Hopkins study of persuasion, people who are unable to use nonverbal communication techniques such as "smiling, gazing, interpersonal distance, and physical contact" have trouble getting their messages across.[23]

The salesperson must be a master communicator, both verbal and nonverbal.

Table **5-3** Important Body Language

Gesture	Meaning
Open hands, sit on edge of chair, open coat	Openness
Stroking chin, tilted head, hand to cheek	Evaluation
Slouching, no eye contact, unfocused	Indifference
Crossed arms and/or legs, touching nose	Rejection
Erect, steepling hands, hands behind head	Confidence

Can you identify the emotions protrayed?

T a b l e **5-4** **The Use of Eyes in Selling**

While listening, the salesperson must maintain eye contact.

The general rule is that the speaker occasionally finds time to break eye contact.

The listener should spend more time looking at the speaker.

In the United States, eye contact for short periods of time is appropriate.

Good contact is called the "glance away"—don't stare.

The salesperson should glance away periodically, but not during important points.

If a speaker pauses and looks away, she isn't finished speaking.

A locking of gazes indicates that the listener can now become the speaker.

5-2d Eyes

In U.S. culture, eye contact for short periods of time is appropriate, although prolonged eye contact is taken to be threatening. A study of the effects of nonverbal behavior conducted at the College of Charleston showed that those who gazed steadily (but did not stare) during a social interaction were judged to be more sincere.[24] In a similar British study, a team of investigators studied the effects of eye contact in a real-life setting in which a person soliciting money for charity alternately looked the prospective donor in the eye and looked at a money tin. Significantly more money was donated in the former situation.[25]

As explained in Table 5-4, in American culture, good eye contact is called the "glance away." Americans don't like others to stare at them. If a salesperson locks eyes with a prospect, stares the prospect right in the eye, never blinks, and never looks away, then the prospect will begin to feel very uncomfortable. When interacting with American customers, it is best for the salesperson to occasionally let his or her eyes drift away from the customer's face.[26] It is critical, though, for salespeople to maintain eye contact when listening. In our society, the general rule is that the speaker should find ways to break eye contact and look away. The listener is expected to spend relatively more time looking at the speaker. Looking away too often signals to the speaker: "I am not completely satisfied with what you are saying. I have some qualifications." Moreover, listeners should be careful in picking the moment to begin speaking. If speakers pause but look away, they are signaling that they are not finished and should not be interrupted. A locking of their gazes at this point, however, would signal that the listener can begin speaking.

5-2e Facial Expression

Charles Darwin maintained that facial expressions are universal and are based on the process of biological evolution. He believed the face to be a sensitive tablet upon which are written universally recognized emotions.

It is important for salespeople to understand facial expressions. If a prospect's mouth is relaxed without a mechanical smile and the chin is forward, the salesperson's presentation is being closely followed. If prospects maintain eye contact with the salesperson for seconds at a time, with a slight smile angled upward toward the nose, they are weighing the proposal. If the smile becomes relaxed and they appear enthusiastic, the sale is almost assured. However, if the jaw muscles tighten and the lips become pursed, then they have taken a defensive position and may reveal and react as little as possible. All of us have noted this tight-lipped expression in others at one time or another.

T a b l e **5-5** Body Language of Receptive and Unreceptive Listeners

Body Channel	Receptive (Positive Cues)	Unreceptive (Negative Cues)
Facial expressions and eyes	Smiles, much eye contact, more interest in the person than what is being said	No eye contact or squinted eyes, jaw muscles clenched, cheeks twitching with tension, eye contact is a sidelong glance
Arms and hands	Arms spread; hand open on the table, relaxed in the lap, or on the arms of a chair; hands touching the face	Hands clamped together, arms crossed in front of the chest, hand over the mouth or rubbing the back of the neck
Legs and feet	Sitting: legs together, or one in front of the other	Standing: crossed legs, pointing away from the speaker
	Standing: weight evenly distributed, body tilted toward the speaker	Sitting or standing: legs and feet pointing toward the exit
Torso	Sitting on the edge of the chair, unbuttoning suit coat, body tilted toward the speaker	Leaning back in the chair, suit coat remains buttoned

5-2f Summing It Up for Customers

Putting together what we have said so far, Table 5-5 provides clues as to differentiating receptive from unreceptive listeners.

5-2g Body Language Tips for the Salesperson

Salespeople, as well as clients, put out visual signals based on their body language. Often they are not even aware of doing so. An effective salesperson needs to know how to master the subtle cues of body language before he or she can be successful. Visual signals can make you appear not to be in control and will detract from your overall presentation . . . and the sale.

1. *Posture.* Next time you notice you're feeling a bit down, take a look at how you're standing or sitting. Chances are you'll be slouched over with your shoulders drooping down and inward, making a bad impression. If standing, stand up straight and face your prospects head-on. Keep your posture open with arms relaxed and hanging down at your sides. If your hands are clasped firmly in front of you, your feet are crossed, and your body is tight, then you are not exactly exuding confidence. Other "don'ts" include:[27]
    -   Hands on hips: You look too condescending or parental.
    -   Crossed arms: You are not conveying a look that says, "Let's talk."
    -   Hands crossed in front of you (otherwise known as the "figleaf" stance): This makes you look weak and timid.
    -   Hands joined behind your back: This stance (the "parade rest") makes you seem like you have no energy.
    -   Leaning back in a chair, if seated: You look like you're ready to pass judgment.
    -   Putting your hands in your pockets: This makes you seem nervous and can result in jingling any change or keys that might be there.
2. *Head position.* When you want to feel confident and self-assured, keep your head level both horizontally and vertically. You can also use this straight-head position when you want to be authoritative and want what you're saying to be taken seriously. Conversely, when you want to be friendly, listening, and

receptive, tilt your head just a little to one side or other. You can shift the tilt from left to right at different points in the conversation.[28]

3. *Arms.* Arm position indicates how open and receptive you are to everyone you meet and interact with, so keep your arms out to the side of your body or behind your back. This shows you are not scared to take on whatever comes your way and you meet things "full frontal." Generally, the more outgoing you are as a person, the more you tend to use big movements with your arms. The more quiet you are, the less you move your arms away from your body. Try to strike a natural balance and keep your arm movements midway. When you want to come across in the best possible light, crossing the arms in front of others is inadvisable.

4. *Legs.* Legs are the hardest parts of our bodies to control consciously. They tend move around a lot more than normal when we are nervous, stressed, or being deceptive. The best bet is to keep them as still as possible. Be careful too in the way you cross your legs. Do you cross at the knees, ankles, or bring your leg up to rest on the knee of the other? Be aware that the last position mentioned is known as the "figure four" and is generally perceived as the most defensive leg cross.

5. *Angle of the body.* Angle of the body in relation to others gives an indication of our attitudes and feelings toward them. We angle toward people we find attractive, friendly, and interesting and angle ourselves away from those we don't!

6. *Hands.* Hand gestures are so numerous that it's hard to give a brief guide. Palms slightly up and outward is seen as open and friendly. Palm-down gestures are generally seen as dominant, emphasizing, and possibly aggressive, especially when there is no movement or bending between the wrist and the forearm.

7. *Mouth.* Mouth movements can give away all sorts of clues. We purse our lips and sometimes twist them to the side when we're thinking. We also might use this movement to hold back an angry comment that we don't wish to reveal. Nevertheless, it will probably be spotted by other people, and although they may not know the comment, they will get a feeling you were not too pleased.

8. *Facial expressions.* Be aware of any artificial, unfriendly, or deadpan expressions you may be making. Do you squint, frown, or make strange faces? Once you are aware of any expressions you may make, it will be easier to eliminate them. Practice smiling and looking pleasant. That's how you want to look when meeting clients or prospects.

    Some facial expression "don'ts" include:
    - Arching eyebrows: This makes you seem surprised or questioning.
    - Frowning: Your moodiness will be the only thing the other person remembers.
    - Grimacing: Your prospect will wonder where it hurts.

9. *Handshake.* A handshake can be soft, firm, brief, long, or even painful. The way you shake hands provides clues to your personality. Aggressive people have firm handshakes. People with low self-esteem often have a limp handshake. A domineering man often squeezes the hand of a woman during a greeting. The woman can move her index and little finger in toward the palm to prevent a crushing handshake. This negates his dominant act and keeps her in equal control. So adopt a handshake that is firm, yet not crushing. Convey confidence and professionalism, not dominance.

5-3 Dress As a Form of Communication

The moment you meet prospective clients, they judge you by what they see and feel. The process takes less than 10 seconds, but the impression is permanent. Whether you make or break a sale can literally depend on the silent signals that you send during this first contact. We have already discussed the importance of nonverbal behavior to making that initial impression. Your dress is as critical—perhaps even more so—when making that first impression. As the old saying goes: You never get a second chance to make a first impression! Not only is clothing important to how others perceive us, but it also affects our view of ourselves and our confidence. We often estimate how we are perceived by others and incorporate this image into our own self-perception. Clothing, then, can affect confidence, and salespeople should take note.

For the past few years there has been a loosening of corporate dress codes, originating with "Casual Friday." This evolution is portrayed and humorously carried through to its possible conclusion in the photo. The nation's workplace shift from Casual Friday to Casual Every Day may be shifting again—back to Casual Friday.[29] The latest trend in men's business dress is best summed up in a word coined by Ford Motor designers: *retrofuturism.* It involves taking classic design and updating it with modern technology. You see it on the 2003 Ford Thunderbird, revitalized with twenty-first century engineering and creature comforts while remaining true to its 1955 styling. You also see it in men's suits, shirts, and ties that marry innovative fabrics and inspiration drawn from past eras of elegance.[30] The traditional single-breasted, gray suit, for instance, may now have lapels that are peaked rather than notched, and a more fitted jacket than the "sack" suit of yesterday. Yet comfort is foremost, in part thanks to the technology used to create the lightest-weight wools ever. In keeping with the retrofuturist trend in tailored clothing, the best shirts and ties feature Old World design elements in traditional and updated colors and fabrics—a solid color shirt in a microherringbone weave, for instance. What one would have formerly thought of as sporty—tattersalls, gingham checks, and subtle plaids—now come in dressed-up versions with French cuffs. In ties, classic patterns such as regimental stripes, understated geometrics, or even solids are worked in luxurious, textured silks. Such change returning to the traditional is understandable through surveys. According to a recent S&MM/Equation Research survey of 361 executives, 30 percent of executives say that customers have commented negatively on a rep's appearance or grooming. And 49 percent say their salespeople have encountered prejudice from customers because of the way they look. In fact, 48 percent say salespeople's physical image has become more important since the economic boom of the late 1990s. In addition, 38 percent believe their companies have lost business because of a sales rep's negative appearance. "When things are slow, companies are looking for a safe harbor," says Scott Testa, COO of Mindbridge Software, Inc., an intranet software company based in Norristown, Pennsylvania. "They are looking for companies they can feel comfortable with, and part of that comfort comes from a level of professionalism that is the result of good physical presentation."[31]

Has Casual Gone Too Far?

With a loosening of dress codes, sales and marketing personnel are caught in the middle, as they have to travel between their offices and that of their customers or prospects, each of which may have its own dress code. Because of this dilemma, perhaps the place to start is with the orthodox.

In *New Dress for Success* and *New Women's Dress for Success,* John T. Molloy writes, "In almost any situation where two men meet, one man's clothing is saying

What would you wear to work?

to the other man: 'I am more important than you are, please show respect' or 'I am your equal and expect to be treated as such.' "[32] Of these two situations, salespeople should dress for treatment as equals. Both overdressing and underdressing are to be avoided. Overdressing might cause customers to be uncomfortable and hesitant about disclosing their needs and wants. Underdressing could cause them to distrust salespeople as lacking in expertise. How, then, should salespeople dress to appear credible?

According to Molloy, the most important garment for both men and women in any business situation is the suit. It will most influence any viewer's stereotyped judgment of the wearer. The suit immediately conveys authority, credibility, and likability, qualities that are critical in business interactions. Molloy has specific guidelines for how business suits should look. In actual practice, although this image has changed somewhat for men; it has changed much more dramatically for women, who are more prevalent than in the past in the executive suite and as sales reps.

5-3a Male Salespeople

Standard attire for men is a conservative dark navy or gray two-piece business suit (of natural fibers, such as wool, if possible), a white long-sleeved button-down dress shirt, a conservative silk tie (that matches the colors in the suit), and nicely polished dress shoes. If you do not own a suit, or the company is a bit more informal, then you should wear a conservative sports coat (no plaids or wild patterns and preferably a dark color), nicely pressed dress slacks, a white long-sleeved button-down shirt, a conservative silk tie, and nicely polished dress shoes. Your belt should match your shoes.

If you have a beard or mustache, it should be neatly trimmed. If you have any visible body parts pierced, most experts recommend removing all jewelry, including earrings.

5-3b Female Salespeople

Standard attire for women is a conservative dark navy or gray skirted wool blend suit. Job experts and employers seem split on the notion of pantsuits, so a skirted suit is a safer choice. Other conservative colors—such as beige or brown—are also acceptable. A blazer with blouse and skirt is a possible second choice to a suit. Skirt length should be a little below the knee and never shorter than above the knee. Avoid wearing a dress. Blouses should be cotton or silk and should be white, or some other light color. Shoes should be low-heeled.

Types of attire for business occasions.

Makeup should be minimal, with lipstick and nail polish in conservative tones. Pantyhose should be flawless (no runs) and conservative in color. You should opt for a briefcase rather than a purse.

5-3c Advice for Both Men and Women

Good advice for both men and women is shown in Table 5-6.

Despite the "retro" trend in dress, many companies still have retained a more casual dress code. So what is the salesperson to do? Rule number 1 is to consider the nature of the client's work. If you're calling on someone in the financial business, the "dress for success" suit is appropriate. For the advertising business, more casual attire is suitable. If you are uncertain, especially with a new prospect, call ahead and inquire about their dress code. Above all, be adaptable. Michael Canney, a sales rep for Becton, Dickinson and Company, a medical devices firm in Franklin Lakes, New Jersey, rarely wears a jacket in his territory of Austin, Texas, because it's just too hot. "In the summer, wearing a nice button-down and khakis is fine." Canney often visits nurses in hospitals between 5 A.M. and 6 A.M. and showing up clad in a suit and tie would just be impractical. "I'm working with people who are hands-on. As long as you look professional, that's the most important thing."[33]

5-3d Guidelines for Casual Dress

So how does the salesperson dress casually?[34] (*Note:* "Dress casual" means going with a coat but no tie, or with a tie and no coat.)

For men:

- Try a blazer with an open-collar shirt. Choose a polo-style knit or band-collar woven shirt.
- Sport cotton trousers in khaki, navy, or hunter green.
- Loafers and socks with a subtle pattern that matches your pants.

T a b l e **5-6** Checkpoints for Appearance

Men	Women
Minimal or no cologne	Minimal perfume
No food, gum, or cigarettes	No food, gum, or cigarettes
Empty pockets	Empty pockets
Clean, trimmed nails	Light-colored nail polishes or clear polishes only; short nails
Matching socks	Dark or nude hose with no runs
Shined, conservative shoes	Clean, polished, conservative shoes with heels no higher than 2 inches
No visible body piercings (nose, eyebrow, lip, labret, etc.)	No visible body piercings (nose, eyebrow, lip, labret, etc.)
Clean, trimmed head and facial hair	Attractive, controlled hairstyle—long hair should be pulled back or up
Fresh shave	Light makeup
Conservative tie	Moderate, conservative jewelry
Clean, pressed business suit in blue or gray	Clean, pressed business suit in blue or gray or tailored dress
Light shirt	Well-tailored shirt—no low necklines or straining buttons
Light portfolio or briefcase	Light portfolio or briefcase

For women:

- Cotton or silk shirts. Add a vest to dress up a plain shirt.
- Mix jackets with your career suits with separates.
- Try softer fabrics in slim or full skirts. Skirts should be slightly above the knee to ankle length.
- Dress down with trousers or soft pants.
- Take a break from high heels and wear flats, oxfords, or loafers.
- French blue and tan are the contemporary casual colors.
- The sport coat is a bridge. It can be worn with khakis, various dress slack fabrics, mocks and polos, and dress shirts and ties.
- Just remember, without further information, on the first call, dress conservatively; you never get a second chance to make a first impression!

5-4 Time and Space "Speak"

If someone is late for an appointment with you, how does it make you feel? In our society, being late conveys the message: "You aren't important. I don't need to hurry to be on time for you." Interestingly enough, this isn't true in all cultures. In the United States, it is mandatory that the salesperson be on time for an appointment, but in South America, where one expects to wait and wait, being on time is not that critical.

proxemics
The distances at which people interact.

Distance, or more formally, **proxemics**, also communicates. We interact with people at different distances. We don't talk with customers at the same distance that we do with our spouses. Neither do we interact with strangers at the same distance that we do with friends. To verify this, the next time you go to a doctor's office where there is just one other patient, sit next to that person and watch his or her reaction.

Research has demonstrated that everyone has an invisible bubble of space around them that contracts and expands. This bubble is a kind of mobile territory that the individual will defend against intrusion. In crowded public places, we tense our muscles and hold ourselves stiff, communicating to others our desire not to intrude upon their space and, moreover, not to touch them. At all costs, we try to avoid eye contact. Walking along the street, our bubble expands slightly as we move in a stream of strangers, taking care not to bump into them. In a work situation or in a restaurant, our bubble changes as it adjusts to the environment.

People in the United States employ four main distances in their business and social relations: intimate (up to 2 feet); personal (2 to 4 feet); social (4 to 12 feet); and public (more than 12 feet) (see Figure 5-3).[35] Each of these distances has a near and a far phase and is usually detectable by changes in the volume of the voice. The intimate distance is used for the most private activities, such as showing affection to another person. Even at the far phase of the intimate distance, one is within easy touching distance of the other person. In general, the use of intimate distance between adults is frowned upon in public places. It is also far too close for strangers, except where crowding forces it.

In the second zone, personal distance, the close phase represents the distance at which spouses interact in public. If another person moves into this zone, the spouse may not look kindly on the gesture. The far phase is the most common spacing for people in conversation. But this distance is not all that intimate; the phrase at "arm's length" accurately describes the nature of this distance.

The social distance is reserved for business transactions. People who work together tend to use close social distance, 4 to 7 feet. This is also the common distance

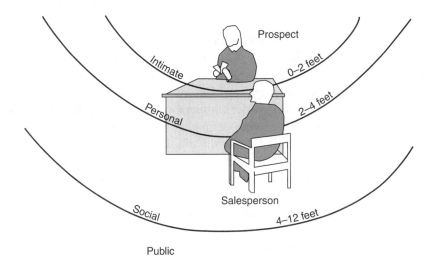

Figure 5-3
Proxemic Zones

for conversation at social gatherings. To stand at this distance while facing someone who is seated has a dominating effect (for example, teacher to pupil, boss to secretary). The far phase of social distance, 7 to 12 feet, lends a formal tone to business or social discourse. In an executive office, the desk serves to keep people at this distance.

The social distance, especially the close phase (4 to 7 feet), represents the distance at which salespeople should approach clients they have never met. Imagine the reaction of a buyer if a sales representative were to pull up a chair 2 to 4 feet away and begin a presentation. Although this is not quite as forward, what reaction do salespeople encourage when they enter an office and immediately take over part of the client's desk for their samples? The general rule for salespeople is to begin at the close phase of the social distance and not to approach closer until friendly relations are established. Invading the client's space too soon will cause the client to draw up a defensive barrier that may never be broken.

The fourth and final zone, public distance, is used by teachers in classrooms or speakers at public gatherings. Its farthest phase, 25 feet and beyond, is used for important public figures. Although it is dangerous for the sales representative to approach too closely too soon, it is equally dangerous to begin at too far a distance. Starting from the public distance may create an image of unsociability or conceit.

Psychological proxemics also exist. Your ideas and language may be formal, as in the public zone ("How do you do?"); casual, as in the social zone ("Hi!"); friendly, as in the personal zone ("How's the family, Joe?"); or intimate ("Hi, sweetie"). As with distance zones, salespeople may intrude upon their customers' psychological zones by speaking too familiarly too soon.

Interestingly enough, people can be classified into two major proxemic groups: contact and noncontact. When two people from contrasting groups get together, misunderstanding is almost inevitable. Contact people get too close, both physically and psychologically, to their noncontact counterparts, and vice versa, resulting in unpleasant feelings for both parties. The noncontact people are seen as cold, unfriendly, or impolite by the contact people. On the other hand, noncontact people perceive contact people as overly friendly, obtrusive, and smothering. Desire for contact or lack of the same is directly related to one's personality style. Analytics and Drivers prefer noncontact behavior, while Expressives and Amiables desire contact in their relationships. Interestingly enough, for contact-oriented customers, research shows that a light, brief (half-second) touch by a salesperson on the upper arm of customers caused them to extend the appointment by 63 percent and buy 23 percent more. Timing here is critical. Touch the customer shortly before you want them to do something—agree to another appointment, buy, etc.[36]

Proxemics also extend to possessions and territory (or "turf"). Have you ever become upset because someone picked up your tennis racket or golf clubs without asking? Or sat in your favorite chair? Buyers, too, have their territory; when threatened, they are not likely to give the salesperson a fair hearing. So salespeople should never stop by a client's office without an appointment and stick in their heads without knocking. Nor, when in buyers' offices, should they examine personal objects without permission. And they certainly should not march haughtily into a customer's office and immediately plop their briefcase on the buyer's desk. All of us have our territory, and we like to keep it to ourselves, unless we decide otherwise.

So far we have cautioned salespeople not to invade buyers' space, psychological and territorial, too soon. It is also true that salespeople should move forward under the proper set of circumstances. If a buyer indicates that a friendlier relationship is desired and the salesperson does not reciprocate by moving closer, the buyer may be offended by the salesperson's remaining distant.

5-5 Vocal Intonation

Much can be learned about prospects from the way they speak. Vocal intonation is particularly revealing about prospects' intentions. For example, a salesperson will have to choose a different approach depending on whether a prospect has said, "What do you mean!" or "What do you mean?" Salespeople misinterpreting these statements are likely to find themselves in an awkward position.

The salesperson's own voice is a critical factor in how he or she will be received. If you know enough about your own voice, you can regulate it to make the impression you want, as indicated in Table 5-7. Who has a good voice? Americans love deep, throaty voices like Ronald Reagan's, but some low voices don't work well: ex-President Clinton (too low and hoarse).[37] Bad voices, according to experts, generally fall into two categories: too nasal and too low. Although there exists little empirical data on vocal characteristics in a selling context, one study is very elucidating.[38] In comparing the speech of successful sales performers, Peterson et al., found that speech rate somewhat more rapid than that of normal conversation was correlated with superior performance. The increased rate should not come, how-

T a b l e **5-7** **Vocal Intonation**

Loudness	Adjust to loudness of buyer
Pitch	Lowness or highness of voice
	Lessen pitch at the end of a sentence, implying certainty
Vocal quality	Watch for nasality
	Eliminate breathiness
	Eliminate harshness
	Two elements to achieving quality: posture and diction
Enunciation	Sound out every vowel and consonant; if you have a strong regional accent, make sure you are understandable by people from outside of the area
Hesitation	Avoid long pauses
Fillers	Avoid "uh," "um," "you know," "really," etc.
Emphasis	Pick words to stress

ever, solely from articulating words more rapidly than normal, but by a variety of vocal behaviors, such as compressing pauses between words, phrases, and sentences in conjunction with appropriate phonetic contraction strategies (e.g., *They're* instead of *they are; D'ya* instead of *do you,* etc.). Lowering one's voice at the end of a sentence also was more successful, projecting an aura of authority and credibility. In contrast, rising inflection gives the impression of uncertainty and questioning. Finally, at least a modicum of vocal variability was associated with sales success. Loudness was not correlated with sales success.

Try taping your voice and analyzing it, using the material already presented and that which follows:

1. *Loudness.* Though not significant in the Peterson study, loudness, as we know from our everyday experiences, can be irritating. As you listen, try to remember whether others often ask you to speak up or repeat things or whether they back off or lean back, indicating you are too loud. You can achieve proper volume control by listening to your prospect's voice. Speak quietly to the quiet. Speak a little louder to the loud. If you have an angry customer, use a low tone of voice; this will tend to calm him or her.

2. *Pitch.* The lowness or highness of your voice—its overall tone—does much to form people's impression of you. As mentioned already, watch out for a rising or upward inflection at the end of sentences, signaling tentativeness. The tone should go down, indicating completion and certainty. Avoid singsong variation in your voice, or you will sound like a kindergarten teacher, not a professional salesperson. But don't go to the other extreme and talk in monotone; some amount of variation is good, as the Peterson study demonstrated. Use a slightly higher pitch when talking about something new and exciting. A lower pitch generally reassures the listener; it should be used to emphasize quality, service, and warranty.

3. *Vocal quality* (or *timbre*). Watch for "talking through your nose." Nasality is appropriate only for the sounds *n, m,* and *ng.* If you are too nasal, open your mouth more to get out vowel sounds. Look out for breathiness, or you will give an impression of bewilderment, delicacy, or conspiracy. Also watch for thinness; it is hard to convey authority if your voice sounds childlike. Steer clear of stridency—a sharp, metallic sound with a high, squeaky pitch. It conveys tension and nervousness. Harshness is another vocal quality to be avoided. When you are angry or irritable, your voice may take on a rough, hard, low-pitched quality. Others' first impressions of you may be that you are unsympathetic, sarcastic, or overbearing. Two basic elements determine voice quality: (a) posture—which affects the way you use your breath, and (b) diction—which determines clarity, fluency, and (surprisingly) strength. When either posture or diction is poor, pressure builds in the chest or strains your throat. You should learn to deliberately exhale and inhale with the abdominal muscles and ribs and to maintain proper posture, avoiding rounded shoulders and curvature of the lower back, which creates constant downward pressure on the chest and ribs. Diction also helps reduce tightness in the throat by focusing your speaking away from the throat and toward the front of your mouth. Seventy percent of consonants are formed with the lips, tip of the tongue, and the upper front teeth.[39]

4. *Enunciation.* Salespeople often are so eager to tell prospects about the wonderful features of their products that they forget all about proper enunciation. Sound every vowel and consonant meant to be sounded.

5. *Hesitation.* Leaving long pauses between words and sentences is a bad speech habit. This distracts from the sales presentation and gives the prospect time to build up doubts in his or her mind about the salesperson, the product, and the company. It usually makes the listener wonder if the speaker knows what he or she is talking about.

6. *Fillers.* These are words used to fill uncomfortable silences; they should be eliminated. They might include single-syllable sounds (e.g., *uh, um, ah, eh,* and *oh*); phrases that add nothing to the meaning of the sentence (e.g., *you know, you see, well so then, ya understand, so really,* and *OK?*); hedge words, such as *I guess, maybe, perhaps,* qualifiers like *just, that's all,* and *only*; and noises (e.g., throat clearing, shuffling, tongue clucking, sighs, yawns, and coughing). Clients judge the salesperson's level of confidence and product knowledge by his or her fluency of speech, and fillers are interpreted as nervousness or uncertainty.

7. *Emphasis.* Be aware of what words you emphasize, because this can change the meaning of what you say dramatically. Consider how the statement, "I didn't say he took that" changes dramatically with differing emphases. " *I* didn't say he took that" (*she* said it). "I didn't say he took *that*" (he took *something else*). "I didn't say he *took* that" (he *borrowed* it).

5-6 A Final Word

Several times we have mentioned the importance of not overanalyzing nonverbal behavior. Some nonverbal signals have several meanings. Crossed arms can indicate defensiveness, or simply a comfortable position. Touching the nose can suggest doubt in what the person is hearing, or it could be a response to an itch or soreness from a recent cold. Likewise, an unbuttoned jacket can signify openness and cooperation. It could also be an overweight person trying to fit into an old jacket.

Research also indicates that different people have widely different abilities to identify nonverbal behavior. So it is a good idea to be careful about your conclusions from observing nonverbal behavior until you gain experience. Salespeople should pay attention to both verbal and nonverbal communication. Together they provide a more complete picture of communication.

It is also true that individuals are rarely clear prototypes of any one personality style; all of us usually demonstrate traits across the spectrum. Still, in most instances, there is a distinct dominant personality for each of us, but it isn't always that easy to discern.

Notwithstanding, this discussion should not be interpreted as belying the importance of nonverbal behavior. It merely suggests that its interpretation requires skill and practice. It also suggests that people should not have absolute reliance in their ability to interpret nonverbal cues accurately. The salesperson has to work hard at effective two-way communication; it does not come automatically.

Chapter Summary

This chapter covered the importance of communication, beginning with the elements of the communication process: source, encoding, message, decoding, receiver, and feedback. Salespeople should do everything possible to facilitate clients' understanding. They should avoid using big words that sound impressive but mean little to the prospect. It also is wise to use active rather than passive descriptions and to recognize that even subtle differences between synonyms can evoke contrasting emotional reactions.

The advantages of two-way communication over one-way communication in selling, plus the importance of active listening, were explained, along with some tips for improving one's listening skills. The critical relationship between questioning and communication was also mentioned, although a complete discussion was postponed until Chapter 9.

A description of nonverbal behavior constituted a major portion of this chapter. The important contribution of dress to the salesperson's credibility was explained, along with dress suggestions. Other elements of nonverbal behavior include time, space, body language, eyes, facial expression, and vocal intonation. The importance of being able to interpret these nonverbal cues becomes evident when one considers that experts believe language itself composes only 35 percent of all communication. However, students are warned to avoid jumping to immediate conclusions from interpreting nonverbal behavior. Interpretation is an art, not a science; not every nonverbal cue means something, and expertise in interpretation comes only with experience.

Discussion Questions

1. What are the elements of the communication process?

2. Why is two-way communication preferable to one-way communication for salespeople?

3. Why is it necessary for sales representatives to be active listeners?

4. How does one become an active listener?

5. What is source credibility? What factors affect it?

6. Why is nonverbal communication important? What are some of the elements of nonverbal behavior?

7. How does one dress so as to convey credibility?

8. Of what value is color to dress?

9. How does distance influence social interaction? How does time influence it?

10. What is body language? What are some characteristic poses that are important for salespeople to recognize?

11. How is communication evident in facial expression?

12. What is the importance of vocal intonation?

13. "Nonverbal communication is far more important to salespeople than language itself." Defend or refute this statement.

14. It has been said that the common outcome of communication is misunderstanding. Do you agree?

15. Explain what the following instances of body language mean:
    a. A person talking with his or her hands open
    b. A person sitting in a meeting with crossed legs and arms
    c. Someone tapping his or her fingers on a desk
    d. Someone leaning forward with hand to cheek

16. What does the distance at which others deal with us reveal about their feelings toward us?

17. How good are most people at listening?

18. To be a good listener, one should attend only to the words themselves and ignore all distractions. Discuss.

19. It is important to listen just for facts. Discuss.

20. As one listens, it is important to make assumptions in order to prepare one's rebuttal. Discuss.

21. Explain psychological proxemics. What sorts of people can you approach from a closer distance more rapidly?

22. How should salespeople use eye contact, as both speakers and listeners?

23. Explain pacing.

24. Try watching a TV program while the sound is turned off. From the nonverbal behavior of the actors, determine what is taking place. Then turn up the volume and see if you are correct.

25. Listen to your professors' lectures. How do they use vocal emphasis to indicate the main ideas? How do their voices communicate their attitudes toward their subjects? Can you tell if they are enjoying themselves? Compare different styles. How is your enjoyment of class affected by contrasting vocal styles?

26. Go into the library and look for a table at which there is only one person studying. Take a seat next to the person. Repeat this several times. What is the typical reaction?

27. Keep a record for three or four days of all the clothing, jewelry, and other adornments you wear. Record any changes in clothing you make during the day. Once completed, explain why you made these changes and what the clothes might communicate to others.

28. What are the guidelines for casual dress?

Chapter Quiz

1. _____ is when people not only interpret things in terms of their existing attitudes but they also sometimes fail to notice information in opposition to their existing beliefs.
   a. Noise
   b. Decoding
   c. Egocentricism
   d. Selective perception

2. One method of active listening is amplification, which is
   a. watching for nonverbal communication cues.
   b. inviting additional comments.
   c. establishing and maintaining eye contact.
   d. encouraging the other person to talk about themselves.

3. _____ involves presenting to another person those aspects of yourself that are most nearly like those of the other.
   a. Body language
   b. Amplification
   c. Pacing
   d. Source credibility

4. According to an expert, Albert Mehrabian, 55 percent of our communication is through
   a. posture, gestures, and facial expressions.
   b. our tone of voice.
   c. words themselves.
   d. the written word.

5. In terms of nonverbal communications, Mehrabian indicates that nonverbal communication indicates the degree of all of the following *except*
   a. personality.
   b. liking.
   c. status.
   d. sheer responsiveness.

6. It is important for salespeople to understand what is being said through a buyer's body language. Crossed arms and/or legs and touching the nose would indicate
   a. openness.
   b. indifference.
   c. rejection.
   d. evaluation.

7. All of the following body language gestures would indicate a receptive listener *except*
   a. hand over the mouth or rubbing the back of the neck.
   b. sitting legs together or one in front of the other.
   c. arms spread, hand open on the table.
   d. standing with weight evenly distributed, body tilted toward the speaker.

8. Which of the following statements about the dress or attire of salespeople is false?
   a. Overdressing may cause customers to be uncomfortable and hesitant about disclosing their needs and wants.
   b. Underdressing could cause customers to distrust salespeople as lacking in expertise.
   c. Although it is acceptable for women to have visible body parts pierced, most experts recommend removing all jewelry, including earrings, for men.
   d. Women should avoid wearing a dress, and blouses should be cotton or silk and should be white, or some other light color.

9. People in the United States employ four main distances, or proxemics, in their business and social relations. The distance at which salespeople should approach clients they have never met should be
   a. personal (2 to 4 feet).
   b. personal (4 to 6 feet).
   c. social (4 to 7 feet).
   d. social (6 to 9 feet).

10. In terms of psychological proxemics, which statement indicates a salesperson speaking in the social zone?
    a. How do you do?
    b. Hi, honey
    c. How's that good-looking family, Joe?
    d. Hi, sweetie

Web Exercise

How good are your listening and speaking skills? One place to assess your listening skills is www.queendom.com/cgi-bin/tests/transfer.cgi. Take the communication test and see how you do. Do you agree with the assessment? How can you improve your skills?

Notes

1. Stephen X. Doyle and George Thomas Roth, "Selling and Sales Management in Action: The Use of Insight Coaching to Improve Relationship Selling," *Journal of Personal Selling and Sales Management,* Winter 1992, p. 62.
2. David W. Johnson and Frank P Johnson, *Joining Together,* Englewood Cliffs, NJ: Prentice Hall, 1991, p. 110.
3. "Question First, Then Present," *SellingPower.Com, Presentation Newsletter,* April 26, 2004.
4. "Ways to Anger Customers," *Sales & Marketing Management,* August 2002.
5. Jay Amberg, *Study Skills Handbook,* Tucson, AZ: GoodYear Books, 1993.
6. Tony Alessandra, Phil Wexler, and Rich Barrera, *Nonmanipulative Selling,* Englewood Cliffs, NJ: Prentice Hall, 1997.
7. "Rephrase," *Training: Professional Sales,* http://demo.apogee.net/ccit/train/tpmen.htm, June 2004.
8. "Interaction Rate," *Training: Professional Sales,* http://demo.apogee.net/ccit/train/tpmen.htm, June 2004.
9. Tony Alessandra, Phil Wexler, and Rich Barrera, *Nonmanipulative Selling,* Englewood Cliffs, NJ: Prentice Hall, 1997.
10. Ibid.
11. Annie Murphy Paul, "Self-Help: Shattering the Myths," *Psychology Today,* March 1, 2001.
12. Albert Mehrabian, *Silent Message,* Belmont, CA: Wadsworth Publishing Co., 1981, pp. 248–257.
13. Ibid.
14. Robert C. Brenner, "Body Language in Business: How to Sell Using Your Body," www.brennerbooks.com/bodylang.html, 1998.
15. Jerry Richardson and Joe Margolies, *The Business of Negotiation,* New York: Avon, 1984, p. 26.
16. *Harvard Business Review on Effective Communication,* Boston: Harvard Business School Press, October 1999.
17. William S. Condon and L. W. Sander, "Neonate Movement Is Synchronized with Adult Speech: International Participation and Language Acquisition," *Science,* January 11, 1974, p. 99.
18. Edward T. Hall, *Beyond Culture,* New York: Anchor Books, 1990.
19. Ibid.
20. Donald J. Moine and Kenneth L.Lloyd, *Unlimited Selling Power: How to Master Hypnotic Skills,* Englewood Cliffs, NJ: Prentice Hall Press, 1990.
21. Susan Goldin-Meadow, *Hearing Gesture: How Our Hands Help Us Think,* Boston: Harvard University Press, 2003.
22. John A. Quatrini, "The Right Touch," *Personal Selling Power,* March 1995, p. 68.
23. John E. Gibson, "Can Your Expression Make or Break an Impression?" *Family Weekly,* March 28, 1982, p. 23.
24. John E. Gibson, "Does It Pay to Look Someone in the Eye?," *Family Weekly,* January 23, 1983, p. 10.
25. Ibid.
26. Anthony J. Allessandra, James Cathcart, and Phillip Wexler, *Selling by Objectives,* IndyPublish.com, December 1998.
27. Marjorie Brody, "Does Your Body Language Stop a Sales Presentation before It Starts?," www.powerpointers.com, June 18, 2004.
28. Robert Phipps, "Top Ten Body Language Tips," www.selfgrowth, June 18, 1004.
29. Joyce Lain Kennedy, "Business Fashions Shifting to a More Formal Look," *Milwaukee Journal-Sentinel,* November 12, 2003.
30. "Dress Smart: The New Wardrobe Intelligence," *Business Week,* September 8, 2003.
31. "Image Is Everything," *Sales & Marketing Management,* October 2003.
32. John T. Molloy, *John T. Molloy's New Dress for Success,* New York: Warner Books, 1988.
32. John T. Molloy, *New Women's Dress for Success,* New York: Warner Books, 1996.
33. "Image Is Everything," *Sales & Marketing Management,* October 2003.
34. Sandy Mickelson, "Simple Fashion Trends Make Big Impact," *Oshkosh Northwestern,* August 16, 2002, p. B8.
35. Tony Alessandra, Phil Wexler, and Rich Barrera, *Nonmanipulative Selling,* Englewood Cliffs, NJ: Prentice Hall, 1997.
36. John A. Quatrini, "The Right Touch," *Personal Selling Power,* March 1995, p. 68.
37. Robert Sharoff, "Speech Therapy," *Selling,* December 1994, p. 13.
38. Robert A. Peterson, Michael P. Cannito, and Steven P. Brown, "An Exploratory Investigation of Voice Characteristics and Selling Effectiveness," *Journal of Personal Selling and Sales Management,* Winter 1995, pp. 1–14.
39. Morton Cooper, "Don't Put Up with Voice Fatigue," *Wall Street Journal,* September 28, 1992, p. A12.

Case 5-1

Peggy Leisering, sales representative for Aquaflex Corporation, is calling on Mark Grassman, optometrist and owner of Eyewear Professionals in Aspen, Colorado. Peggy wants to convince Mark of the merits of carrying extended-wear contact lenses in his store.

Peggy: Mark, I'd like to talk to you about our new line of extended-wear contact lenses. I'm sure you've heard something about them.

Mark: Yes, I have. Only last week, I read an article in *Ophthalmologist' Quarterly* about some studies being done and . . .

Peggy: Good! Then you know about some of the advantages of extended-wear contact lenses for your customers—the fact that they offer improved visual acuity, fit, and durability.

Mark: Yes, fit certainly is important. I . . .

Peggy: Yes, it is. And customers are really happy about their improved vision, if they are used to hard contact lenses. Not only that—many people who were always afraid of contacts are now interested.

Mark: I'm sure that's true.

Peggy: To make carrying our lenses attractive to you, Aquaflex is offering some really competitive marketing programs. We're offering a consignment program with built-in discounts to improve penetration among large-volume practitioners who fit 10 or more pairs of extended-wear lenses a month.

Mark: Consignment program?

Peggy: Yes, I knew you'd be excited about the possibilities. Additionally, Aquaflex has established a VIP program for large purchasers of extended-wear contact lenses. This program will really save you money.

Mark: That sounds fine. Tell me, what experience have other optometrists had with the extended-wear lenses?

Peggy: Just great! They're happy with the profit margins and sales volume especially.

Mark: And their customers have had good experiences with the lenses?

Peggy: Excellent reports. Can I put you down for an order?

Mark: Well, I'm kind of busy today. Can you leave some material that I can read and then get back to you?

Peggy: Sure, I've got some right here in my briefcase. Can we set up an appointment in the near future?

Mark: Well, I'd better call you. You know how business is.

Questions

1. What evidence is there in the dialogue that Peggy has much to learn about communication? Is she a good listener?
2. Rewrite the dialogue to show how you think Peggy should have handled matters.

Case 5-2

James Grunloh, sales representative for Appleton Office Supplies Company, has just entered the office of Bob Croze, office manager for Old Orchard Candle Makers. James, who has just graduated from college and begun selling for Appleton, is dressed in a two-piece brown suit. As James enters the office, Bob, a large man about 50 years old, sits behind a large wooden desk with his arms and legs crossed.

James (walking around Bob's desk to extend his hand): Good morning, Bob. It's a pleasure to meet you. How are you today?

Bob: Fine, just fine. You're a little late.

James: Just five minutes. I got delayed at the bank.

Bob (rubbing his nose with his index finger and crossing his arms and legs): Well, okay. What can I do for you?

James: I'm here to tell you about our new office forms. I think you'll be quite pleased with them.

Bob: Before you go any further, let me tell you that we've just placed an order with one of your competitors.

James (crossing arms and legs, his voice increasing in speed and pitch): I'm sorry to hear that. You should have waited until we got here. Appleton's prices have just been lowered by 10 to 20 percent.

Bob (uncrossing arms and legs and stroking his chin): They have?

James (buttoning his coat and starting to rise): Well, I guess it's too late if you've already placed the order. Next time, give us a chance, will you?

As James leaves, Bob sits at his desk with his elbows propped on his desk and holds both hands together in front of his mouth.

Questions

1. What mistakes in his own nonverbal behavior has James made?
2. What nonverbal cues in Bob has James failed to recognize?

Beginning the Relationship Selling Process

Key Terms

after-marketing
allowances
assurance
benefit
candor
cash discounts
C.B.D. (cash before delivery)
C.O.D. (cash on delivery)
competence

customer-orientation
C.W.O. (cash with order)
dependability
discounts
discrete transaction
empathy
E.O.M. (end of month)
feature
F.O.B. destination

F.O.B. plant (or F.O.B. origin)
just-in-time (JIT)
likability
list price
quantity discounts
reliability
tangibles
trade discounts

Learning Objectives

Learning Objectives

After studying Chapter 6, you will understand:

- The definition of relationship selling
- Why it makes sense
- Differences between transactional and relationship selling
- How to create "value-added"
- Critical relationship variables
- The process of relationship selling
- Successful after-marketing

- The basic principles of relationship selling
- Important elements of precall preparation with regard to industry, company, product, customer, and competition
- How to conduct a target market analysis

This chapter presents opportunities to integrate material already covered and to outline the future course of the text. Until now, the discussion has centered on presenting necessary background information for sales representatives. In the course of the discussion, an approach to selling emphasizing interaction, two-way communication, and relationship-building has been implicit. With sufficient background material, it is now time to present a formal statement of the relationship philosophy of selling. This statement will compose the first portion of the chapter, and it is followed by a discussion of the first step in the process, precall preparation.

6-1 Definition of Relationship Selling

As we explained in Chapter 1, a new term has been introduced into marketing terminology, *relationship marketing*. Although some might argue that customer relations and after-sale service have always been critical, there is a fresh recognition of the value of maintaining a long-term relationship or partnership with certain customers. Though really an extension of the marketing concept (the basic idea is to understand and solve a customer problem and you've already deepened the relationship), it has only recently become a driving marketing focus. The traditional focus has been a transactional one, emphasizing getting the sale and mostly ignoring the period afterward. The traditional assumption of the selling organization after the sale is that the product will not break down during the warranty period and, hence, little follow-up will be needed. Although some after-sale communication might have occurred, it is nothing compared to what is expected in relationship management. Relationship marketing goes further than sellers have ever gone to bind the buyer and seller together for the long term. In relationship management, buyer and seller are not viewed as opponents, but as partners. The payback? One study estimates that a decrease in the customer defection rate by 5 percent can boost profits by 25 percent to 85 percent.[1] Accordingly, relationship marketing is defined as

> Long-term agreements between buyers and sellers that reduce conflict and promote mutually beneficial ties between two firms. Using purchasing partnerships, buyers are supposed to receive a continuous stream of quality products and services, while suppliers are assured of a significant portion of buyers' orders. The relationship enables the partners to plan requirements on a mutually beneficial time schedule with mutually satisfactory pricing.[2]

6-2 Comparing Transactional and Relationship Selling

Perhaps the best manner in which to explain this significant shift in thinking of customer relationships is to contrast it with transactional marketing. Table 6-1 outlines these differences.

As indicated in Table 6-1, it is useful to think about possible marketing approaches or strategies along a marketing strategy continuum. Relationship marketing is placed at one end of the continuum. Here, the general focus is on building relationships with customers (or other parties as well, although only customers are discussed in this context). At the other end of the continuum is transaction marketing, where the focus of marketing is on one transaction at a time. Transactional marketing revolves around creating single transactions or exchanges at a time and not around building long-term relationships.[3]

To draw a complete contrast, it is necessary to draw a distinction between transactions (in particular, discrete transactions) and relational exchange:

T a b l e **6-1** A Comparison of Transactional and Relationship Selling

Strategic Element	Transactions	Relationships
Timing	Short-term	Long-term
Dominant quality dimension	Product quality	Quality of interactions
Price elasticity	More sensitive	Less sensitive
Obligations	Offers and claims regulated by law	Primarily promises between parties plus customs and laws (i.e., self-regulation)
Expectations for association	Little, unless failure	Any conflicts of interest balanced by trust and efforts at unity
Primary personal relations (i.e., social interaction and communication)	Minimal	Important personal, noneconomic satisfaction derived
Cooperation	No joint efforts	Joint efforts
Planning	No future anticipated	Detailed planning for future exchange
Measurement of performance	Little, if product works	Significant attention to specifying, quantifying, and measuring all aspects of performance (including service)
Power (imposing one's will on others)	May be exercised until obligations met	Interdependence
Division of benefits and burdens	Sharp division	Likely to include some sharing over time
Emphasis in selling process	Closing	Problem recognition
Personnel involvement	Marketers and buyers	Integration of personnel from many functional areas
Importance of internal marketing	Minimal	Critical

Sources: Adapted from C. Gronroos, "The Marketing Strategy Continuum: Towards a Marketing Concept for the 1990s," *Management Decision,* 1990, pp. 3, 9; Youngme Moon, *Interactive Technology and Relationship Marketing Strategies,* Boston: Harvard Business School Publishing, 1999; F. Robert Dwyer, Paul H. Schurr, and Sejo Oh, "Developing Buyer–Seller Relationships," *Journal of Marketing,* April 1987, pp. 11–27; Thomas Wotruba, "The Evolution of Personal Selling," *Journal of Personal Selling and Sales Management,* Summer 1991, pp. 1–12; B. A. Weitz and K. D. Bradford, "Personal Selling and Sales Management: A Relationship Marketing Perspective," *Journal of the Academy of Marketing Science,* Vol. 27, No. 2, April 1999, pp. 241–254.

discrete transaction
Money on one side and and an easily measured commodity on the other. No further interactions between buyer and seller are expected over time.

Discrete Transactions

The prototype of a **discrete transaction** is money on one side and and an easily measured commodity on the other:[4]

> Discreteness is the separating of a transaction from all else between the participants at the same time and before and after. Its [pure form], never achieved in life, occurs when there is nothing else between the parties, never has been, and never will be.

Note that relational elements are explicitly excluded. A one-time purchase of un-branded gasoline out of town at an independent station paid for by cash approximates a discrete transaction.

Relational Exchange

Discrete transactions are differentiated from relational exchange along several dimensions. Most important is the fact that relational exchange occurs over time; each transaction must be viewed in terms of its history and its anticipated future. The basis for future collaboration may be supported by expectation assumptions, trust, and planning. Relational exchange participants can be expected to derive complex economic, personal, and noneconomic satisfactions and engage in social exchange. Because duties and performance are relatively complicated and occur over an extended time period, the parties may direct much effort toward carefully defining and measuring the items of exchange.[5]

Consistent with the preceding discussion, another example of a discrete transaction would occur when a consumer might buy peaches at a farmer's market or a grocer may buy bags in quantity from any of several sources. The products can be easily evaluated, paid for with cash, and carted away. There is no prolonged negotiation, paying by cash ends the transaction, and mutual dependence quickly ends.

Relational aspects begin to appear when the buyer pays by check or the seller schedules delivery by next week. That is, dependence is extended, performance is less straightforwardly evaluated, uncertainty leads to protracted communication, the beginnings of cooperative planning and anticipation of conflict arise, and expectations of trustworthiness may be implied by personal characteristics.[6]

More extended relationships enable companies to design services that differentiate their offerings and attract long-term customers. Bandag, which sells truck-tire retreads to more than 5,009 dealer-installers, offers extensive extra services. For example, it assists dealers in filing and collecting on warranty claims from manufacturers and will soon begin offering comprehensive fleet-management services to its largest accounts. Bandag plans to embed computer chips in the rubber of newly retreaded tires to gauge each tire's pressure and temperature and to count its revolutions. That information will enable the company not only to tell each customer the optimal time to retread each tire (thus reducing downtime caused by blowouts) but also to help it improve its fleet's operations.[7]

Respecting the strategic elements in Table 6-1, timing differs depending on where on the continuum a firm is. As transaction marketing means that the firm focuses on single exchanges or one transaction at a time, the time perspective is rather short. The unit of analysis is a single market transaction. Profits are expected to follow from today's exchanges, although sometimes some long-term image development occurs. In relationship marketing the time perspective is much longer, as with Bandag. The marketer does not plan primarily for short-term results. His or her objective is to create results in the long run through enduring and profitable relationships with customers. In some cases, single exchanges may even be unprofitable as such.

For a firm applying a relationship strategy, the traditional marketing mix often becomes too restrictive. Many important customer contacts from a marketing success point of view are the ones outside the realm of the traditional marketing mix and marketing specialists. The marketing impact of the customer's contacts with people, technology, and operational systems and other nonmarketing functions materially determines whether he or she (or the organizational buyer as a unit) will continue doing business with a given firm. All these customer contacts are more or less interactive. Relationship marketing and selling thus involves people who have dual responsibilities. Their main duties are in operations or some other nonmarketing tasks, but they also perform a crucial marketing task because of their vital customer contacts. They have responsibilities as "part-time marketers." This is the case, for example, in most industrial marketing and services marketing situations. A successful interactive marketing performance requires that all parts of the firm that are involved in taking care of customers collaborate and support each other in order to provide customers with good total perceived quality and service satisfaction. Thus, for a firm pursuing a relationship marketing strategy, the internal association between marketing, operations, personnel, and other functions is of strategic importance to success. In relationship marketing, interactive marketing becomes a critical part of the marketing function.[8]

Consequently, part-time marketers have to be prepared for their marketing tasks. Internal marketing is needed to ensure the support of traditional nonmarketing people. They have to be committed, prepared and informed, and motivated to perform as part-time marketers. As Jan Carlzon of SAS noticed, "Only committed and informed people perform." This does not go for the back-office and frontline employees only. It is, of course, equally important that supervisors, middle-level, and top-level managers be equally committed and prepared. The internal marketing concept states that "the internal market of employees is best motivated for service mindedness and customer-oriented performance by an active, marketing-like approach, where a variety of activities are used internally in an active, marketing-like and coordinated way."[9] In transaction marketing, there is not much more than the core product, and sometimes the image of the firm or its brands, which keeps the customer attached to the seller. When a competitor introduces a similar product, which is quite easily done in most markets today, advertising and image may help retain customers, at least for some time, but price eventually becomes a critical issue. A firm that offers a lower price or better terms is a dangerous competitor, because in transaction marketing the price sensitivity of customers is often high. A firm pursuing a relationship marketing strategy, on the other hand, has created more value for its customers than what is provided by the core product alone. Such a firm develops over time more and tighter ties with its customers. Such ties may, for example, be technological, knowledge-related or information-related, or social in nature. If they are well handled, they provide customers with added value, something that is not provided by the core product itself. Of course, price is not unimportant, but is often much less of an issue. Skillful relationship marketing makes customers less price sensitive.

A transactional marketing approach includes no or minimal customer contacts outside the product and other marketing mix variables. The benefits sought by the customers are imbedded in the technical solution provided by the product. The customer will not receive much else that will provide him with added value, other than perhaps the corporate or brand image. Hence, the technical quality of the product is the dominant quality-creating source in transaction marketing.

In relationship marketing, the situation is different. The customer interface is broader and the firm has opportunities to provide its customers with added value of various types (technological, information, knowledge, social, etc.). Hence, how the interaction process is perceived grows in importance. When several firms can provide a similar technical quality, managing the interaction processes also becomes imperative from a broader quality perspective. Thus, in relationship marketing, the perceived quality dimension grows beyond the core product in importance and often becomes dominating. Installing goods, technical service, advice on how to use a physical good or a service, just-in-time logistics, customer-adapted invoicing, technical know-how, information, social contacts, and a host of other elements of bigger or smaller magnitude are added to the relationship, as described in Box 6-1, so that it becomes more attractive and profitable for the customer to engage in an on-going relationship with a given partner in the marketplace. All such elements are different types of services. Of course, this does not mean that product technical quality can be neglected, but it is no longer the only quality dimension to be considered as one of strategic importance.[10]

A typical way of monitoring customer satisfaction and success is to look at market share and to do ad hoc customer satisfaction surveys. A stable or rising share of the market is considered a measure of success and, indirectly, customer satisfaction. When the customer base remains stable, market share is a good measurement of satisfaction. However, often one does not know whether it is truly stable or whether the firm is loosing a fair share of its customers, which is replaced by new customers through aggressive marketing. In such situations, just following market share statistics may easily give a false impression of success, when in fact the number of unsatisfied customers and ex-customers is growing and the image of the firm is deteriorating.

For a consumer packaged-goods marketing firm, which typically would apply a transaction marketing strategy, there are no ways of continuously measuring market success other than monitoring market share. A service firm and many industrial marketers, on the other hand, that can more easily pursue a relationship marketing strategy, have at least some kind of intimate interaction with almost every single customer, even if they serve mass markets. Thus, customer satisfaction can be monitored directly. A firm that applies a relationship-type strategy can monitor customer satisfaction by directly managing its customer base. Managing the customer base means that the firm has at least some kind of direct knowledge of how satisfied its customers are. Instead of thinking in anonymous numbers, or market share, management thinks in terms of people with personal reactions and opinions. This requires a means of gathering the various types of data about customer feedback, which arrives every day; this data is collected by many employees in large numbers of customer contacts. In combination with market share statistics, such an intelligence system focusing on customer satisfaction and customer needs forms a valuable source of information for decision making.

Consequently, in a relationship marketing situation, the firm can build up an online, real-time information system. This system will provide management with a continuously updated database of its customers and continuous information about the degree of satisfaction and dissatisfaction among customers. This can serve as a powerful management decision-making tool. In a transaction marketing situation it is impossible, or at least very difficult and expensive, to build up such a database.

6-3 Rationale for Relationship Marketing

One obvious question at this juncture is why the sudden interest in relationship marketing? The answer is lifetime value. Lifetime value is the sum of the future stream of earnings and other benefits attributable to all purchases and transactions with an

Box 6-1

Ten Ways to Augment the Product for Collaborative Relationships

- *"Pull" promotional programs* can be directed at the customer firm's customers. This might involve trade journal advertisements touting the value of products made from or with the suppliers firm's components.

- *Warranty, maintenance, and repair agreements* can be offered to customer firms to reduce the risk associated with usage of a supplier's products.

- *Cooperative advertising and promotional allowances* can serve the dual purposes of enabling smaller customer firms to advertise regularly and coordinating customer and supplier market communication efforts.

- *Joint sales calls* can be utilized to assist customer firms in developing new markets, or to deal with problem accounts.

- *Coordinated cost-reduction programs* can be implemented to dramatically pare the customer firm's real costs of doing business. Joint material requirements planning (MRP) systems, computer-to-computer order entry systems, just-in-time inventory programs, and statistical process control are some examples.

- *Technical assistance* can be provided to augment customer firm's technical product and application knowledge. Supplier firm technical and production experts can make suggestions on how the customer firm could gain cost savings through substitute materials and alternative production processes.

- *Logistics and delivery systems* can be used to create value. For instance, a manufacturer of paint pigments in "slurry form" rather than in "dry bag" form created greater value for the customer. This enabled customer firms to reduce costs in the production process because they no longer had to emulsify the pigment before use. As a side benefit, the manufacturer was able to gain logistical cost savings because greater quantities of pigments were ordered at a time, and the slurry could be delivered more economically.

- *Computer networking capabilities* can be used to troubleshoot customer problems from a remote location. For instance, a manufacturer of scientific testing equipment uses its network to solve customer problems more quickly. Data and computer software can be downloaded from the equipment on-site and transferred to the manufacturer's simulation computers via telephone interlink. The supplier can troubleshoot the software and make corrections in the case of problems. The corrected software can then be sent back to the customer firm via telephone interlink.

- *Shared expertise programs* in which information is more openly shared between supplier and customer firms is another option. In the marketing area, one manufacturer of chemicals and plastics not only shares information on economic trends with customer firms but also performs market research studies for those customers that lack in-house research expertise. On the technical side, one manufacturing company has a "scientist exchange program" in which its own scientists spend time working in the research and development labs of customer firms.

- *Value-enhancement and codesign programs* can be put in place to upgrade the value of current customer firm products as well as to jointly design new products. Considerable value can be added to the product offering at times simply by a reallocation upstream of processing and production functions. For instance, many steel service centers now perform the functions of stamping doors and window panels for automakers, resulting in a lower overall cost. The assembly of electronic components into modules or boards by electronic component manufacturers is another example of this process.

individual customer, discounted back to its present value. As illustrated in Figure 6-1, the longer customers are retained by a company, the more profitable they become because of increased purchases, reduced operating costs, referrals, price premiums, and reduced customer acquisition costs. To this can be added the insights provided, which may result in new capabilities that can be applied to other customers.[11]

As Figure 6-1 indicates, acquiring new sales is more expensive than selling to an existing customer. In one survey, respondents reported that it took an average of seven calls to close a first sale, compared with only three calls to close a sale to an existing account. By multiplying the difference of four sales calls by the average cost of a sales call ($250), we can see that it's more than twice as expensive to land a new account than it is to penetrate an existing account. Specifically, the cost of a sale to a new account comes to $1,750 versus $750 for an existing one, a 235 percent premium on the cost of a new sale over one to an existing account. Moreover, survey participants reported an average of only 17 percent of their companies' sales volume coming from sales to new accounts. That figure isn't surprising when one considers that managers at most firms indicate that the margins accepted "to get a foot in the door" are often lower than those for subsequent sales, making new-account business the least profitable as well as the most expensive. Moreover, additional research indicates that the average company loses half its customers every five years; reducing customer defections by 5 percent can increase profits by 25 to 85 percent; as many as 85 percent of customers who defect say they were satisfied with their current supplier; extremely satisfied customers are six times more likely to repurchase than those merely satisfied; and a satisfied customer will tell five people, while a dissatisfied customer will tell nine.[12]

Figure 6-1 also portrays how consumers use the product or service slowly at first, but as their satisfaction grows, so do their purchases and usage. Moreover, as their purchases rise, operating costs decline. It costs money to process new customers, checking their credit and adding them to the corporate database. Existing

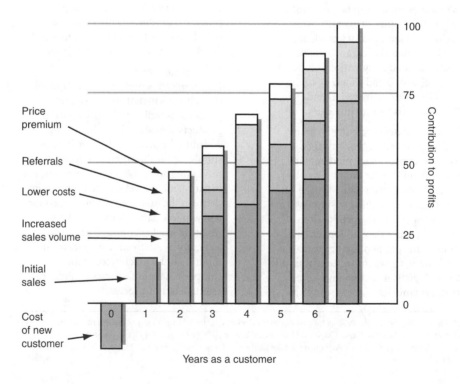

Figure 6-1
Why Loyal Customers Are More Profitable

customers, in contrast, are only added once. Also, as the seller gains experience with its long-term customers, it can serve them better and more efficiently. Not only do they buy more because of the seller's superior knowledge of them, but they also have fewer questions or problems. Yet a further benefit is the seller's ability to charge more for its products or services. Customers will pay more for a known quantity than risk change to a cheaper but unknown competitor. If satisfied, happy customers also do a lot of talking over the years, yielding many referrals.

Increased customer retention drives job satisfaction among the seller's own employees (i.e., job pride), which leads to higher retention; longer employee tenure, in turn, leads to higher productivity. The very idea of customer satisfaction helps align employees behind a common goal that everyone can understand. One of the biggest hurdles to building customer loyalty is the problem of employee turnover, but high employee retention means a workforce that understands what customers need and has higher productivity. Even in retailing, which typically pays front-line employees minimum wage, companies are rethinking the practice. Home Depot, for example, pays significantly more than the industry average and has been very successful with this approach as an essential element of its marketing strategy and well-publicized success.[13]

Other factors have also accelerated the trend toward relationship selling. Many American firms are adopting Japanese practices such as **just-in-time (JIT)** inventory handling. In contrast to the traditional American practice of competitive bidding for large supply contracts, JIT calls for frequent deliveries with small lot sizes synchronized with manufacturer production schedules. Often, deliveries are made right from the truck or boxcar to the assembly line. In such a system, there is little tolerance for defects, and closer ties between manufacturers and their suppliers is the rule. The traditional adversarial relationship between supplier and customer must be replaced by a partnership philosophy. It is not possible for the JIT producer to work with multiple materials or parts suppliers; rather, one or a few suppliers virtually integrate their own order systems with the production schedules of the producer to make the requisite frequent deliveries of JIT. Producer and supplier must have an intimate knowledge of the needs and capabilities of one another. The salesperson has to manage the relationship of his or her company's design engineers, quality assurance engineers, and production personnel with those of the buyer. Without backup stock to replace defective parts, there is little room for error in JIT; the supplier must approach near-perfect quality consistently. This has often assumed more importance than price in the vendor selection decision.

As illustrated in Figure 6-2, the impact of JIT has been to drastically reduce the number of suppliers with which companies do business. Companies around the country are cutting back the number of suppliers they use by as much as 90 percent. Motorola has cut its 10,000 company supplier base by 70 percent and is still slashing. Xerox has reduced its supplier base to about 500 (from 5,000) and has seen its reject rates on parts go down by a factor of thirteen. Companies are demanding higher levels of service and product quality from the survivors, and they are willing to pay a premium on the theory that getting things right initially is cheaper in the long run.[14]

Of course, another driving force between forming relationships has been globalization. Recognizing the more rapid growth overseas, many companies have found it less costly and more profitable to forge alliances with foreign partners. Besides minimizing costly investments, foreign partners know their markets more intimately, reducing the risk for American companies.

just-in-time (JIT)
Frequent deliveries with small lot sizes synchronized with manufacturer production schedules.

Many companies are cutting back the number of suppliers they use and demanding higher quality from those they keep.

	Number of Suppliers		
	Current[1]	Previous[2]	% Change
Xerox	500	5,000	−90%
Motorola	3,000	10,000	−70
Digital Equipment	3,000	9,000	−67
General Motors	5,500	10,000	−45
Ford Motor	1,000	1,800	−44
Texas Instruments	14,000	22,000	−36
Rainbird	380	520	−27
AlliedSignal Aerospace	6,000	7,500	−20

Figure 6-2
Diminishing Suppliers
Source: John R. Emshwiller, "Suppliers Struggle to Improve Quality As Big Firms Slash Their Vendor Rolls," *Wall Street Journal,* August 16, 1991, p. B1.

[1]Companies have different ways of counting their supplier base. For example, some count only direct manufacturing suppliers, while others count service and support suppliers.

[2]Number of suppliers firm had prior to starting reduction programs.

6-4 A Theory of Relationship Selling

Some people, including many practicing salespeople, maintain that selling cannot be taught; it must be learned through hard work and experience. Certainly, experience can teach much about selling, but it is not the only teacher, or even conceivably the best.

6-4a Why a Theory of Selling

Experience is a good teacher for salespeople, as long as a framework has been provided against which to assess performance. Any salesperson who learned to sell exclusively through observing others knows how difficult this can be. Unless the student already knows what to look for, mere observation will provide limited information. Frequently, practicing salespeople themselves do not know the reasons for their success, which of course makes it difficult to teach anyone else.

The need for a theory of selling is analogous to a sharpshooter's need for a means of marking the target. A sharpshooter may fire thousands of rounds at a target but never improve; he or she might even get worse. If a flag is raised after each shot, however, the necessary adjustments can be made and the score improved. Salespeople, like sharpshooters, need a method of determining whether they have hit the target. Even if it is less than perfect, a theory or philosophy of selling gives salespeople a target at which to aim and a means for assessing their performance. If they miss with one call, they can determine what went wrong and adjust their technique the next time around.

6-4b Principles of Relationship Selling

Relationship selling is not a series of mandatory sequential steps that must be followed religiously to final success. Rather, it is a philosophy of selling: a fundamental, comprehensive way of dealing with clients. This is not to say that there is an absence of formal tactics with relationship selling; to be sure, there are objections-handling techniques, closing techniques, and the like. But the essence of relationship selling is a philosophy the salesperson should internalize and use as a general guide in all dealings with clients. As such, relationship selling includes the following basic principles:

1. What does the sales rep have to do in terms of specific words and actions to establish a relationship with a client? As mentioned in Chapter 5, the key is

T a b l e **6-2** **Building the Relationship: "The Five Trust-Builders"**

Candor: (Words)

- Your presentations are balanced and fair (e.g., product limitations as well as advantages are discussed).
- What you say agrees with what the buyer knows to be true.
- The proof you use to support your words is credible.
- Subsequent events prove your statements to be true.

Dependability: (Actions)

- Your actions fulfill your prior (verbal) promises.
- Your action fits a pattern of prior dependable actions you have established.
- You refuse to promise what you can't deliver.

Competence: (Ability)

- You display technical command of products and applications (i.e., you are accurate, complete, and objective).
- You have the skill, knowledge, time, and resources to do what you promise and what the buyer wants.
- Your words and actions are consistent with a professional "image."

Customer-Orientation: (Intent)

- You understand the buyer's needs and place them on a par with your own (and your organization's).
- You give fair and balanced presentations (pros and cons) and clear statements of benefits.
- You advise rather than "sell." (You won't push a product the buyer doesn't need.)

Likability: (Personality)

- You make efficient use of the buyer's time.
- You are courteous and polite.
- You and the buyer share and talk about areas of commonality: goals, interests, even comparable intelligence. This extends to nonbusiness topics.

Note: There is an emotional component to likability that is difficult to define.

Source: From *Journal of Personal Selling and Sales Management,* Vol. XII, No. 1 (Winter 1992): 62. Copyright © 1992 by Pi Sigma Epsilon. Reprinted with permission of M. E. Sharpe, Inc. All rights reserved. Not for reproduction.

trust. The fundamental reality in a relationship is that the client is dependent on what the salesperson has said or promised. The buyer faces risk if what the salesperson has said turns out to be false or what is promised is not delivered. If a vendor has been selected as the sole supplier in a just-in-time manufacturing role, failure of the supplies to arrive on time will result in shutting down the production line, a very expensive proposition for both the manufacturing organization in general and the decision maker(s) who selected the vendor. Table 6-2 enumerates detailed techniques for eliciting trust on the part of the buyer. They are: **candor, dependability, competence,** a **customer-orientation,** and **likability.**[15]

2. Relationship selling is participative. Many salespeople and their managers view selling as a conflict between buyers and sellers, with salespeople using superior strength and determination to impose their wills on their customers. They see selling as a struggle that the salesperson must win. When salespeople use this approach, it is no wonder that many customers become defensive and refuse to buy, even if it is in their best interests.

Relationship selling sees the salesperson's task as fundamentally different. Psychology suggests that the greatest pressure for change comes from within the individual. Once people recognize the existence of certain needs, they begin to act to satisfy those needs. Until individuals have gained insight into their needs and problems, even the most effective sales

candor
Your presentations are balanced and fair (e.g., product limitations as well as advantages are discussed).

dependability
Your actions fulfill your prior (verbal) promises.

competence
You display technical command of products and applications (i.e., you are accurate, complete, and objective).

customer-orientation
You understand the buyer's needs and place them on a par with your own (and your organization's).

likability
You and the buyer share and talk about areas of commonality—goals, interests, even comparable intelligence; this extends to nonbusiness topics.

presentation will fall on deaf ears. The salesperson who seeks to dominate customers may find them so busy resisting domination that they have little time to think about their needs. So with relationship selling, the salesperson encourages prospects to talk so they can uncover their own needs. Problems do not get solved by salespeople; they are solved by the person who has the problem. The salesperson may support the prospect in this process by offering encouragement and suggestions for solutions, but the basic pressure for change comes from within buyers themselves. A salesperson will have difficulty telling customers to buy because of features and benefits. However, prospects who have been helped to discover the features and benefits for themselves are much more likely to respond favorably. People like to buy; they do not like to be sold.

A participative approach to selling is advantageous from another standpoint—that of attention. The more that people participate in the communication process, the easier it is for them to be attentive. When you are just listening to a speaker and have no opportunity to respond, how long is it until your mind begins to wander? How often does this happen to you in class, for example?

VIDEO

3. Relationship selling encourages active listening and questioning. Telling prospects what they need doesn't work; instead, prospects must be encouraged to talk. The salesperson does this through active listening. To discover a prospect's needs, the salesperson listens carefully, makes a tentative conclusion, and tests carefully with a question. Through nonverbal and verbal feedback—positive, neutral, or negative—the salesperson appraises an initial conclusion and readjusts if necessary. In this manner, as imperfect as it may be, prospect needs are discovered.

In the traditional transaction-oriented approach to selling, much effort is expended on closing. In relationship selling, most of the sales call is spent solving the customer's problem, and only with active listening is there a suspension of the salesperson's own thoughts and feelings and complete attention to the prospect's. This means not thinking about what to say next but attempting to understand the prospect's needs, problems, and emotions. Which of the following responses by the salesperson illustrates active listening?

Prospect: What I really need is a way to reduce downtime due to equipment breakdowns. You can't imagine how many hours I've stayed late because of this.

Salesperson: Yeah, I can understand that. Let's see, uh, let me explain the third feature of our product, its ease of operation. (I wonder if I can still get lunch reservations at Le Bistro?)

or

"Could you tell me more about the sort of machine breakdowns you've had that caused excessive downtime? What sort of design changes would you want in a new machine?"

Prospects often are unaware or unsure of their needs. Without the aid of salespeople, how many life insurance buyers would be certain about their insurance needs? How many homeowners would know, without help from a salesperson, whether they needed a lawnmower with a rear bagger, electronic ignition, and mulcher? Through tentative listening and careful questioning, the sales representative can determine buyer needs, help buyers recognize those needs, and crystallize the needs so that both salesperson and prospect agree on them.

Different selling skills are emphasized in transaction (i.e., traditional) versus relationship selling. In the traditional approach, salespeople are expected to move and persuade the buyer. Hence, verbal skills are stressed. In the relationship approach, salespeople are problem-solvers; listening and analytical skills are preeminent.

4. Relationship selling is buyer-oriented. Interactive salespeople are people-oriented rather than product-oriented. They recognize that people do not buy the product for itself but for what it will do for them.

    This means that the sales representative must translate product facts into people benefits. Witness the following two exchanges between parent and child, and see how the parent uses this principle in the second instance.

    Exchange 1:

    Parent: Johnny, take this medicine. It will help your cold!

    Johnny: No!

    Exchange 2:

    Parent: Johnny, take this medicine so your cold will go away, and you'll be able to go back outside and play with your friends.

    Johnny: Okay.

    A buyer orientation implies that salespeople must be sensitive to buyer behavior. They must be able to recognize prospects' needs and demonstrate how the product resolves these needs or problems.

5. Relationship selling is empathetic. A story about Ben Duffy, the legendary life insurance salesperson, helps illustrate the meaning of empathy. As a young sales representative, Ben made an appointment at a large company to discuss its insurance needs. As might be imagined, Ben was apprehensive the night before the call, so he sat down and asked himself, "What questions would I have of any insurance agency before I hired them?" Responding to his own question, Ben proceeded to write down the questions he would ask if he were in the buyer's position. The next day, Ben explained to the prospect's president what he had done the previous evening. As it turned out, the president had prepared his own list, and, in comparing it with Ben's, the two men found few differences between the two lists. To make a long story short, the net result for Ben was a $12 million contract.

    As with Ben, relationship selling requires that salespeople go beyond merely understanding customer needs and put themselves mentally in the customer's place. This projection will be evident in the salesperson's manner and words, something that cannot help but be noted by buyers, who will develop a feeling that the salesperson understands them and their problems and cares for their needs. To a great extent, people buy not so much because they understand the product but because they feel understood by the salesperson. Empathy is not without its costs to the salesperson, however. To develop empathy, salespeople must agree to themselves, "I will never sell customers a product or service they don't need." This might cost a few sales in the short run, but the salesperson will have more success in the long run and feel better about it. Sales representatives are often afraid to ask for an order because they feel they are deceiving the buyer. However, if they have contracted with themselves never to sell an unneeded product, then they won't experience this self-doubt.

A story helps to illustrate this point. Julie Yunowich, a paper tissues sales representative, called on a little grocery store in northern Michigan for the first time and explained a promotional offer on tissue. The buyer ordered twice as many rolls as Julie felt were needed, but rather than tell the buyer outright that he was wrong, Julie placed the order for only half as many rolls. When Julie made her second call, the buyer exclaimed, "I'm sure glad your company shipped short on me. I'd never have sold what I ordered." Julie then explained what had really happened. As a result, competitive salespeople don't receive the same treatment Julie does at that store—or the same amount of business!

6. Relationship selling requires maturity. Salespeople must understand and accept themselves. Whenever people become less concerned with themselves, they become more concerned with others. Our ability to perceive is in inverse proportion to how much we worry about ourselves. If we are unnecessarily afraid, worried, anxious, or concerned about ourselves, we have little time to perceive what is happening around us.

   A mature approach to selling further requires an uncritical approach by the salesperson. Most of us have a tendency to judge others from our point of view rather than to try to understand them from theirs. Often this leads to criticism, because from our perspective their decisions make little sense.

7. Likability is critical to the establishment of a relationship. This means being courteous and polite (not dominating, as recommended in much classic selling literature), making efficient use of the buyer's time, and ascertaining common ground. Research has demonstrated again and again that commonality of interests facilitates communication and friendship. Be personally interested in customers, not just as commodities or business partners. Find out their hobbies and interests. The more you take an interest in your customers, the more impressed they'll be by your selflessness and genuine caring. Advises one veteran sales rep:[16]

   > To encourage a lasting, profitable relationship, I always strive to learn more about my customers on a strictly personal level. With this in mind, I have found it tremendously effective to ensure that at least every third phone call to my accounts is not business related, but simply a call to see how the person—not the account—is doing. Encourage your customers to talk about their families, hobbies, and activities outside their office. Even the busiest buyer welcomes this brief social call, and we both enjoy discovering each other's outside interests. An unexpected benefit: a much greater percentage of my first phone calls are accepted, virtually eliminating unnecessary "phone tag."

   Individuals among the partners may obviously develop strong personal friendships that tend to hold the relationship together. Studies have demonstrated that buyers and sellers who have strong personal relationships are more committed to maintaining the relationship. *Social bonding* is defined as the degree of personal friendship and liking shared by buyer and seller.

   The professional relationship salesperson will recognize these factors crucial to a relationship and use them to select prospective partners, establish the relationship, build upon it, and enhance it. In the long term, relationship salespeople will satisfy themselves, both monetarily and personally, and their companies; transactional salespeople will find it difficult just to "run in place." They'll always find themselves frenetically prospecting for new accounts, engaged in threatening competition, and being stressed to meet the needs of ever more demanding accounts. To secure the benefits of long-term customer relationships, sales reps develop the relationship intelligently, making use of the critical relationship variables.

8. Deliver impeccable service and resolve problems quickly. Use problems as an opportunity to demonstrate your company's customer service talents. Problems separate good companies from great ones, not just by the infrequency of mistakes, but response time and attention to resolving problems to client satisfaction. Has your company set up systems to correct problem situations quickly?

Ask for feedback on service. Let your customers tell you how your service measures up and where you need to improve. Oftentimes, your employer will do this; if not, make sure that you do.

Go out of your way to provide good service. "It was a cold, icy, January morning when a customer called our office in a panic," recalls David Lubetkin, president of Industrial Edge USA, an apartment house supplier in Orange, New Jersey. "He urgently needed 60 pounds of rock salt to be delivered to one of the properties his company manages—100 miles away in Pennsylvania. We had a good supply of salt, but our trucks were already on the road. None were due back before 8 or 9 P.M." So Lubetkin and company CEO Stephen Weintraub rented a truck and made the delivery themselves. Averaging 20 miles per hour through the ice and snow, a typical 1½ hour drive turned into a 4½ hour icy crawl. They dropped off the salt and drove back for an even longer ride. The two executives left their office at 11:30 A.M., and didn't return until 10 P.M.[17]

9. Real relationship selling means delivering more than what's been promised; that is, value-added is part of that relationship. For Jeff Multz, director of sales and marketing at Firstwave Technologies, Inc., a web-based customer relationship management firm in Atlanta, hanging onto customers is simple, even in the notoriously saturated customer relationship management (CRM) market. "It's so basic, it's scary," he says. "We find out what our customers' needs and wants are, and then we overdeliver." At Firstwave, overdelivering on a deal typically means doing small but meaningful favors, such as issuing software upgrades to existing clients before they are requested or fulfilling orders earlier than expected. Multz also pushes salespeople to heavily research customer needs, document what they find, and use that information to manage a long-lasting relationship with the client. "Customers rarely see delivery in abundance because we all seem to live in a land of mediocrity," Multz says. "To keep our customers, they need to feel like they're getting a $1.50 back for every dollar they spend." For Multz's sales force, giving back more means going beyond expectations, like promising product delivery in a month and then sending it in a week, for example. "Our reps understand that they're not in sales—they're in service," he says. "They can't push to sell now. They have to create relationships instead."[18] At Toll Company in Minneapolis, Tony Litwinchuk oversees 12 salespeople who sell oxygen, nitrogen, and argon, the kinds of compressed gases that stock hospital intensive care units and power steel cutters. "If we go ahead and just sell our commodity, then the competition will come in with the lowest price and just eat us up," Litwinchuk says. That's why in addition to selling pressurized air, Litwinchuk's reps focus heavily on customer care, teaching clients about new applications for the products and sometimes referring customers to technical service agents when they have more complex problems.[19]

VIDEO

The points mentioned here describe the philosophy of interactive selling. Later, this philosophy will be described in more detail with suggestions for implementing it at each stage of the selling process.

6-5 Precall Preparation

In Chapter 1, "The Role of Personal Selling," we outlined the seven steps in the selling process: preparation, prospecting, approach, problem recognition, presentation, handling objections, and closing. Some might question making precall preparation the first step in selling, but the fact is that preparation is critical to communication. Interactive selling requires the salesperson to have some prior general understanding of the prospect's potential needs and problems. Otherwise, formulating questions to determine specific individual needs becomes very difficult. Precall preparation also assists in developing empathy. Effectively putting oneself in the customer's place requires in-depth knowledge about industry, company, product, and competition. Often salespeople are astonished when the prospect refuses to buy following what they consider to have been an outstanding presentation. If they were able to put themselves in the customer's position (which precall preparation helps them to do), they would better understand the reaction and be prepared to begin anew.

Precall preparation is important from another standpoint. It allows the sales representative to present a more credible image. We stated earlier that trust (which is the foundation of customer relationships) depends on the salesperson's candor, dependability, competence, customer-orientation, and likability. The last three of these especially relate to precall preparation. Demonstrating competence demands technical command of products and applications, much of which is learned before the call ever takes place. With today's increasingly technical products and services, sales reps are unlikely to pick up knowledge "on the fly." Sure, observing applications is important, but there is no substitute for disciplined study. Salespeople who are knowledgeable will always have the advantage, because they will be believed. The salesperson who fails to prepare will make few sales. For example, how do you feel about retail sales clerks who know little about the suit, shirt, or blouse they are trying to sell you? The conclusion is evident: There is no substitute for competent product knowledge. Another aspect of trust-building is customer-orientation. Again, precall preparation is essential here. Even with an identical product, application by industry and customer can be dramatically different. The manner in which a computer is used in manufacturing—forecasting, materials requirements planning, inventory control—is entirely different from its use in a financial institution—tracking checks, savings accounts, loans, or trust accounts. Even though he or she might know the equipment, the sales rep well versed in manufacturing would have a difficult, if not impossible, time conversing with a customer in a financial institution. As respects likability, an important aspect is commonality of interests, both business and nonbusiness. Harvey McKay, owner of McKay Envelope and author of *Swim with the Sharks Without Being Eaten Alive: Outsell, Outmanage, Outmotivate, and Outnegotiate Your Competition*, insists that his salespeople maintain 66 items of information on each client, including educational background, career history, family, special interests, and lifestyle (including vacation habits). Why is this important? To establish a relationship! To say, "We care!" For example, respecting vacation habits, what is going to be the reaction of the outdoors lover who receives a book of photographs of Yosemite by the famous photographer Ansel Adams?[20]

6-5a Know Your Industry

The more that salespeople know about the industry they serve, the better their position to serve customers. Customers view a good sales representative as a source of valuable sales information, because they are often too busy to keep abreast of changes themselves. Without pharmaceutical detail people, how would doctors find time to learn about new drugs and new techniques? Without the computer sales representative, how would users learn about the availability of new hardware and software? To accomplish this, salespeople must have an intensive knowledge of their industry. This requires knowledge of all the forces that may affect it—legal constraints, technology, customs, attitudes, and economic conditions and expectations. For example, knowing that the government requires automobiles to meet certain minimum mileage standards will help the aluminum salesperson convince auto manufacturers to use more aluminum than steel in the assembly process, because the weight saved will assist in meeting these standards. An understanding that supermarkets are losing business to fast-food chains will assist trade sales representatives seeking shelf space for their gourmet, microwaveable pasta dishes, ready to eat within minutes. As fast-food restaurants draw people away from cooking at home (and buying at the supermarket), smart salespeople will persuade grocery store managers that stocking such products will bring in traffic that might otherwise be lost to eating out. The greater their industry understanding, the more these sales representatives will be seen as consultants by customers.

Industry knowledge is valuable in another respect. Unless the sales representative works for a large company with a wide product line, it is usually impossible to be competitive with all customers. The needs of the mass market are so diverse that no one product or service will appeal to all parties. Seven Up does not try to do head-on battle with the leading cola brands; it seeks buyers among those who desire a noncola soft drink. Apple Computer does not attempt to compete for the Windows-based PC market; it concentrates on a graphics and multimedia niche. While such firms as Canon, Sharp, and Ricoh battle it out in the low-end fax machine market; Pitney-Bowes found a profitable niche among corporate clients for higher-end fax machines. In contrast to cheap faxes, Pitney-Bowes integrated fax equipment with other office technologies, such as computer networking and voice processing. Then it developed features that permit users to store up to 1,200 pages of text and 1,000 telephone numbers in the fax machine, giving customers the capability to send time-sensitive information whether it's short items, such as inventory and shipping data, or long text, such as technical reports.[21] The managers of ScrubaDub, a small family-owned chain of car washes in the Boston area, sought to determine its target market. Upon reflection, they decided their target market was upscale ($85,000 annual income), lived close to one of their outlets (within 3 miles), and owned new cars (3 years or newer). By redesigning their business to provide precisely what this target segment wanted—personalized service, guarantees, an attractive environment—ScrubaDub has grown to become one of the top 20 car-wash operations in the United States.[22] Smart sales representatives, like those for Pitney-Bowes, will take the time to sit down and analyze which of their potential customers are most likely to buy. There is no sense wasting time on prospects who have little interest in the salesperson's products. Professional salespeople will identify a target market or group of customers with a set of characteristics that makes them especially likely to buy the salesperson's product or service.

6-5b Know Your Company

When competing products and services are just about equal, often the salesperson with the most knowledge about his or her company is the one who gets the order. By knowing the special credit terms, shipping procedures, and merchandising assistance his or her company provides, this salesperson is able to offer a total package of greater value than that of a competitor with an essentially equivalent product.

It is also true that many times customers do not have the expertise to judge the quality of a product directly. In these instances, the reputation of the manufacturer may be the critical factor in the sale. In the financial industry, for example, comparing the quality of various funds may be so difficult that buyers base their ultimate decision on the vendor's reputation.

Company reputation is not the sole factor in every buying situation, but its importance is not to be ignored. Sales representatives should take care to study their company's history, finances, policies, and procedures.

Company History

Past performance is valuable in promoting a credible image of the company. If the company is the first to introduce a product or is the largest manufacturer in an industry, these facts should be presented to prospects because they indicate expertise and quality. Being able to present a long and stable company history is another way of demonstrating quality. Successful case histories are also important to relate. If a computer vendor has successfully designed and implemented a reservations system for a major airline, salespeople should be sure to point this out to prospects.

Company Finances

The financial strength of a company can be important to the buying decision. Organizations of questionable financial strength may fail, leaving their customers without a dependable source of supply. However, with financially strong companies—ones with a sound balance sheet and income statement or record of growth in the value of company stock—customers need not worry.

Company Management

One sales manager tells the story of how he lost a sale as a young sales representative by not knowing his company's top management. Calling on a large ball-bearing manufacturer, he was greeted by the company vice president, who asked, "What do you think about the news? Do you know Red at all?" Not wishing to appear ignorant, he feigned knowledge. Upon being pressed for additional information, however, he was finally forced to admit his ignorance of Red. As it turned out, Red, who was an old college buddy of the manufacturer, had recently been named president of the salesperson's company. Needless to say, no order was forthcoming. Although such a scenario is unlikely to transpire often, salespeople should be aware of the top executives in their organizations and the reasons for their having attained their success. An industry leader, a top research person, or a financial wizard can greatly impress a customer. A well-known company president like Bill Gates cannot help but impress potential Microsoft customers.

Company Size

The advantages enjoyed by a large manufacturer are fairly obvious—economies of scale, buying power, ability to work on a smaller margin, and so forth. In contrast, some customers may prefer to deal with smaller concerns, believing that their business will be unimportant to big companies. The salesperson can point out that a small company can bring more personal attention to each order and can specialize in areas where it is most expert. A. Schulman, Inc., a maker of plastics used in such diverse products as furniture, moldings, and auto dashboards, is small compared to industry leaders Dow Chemical, Monsanto, Quantum, and BASF. Yet, Schulman has made its smallness a virtue. For example, Schulman can still fill rush orders by scheduling special weekend production runs, something impossible for its giant rivals. By touting this feature as a unique benefit, the sales force avoids head-on conflicts with stronger competitors and competes on quality, not price. Schulman also aims at smaller organizations neglected by market leaders.[23]

Company Policies and Procedures

Hearing a salesperson admit ignorance of company policies and procedures is unlikely to build a customer's trust in the salesperson. It is an even greater sin for a salesperson to promise performance and delivery, only to discover later that the promise cannot be met. So salespeople are well advised to learn policies and procedures regarding prices, discounts, credit terms, delivery, and related matters.

The basis for most company price quotations is **list price,** the rate usually cited to customers. However, as with the sticker price on cars, buyers may not pay the list price.

In many instances, **discounts** and **allowances** reduce list prices. These deductions typically are offered when buyers have performed an activity of value to the seller. Discounts can be classified as cash, quantity, or trade discounts. **Cash discounts** are the reductions in price that are provided to buyers for early payment of their bills. Cash discounts usually specify a time period during which the discount can be obtained. A typical cash discount might be "2/10, net 30," indicating the buyer can subtract 2 percent from the bill for payment within 10 days. Otherwise, payment of the full amount is due within 30 days. If the list price was $500, for example, and the purchase was made October 1, then $490 would be due the seller at any time up to October 10. Payment any later would require a check for $500. **Trade discounts** are deductions from list price offered to members of the channel of distribution. Manufacturers, for example, may offer retailers a trade discount of 40 percent from the list price, and if they further wish to encourage activities by wholesalers, an additional discount of 10 percent may be granted. In the latter instance, wholesalers pass the 40 percent discount on to their customers (retailers) and keep the additional 10 percent as payment for services such as storage and transportation. The theory behind trade discounts is that they reward intermediaries for activities that otherwise would have to be performed by the manufacturer. **Quantity discounts** are reductions granted for purchasing in large amounts. They may be either noncumulative or cumulative. *Noncumulative quantity discounts* are one-time discounts offered for buying in volume. *Cumulative quantity discounts* are reductions offered over a longer period of time.

Allowances are similar to discounts in that they are deductions from the list price. Advertising allowances are provided by the manufacturer to encourage retailers to promote the manufacturer's goods through local advertising. The manufacturer designs the advertising program, establishes rules and controls, prepares the ads, and encourages retailers to use them. The typical arrangement for sharing costs of the advertising program is for manufacturer and retailer to split the costs equally. Proof of performance is required before payment; the proof commonly consists of a tear sheet of the retail advertisement showing the manufacturer's product, or a radio or television affidavit certifying the advertising was done.

list price
Rate usually cited to customers.

discounts
Reductions in list price for paying in cash, for services rendered as a member in the channel of distribution, or buying in quantity.

allowances
Similar to discounts in that they are deductions from the list price. For example, advertising allowances are provided by the manufacturer to encourage retailers to promote the manufacturer's goods through local advertising.

cash discounts
The reductions in price that are provided to buyers for early payment of their bills.

trade discounts
Deductions from list price offered to members of the channel of distribution.

quantity discounts
Reductions granted for purchasing in large amounts; may be either noncumulative or cumulative. Noncumulative quantity discounts are one-time discounts offered for buying in volume. Cumulative quantity discounts are reductions offered over a longer period of time.

F.O.B. plant (or **F.O.B. origin**)
The buyer must pay for all the freight charges.

F.O.B. destination
The buyer pays no transportation charges whatsoever; the seller pays for everything.

C.O.D. (cash on delivery)
Probably the most common credit term.

C.W.O. (cash with order)
A credit term.

C.B.D. (cash before delivery)
A credit term.

E.O.M. (end of month)
Regardless of the time during the month when the purchase is made, the credit period under E.O.M. terms will not begin until the end of the month.

The seller has several alternatives in handling transportation charges. *F.O.B.* (*free on board*) pricing is fairly common. **F.O.B. plant** (or **F.O.B. origin**) pricing means that the buyer must pay for all the freight charges. The seller pays only for costs associated with loading the shipment aboard the carrier selected by the buyer. Legal title and responsibility pass to the buyer once the goods are loaded on the carrier.

F.O.B. destination means that the buyer pays no transportation charges whatsoever; the seller pays for everything. The seller permits the buyer to subtract transportation expenses from the bill. The amount credited the buyer varies with the freight charges. This method of handling transportation charges is sometimes called *freight absorption.*

Credit terms vary widely by industry, by company, and by the financial condition of the buyer. Still, some common policies can be indicated. When a sales representative sells to a customer with questionable finances, certain terms may be quoted. **C.O.D. (cash on delivery)** is probably the most common, although **C.W.O. (cash with order)** and **C.B.D. (cash before delivery)** are sometimes required.

Dating programs are commonly employed to encourage business. They represent extensions of the time when payment is due and also the period when the cash discount is available. One common dating program is **E.O.M. (end of month)** terms. Regardless of the time during the month when the purchase is made, the credit period under E.O.M. terms will not begin until the end of the month. If the customer were to make purchases on October 9, 12, and 23, under "2/10, net 30, E.O.M." terms, the cash discount would be good until November 10 for all of October's purchases, and the net amount would not become due until November 30. In certain businesses, the extension of terms may stretch to several months. Orders placed in January may not be billed until May or June. Such terms help generate orders during seasons of slow demand.

Another area of company knowledge that pays dividends for the salesperson is order processing. The more that salespeople know about procedures here, the less likely they will be to promise something that cannot be delivered. They will be in a position to discuss realistically with the customer what can and cannot be done and why. In any situation, they will know what options and changes are possible.

6-5c Know Your Product

There is no substitute for product knowledge. Some salespeople reputedly have enough natural ability to sell an icebox to an Eskimo, though, in truth, most salespeople require product expertise to be successful. How can an insurance salesperson succeed without in-depth knowledge of term and whole life policies and various annuity plans? How can the pharmaceutical salesperson detail a drug to doctors without knowing what the drug will do, what it will not do, and any possible side effects?

Customers rely on salespeople to supply information for their buying decisions. If salespeople are unable to provide adequate information, customers will buy from the competition. Salespeople should set up their own training program, composed of the following steps:

1. Read all company product literature and attend all the company-sponsored training programs they can.
2. If they sell many products, pick one product each day to learn as much about as they can and try selling it.
3. When they have acquired a basic knowledge of their company's products, they should start comparing them with those of competitors. In most sales calls,

reps need not only extensive knowledge of their own line but also enough knowledge to defend their line against the competition's.

4. Seek out accounts where their product (or even a competitor's) is used. Talk to users to gain insight into important features that they should emphasize in their sales calls.

5. Take a tour of their company's plant to see how the product is made. Reps typically will be surprised at how much care goes into the product's production, and their enthusiasm will carry over into sales calls.

6. If possible, they should use the product themselves or give it to a friend for trial. (Obviously, not all products lend themselves to this step.)

Product knowledge has additional benefits. Expertise manifests itself in the interview. The knowledgeable sales representative is perceived as believable, a person on whom the customer can rely on with few doubts. From the salesperson's standpoint, product knowledge inspires confidence and enthusiasm. If salespeople are convinced of the product's merits, they will be enthusiastic about it. Enthusiasm is infectious; if the sales representative has it, the customer is likely to catch it, too.

Product knowledge is not just a matter of being able to enumerate technical details. The sales representative must be able to relate product features to customer needs. Much criticism of salespeople centers around their failure to determine customers' needs and problems, when, after all, the real reason people buy is to fulfill a need and solve a problem.

It is critical that salespeople make a distinction between features and benefits. A **feature** of a product or service is any fact about it that will be true, whether or not that product or service is ever bought and used. The feature may be tangible, such as part of the physical makeup of the product itself. Important features of an automobile, for example, might include air-conditioning, front-wheel drive, and disc brakes. Features may also be intangible. Service, delivery, and price represent important intangible features. A **benefit** is how the feature helps satisfy a need or problem for the customer. A feature describes the product; a benefit relates it to the user. It tells the customer "What's in it for me?" Millions of paper clips will be sold this year, but people don't want to buy paper clips. What they want to do is hold paper together. Actually, they don't even want to hold paper together as much as they want to avoid the problems that would arise if they didn't hold papers together. The 15.1 cubic feet of trunk space in a new car means nothing unless that car salesperson translates this feature into the capacity for two 2-suiter suitcases, three garment bags, and a set of golf clubs. Unless features have been related to user needs, no benefit has been demonstrated. The customer isn't especially interested in the speed of a drill; he or she is interested in its ability to help build something, or as one salesperson put it, "The customer isn't interested in the drill; they want the hole it will make." Citing a bicycle's 10 speeds means little until it is explained that climbing a hill, going down a hill, or just pedaling on a flat road can be done with a minimum of effort and maximum safety. People don't buy life jackets; they buy safety. Professional salespeople don't sell diamonds; they sell love and romance.

A story told by a veteran salesperson about an event in his youth illustrates the important difference between features and benefits. Working in a department store, he was faced with selling a truckload of folding aluminum chairs with plastic webbing that no one seemed particularly interested in buying. While the young salesperson was marking down their price, his father happened by and remarked, "I've got a chair just like those. Makes a great seat when you're fishing from a muddy

feature
Any fact about a product or service that will be true, whether or not it is ever bought and used; may be tangible or intangible.

benefit
How the feature helps satisfy a need or problem for the customer; relates a benefit to the user.

creek bank." Knowing the numbers of retired and semiretired people in town who fished, the salesperson, filled with inspiration, pulled more of the chairs from the warehouse, mass displayed them, and attached a sign: Fishing Chair—$6.95. In two days, they were sold out—at the regular undiscounted price.

Of course, determining benefits presumes that product features have already been identified. Although most companies provide much information, there is no guarantee that it will necessarily be complete or even relevant to each and every customer's needs. To identify relevant features, salespeople may wish to ask themselves the following questions:

1. What led to the development of the product? Knowing why the product was introduced will reveal much about important features. Automated teller machines (ATMs), for example, were developed because bank patrons wanted to complete their banking activities as quickly as possible. The sales representative should recognize this need for the product and concentrate on features that facilitate this overriding customer desire. The speed of the system and the ability to bank wherever the ATM sits (be it on bank premises or in a grocery store) are critical features. Knowing that jogging shoes were designed to minimize stress on the runner's feet tells much about significant product features. In this light, wide heels and extra padding in the soles become significant product features.

2. Of what is the product made? The materials composing a product may be critical to its sale. A common customer objection concerns price, but one way of handling the objection is to point out the quality of material present in the product. If a competitor is offering an office desk that is $50 cheaper but made of pressed wood, salespeople may emphasize to customers that their desk is made of thick-gauge steel that will last longer and resist dents. Pointing out that a certain type of contact lens is made of hard plastic that requires replacement only after 8 to 10 years demonstrates real customer value. Relating how a set of golf clubs has graphite shafts to increase distance and accuracy will make any golfer take note.

3. How is the product made? The care taken in the manufacturing process can be a significant feature. If the product is fashioned by hand rather than by machine, this should be pointed out to customers. Certain high-quality makes of motorcycles, for example, are handmade. Quality control is a significant part of the manufacturing process. A refrigerator's being opened and closed 100 times before it is released from production, ensuring it won't stick, is an important feature. If a product is built within very tight tolerances, this fact will be important to customers using the item to manufacture their own product.

4. What is there about the product itself that makes it stand out? Is it especially appealing? What about the styling? Are there any unique features? Product appearance may be critical to the sale. How many automobiles are sold primarily on the basis of appearance and styling? Unique features—those that make the product stand out from the competition—should be identified. Recently a couple purchased a new stove. The feature that clinched the sale was the incorporation of fold-down counters that could be placed over the burners when the stove was not in use. This one feature prompted the purchase, because the couple wanted more counter space in the kitchen and the fold-down counters could hide any dirt on the stove when unexpected guests stopped by.

5. What about product use? What will the product do? How can it be used? Convenience, flexibility in use, repair record, required operator skill, safety features, durability, and ease and speed of operation all represent significant product features. The multifunction computer peripherals that also send and receive faxes on plain paper, make copies, and scan in addition to printing exhibit value in their multiple usages. Not only is the Nokia 6630 imaging smartphone a 1.3 megapixel digital imaging device, but it's also a portable office and a modern rich-media machine. Email can be downloaded directly to the Nokia 6630 imaging smartphone. Plus, it has Quickoffice document viewer applications that allow viewing important documents in formats like Microsoft Word, PowerPoint, and Excel while away from the office. The smartphone can be plugged into the stylish Nokia Video Call Stand PT-8 (sold separately) for a video call.[24] Whatever the product, there should be some inherent advantages present, and the sales representative must recognize them.

6. What is the price? Is it cheaper than the competition? Is it more expensive? If so, can this be balanced against higher quality? Can the product more than pay for itself—with immediate or long-range savings, avoidance of obsolescence, greater protection against breakdowns, or reduced or eliminated upkeep or repair costs? An inkjet printer might cost less in the short run, but a laser printer will save over the long-term because of the fewer ink cartridges consumed and machine longevity. Can you offer special terms to buyers, such as delayed billing, leasing arrangements, or financing? What does your company offer that most competitors do not—guarantees, frequent deliveries, trade-ins?

7. Is service readily available? This is a crucial factor in many buying situations. Several mainframe computer vendors that have since failed were caught in a classic dilemma regarding service. To acquire additional business, they needed to establish more service facilities, but to do so before getting the accounts made the costs prohibitively high. Having to get service for a new system in Kansas City out of the Omaha branch wouldn't satisfy potential customers in Kansas City, who probably would buy from competitors instead. But if the vendor first builds and stocks a service center in Kansas City, it might mean that several years will pass before enough business can be generated to cover the costs of the center.

   In the computer industry, as with many others, service is critical. Often, competitive products are similar, so service (i.e., personnel, parts availability, and speed of delivery) determines the choice of supplier.

8. Is there recognition by outside authorities? Reports of product performance conducted by independent bodies, such as *Consumer Reports* or Underwriters Laboratories, should be related by sales representatives without fail. Case histories of satisfied customers are also valuable. In the sale of business machines, for example, the presence of successful installations in an area is a strong selling point. Another effective tactic is to supply potential customers with the names of satisfied accounts whom the prospect may subsequently call.

9. Is there breadth and depth to the product line? Product breadth—the number of different models, sizes, or capacities—and depth—styles, colors, etc.—are important. Satisfying customer need is easier with breadth and depth than in their absence. When selling automobiles, it helps if numerous colors,

interiors, engines, and additional features are available. Having to sell one basic model to all customers would be an arduous task for even the most accomplished salesperson. In selling tennis racquets, it helps if the customer has a choice among different grip sizes, string tensions, compositions (e.g., metal, ceramic, or graphite), and design (e.g., open versus narrow throat, head-heavy versus head-light). In an industrial setting, breadth and depth are important from another standpoint. If a company plans to grow, buying from a supplier with a limited line may be costly. When the time for upgrading arrives, the company may have to go to another vendor with all of the transitional problems that might occur—different parts, different power requirements, and differences in operator handling.

6-5d Know Your Competition

When identifying product features, sales representatives should be aware of the competition. They should determine which features are present in competitive products, which are absent, and which are superior in comparison with their own.

Where is competitive information available? To the enterprising sales rep, this is never a problem:

1. *Customers.* Talk to whomever you can: buyers, sales clerks, switchboard operators, office personnel, and production workers. Often, you can inspect competitive products in action at customers' offices. It is in the customer's best interests to make you competitive. Ask them what they like and dislike about competitive equipment, the strengths and weaknesses, inefficiencies, and so forth.

2. *Competitors.* Often you will find yourself in contact with competitive sales personnel, perhaps at a customer's office or a professional meeting. You don't have to come right out and ask for trade secrets, but who more than salespeople are likely to talk? One word leads to another; engage them in conversation.

3. *Newspapers and magazines.* The business press and especially trade journals are sources of all kinds of useful tips—news events, hirings, employment shifts, site preparation, acquisitions, and the like—that can be revealing.

4. *Advertising.* Although advertising concentrates on the good points of products, competitive advertising nevertheless provides useful information.

5. *Trade shows.* Trade shows are a rich source of information. Reps who are too well known to drop by a competitor's booth can ask a friend or lesser-known associate to do this.

6. *Internet.* Of course, the easiest route is to log onto the Internet and look at the competitor's website. There are numerous sites for business research, such as http://finance.yahoo.com, www.hoovers.com/free, and www.thomasregister.com.

Once salespeople have obtained enough information, they will find it useful to write out a systematic comparison (perhaps on a spreadsheet) of their product with that of the competition. Table 6-3 represents one such analysis of competing manufacturers of steel buildings. Such analysis better prepares salespeople for the interview. They will not be caught by surprise, make a poor presentation, or be unable to answer consumer objections arising from comparisons. They also will have a better appreciation for the capabilities of their own product. Knowing a product feature is important; knowing that no competitive product has the same feature can be decisive.

T a b l e **6-3** Sample Analysis of Competition in Steel Buildings

Porta-King Durasteel™ and PC Series Buildings	Competition	The Porta-King Advantage
FRAME AND BASE	**FRAMEWORK AND WALLS**	**FRAMEWORK AND WALLS**
Frame: 2" x 2" x 11 gauge structural steel tubing.	**Frame:** 2" x 2" x 14 gauge. 2" x 2" x 15 gauge. 1" x 1" x 16 gauge. No frame provided.	**Frame:** Porta-King framing material ranges from 45% to 85% THICKER than the competition. One competitor uses NO vertical frames at all, relying solely on welded panels for strength.
Base: 12 gauge galvanized steel.	**Base:** 14 and 13 gauge galvanized steel.	**Base:** Porta-King base frame ranges from 16% to 38% THICKER than the competition.
Walls, Int: 16 gauge galvanized steel.		
Walls, Ext: 14 gauge galvanized steel.	**Walls, Interior:** 16 and 18 gauge steel.	**Walls, Interior:** Porta-King wall material ranges up to 23% THICKER than the competition.
Insulation:		
Durasteel-	**Walls, Exterior:** 14 and 16 gauge steel.	**Walls, Exterior:** Porta-King wall material ranges up to 23% THICKER than the competition.
R-10 walls and R-19 ceiling.		
Durasteel-PC-		
R-9 walls and R-17 ceiling.	**Insulation (Walls and Ceiling):** R-0 walls and R-0 ceiling. R-4.3 walls and R-17.4 ceiling. R-10 walls and R-0 ceiling.	**Insulation (Walls and Ceiling):** If you don't ask the competition for insulation, in many cases you won't get it. With Porta-King, insulation is always standard.

Durasteel   **Durasteel PC**

Source: From Porta-King Building Systems.

6-6 Target Market Analysis

The culmination of intensive preparation regarding industry, company, product, and competition is the specification of a target market—those potential customers with the greatest probability for buying the salesperson's offerings.

Such a specification greatly aids salespeople in prospecting, the next stage in the selling process. When prospecting, sales representatives must identify individual accounts that might have need for their services, especially those with whom the sales rep can establish a profitable long-term relationship. It's a lot easier selling to existing customers than all new ones. Calling on those with little need is a waste of the salesperson's precious time. Specification of a target market helps reduce such waste, and it provides further assistance at subsequent stages of the selling process, particularly the preapproach, approach, and presentation. A profile of the target customer helps the salesperson initiate a discussion. An absence of knowledge about potential customers impedes the relationship selling process of asking questions and listening. Without at least a general understanding of customer needs and likely responses, it's difficult to formulate questions.

How does one go about the process of identifying a target market? The answer is by thoroughly studying industry, company, product, and competition. Then, and only then, is the salesperson prepared. After studying those areas, salespeople should sit down and analyze the total business environment for their products and services in the following sequence:

1. List all the features and benefits associated with the product or service. No product feature, no matter how seemingly small, should be ignored. It is surprising sometimes how minute distinctions between products can make

the difference between success and failure. Besides, it is the customer's estimation of differences, not the salesperson's, that is critical; to customers, the differences may be large. Rank the importance of these benefits from the viewpoint of customers.

2. Enumerate your company's strengths and weaknesses. Is the company financially strong? Does it have a strong reputation? Is it known for its service and quality control? Are its plants close to customers? Are credit terms favorable? Are discounts substantial?

3. What are competitors' strengths and weaknesses, especially respecting the ranking of benefits completed in step 1? Are they major or minor? Which features and benefits do they concern? Is the competition large or small? If large, what are the chinks in their armor? It is usually difficult to attack the leader head-on. If the competition is weaker, how have they managed to survive? Have they selected a particular market segment for special attention? Can this market be satisfied better, or is it wiser to concede it for another niche?

4. Describe the typical customer in the industry with regard to all major characteristics. Remember, not all customers are created equal. Some are profitable and some are not. The first step is to analyze one's existing customers and answer the following questions: Who are my current customers (e.g., location, size, SIC code, etc.)? How are they segmented on such factors as purchase behavior? Volume? Growth rate? Relationship duration? Profitably? Often, the results of such analysis are surprising. Frequently, the 80/20 rule operates: 20 percent of your customers account for 80 percent of your sales volume and profits.

5. Are there certain groups, not currently being marketed to, who could use the product or service? Be prepared to challenge the status quo here. When fellow Xerox sales reps advised Tonya Turner that banks didn't buy facsimile machines, she opted to ignore them. She was determined to find a problem that fax machines could solve for the potentially lucrative banking market. After poring over newspapers and annual reports, Turner discovered that banks were having difficulty processing large numbers of new loan applications because it took so long to mail the information to the central processing sites. Turner reasoned that the information could be faxed, allowing the transfer to transpire in one hour instead of several days. Now her earnings are in the 6-figure category.

6. Given product features and benefits and their ranking in importance, company strengths and weaknesses, and the nature of the competition, which customer subclass or classes does the salesperson's product or service best fit? Illinois Tool Works (ITW) is a $10 billion company based in Glenview, Illinois. It is an organization that has turned the use of the 80/20 rule into a science. ITW does an 80/20 analysis of everything to determine where to get the biggest bang for the buck. As a result, ITW is an incredibly lean and efficient organization. CEO W. James Farrell stated recently in a *Business Week* interview, "Intellectually it's easy (80/20) to understand, but it's very difficult to put into practice. You will hear people in the organization say that you can't get rid of products because you need a complete product line to sell. Others will argue that the volume is needed to absorb fixed costs." Mr. Farrell claims that ITW's costs are lower than those of 75 percent of comparable companies as a result of using the 80/20 principle as a decision-making tool. At ITW, lean isn't a recent fad or program-of-the-month—it is a way of life.

Business Week proclaimed ITW as "the Dean of Lean" with respect to manufacturing organizations.[25]

To illustrate how a salesperson might undertake a target market analysis, let's follow the activities of Ron Friendly, sales representative for the Superior Hospital Uniform Company. Ron has just received samples of a new uniform to be used by doctors and nurses in hospital operating rooms. In contrast to prior uniforms, this new garment has a number of advantages, primarily stemming from the incorporation of a polyester-cotton blend in its manufacture. Older uniforms were made of 100 percent cotton. Such uniforms had a number of disadvantages: They required ironing in hospital laundries, they wore out much faster than a blended garment, and their appearance left much to be desired in comparison with a blended uniform. However, until the introduction of Superior's new polyester blend, only 100 percent cotton uniforms had been allowed in operating rooms because of problems with static electricity. Cotton uniforms absorb body moisture, providing a path for the electric charge to be conducted and eventually grounded. Polyester, however, does not absorb moisture, and a buildup of static electricity might cause an explosion in the atmosphere of operating rooms, which often are filled with flammable anesthetics. Superior solved this problem, however, by weaving stainless-steel thread throughout the uniform, providing a conductive path for the static electricity. The uniform presents only one problem to a Superior sales representative like Ron Friendly: It costs about 50 percent more than competing cotton garments.

From his product analysis, his knowledge of hospitals' use of operating room uniforms, and his knowledge of his own company's strengths, Ron identifies the following factors that will affect his ability to sell the new Superior uniforms:

1. Ron believes that larger hospitals should be approached first, because smaller ones usually do not have the resources to spend on a more expensive uniform.

2. Ron also targets his market to the larger hospitals because they usually have extensive laundry facilities with higher labor costs. A blended uniform that needs no ironing will be attractive as a means of cutting labor expenditures.

3. Ron believes that hospitals where the decisions are made by the functional department, rather than by purchasing, will make the best customers. Those hospitals where the purchasing department tightly controls the purse strings are not as likely to buy a more expensive uniform, regardless of the technical advantages. A hospital where the operating room administrators make their own buying decisions without interference from the purchasing department will be best.

4. Hospitals that are less concerned with speedy service represent better potential buyers. Ron's major competitor is based in his geographic sales territory, enabling them to provide faster delivery. Superior's factory and warehouse are on the East Coast, contributing to a lengthier delivery time.

5. The Superior Hospital Uniform Company has a reputation for producing high-quality uniforms. This should assist Ron's sales calls, especially with current customers. Additionally, the uniform has received a good evaluation from an independent rating firm, which should further facilitate sales.

Another good example of identifying a target market is presented by David Mercer in his book, *High-Level Selling*.[26] While Mercer was working for the IBM Biomedical Group, it became clear to him very early on that IBM's blood-processing machines would be bought by hematologists (doctors who specialize in blood disorders). After a while, it became clear to Mercer that within this overall group the main buyers were those who saw themselves as "clinical" hematologists—that is, hematologists who are concerned with not just analysis but also treatment. Furthermore, the hottest prospects were young (typically under the age of 30), and they tended to have trained in just a handful of teaching hospitals. This allowed Mercer to concentrate on only a limited number of prospects; it also allowed him to concentrate special effort on penetrating those relatively few teaching hospitals, which he also could use as powerful references.

6-7 After-Marketing

after-marketing
Applies marketing principles to customers after they've made a purchase.

Retaining customers requires marketers to exhibit care and concern for them *after* they've made a purchase. This is part of **after-marketing,** which applies marketing principles to customers after they've purchased a company's goods or services. The rationale for after-marketing is firmly grounded in psychology. Following purchases, many buyers experience *cognitive dissonance*—the mental recognition that one has purchased something that may not have been the smartest, most rational alternative. The customer's need for reassurance does not go unnoticed by smart salespeople. They are wise in reassuring customers that they have made a good purchase decision and are getting their money's worth. There is a second psychological principle that reinforces the importance of postpurchase feedback. Learning theory suggests that the increased likelihood of repeating behavior is associated with reward. Unfortunately, with all too many products or services, consumers don't overtly experience any direct or immediate reward. Marketers often naively assume that consumers will automatically recognize the benefits inherent in their products or services. They would be well advised to actively direct their customers toward discovering reward through active after-marketing.[27]

After-marketing includes the following elements:

- Participating in activities and making efforts to keep customers satisfied after the purchase
- Doing everything possible to increase the likelihood that current customers will buy a company's product or brand on future occasions
- Increasing the likelihood that current customers will buy the same company's complementary products rather than a competitor's
- Repeatedly measuring customer satisfaction

Moreover, if one needed further confirmation of the importance of after-marketing activities, there are these staggering statistics. Studies of customer dissatisfaction show that customers are dissatisfied with their purchases about 25 percent of the time. How often do they complain? The surprising finding is that is that only 5 percent complain. The other 95 percent either feel that it is not worth the effort to complain or they don't know how or to whom to complain.

Of the 5 percent who do complain, only about 50 percent report a satisfactory problem resolution. Yet, satisfactory resolution is essential, because a satisfied customer tells on average three people about a good product experience; the dissatisfied one tells 11 people. If each of them, in turn, tells others, the number of people exposed to bad word of mouth grows exponentially. In contrast, customers whose complaints are resolved to their satisfaction often become more loyal than customers who never complained. About 34 percent of customers who register major complaints will buy again from the company with complaint resolution, and this rises to 52 percent with minor complaints. If the complaint is handled quickly, between 52 percent (for major complaints) and 95 percent (minor complaints) will buy again from the company.[28]

6-7a The Five Components of Service Quality

Of course, to ensure good service, it is important to know its components. These attributes are presented in order of importance as rated by consumers (allocating 100 points):[29]

1. **Reliability:** The ability to perform promised service dependably and accurately (32 points)
2. **Responsiveness:** The willingness to help customers and to provide prompt service (22 points)
3. **Assurance:** The knowledge and courtesy of employees and their ability to convey trust and confidence (19 points)
4. **Empathy:** The provision of caring, individualized attention to customers (16 points)
5. **Tangibles:** The appearance of physical facilities, equipment, personnel, and communication materials (11 points)

As shown here, reliability is the most important aspect, approximately three times as important as tangibles, the least important of the five. The definitions of quality service are repeated and expanded in Table 6-4, along with examples of each element.

reliability
The ability to perform promised service dependably and accurately.

assurance
The knowledge and courtesy of employees and their ability to convey trust and confidence.

empathy
The provision of caring, individualized attention to customers.

tangibles
Regarding service quality, the appearance of physical facilities, equipment, personnel, and communication materials.

T a b l e **6-4** Definitions of Quality Service Elements

Element	Definition	Examples
Reliability	The ability to perform the promised service dependably and accurately	Is the credit card statement free of errors? Is the washing machine repaired right the first time?
Responsiveness	Willingness to help customers and provide prompt service	Does the company answer letters or phone calls? Is the stockbroker willing to answer my questions?
Assurance		
Competence	Possession of the required skills and knowledge to perform the service	Does the repairperson appear to know what he is doing?
Courtesy	Politeness, respect, consideration, and friendliness of contact personnel	Does the bank teller have a pleasant demeanor?
Credibility	Trustworthiness, believability, honesty of the service provider	Does the bank have a good reputation?
Security	Freedom from danger, risk, or doubt	Is the credit card protected from unauthorized use?
Empathy		
Access	Approachability and ease of contact	Does the company have a 24-hour toll-free telephone number?
Communication	Keeping the customers informed in language they can understand and listening to them	Can the customer service representative clearly explain the billing procedures?
Understanding the customer	Making the effort to know customers and their needs	Do communications from the company acknowledge the customer's unique needs?
Tangibles	Appearance of physical facilities, equipment, personnel, and communication materials	Are the bank's facilities attractive? Do the tools used by the repairperson look modern?

Source: Adapted with the permission of The Free Press, a Division of Simon & Schuster Adult Publishing Group, from *Delivering Quality Service: Balancing Customer Perceptions and Expectations* by Valarie A. Zeithaml, A. Parasuraman, Leonard L. Berry. Copyright © 1990 by The Free Press. All rights reserved.

6-7b After-Marketing Activities

To ensure the implementation of these service components, certain activities are necessary. They are (1) building a database, (2) acknowledging customers, (3) maintaining contact with customers, (4) measuring customer satisfaction, and (5) reclaiming lost customers. Although several of these activities depend (to one degree or another) on the salesperson's employer, the smart rep is advised to make up for any corporate deficiencies with his or her own after-marketing endeavors.

Building the Database

Many companies have recognized the importance of computerizing customer profiles and providing this information to sales reps. If not, the power and availability of personal computers and "contact management" software allow the individual salesperson to do so with reasonable effort. Every other after-marketing activity becomes more efficient and more effective with automation; paradoxically, it also allows for greater personalization. The account-tracking and customer service software of Wells Fargo helps it to focus on the highly profitable but underserved small-business segment and to offer companies in it rapid credit approval, electronic loan repayment, and other special services that propelled the bank from 11th to first place in small-business-loan volume in only three years.

Acknowledging Customers

At a minimum, the buyer should receive thanks for an order—a handwritten note immediately following a purchase has immeasurably favorable reactions. Being on-site for installation and training is guaranteed to have a favorable impact. Beyond this, go through your contact file and jot a note, send a card, or make a note to call anyone you haven't seen in a long time. Keep up to date with newspapers and trade magazines. Send article clippings to clients who would be interested in the news. If a client was promoted or won an award, send a note of congratulations. If the event appears in the press, send the clipping along. Send a note or card for special occasions like birthdays; clients will be pleasantly surprised. Think of ideas you can pass along, like ways to merchandise products, save money, improve productivity, and, of course, new company products of special value to the client. Create user groups of clients to share ideas. Many companies send out newsletters to customers; if not, compose your own. As might be expected these days, technology can help. Joel Block may not be the world's most well-informed consultant, but to his clients he sure looks that way. Block, rep for Growth-Logic, a company based in Agoura Hills, California, uses software that scours the Internet and plucks out news items relating to his customers, which are typically midsize companies that need help expanding their businesses. That gives him an excuse to contact each one, boosting his chances of closing a deal. "The key is to be top-of-mind all the time," Block says. "If I call just to say, 'Hi, how are you?' it's not going to be long before we run out of things to talk about." Block uses software developed by Irvine, California–based Client Dynamics to track items of interest to his top 40 customers. All he had to do to set up the system was fill out a web-based profile and a series of search terms for each client. Now, each morning, the software searches 6,000 news sources and delivers a list of hits. Block can forward items to clients, call them, or drop them a quick note. He uses the software to keep track of it all.[30] "To be able to send an email to someone and say, 'Congratulations, you got some great press,' is a way of touching someone that's nonthreatening but very powerful," Block adds. "A lot of times we end up doing a deal."

Maintaining Contact

Not only should the salesperson initiate outbound communication, but he or she should also make it as easy as possible for customers to get a hold of them. Cellular phones, pagers, answering services, Internet addresses, 800 numbers, and the like, are essential. Note that accessibility is one of the critical service elements. Accessibility is vital to handling complaints. The longer the customer waits for a reply, the madder they get. Yet, properly handling the problem represents a significant opportunity for cementing the relationship. Thanks to the emergence of websites that allow customers to serve themselves, the Internet has great potential for improving customer service. Web-based customer service not only saves money but, by involving the customer in the process, it also often leads to greater customer satisfaction. Unlike a phone call, visiting a website can provide access to extensive database information. Websites also enable companies to learn more about their customers. It's possible to learn a user's preferences just by tracking where he or she goes on a site. Ultimately this information can be used automatically to develop a profile of the customer. Some companies see web technology as an opportunity to put certain aspects of customer service on a do-it-yourself basis. "Providing customer service online is our equivalent of the automated teller machine," says Doug Topken, managing director, electronic commerce services for Federal Express. "It lets people service themselves when it's most convenient." FedEx, an early adopter of the web, has created a variety of methods that not only let users track their packages electronically but also enable them to pass along data to recipients so they can track the shipment as well. Thus, a company using FedEx can enhance its customer service by automatically providing clients with peace of mind about their orders.

Handling customer inquiries at call centers is another task that can be improved by technologies found on the Internet. Rather than having an individual log in and retrieve the email messages, email response management systems (ERMSs) retrieve and route them into pools based on their address, subject, and content.[31] From there, agents answer them on a first-come, first-served basis. The system includes real-time monitors and reporting capabilities that help companies measure, track, and manage the flow of email. The value of ERMS evolves from efficiency—the staff can create a library of commonly used responses that frees them from having to type responses to frequently asked questions repeatedly; tracking—now that managers have the tools to measure email service levels, they can make critical decisions regarding staffing needs, analyzing how much time is being spent responding to email and evaluating the effectiveness of each individual or department; and customer satisfaction—companies are able to cut the turnaround time drastically on email and web-based inquiries. Commented one user of ERMS, "Previously, we had to dedicate valuable employees to sort through all the messages generated by forms or links on our website and forward them to the appropriate personnel. That added to the response time, costing us money and aggravating customers who were anxiously awaiting a reply." But with ERMS in place, the average response time has dropped from one or two *days* to a little less than two *hours*. Table 6-5 details additional techniques for delivering customer service.[32]

With such technology, a customer at Lands' End, for example, can receive a catalog by mail, investigate a purchase on the website, and either call the telephone center or activate a chat session to ask a question. The Lands' End customer service rep can push additional information to the customer immediately or open a web page they can cobrowse (i.e., browse together).

Table 6-5 Technology Facilitators for Customer Service

- Email: For customer service as well as promotions
- Telephone-information-driven call center technology
- Chat: Using instant-messaging technology to permit two-way dialogue between customers and reps
- VoIP (Voice over Internet Protocol): Telephone over the Internet or private intranet
- Push: Automatic delivery of content to a user's computer as part of a planned schedule of communications or triggered by an event
- Cobrowsing: Technology that allows a customer and a rep to view the same web page at the same time
- Embedded module: A chip embedded in a piece of equipment (from a copier to a refrigerator) that can send automatic notification of required service

Measuring Customer Satisfaction

Increasingly, many companies are systematically measuring customer satisfaction by sending out formal customer satisfaction surveys periodically. Tracking customers who have broken earlier patterns of consistent ordering are also indicative of possible satisfaction problems.

Reclaiming Lost Customers

Customers may defect for a number of reasons, not all of which are under the control of the marketer. The customer may have disconfirmed expectations, contacted a rude customer service rep, moved to another location, or received a perceived better deal from a competitor. Yet, curiously enough, it often is still more cost-effective to contact a former customer than a new prospect. Rarely have they totally negative images of their former vendor; they may no longer be devoted, but they are usually still accessible. They may even have some remnants of brand or vendor loyalty. It's also quite possible they aren't all that enamored of new vendors and are ready to return.

Chapter Summary

The chapter began with a definition of relationship marketing as a focus on maintaining long-term customers as partners. This contrasted to the traditional transaction-oriented view of marketing, wherein the emphasis is on getting the sale and deemphasizing the period thereafter. The reasons for this new emphasis upon relationships were explained in terms of reduced long-term costs, diminishing vendors, and just-in-time manufacturing systems.

This chapter integrated material presented in earlier chapters into a formal statement of the relationship selling philosophy. The principles of this philosophy follow:

1. Relationship selling is participative.
2. Active listening and questioning are encouraged.
3. Relationship selling is buyer-oriented.
4. Empathy is crucial.
5. Maturity is required of the salesperson.
6. Likability is critical.
7. Deliver impeccable service.
8. Value-added is important.

Precall preparation, the first step in interactive selling, includes learning about one's industry, company, product, and competition. Industry knowledge provides sales representatives with a better perspective of their customers and allows them to determine their strongest markets. Company knowledge, including its history, finance, and reputation, is important because the customer buys not only the product but also the company that stands behind it. Company policies and procedures (including cash discounts, trade discounts, quantity discounts, allowances, transportation charges, and credit policies) also influence sales. The importance of product knowledge to the salesperson was discussed, along with a delineation of the differences between a product's features and its benefits. Features are facts about the product or service that will be true whether or not it is ever bought and used. Benefits are the way features help satisfy a buyer's specific needs or problems. Although a feature describes the product, a benefit relates it to the user. It tells the customer "What's in it for me." Some suggestions for identifying product features were offered. Completing the section on precall preparation was a discussion on ways to learn about and assess competitors.

The chapter described a salesperson conducting a target market analysis. This process represents a culmination of the precall preparation stage. By sitting down and systematically analyzing industry, company, product, and competition, salespeople are able to identify the general profile of customers who are most likely to buy their goods or services. Chapter 7, "Successful Prospecting," will explain methods for finding specific customers with this profile.

The chapter ended with a discussion of after-marketing, which applies marketing principles following the purchase. Important after-marketing activities are (1) building a database, (2) acknowledging customers, (3) maintaining ongoing contact with customers, (4) measuring customer satisfaction, and (5) reclaiming lost customers.

Discussion Questions

1. Define relationship marketing.

2. Draw distinctions between transactional and relationship marketing.

3. Describe a discrete transaction.

4. Why is "internal marketing" so important to furthering the relationship?

5. What are some ways of bringing value-added to the relationship?

6. How do transactional and relationship marketers differ in their measure of market satisfaction?

7. What trends have contributed to the growth of relationship marketing?

8. Why is it cheaper to do business with existing customers?

9. Explain ways of augmenting the product offering.

10. Why is it necessary to have a theory of selling?

11. Describe relationship selling. What is it? What are its principles?

12. What is the reason for precall preparation?

13. Of what value is preparation regarding the salesperson's industry?

14. How does company knowledge assist the efforts of salespeople?

15. Define the following terms: cash discounts, trade discounts, cumulative quantity discounts, noncumulative quantity discounts, advertising allowances, F.O.B. plant, F.O.B. destination, uniform delivered price, C.O.D., C.W.O., and E.O.M.

16. Explain the differences between features and benefits.

17. Indicate some ways for sales representatives to identify product features.

18. How does knowledge of the competition help the salesperson? How can one find out about the competition?

19. What is a target market analysis? How does it assist the salesperson?

20. The marketing club at your school, of which you are a member, has initiated a money-making project. The club plans to give out desk blotters to students and faculty at registration. The costs (and hopefully a profit) will be furnished by businesses that will pay for advertising space on the blotter. Who would you identify as the target market for the blotter? Who is the competition?

21. When should salespeople stress their company over the features of their product or service?

22. The list price for ladies' blouses is quoted at $20. Trade discounts of 30 and 20 percent are offered to retailers and wholesalers, respectively. If the blouses are ordered in quantities of a dozen or more, the cost per dozen is $18. Transportation charges are F.O.B. origin. A wholesaler in Little Rock orders 12 dozen blouses from the manufacturer's plant in St. Louis. What does the wholesaler pay?

23. Tom Jones works for his father, who owns Struensee Siding Company. Struensee specializes in aluminum siding for houses. Until now, Tom's father has concentrated on advertising to draw in business, but recently business has fallen off. Tom has suggested to his father that Tom act as an outside salesperson. What suggestions could you make to Tom before he begins selling? What are some identifiable features and benefits associated with the siding?

24. Define after-marketing.

25. Why is after-marketing important?

26. What are the five components of service quality?

27. Explain the essential activities of after-marketing.

28. Do research and identify some major corporate partnerships. What do the partners gain with their relationship?

Chapter Quiz

1. All of the following are strategic elements of relationship selling *except*
   a. timing is long-term.
   b. the dominant quality dimension is the quality of interactions.
   c. emphasis in selling process is problem recognition.
   d. price elasticity is higher.

2. The longer customers are retained by a company, the more profitable they become because of all of the following reasons *except*
   a. price discounts.
   b. increased purchases.
   c. reduced operating costs.
   d. referrals.

3. Acquiring new customers is more expensive than selling to an existing customer. In one survey, respondents reported that it took an average of _____calls to close a first sale, compared with only three calls to close a sale to an existing account.
   a. 12
   b. 10
   c. 7
   d. 5

4. In building relationships, trust is essential. When your presentations are balanced and fair (e.g., product limitations as well as advantages are discussed), you are building trust through
   a. demonstrating competence.
   b. your candor.
   c. offering dependability.
   d. using a customer-orientation.

5. Relationship selling involves all of the following principles *except*
   a. it encourages active listening and questioning.
   b. it is focused on closing the order.
   c. it is buyer-oriented.
   d. it is empathetic.

6. Deductions from the list price offered to members of the channel of distribution are called
   a. trade discounts.
   b. cash discounts.
   c. quantity discounts.
   d. allowances.

7. It is critical that salespeople make a distinction between features and benefits. Which of the following statements illustrates a benefit?
   a. This window air conditioner comes with a money-back guarantee.
   b. This window air conditioner is made from 98 percent aluminum alloy.
   c. This window air conditioner is rated as the most energy efficient by *Consumer Guide.*
   d. This window air conditioner is large enough to keep your office cool even during the hottest days of summer.

8. The process of identifying a target market involves thoroughly studying all of the following *except*
   a. industry.
   b. marketing.
   c. product.
   d. competition.

9. The ability of the salesperson to put himself or herself in the buyer's shoes and understand their viewpoint is
   a. empathy.
   b. reliability.
   c. assurance.
   d. responsiveness.

10. To ensure the implementation of quality service in the after-marketing activity stage, certain activities are necessary. They include all of the following *except*
    a. building a database.
    b. acknowledging customers.
    c. locating new customers.
    d. measuring customer satisfaction.

Profiles

Product Description for Role-Playing

Here are some product descriptions that your instructor may assign for videotaping or presentation before the class. In the exercise, students will have opportunities to play both salesperson and buyer (described at the end of Chapter 8, "The Approach"). In succeeding chapters, you will be assigned tasks to prepare for the experience (e.g., preparing

questions to ask, composing a sales presentation, formulating responses to likely objections, and planning closes). By the end of Chapter 13, "The Art of Closing," you should be prepared to play a salesperson and sell to a student playing the part of one of the described customers. This student will have received additional instructions from the instructor on his or her own unique buying motives, objections to raise, and circumstances under which he or she should agree to purchase. Instructors should consult the *Instructor's Manual* for further information about this role-playing experience.

Radio Station WEAU

Radio station WEAU is a 250-watt radio station in Eau Claire, Wisconsin, reaching a broadcast area of approximately 15 miles. In contrast to several competitors in the city that appeal to teenagers and college students with a "top 40" format, WEAU seeks an adult audience of higher income and education. Its format strikes a balance between "middle of the road" and "good" music by playing show tunes, old standards, popular nonrock tunes, well-known vocalists, news and information programs, and semiclassical music, mostly instrumental. Though not as recognized an advertising medium as newspapers and television, radio has a number of distinct advantages to offer. First, it is a very selective medium; each station appeals to a relatively narrow audience, who tends to be more loyal than television viewers, who are continually switching channels. Radio is a low cost-of-entry medium, especially in comparison with television. The combination of selective appeal, listener loyalty, and low cost allows an advertiser to deliver an inexpensive message several times for the same cost as television and newspapers. Moreover, the latter appeal to, and charge for, a broader audience, both demographically and geographically, than a local retailer often desires. Radio is extremely mobile. It goes from room to room with listeners, to the beach, and in the car. Two of the highest times for radio listenership are during the morning and afternoon commuting times, when radio reaches working people like no other medium can. From 6 A.M. to 10 A.M. and from 3 P.M. to 7 P.M., captive commuters have little to do besides tune in, and nearly 90 percent of them listen at least once a week.

Radio is very personal; disc jockeys develop a great deal of rapport with their audiences by speaking their language. Advertisers take advantage by allowing radio personalities to deliver the advertising message in their own distinctive style. Or the advertiser may decide to deliver the message personally, adding believability and "folksiness." Radio commercials can be produced on very short notice. For commercials delivered live, the production process requires only preparation and delivery of a script. Even with recorded messages, production time is short. Commercials usually are produced in a recording studio, and audiocassettes are mailed to the station, requiring as few as one or two days. As might be expected, the cost of production is low. Live commercials have no production costs. For recorded commercials there are charges for recording studios, talent employed, and script writing, but some radio stations, like WEAU, will record messages for their stations with their own talent at no extra charge.

RADAR (radio's all-dimension audience research) studies, as well as other research, has provided some interesting information about how radio is used:

1. There are 5.7 radios per family in the United States, in both the home and the automobile.
2. During an average week, 96 percent of all persons 12 years old or older listen to radio. On an average day, more than four out of five adults listen to radio.
3. The average adult's listening time is 3 hours, 27 minutes per day, and this figure averages higher for key advertising targets—adults 18 to 49 years of age, upscale working women, and professional/managerial males.
4. Nearly 9 out of 10 consumers are reached by radio on a weekend, with individuals averaging 3 hours of listening every Saturday and Sunday.
5. Radio is a leader in morning and afternoon "drive times," and new research puts radio as the number one daytime medium between 10 A.M. and 3 P.M. This is because TV doesn't penetrate the workplace much, but millions of workers do keep the radio on at various times throughout the workday.

Yet for all its favorable aspects, radio does have its disadvantages. It lacks the visual impact of television, and its message is more fleeting than that of the newspaper; people cannot sit and absorb an advertisement at their leisure. Nor does radio lend itself to complex messages as print media does. From the standpoint of attention, people are often engaged in other activities while listening to the radio—preparing for work, eating breakfast, driving, eating dinner, and reading.

Copies of rate cards for both WEAU and the local newspaper, the *Eau Claire Northwestern*, follow, along with information on interpretation.

Radio: How to Interpret Rates

Standard Entry

The AM/FM commercial station entry typically includes the station's address, phone number, website, the program format (i.e., oldies, talk, classic rock), audience profile (i.e., persons 35–64 years of age), personnel contacts, network affiliation(s), special programming, facilities, and operating schedule. Program format and audience profile information are key for advertisers trying to reach their target customers.

Using Estimated Rates for Planning

Rates for radio advertising are subject to frequent fluctuation and are dependent on factors such as the time of day when an ad runs, the station's ratings, and the level of demand from advertisers for air time.

The time of day is segmented into "day parts," such as morning drive time (6 A.M.–10 A.M.), midday (10 A.M.–3 P.M.), afternoon drive (3 P.M.–7 P.M.), and evening (7 P.M.–12 A.M.).

As stated earlier, advertising costs are also contingent on a station's ratings. Basically, the higher the ratings, the higher the advertising costs. Thus, a station's price for advertising is listed as a cost-per-point (rating point) figure (i.e., $5 per rating point). A single rating point is equivalent to 1 percent of the target population.

The SPARC cost-per-point entry for WEAU contains the following information:

Cost-per-Point—Eau Claire

Day Part	4th Quarter 2006
AM	47 (e.g. $5 \times 47 = 235$)
Day	39
PM	46
Eve	50

(Cost is for 30-second commercial lengths. Day parts are AM, m-f, 6-10; Day, m-f, 10-3; PM, m-f, 3-7; Eve, m-f, 7-12.)

Newspapers: How to Interpret Rates

SAUs and "Inches"

Most newspapers use the standard advertising unit (SAU) system in selling advertising space. This system utilizes 56 fixed sizes for broadsheet newspapers participating in the system and 32 for tabloids.

The size of SAUs ranges from one column ($2\frac{1}{16}''$ wide) to six columns in width, and from 1″ to 21″ ("full depth") in depth. The following chart indicates the various sizes of SAUs for a broadsheet newspaper. For example, an SAU of dimensions 2 × 3 is two columns wide and 3″ in depth. Note that this chart indicates all 56 options for a broadsheet.

Rates

Some papers list their rates for each standard advertising unit. However, because advertisers often buy space in bulk, most papers list their rates in terms of column inches (which are labeled "inches") rather than in terms of SAUs. One "inch" actually equals one column ($2\frac{1}{16}''$ wide) by 1″ in depth.

There are about 132″ per page in a broadsheet newspaper. Rates are usually quoted in dollars per inch (i.e., column inch). The basic rate is generally listed under the designation "SAU open, per inch." This is the rate you would pay if you bought one ad, one column inch in size, to run one time.

Discounts for Bulk Purchases

Often, advertisers commit themselves to buying a certain number of inches or pages over the course of a certain period of time (e.g., one month or a year). In such cases, the newspapers give a discount to the advertisers, and the dollar amount per inch decreases. Sometimes the percentage of the discount from the basic rate is indicated following the standard rates. The following example shows excerpts from the *Eau Claire Northwestern* sample calculation.

Figure 6-3 illustrates how the cost of radio and newspapers compare, as the number of ads increases.

S.A.U. Nomenclature

Width	1 Column ($2\frac{1}{16}$ in)	2 Columns ($4\frac{1}{4}$ in.)	3 Columns ($6\frac{7}{16}$ in.)	4 Columns ($8\frac{5}{8}$ in.)	5 Columns ($10\frac{13}{16}$ in.)	6 Columns (13 in.)	Double Truck ($26\frac{3}{4}$ in.)
Depth in Inches							
1	1 × 1						
$1\frac{1}{2}$	1 × 1.5						
2	1 × 2	2 × 2					
3	1 × 3	2 × 3					
$3\frac{1}{2}$	1 × 3.5	2 × 3.5					
$5\frac{1}{4}$	1 × 5.25	2 × 5.25	3 × 5.25	4 × 5.25			
7	1 × 7	2 × 7	3 × 7	4 × 7	5 × 7	6 × 7	
$10\frac{1}{2}$	1 × 10.5	2 × 10.5	3 × 10.5*	4 × 10.5	5 × 10.5	6 × 10.5*	13 × 10.5
13	1 × 13	2 × 13	3 × 13	4 × 13	5 × 13		
14	1 × 14	2 × 14	3 × 14	4 × 14	5 × 14	6 × 14	13 × 14
$15\frac{3}{4}$	1 × 15.75	2 × 15.75	3 × 15.75	4 × 15.75	5 × 15.75		
18	1 × 18	2 × 18	3 × 18	4 × 18	5 × 18	× 18	× 18
21	1 × FD**	2 × FD**	3 × FD**	4 × FD**	5 × FD**	6 × FD**	13 × FD**

*An ad that fills one quarter of a page measures 3 × 10.5 or 31.5 standard column inches. A horizontal half page is 6 × 10.5 or 63 standard column inches.

**FD (Full Depth) can be 21″ or deeper. An ad that fills an entire page is 6 × FD (132 in.).

Total cost for a 1/2 page (or 63 column inches) in the Sunday *Northwestern* is $133.79 × 63 = $8,428.77.

Morning, Saturday and Sunday

Commission and Cash Discount

15 percent to agencies; no cash discount

Policy—All Classifications

30-day notice given of any rate revision.

Alcoholic beverage advertising accepted.

Advertising Rates

Effective January 1, 2006

Rates verified April 14, 2006

Black/White Rates

	Morn.	Sun.
SAU open, per inch.	100.74	133.79 ← Basic rate, per column inch

Inches charged full depth: col.21; pg.126 dbl truck 273.

YEARLY CONTRACT

	Per inch	
	Morn.	Sun.
$\frac{1}{4}$ pg	100.74	133.79
$\frac{1}{2}$ pg	100.74	133.79
1 pg	95.93	127.69 ← Contract rates, per column inch. Note that the rate decreases as space increases.
2 pgs	94.83	125.80
4 pgs	92.74	123.98
6 pgs	92.62	123.35

Discounts

Multi-insertion discounts (pickup rates): 1st ad contract rate, 2nd ad 15% discount, 3rd ad and successive ads 25% discount. Discounts apply to ROP weekday ads only (color and black & white with no changes). When a Sunday/Holiday insertion is involved, it will count as part of the sequential schedule but will not be discounted. Discounts apply to full run or two-zone or more zone buys. For each ad series, at least one insertion shall be at regular nondiscounted rates.

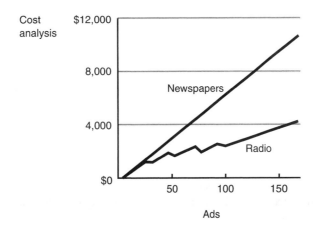

Figure 6-3
Contrasting Costs of Radio versus Newspapers As Ads Increase in Number

Ergo Futura Furniture

Ergo Futura is a technically advanced line of office chairs and desks designed to maximize the comfort of office workers and, hence, their productivity. Although scientific study has long been applied to the jobs of production workers, only recently have the same analytical techniques been transferred to the office environment. One surprising finding has been the dramatic effects on productivity of such seemingly mundane factors as lighting, ringing phones, inadequate ventilation, and, most of all, poorly designed desks and chairs that at best are uncomfortable and at worst contribute to bad backs, sore knees, and stiff necks. "By eliminating repetitive stress injuries, American companies could save $20 billion each year in workers' compensation," former U.S. Labor Secretary Robert B. Reich said. Musculoskeletal disorders are the country's most costly category of workplace injuries and illnesses. In addition to spending $20 billion annually on workers' compensation costs due to repetitive stress injuries, the United States spends another $100 billion on lost productivity, employee turnover, and other indirect expenses. One study by the National Institute of Occupational Safety and Health, a research arm of the federal government, found that a well-designed desk and chair added 25 percent to the productivity of data-entry clerks, who generally average $24,000 in salary and benefits. Moreover, in another study by HumanTech, a Toronto-based office design firm, absenteeism fell from 4 percent to 1 percent, error rates in documents were cut in half, and employees began using computers more often during the workday following the installation of ergonomic furniture. In a survey of working conditions, white-collar workers placed having a comfortable chair only second in importance to adequate lighting. Experts in office design estimate that a properly designed office can add an hour or more a day to worker output. Sitting is blamed for most of the lower back pain that strikes 90 percent of Americans sooner or later at an estimated cost of $70 billion a year. Deborah Kearney, a consultant in ergonomics, writes that pressures on spinal disks measure about 35 percent less while people stand than while they sit unsupported.

The Buckstaff Company of Brockton, Massachusetts, recently introduced a line of chairs and desks, Ergo Futura, that it markets for those who work with data terminals and PCs. The name for the line evolved from the science of ergonomics, which studies the relationships between people and machines. The word comes from the Latin *ergo* (work) and *nomics* (law or management) and includes determining where to locate controls on a dashboard or any other machine, how high to make a desktop, and where a chair's backrest should be to maximize support.

Studies indicate that bad backs are the second leading cause of absenteeism among office workers and, overall, afflict an estimated 50 to 80 percent of the general population. A Louis Harris poll conducted for Steel-Case, the largest U.S. manufacturer of furniture, found that 54 percent of surveyed workers felt that the comfort of their chairs affected their performance. States Niels Different, an industrial designer who has won awards for his chair designs, says, "Sitting is an athletic activity. Tasks such as typing put a 30 percent additional load on the spine." Most office chairs were never designed for use over long periods of time—certainly not a full 8-hour day. Besides contributing to back problems, a chair can restrict blood flow to the legs with an improperly designed cushion, put pressure on hip joints with too soft a seat, and fail to dissipate body heat with the wrong type of material, especially if workers are wearing blended polyester garments. Consequently, workers are continually getting up and stretching to relieve stiffness, further restricting productivity.

Aetna Insurance Company estimates that 45 percent of workplace injuries—and 63 percent of total injury-claim payments—are for cumulative trauma disorders such as carpal tendonitis and carpal tunnel syndrome (CTS), which strike people who do a lot of typing and other repetitive hand movements at the keyboard. "Repetitive stress injuries (RSIs) cost American businesses about $10.8 billion in 1995, or an average of $12,000 for every case of RSI," according to *CDT News*, May 1996. Symptoms of CTS include intermittent numbness, pain, or a tingling sensation in the thumb, index finger, or middle finger. According to the Bureau of Labor Statistics, repetitive stress injuries have nearly tripled in recent years.

In December 1990, San Francisco passed an ordinance requiring employers to provide office workers with adjustable desks and chairs. The penalties for noncompliance are up to $500 per day.

Through intensive analysis with the help of machines that measure blood flow through extremities, muscle contraction, and changes in the angles of body segments, Buckstaff engineers have designed the Ergo Futura chair with the following features:

1. A scroll edge, meaning that the front of the chair is rounded off.
2. Support at the base of the chair, helping the back to hold a slight forward arch.
3. A lightly padded seat cushion.
4. A backrest that hits the lower few inches of the shoulder blades, facilitating relaxation.
5. Adjustable seat height, allowing changes within a 6"–9" range.
6. Accessory footrests that eliminate dangling feet for shorter people, who must raise their chairs to reach desktops.

Ergo Futura chairs begin at $300, and the highest-priced chair is just over $1,000. The latter top-of-the-line model is made of "Pellicle"—as opposed to the traditional foam-and-fabric office chair construction—allowing air to pass through it so body heat doesn't build up. Moreover, this chair tilts with the body as it moves, and armrests can be adjusted both vertically and laterally. This makes them approximately $100 to $150 more expensive than comparable conventional chairs. On its own, a properly designed chair can add as many as 40 productive minutes a day—21 productive days a year—for most office workers, according to E. R. Tichauer, a professor of human factors engineering at New York University.

In their research, Buckstaff engineers have found that desks also have great impact on the productivity of those working with data terminals. Machines that have the keyboard attached to the screen force users to adjust their posture to the machine, rather than the other way around. This is especially true for people with glasses—bifocals in particular—who read out of only a part of their glasses and must tilt their heads to read the screen. To avoid glare, workers often lean forward, backward, or sideways, wreaking havoc on backs, wrists, arms, and necks. Furthermore, eyestrain is likely if there is too much distance between the worker and the screen.

Ergo Futura desks have been designed for maximum flexibility. The desktop is split: one-half for the screen and the other half for the keyboard. Each half moves independently of the other and can be tilted either forward or backward. Movement is effected with cranks located under the desk; some models even have electric controls that move the desk up or down at the touch of a button. New enhancements included retractable keyboard trays and separate shelves for monitors, keyboards, and peripherals.

Ergo Futura desks begin at about $500 and can run as high as $2,000. This makes them approximately 1½ to 2 times as expensive as more conventional desks. Of course, Buckstaff believes that productivity gains will more than compensate for the extra cost, and these savings should be present for a long time, because both desks and chairs are built to last at least 20 years.

Buckstaff believes that the potential for its new line of office furniture is immense. In Sweden and certain other countries, use of ergonomic desks and chairs is already required by law for workers who sit at computer terminals. Just recently, the Communications Workers of America (CWA) negotiated a deal with Wisconsin Bell to buy $350,000 worth of new chairs as part of CWA's employment contract negotiations with the telephone company.

Activity

1. Write down a list of features and benefits for Ergo Futura office furniture.

Pip Pop

After extensive research and development, the Peter and Greer Company of Cincinnati, Ohio, has created a unique new consumer product—a carbonated, powdered soft drink, sold in packets of six. All consumers need do is open a packet, pour the powder into a glass, and add water. Numerous blind taste tests have proved the inability of consumers to distinguish Pip Pop from traditional bottled soft drinks. Pip Pop comes in either regular or diet form and all the multitude of flavors of a typical bottled or canned soft drink. The product has a number of distinct advantages. It is vastly cheaper: $1 per 6-pack versus approximately three times as much for traditional carbonated soft drinks. For this reason alone, parents should find Pip Pop very appealing, and kids will be enthralled with the novelty of the product. Of further convenience, Pip Pop will do away with the need to return empty bottles or to dispose of cumbersome aluminum cans. The paper packet in which Pip Pop is sold is totally recyclable and ecologically sound, which should appeal to consumers increasingly concerned with maintaining the environment. Besides liking the product's consumer appeal, supermarkets and other mass merchandisers will be lured by the savings in storage space required by Pip Pop, and the extra profits it will generate per foot of shelf space over conventional soft drinks. Labor costs will also be less for Pip Pop. Supermarket personnel currently must sort out returned empty bottles to be picked up later by local bottlers.

Pip Pop has been introduced in test markets in Kansas City, Missouri and Green Bay, Wisconsin. In six months, it has done very well, capturing nearly 5 percent of the soft drink market. On a national basis this translates into millions of dollars of sales and profits.

Pip Pop represents the first foray of Peter and Greer into soft drinks, though they have a well-deserved reputation for merchandising excellence in other product categories. Their several brands of detergents, for example, control well over 50 percent of that category's sales. Their sales of disposable diapers represent a full 75 percent of all disposable diaper sales, and their toothpaste brands have captured approximately a 40 percent share. As with all of their other products, the Peter and Greer Company plans to support Pip Pop with all of its considerable marketing expertise and resources. On "rolling out" the product for national distribution, Peter and Greer will invest a million dollars in network television ads. Targeted for Saturday mornings and from 4 P.M. to 6 P.M. weekdays, prime youth-viewing times, 30-second commercials will feature prominent sports personalities drinking Pip Pop and kids having fun making the drink. In one of the ads, Michael Jordan, the popular basketball player, is shown preparing glasses of Pip Pop for several of the children in his neighborhood. Concurrent with media advertising, coupons will be offered in local newspapers, mailed directly to homes and enclosed in each package of Pip Pop. The coupon, worth 20 cents off each 6-pack, will be in effect for 90 days. Special dealer offerings will become effective following the initial consumer couponing program and will last for 90 days. Supermarkets and other retailers can take advantage of a 20 percent reduction in the price of each case and of free-standing displays made available by Peter and Greer. As with all other Peter and Greer products, there will be the normal allowances for coop advertising—50 cents off per case when the retailer meets requirements for local newspaper advertising.

The profit margin for Pip Pop is comparable to that of conventional soft drinks. Although its lower price will mean less profit to retailers per sale, the unique savings of the product versus conventional soft drinks should more than compensate.

Activity

1. Write down a list of features and benefits for Pip Pop.

Multicard, the All-Purpose Credit Card

Multicard is an all-purpose credit card with a worldwide circulation. By presenting the card to merchants, holders can gain immediate credit. The advantages of the card to retailers are varied and significant. It expands their customer base beyond those consumers who carry just the retailer's own card or charge account, which significantly increases the number of potential customers. One of the more telling arguments in favor of Multicard, given its large customer base, is that surveys show retailers losing sales if they fail to display signs showing they accept certain cards. These studies show that many consumers are too embarrassed to ask if their card can be used to make a purchase. Shoppers simply leave the store without buying anything at all. It is also true that those who have Multicard tend to be younger, upscale consumers who have a college education and are employed in professional or business work. Multicard assumes the cost for collecting any unpaid accounts, which total some 5 to 7 percent of accounts receivable for the typical store, eliminating the costs for retailers of maintaining their own credit and collection departments. Sales clerks are able to take advantage of Multicard's sophisticated computer system by dialing directly into the system to verify customer credit. Because of the nearly instantaneous reply, customers are saved lengthy embarrassing waits until their credit is approved, which usually requires phoning the local credit bureau and waiting for a clerk to look up the customer's record. Because retailers receive immediate credit for the amount of sale as soon as they deposit Multicard slips, their cash flow is improved; they need not wait for customers to pay their bills. Of course, this frees retailers of the overhead of keeping track of payments, printing bills, and mailing them out, tasks typically calling for some sort of data-processing system. Because Multicard advertises in local newspapers, on television, and on radio, promoting the use of the card along with the names of stores where it is honored, retailers profit from free advertising. Consumers themselves like the idea of needing only one universal credit card rather than keeping track of numerous single-purpose cards. For all of these benefits, Multicard deducts 2 percent from the face amount of purchases made with the card. That is, if the customer's bill totals $100, Multicard immediately credits the merchant's account for $98.

Besides the convenience and additional credit it offers, Multicard also attracts consumers with other incentives. Multicard offers a 5 percent rebate on airline tickets and a 10 percent rebate on hotel charges. The cardholder, his or her spouse, and other members of the family receive up to $500,000 in airline/common carrier insurance when each fare is charged. If a customer's auto-insurance policy doesn't cover rental cars, Multicard will, saving approximately $10 a day in extra fees. Multicard offers discounts toward merchandise purchases from its own biannual catalog. Multicard will double (up to one year) the free repair period offered by manufacturers' warranties for purchases made on its card and registered at the time of purchase in its Buyer's Assurance Protection Plan. Through another program, Purchase Protection, it also insures retail purchases against theft, fire, damage, or loss for 90 days from the date of purchase, up to $50,000 per cardholder.

A new Multicard feature is its price protection feature. If customers buy a product with the card, then find it elsewhere at a cheaper price, Multicard will refund the difference. The customer, though, must provide proof within 60 days that the lower price was advertised in print.

Activity

1. Write down a list of features and benefits for Multicard.

Falcon King Air

Many companies have grown dissatisfied with the cost and especially the inconvenience of commercial air travel. Executives must reserve trips in advance of flying on commercial flights; they cannot leave on short notice as with a corporate plane. Commercial trips often involve time lost waiting for flights (even greater with delays), switching planes to make connections, and commuting from airports far from city centers. Costs rise even further if employees are forced to stay overnight because air service is limited. All this is compounded by ensuing ruined schedules, delayed meetings, and even deals blown in today's fast-paced business world. Moreover, all this presumes that the final destination has an airport. Airline trunk routes serve only 250 airports nationwide. Since 1984, major carriers have clipped 65 airports off their schedules, and regional airlines even more. Since "9/11" this trend has accelerated.

Business aircraft can often avoid the airline hub airports and use noncongested reliever airports. The fact that business aircraft have many choices of airport locations at many destinations represents a major factor in the time-saving capability of business aircraft. Note in the map of Atlanta (see

Figure 6-4) the large number of landing-site choices for the traveler with a business aircraft over Hartsfield International. Clearly, reaching an airport from one's residence or office and returning from the airport generally are more convenient for the traveler using business aircraft than for the traveler restricted to flying on a commercial airline.

When one looks more closely, the difference in trip time becomes more apparent for four reasons: (1) commercial air carrier schedules may not be compatible with business appointments; in contrast, with a company aircraft, little notice is necessary before taking off; (2) intermediate en route stopovers may be at distant hub cities conveniently located for the airlines, not the executive; (3) large, regional air terminals may be hours away from one's business destination; and (4) airlines would like passengers to check in 90 minutes before an international flight and 30 minutes before a domestic flight.

The impact of these four factors on overall trip time is compounded on multiple-leg trips. If one calculates the average value of a top executive's time, assuming 1,500 productive hours of work per year, the savings can be significant.

As stated, the most directly measurable tangible benefit from business aircraft is time savings. It is generally recognized that the value of an individual's time is greater per hour than just the direct salary he or she receives. Such values have long been recognized and appraised in the insurance industry in the offering and underwriting of "key man" insurance policies for business. A key person may be thought of as a valuable asset who is insured by his or her firm against possible loss in the same way that a building is insured against physical damage. To estimate total employment costs from salaries or wages, businesses usually use a multiplier to account for additional compensation and fringes. Several methods of analysis are used to determine multiplier values. The most accepted of these would conclude that a multiplier of 5.72 is appropriate for a senior corporate executive and 3.76 for middle-management and professional personnel. For example, a senior executive with a salary of $200,000 per year (approximately $100 per hour) has a time value to his or her company of approximately $572 per hour. The respective figure for middle managers and professionals (at a $100,000 annual salary) is $163 per hour. Savings for managers can be considerable, then, since it is estimated that on the average trip three extra hours are spent on commercial air flights versus the comparable flight on a corporate aircraft. If one knows, then, how many company executives (upper- and middle-level) fly during the year, the number of flights they make, and the average airfare, one can calculate the savings of buying a company plane.

Moreover, for most corporate travelers, time spent traveling is time lost—incredibly expensive executive time. Time spent getting to the airport, waiting at boarding areas, sitting on crowded planes, waiting at luggage counters, and leaving the airport, is all valuable time lost in the shuffle.

But for some lucky travelers, the time spent traveling is just the opposite. It's markedly more productive. These are people traveling in company aircraft. They go straight from their office on the ground to their office in the air—on schedule. On board, they can discuss, plan, prepare, and rehearse in complete privacy. With an optional airborne telephone, they can stay in touch with subordinates on the

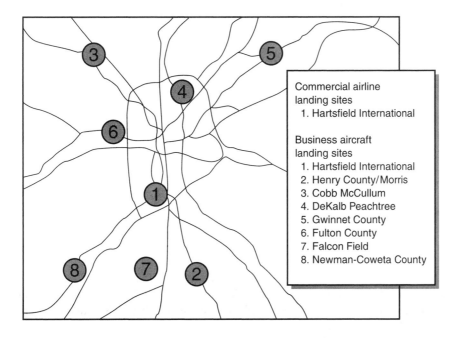

Figure 6-4
Map of Atlanta Landing Sites

ground. Comments James D. Robinson, CEO for American Express, "I can do some of my preparation work for my next appointment on the airplane. The onboard office is quiet and there are few interruptions. If we need to have meetings or conferences on board, we have room for that. We are always prepared when we land. As they say, wherever we go, we hit the ground running."

Companies also get strategic and operational trip results from owning their own aircraft. Recently, AT&T acquired McCaw, requiring senior AT&T executives to sit down with institutional investors and large financial houses worldwide to describe the value in AT&T stock for their pension plans, mutual funds, trust funds, and so forth. "Our teams made presentations in two or three cities each day," related AT&T's CEO. "This went on for a week. Not only did they have grueling presentation schedules, but they also had to travel and show up fresh for each meeting. They did it using their own aircraft. They could not possibly have done it on the airlines."

To handle the needs of companies understandably desiring their own planes, the Falcon Company of Wichita, Kansas, has developed the King Air, an economical two-engined turbo-prop aircraft. The King Air has 607 cubic feet of cabin space, some 37 percent more than its direct competition—enough room for up to six passengers and their baggage. This extra cabin space also allows amenities not often found in smaller business aircraft, such as a pressurized, accessible baggage compartment, a galley, a private lavatory, a couch, conference/dining tables, and a television. The range of the aircraft with a full load is up to 1,407 nautical miles; the comparable figure for a jet is 1,528 miles. The plane cruises at 350 mph, competitive with all other turboprop business aircraft. At this speed, you could schedule a 9 A.M. meeting 350 miles away (say, Chicago to Minneapolis) and still get a good night's sleep, because flight time would be only one hour. The commercial airliner between Chicago and Minneapolis is scheduled for an hour and ten minutes, to allow time for taxiing, climbing to altitude, time in flight pattern, and so on. On longer trips, of course, the higher speed of the jet will work to advantage, but studies show that the length of the average business trip is only about 350 miles. On such a trip, the most closely priced, comparably sized private jet competitor would get you there 11 minutes sooner, while consuming 67 gallons more fuel and offering a much smaller cabin. In fact, the King Air delivers more passenger miles per pound of fuel than any other airplane of its size, propjet or jet. It's no wonder that more than two-thirds of all business airplanes are King Airs. The King Air can help passengers reach customers or plants that more expensive executive aircraft cannot. It lands and takes off in under 3,000 feet, meaning it can land on 94 percent of the airstrips in the world, including unpaved strips. Often this capability allows it to land closer to the site of the passengers' business trip than with the typical regional airport.

The King Air has been designed for maximum safety; it can safely fly and land with just one engine. Every King Air is flight tested for 12 hours. Every airframe, every wing, and every system is tested and retested. All metal parts have been thoroughly protected against corrosion with an 11-step polyamide epoxy process. Moreover, controls for the aircraft are simply designed and easily learned by any qualified pilot within a short period of time, even those without commercial airline experience. The King Air has a warranty of 12 months or 150,000 miles, whichever comes first, and many components have their own special longer warranties. Additional Gold Card warranty protection on the entire plane can be purchased for two more years. The Falcon Company maintains a training school in Wichita for flying and ground personnel. The school is open virtually the entire year. The King Air possesses such a strong record of durability and safety that it qualifies for the most favorable rates on hull insurance. The cost of the plane is $4.2 million, approximately $250,000 more than direct competitors but considerably less than jet aircraft, which, while faster and less noisy, typically cost at least $0.5 million more. Moreover, the King Air uses about one-third less fuel than the average comparably sized business jet. In three years, a jet uses as much fuel as the King Air does in four, so, in comparison, the King Air flies every fourth year free. Although the King Air is slightly noisier than jets, everything has been designed to make it the quietest turboprop on the market. This is the result of four steps:

1. The engines have been moved nearly half a foot forward.
2. Four-blade propellers turn more quietly.
3. The inner shell of the cabin is shock-mounted to dampen sound and vibration.
4. The inner shell is wrapped in both thermal and acoustical insulation.

Another choice available from private leasing and maintenance companies is "fractional ownership." In simplified terms, a company can buy a share of a professionally operated and maintained aircraft and leave the "driving and hassles to them." Table 6-6 enumerates prices for fractional ownership.

Activity

1. Write down a list of features and benefits for the Falcon King Air.

Financial Services Exercise

Your task here is more unstructured than for the products and services just profiled. You are to assume that you have been employed by a large financial services company (one of your choice) to sell financial plans to the Swanson family, who will be described in Chapter 8, "The Approach."

Table **6-6** Prices of Fractional Airplane Ownership

Share Level	1/16	1/8	3/16	1/4	5/16	3/8	7/16	1/2
Purchase price	$264,000	$528,000	$792,500	$1,056,000	$1,320,000	$1,584,000	$1,848,000	$2,112,000
Operating costs								
Monthly management fee	$3,975	$5,790	$8,685	$11,580	$14,475	$17,370	$20,265	$23,160
Occupied hourly fee	$725	$725	$725	$725	$725	$725	$725	$725
Allocated hours per year	50	100	150	200	250	300	350	400
Five-year utilization	250	500	750	1,000	1,250	1,500	1,750	2,000

Your first endeavor should be researching a financial services company and learning its product line. Any brokerage house, insurance organization, or other financial specialist is a legitimate choice. Among the companies you might research are Aetna Casualty & Life, IDS/American Express, Merrill Lynch, Prudential/Bache Securities, the Sears Financial Network, Shearson/Lehman Brothers, and E. F. Hutton.

Web Exercise

Go to http://finance.yahoo.com, www.hoovers.com/free, or www.thomasregister.com and look up business information for three companies whose products you use weekly: your cell phone company, Coca-Cola, your favorite frozen pizza brand, sports equipment, or computer equipment. What kind of information is provided? How in-depth is the information about the companies? What kinds of things did you find out that would be of use to you if you were selling to these companies?

Notes

1. Frederick F. Reicheld and W. Earl Sasser, Jr., "Zero Defections: Quality Comes to Services," *Harvard Business Review,* September/October 1996, pp. 105–111.
2. Eugene H. Fram and Martin L. Presberg, "Customer Partnering— Suppliers' Attitudes and Market Realities," *Journal of Business & Industrial Marketing,* Vol. 8 (4), 1993, pp. 43–51.
3. Christian Groonos, "From Marketing Mix to Relationship Marketing: Towards a Paradigm Shift in Marketing," *Asia–Australia Marketing Journal,* August 1994, pp. 9–31.
4. Ian R. Macneil, "Contracts: Adjustment of Long-Term Economic Relations under Classical, Neoclassical and Relational Contracts," *Northwestern University Law Review,* 1978, pp. 854–902.
5. Ian R. Macneil, *The New Social Contract, An Inquiry into Modern Contractual Obligations,* New Haven: Yale University Press, 1980; B. A. Weitz and K. D. Bradford, "Personal Selling and Sales Management: A Relationship Marketing Perspective," *Journal of the Academy of Marketing Science,* Vol. 27, No. 2, April 1999, pp. 241–254.
6. F. Robert Dwyer, Paul H. Schurr, and Oh Sejo, "Developing Buyer–Seller Relationships," *Journal of Marketing,* April 1987, pp. 11–27.
7. B. Joseph Pine, II, Don Peppers, and Martha Rogers, "Do You Want to Keep Your Customers Forever?" *Harvard Business Review,* March/April 1995, pp. 103–114.
8. C. Groonos, *Service Management and Marketing: Managing the Moments of Truth in Service Competition,* Lexington, MA: Free Press, 1990.
9. J. Carlzon, *Moments of Truth,* New York: Harper & Row, 1987.
10. Christian Groonos, "From Marketing Mix to Relationship Marketing: Towards a Paradigm Shift in Marketing," *Asia–Australia Marketing Journal,* August 1994, pp. 9–31.
11. Frederick F. Reicheld and W. Earl Sasser, Jr., "Zero Defections: Quality Comes to Services," *Harvard Business Review,* September/October 1996, pp. 105–111.
12. Joe Giffer, "Capturing Customers for Life," Cambridge Technology Partners, www.ctp.com, 2004.
13. Rahul Jacob, "Why Some Customers Are More Equal Than Others," *Fortune,* September 19, 1994, pp. 215–224.
14. John R. Emshwiller, "Suppliers Struggle to Improve Quality As Big Firms Slash Their Vendor Rolls," *Wall Street Journal,* August 16, 1991, p. B1.
15. Stephen X. Doyle and George Thomas Roth, "Selling and Sales Management in Action: The Use of Insight Coaching to Improve Relationship Selling," *Journal of Personal Selling and Sales Management,* Winter 1992, pp. 59–64.
16. John Alofs, "I Just Called to Say 'How are You?' " *Personal Selling Power,* July/August 1995, p. 60.
17. Ginger Trumfio, "Anything for a Client," *Sales & Marketing Management,* June 1994, p. 102.
18. Erin Strout, "Keep Them Coming Back for More," *Sales & Marketing Management,* February 2002.
19. Kathleen Cholewka, "Service Slowdown," *Sales & Marketing Management,* November 2001.
20. Harvey McKay, *Swim with the Sharks Without Being Eaten Alive: Outsell, Outmanage, Outmotivate, and Outnegotiate Your Competition,* New York: Ballantine Books, August 27, 1996.

21. "Fax Networks," www.pb.com.

22. Duncan McDougall, "Know Thy Customer," *Wall Street Journal,* August 7, 1995.

23. Norton Paley, "Choose Competitors Carefully," *Sales & Marketing Management,* June 1994, pp. 57–59.

24. www.nokia.com, 2004.

25. Marvin Schiedermayer, "The 80-20 Rule: A 100-Year-Old Tool for Today's Lean Management Decisions," www.madisonconsultants.com/articles/80-20rule.html.

26. David Mercer, *High-Level Selling,* Houston, TX: Gulf Publishing Co., 1991.

27. Terry Vavra, *Aftermarketing,* New York: Irwin Publishing Co., 1992.

28. Roland T. Rust, Subramanian Bala, and Mark Wells, "Making Complaints a Management Tool," *Marketing Management,* 1992, pp. 41–45.

29. V. Zeithami, A. Parasuraman, and L. Berry, "Understanding Customer Expectations of Service," *Sloan Management Review,* Spring 1991, p. 28.

30. Daniel Tynan, "Something to Talk About," *Sales & Marketing Management,* 2004.

31. Marshal M. Rosenthal, "Using the Internet to Improve Customer Service," Sales Marketing Network at info-now.com, 2004.

32. Mary Lou Roberts, *Internet Marketing,* New York: McGraw-Hill, 2003.

Case 6-1

Analyze the following dialogue and determine if you think the salesperson is practicing interactive selling. Kyle, the salesperson, is trying to sell a new car to Karla, who has just walked into the showroom and looked around a little.

Kyle: My name is Kyle Mueller. Come on into my office and have a cup of coffee. Let's talk things over.

Karla: Thanks. Could I have a little cream in mine?

Kyle: Sure thing! (*shouting to a secretary*) Jennie, get us two coffees, one with cream, one black, please. (*turning back to Karla*) Let me ask you a few questions. (*filling out an order form*) How about giving me your name, address, and telephone number?

Karla: Karla Bowditch, 1213 Washington, 233-2165.

Kyle: Okay, Karla. Tell me what kind of car you want.

Karla: Well, I was basically thinking in terms of a small car, one that . . .

Kyle: Excellent! Let me tell you something about our new Contour. It has front-wheel drive, a transverse mounted engine, rack-and-pinion steering, and disc brakes. Now how about that?

Karla: Well, it sounds nice. I have a family and I have to do a little traveling now and then.

Kyle: The Contour will hold four people comfortably, and its gets 30 miles per gallon according to the latest EPA ratings. That should handle you. What kind of car are you driving now?

Karla: (*hesitantly*) Well, I'm driving a 1995 Pontiac Grand Prix. It's a good car with lots of room and lots of trunk space.

Kyle: What's it going to take in trade-in on your Grand Prix to get your order for a new Contour today?

Karla: Well, I think I need to shop around a bit more. I'm really not all that sure . . .

Kyle: Let me tell you, you'll get no better deal than here at Dolgin Motors. We have the finest reputation for integrity and service in the entire area. No one, but no one, undersells Dolgin. I tell you what. Let's knock $500 off the sticker price, and I'll see what my manager says. If he knows that we can get your business today, maybe he'll go for it.

Karla: (*getting up to leave*) I'm just not in a position to make a commitment today. I need to look around some more before buying.

Kyle: Don't leave yet. Maybe I can get my manager to agree to even more.

Karla: (*walking out of Kyle's office*) No, I'll get back in touch with you later after I've had more time.

Kyle: Okay, but you're making a mistake. I could get you a great deal today.

Questions

1. What principles of interactive selling did Kyle violate?
2. How would you have handled matters differently?

Case 6-2

Dave Ward, sales representative for Green Mountain Micro Brewery, is responsible for sales in a territory in New England. Recently, Dave has run into some problems in getting local beer distributors (beer wholesalers), liquor stores, and supermarkets to stock Green Mountain. In addition, they usually don't give it prime shelf space. A conversation with Richard Rouse, a distributor in Braintree, Massachusetts, follows.

Dave: Rich, I've noticed that you haven't been ordering Green Mountain these days. Certainly not like you used to. What's the problem?

Rich: I'll tell you what the stores we sell to say. They say people don't come into the store asking for Green Mountain like they do the national brands. Budweiser, Coors, Miller, and the rest put a lot of money into advertising, and that adds up when customers come into the store.

Dave: That's true to some degree, but people in this area are getting interested in unique-tasting, fresh, non-traditional beers.

Rich: Maybe, but you've still got to get the name of the beer out in front of the public, even if it's just locally.

Dave: Anything else? I'll be talking with my manager next week and maybe he'll listen to some recommendations.

Rich: Something else that bothers me. We distribute to a lot of stores in the area, but Green Mountain doesn't offer us that additional discount that other brewers do. We might do more business with you if we got that discount.

Dave: You've got to admit, we do offer some pretty healthy discounts for large orders, though.

Rich: True, but some brewers also offer discounts for volume that add up over the course of a year. Green Mountain doesn't.

Dave: We do have some healthy terms regarding transportation charges, however.

Rich: As good as some brewers, but your terms for early payment of bills leave something to be desired.

Dave: Is that it? Anything else?

Rich: Well, one last thing. You know winter lasts awhile up here, and beer is a seasonal item. So maybe Green Mountain can think of something to help us during the cold months.

Dave: Okay. Thanks, Rich. I'll see you again next month, when I get back in Braintree again.

Question

1. If you were in Dave's position, what recommendations would you make to your manager?

Successful Prospecting

Key Terms

centers of influence	endless chain	outbound telemarketing
cold-calling	inactive ("orphan") accounts	preapproach
contact management software	inbound telemarketing	tickler file

Learning Objectives

Learning Objectives

After studying Chapter 7, you will understand:

- The critical role of prospecting in sales success
- How to qualify prospects with regard to need, ability, and authority
- The major techniques of prospecting
- The importance of the preapproach
- How to set up and maintain prospect files
- How to plan for successful prospecting
- How technology has dramatically impacted prospecting

Bob Harris has just completed two months of training with the Everlive Insurance Company, learning the ins and outs of selling term, whole life, and property insurance. It is Monday morning, and Bob has just arrived at the office to begin his new career. After clearing his desk and filing his notes from training school, Bob decides to contact some people who might be interested in buying insurance. However, Bob is at a loss about how to begin. Whom should he contact? By what means? How will he know if the people he contacts are eligible to buy—and, moreover, if they are likely to buy?

7-1 What Is Prospecting?

The answer to this question and the answers to other questions come from knowledge of effective prospecting techniques. In personal selling, *prospecting* is the process of identifying potential buyers who have:

1. A need for the product or service
2. The ability to pay for it
3. The authority to buy it

Quite often, salespeople can put together a list of potential prospects, or names of individuals who might buy. However, for every 10 prospects, two may not have a need, three may not have enough money, and two may not have the authority to buy. It's no wonder that by some estimates fully 65 percent of all sales calls are made on the wrong person.

Before beginning the arduous task of prospecting, it is important to consider these numbers from Figure 7-1:[1]

- 2 percent of salespeople close the sale on the first call.
- 3 percent close on the second call.
- 4 percent close on the third call.
- 10 percent close on the fourth call.
- 81 percent close the sale on the fifth call.

Obviously, salespeople must not give up easily, but they should also be careful in choosing their prospects. Moreover, the reality is that it is three times as expensive to sell to a new account as it is to sell to an existing one.[2] Not only does it require more calls (3 versus 7, on average) but the list price is usually discounted dramatically, also. Of course, this is an academic question to the new sales rep just entering a territory with few, if any, accounts, or the new business salesperson who must continually prospect for much new business. Yet, it does imply that the smart

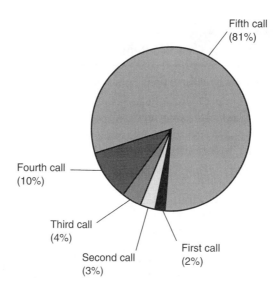

Figure 7-1
Calling and Closing
Most closes aren't made until later calls.

Fifth call
(81%)

Fourth call
(10%)

Third call
(4%)

Second call
(3%)

First call
(2%)

salesperson will search for those prospects with whom he or she can establish a long-term relationship rather than merely engage in a one-time transaction.

Unfortunately, most salespeople want to "ready, fire, aim," rather than the inverse. It is far better to do some work up front, determining those prospects with lasting power—the ones with whom a relationship can be established. Fortunately, there are numerous resources available to help the sales rep get the inside line on prospects—many costing nothing more than a little time and effort. Most of the sources that follow are readily available on the Internet, examples of which can be found in Box 7-1. Michael Shanley, outside salesperson for Liebovich Bros., Inc., in Rockford, adds that although his business customers use the Internet to purchase, he also uses it to determine prime sales prospects. "A salesman spends a lot of time qualifying customers, or figuring out whether a business manufactures products that would entail the use of our products. We used to have to look in manufacturers' directories. Now, you can easily pull this kind of information off the Internet, and you can do it quickly."[3]

7-1a Does a Need Exist?

Obviously, it is useless to call on people with little need for the product or service. However, salespeople waste much time with the wrong prospects, which is no laughing matter. The sales representative's overall efficiency and income are very much affected by the ability to assess prospect need.

One way of determining prospect need is to compare a prospect with the salesperson's previously determined description of a target market. If there is great dissimilarity, the prospect is unlikely to have need. Remember Ron Friendly in Chapter 6, "Beginning the Relationship Selling Process,"—the sales representative for Superior Hospital Uniform Company? Ron is trying to find out whether Mercy Hospital has a need for Superior's polyester-blend surgical uniform. Mercy is a large hospital (500 beds) with extensive laundry facilities and 12 operating rooms. Surgical personnel are knowledgeable and are likely to appreciate the technical advantages of the new uniform. In the past, Mercy Hospital has placed many orders with Superior and has been satisfied with the quality of the garments. Mercy has ordered little from Superior's major competitor, despite that firm's ability to deliver sooner. On the basis of this target market comparison, Ron decides that Mercy is likely to have a need for Superior's new surgical uniforms.

Box 7-1

Resources for Sales Reps

Here is a brief list of online sources.

General Company, Industry, and Geographic Information

Hoover's Online: www.hoovers.com: Timely and detailed information on more than 50,000 public and private companies.

Galileo Internet Resources: www.galileo.usg.edu/cgi-bin/homepage. cgi?_cc=1&_id=42315782-1120302296-0115
A listing of company directories and other competitive analysis sites on the Internet.

Michigan State University's MSU-CIBER: http://ciber.msu.edu/busres.htm: U.S. and international news and periodicals, statistical data and information resources, international trade information, company directories, and much more.

Corporate Information: www.corporateinformation.com
Provides U.S. and international company information, including research reports, company profiles, earnings information, and analyst reports.

Public Record Databases: www.searchsystems.net
Private company resources, compiled by Pacific Information Resources, Inc.

Investigative Resources International: www.factfind.com/database.htm

Links to searchable databases and research sites, including newspapers, journals, NGOs, privacy and security information, open-source records, public agencies, legal information, and more.

U.S. Census Bureau: www.census.gov: A wealth of information on everything from state demographics to average sales of businesses in your community to stats compiled in the 1997 economic census.

Federal Statistics: www.fedstats.gov: The gateway to statistics from over 100 U.S. federal agencies.

Corporate Annual Reports and Financial Information

Barron's Annual Report Service: http//barronsonline.ar.wilink.com/asp/BAR5_search_eng.asp
A service that gives you access to annual reports, for select companies, provided by World Investor Link and Barron's Online.

SEC's Edgar Database: www.sec.gov: A database of annual and quarterly reports of all publicly traded companies.

State-Specific Data

State Data Center Program: www.census.gov/sdc/www
A cooperative program between the states and the Census Bureau. The Business and Industry Data Center Program, also found here, is intended to meet the needs of local business communities for economic data.

Whatever the product or service, the salesperson should spend time assessing prospect need. The automobile salesperson should find out about prospects' current cars—make, year, model, and what they like and don't like about them. The salesperson might also ask about the size of prospects' families and whether they use their cars for both recreation and work. Answers to these questions will help salespeople decide which of their models will best satisfy prospect need. One sales representative for the Institutional Division of Economics Laboratory, Inc. (EL), has a unique method of determining prospect need. He calls it his "back door" method. Whenever he makes an appointment for selling one of his dishwashers to a restaurant or hotel, he enters through the back door. By going through the back, he can look at the setup in the kitchen area, examine some glasses and silverware for cleanliness and spots, and see which competitor's dishwasher is currently installed. In this manner, he can decide if need is present and, if so, show through tests how EL's equipment will solve these problems.

7-1b Can They Pay for It?

There is not much point in spending time with prospects who cannot pay for the product or service. The automobile salesperson might ask about clients' occupations and the amount of their current car payments. Showing them a $45,000 car they cannot afford makes little sense. They might want the car desperately, but they aren't legitimate prospects. All too many salespeople evaluate clients by their expressed desire rather than by their ability to pay.

When selling to the industrial market, sales representatives will find it worthwhile to check with credit rating services such as Dun and Bradstreet, the Better Business Bureau, chambers of commerce, banks, or other sources.

7-1c Do They Have the Authority to Buy?

The salesperson must be sure to call on prospects who have the authority to buy. Often, this is not easy. When selling e-learning via the Internet (MIS or "soft skills" training), salespeople may have problems determining who is the primary decision maker. In larger companies, decision-making power may lie with the vice president of corporate training, the human resources manager, or both. Very rarely does the chief executive officer become involved—they may not even use PCs. In some instances, especially small and medium-size companies, the decision often rests with the owner of the company. Now, there is the additional problem of outsourcing, in which companies hand over broad swaths of activities, such as their finance, human resources, and IT departments, to outside companies. Software vendors, for example, might call on who they think would be a prime customer for their product, only to find out that it has been outsourced to a company handling IT services for a number of organizations. It then becomes problematic to identify and contact these buyers, who are in a position to negotiate and buy in volume at large discounts.[4]

Some advise beginning at the top of the organization, even the CEO, because it is far easier to move down the hierarchy than up it. If you're dealing with a mid-level manager, how do you say, "I need to talk with your superior, because I have learned that you really don't have final authority"? The answer, of course, is that instead you can tactfully ask, "Is there anyone else I need to talk with about this purchasing decision?" However, there is no guarantee that the mid-level manager will do so, or even realize or admit that he or she does not have full authority. It is easier, though easier said than done, to start at the top, firmly identify the decision maker, and use his or her referral for an appointment. Is an underling going to refuse a request for an appointment suggested by a superior?

To return to the example of Ron Friendly, Ron will have to determine Mercy Hospital's balance of power between surgical personnel and the purchasing department. If the former have the most power, Ron can concentrate on demonstrating the technical advantages of his uniforms. On the other hand, if purchasing has more control over the decision, Ron will face a difficult task. Price, not quality, will influence the purchasing people.

Unfortunately, there are no definite ways to identify the key decision maker consistently. If one is able to call on the president, for example, identifying the decision makers should not be a problem. Oftentimes, users of the product or service can identify who is a decision maker, if not themselves. 3M's popular Post-its® made no headway with executives until 3M began promoting the product to secretaries. If the salesperson is still unsure, sometimes a candid, direct approach is best. An industrial machinery sales representative might ask, "Mr. White, will you be the one making the decision, or will others be involved?" Or, "Who do you report to?" "What budget do you have responsibility for?" "Who else is responsible for that budget?" It is quite possible that Mr. White is not the major decision maker, and the salesperson needs to get to who is.

7-2 The Importance of Prospecting

Selling works by the law of averages. Good salespeople know that a given number of calls will result in a certain number of orders. They plan accordingly and feel confident that the law of averages will eventually produce the desired results.

The law of averages, however, works only when there are enough qualified prospects for the salesperson to contact. Accordingly, the salesperson must prospect continuously and persistently. Neglecting this area is dangerous, even though the consequences may not be immediate. When current prospects are exhausted, the salesperson is left in the unhappy position of starting all over again. The first step in successful selling, then, is to make prospecting an automatic daily activity. That way, a steady flow of qualified prospects will be maintained.

Although persistence will bring results, salespeople can increase their success even further by improving the quality of their prospecting. Let's take a look at the numbers to demonstrate this. Suppose we have a salesperson who has collected the names of 20 potential prospects. Of these, 10 turn out to be qualified prospects. Three interview appointments are made, from which one sale of $500 results. This is illustrated in Figure 7-2.

Now suppose that the same salesperson improves the quality of the prospecting effort. As depicted in Figure 7-2, from another body of 20 potential prospects, 15 turn out to be truly qualified as to need, authority, and ability to pay (in fact, they are able to pay more). From these 15, 5 interviews are made, and 2 sales of $1,000 each result. In this instance, the salesperson has increased dollar sales some 400 percent through better prospecting. Even without an improvement in persuasive ability, the salesperson has dramatically increased sales volume.

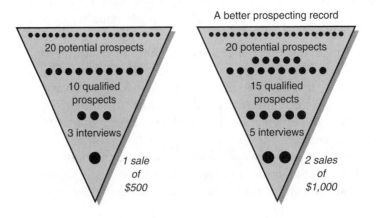

Figure 7-2
Prospecting Records

7-3 The New Technology of Prospecting

Before discussing specific methods of prospecting, it is important to first indicate how dramatically technology has transformed sales and marketing, especially prospecting. The relatively low cost of Internet services, telemarketing, and of sales and marketing automation makes it possible for any company to compete at a significant savings in time and money. Accordingly, sales organizations will require fewer high-paid "closers."

Obviously, the more salespeople prospect, the more business eventually comes in. However, most salespeople dislike the forbidding task of finding the names of decision makers, writing letters, and following up with telephone calls, not to mention being rejected eight times out of ten. The more senior the salesperson, the less willing he or she is to prospect. The result: Most organizations don't do enough prospecting.[5]

One reason the new technology is so successful is that it divides responsibility for these five basic steps of the selling process: identifying a decision maker, making contact through letters or phone calls to get an appointment, making the presentation, closing the sale, and maintaining the customer. With traditional marketing, the same people perform all five tasks, but new marketing technology allows stratification of the sales force, often using part-time employees to do the basic job of identifying decision makers. In many cases, a junior salesperson follows up on sales letters and calls to get appointments. Making presentations and closing the sale, however, is generally reserved for high-level salespeople. Depending on the status of the account, postsale contact often is shared by junior and senior salespeople along with customer service representatives. For example, when Xerox rolled out DocuShare, its new web-based knowledge-sharing product, the amount of lead generation needed "outstripped our capacity," stated Mark Simmons, general manager of Xerox Corporation's Customer Care Center in Palo Alto, California.[6] So Xerox turned to Techmar Communications, which supplied outsourced salespeople who help prequalify leads and create prospect relationships via telephone. These telereps encouraged prospects to download a limited version of DocuShare from the web, enabling them to demo the product before making a decision. "By helping prospects try the product first, [the telereps were] making them more excited about it," Simmons explained. These expanded capabilities have paid off for Xerox, which is seeing a doubling of business [for DocuShare] on a quarter-by-quarter basis.

Sales automation software, whether "contact management" or more sophisticated customer relationship management (CRM) programs with database analysis capabilities, makes it easy and inexpensive to enable the sales force for automated prospect-tracking. The key processes to be automated include keeping track of potential prospects by source, buying qualifications, and timing; communicating with potential prospects at the right time by telephone or mail; and tracking what happens to each prospect over time.

With these programs, salespeople maintain prospect information on their laptop computers and regularly upload information into a central database. Every contact with a customer should be regarded as an opportunity to get more information to serve that end. Once the organization has the appropriate software and hardware, every contact with the prospective customer should be entered into the database. Analysis of the database allows identification of only those prospects with the highest likelihood of buying. Prospective customers are so barraged with information and have so little time, they show little interest in any marketing pitch unless they're in a buying mode. Under these circumstances, the new technology works well because it is dedicated to addressing the optimal prospective purchasers at just the right time.

CRM software collects and interprets customer-based data from internal (marketing, sales, customer support) and external (market research, competitive intelligence) sources. It allows for better customer service by giving every employee the complete history of a customer's needs, problems, and purchases and targets potential sales by identifying the most lucrative customers and designing products for them. Mercedes-Benz successfully implemented CRM across its European divisions. The main driver was to understand the customers and offer them an individualized experience of consistent quality and to shift from mass marketing to one-to-one marketing. Mercedes-Benz now has a database of 10 million European customers whom it can contact individually and has improved customer retention and loyalty through improved customer care and insight. Sales effectiveness and efficiency also improved. Loyalty rates across Mercedes-Benz's markets in Europe are expected to rise as a result.[7]

Moreover, once a sale is made, relationships can be built with these customers, who are more likely to buy again (if satisfied) with much lower costs than prospecting for new customers. Marketers that want to build genuine credibility use the following relationship-building strategies, varying their selection according to the economics of the product line and the number of potential customers: newsletters; special offers and promotions tied, if possible, to the level of loyalty; eligibility to participate in special sponsored events or "customer councils"; exclusive information services via the Internet; and access to advanced levels of education in the field. Improved technology has transfigured prospecting.

7-4 Prospecting Methods

Over the course of time, salespeople have developed numerous methods for generating prospects. The following discussion of methods is by no means complete; there are probably as many variations of prospecting methods as there are salespeople. But the discussion does include most of the major recognized prospecting techniques. These can be discarded, altered, or combined, depending on the needs of the individual salesperson. The type of selling position will greatly influence this choice. An insurance salesperson might be able to use almost every method, while a business machines representative would be much more restricted. Whatever the final choice, the sources of prospects discussed here are as follows:

1. Friends and acquaintances
2. The endless chain
3. Centers of influence
4. Noncompeting sales personnel
5. Cold-calling
6. Observation
7. Lists and directories
8. Direct mail
9. Advertising
10. Seminars
11. Telemarketing
12. High-tech prospecting
13. Inactive accounts
14. Trade shows

7-4a Friends and Acquaintances

Friends and acquaintances constitute a rich source of prospects. Much of the business written by beginning insurance agents and securities brokers comes from people they knew before they entered the business. Industrial salespeople are likely to develop acquaintances and friendships after selling for awhile, and these friends provide sources for leads. Bankers, trade association personnel, and members of organizations such as the chamber of commerce represent other valuable acquaintances for industrial sales representatives.

A helpful technique for building prospect lists from friends and acquaintances is for salespeople to ask themselves, "Whom do I know?" They may know people from:

1. A previous job
2. Schools and colleges attended
3. Hobbies and sports activities
4. Participating in public service organizations and charities
5. Their neighborhood
6. Their church or other religious organization
7. Organizations of which they are members

Once such a list is developed, it is important to update it periodically as the salesperson continues to meet new people.

7-4b Endless Chain

An especially valuable method of prospecting is the **endless chain.** After each interview, the salesperson asks the client for the names of other people who might be interested in the product or service. As Figure 7-3 depicts, it does not take long to develop a lengthy list of prospects. A first interview may provide the names of two other prospects; two more names may be obtained from each of them for a total of four; these yield eight, and so forth. When asking for leads, the sales representative does not necessarily have to have made a sale, although it certainly helps. Even if the prospect does not need the product or service, the salesperson can ask for the names of those who do.

The endless chain is especially valuable in the sale of intangibles such as insurance and securities, but it is also useful in industrial selling. Executives in the same type of business or with the same professional specialty are in a good position to know of other prospects with similar needs and problems.

endless chain
A method of prospecting in which the salesperson asks each client the names of other people who might be interested in the product or service.

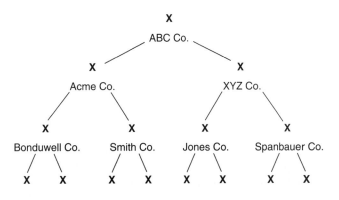

Figure 7-3
The Endless Chain

The endless chain method requires the use of referrals. That is, in making the next call, the salesperson can use a name from a previous interview. The referral will gain the salesperson more immediate acceptance from a prospect and diminish the chances of a quick refusal. Salespeople with referrals carry more credibility with them and feel more confident because they know more about the prospect and may already have been able to do some qualifying.

The prestige of a referral is not to be underestimated. Two sales representatives of equivalent expertise may call on the same prospect, but if one bears referrals from the prospect's acquaintances, this salesperson will have a greater chance for success. Prestige and credibility have a dramatic effect on the outcome of an interview, and a referral strengthens credibility. When a sales representative is recommended to a buyer, the salesperson can be assured that the interview will occur under favorable circumstances.

If possible, it helps if the salesperson can secure an introduction by email, letter, card, telephone, or luncheon meeting. A personal introduction, especially at a luncheon meeting, is perhaps the best means of referral, but it is difficult to set up. A telephone call may be easier to get and is probably as effective as a letter, because the caller's enthusiasm will be evident in his or her voice. Once you get the referral, it's not sufficient just to say "thank you" and leave. After calling the referral, report back to the person who gave it to you. Tell your referral source how things went, whether the person was interested, whether you closed a sale, or even whether there was no interest. Reporting back to the source of the referral keeps that person in the loop and increases the chances of receiving yet others from them.[8]

Using the endless chain method, salespeople may eventually build their own "nest" of prospects. *Nest prospecting* means prospecting and selling within a group until the salesperson is sufficiently well known in that group to be considered its own sales representative. An insurance salesperson, for example, might become known as the agent for all the dentists in a town. Nests may be composed of any people with a common set of interests: the employees of a store or plant; people in the same business (e.g., building contractors, store owners, and service station operators); people in the same profession (e.g., druggists, doctors, lawyers, teachers, and accountants); or members of the same social, civic, or religious group.

As might be expected with the rapid development of technology, "social networking" software exists for discovering referrals. A sales rep, for example, might struggle to get in the door at A-Plus Client, Inc., but every time he or she approaches them, all they get is a "Thanks, but no thanks." Then the rep discovers that Sally in accounting went to college with the CFO. Had this been known earlier, the deal might have been closed. "Selling through relationships is a thousand times more effective than cold-calling," according to Boston-based Contact Network Corporation, a maker of software that collects data about your company's "social network" to expand the salesperson's circle of potential customers. Contact Network's software does its job by scanning a firm's email logs, contact databases, and online resumes. When the name of a prospect is keyed into the software's search engine, a list of people who know someone at that company appears on the screen. The salesperson can then email colleagues to get the low-down and reference for the company before calling.[9]

7-4c Centers of Influence

centers of influence
People who, because of their position, responsibility, accomplishment, and personality, exercise more than ordinary influence and can direct salespeople to prospects.

Centers of influence are people who, because of their position, responsibility, accomplishment, and personality, exercise more than ordinary influence. They are opinion leaders, with their influence radiating in all directions like the spokes of a wheel. Research has demonstrated that the adoption of a product or service first requires trial by an innovative group of firms or individuals who relate their experiences to others. This has been found to be true for physicians in the adoption of new drugs and for farmers in trying new seed hybrids. In business, centers of influence are also important. It is critical to secure adoption by an innovative firm so that others may see the new product in operation. Once this occurs, rapid adoption usually follows.

Centers of influence may be found in four areas: the business, social, political, and religious realms. A few places to find these key people are trade association meetings, trade shows, or any business-related social event. They may be someone who is well respected because of financial expertise—a bank officer usually has prestige and contacts with businesspeople, borrowers, and depositors. An owner of a business employing many workers would also fall into this category. Prominent accountants, attorneys, and consultants constitute additional business centers of influence.

An office-furniture salesperson can use centers of influence by cultivating the managers of large office buildings, who tell the salesperson what firms are moving in or out. Chances are the firms will need new furniture. CPAs are centers of influence for financial sales reps. Calling them, rather than potential clients themselves, yields many more referrals. Centers evolving from social position include officers in the local country club; members of local school boards, hospitals, and charities; and people with old, respected family names. Those involved in church affairs—ministers, rabbis, priests, and presidents of church clubs—represent religious centers of influence. Politicians also are not to be ignored as centers of influence.

A referral from a center of influence is especially effective because of the authority it carries. The principle of a "power lead" operates here. When the name of the president of a company is employed in selling to a subordinate in the organization, leverage is obviously increased. Similarly, referral by the president of the local bar association is sure to carry much weight with a younger, less established attorney in the community.

Be sure to stay on their minds. If you find an article that a center of influence might enjoy, send it. Send them something every month as a reminder; a notepad with your name and picture on it that sits on their desk acts as a constant reminder. Send them leads. That way, reciprocity on their part is impelled. Send a handwritten thank-you note whenever you receive a lead from them, regardless of whether it ends in a sale.[10]

7-4d Noncompeting Sales Personnel

Salespeople for noncompeting products are an excellent source for getting prospect names. These sales representatives are likely to have information on new business openings, changes in personnel, and other kinds of valuable facts. Noncompeting sales personnel can strike agreements to exchange information, the operating principle being "you scratch my back, and I'll scratch yours." A computer salesperson, for example, can agree to exchange intelligence with a copying machine representative. A salesperson stocking detergent can learn much from salespeople stocking the panty hose display at the same supermarket. Even without a formal arrangement for exchanging information, the observant sales representative can learn much by listening to other salespeople waiting in the reception room of the purchasing agent's office. Whenever and wherever you meet a noncompeting sales representative, the opportunity for prospecting should not be lost.

7-4e Cold-Calling

cold-calling
Method of prospecting in which the salesperson goes door to door, office to office, or factory to factory searching for potential clients face-to-face.

At one large business machine company, beginning salespeople are given a small fax machine and told to go prospecting office to office. This describes the **cold-calling** method of prospecting. A sales representative identifies a geographic area where prospects are likely to be found and starts going door to door, office to office, or factory to factory.

Certainly cold-calling has worked effectively for the securities firm Edward D. Jones & Company. Jones forgoes big-city offices, instead choosing sites such as Spearfish, South Dakota; Whitefish, Montana; and Festus, Missouri. The firm assigns only one broker to an office, so he or she has to hustle hard to succeed. It also places its sales representatives in towns where they have not grown up, finding it easier for the rep to become known as a financial expert if he or she is not remembered there as a schoolchild. To ensure that the broker does not sit in an office waiting for business to come his or her way, Jones does not even give reps an office until they have made a thousand cold-calls on local residents.[11]

Quite often, however, the cold-call will result in an appointment at a later date. In this respect, the cold-call may be more effective than a phone call, because it is easier to turn down a salesperson over the phone than in person. As one sales rep for a commercial real estate firm indicates, you learn a lot by just chatting with the receptionist in person, rather than over the phone, such as how long the company has been in the office, how well the employees like the setup, whether there's talk of moving to new space because it's a tiny office where employees are tripping all over one another. Also, this sales rep comes away with the name of the decision maker and, when he calls on the phone, he's remembered because of his visit.[12] But there is no question that cold-calling is time-consuming; calling over the phone can cover a lot more ground than canvassing in the same amount of time. Considerable time may also be spent in qualifying, since the sales representative typically cold-calls with little if any information about prospects.

For maximum success, the salesperson should be selective in choosing areas for cold-calling. The insurance representative should select a subdivision with moderate to expensive homes, since calling in poorer areas is unlikely to result in many sales. The copier sales representative should call in an area with many business offices, especially large ones where multiple orders are likely. For salespeople with more specialized products, it may be advisable to secure a list first. A representative selling to air-conditioning contractors, for example, might look in the yellow pages to identify those to be canvassed.

At the end of a cold-call, the salesperson should be sure to leave a business card. The more cards that are given out, the more sales will result. Some people who are not interested during the cold-call might develop interest later. It is also important to ask for referrals when cold-calling, as this adds to the total number of leads generated.

Cold-calling is not effective in the sale of all products and services. It is valuable with tangible consumer items in general use (such as encyclopedias and cutlery) and in industrial selling for standard items such as copiers, calculators, and faxes. But for the sale of specialized products, cold-calling may be an inefficient use of time. A sales representative selling spindle-forming machinery to the woodworking industry, for example, will not find cold-calling very productive.

7-4f Observation

Prospecting by personal observation basically involves looking around for the type of prospects needed. A salesperson selling roofing, for example, can drive down the street looking for homes with missing shingles. A real estate agent can drive around looking for homes with "For Sale by Owner" signs in the front yard. Even when not intentionally looking for prospects, salespeople should be alert for any information they might overhear in conversations. An insurance salesperson, for example, should be alert to mentions of weddings, births, and other sales opportunities. To maximize the chances of obtaining such information, sales representatives can frequently change the places where they eat, shop, and have their hair cut.

One consultant has even added high tech to observation prospecting. Driving in his car, noticing substantial companies in office towers, he plugs his IBM notebook PC into his car's cigarette lighter and his cellular phone into the computer and starts faxing letters to the training department of each business he passes. He waits a few minutes and then follows up with a phone call. "I'm in my car next to your office," he says, "and I was wondering if I could stop by and introduce myself." In one instance, the training director walked downstairs to see the salesperson for himself. In most, he arouses enough curiosity to secure a subsequent appointment.

Some salespeople enlarge on the observation technique by using sales associates or "bird dogs," as they are sometimes called. An automobile salesperson might make arrangements with service station personnel or car insurance salespeople to provide leads in return for cash bonuses. Some companies even use junior sales representatives to cold-call areas and set up appointments for senior salespeople.

Because they are in a position to recognize when equipment needs replacement, company service personnel are excellent bird dogs. They will also be able to do some advance qualifying for the salesperson, because they will have a good idea of the customer's need and financial ability and may also know who in the organization should be contacted. One Des Moines office-supplies sales rep says, "My personal sales force is made up of about 20 people." This includes data-processing service engineers, office-machine repair personnel, and vending-machine service people. Smart salespeople take pains to be on good terms with service people.

7-4g Lists and Directories

When salespeople take over a territory, their company usually provides them with a list of customers. Although this represents a valuable starting point, the sales representative should be aware of other sources: newspapers, trade publications, and various commercial lists and directories.

Newspapers provide a wealth of leads. Just think of the features that regularly appear in local newspapers:

- Births
- Weddings and engagements
- Society news
- Changes in management and promotions
- New arrivals in town
- New businesses starting up
- Real estate information
- Building plans and permits issued
- Community events and participants

All of these may signal the need for products and services. The start of a new business provides opportunities for the sale of office equipment, fixtures, and furniture. A birth or wedding probably indicates a need for increased insurance. The award of building contracts provides leads for construction-equipment salespeople. The leads generated from the newspaper are limitless. Looking for such leads can be outsourced also. Robert Smith, the owner of Robert Smith and Associates, a publicity and venture-capital-raising firm in Rockford, Illinois, recently discovered a way to pinpoint customers who would need his services. He uses a media clippings service, CyberAlert.com, to receive emails of articles that contain his chosen key words: "IPO" and "raising capital funding." Smith takes those stories (about 45 a day), locates the company's CEO through a search engine, faxes an introductory letter, and often hears back the same day. "I have a letter that's headlined, 'Get up to $40 million in funding.' Then the first line says, 'I read about you in *X* publication.' And I offer a free consultation with the first letter. I've had calls back within 10 minutes of faxing a letter," Smith says. Since using this tactic, Smith's sales have shot up from one deal a quarter to two deals a month, averaging $50,000 apiece—all for a service that costs him $19.99 a month.[13]

Commercially available directories and lists, whether printed or on the Internet, represent yet another source of prospect information. The telephone directory, both regular and classified, furnishes many leads. Because it is organized by product or service, the classified section is particularly valuable to the salesperson. It also lends itself to creative use. For salespeople interested in new businesses, a comparison of two consecutive years' phone books reveals much. The city directory is valuable in providing a list of businesses and individuals by address on a street-by-street basis. A state industrial directory supplies a listing of industrial firms within a state by geographic area, by product or service, and in alphabetical order. Specialized lists are also available for purchase from commercial reporting organizations. In the paper industry, for instance, *Walden's Book of Manufacturers* lists all manufacturers of paper and flexible packaging.

It also is relatively easy and inexpensive to secure highly selective computer-generated lists. Donnelley Marketing in Oak Brook, Illinois, maintains one of the largest consumer databases in the country—85 million names, complete with extensive profiles on buying habits and more. An example of what can be accomplished with such lists is illustrated by a recent promotion sponsored by the Milwaukee division of Ford Motor Company. Ford mailed Taurus test-drive invitations to 10,000 area drivers, offering to deliver the cars to their front doors, if necessary, and pick them up later. The upscale invitees had to meet six qualifications: residency in the Milwaukee metropolitan area; 35 to 55 years of age; a minimum household income of $60,000; employment as a doctor, lawyer, high-level executive, or business owner; driver of a 2- to 4-year-old car; and married. R. L. Polk & Company of Taylor, Michigan, generated the list from its Totalist file, which profiles 90 million households nationwide.[14]

Donnelley will even take a file of 200 of a company's customer phone numbers and

- Analyze their customers.
- Tell how many new prospects there are in the geographic area of your choice.
- Generate a $99 report.

7-4h Direct Mail

Prospecting by direct mail can be an effective method. Prospects are mailed a letter inviting a reply if they are interested in the product or service described. Though response rates are typically low, direct mail can still be valuable. Even if only one or two sales are made for every hundred letters mailed, the costs are such that direct mail can be profitable, particularly for expensive products or services.

Response rates will never be high with direct mail, but several methods exist for improving the percentage of returns. When composing a letter or postcard, it is best to personalize it. Identifying the prospect by name is a good idea, because no one likes to receive mail addressed to "Resident" or "Occupant." Market research among personal computer buyers shows that between 60 and 80 percent of them will read a letter addressed to them by name (the range being due to how much the letter looks typed, at the top end, or obviously word-processed, at the lower end), whereas less than 40 percent will read one addressed to them by title, and only about 20 percent will read one addressed to the company. Personally signing the closing of the letter is helpful, and, if numbers permit, writing postcards by hand is desirable. Specializing the message for a particular type of recipient helps. When mailing to newlyweds (see Figure 7-4), for example, the letter might begin, "May we see you after you return from your honeymoon, please?" Note that immediately thereafter, the writer "fires the biggest gun first." That is, without delay the sales rep gets into the typical needs young clients might have about life insurance and its benefits.

It is a good idea to include a "P.S." at the end of the letter. That little addendum is the most frequently read part of a letter, according to several industry surveys. You should put your most important selling point or notice of a timed offer there. In fact, the time limit on any offer need not be mentioned anywhere else in the letter. A major

---

THE EVERLIVE INSURANCE COMPANY

John G. Smith, Special Agent
January 2, 2006

Mr. Mark Anderson
666 Main Street
Rockford, IL 66660

Dear Mr. Anderson:

I understand that you and Pamela Larsen recently became engaged.

Many young couples I've spoken with have told me that I was able to answer their questions about life insurance, questions such as: "Do we really need life insurance?," "How does it work?," "How much does it cost?," and "Will the money be refunded if I live beyond age 65?" I've also found that many couples hesitate to ask about life insurance for fear an agent will try to sell them something they don't understand, can't afford, or don't know if they want it.

Whenever I visit an engaged couple, I do four things: I show them how life insurance works; I answer any questions they may have; I explain how they can buy some life insurance now, if they're interested; and I explain how they can receive up to $5.00 or more at age 65 for each $1.00 invested.

When you do buy life insurance, Mr. Anderson, you'll be investing money you earned by hard work. Doesn't it make sense to find out as much as you can about insurance now, so that when you do decide to buy some you'll make a well-informed decision? I hope your answer is yes.

Fill out the enclosed card to receive a free appointment calendar for 2006 and schedule an appointment for us to meet and decide if I can be of any service to you and Ms. Larsen.

Sincerely,

John G. Smith

P.S. Rates are really attractive for those under 25. Now is the time to purchase insurance while it still is cheap!

Figure 7-4
Sample Prospecting Letter

purpose of a sales letter is to get the reader to do something, no matter how small a step it is. Some ask for an immediate order, but big-ticket and complex items often ask the reader to send for more information or to authorize a call by a sales representative.

Try to persuade the reader to take immediate action. Too often, people who read sales letters put them away so they can act on them later, and then they never get back to them. So you need to convince readers to act immediately. Guarantees of a delivery date, discounts for orders placed by a certain date, prizes or special offers to the first group to respond, a free trial, an unconditional guarantee, or a no-strings-attached request card have all proved successful.

A sample letter incorporating some of the preceding suggestions is presented here. Would you expect the techniques to increase the rate of return?

Repetition and follow-up procedures increase the rate of response. Some authorities recommend at least two mailings to each prospect. With the large amount of commercial mail received by most people, multiple mailings may be required before the message has an impact. Follow-up with other methods helps. A letter or postcard makes an excellent preconditioner for follow-up contact by telephone or in person.

contact management software
Software that facilitates keeping track of potential and current customers, including their purchase history.

Of course, these days the direct mail process is easily automated with the ubiquitous **contact management software** available, such as *ACT!*, *Telemagic*, and *Goldmine*. (A demo for ACT software can be seen at www.act.com/products/2005/demo/?campaign=h_cta1.) Templates can be designed for each target market (and even personalized for individual customers) and addresses mail merged, so that letters are printed, including the envelopes, and mailed in quantities that would have taken days or months 20 years ago. It is also possible to substitute faxes for letters these days. In a fraction of the time it takes to mail out prospecting letters, contact management software allows the salesperson to transmit "broadcast" fax over computer modems. In composing the fax, all of the rules regarding writing a prospecting letter also applies. It is important to have the specific fax number of the desired prospect. The Telephone Consumer Protection Act of 1991 (TCPA) and Federal Communications Commission (FCC) rules prohibit sending unsolicited advertisements, also known as *junk faxes,* to a fax machine. This prohibition applies to fax machines at both businesses and residences. An *unsolicited advertisement* is defined as "any material advertising the commercial availability or quality of any property, goods, or services which is transmitted to any person without that person's prior express invitation or permission."[15]

7-4i Advertising

Many large companies make extensive use of advertising to develop prospects for their sales forces. A coupon may be provided at the bottom of a magazine ad for the reader to mail in and receive information. Industrial trade magazines usually include a section in the back where the reader can check a box to receive more information from the advertiser. The "bingo" card at the back of the magazine will often include a phone number instead of a return mail address. When the number is dialed, a user follows a series of voice prompts a voice mail system. The caller can select one or more documents or a complete catalogue to be mailed. A caller can also be prompted for his or her fax number and the requested document sent within minutes.

Although advertising can generate many leads, it may take considerable time for salespeople to qualify them. One example of a qualifying procedure is that of Micro Motion, a $200 million company based in Boulder, Colorado. Leads are generated from trade publication advertisements, direct mail campaigns aimed at purchasing managers, and trade shows in such target industries as chemicals, oil, and pharmaceuticals. These leads are followed up with a personalized letter from Micro Motion's director of marketing and a questionnaire asking for information on the respondent's purchasing authority, time frame, and budget. Letting people reply themselves proves their qualifications. If a prospect asked for information and was sent a questionnaire, but didn't return it, why would a salesperson be given that lead? Upon receiving the returned questionnaires, answers are categorized into leads by interest level. Prospects who are very interested in purchasing a Micro Motion product, or who request more information, are categorized as "hot." All hot leads are sent back and forwarded to the appropriate salesperson.[16] Last year the program spurred a 5 percent increase in sales, or about $180,000 in additional revenue.

7-4j Seminars

Long used in the sales of intangibles such as insurance and securities, seminars are used by more and more companies for prospecting. Without question, they have a number of advantages: They maximize time by presenting to more than just one prospect, there is a guaranteed amount of time for a presentation, there is the possibility of attracting some prospects who are difficult to see by personal appointment, and they come prequalified (i.e., if they come, they're interested). A seminar also can bring together prospects and satisfied customers.

The best site to choose to maximize attendance is usually a neutral one, such as a hotel, restaurant, or college. Having a seminar at a company's office, for example, will deter many prospects from attending. Also, offering the seminar on two consecutive days increases the number who will attend; those who are unable to attend one day might the next. The best way to get prospective customers to attend is by using a 3-step approach of direct mail, phone follow-up, and last-minute reminder:

1. Mail out written invitations, with postpaid return response cards enclosed.
2. After allowing sufficient time for response, follow up with telephone calls, asking if the invitations were received. To those who respond that they have not received the invitation, the phone call provides the salesperson with a chance to solicit their attendance with an explanation of the benefits of attending. If they say they aren't interested, the salesperson has one more chance to enumerate seminar benefits.
3. On the day before the seminar, the seminar holder can call prospects who have expressed an interest in attending and remind them of the date and time.

The sales presentation at the seminar should be professional, with high-quality audiovisual aids and eye-catching demonstrations. If there are no more than 15 to 20 people in attendance, asking each attendee what he or she wants to learn from the seminar will optimize attention by enabling the salesperson to present benefits from their viewpoint. Writing them down on a chalkboard or an overhead reinforces this. Inviting satisfied and enthusiastic customers to share their experiences at the seminar provides effective endorsement of the salesperson's product or service. Once the formal presentation is finished, refreshments can be served, giving the salesperson time to talk personally to as many attendees as possible.[17]

At this juncture, it is critical to get attendees' names and addresses. One way is to do a drawing for a free book, video, or cassette, asking attendees to simply submit their business cards. Another approach is to have everyone complete a brief questionnaire.

Some companies have brought high tech to the seminar idea with videoconferencing. Zimmer, Inc., a medical equipment manufacturer, recently demonstrated its new arthroscopic instruments in a delicate knee operation witnessed by 1,000 orthopedic surgeons at 26 videoconference sites throughout the country. In addition to broadcasting the surgery, Zimmer produced a 3-hour program on the latest advances in diagnosis and surgical techniques and conducted local workshops at each site.

7-4k Telemarketing

There are many forms and applications of telemarketing. The most inclusive categorization is to differentiate between **inbound telemarketing** and **outbound telemarketing.** As the terms imply, in inbound telemarketing the prospect calls the company; in outbound telemarketing, the salesperson contacts the prospect. There are many advantages to adding telemarketing to the marketing mix. On the business-to-business side, with the cost of a field sales call rising steadily, telemarketing can be a cost-effective alternative. In some cases, it can be used to replace face-to-face selling on smaller accounts. In others, telemarketers qualify leads before handing them off to field salespeople. In both business-to-business and direct-to-consumer marketing, a telephone call is more attention-getting than a direct mail piece. Also, it provides a faster response than the mail, and it is more certain: You not only know that the call was received, but you also know *when* it was received. Telemarketing can be used for many purposes. Among them are generating and qualifying leads, providing service to existing customers, managing and screening inquiries, setting appointments, announcing new products, cross-selling or upgrading existing customers, building a database, taking reservations, and making direct sales.[18]

For example, as a marketing agent for insurance companies, National Marketing Systems (NMS) has two functions. First, it recruits agents to sell insurance for the companies with which it is affiliated. Then, it supports those agents by giving them information about the insurance companies and their products plus names of prospects. NMS had been recruiting agents by using a combination of direct mail, ads in industry publications, and postcard decks. Recently, the company decided to experiment with telemarketing, and the results have been dramatic. "The cost-per-contact to communicate with agents is substantially less," says the president and CEO of the Albany, Georgia, company. Using telemarketing, the cost-per-agent-contact is about $6.50. That compares with about $20 per contact using direct mail, $30 per contact for ads in industry magazines, and $35 per contact with a postcard deck. With telemarketing, "the return is much better, and the quality of agents is higher."[19]

The key to successful inbound telemarketing is the use of mass media advertising, direct mail, and other promotional activities to stimulate calls from prospects and customers. By including a toll-free 800 number in its promotional material, a company encourages consumers and business prospects to call for added information or to place orders. If the order is not placed, sales leads can be followed up by either additional telemarketing sales personnel or field sales representatives.

There are many examples of companies that use inbound telemarketing effectively. The travel industry is replete with examples. Airlines, hotel and motel chains, rental car companies, and other travel services have used inbound telemarketing to stimulate reservations. Toll-free phone numbers are featured prominently in travel advertising, encouraging customers to call for information and to make reservations.

The second major use of inbound telemarketing is customer service. Buyers are encouraged to call with requests for product information, suggestions, and complaints. Not only will inbound telemarketing help a firm process customers' orders quickly and improve customer service but telemarketers can also take further advantage of a customer's call to cross-sell additional products and services. For ex-

inbound telemarketing
The prospect calls the company.

outbound telemarketing
The company calls the prospect.

ample, when a customer calls one of AT&T's consumer market sales centers to obtain credit for a wrong number or to correct another problem, the customer service representative is able to examine the caller's records and suggest "Reach Out America" or some other service plan appropriate for that customer.

Outbound telemarketing is the other major approach used. This involves initially contacting customers through an outbound telephone call. Many successful direct marketers have combined two forms of communication. A direct mail piece, for example, sent prior to a telephone call increases the customer's receptivity to a follow-up phone call and provides a frame of reference for the call.

Salesnet, a service bureau that specializes in telemarketing, has mounted an extensive outbound telemarketing campaign for Avis. After first purchasing mailing lists and consulting with Avis to identify the profile of companies most likely to be interested in leasing, Salesnet puts together an effective sales approach. This accomplished, Salesnet telephone operators, using computer-dialed telephones, phone prospects and follow verbatim the sales approach that appears in front of them on their CRTs. The results have been very satisfactory. Not only has valuable sales force time been saved but more appointments have also been made with higher-echelon executives. Given leads for qualified prospects who are already sensitive to Avis offerings, Avis salespeople find that the time it takes to close a sale has been reduced by 30 days.[20] Avis's findings parallel those of other companies using sophisticated telemarketing systems. With a solid telemarketing program, all leads can be worked through the initial qualification and need-analysis stages at a fraction of the cost of field sales lead qualification. And *all* leads are followed up, not just the few intuitively appealing to the field sales rep.

MCI, the long-distance phone company, has taken telemarketing one step further by scheduling the field sales force's personal appointments. On a daily basis, regional field sales managers supply the telemarketing group with time availabilities when salespeople are not scheduled. When a telemarketer comes across a good business prospect in Chicago, for example, the computer matches the prospect's zip code with the correct salesperson's territory. The prospect is then told that the salesperson can stop by for a visit at, say, 10 A.M. next Thursday. When the salesperson checks the automated call schedule later, he or she finds the scheduled calls.

The most advanced forms of telemarketing are found in business-to-business applications that involve total account management. This form of telemarketing involves consultative selling in the same way as field sales. A number of large companies, such as A.B. Dick, IBM, 3M, Xerox, and Massey-Ferguson, provide full account services to small accounts through telemarketing. Massey-Ferguson, a giant producer of farm and industrial machinery, instituted telemarketing to serve 600 low-volume dealers. Sales analysis had revealed that these 600 dealers accounted for only 10 percent of Massey-Ferguson's sales, but the costs of servicing them were almost identical to those of a high-volume dealer. In addition to cost savings, Massey-Ferguson has been able to increase the number of contacts with its smaller dealers, to improve the quality of contacts, and to provide these dealers with faster responses to inquiries and requests.

Even in the absence of a systematic telemarketing operation on the part of their companies, salespeople should still make extensive use of the telephone in their prospecting. It has tremendous reach, saving much time and legwork. It is immediate; it gets the message across quickly; and, unlike direct mail, the sales representative can answer objections and set up appointments.

Perhaps the greatest advantage of the telephone in prospecting is the speed with which calls can be made. It is realistic, even in professional selling, to make 50 calls in a day (compared with perhaps 300 face-to-face cold-calls in a year). Moreover, as a means of making mass contacts, it is significantly more successful than mailings. The conventional wisdom is that the phone is 10 times more productive than mailings.[21] The biggest disadvantage of the telephone is that compared with a personal visit, it is more difficult to be persuasive with only your disembodied voice to work with. For this reason, many (perhaps most) sales professionals find using the phone awkward. Even the most experienced reps find it daunting to face a cold telephone and the need to make a half-dozen appointments.

The Internet makes call centers more important than ever. Customers expect a company's website to list a toll-free telephone number. And they expect a company that is sufficiently up-to-date technologically to have a website to have an equally up-to-date call center with well-trained telephone sales representatives. Voice over IP technology will allow reps to talk with prospects directly while both are online, forgoing text-based chat.

7-4l High-Tech Prospecting

Earlier, we alluded to how technology has transformed prospecting. CD-ROMs are helping marketers reduce the cost of personal sales while also making such calls more valuable. What makes CDs especially attractive to marketers is their ability to personalize—users can input data and receive a calculation, do competitive comparisons, cost justify, plan, or receive advisement on the spot if a modem is available to call the sender. Disks permit the customer to design the message through the use of simple menus. With a disk, customers choose the price, range, color, design, performance, and other special features they want to see, and they can often input data and receive calculations, plans, or advice back. Moreover, a demo that includes color, animation, and music is more memorable than a printed presentation. For example, a recent CD promotion mailed to 5,000 senior executives generated a 10 percent response rate. A subsequent survey of recipients indicated that 85 percent played the demo and 60 percent spent more than 5 minutes reviewing it. A demo CD has a greater impact than print; in addition, the cost of producing and distributing a demo CD is competitive. The cost of paper continues to rise, while that of CDs is falling. The postage for a demo disk is significantly less than that for sending a comparable amount of printed information. A significant further advantage of diskettes over print is the prospect's ability to order the product directly from the seller over the phone, using on-disk software and a modem.

Citicorp, in selling its *Global Report* to financial information users, cut the costs of generating leads 90 percent. Originally, it sent out a direct mail piece and followed it with presentations by salespeople; later, Citicorp replaced that method with a letter offering a preview CD. When a prospect asked for the CD, a telemarketer made an appointment for a phone interview by a salesperson. The salesperson walked the prospect through the demo disk, stressed certain advantages, pointed out features that might not be noticed, and answered questions. With the development of the Internet, especially with broadband connections becoming more prevalent, steaming video can substitute for a CD without the costs of CD duplication.

Another high-tech tool is email.[22] Over the last few years, targeted email promotions have grown enormously. An effective email promotion drives traffic and often generates sales. To be effective, email promotion needs to be targeted to a specific, well-defined group of prospects. Promotions for products and services with broad appeal, such as modems or Internet service providers (ISPs), are harder to execute profitably than those with a more focused market, such as small business inventory software or horror-movie posters.

The best email addresses come from existing prospects, customers, and web visitors. Those people are already qualified. They know your company and, if they volunteer to give you their email addresses, they want to hear more from you. Building an email list is the most effective way to get people to return to your site after they've visited it. It is also the cheapest. Just put a sign-up form in a prominent location on your site. Ask visitors to provide their email addresses if they'd like free news about additions to your site. Then send messages when you add or change your site or your products. In addition to building your own lists, you can rent them. Rented email lists can succeed for you if you watch for two key factors. Entries can be selected by employee size, sales volume, job title, one email per company or all emails per company, type of business, credit rating, and more. It is advisable to use only "opt-in" lists, those made up of people so interested in a topic that they have explicitly *asked* to receive email from strangers. Second, double-check the list topic to make sure that it matches your category of product or service exactly.

A high-tech prospecting opportunity causing a great deal of interest among businesses is the Internet. The Internet is the backbone of the information superhighway. The highway itself consists of mostly "land lines," telephone, cable, or fiber-optic wires. The information is virtually anything—voice messages, typed words, numbers, charts, catalogs, brochures, or even moving and talking pictures. One of the Internet's big advantages: Three fourths of all consumers and most businesses and nonprofits are already hooked up.

How can the Internet be useful to salespeople? Here's a short list of some of the ways being used right now:[23]

1. Targeting people searching for information about your product or service category for much less than traditional marketing. It allows users to get specific information on demand when they need it, any time, day or night.

2. Getting the names, addresses, and telephone numbers of qualified prospects.

3. Contacting these prospects.

4. Finding out something about the prospect's needs and plans. The Internet represents a low-cost way to build a database of people specifically interested in what your company sells. When your website works properly, people voluntarily provide your company with information about themselves in a format that's automatically added to your database for future communication. These are the people you really want to know: prospects or customers keenly interested in your company or in your product or service category. The truth is that some of the nation's most successful sites achieve excellent results with an annual investment of as little as $10,000.

5. Using the website as a relationship marketing tool by giving people such things as access to proprietary information or special pricing and services. Reward your best prospects for providing their names, addresses, and email addresses. After all, their willingness to reveal information about themselves can reduce your marketing costs. Scheduling conflicts can be minimized because the client can choose the time to go online and observe a presentation that employs the kind of multimedia techniques once reserved for elaborate dog-and-pony shows. A salesperson calling on a customer can tap into the company network for the latest information on products, applications, and prices.

6. Taking an order from the prospect and making sure it is filled promptly and correctly and at a lower cost. Office Depot, the largest office supply retailer on the Internet, has found that processing an order over the Internet costs less

than $1 per $100 of goods sold versus twice that for orders faxed into a customer service center. The cost impact of migrating customers to the web for service requests is even more dramatic. "The costs of an [800-number] service transaction is about ten dollars," says the chief technology officer for Traveler's Life and Annuity Insurance. "When this same transaction is processed over the web, it can be completed for about one-hundredth the cost."

Along with cost savings, the other benefit of shifting transactions to the web is freeing up sales reps from administrative tasks, like shipping catalogs or tracking orders, to concentrate on strategic selling activities. Dell Computer, for example, estimates that the introduction of its online Premier Pages for its corporate clients has reduced the average number of phone calls needed to complete a sale from three to one and a half. The focus on strategic selling also leads to a better customer experience as salespeople take a more consultative approach.[24]

7. **Capability of live chat.** Visit online superstore Technobrands.com, for example, and a coupon pops up offering an immediate discount. Click the coupon, and you're engaged in a live chat with a Technobrands sales rep. This kind of personal interaction pays off big, says Joel Skretvedt, the store's director of Internet operations. "Shoppers who chat are 13 percent more likely to buy something, and they spend an average of $60 more per transaction," he says. With Voice over Internet Protocol, telereps will be able to actually talk with customers, not just chat with text messages.[25]

As one example of optimal website usage, J. P. McHale Pest Management has as its goal to generate leads for metropolitan New York area business via a website. To make sure it attracted only those concerned about pests, the company created a pest-control information service and called it www.nopests.com. It hired editors and writers to create useful, authoritative articles on such topics as major pests in the region, how to combat them, and the use of integrated pest management. A "viewer" enables people to see four-color pictures of common household pests. The site includes an ask-the-expert section, a seasonal pest update, and details about a free home inspection. J. P. McHale mentions the site in its advertising and brochures and has registered it on major search engines. By following up with people who "asked the expert" or who requested a free inspection, the company made enough sales in four months to recover the $8,000 it spent to develop the site. Leads continue to come in at hardly any additional cost.[26]

7-4m Inactive Accounts

inactive ("orphan") accounts
People who have bought from the vendor before, but currently do not have an assigned salesperson.

Inactive ("orphan") accounts are often a good source of leads, any preconceptions against them by salespeople notwithstanding. They do not represent just discontented former customers. There may be a number of reasons, not all bad, why the customers stopped ordering. Often it is nothing more than that the previous salesperson in the territory stopped calling on them. Perhaps a new buyer took over, a new product line created different requirements, or new production techniques required changes from suppliers. Inactive accounts may be ready to begin reordering if the salesperson takes the time to call on them. In the insurance business, for example, there may be "orphan" accounts consisting of policy buyers not currently assigned to a salesperson. Another rep might call them for "free needs analysis" to update current financial requirements. Because they have already bought from the company, they likely already have a favorable attitude and are more likely to buy than "cold" contacts.

7-4n Trade Shows

Many companies rely on exhibits at trade shows to generate prospects. For example, companies who sell to the hospital industry can exhibit their wares at the annual meeting of the American Hospital Association. Trade exhibits have a number of advantages. Companies (especially small and new ones) can gain instant recognition with the large numbers of prospects who visit their booths and spot their products for the first time. As one exhibitor commented, "A trade exhibit gets your name out there right away as opposed to some of your other marketing options."[27] Especially advantageous is the fact that potential buyers can actually see the equipment in operation, which may not be true if the sales rep is working out of his or her car and visiting the prospect's office. Because the booths are usually staffed by members of the sales force, prospects can meet them in a setting that is less intimidating than a personal call. When the sales reps call later for an appointment, there is less apprehension among prospects because they have already met the caller.

7-5 The Preapproach

Formally, the **preapproach** includes all those activities that precede actual personal contact and that provide additional personal and business information about the prospect. It is difficult to distinguish when prospecting ends and the preapproach begins. Often they occur simultaneously. Basically, the preapproach seeks to obtain information in depth about prospects as individuals, as well as about their companies, along with any other factors likely to affect the sale. By completing a target market profile, the salesperson will have in mind a general picture of a prime prospect. From prospecting activities, the salesperson will gather still more facts. However, the picture may yet be incomplete, and this constitutes the need for the preapproach.

preapproach
All those activities that precede actual personal contact and that provide additional personal and business information about the prospect.

7-5a Preapproach to the Individual Customer

An important rule of communication is that the process is facilitated if both participants know something about one another. From your own experience, you know how difficult it is to meet people for the first time when you know absolutely nothing about them. It is not nearly so uncomfortable talking with a stranger if you know something beforehand about his or her occupation, friends, hobbies, and family. The preapproach is intended to facilitate communication for salespeople. The more they know about the prospect, the better off they are.

In a classic study, Franklin Evans demonstrated that similarity between an insurance salesperson and prospect increased the likelihood of a sale. Evans studied successful and unsuccessful sales calls and concluded that the successful ones were much more likely to be characterized by similarity between buyer and seller. The successful percentage is consistently higher for dyads, or pairs, with the same characteristics than for dyads with differences. This is true for height, age, income, religion, politics, and even smoking habits.[28]

The implications of Evans's study are straightforward. Salespeople should find out as much as possible about the buyer before the interview takes place. Salespeople should take care to avoid points of difference between themselves and buyers. Commonality leads to likability, a critical factor to building a relationship. If prospects do not smoke, salespeople should avoid lighting a cigarette. If prospects are political conservatives, liberal sales representatives should steer clear of political discussions. By the same token, sales representatives should be sure to emphasize points of similarity. Research has demonstrated that persuasion is augmented if points of agreement are established early in the interview.[29]

Harvey Mackay, author of the *New York Times* best seller *Swim with the Sharks without Being Eaten Alive* and CEO of Mackay Envelope, credits his company's success in the highly undifferentiated envelope business to just one factor: "salesmanship—inspired, energized, superior salesmanship." Mackay has his salespeople meticulously collect information on their customers, including seemingly trivial facts, such as their hobbies, lifestyles, and special interests. No matter how seemingly trivial, this establishes the salesperson as an effective listener, according to Mackay. Effective listeners remember order dates and quality specifications. They are easier to talk with when there's a problem with a shipment. In short, effective listeners sell to more customers . . . and keep them longer.

For 30 years at Mackay, salespeople have been required to collect this kind of information on a questionnaire popularly referred to as the "Mackay 66" (because it has 66 questions). Salespeople complete one form for every customer. It lists all vital statistics, such as the contact's educational background, career history, family, special interests, and lifestyle. It is updated continually and studied to death at Mackay. The company's overriding goal is to know more about its customers than they know about themselves. For example, question 48 asks about the customer's vacation habits. Vacation choices say a lot about people. Is he the outdoors type who loves to white-water raft on the Colorado River or does he prefer to travel Europe and Japan by bus? Is she a tennis enthusiast who plans her vacation around major professional tournaments? How would that lover of the outdoors react to a book of photographs by Ansel Adams? What would the sightseeing type say on receiving an array of hard-to-get brochures about unusual and exotic tours? Imagine the reaction of that tennis buff as she reads the previews of Wimbledon and the U.S. Open that a salesperson sent her a few weeks before the events.[30] Besides talking with acquaintances of the prospect, the salesperson can pick up much preapproach information by being observant and by researching companies on the Internet.

7-5b Preapproach to the Organizational Customer

Preapproaching the customer organization involves gathering information over and above that already available from prospecting. Among the facts that might be obtained are facts about company operations. Sales representatives will be in a much better position to sell if they can answer the following questions regarding the customer company's operations:

1. To what market does the company sell?
2. What does the company make or sell?
3. What are its future plans?
4. What problems does it face?
5. What is its sales volume?
6. What is the quality of its product or service?
7. What materials are used in manufacturing?
8. How are products manufactured?

The sales representative must also understand company buying practices. Here are some important considerations:

1. Does the company order only from a single vendor or does it prefer multiple vendors?
2. Who are its current suppliers? Is the company satisfied with them? If not, why?

3. In what volume does the company buy? How often?
4. What are the contract termination dates?
5. What are the prices paid?
6. What is the company's credit rating?
7. Does the company practice reciprocity?

7-6 Getting the Most from Prospecting

Successful selling requires planned and organized prospecting. Failure to prospect or halfhearted efforts to do so will inevitably have an adverse effect on sales performance. The salesperson should always take care to maintain an adequate pool of prospects. As sales are closed, the maintenance of production requires the availability of enough qualified prospects to call on next. This necessitates careful planning and the maintenance of useful records.

7-6a Establishing a Plan

Successful sales representatives establish specific prospecting objectives and then make plans for their execution. Table 7-1 shows one such plan. Notice that the salesperson has established prospecting goals for each day of the week and, further, that these goals have been specified by method: direct mail, telephone, cold-calls, and referrals. In this way, the salesperson can assess prospecting performance on a daily, weekly, and monthly basis. Additionally, the very act of writing down a plan improves the likelihood of its being carried out.

It is advisable to set aside a specific time every day for prospecting. Many successful salespeople do their prospecting early in the morning, leaving the afternoon for interviews, while others prefer the afternoon for prospecting. Whatever the preference, the important thing is that it be done. Prospecting is based on the law of averages. The more regularly it is performed, the more prospects are found, and the better the odds of success.

7-6b Maintaining Records

After a prospect is identified, a prospect card should be prepared and placed in a prospect file, one of the most important files in the salesperson's office. Prospect cards should contain information on individuals, their companies, and other facts that might be important. These cards will prove invaluable when reviewed before

T a b l e **7-1** A Prospecting Plan

Daily Activities	Direct Mailings	Phone Calls (Cold)	Canvassing	Referrals (Follow-Up)
Quotas	Daily–20	Daily–10	Daily–5	Daily–2
Actual				
Monday	15	9	3	2
Tuesday	22	8	2	2
Wednesday	18	15	1	2
Thursday	19	10	6	2
Friday	21	10	4	1
Week's Total	95	52	16	9

each sales call. Imagine the prospect's reaction when the salesperson inquires about his or her spouse and children by name or when the salesperson refers to an incident that happened months ago. In both instances, the salesperson's image is likely to grow larger in the prospect's mind. For such facts, salespeople should not trust their memories. It is much easier to refer to a card such as the one illustrated in Figure 7-5.

A **tickler file** can help sales representatives remember when to approach customers. A small card file with 4″ × 6″ cards works well. There should be a section for each month, which should be divided into four weeks or by numbered tab (1 through 31). For each client or prospect there will be an index card on which the salesperson writes the client's name and contact date. As the salesperson plans contacts and follow-ups, he or she simply puts the card in the appropriate week or day. After talking with a customer, the salesperson writes notes on the prospect card and puts the tickler file card in the week of the next contact. There is a good reason to keep master files and tickler files separate. If a client calls, the salesperson has to quickly dig up information on the account. If that information is in alphabetical order in the master file, it is easy to locate. If it were attached to the tickler card and filed under a date somewhere in the future, it would be difficult to find unless the salesperson just happened to remember when he or she planned to talk to that person again.

A salesperson who has a personal computer can keep this information stored in one of the many software packages available to record prospect information. Among the capabilities of today's systems are providing easy access to customer and contact information; improving customer communications by automating letter-writing, faxing, emailing, and even dialing the telephone in telemarketing operations; rapidly generating many reports, including lead sources, closing ra-

tickler file
File maintained by week or month in which the sales rep can place the name of the prospect for follow-up activities.

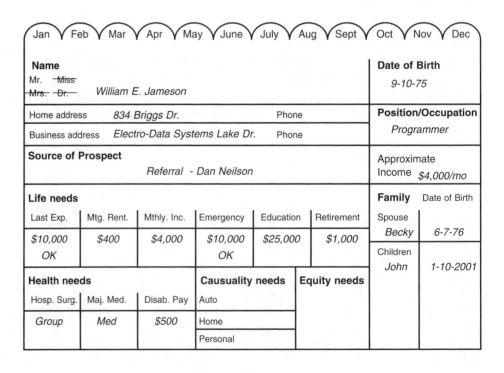

Figure 7-5
Sample Prospect Card

tios, and so forth; easily planning sales trips geographically; and keeping track of customer needs and buying schedules.[31] With contact management software, the sales rep can even set the tickler date and time to recontact a prospect, and the computer will automatically alert the sales rep to make the contact at the appropriate moment.

Among choices of software are *ACT!, Goldmine, Sharkware,* and *Telemagic.* The information contained on prospect cards or in the computer has an additional benefit: It eases the approach, the first occasion when salesperson and prospect make personal contact. During the approach, it is the sales representative's task to gain the attention and interest of the prospect. The information in prospect files provides material for formulating the approach.

VIDEO

Chapter Summary

Critical to successful selling, prospecting is the process of identifying potential buyers with the following:

1. A need for the product or service
2. The financial resources to pay for it
3. The authority to make a buying decision

In the absence of need, there is no point in calling on a prospect. Despite myths to the contrary, no salesperson is so skilled as to be able to sell something that a buyer does not need. Nor does it make sense to expend time on prospects who do not have the ability to pay for the product or service. Finally, sales interviews should be reserved for those who have the ability to make a buying decision or, at least, have an important influence on the final decision.

Prospecting must be performed persistently because of the law of averages. The painful reality for salespeople is that not everyone is going to buy their products. For every ten people, two may not have a need, three may not have enough money, and two may not be in a position to make a decision. So salespeople should do everything possible to maximize their chances of success. They should set aside some portion of each day for prospecting. They should seek out potential buyers with the greatest need and ability. And they should be sure to maintain accurate and complete prospecting records.

Given the wide variety of types of selling positions, there are literally thousands of prospecting methods, and technology has dramatically improved the effectiveness of all methods. Nonetheless, prospects are generally obtained from the following sources:

1. Acquaintances and friends
2. The endless chain
3. Centers of influence
4. Noncompeting sales personnel
5. Cold-calling
6. Observation
7. Lists and directories
8. Direct mail
9. Advertising
10. Seminars
11. Telemarketing
12. Inactive accounts
13. High-tech prospecting
14. Trade shows

Immediately following prospecting (or while prospecting is underway), the salesperson gathers preapproach information. Basically, the preapproach seeks to obtain in-depth information about prospects as individuals, about their company, and any other factors that can affect the sale. With regard to the individual, preapproach information can include facts about occupations, friends, hobbies, and families. Preapproach information about a company may include facts about company operations—e.g., markets, plans, and manufacturing processes—and buying practices—e.g., vendor relations, buying volume, and credit rating.

Chapter 7 concludes with a discussion of ways to get the most out of prospecting. This requires that the salesperson establish an organized plan for prospecting with numeric targets specified for each prospecting method. It also means that the salesperson should organize a filing system with useful information written on prospect cards or stored in the computer. This assists prospecting and also aids in the approach, the next step in the selling process.

Discussion Questions

1. What is prospecting?

2. Why is prospecting important to a salesperson's success?

3. How does one go about developing a list of acquaintances for prospecting purposes?

4. Describe the endless chain method of prospecting.

5. What is a center of influence? Name some typical ones.

6. Why are noncompetitive sales personnel a good source of prospects?

7. What are the advantages of cold-calling? What are the disadvantages?

8. How is observation used as a method of prospecting?

9. Name some valuable sources for lists and directories.

10. What are some rules for putting together a good prospecting letter? How can the response rate of a direct mail campaign be increased?

11. What are the advantages of prospecting by seminar?

12. Define telemarketing.

13. What is the importance of the preapproach?

14. What can the salesperson do to maximize prospecting success?

15. Explain some ways of doing high-tech prospecting.

16. What are the advantages of trade shows as a method of prospecting?

17. You have just accepted a position as campus sales representative for the Everlive Insurance Company. Establish a prospecting plan to begin your career.

18. Your roommate has just taken a job selling advertising for your college paper. The night before beginning, she inquires, "Where do I start?" What would you tell her?

19. Explain how you would begin qualifying prospects for buying a new home.

20. How would you qualify the following prospect for a life insurance policy?
    Age: 35
    Sex: Female
    Marital status: Recently married
    Dependents: One 12-year-old daughter from a previous marriage and a husband who works in a bank
    Education: Master's degree
    Occupation: Speech therapist in school system
    Approximate household income: $60,000 per year
    Residence: Owns house
    Health: Good

21. Differentiate between inbound and outbound telemarketing.

22. Describe methods for so-called high-tech prospecting.

23. What is the preapproach and why is it important?

24. Explain the potential of the Internet for prospecting.

25. Explain how technology has impacted prospecting

26. What is contact management software? Use links to the websites for ACT!, Goldmine, Sharkware, and Telemagic to illustrate your explanation.

Chapter Quiz

1. In personal selling, prospecting is the process of identifying potential buyers who have all of the following *except*
   a. need for the product or service.
   b. ability to pay for the product or service.
   c. current ownership of a competitive product or service.
   d. authority to buy the product or service.

2. Although salespeople put together a list of potential prospects, or names of individuals who might buy, it is estimated that 65 percent of all sales calls
   a. do not result in a product or service demonstration.
   b. are made on the wrong person.
   c. are made on individuals who do not need the product or service.
   d. result in additional visits because of lack of proper prospecting techniques.

3. An especially valuable method of prospecting is the endless chain, which involves the salesperson
   a. asking after each interview for names of other people who might be interested in the product or service.
   b. calling his or her friends and acquaintances.
   c. asking each person who makes a purchase for names of other businesses that need the product and have the ability to make a purchase.
   d. developing a list of people who, because of their position, responsibility, accomplishment, and personality, exercise more than ordinary influence on others around them.

4. An especially valuable method of prospecting is the center of influence, which involves the salesperson
   a. asking after each interview for names of other people who might be interested in the product or service.
   b. developing a list of prospects from his or her friends and acquaintances.
   c. asking each person who makes a purchase for names of other businesses that need the product and have the ability to make a purchase.
   d. developing a list of people who, because of their position, responsibility, accomplishment, and personality, exercise more than ordinary influence on others around them.

5. A real estate agent might drive around, looking for "for sale by owner" signs in front of houses. This method of prospecting would be classified as
   a. cold-calling.
   b. observation.
   c. noncompeting sales personnel.
   d. endless chain.

6. Although advertising can generate many leads,
   a. most do not have the authority to make a purchase.
   b. telemarketing can produce leads faster and cheaper.
   c. it may take considerable time for salespeople to qualify them.
   d. the cost per lead is more expensive than cold-calling by salespeople.

7. Perhaps the greatest advantage of the telephone in prospecting is
   a. the success of telemarketing versus face-to-face sales calls.
   b. the superior success of telemarketing versus cold-calling.
   c. the speed with which calls can be made.
   d. the ability to use bird dogging.

8. In terms of collecting email addresses of prospects, the best email addresses come from all of the following sources *except*
   a. advertising in the newspaper or magazines.
   b. current prospects.
   c. customers.
   d. web visitors.

9. _____ includes all those activities that precede actual personal contact and that provide additional personal and business information about the prospect.
   a. Prospecting
   b. The preapproach
   c. The approach
   d. The presentation plan

10. In the preapproach to the organizational customer, all of the following questions except one indicate facts the salesperson should obtain about a prospect's operation. Which question is the exception?
    a. To what market does the company sell?
    b. What does the company make or sell?
    c. What problems does the company face?
    d. What is their Morningstar fund rating?

 **Profile**

Role-Playing Exercise

For the products and services described in Chapter 6, prospect in your community for qualified customers and prepare a preapproach for each.

Web Exercise

Go to www.abii.com. What kinds of lists are available? What kind of information is offered? How detailed is the information?

Notes

1. Jacques Werth, "Closing Sales," www.highprobsell.com, 2004.
2. William A. O'Connel and William Keenan, Jr., "The Shape of Things to Come," *Sales & Marketing Management,* January 1990, pp. 36–41.
3. Marilyn Kennedy Melia, "The E-Volving Salesman," *Chicago Tribune,* June 11, 2000.
4. Kevin Delaney, "Business Software: Where Did the Buyers Go?" *Wall Street Journal,* December 19, 2003, p. B4.
5. Bruce Bolger, "The New Marketing," Sales Marketing Network at info-now.com, 2003.
6. "Channels by Industry," *Sales & Marketing Management,* December 1998.
7. S. Tamer Cavusgil, "Extending the Reach of E-Business Technology Continues to Change the Corporate Playing Field," *Marketing Management,* March/April 2002, pp. 24–29.
8. Debby Peters, "How to Close That Referral Circle," *Personal Selling Power,* January/February 1995.
9. "Leveraging Your Leads," *Sales & Marketing Management,* 2003.
10. Ginger Trumfio, "Cultivating Your Network," *Sales & Marketing Management,* January 1994, p. 57.
11. Sanford L. Jacobs, "To This Broker, Paris in Illinois, New York in Limbo," *Wall Street Journal,* June 12, 1996, p. 1.
12. Francy Blackwood, "The Arctic Circle of Calls," *Selling,* August 1992, pp. 18–20.
13. "Lead Generator," *Sales & Marketing Management,* June 2004.
14. Cathy Fitzpatrick and Lee Bergquist, "Direct Marketers Have Little Trouble Building Dossiers," *Milwaukee Sentinel,* June 18, 1991, p. 1A.
15. "Unwanted Faxes: What You Can Do," Federal Communications Commission, Consumer and Governmental Affairs Bureau, 2004.
16. "Channels by Industry," *Sales & Marketing Management,* December 1998.
17. Milt Grassell, "Selling by Seminar: Let the Prospects Do the Walking," *Personal Selling Power,* September 1994, p. 11.
18. Rayna Skolnik, "Call Center Overview," Sales Marketing Network at info-now.com, 2004.
19. Ibid.
20. Steven Mintz, "Sales Lead Specialists to the Rescue," *Sales & Marketing Management,* June 6, 1993, pp. 79–83.
21. David Mercer, *High-Level Selling,* Houston: Gulf Publishing, 2000, pp. 69, 90.
22. Vince Emery, "Driving Qualified Traffic to Your Web Site," Sales Marketing Network at info-now.com, 2004.
23. Philip Holmes, "Relationship Marketing via the Internet," Sales Marketing Network at info-now.com, 2004.
24. "Harnessing the Internet's Potential," *Sales & Marketing Management,* 2003.
25. "Don't Ask, Don't Telemarket?" *Sales & Marketing Management,* 2003.
26. Philip Holmes, "Relationship Marketing via the Internet," Sales Marketing Network at info-now.com, 2004
27. Bill Kelly, "Trade Show Tips and Travails," *Sales and Marketing Management,* July, 1991, 42–47
28. Franklin B. Evans, "Selling As a Dyadic Relationship—A New Approach," *American Behavioral Scientist* 6, May 1963, pp. 76–79.
29. Harvey B. Mackay, "Humanize Your Selling Strategy," *Harvard Business Review,* March–April 1988, pp. 36–47.
30. Ibid.
31. George Colombo and Leanne Benfield, "Sales Automation," Sales Marketing Network at info-now.com, 2004.

Case 7-1

Tom Tracy, a junior at Emory University, has just accepted a summer position with ACG, Automobile Club of Georgia. Tom is attending his first sales meeting, where the manager, Lisa Wolf, is explaining what she expects of the sales force.

Lisa: Now, I know you were told what is expected of you when you were hired, but there's no harm in going over it again. Besides, there are probably some things that need elaboration. So here goes. If you have any questions, go right ahead and ask. Your first responsibility is to sell membership in ACG. Each membership costs $50 . . .

Tom: How much commission will we receive from each sale?

Lisa: From each membership sold, you'll get a commission of 20 percent, or $10. That membership allows the person to get trip-planning services, free towing, reports on motel and gasoline availability, and, most important for you salespeople, the right to sell automobile insurance and life insurance at reduced rates. Now, these insurance plans will give you higher commission rates than the sale of the membership, with the dollar amount you receive depending on the specific policy sold.

Tom: So, in other words, the real objective is to sell the membership and then follow up by selling insurance.

Lisa: That's correct. Also, if you meet your quota on memberships and insurance policies, you will receive a substantial bonus.

Tom: How do we find potential buyers for ACG memberships?

Lisa: That's completely up to you. I will say this, however. Prospecting is crucial to your success. We've discovered in the past that for every 10 names you come up with, you'll get three interviews, and ultimately one sale.

Tom: Will we get reimbursed for expenses?

Lisa: Each week you'll get a check in the mail for $75.00. It's up to you to decide how to spend it.

Questions

1. On what target market should Tom concentrate?
2. How should he go about prospecting for members?

Case 7-2

Sonya Cox sells copiers for the SMC Corporation. SMC has managed to carve out a niche in the copier market by concentrating on small to medium-size accounts. SMC's machines can be purchased for between $1,000 and $15,000. If leased, the rent can be as low as $50 per month, depending on the length of the lease. In the course of planning calls for the following week, Sonya is reviewing the prospect cards in her file. Information on these accounts is as follows:

Dr. James T. Lipscomb. Dr. Lipscomb is a dentist in Tacoma, Washington. Dr. Lipscomb has been in practice five years, and his number of patients is growing rapidly. Currently, billing is handled by office help, who copy charges from ledger cards to invoices, which are then mailed. On the average, more than 1,000 invoices a month are mailed out, and one clerk's work is dedicated to this task.

Lennox Candles, Inc. Lennox employs more than 500 people in the manufacturing of decorative candles. Xerox already has many large machines installed with Lennox, but some of the smaller departments might have a need for copiers. Mr. John T. Henry is the purchasing agent responsible for placing orders, but the department heads would probably be responsible for actually deciding if a copier were needed. Lennox sales have been increasing over the past two years, but with a downturn forecasted for the economy, management is scheduling a decrease in production and is watching expenditures closely.

Scott T. Yakes. A recent graduate of the University of Washington Law School, Scott has established a practice in Seattle, Washington, where he specializes in family law—wills, house closings, and uncontested divorces. Scott's clients tend to come from low- and medium-income families, and business is increasing. Currently, Scott's one secretary is responsible for all office duties, including typing, filing, and billing.

Michael Condon. Michael Condon operates an accounting business in Yakima, Washington. Michael has been in business for 20 years and does the taxes for some of the largest businesses in town. Michael employs 10 CPAs and 5 office personnel. Michael himself is spending less time with the business as he nears retirement age. Michael's two sons, Bob and Ed, are taking increasing control of the business. Bob tends to be involved with the business, while Ed spends more time with community affairs. However, for any major decision, both Bob and Ed must consult with their father.

Questions

1. Which of these accounts represents qualified accounts? Why?
2. Which is the least qualified account? Why?

The Approach

Key Terms

screener
small talk
telephone track

Learning Objectives

Learning Objectives

After studying Chapter 8, you will understand:

- The best ways for gaining entry to the prospect's office
- Effective techniques for telephoning the prospect and selling the interview
- Proper sales etiquette

- How to make a good first impression with the client
- Ways for getting the prospect's attention at the beginning of the interview

The *approach* is the first time the salesperson and the prospect come into actual contact with one another. For this reason, many experts call it the most important 30 seconds in the selling process. At this time, salespeople must establish rapport and attract the prospect's attention. If they fail to do so, the rest of the presentation may well be for nothing. But it is not always that easy. Prospects may be thinking about getting a promotion, cutting departmental costs, or even playing golf later that afternoon. Yet the sales representative must somehow penetrate their train of thought and get them to focus on the salesperson's proposition. To solve this problem, numerous tactics have been developed, some of them showy and gimmicky and some even downright crude. In interactive selling, the basic way of gaining attention is by getting the prospect to participate in the opening. As we have said, nothing gains attention better than participation.

But before we get into some of these techniques for securing prospect attention, it is important to talk about arranging the face-to-face meeting between prospect and salesperson. There is no point in a sales representative's being the best "opener" around if he or she cannot get an appointment. The approach then consists of three steps: gaining entry, establishing rapport, and winning the prospect's attention once the face-to-face interview has begun.

8-1 Gaining Entry

Getting an appointment is easiest with an existing customer. At the other extreme is a first call. There are three basic ways for getting this initial interview: letter, telephone, and cold-call. Each has its advantages, disadvantages, and methods of application that improve effectiveness. Discussions of each method follow.

8-1a The Letter (or Email)

Compared with the telephone and cold-call, the letter (or email) is the least valuable means of gaining entry. It is the easiest to ignore or turn down. Because the salesperson is not present (or even on the telephone), the letter can quickly be thrown away. There is no guarantee that the letter even got to the right individual; a secretary may have pitched it as junk mail. To this end, the sales representative should address the letter to a specific individual, suggest some possible appointment dates and times, and then follow up with a phone call.

8-1b The Cold-Call

The primary decision that salespeople face with the cold-call is whether they are willing to trade the impact of a personal visit for the extra time expended. Although the advantages and disadvantages of the cold-call were discussed in Chapter 7,

"Successful Prospecting," one important matter not discussed is the necessity of getting past a number of subordinates—"buffers," so to speak—in order to see the decision maker. Inevitably, with a cold-call, the salesperson first has to see a subordinate, usually a secretary or receptionist. In some instances, junior executives may be an additional obstacle. However, surprise long-run benefits sometimes arise from talking with these subordinates.

First, stride purposefully and confidently to the receptionist's desk. Smile and make eye contact. All of these activities communicate confidence, honesty, and sincerity—a professional image, in other words. Have your business card ready, without losing eye contact and without fumbling for the card. Pause to provide the receptionist time to start listening. Present your card, introduce yourself, and speak slowly and clearly. Ask for assistance by suggesting, "Perhaps you can help me." These words give the receptionist a feeling of importance and control, and help build a friendship. Ask for the name of the person you need to speak with: "Could you tell me who is in charge of. . . ?" Be polite and patient; arrogance and aggressiveness can ruin your chances at this juncture. If you receive the name, ask if that person is currently available. If not, phone later to make an appointment; an immediate meeting is unlikely. If you get to see the prospect on the spot, without a prior appointment, be grateful for even 5 or 10 minutes. One of the biggest advantages of cold-calling is simply getting your foot in the door, so be satisfied with that. If the prospect is unavailable, find out when they will be. Ask if the secretary schedules their appointments. Ask about convenient times to call back. If not available, use this time to make inquiries about the prospect's business situation. Finally, thank the receptionist by name. This demonstrates your caring and that you do not regard the receptionist as merely an annoying gatekeeper, but an important person.[1] This will help the receptionist remember you, especially over other salespeople who are not as considerate.

One last word about cold-calling: Sometimes the salesperson has to accept a firm turndown and move on to the next call. Many companies have a policy of not receiving salespeople without appointments. If the sales representative did not know this before calling, then it is best to exit gracefully, taking time to leave a card, samples, or any promotional material. Too, it is important to follow up a call—even a negative one—by sending a letter thanking the prospect for their time and cooperation.

8-1c The Telephone

A salesperson's business use of the telephone has two primary purposes: (1) to make appointments with new prospects and current customers and (2) to take care of some routine contacts that do not require a personal visit. Our consideration here is to discuss the use of the telephone for making appointments with new prospects.

Many salespeople find the telephone awkward at first. Because it cuts them off visually from the prospect, it is hard to judge the prospect's reactions in the absence of nonverbal behavior. Salespeople will find it helpful to create a positive mental picture of the prospect before calling by imagining they are about to talk to a friend or acquaintance whom they especially like.

A cardinal principle when approaching new prospects on the telephone is that the sole objective of the phone call is to secure an appointment and not to sell, which is the job of the interview. The secret of effective telephone selling is to arouse interest and introduce the proposition without forcing a premature decision. With rare exceptions, attempts to use the telephone to conduct an interview—or any part of it—will be a disappointment and a waste.

8-2 The Telephone Track

The telephone approach (or **telephone track**) is organized so that certain standard phrases can be used in most any conversation. Yet, a "canned" approach—one used on every occasion—is not recommended. Some variation obviously will have to be made because of different products. But standard phrases that salespeople may select (and alter) to fit their own tastes and those of their prospects can be prepared.

The six steps of the telephone track follow. There is nothing magical about these steps. Leaving out one step will not necessarily eliminate getting an appointment, but they have proved generally effective in the hard test of field experience.

1. Precall planning and organization
2. Identifying yourself and your company
3. The lead-in statement
4. An interest-capturing statement
5. Stating purpose of call and asking for an appointment
6. Handling objections

8-2a Precall Planning and Organization

Before picking up the telephone and making the call, salespeople should ask themselves if all homework has been completed. There should be a list of prospects to call, giving each prospect's full name, address, and phone number. This material should be available from the preapproach activities described in Chapter 7. The full name is important because it is surprising how many times the request to speak with "Mr. Smith" is followed by a question like "Which Mr. Smith? R. B. or T. J.?" When the salesperson does not know the buyer's name, it is best to get it from a switchboard operator before being connected to a secretary. Ask the operator, "Who is in charge of. . . ?" and then let him or her connect you. That way, when a secretary answers, you can ask for the buyer by name, increasing the odds of talking to that individual. It is helpful if qualifying has already been completed prior to the phone call; otherwise, it can increase the length of the conversation and decrease the probability of securing an appointment.

Picking the right time to call is important; some prospects are more available at certain times of the day (accountants, for example, are difficult to contact during tax season and doctors are harder to reach in the morning when they may be performing operations). Often secretaries have been instructed to screen calls to their bosses. They are told to give an excuse (e.g., "He is out of the office" or "She is in a meeting now") and take any caller's name and number for the executive to return the call if so desired. They are especially wary of salespeople.

Get the **screener**'s name, and ask if it is okay to call them by their first name. You will seem less like a stranger the next time you call. Act like an important person and project that image. When the screener relates, "Ms. Jones is in a meeting," don't ask, "When can I call back?" Instead, try, "Ann, I'm busy today, too, and really would like to speak with her. I can call back at 2:15 or 3:30. Which is better?" Having done this, when you call back, Ann feels almost obligated to put you through because she suggested which time to call.

It's best not to leave your number for a callback unless all else has failed and this is your last attempt; in that case, you have nothing to lose anyway. You should not leave your number for two reasons:

1. The decision maker probably won't call you back and you are compelled to allow him or her sufficient time to do so, which, in any regard, takes you out of control of the situation. When you do call back, there's also a little awkwardness or embarrassment on their part because they didn't return your call.

2. If the decision maker does call you back, you might be on another call or preoccupied in some way and unprepared to make a good presentation. Again, you've lost control.

Another common response from screeners [besides "He (or she) isn't in"] is, "What is this in reference to?" Your response to this question will determine whether you get through to the decision maker. Don't reply with a phrase that makes it obvious you want to sell something:

I just wanted to ask Mr. Jones if he would be interested in a new fax machine.

That will invite the reply:

Mr. Jones isn't in right now.

Instead, lead with the benefits of your product or service:

I have to let Mr. Jones know that he will save with the new Lexmark multifunction unit that does the job of a printer, copier, and fax machine. Is he in, please?

Even better, if Mr. Jones has responded to your prospecting letter or some advertising (for example, a reply card, magazine circling, and so on), you can honestly respond, "Mr. Jones asked us to give him a call. Would you please tell him I'm on the line." You might try a novel approach. "This is Ron Marks. I just read the article about Jim in *Forbes* magazine and have a business opportunity to discuss with him. Is he available?"

One way of winning screeners to your side is by asking their advice. They can usually give you inside information on their companies' goals and needs, so you might say to the gatekeeper, "Kathy, it would help matters if you could tell me a little about your company and its use of faxes before I set an appointment to see your boss." Asking for their advice demonstrates that you value their opinions. Compliment screeners for their help (even a small gift is appropriate) and once you visit their boss, be sure and praise them to him or her.[2]

If all else fails, here are a few tactics used by sales professionals to get past executives' administrative assistants:

- *Sell to the gatekeeper.* A 2000 survey by the Menlo Park, California–based Office Team, a leading specialized administrative staffing service, revealed that 91 percent of executives consider their assistant's opinion an important factor in the employee selection process. Just five years earlier, only 60 percent of executives had felt this way. Imply subtly to the gatekeeper that he or she is absorbing more decision-making responsibility. Suggest that the real buyer get more involved so that if an incorrect decision is ultimately made, the responsibility will be shared. When you're finished, let the gatekeeper know you enjoyed the chat, especially because you know how busy he or she might be.

- When the admin says, "Does Mr. Buyer know you?" you need a compelling answer. If the admin has been instructed *never* to allow someone like you to be put through in a situation like this, you may not have a chance. You'll need a plan B that must include selling to the gatekeeper. Some salespeople will send a letter to the gatekeeper with a letter to the real buyer attached. The letter to the gatekeeper reminds them of the call that was previously made and asks them to put forward the attached letter to their boss.

- Have your boss call the real buyer for the purpose of requesting a meeting, which you will attend. The gatekeeper will be angry and so might the buyer, but you may get your meeting.
- Figure out how to meet the real buyer in another venue, for example, at an industry association meeting or an investor conference.
- Ask an existing customer executive who may know this person to call on your behalf, suggesting a meeting.
- Above all, don't lie. You may get past the administrative assistant, but when she finds out what you did, you've got an enemy on your hands with a lot of influence.
- *Request information from the gatekeeper that will tax their ability to answer. Suggest both of you call on the real buyer to get the answers to those questions.*[3]

The salesperson may want to keep a text of the telephone track close by, especially if he or she is new to the job. This inspires confidence and makes for a smoother presentation. Practice is also a good idea for improving the effect. One of the best ways of practicing is to drill and rehearse the entire track with a tape recorder. While playing back the tape, the salesperson should pay particular attention to delivery. Some suggestions regarding delivery are presented in Table 8-1.

T a b l e **8-1** Suggestions for Telephone Delivery

1. Above all, remember that visual communication is lost over the phone. To compensate, oral skills and listening habits must improve.

2. Your lips should be half an inch from the telephone mouthpiece for maximum effectiveness. Open your mouth wider when speaking on the phone to allow you to enunciate more clearly and to avoid any tendency to mumble. Use simple language and avoid technical terms and slang.

   On the phone, people have a tendency to copy the tone of the other person. Your voice should say, "I am friendly, understanding, and competent." As unconventional as it may sound, one way of doing this is to smile into the telephone. People will note the difference in vocal intonation.

3. Be aware of your rate of speech. Talking too fast creates misunderstanding and mistrust; talking too slow encourages daydreaming by the listener and makes you sound boring and unenthusiastic. Experts think 140 words per minute is about the right pace for the phone. The timing or pace may communicate important clues. A long, drawn-out pace may project indifference, while a short reply can indicate impatience.

4. Use plenty of variation in your tone; people like talking to people, not machines.

5. Let the customer know you are listening by interjecting "yes," "uh-huh," "I see," etc.

6. Voice tone or *vocal factors* include pitch, tone, volume, rhythm, and inflection and are a critical part of the message conveyed on the phone. If the voice is "raised," an emotion of frustration or anger may be communicated.

7. Voice pitch can communicate a lot about style and emotions. Anger and excitement tend to cause the voice to rise, which may communicate frustration and anger. A low-pitched voice or speaking in a monotone may communicate indifference, laziness, or even incompetence. Make sure your voice is neither too low nor too high-pitched (i.e., squeaky).

8. Positive language includes the use of such words as "can," "will," "shall," and "certainly." Energy and expression should be put into the voice.

9. If the rhythm of the voice is unsteady or too fast, the greeting will be hard to follow or even lost entirely. Therefore, the rhythm should be comfortably paced and steady. Friendliness is conveyed through voice tone—by inflection at the end of statements with a lilt in the voice. The voice should have clarity so the caller will have no trouble understanding. The deliberate clarity of the voice is necessary for the communication of a friendly greeting with an offer of help.

Sources: Darryl M. Smith, "What Do You Say after You've Said Hello," *Sales & Marketing Management,* 1977; Leon A. Wortman, "Eight Keys to Telephone Sales," *Marketing Times,* September–October 1981; Art Sobczak, "How to Be a Success in Telephone Sales," *Personal Selling Power,* March 1990, p. 41; Mark Edward Jensen, "Enhancing Telephone Communication in the Dental Office," *The Journal of Contemporary Dental Practice,* Volume 1, No. 1, Fall Issue, 1999.

8-2b Identification

The attention-getting effort begins when the prospect answers the phone and the salesperson introduces himself or herself. The introduction contains three elements: the prospect's name, the salesperson's name, and the salesperson's company. Personally, I recommend that the company's name be emphasized slightly more than the other two, as it will carry the most prestige and credibility at this stage of the call. Given my experience, I also suggest that the salesperson's last name be mentioned twice. Otherwise, it tends to easily be forgotten by the prospect. Accepting these two recommendations, an introduction might be phrased as follows:

> *Mr. Jones?* (slight pause) *My name is Friendly, Ron Friendly, of* (emphasize) *the Superior Hospital Uniform Corporation.*

All of this may sound like no big deal, but if you don't say it correctly or clearly, then while you are talking, the prospect will be thinking, "Who is this?" Needless to say, your well-thought-out presentation will be for naught.

The introduction's delivery is especially important. Enthusiasm and a clear, audible delivery are especially critical at this early stage of the phone interview. Once the introduction is concluded, the salesperson should speed up the rate of conversation. The likelihood of getting a "no" or "I'm not interested" is particularly great at this point, and the salesperson can decrease this probability by accelerating into the lead-in.

8-2c The Lead-In

This is a critical part of the telephone track. A request, such as, "Hi, I'm just calling to check in with you" or "I'm Ron Marks, sales representative for Northern Life Insurance" are sure to end without an appointment.[4] A lead-in statement should immediately follow the introduction. Material in the lead-in may include:[5]

- A third-party reference
- Literature sent to the prospect by the salesperson or the company
- The prospect's or the salesperson's recent company advertising
- A statement of a known problem in the prospect's industry or profession
- Pertinent points made by a recognized figure in the prospect's industry at a recent conference or in an article
- The inactive account approach

A good third-party reference is probably the best lead-in. For instance: "Mr. Holiday [purchasing agent for Mercy Hospital]? My name is Friendly, Ron Friendly of the Superior Hospital Uniform Company. I was with Sam Barry over at Baptist Hospital yesterday, and he mentioned that you might be interested in our new surgical uniforms."

Third-person references can be business friends or acquaintances of the prospect. It is helpful if the third party is at least at the same career level as the prospect. References of a lower rank will not carry nearly as much weight. The best sources of references are, of course, current customers—satisfied ones. The worst thing a salesperson can do is mention customers only to find out that they are dissatisfied, so it is mandatory to check with them first. A phone call or letter to these references also may reveal important qualifying or preapproach information about the prospect.

Another effective basis for the lead-in is mail from sales representatives or their company. Asking if they have had a chance to read the literature (whether or not they have) compels prospects to at least answer the question. Their answer allows the salesperson more time to develop the presentation. For example, after the introduction, the salesperson might proceed:

> **Salesperson:** Within the last couple of weeks, you received a letter concerning our new surgical uniforms. Did you get a chance to read through it, Mr. Jones?
>
> **Prospect:** No, I didn't.
>
> **Salesperson:** OK, well as long as you have it there, why don't you grab it and let's go through it together.[6]

(Now the salesperson makes an interest-capturing statement.)

Lead-ins based on media advertising or industry problems also may be effective, and readers may wish to create such messages in their minds. If they are well done, they can be as effective as the third-party reference or mail approach. If none of these lead-ins is possible, then the salesperson might choose to rely on the company's reputation to capture the prospect's attention. This may be effective if the company is well known, but the salesperson should use other lead-ins if possible.

In spite of what you might think, inactive accounts can often lead to renewed business. A company's new supplier, for example, may not have worked out as hoped. If there were problems in the past, a salesperson could say, "I was looking over our records recently, and I notice we have not done any business with you lately. Is there a reason for this? Can I stop by and discuss matters with you?" You will be surprised at how many inactive accounts can be revived.

8-2d Interest-Capturing Statement

Once the salesperson has attracted the prospect's attention with a lead-in, a short statement is needed to arouse interest. The objective is to give the prospect a reason to continue the conversation.

The statement might be a benefit statement, which would include (1) a major benefit of the product or service and (2) the product feature from which this benefit evolves. For instance, the sales representative might say:

> *Mr. Jones, the new Superior polyester-cotton blend uniform will substantially reduce your hospital laundry costs because of its "no-iron" feature.*

Hopefully, the benefit mentioned will be the prospect's most pressing need, but there is no guarantee that it will be. A good preapproach may reveal some clues, but in the final analysis salespeople must make an educated guess and take their best shot.

A statement is not the only method of capturing the prospect's interest. The salesperson might also ask a question, such as, "Mr. Jones, if you could have the perfect surgical uniform, what would it be like?" This only represents one possibility. The salesperson might wish to phrase the benefit statement as a question, such as, "Would you find it valuable if you didn't have to iron your uniforms?" There are a great many opportunities for creativity here. One software company discovered the value of using questions. The software was designed for graduating high school seniors to show them sources of loans, grants, and scholarships. They had been using a one-way, 15-minute presentation with limited success. Instead, they changed the whole format to begin with a congratulatory opener: "I understand Johnny's graduating from high school. Congratulations. That's a pretty big event, isn't it?" (After the reply) "I just wanted to share a little information. We've been able to help high school seniors finance their education more comfortably. What college is Johnny thinking of attending?" (After reply) "About how much do you think that's going to cost you each year?" (After the typical reply of "too much") "If I could show you some sources of loans, grants, and scholarships, how much more comfortable would that make financing Johnny's college career to you?" The result: a tenfold increase in sales.[7]

Some additional examples of interest-capturing statements follow:

Mr. Doe, we have a special offer on case lots of ABCs this month. You'll save more money by ordering by the case.

Our new . . . can save you lots of time and work space for your . . . , Ms. Whitehall.

You know, Ms. Smith, we have redesigned our . . . packaging. Now it's a perfectly round cylindrical shape that tapers toward the bottom. The increased attractiveness has improved sales 25 percent in most of our stores.

Mrs. Brooks, I've worked with many banks in the area and have shown them how to increase their bottom-line profits by decreasing their accounts-payable expenses.

How would you like to cut your automobile insurance in half?

8-2e Stating Purpose and Asking for an Appointment

Following an interest-capturing statement, the salesperson should state the purpose for making a personal visit and ask for the appointment. Typically, the former follows logically from the interest-capturing statement. Continuing with the interest-capturing statement used earlier, Ron Friendly might say:

Mr. Jones, the new Superior polyester-cotton blend uniform will substantially reduce your uniform laundry costs because of its "no-iron" feature. (interest-capturing statement) Can we meet next Wednesday at 3 or Thursday at 10 to discuss this feature and the many others you should find attractive?

In stating the purpose, it is important to remember that the objective of the phone call is to secure an appointment. Giving away too much of the proposition over the phone runs the risk of a turndown before the salesperson can make a proper presentation in person. The rule is to provide just enough information to create a desire to learn more. Should the prospect ask for more information, the salesperson can respond with something like, "For full development of the idea, I frankly need more time. Investments have become such a complex subject these days that I really need to talk with you in person." When seeking an appointment time, as Ron did, it is advisable to offer two choices. Should you propose only one date, you give prospects the choice between meeting you that day or not at all. They can always say they are too busy to see you, but if you offer two dates, experience demonstrates that you increase your odds of getting an appointment. Moreover, suggesting next Wednesday or Thursday implies that the salesperson is a busy person. A prospect thinks, "Busy people are more successful than people who have a lot of time on their hands." Having once secured the appointment, the salesperson should end the conversation, confirming the date and time: "I'll see you Thursday at 10, then." This serves as a reminder to the prospect and allows a graceful cessation of the conversation. Continuing might only end with a cancellation of the appointment.

When seeking an appointment, it is critical to avoid the use of "weasel" words such as *maybe, if, could, possibly, perhaps,* and *like.* Imagine what the prospect thinks when these words are used. For example, you might call for an appointment and say," *Maybe* I could stop by on Thursday?" This is too weak; the prospect is probably saying to himself or herself, "And then again, maybe not!" To emphasize the point, let's put all these weasel words together.[8]

"*Perhaps* we *could* get together *if* you *might* have a few minutes, and *possibly*, we *may* be able to see how my product *could* be of benefit, and I'd *like* to stop by tomorrow, *if* you don't mind."

8-2f Handling Any Objections

Any reason that the prospect might give for not granting the interview is considered an objection. Chances are the salesperson will not be able to overcome the objection without revealing much about the proposition, so the goal in a telephone approach is to set up an appointment rather than solve the customer's problem. Instead of answering the objection, the objective then is to use it as another reason for granting the interview. (Table 8-2 details some common objections and ways of handling them.)

However, realistically, the timing may not always be right for prospects. Wouldn't it be great if every prospect became a new customer around our time line? It's a safe bet that some of the prospects you call on will not be ready to take that next step with you, at least not just yet. Better to respond to a real objection about bad timing: "Mr. Prospect, thanks again for your time today. Before we wrap up this conversation, I've noticed that in the past, when I have attempted to reconnect with someone months after our first contact, many things have happened. Changes in their position, in their company, or in their life often have the tendency to divert even the best-laid plans. Since there are so many things that can happen in two months, I was hoping that I could stay in contact with you without stepping over the line and being annoying about it. With your permission, can I contact you from time to time with updates about our product or valuable information that you may find of interest as it relates to your business?" A monthly newsletter (perhaps via email), an article of interest, collateral material, or a great new product feature are just a few ways to deliver value during this "downtime" and keep your finger on the

T a b l e **8-2** **Some Common Telephone Objections and Ways of Handling Them**

1. Objection:

   "*Can't you mail the information?*"

   Reply:

   "*Well, everyone's situation is different, Ms. Smith, and our plans are individually designed to meet the needs of each customer. Now . . .*" (Go on to a benefit statement and request an appointment.)

2. Objection:

   "*What is it you want to talk about?*"

   Reply:

   "*Mr. Prospect, this is an idea that is difficult to explain on the telephone and . . .*"

3. Objection:

   "*You'd only be wasting your time*" or "*I'm not interested.*"

   Reply:

   These objections are general, and they may be hiding a specific objection that the salesperson should attempt to uncover with a reply such as: "Do you say that because you're not in the market for a new copier, Ms. Donovan?"

   Such a question may uncover that prospects have had bad past experiences with the salesperson's company, that they think prices are too high, etc. These specific objections may then be dealt with individually by the salesperson. But remember, don't go too far. Your main objective is to get an appointment!

pulse of every prospect you speak with.[9] This way, if things change on the prospect's side, you won't be the last person to find out.

8-2g Voice Mail

For Lauren Januz, it seemed like a sure sale. She got a tip that a major Chicago college could be a good prospect for the monogrammed pens, pencils, tote bags, and other advertising specialties her firm markets. She called the director of marketing services at one university, received a voice mail message, left her name and phone number, and awaited a reply. After no response, she called again, got voice mail once again, left a message, and received no return. Becoming frustrated, she sent a customized introductory letter. Still no response. After two weeks and 14 voice mail messages, she had still to make contact.[10] Says Januz, "Voice mail has done a horrible disservice to the selling profession. Middle managers are using voice mail as a way to shield themselves from phone calls. And instead of callbacks, they just ignore the messages."

The reality, as this story relates, is that it's getting more and more difficult to contact prospects in the age of voice mail. Middle executives and purchasing managers, swamped with additional responsibilities because of downsizing, have less time to meet with salespeople in person, let alone on the phone. Like it or not, sales reps have no choice but to seek the best ways of dealing with voice mail. How can they increase their chances of receiving return calls? What types of greetings increase their chances? Unfortunately, there are no easy answers.

First, some mechanics. If you get an automated attendant ("If you know your party's extension, please press it now," etc.), just press the "0" button to get the operator. Get the direct phone number of the person you are calling, and then dial it. If you get the secretary, find out when the person will be back or the best time to reach that person. Failing this, if no secretary is available and you have to leave a voice mail message, use a referral or explain a special, individualized benefit your product or service can offer, or even better, both.

If you have to leave a voice mail message (or answering machine message, for that matter), make sure it has impact and gets your prospect's attention—enough to return your call. Give them a strong reason (one that's important to them) to return your call. Usually this means providing a referral and a benefit. For example, compare the impact of the following two messages:

Message 1:

"This is John Smith, sales representative, at ABC Corporation. Give me a call at 233-2165 when you return."

Message 2:

"Hello, (insert name). This is Tim Neumann, TBN Sales Solutions, (920) 555-1306. I'm sorry I missed you. I'm calling to introduce my company to see if we can help. TBN Sales Solutions increases commissions for salespeople and profits for businesses through customized training, coaching, and consulting. We establish structures and procedures, through classroom workshops and individual sales coaching, to teach reps to control their own destiny, thereby impacting the bottom line. Please call me. I've cleared my schedule tomorrow morning at 9:30 and tomorrow afternoon at 1:45 to provide the details to you. Your friend Bob Smith at Butler has taken advantage of this opportunity and invested with us. Again, Tim Neumann, TBN Sales Solutions, (920) 555-1306. Thank you."

A few quick tips for leaving voice mail, as evident in message 2:[11]

1. Speak slowly, but enthusiastically. If you aren't excited, the prospect won't be.
2. State your name, company, and phone number at the start and at the end. Nothing is worse than when someone is interested in your product and they have to play the message 10 times to catch your name and number.
3. State your desire to "help." As we said last month, it's a powerful word.
4. Provide a choice of times. If the caller expects a response at specific times, the listener is likely to feel more of an obligation to return the call.

8-2h Think about Selectivity (Knowing When to "Back Off")

On average, salespeople close 17 percent of their appointments. In many industries, closing rates are much lower. However, most salespeople keep hoping that they'll get better at persuading interested prospects to buy. When you're doing something that has a small probability of producing a positive result, an occasional payoff will get most people to keep doing it. The vast majority of people who keep putting their money in slot machines will lose all of their money in a short time. The lure of the big win combined with a few small wins keeps them hooked. They keep hoping that they'll become more skillful and learn how to beat the odds. That's the principle that enables gambling casinos to earn billions of dollars a year.

If you spend your time only with prospects who want what you're selling and who will make a commitment to buy if it meets their requirements, you have broken this pattern. You should stay in touch with a large number of prospects by frequently calling them all or send "opt-in" email. For most industries, the best frequency is every four weeks. Each time you call your prospects, you should present them with a different prospecting offer than the previous one. That will minimize the likelihood of their being annoyed with your calls. New information isn't annoying unless it's used for manipulative purposes. Each time you call, you must be willing to accept "No" for the answer and be willing to move on to your next call, quickly. Each successive time that you call, your chances of contacting the prospects who want to buy increases.

The best time to visit with a prospect is when they are ready to buy (or specify) your type of product or service. If you visit with prospects when they are not ready to buy, your chances of selling to them are small. If you wait to visit them when they are ready to buy, it's more likely that you will get their business.[12]

8-3 Establishing Rapport

After gaining entry to the prospect's office, the second major task of the approach is to establish rapport with the client, as outlined in Table 8-3. Relationship selling requires a free and honest exchange of ideas and feelings between prospect and salesperson. This cannot occur unless a receptive communications climate has first been established. In an unreceptive climate, one or both of the partners has set up barriers to communication. Most frequently, this happens because the prospect does not completely trust the salesperson. At the first sign of insincerity, the prospect establishes a barrier and refuses to interact further with the salesperson.

T a b l e 8-3
Physical Gestures toward Establishing Rapport

This is a Largely Nonverbal Art, so be Mindful of Your:

- Appearance
- Handshake
- Posture
- Eye contact
- Small talk
- Etiquette

The trouble is, you don't have much time to establish a credible image. Some experts suggest as short as 10 to 15 seconds; others, up to 4 minutes.[13] During these few seconds (or minutes), prospects form immediate impressions about whether salespeople are worth getting to know better. Although frequently unconscious of why they instantly like or dislike a rep, experts attribute it to the nonverbal messages reps send—appearance, posture, eye contact, smile, handshake. If bad signals are sent out, as the old adage goes, "You never get a second chance to make a good first impression!"

Young sales reps—and even older reps who appear to be very young—have trouble earning respect in today's competitive sales landscape. As a result of such circumstances, one young female rep goes to great lengths to look older. She wears an ultraconservative suit and pulls her hair back in a ponytail at the nape of her neck when visiting clients. She covers her freckles with makeup. And she makes sure to flash her wedding band and talk about her husband, tactics that she hopes are proof she's older than she looks. Indeed, cultivating a mature look can help young-looking sales reps to gain more clout. "Like it or not, prospects judge you in the first 10 seconds you walk through the door," says Kelley Robertson, president of The Robertson Training Group, a sales training firm. "If you look like a kid, they're going to ask themselves, 'Is this person qualified to help me with my purchase?'" The biggest mistake youthful-looking salespeople can make, Robertson says, is dressing too trendily. He recently coached a sales rep in his twenties who worked for the Sony Corporation on how to tone down his attire. Another way for young-looking reps to earn respect quickly is to talk the part of a mature salesperson. That means avoiding slang, speaking with a deeper voice, and talking slowly.[14]

8-3a Appearance

Appearance is critical. Although casual wear may be inching into the corporate world, sales reps should be very cautious. They should know the prospect's (and his or her company's) style, before throwing on their favorite khakis. "I am not impressed by someone who shows up in a warm-up suit or jeans," says Joe Weldon, marketing manager of cellular equipment at BellSouth in Atlanta, who makes million-dollar purchase decisions. "They are representing their company, and if they create a less than professional image, I tend to perceive their company that way."[15] Appearance also extends beyond just the salesperson's dress. For example, a sales representative may create a poor impression by handing the receptionist a grimy business card instead of a crisp new one or by pulling an obviously worn sample or a crumpled flyer out of his or her briefcase. Something as small as an appointment book may detract from a positive overall image. If it bulges with scraps of paper that fly off in the prospect's office, it is distracting at least and self-defeating at worst. Another way to create a poor impression is to take a prospect to lunch in a cluttered car. Trash and samples scattered indiscriminately throughout the vehicle will not give the impression that the sales rep is a professional. In selling, everything about you adds to—or subtracts from—the total impression you make. Even small things can make a big difference.

8-3b Handshake

What a sloppy handshake says about the person behind the hand is that he or she just doesn't have things together. If you're the sloppy shaker, you're telling the client, boss, or interviewer that you have problems. That conclusion can lead him to make a subconscious decision that he doesn't want to do business with you—or that you won't make a good representative of his company. What is a proper handshake?

The act seems so simple, yet people get confused over how to do it. In the United States, you're expected to offer a firm handshake and make eye contact at the same time. A firm handshake with good eye contact communicates self-confidence.

In U.S. etiquette, an appropriate handshake begins with the introduction:

VIDEO

1. Extend your hand and grip the other person's hand so that the webs of your thumbs meet.
2. Shake just a couple of times. The motion is from the elbow, not the shoulder.
3. End the handshake cleanly, before the introduction is over.
4. If you want to count, a good handshake is held for three or four seconds.

Shaking hands can be awkward in some situations. Should you be introduced to someone when your hands are full, carrying files or other packages, don't try to rearrange everything. Simply nod your head as you respond to the introduction.

If you have a tendency to have cold hands, stick your right hand in your pocket to warm it up as you approach a situation in which you'll have to shake hands. If you have perennially clammy hands, try the high school prom date approach and take a quick swipe of your right hand on your skirt or trousers, so that when you present it, it's dry. You can do so quickly and gracefully, and no one will be aware that you made the gesture.[16]

If the prospect's hand is offered, be sure not to abuse the privilege. Many salespeople practice such abominations of the art of handshaking as "the bone crusher, the pump handle, the limp digits, the wet rag, and the no-release clamp." Shake hands firmly but without these abuses. Be aware of how much of the hand is involved in the shake. Only offering the front half of the fingers says, "I don't want to become too involved with you." Palm to palm, web to web is a safe choice, and, of course, no sweaty palms.[17]

8-3c Posture

Posture can be interpreted as a window into how salespeople view themselves and the products or services they are selling. When the body is held in an upright position—erect stance, head straight, shoulders pulled back—it projects confidence, competence, dignity, and enthusiasm. In contrast, a slumped body—rounded back, bowed head, slack shoulders—sends out the wrong image (i.e., insecurity, disinterest, and lack of conviction). It is of further import how weight is distributed. Feet should be shoulder-width apart, knees slightly bent and relaxed; do not rock or sway.[18]

8-3d Eye Contact

Eye contact is a further important element of first impressions. In our society, the salesperson should make immediate eye contact. If handled correctly, early eye contact projects honesty, sincerity, and attentiveness. In contrast, failure to make eye contact may be interpreted as sneaky, dishonest, or insincere. Furthermore, a relationship can begin badly if eye contact is held either for too long or too short a time. Rapidly moving one's eyes is perceived as sneaky; a prolonged gaze is perceived as threatening. What is the right amount of time? No more than three seconds on average. Then, break contact briefly.[19]

8-3e Small Talk

Often there is tension present in the first meeting between prospect and salesperson. For this reason, many sales representatives begin their conversation with **small talk**—a discussion of topics such as hobbies or sports that are basically unrelated to the sale itself. If the sales representative knows from the preapproach that the prospect is an avid tennis player, there is no harm (and probably much good) in discussing Andy Roddick's chances at Wimbledon. Behavioral research supports such a strategy. Finding an initial point of agreement with people improves the chances of persuading them to your way of thinking regarding a later point of discussion.

It is also true that prospects may reveal more about themselves and their company in small talk. Often they are less guarded and more open than in a strictly business conversation. Clues about quality concerns, price expectations, and service desires can appear in small talk. For example, when Mary Baker, sales representative for a textile company, first called on a buyer at a furniture upholstering company, she noticed the man's desk was littered with new-car catalogs. She began, "It looks as if you're getting ready to buy a new car." After a short conversation that revealed the buyer's concerns about fuel economy, "sticker shock," and whether a certain salesperson would call back with a better deal, Mary decided she had a price-sensitive buyer on her hands. Similarly, if the man had concentrated on the quality of German cars, the importance of the dealer's service department, and extra features, such as air-conditioning, a sunroof, or white sidewalls, she might have concluded differently.

Accordingly, topics for icebreaker conversations can be:

- A personal interest of buyers or their families, if the salesperson has such information from the preapproach
- A sincere—and deserved—compliment about the prospect's plant, products, office, or community activities
- Some pleasant news about the industry—favorable legislation, economic upturns, or new technology

If small talk is engaged in, there is always the problem of making the transition to business matters. It is important to recognize when the prospect wishes to change the conversation to business. Nonverbal clues should be noted. The salesperson should not wait for prospects to say, "Let's get down to business," by which time they may be annoyed. It is better to let small talk lead logically into discussing business. For example:

> Speaking of box scores and batting averages, Dave, I brought along some statistics on the wear quality of the new uniform I showed you a couple of weeks ago . . .

> If you're right and the stock market does rebound next month, you'll probably see an increase in machine tool orders. We've already had some inquiries from customers who had things on hold, so . . .

> I could sit and talk golf for hours, Bob, but I know you're busy, so let me show a new item in our line that should increase your impulse-purchase sales . . .

Sales representatives should be careful before automatically plunging into small talk in each and every sales call. Some buyers do not appreciate discussion of anything but business matters. With regard to the personality profiles introduced in Chapter 4, "Buyer Behavior," Drivers are interested in the job and nothing else. A sales representative who spends time discussing golf or tennis will

VIDEO

small talk
A discussion between sales rep and customer on such topics as hobbies or sports that are unrelated to the sale itself.

appear a lightweight in a driver's eyes. Even with buyers typically interested in discussing unrelated matters, not every interview presents an opportunity for small talk. They might be pressed for time and want to complete the interview as swiftly as possible.

Small talk, when used appropriately, is but one effective way of reducing tension during the approach. Some other suggestions follow:

- Assure the prospect that no high-pressure or manipulative techniques will be used.
- State that the interview will not take long.
- Discuss a mutual acquaintance with the prospect.
- Ask the prospect's advice on a particular matter.
- Use humor.
- Flatter the prospect (do this carefully).[20]

There are other more general ways to put people at ease. As indicated in Table 8-4, these apply to any social situation, sales call or otherwise.

8-3f Etiquette

Salespeople should follow certain standards of etiquette while interviewing clients. Some are basic, but it is surprising how often salespeople abuse them—to their disadvantage.

We have already discussed the importance of appearance with regard to the salesperson's clothing. The car the sales representative drives also contributes to appearance. Driving a nice but not flashy car is a good idea. Flashiness awakens in the buyer's mind those harmful elements of the sales representative's stereotype. It also makes the buyer question whether salespeople and their companies are overcharging their customers.

It is a matter of courtesy not to demand to see the buyer. Professional buyers will see the salesperson as soon as possible. Pushing them will only lead to their finding reasons not to see the sales representative.

A critical part of sales etiquette is remembering the buyer's name. Forgetting a name may be interpreted by buyers to mean that in the salesperson's eyes they are

T a b l e **8-4** How to Put People at Ease

Putting people at ease is a basic step in getting people to react favorably toward you, says Dr. Arnold Lazarus, a psychologist at Rutgers University. He offers these suggestions:

- Let people hear your voice. Don't just nod. The sound of the voice is like a calling card or introduction.
- Avoid talking too much or too little. If you tend to be too quiet, use more words. If you are a compulsive talker, try to summarize. Others often like to hold the floor themselves.
- Use the word "I" in your conversation. You are much less of a mystery when you disclose something about yourself.
- Look for something you can comment on positively. Pick something that you genuinely like about the other person and point it out to him or her.
- Be able to laugh at yourself. If you tell a story in which you do not come out in a particularly good light, other people will immediately warm up to you.
- Let your face express your feelings. If it is a mask, you are not going to put anybody else at ease.
- Make eye contact with the other person. By looking up at the ceiling or down at the floor while speaking, you make your listener feel ill at ease.

not worth troubling with or are not important. Yet, it is difficult for salespeople to remember the names of all the people with whom they come in contact. Here are some suggestions for easing this arduous task:

1. Hear the name.
2. Ask the person to spell it.
3. Say something about it.
4. Use the person's name in the next few minutes.
5. When you depart, say the name.

As a further aid to remembering, make a pictorial image of the buyer's name. To be effective, the image should be (1) ridiculous, (2) vivid with motion, (3) exaggerated, and (4) tied to the person's dominant feature. If he is a bit on the portly side, Mr. Earl becomes "the Earl of Ham," and so much the better. "Gordon" can become "garden," and if Mr. Gordon has a large nose, an image can be formed of a garden growing over his nose. If the prospect looks as if he has a pit in his head like an olive, then it is easy to remember his name as Oliver.

If making a picture is difficult for you, another way you can remember a name is to tie it to one you have already run across. Mr. Moriarty might be remembered because you ran across the villain Professor Moriarty in Sir Arthur Conan Doyle's Sherlock Holmes novels. Similarly, if Ed Cruise bears a striking resemblance to movie star Tom Cruise, then recalling his name should be relatively easy.

Don't treat someone's office as your home turf. Wait until you're invited to sit down, and then ask the other person where they prefer for you sit. Don't fiddle with things on their desks, and watch where you put yourself and your belongings. If you're going into someone's space, you really need to be respectful. Do put cell phones, pagers, and BlackBerrys on hold. Checking messages, taking calls, or checking email are to be avoided. How are you going to solidify relationships or build business if you're giving the impression that everything in the world is more important? If you are expecting an urgent call, alert your companion to the fact beforehand, ask for permission to handle the call, and then excuse yourself when the call comes in.[21]

It is further a part of sales etiquette for sales representatives to thank prospects for taking time to see them, and salespeople should be properly appreciative. This should help establish a receptive communications climate and an image of the salesperson as an empathetic individual. But this appreciation should not be delivered apologetically. Remember, the salesperson is providing a benefit to the buyer!

The salesperson should be attentive to certain habits and mannerisms that are potentially annoying to prospects. Continually using words and phrases such as *now, well, frankly,* and especially *you know* is enough to distract even the most forgiving buyer. Certain physical mannerisms fall into the same category: pulling one's chin, mouth, or nose; drumming one's fingers; straightening one's tie or skirt; or clicking a pen. Although it is easy to overemphasize the importance of these distractive habits, there is no question that professional salespeople rarely manifest such characteristics. Through practice and experience, they have gained the confidence that curbs such nervous mannerisms.

Though the salesperson should be friendly, there is such a thing as overdoing it. A buyer should not be addressed by his or her first name unless so requested. Salespeople should not take a chair until invited to do so. Buyers should not be touched on their shoulders, arms, or legs. Nor is it professional to engage the prospect's employees in idle conversation that keeps them from their duties. Should the salesperson need to use a prospect's equipment for a demonstration, permission should be sought first and an effort should be made to protect it from damage.

Honesty is another important part of sales etiquette. If the salesperson does not know the answer or does not have the solution to the buyer's problems, honesty is the best policy. Telling buyers the truth is much better than making the buyers look bad later in the eyes of their own management because they were sold a solution that failed. Candor is an element of trust and must be cultured to develop the relationship.

The professional salesperson does not waste a buyer's time. Sales representatives should learn to tell how busy the buyer is and adjust the length of the sales call accordingly. They should learn the buyer's procedures to find the best time of the day or week to call. It is important for salespeople to establish sure ways by which buyers can reach them. Nothing is more discouraging to a buyer than to hear an answering service announce several days consecutively that the salesperson cannot be reached. If prospects are likely to have a problem requiring immediate attention in the near future, the sales representative should arrange to reach them personally before going out of town.

8-4 Gaining Attention

Having established a receptive communications climate, the task of the salesperson is to capture the prospect's attention. The sales representative must say or do something that will compel prospects to stop whatever they are thinking or doing and pay heed. The opening statement is like the headline of an advertisement—it should project an important reason for listening so that the prospect will believe that not listening to salespeople carries a greater risk than attending to what they say.

But gaining the client's attention is not always easy. Many buyers, especially professional ones, have learned to sit upright at a desk, look intently at visitors, and nod from time to time, while all the while their minds are far away. Prospects (be they purchasing agents, executives, or shoppers) have countless things on their minds. Although the body may be present, the mind of the prospect can be somewhere distant.

If you were a buyer, think about how you would react to a salesperson who opens with, "I happened to be passing by and thought I'd drop in for a minute" or something similar. It almost says, "What I have to say isn't very important, but I have nothing better to do and you probably don't either, so here goes . . ." Not only does such an opener detract from the presentation that follows but it is also disrespectful of the buyer's time—and it is decidedly unprofessional. In a very real sense, a sales call is like a novel. If the reader's attention is not piqued early, he or she may never finish the book. The salesperson must do or say something that will pique the buyer's immediate interest. But it is important not to go too far in this direction. If the mindless opener characterizes one extreme, then showy or gimmicky approaches represent the other. They may attract immediate attention, but the wrong kind.

The classic in this regard (not to mention outright gall) comes from the early days of cash register sales. Salespeople used to be taught to walk into a prospect's store, deliberately go over to a hook where charge slips were stuck, tear off one, and throw the slip onto the floor. After the storm subsided, the salesperson would express surprise that the merchant was so concerned with one charge slip, when more money was undoubtedly lost through the loose cash management that characterized merchants of that time.

Another common approach is for the salesperson to announce some sort of benefit that the prospect will gain from the product or service. The salesperson might state, for example, "I can save you X amount of dollars by your using our machine." Such a statement implies that the sales representative knows how to perform the prospect's job better than the prospect does. Although this might be all right in those rare instances when prospects look up to the sales representative as an expert, in most cases they are unlikely to react favorably to such a patronizing declaration.

Most people are turned off when someone implies superiority over them. In the approach, it is not a good idea to imply that the salesperson knows all about the prospect and what is good for him or her. One sales representative related how, as a young man, he called on an architect. After hearing the architect's plans for a building, he replied, "You can't do that." The customer answered, "Young man, never tell people they can't do something."

Besides the problem of implied superiority, both the showmanship and declaration approaches smack of the old stereotype. They make the prospect think about all those old stories about lying salespeople, and this establishes a barrier in the prospects' minds. They become doubly wary of placing their trust in the seller.

For these reasons, it is recommended that salespeople use questions in their approach, if at all possible. There are a number of advantages associated with this technique. First, the use of a question does not suggest superiority—you are asking, not telling. Moreover, there is nothing more attention-getting than participation. Merely listening to a presentation versus participating in it makes a world of difference in attentiveness. There are few things that grab our interest more than talking about ourselves and our own projects. This human tendency provides a further advantage to the questioning approach—prospects are likely to reveal much about their needs and problems and this, of course, is what the salesperson is after in the early stages of the interview.

To illustrate the value of questioning over telling in openers, compare the following two approaches for an office-machine salesperson.

I'd like to tell you about a laser printer that comes as close as possible to being the perfect printer—certainly the best on the market.

Versus

If you could design the perfect printer, what would it be like?

Which approach do you think would gain more attention? Which would the buyer find less offensive? Which would leave him or her more open-minded?

Openers exist in an infinite variety. Although the following collection is not complete, enough are presented so that the student of selling should never suffer for want of an opener. In most instances, the openers have been structured in the form of a question.

8-4a The Introduction Approach

In this simplest—and probably weakest—of approaches, a salesperson announces his or her name and company and perhaps hands the prospect a business card. The introduction approach may also extend to a mention of the topic for the call, such as follows:

Mr. Prospect, my name is John Bleak and I'm with Fox Papers. My company has just introduced a new coated paper of especially high quality. May I tell you about it?

Such an opening is unlikely to generate much attention and enthusiasm. Unless the introduction is followed by another attention-getting statement, it usually is not sufficient in and of itself.

Handing the prospect a business card at this point helps them remember the salesperson's name and company. Others think a business card can be distracting and recommend giving the card at the end of the sales call. Innovative sales reps are beginning to use business cards that are also mini-CD-ROMs, holding up to 600MB of information and may include video clips and HTML links.[22]

V I D E O

8-4b The Referral

Citing the name of a third party, especially a satisfied customer, is an effective method of face-to-face approach, just as it is when phoning for an appointment. It is even more effective if the reference is an acquaintance of the prospect, in which case the prospect feels obligated to pay attention. A salesperson might phrase such an opener like this:

The Acme Company just leased a system from us, and Sue Jones, their data-processing manager, suggested that your situation might be similar to theirs.

The referral may be embellished with a written testimonial letter that the sales representative hands the prospect. One creative sales representative even tape recorded a message from a reference.

In the event the salesperson does not have a referral from a friend of the prospect, he or she can use the name of one of the prospect's competitors who is already a client: "Mr. Brown, has Fred Miller ever mentioned my name to you?" Now, it isn't likely that Miller, his competitor, would have talked about him or her; however, mentioning Miller is an icebreaker, and Brown is probably interested in knowing what his competitor is up to.

8-4c Offering a Benefit

Offering a benefit is probably the most widely used type of opening, and it is a good one if the benefit is of real interest to the buyer. An example follows:

XYZ has some exciting new copiers you may want to look into, because we're now designing copiers for specific jobs done in businesses such as yours. The benefit to you is that equipment designed for your business makes your employees more efficient. Wouldn't you like to see happier employees who get their work done sooner and can then work on other jobs you normally have to let slide or pay extra to have done?

The benefit approach is especially valuable if it is addressed to the buyer's dominant buying motive, because this leads logically into the presentation.

Statements that combine mention of a satisfied customer along with a benefit are an effective form of benefit statement; they offer evidence of the benefit. For example, a salesperson for a plastic container company talking with the purchasing agent for a food firm might say:

> *Linda Fitch, marketing manager for Farmland, was telling me just yesterday that they've increased their sales in certain items because of packaging in plastic containers. She says buyers find the containers easier to store on crowded pantry shelves and easier to dispose of after use.*

The salesperson can turn the statement of the benefit into a provocative question: "How would you like an extra secretary for just $30 a week?" So asks the salesperson for a digital copier, who then proceeds to show how two of his or her machines will increase the output of two secretaries by 50 percent.

8-4d The Curiosity Approach

Another effective approach is through appeal to the prospect's curiosity. A salesperson might ask the prospect, "Would you like to see the product your neighbors are buying?" or, "This bit of wire cost the Blank Company more than $250,000 last November. Want to hear about it?" Wouldn't you? The salesperson can then proceed to tell how a short circuit caused a $250,000 blaze.

An investment salesperson I recently met handed me his business card. In the lower left-hand corner, the number *12,639* was printed in boldface. When asked about it, he replied, "That happens to be the number of meals you'll buy after age 65 if you live a normal life expectancy. If you pay just $4 per meal, you'll need at least $50,556 for you and your spouse. Would you care to spend a few minutes discussing retirement investments?" We did.

8-4e The Compliment Approach

A compliment represents still another approach, but the salesperson must be careful in employing the opening. Nothing is more obvious or more offensive to prospects than an insincere attempt to flatter them. The ideal compliment is sincere, specific, and something of real interest to the prospect.

The sincerity of the compliment is in direct proportion to how specific it is. To say, for example, "Mr. Smith, you are known as someone who is really an expert in your field," may make him wonder what is referred to and who has been talking. To mention specifically, however, that other store managers consider him to have been highly innovative in carrying new lines may greatly increase the perceived sincerity of the compliment. Remember that the compliment has the most value when it refers to an area in which the prospect has the most interest and pride. A sales representative's use of the compliment approach might be:

> *Ms. Taylor, I see you've redone the decor of the women's department. I think it looks just great. It blends in perfectly with the decor and theme of the rest of your store. Would you like to know what other people in your business have done to double their return from the women's department?*

Compliments should always be sincere. Possible topics for putting together a compliment approach follow:

1. Plaques or other mementos of achievement on the prospect's wall
2. The appearance of the prospect's business—interior or exterior
3. An especially pleasant receptionist
4. The prospect's recent promotion to a position of higher responsibility

5. The prospect's family (e.g., perhaps a child was just named to the all-city basketball team or received an academic scholarship to a college or university)
6. Recent news of business successes by the prospect's company
7. Pictures of the prospect

Regarding the last of these, one salesperson was able to sell a notoriously difficult record-industry executive. The man's office was vast and intimidating, with one wall literally a photo gallery of rock stars and musicians. The sales rep had no idea who the musicians were, but he noticed that the executive was much heavier in the photos. Assuming that all of us worry about our weight, the rep began, "Before we discuss anything else, I have to know how you lost 40 pounds." Within minutes, they were sharing diets and exercise routines.[23]

VIDEO

8-4f The Product Approach

A physical demonstration of the product itself (or some aspect or benefit of the product) can be a dramatic opener. For example, a glue salesperson might say to a prospect, "These two pieces of wood are held together with our glue. Try to pull them apart."

The advantage of the product approach is that it appeals to more than just one of the prospect's senses, and this increases attention. Even with products too large for the sales representative to bring along, it is still possible to hand buyers something to grab their attention. When Charles Ward was vice president of manufacturing for Brown & Bigelow, a calendar printing company, he purchased one of the first rotogravure presses in the United States. Even though such presses had been used in Europe for several years, U.S. customers initially shied away from their use because of the higher cost. Convinced that the press's higher quality would be attractive if given a fair hearing, Ward decided to try selling a rotogravure on his own. Getting the name of an "impossible" account from one of his salespeople, Ward handed the receptionist a painting reproduced by rotogravure and asked her to take it to the president along with this message: "A Mr. Ward wants to talk to you about pictures like this one." The president was impressed enough with the picture to invite Ward in. Ward described the new European process and reminded the president that the calendars his firm sent out were reproduced from original art. "Aren't the high-quality paintings you buy each year worth the best reproduction possible?" he asked. Ward received his order shortly. Similarly, the computer salesperson might give prospects a printout specially designed for their needs. A salesperson for a truck-leasing firm might hand a color photograph to a transportation manager and ask, "How would you like to have your trucks look this good all the time?"

VIDEO

8-4g Getting Agreement on a Problem or Situation

If buyers have no problems, needs, or wants, they probably will not be interested in the salesperson's presentation. Accordingly, the sales representative may begin with a question to confirm the existence of a need that the product or service can resolve. Often the preapproach will reveal clues to a problem, in which case the salesperson can ask a verification question to confirm the accuracy of this information:

Mr. Smith, I understand that you just bought out the Acme Company. Doesn't that require an increase in your mill-working capability?

In the absence of hard facts, the sales representative may inquire about a need that is common to businesses like the prospect's:

Ms. Jones, other people in your industry tell me they are finding that their business forms keep increasing in cost. Is that true of your company also?

8-4h Qualifying the Buyer

Without prior information, the salesperson may want to qualify the prospect first before proceeding further into the interview. There's no point in continuing, after all, if there is no need. A mutual-funds salesperson might open:

Mr. Hardy, if I can satisfactorily demonstrate a way of investing your money for both a high yield and security, would an investment of $100 a month be a problem for you at this particular time?

With the qualifying approach, the salesperson must be careful not to antagonize the prospect. Asking abruptly about need, ability, and authority will alienate even the most even-tempered prospect. So the salesperson should preface the qualifying question with a reason, such as the benefit statement earlier. Another good prefacing statement would be:

Mr. Hardy, I wouldn't want to waste a moment of your valuable time, so I wonder if I might ask you a few questions about . . .

8-4i The Survey Method

VIDEO

The survey method is widely used in large-unit industrial sales. Business machine companies such as IBM, Unisys, and National Cash Register are extensive users of the survey method.

When using the survey method, the sales representative begins by seeking permission to survey, or gather information on some aspect of the prospect's business in which the salesperson may be of service. It is, in effect, a formal method of exposing problems and formulating a solution to these problems. The survey method is attractive to industrial prospects because they realize that their company's problems may be so unique that no sales representative can recommend a solution without extensive study of the firm's system. Yet receiving permission to conduct the survey may involve a considerable effort on the part of the salesperson. In some respects, the survey approach requires two sales: selling the prospect on the idea of a survey and the actual sale itself. Sometimes the former involves more effort, and the order follows as a logical result.

The survey approach offers advantages to both prospect and salesperson. To prospects, it represents an opportunity to have their business studied by experts but with no commitment on their part to buy. From the salesperson's side, the survey represents opportunities to uncover deficiencies within the prospect's operation, match exact solutions with needs, develop cost justifications, further qualify the prospect, meet with top management, and enhance prospect confidence in the salesperson. But the salesperson should not automatically employ the survey with each and every prospect. Because it is so costly and time-consuming of company resources (especially the technical personnel that have to carry out the survey), it should be used only for large accounts with complex operations.

The efficacy of the survey method is based firmly in the principle of reciprocity. That is, we feel obligated to reciprocate when we receive a favor. A customer who feels indebted to a particular company may buy its services to repay the favor of a free examination or survey. The salesperson should be cautioned again, however, that the high cost of the product or service can reduce or negate this tendency.[24]

8-5 The Next Step

Once the approach is completed, salespeople should spend time with prospects, discovering their needs and problems. This is an important stage, perhaps the most critical one in the selling process. Often prospects fail to buy not because they do not understand the product but because they do not understand the need for it. This crucial problem-recognition process is discussed in Chapter 9, "Problem Recognition."

Chapter Summary

The approach represents a critical stage of the selling process because it is the first time prospect and salesperson meet face-to-face. For this reason, many have called the approach the most important 30 seconds in selling. During the course of the approach, the sales representative has to gain entry to the prospect's office, establish rapport with him or her, and gain the prospect's attention for the remainder of the interview.

There are three basic ways of gaining entry: a letter, a cold-call, and a telephone call. Because the sales letter and cold-call were extensively covered in Chapter 7, "Successful Prospecting," most of the discussion in this chapter centered on the use of the telephone in the approach. The basic objective of the telephone call is to sell the interview, not to sell the product or service itself. As such, there are six steps in the telephone track:

1. Precall planning and organization
2. Identifying yourself and your company
3. The lead-in statement
4. An interest-capturing statement
5. Stating the purpose of the call and asking for an appointment
6. Handling any objection

Once the salesperson has gained entry, a major task is to establish rapport with the prospect. The importance of establishing rapport (i.e., dress, eye contact, shaking hands, posture, etc.) with the buyer was emphasized. Other aspects of sales etiquette were discussed, such as how to remember the buyer's name and how to avoid certain mannerisms that may annoy buyers.

The final portion of the chapter concentrated on ways of gaining prospect attention using openers such as the introduction approach, the referral, offering a benefit, appealing to curiosity, the compliment approach, the product approach, problem agreement, and the survey method. Sometimes an approach will consist simply of qualifying the buyer.

Discussion Questions

1. What are the three major ways of gaining entry to the prospect's office? Which is preferable and why?
2. What is the primary objective of the telephone call?
3. What are the six steps in the telephone track?
4. Why is precall planning important? What can be done to improve it?
5. What are some suggestions for improving telephone delivery?
6. What are some effective lead-in statements? Which are best?
7. What are some interest-capturing statements?
8. How far should the sales representative go in stating the purpose of the phone call?
9. What are some common objections heard over the telephone, and how can the salesperson handle them?
10. What are the elements of gaining prospect rapport?
11. What are the elements of making a good impression on the prospect?
12. When should the sales representative shake the prospect's hand?
13. What are some topics for small talk to open the interview? Are there any hazards with small talk?
14. What are some ways of reducing tension at the onset of the interview?
15. What are some suggestions for remembering a prospect's name? Why is it so important to remember?
16. What are some openers to gain the prospect's attention?
17. What is the survey method? When is it used?
18. Describe how the salesperson should respond to voice mail.

19. Lisa Carter, account representative for WOKY television station in Green Bay, Wisconsin, has an appointment with Bob Thomas of the newly opened Carleton Supper Club. The Carleton offers gourmet food along with big-name entertainment. Until now, Bob has restricted his advertising to newspaper and radio. Making use of the following techniques, formulate approaches that would be useful to Lisa:

    a. Introduction approach
    b. Referral approach
    c. Offering a benefit
    d. Curiosity approach
    e. Compliment approach
    f. Product approach
    g. Getting agreement on a problem
    h. Survey method

20. Craig Baker, sales representative for the BMI Company, has identified the Western State Bank as a prospect for BMI's automatic tellers. The president of the bank is Terrence Noone, who is noted in town for his conservative ways. Plan a telephone call for Craig that will secure an appointment with Mr. Noone.

Chapter Quiz

1. The approach is the
    a. first time the salesperson and the prospect come into actual contact with one another.
    b. process of gathering personal information about the prospect.
    c. method the salesperson will use to present the product or service to the prospect.
    d. process of making an appointment to see a prospect.

2. The least valuable means of gaining entry to see a prospect is the
    a. telephone.
    b. cold-call.
    c. mail or email.
    d. in-person visit.

3. The introduction by the salesperson during the identification step of the telephone track contains all of the following elements *except*
    a. prospect's name.
    b. salesperson's name.
    c. gatekeeper's or screener's name.
    d. salesperson's company.

4. Of the following lead-ins, probably the best is
    a. literature sent to the prospect by the salesperson.
    b. third-party references.
    c. a statement of a known problem in the prospect's industry or profession.
    d. the inactive account approach.

5. In the telephone track, once the salesperson has attracted the prospect's attention with a lead-in, the next step is
    a. stating the purpose of the contact and asking for an appointment.
    b. handling any objections.
    c. identification.
    d. an interest-capturing statement.

6. After gaining entry to the prospect's office, the second major task of the approach is
    a. gaining the prospect's attention.
    b. to establish rapport with the prospect.
    c. to state the purpose of the visit.
    d. to present the benefits of the product.

7. Eye contact is an important element of first impressions. All of the following statements about eye contact are true *except*
    a. prolonged eye gaze is perceived as confident and assertive.
    b. correct eye contact projects honesty, sincerity, and attentiveness.
    c. failure to make eye contact may be interpreted as sneaky, dishonest, or insincere.
    d. rapidly moving one's eyes after initial eye contact is perceived as sneaky.

8. In terms of gaining attention, _____ is probably the most widely used type of opening.
    a. offering a benefit
    b. the introduction method
    c. the referral method
    d. the compliment approach

9. "Ms. Taylor, I see you've developed a new point-of-purchase display. I think it looks just great. Would you like to know what other people in your business have done to double their return from their point-of-purchase displays?" This is an example of the _____ approach to gaining attention.
   a. referral
   b. curiosity
   c. product
   d. compliment

10. "Mr. Smith, other people in your type of retail business tell me they are finding that their storage costs keep increasing because of potential food spoilage. Is that true of your company also?" This is an example of the _____ approach to gaining attention.
   a. gaining agreement on an industry problem
   b. survey method
   c. referral method
   d. getting agreement on a problem or situation

Profile

Customer Profiles for Role-Playing Exercise

For the following prospects, prepare a telephone track that will secure you a personal appointment. Additionally, write down approaches you believe will be effective for the beginning of a sales call. You may need to review the product descriptions provided at the end of Chapter 6, "Beginning the Relationship Selling Process." Please note that two names are provided for each buyer, allowing either a male or a female student to play the described buyer role.

Sales Representative's Background Information, Radio Station WEAU

You have identified the Down to Earth Restaurant in Eau Claire, Wisconsin, as a prospect for WEAU radio station. The restaurant has been in business five years and serves unique, good-tasting natural food. Some menu items are of the unusual sort expected in such a restaurant, but many are traditional, including sandwiches, soups, and salads, though these are still made with all-natural ingredients. It is not surprising that Down to Earth's clientele tends to be young and well educated. In fact, most customers are students and faculty from a major, 4-year, urban university only two blocks away. Down to Earth is also within three blocks of the downtown area, where many offices and retail stores are located. Service is limited; patrons must place their own orders and take their trays to their table. Of course, this holds prices down, and younger customers do not seem to mind. Parking is limited, although the restaurant is within easy walking distance for most customers. From your own observations, you know that the owner, Ted (Tina) Leahy, advertises extensively, and exclusively, in newspapers. You also know that several new restaurants have recently opened up in Eau Claire and that they must be having some effect on trade.

Sales Representative's Background Information, Ergo Futura Furniture

You have identified the Hoosier Mutual Insurance Company of Indianapolis, Indiana, as a prime prospect for Ergo Futura desks and chairs. Because of its rapid growth in the area of casualty insurance, primarily home and auto, the Hoosier Company has computerized its applications and claims processing. In addition to the company's large IBM mainframe, one hundred data-entry clerks sit before CRTs inputting data. Through one of your friends, who sells photocopiers, you have learned that Clarice (Clarence) Jansen, controller at Hoosier, has expressed some dissatisfaction with the computerization process. In fact, you understand that they plan to hire 25 more clerks because of unrealized gains in productivity and expected additional business.

Sales Representative's Background Information, the Falcon King Air

You have identified the Baker Paper Company of Portland, Maine, as a prospect for the King Air. From Dun and Bradstreet, you learned that Baker sells half a billion dollars' worth of assorted paper products per year and that it has plants and sales offices nationwide. You recently heard from one of your existing customers, Wally Bergstrom of Bergstrom Paper, that Baker executives might be interested in purchasing their own aircraft, as they now have none. At a trade association meeting of paper executives, Wally was talking with Edgar Smith, president of Baker, about Bergstrom's recently purchased King Air. Mr. Smith agreed that his recent experiences with commercial airlines could certainly cause one to think about buying a corporate aircraft. Your objective for making an appointment with Smith is to convince him to take a demonstration ride in the plane. From Wally, you have learned that each month upper-level Baker executives make 80 trips and middle-level managers make 45 trips.

Sales Representative's Background Information, Pip Pop, the Powdered Carbonated Soft Drink

You have identified Quick-Stop stores of Miami, Florida, as a prospect for Pip Pop. Some 20 stores in number, Quick-Stop caters to adults in a hurry to make limited grocery and drug purchases and young people looking for snacks and entertainment. To appeal to the latter, Quick-Stop features frozen soft-drink machines, a large candy selection, video games, comic books, and the like. Quick-Stop stores are open 24 hours a day, and, as typical of their sort of operation, their prices are higher than full-service supermarkets. Donna Layton is the purchasing agent for the chain, buying for all 20 stores.

Sales Representative's Background Information for Financial Services Project

The Swansons, George and Marilyn, have two children, aged 4 and 12, and they live in Overland Park, Kansas, a suburb of Kansas City. Their home has been valued at $230,000, and they carry a 30-year, 6.5 percent mortgage on it. The following data describe their financial situation:

- A combined income of $100,000 from George's work in personnel for Butler Manufacturing and Marilyn's job as a teacher in the Kansas City, Kansas, school system

- Assets worth $93,000, including bank certificates of deposit totaling some $53,000, miscellaneous items (including art and antiques) worth about $20,000, and $20,000 in individual retirement accounts and a tax-sheltered 401(k) company retirement plan

- Term life insurance of $25,000 on George and $14,000 on Marilyn

- A company retirement benefit currently expected to provide an annuity of $100 per month at age 65

- Their current investment program consists of $4,000 per year for the IRAs and $2,400 a year to the 401(k) plan

- Debt of $750 on revolving charge accounts

Web Exercise

Go to www.entrepreneur.com/business-coaching/articles/0,6897,298630,00.html and select two or three articles to read on sales techniques and approaches. What kinds of techniques will work well for nearly every industry or business? Which areas need more tailored approaches? Which approaches do you feel most comfortable starting with? Why?

Notes

1. Debby Peters, "A Warm Reception," *Personal Selling Power,* March 1995, p. 50.
2. Jan Gelman, "How to Get Past the Gatekeeper," *Selling,* July/August 1994, pp. 52–57.
3. Dave Stein, "How to Get Past Gatekeepers," *SalesVault,* May 5, 2004.
4. Art Sobczak, "Avoid the 'Probation Officer' Call," *SalesVault,* May 26, 2004.
5. "Lead-Ins: The Snappy Hookers," *Sales & Marketing Management,* August 29, 1977.
6. Art Sobczak, "Selling When They Think They're Not Ready to Talk," *Salesdoctors,* Salesdoctors.com, 1998.
7. Bob Alexander, "Pose the Perfect Question," *Personal Selling Power,* July/August 1994, pp. 58–59.
8. Gary S. Goodman, *You Can Sell Anything by Telephone,* Englewood Cliffs, NJ: Prentice Hall, 1987, pp. 38–39.
9. Keith Rosen, "While You Have Their Attention, Opt-In," *SalesVault,* May 11, 2004.
10. Melissa Campbell, *"Welcome to Voice Mail,"* Sales & Marketing Management, May 1995, pp. 99–101.
11. Todd Natenberg, "Always Leave Voice Mail," *SalesVault,* September 22, 2003.
12. Jacques Werth, " 'Interested' Prospects and Random Negative Reinforcement," *SalesVault,* April 14, 2004.
13. Jan Gellman, "How to Make a Great First Impression," *Selling,* July/August 1995, pp. 58–65.
14. "No Kidding Around," *Sales & Marketing Management,* September 2002.
15. Kim Miller, "Protocol," *Selling,* November 1994, p. 26.
16. Sue Fox, "Handling the Handshake," Adapted from "Business Etiquette for Dummies," Dummies.com, 2000.
17. Ibid.
18. Ibid.
19. Ibid.
20. Joseph W. Thompson, *Selling: A Managerial and Behavioral Science Analysis,* 2nd Edition, New York: McGraw-Hill, 1993, p. 397.
21. Roz Usheroff, "Etiquette for the 21st Century," *SellingPower,* June 1, 2004.
22. Julie Hill, "Getting Carded: Business-Size CD-Rs Find a Niche," *Presentations,* June 2000, p. 15.
23. Mark H. McCormack, *What They Still Don't Tell Teach You at the Harvard Business School,* New York: Bantam Books, 1989, p. 42.
24. Robert B. Cialdini, "Principles of Automatic Influence," *Personal Selling: Theory, Research, and Practice.* Edited by Jacob Jacoby and C. Samuel Craig, Lexington, MA: Lexington Books, 1984.

Case 8-1

Analyze the following telephone conversation and determine how the salesperson could improve future calls:

Salesperson: Good morning, I wonder if I might speak to Mr. Hermann?

Receptionist: Which Mr. Hermann? M. R. Hermann or T. J. Hermann?

Salesperson: Which one is in charge of purchasing?

Receptionist: That's T. J. Hermann. I'll connect you.

Salesperson: Mr. Hermann, my name is Bob Smith. I wonder if I might make an appointment to see you?

Mr. Hermann: What about?

Salesperson: I'd like to explain about our new cleaning services that are now available to businesses in the area.

Mr. Hermann: We already have a cleaning service that handles our warehouse.

Salesperson: That may be, Mr. Hermann, but our company guarantees satisfaction at the lowest cost.

Mr. Hermann: How much do you charge?

Salesperson: We charge $10 for our services.

Mr. Hermann: Our current cleaners charge $8 per hour.

Salesperson: We offer guaranteed quality.

Mr. Hermann: That may well be, but we're not interested in changing at this time. But call back next year. You never know. (hangs up)

Now rewrite the conversation as you think the salesperson should have handled it.

Case 8-2

Ralph VanHandel, a sales representative for WOSH radio, is calling on Jennifer Graham, owner of Darla's Shop, an Arlington, Virginia, clothing store known for carrying the latest and most popular styles. Ralph is meeting with Jennifer to sell her on the idea of buying radio time for advertising Darla's.

Ralph: (extending hand) Good morning, Mrs. Gram. How are you today?

Jennifer: I'm just fine. By the way, my name is Ms. Graham, G-R-A-H-A-M.

Ralph: Sorry. Sure is a nice day today. Wish I was out playing golf. Do you play golf?

Jennifer: No, I don't. Now what can I do for you? I'm kind of busy. It takes a lot of time to keep Darla's going.

Ralph: I bet. You know, everyone says you're the best store in town. Absolutely everyone.

Jennifer: (folding arms across chest) That's nice. I'm glad to hear that. Now let's get down to why you're here.

Ralph: Fine. First, let me introduce myself. I'm Ralph VanHandel with WOSH radio. I hope I'm not intruding on your valuable time today. I would like to talk to you about buying some advertising spots with WOSH.

Jennifer: Well, in the past, we've pretty much restricted ourselves to advertising in the newspaper. We seem to get better results that way.

Ralph: I'm sorry to hear that. Some people feel that way, unfortunately. But you ought to at least give us a try. You might be surprised, you know.

Jennifer: Maybe I will in the future, but right now I really don't have any desire to waste money on radio advertising. Now I must excuse myself, since we've just got in some new shipments.

Questions

1. Did Ralph handle the approach properly? What mistakes did he make?
2. How would you have approached a buyer like Ms. Graham?

Problem Recognition

Key Terms

closed questions
continuing questions
creative silence
direct questions
dissonance

indirect questions
instant replay
lantern principle
open questions
permissive question

problem confirmation
redirecting questions
statement of purpose
third-party questions

Learning Objectives

Learning Objectives

After studying Chapter 9, you will understand:

- Why problem recognition is critical to the selling process
- The importance of questioning in the recognition process
- How to make the transition from the approach step of the selling process to problem recognition
- Questioning techniques for initiating the flow of information, continuing the flow of information, and checking for understanding
- Further guidelines for asking questions: keep the questions simple; retain the burden of responsibility; space out the questions; ask about benefits, not features; and avoid biased questions

---

At this juncture in any discussion of selling, it is traditional to talk about the presentation. We will do that here, too, but in a different way. Many salespeople and their managers view selling as a conflict between buyer and seller, with the successful salesperson being the one who prevails in the struggle. According to this way of thinking, salespeople are urged to be dominant—to "manage" buyers and, in effect, to manipulate them. The salesperson is directed to tell prospects about the product or service and why they should buy it, the assumption being that a complete, well-delivered presentation will automatically end in a sale. Although there is no question that delivery and drama are important factors, this manipulative approach is quite likely to establish barriers in the buyer's mind, for most people want to buy rather than be sold.

With the manipulative approach, the prospect is seen as a robot that will necessarily do as the salesperson says if only the right buttons are pushed, and the buttons are present in the salesperson's presentation. The words of the presentation are the stimuli or buttons to which the prospect can respond in only one manner—signing the order. This process is conceived to be one-way: buyer to seller. Nothing must be allowed to interfere with the process; the salesperson must manage the situation and be in control the whole time.

Some companies (and salespeople) have formalized the manipulative approach to selling into the "canned" presentation. Here the salesperson memorizes a speech for verbatim delivery to every prospect. This speech is organized to include a complete story of the features and benefits of the product, the hope being that at least some of the phrases will strike a responsive note with the buyer. The really sophisticated canned presentations may include a series of statements, after each of which the prospect is asked for agreement. For example:

> **Salesperson:** Ms. Prospect, have you ever sat down with your husband and discussed what would happen if you were seriously ill? I want you to give me an honest answer.
>
> **Prospect:** No, I haven't.
>
> **Salesperson:** You could use up your savings, but if the doctor said, "You will never work again," your savings wouldn't last long enough, would they?
>
> **Prospect:** No, not long.

There is a minimum of prospect participation in this process. Such canned presentations are generally used in low-level selling (especially with inexpensive items) or in situations where it is important to tell the complete story in a short period of time and move on with little intention of revisiting the buyer. As you might well imagine, many prospects object to the canned approach because they feel they are being treated as objects rather than individuals. "Better," as Ben Franklin once said, "to put on the role of the humble inquirer." We all hate the canned sales talk that goes on and on, with no questions about our needs.

In contrast to the traditional view of selling as a contest in which the buyer is to be managed, there is evidence to suggest exactly the opposite. In a classic study, Schuster and Danes found that "question-asking by the salesperson was a significant indicator of success regardless of product category."[1] In a 12-year $1 million study of effective sales performance, the Huthwaite Corporation, a sales consulting firm, found that successful salespeople asked more questions than their lower-performing counterparts (especially the right questions).[2]

This is not to say, however, that there is no value in planning a presentation, for there surely is. But with relationship selling, planning takes a different form. Each buyer is conceived to be different; each has his or her own needs and problems to which salespeople must address themselves on an individual basis. However, sales representatives can formulate a series of carefully preconceived benefit statements, a series of statements blending features and benefits. With a supply of these carefully planned benefit statements in the back of their minds, salespeople are prepared to present a credible picture of their product, but they are also in a position to individualize their presentation, selecting the right combination of features and benefits appropriate for that particular buyer.

9-1 The Discussion Process

In the selling process, telling is not equivalent to selling, and getting told does not equal being sold. Selling is least effective when the salesperson tells the prospect; it is most effective when the two parties are interacting. The first part of this interaction or discussion is the process of recognition—a mutual talking about, analyzing, and discovering the prospect's needs and problems. To a considerable degree this involves questioning, listening carefully, and analyzing buyers' needs and problems. Once buyers' problems are evident to both the buyers and the salesperson, the next part of the discussion process, the presentation, can begin.

In many ways, salespeople resemble doctors. If a doctor writes a prescription without first making a diagnosis, it amounts to malpractice. A doctor uses various instruments to conduct an examination of the patient. Likewise, salespeople should use questions as their instruments to conduct an examination of the prospect.

9-1a The Importance of Recognition

Recognition is very much associated with the process of human motivation. An individual begins with some form of need, which leads to a problem to be solved. The solution makes it possible for the next need to take hold. Then the whole process starts all over again, as A. H. Maslow theorized in his concept of the hierarchy of needs (see Chapter 4, "Buyer Behavior").

A *need*, according to Maslow, is "a feeling which, if left unsatisfied, produces anxiety or tension . . . yet if satisfied, imparts a sensation of well-being."[3] An unsatisfied need creates tension. If immediate gratification is at hand, there is no problem. As portrayed in Figure 9-1, if there is a large difference between what is desired (the ideal) and what is at hand (the actual), then a *problem* is presented. A problem in turn motivates the individual to seek a solution and reduce tension.

Figure 9-1
The Greater the Gap between the Ideal State and the Actual State, the Greater the Need Gap (i.e., problem) & the Greater the Motivation to Solve the Problem

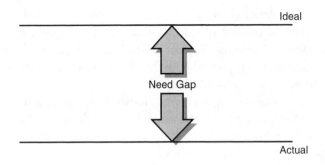

Let's illustrate this process with an example. Let's say you are sitting in front of the television set, when suddenly you realize you are thirsty. There's a hollow feeling in your stomach, and you know you would like a soft drink. If a can is by your side, there is no problem. But if none is immediately available, then there is a difference between the desired situation (drinking a soda) and the current state of matters (not having one). If this difference is great, going to the refrigerator, going next door to borrow, or perhaps getting in the car to go buy a 6-pack could resolve it. In any case, once the solution is found, the whole process begins anew, and the next need—perhaps a pizza—is ready to take hold.

How does all this relate to selling? The answer is that a sale requires buyers to become motivated to buy; they must recognize a need and a problem to compel them to seek a solution. However, recognition is not always easy. Individuals may not be aware that they have an insurance need or that a problem is present because there is a wide contrast between the financial coverage they have for their family and the coverage they require. Hospital purchasing agents may not be fully aware that a problem exists with their current surgical uniform; they may be only dimly aware that some unfavorable comments have been made about current garments. Such situations require recognition before the motivation process can begin. It is up to the salesperson to start the prospect talking so that a need and problem can be recognized. This talking will help prospects become aware of how large a gap exists between their current situation and the one they desire. Once the problem is established, the salesperson can move on to the presentation and illustrate how the product provides a solution to the problem and how desirable the prospect's situation will become after the purchase.

dissonance
The discomfort people feel on recognizing contradictions in their beliefs.

By indicating discrepancies between current situations and more desirable states that prospects could experience, salespeople create **dissonance**. This concept of "cognitive dissonance" is well known in psychology; it was first proposed by Leon Festinger to refer to the discomfort people experience on recognizing seeming contradictions. Festinger contends that people find inconsistencies troublesome and try to resolve these discrepancies (i.e., they try to change their current situations).[4] The marketing implication is that upon encountering prospects too content with their current circumstances to consider change, salespeople need first to invoke discontent to make the prospect receptive to change; the way to do this is by asking the right questions.

There is a well-recognized principle in biology known as *homeostasis*, which says that organisms seek to maintain equilibrium by resisting change and also by reverting to an original state if change should occur. Much the same is true psychologically. Individuals resist change in their thoughts, their feelings, their habits, and even their possessions. The lesson for salespeople is that their customers, too, are characterized by homeostasis; they tend to oppose change from the status quo. Only by drawing out prospect needs and problems through careful questioning can the salesperson disturb the customer's homeostasis. Only when questioning makes customers realize the depth of their current dissatisfaction are they likely to listen attentively to the salesperson's presentation. Change is unlikely until the salesperson's questions have first made customers uncomfortable enough with their current situations to seek relief.

No doctor would think of prescribing treatment without first diagnosing the patient. Yet this is exactly what many salespeople do. They immediately confront their prospects with a tirade about their new "miracle" products without first diagnosing prospect problems. It is no wonder that so many customers resist "miracle cures" and usher such salespeople out of their offices as soon as possible. Much like physicians taking patient histories, if salespeople don't accurately diagnose before they prescribe solutions, they run a risk of providing ones that do not address the clients' true problems. As with doctors, the rule is clear for salespeople: *diagnosis precedes prescription!*[5]

Yet, it is astounding how many sales reps fail to ask questions first, before beginning their presentation. In a recent study of life insurance agents, about one in four failed to inquire about the prospect's investment history, assets, saving objectives, and risk tolerance. Nearly 60 percent did not ask about the prospect's tax bracket.[6] It's no wonder that only about 20 percent of life insurance salespeople are successful.

At this point, the reader might question whether recognition is necessary in every selling situation. The answer is no, not always—but usually. Even when prospects have realized a need, they may not be aware of all the dimensions of the problem. Car buyers may recognize their need for a new car because the old one has broken down, but they may not fully recognize the kind of new car they need. Model, style, color, passenger capacity, and interior remain to be determined. Fulfilling these needs will also require the prospect to go through a recognition process.

How does the salesperson go about assisting the prospect's recognition process? As we have already said, telling is not sufficient. For true understanding, prospects must come to the realization themselves. This requires careful questioning by the sales representative to encourage prospects' talking so that they begin to recognize their needs and problems. This is the fundamental assumption in psychotherapy; when people begin to talk about things, recognition and understanding of their problems become firmer and solutions can be identified.

9-1b The Role of Recognition in the Selling Process

The way recognition fits into the selling process is depicted in Table 9-1. In the approach stage, salespeople seek to gain the buyer's attention. Once the approach is completed, problem recognition begins. This largely involves questioning and listening on the part of the salesperson. Once a problem is established, you can move on to the presentation. Here, the salesperson presents solutions to the prospect in a

T a b l e **9-1** Role of Recognition in the Selling Process

Approach →	Recognition →	Presentation →	Handling →	Closing
		ACTIVITIES		
Getting the interview	Questioning	Offering solutions	Resolving doubts	Signing the order
Relating	Listening			

creative and entertaining manner. Once the presentation is concluded, quite often the prospect still has some doubts and objections about the advisability of buying. It is the job of the salesperson to help resolve these doubts. The final step of the selling process is to close the sale.

Later stages of the selling process cannot proceed satisfactorily without adequate problem recognition. More sales are lost due to prospects' not understanding their problems than to any other factor. The smoothest presentation and most practiced of closes will fall on deaf ears if prospects are expected to relate stated benefits to an unrecognized problem. Attempting to sell a computer to a prospect who has not identified an inventory-control or order-processing problem is unlikely to meet with much success. Neither is trying to sell a cellular phone until the prospect understands how much time is lost due to canceled appointments, stopping to call from pay phones, and having to return to the office to check on inventory order statuses.

In fact, as mentioned in Chapter 1, "The Role of Personal Selling," problem recognition is the *most important* part of the selling process. In contrast to short-term transactional selling that involves one or a few calls, handling objections and closing especially, are much less important in long-term relationship selling. In fact, with relationship selling, preventing objections before they arise and minimizing the number of closing attempts are critical.

9-2 The Value of Questioning

We have already identified how questioning assists the recognition process by encouraging prospects to talk and realize their own needs and problems. Questioning is also advantageous from several other standpoints.

First, questioning aids in holding prospect attention. For the length of time it takes the prospect to answer a question, the salesperson has his or her entire attention. It is not possible for someone to answer a well-structured question and think of something else at the same time. Psychologists have estimated that, on average, people remember 10 percent of what they hear, 50 percent of what they do, and 90 percent of what they see and participate in. Learning (and selling) can be difficult when the listener only sits and passively listens. But when learners participate in the process, their attention increases immeasurably. If we are interested in anything, it is the sound of our own voices speaking our own interests. Remember, the average person speaks at 125 to 150 words per minute, but can think much faster. When the sales rep is talking, the prospect can both listen and think of other matters simultaneously—objections, fears, criticisms, doubts, and personal matters.[7]

Listening to responses to questioning builds trust; every question that salespeople ask implies that they are interested in the prospect. The more the salesperson listens, the more the prospect likes and trusts them, two factors we have identified on numerous occasions as absolutely vital to building the relationship. Each question says in effect, "I want to hear you. I respect your opinion." Once prospects feel that salespeople understand them, salespeople are that much closer to making the sale. As stated earlier, people frequently buy not so much because they really understand the product but because they feel understood by the salesperson.

Questioning also allows sales representatives to test assumptions they have made in the preapproach or during the course of the discussion itself. Without the ability to question buyers about their needs, the sales rep has no guarantee that he or she is on the right track. The salesperson might begin the presentation by stressing that "Acme widgets are 2 cents cheaper than XYZ's." However, if he or she had asked, the prospect might have expressed more interest in delivery, because XYZ's latest shipment had been two weeks late.

Perhaps not as obvious, the one asking the questions has control over the sales process. By asking the right questions in logical sequence, the salesperson can lead the prospect into determining to buy on his or her own. This is especially true of the large, multicall sale, where establishing a long-term relationship is critical.

9-3 Transition from the Approach

In initiating the recognition process, the salesperson must first make a transition from the approach stage of the selling process to the discussion stage. Two techniques facilitate this transition. First, if possible, the salesperson should make a **statement of purpose** (much like that made during the telephone request for an appointment). The sales representative may say something like, "Mr. Jones, I'm calling on you today to determine if our new blended surgical uniform has any application to your hospital's needs." Such a statement helps establish the salesperson as someone of purpose and expertise, someone who is not there to waste the prospect's time. Moreover, expressing a purpose engenders trust on the part of the listener. Too often, one person asks questions of another without giving the reason for asking these questions. As a result, the other person becomes suspicious. The listener feels that the questioner is trying to trap the listener in some way. In the absence of a stated purpose, listeners believe that if they knew why you were asking questions, they would not want to reveal their true desires. Later on, they fear, such information could be used against them, to corner them.

Following the statement of purpose, the sales representative then asks a **permissive question**: "Before I present the merits of our new surgical uniform, Mr. Jones, I wonder if it would be all right if I ask you a few questions about your current uniform uses?" Notice that the salesperson has begun the permissive question in a manner unlikely to offend the prospect. A directive statement to the effect that "I need some facts from you, Mr. Jones" would be offensive to most prospects. But the question prefaced by a "may I" or similar phrase is unlikely to offend prospects, and it will probably encourage them to be more open in talking about their needs. Certainly, it is difficult to refuse a question stated in such terms.

statement of purpose
Before questioning the buyer, the salesperson first states his or her rationale for the sales call.

permissive question
Before questioning the buyer, the sales rep asks for permission to ask questions.

9-4 Identifying Missing Information

Before asking questions, the salesperson must ask himself or herself, "What information am I lacking?" That is, in spite of the most thorough precall preparation regarding industry, company, product, competition, and intensive preapproach, there are bound to be areas where the sales rep's knowledge is incomplete. Of course, it would be impossible to provide a "laundry list" for all possible products and services, but there are a number of generic concerns that are typically "information poor." The salesperson might plan questions respecting:

1. Are there aspects of the current prospect situation that I don't fully understand? For example, "How long have they had their current equipment?" "What are prospect growth plans?" "Are they downsizing or restructuring?" "Who are their current suppliers?"
2. Do I need information on prospect buying needs? If selling to retail accounts, are there economic and demographic factors that will affect ultimate

consumer demand? Before presenting the merits of stocking a new, expensive gourmet coffee, for example, to a supermarket, what are the characteristics of consumers in the trading area? Are there physiological, safety, social, esteem, or self-actualization needs affecting the purchase? Is the prospect a Driver, Analytical, Expressive, or Amiable?

3. Are there problems present? Difficulties? Dissatisfactions? Likes or dislikes about the current set of circumstances? Quality or service considerations? Pricing issues?

4. Have I identified all of the relevant decision makers? In the typical organizational decision, there are multiple buying influences and it is often difficult to uncover all of them. It is absolutely critical to determine who has final approval power (i.e., the one who must actually approve the order). Who will be the actual users of my product or service? What power can they exercise in the decision? Which of these decision makers should I call upon first? Spend the most time and effort?

5. Do I need information on competitors? Because the prospect's frame of reference is influenced by the competition, the salesperson should ask:
   - Who are my competitors?
   - What are their strengths and weaknesses?
   - What is the relative standing of competitive pricing?
   - What are postsale service capabilities?
   - How do competitors rank in the prospect's mind?

6. What objection is the prospect likely to raise: price, skepticism, budget considerations, indifference, satisfaction with the present vendor? The professional salesperson should be prepared to respond to all of these.

7. What is the organizational culture? Are they risk-takers or risk-averters? Are they conservative or flexible? What do they value most? Market share, profitability, stability, stock price, employee satisfaction?

9-5 Questioning Techniques

Once the sales representative has successfully made a transition from the approach, it is time to begin questioning to facilitate the prospect's recognition process. In doing so, the salesperson makes use of two main types of questions: closed and open.

9-5a Closed Questions

closed questions
Specific questions that seek specific answers.

Closed questions are specific questions that seek specific answers. "Do you currently invest in a mutual fund?" is an example of a closed question. As here, responses to closed questions are limited, direct, and to the point: "yes," "no," and the like. Closed questions are useful for opening a dialogue, redirecting the conversation, and checking for understanding. They are also useful for encouraging interaction with reserved customers who do not respond to open questions. Closed questions limit the possible responses to a simple one-word answer like "yes" or "no."[8] Closed questions often begin with *do, are, is, which, have.* "How many" and "How often" are typical closed probes. Closed questions limit possible responses; they have several uses and can be extremely useful in several circumstances. Use them when your customer wanders to steer the conversation back to business. "This is very interesting, but how can I help you resolve your concern?"

Closed questions can also be used to confirm your understanding of a point your customer has made or to confirm needs. You might ask:

Then, we can assume you will send a check for the previous balance today, right?

If I understand you then, you'd like to cut your annual energy costs without changing your comfort, is that accurate?

When you ask questions to confirm needs, your questions should be designed to gain a yes or no response; therefore, they are closed.

Would it be helpful to . . .?

Would it be important to you to . . .?

Do you need to . . .?

Finally, when you just need specific information, closed questions are effective. "How many times did you try to contact us?" or "What is the date you called in to report . . .?"

9-5b Open Questions

Open questions are designed to get customers to respond at length. They are unlikely to be answered with a simple yes or no. Open questions provide lots of room for response; customers may answer in any way they desire. Open questions are good for drawing out feelings, attitudes, likes, and dislikes. Open questions typically begin with *what, how, who, why, where,* and *when.* "What do you think about?" and "How do you feel about?" are examples. Open questions typically begin with words like *what, how, why, where, who.* They can also be statements.

open questions
Questions designed to get customers to respond at length.

Can you tell me more about . . .?

What happened when . . .?

How did you hear about . . .?

You will typically use open questions to explore your customer's situations and to identify needs. They are especially advantageous because they are open to a large range of responses, indicating what's on the customer's mind.

Closed and open questions parallel the sorts of questions you see in exams. True-false, multiple-choice, and other "objective" questions are analogous to closed questions. Essay, case-analysis, and problem-solving questions resemble open questions.

9-6 The Questioning Process

Closed and open questions serve three main purposes: (1) beginning the flow of information, (2) continuing and redirecting the flow of information, and (3) checking for understanding.[9]

9-6a Beginning the Flow of Information

The basic strategy here is to outline the nature of customer problems—to identify the gap between the current situation and that ideal state where the customer would like to be. Salespeople should begin here with closed questions that provide background information about prospects and their business—to basically ascertain "What is the current situation?" Closed questions start the recognition process in a manner that puts prospects at ease because they are easily answerable. Questions that are easy to answer relax the other person. People enjoy giving answers they know are right, and with closed questions you give the other person a chance to give right answers effortlessly. Starting with difficult open questions may well make the prospect evasive and withdrawn. A real estate agent confronted with a prospective home buyer can start the conversation rolling by asking easy things such as the number of rooms in the current house the prospect lives in, the time needed to travel to work, the neighbors, and the schools, rather than leading off with an open question about the sort of home the prospect is looking for. Closed questions basically relate to "what's happening now." They ease the way for open questions and they build confidence and trust in the salesperson. Some examples of closed questions follow:

How many shifts per day do you run in your plant?

How many people in your family drive?

Do you currently have a policy of buying from a single supplier?

Have you ever before considered leasing a data-processing system?

How much insurance coverage do you currently have?

Are you looking for a ranch-style or two-story home?

Will you be making a decision in the next few months?

Have you considered switching to the new Windows XP?

In some instances, closed questions are formulated to verify the accuracy of preapproach information. In other instances, they are formulated on the basis of the sales representative's understanding of businesses similar to the prospect's. In either instance, at this stage of the questioning process, closed questions are intended to determine facts, initiate the prospect's recognition process, and set the direction for asking open questions.

Two phrasing techniques are recommended to ensure that closed questions designed to begin the flow of information do in fact focus on current reality ("what's happening now"). First, always phrase the closed question in the present tense. Second, use key words that signal to the customer that you are asking for information about the present. "Does inventory continue to be a problem?" "Are you still using the B2500 model?" Other key words and phrases that are good here are *remain, as usual, now, currently,* and *at the present time.* Another possibility is making a statement and then ending with the question, "Is this still the case?"

Open Questions for Beginning the Flow of Information

Open questions come into play once the prospect has answered some closed questions. Although closed questions answer "what's happening now," open questions identify the other portion of the problem, "what I want to happen." The spread between the two—"what's happening now and what I want to happen"—reveals the problem. Open questions tend toward the general rather than the specific and allow customers free play in relating their hopes. Open questions tend to begin with *who, what, where, why, when,* and *how.* Some examples of open questions follow:

How do you feel about the new generation of personal computers, Ms. Jones?

If you could wave a magic wand and create a perfect insurance policy to satisfy all your needs and concerns, what would that policy be like?

What advantages do you see for your engineering department workstations, Mr. Smith?

How do you feel about this ranch-style home, Ms. Johnson?

Asking questions is one of the most effective means of maintaining attention. As veteran salespeople say, "Telling isn't selling."

Where are you experiencing the greatest number of problems?

Could you explain why you are doing it that way?

Open questions are of special value in handling resistance from customers whose minds are already made up—but for illogical reasons. In response to open questions, they can begin to examine their own logic, recognize their inconsistencies, and become more receptive to the salesperson's proposition. "What do you like best about . . .?" followed by "What do you like least?" works well in revealing where such prospects are most vulnerable. If the salesperson is referencing a competitor, first asking about preferences reduces the perception that the salesperson seeks only to slander the opposition. For prospects who are satisfied with the status quo, the salesperson might ask, "If you were to make a change, what would be some of the things you would look for?" or "What would be different from the one you have now?"

Two especially good inquiries for getting customers to articulate their desires are "What will happen if . . ." and "Just suppose . . ." For customers who have not yet clearly thought and formulated where they want to be, these techniques are very helpful. "What will happen if the new computer works as you want it to?" "Just suppose you can have another copier anywhere in the office. Where would you put it?"

In both instances, prospects will reveal their prime buying motives and lead the salesperson toward making the sale.

At this juncture it is also useful to use what the industry calls the "Three Golden Questions."[10] Question 1: "Tell me, Mr./Ms. Prospect, what are some of the things you've been proudest of in the past three to five years? What has worked exceptionally well for you?" The idea behind this question is to discover how the prospect defines success. Question 2: "What are some of the things that haven't worked well for you, and why?" This question is framed to discover the gap between "where I am now" and "where I want to be." Question 3: "What areas have you wanted to address or develop, but have been unable to do so due to lack of time or resources or for whatever reason?" Questions 1 and 2 are designed to define success and dissatisfaction, respectively; question 3 addresses future opportunities. This is critical information for the presentation. Other open questions follow: Who are the buying influences? What are their needs? What are buying procedures? Who are new players on the scene? Who is the competition? What are likely buyer objections? In which additional areas is my information weak?

Just as customers have specific buying motives, they also have a consistent buying sequence. That is, they tend to evaluate a product or service in a set pattern or order. The salesperson can seek an **instant replay** to identify this critical pattern. It helps the salesperson discover not only what is important to the prospect but also the sequence in which to present the sales points. In other words, the salesperson determines how the customer makes his or her decision on a step-by-step basis. For example, the salesperson might ask, "How did you decide to buy your last insurance policy?" The sales rep will probably receive answers like, "I bought it because the agent said it provides protection. He said the cash buildup would earn interest rates above what banks pay." It is quite likely that he or she will decide to buy a new policy on the basis of protection and superior interest rates. In other words, if you learn your prospect's buying strategy, and play it back to him, you're going to receive more business.[11]

Open questions are valuable from yet another standpoint. In the course of talking about their goals and feelings, customers will reveal a great deal about their personality styles, something that will assist the salesperson in formulating strategy for the remainder of the sales call. Expressives and Amiables will tend to stress a more personal orientation in their goals (e.g., "I would like better teamwork" or "I would like to keep my employees happy"). In contrast, Analytics and Drivers will emphasize task concerns (e.g., "We need to produce more rapidly and with less waste" or "My chief concern is to track our costs better"). The time taken to respond is another clue for identifying prospect personality styles. Amiables and Analytics will typically take longer to respond and will be quieter in their responses than Expressives and Drivers.

Once they identify the prospects' personality styles by initial open questions, salespeople can structure subsequent questions according to each style. For Drivers, questions can pertain to industry trends, the growth of the company, and the Driver's role in it, and future directions the company might take. For example, "Mr. Jones, competition is fierce in the computer business and yet you remain an industry leader. What would you consider your competitive edge?" Drivers love to talk about themselves and their accomplishments. They also are interested in bottom-line benefits. Accordingly, the salesperson might ask the Driver, "What type of bottom-line benefits would you expect to gain from our product?" For Analytics, questions should focus on facts and details; for example, "Could you tell me about the budget you are working with for the new computer system?" "What are the parameters you have established for the purchase of the computer?" Amiables like to become friends before doing business. Questions such as, "Could you tell me how

instant replay
How the customer makes his or her decisions on a step-by-step basis on the basis of preceding similar buying decisions.

you got into this business?" or "Could you tell me about your business?" will be well received. Expressives, like Amiables, enjoy building a relationship first, so the previous two questions also work well for them. Because Expressives like to further talk about concepts and dreams, a stimulating question would be, "Where do you see yourself and your business in five years?"[12] A summary of effective selling questions for your sales presentation is shown in Table 9-2.

T a b l e **9-2** A Synopsis of Effective Selling Questions

1. What is your main objective?
2. How do you plan to achieve that goal?
3. What is the biggest problem you currently face?
4. What other problems do you experience?
5. What are you doing currently to deal with this?
6. What is your strategy for the future?
7. What other ideas do you have?
8. What role do others play in creating this situation?
9. Who else is affected?
10. What are you using now?
11. What do you like most about it?
12. What do you like least about it?
13. If you could have things any way you wanted, what would you change?
14. What effect would this have on the current situation?
15. What would motivate you to change?
16. Do you have a preference?
17. What has been your experience?
18. How do you know?
19. Is there anything else you would like to see?
20. How much would it be worth to you to solve this problem?
21. What would it cost, ultimately, if things remained as they are?
22. Are you working within a budget?
23. How do you plan to finance it?
24. What alternatives have you considered?
25. What benefit would you personally realize as a result?
26. How would others benefit?
27. How can I help?
28. Is there anything I have overlooked?
29. Are there any questions you would like to ask?
30. What do you see as the next step?
31. Who else, besides yourself, will be involved in making the decision?
32. On a scale of 1 to 10, how confident do you feel about doing business with us? What would it take to get that up to a 10?
33. Are you working against a particular deadline?
34. How soon would you like to start?
35. When would you like to take delivery?
36. When should we get together to discuss this again?
37. Is there anything else you would like for us to take care of?
38. What is your present situation regarding . . .?
39. How do you feel about the . . .?
40. What are some of the things you've been proudest of in the past three to five years?
41. What are some of the things that haven't worked well for you, and why?
42. What areas have you wanted to address or develop, but have been unable to do so due to lack of time or resources or for whatever reason?

Direct versus Indirect

direct questions
Questions that go straight to the point and their intent is obvious.

As the term implies, **direct questions** go straight to the point and their intent is obvious. "Are you the decision maker on the project?" or "How old are you?" and "How much are you willing to spend?" are direct questions. Other examples of such key, sensitive questions include: "Who really makes the decisions?" "What do you really think of my website?" "Why were we really knocked off the plan last year?" "How much money do you really have?" "How deep in the category are you really going?" "What's really going on in this account?" "How much do you really know about your account's business?" "How much of a risk-taker are you really?" "How much will you really fight for my website?" "What's the real objection to advertising with us?" The problem with these is pretty obvious. They can alienate people, but the bigger problem is that direct questions bluntly expose your intent. They often elicit either incorrect information or none at all. A better approach is using indirect questions. With **indirect questions**, the intent is not as obvious. For example, to determine someone's age: "What year did you graduate from high school?" Indirect questions are softer and more comfortable for customers to answer. Information gained from them is regularly honest and useful. As examples, review the two lists of sample questions. The first are direct; the second, indirect.[13]

indirect questions
Questions that are softer and more comfortable for customers to answer.

Direct Questions

- Why is that important?
- Did you make that decision?
- Is the equipment energy efficient?

Indirect Questions

- What do you feel will be most important in the decision?
- Where would you normally go for help with this type of project?
- What would you do if you were in my shoes?
- How is your office's heating and cooling system performing now?
- What do you wish you could change?

third-party questions
Indirect questions asking prospects to relate their opinions in terms of others' reactions (i.e., third parties).

An especially valuable form of indirect questioning, indirect questions asking prospects to relate their reactions to the situations of others, are known as **third-party questions**.[14] Asking car buyers directly about their abilities to afford an automobile may offend them and bring the potential sale to an abrupt halt. But asking prospects whether they think the car is affordable for most buyers will be less offensive but no less revealing, since the salesperson may interpret prospects' answers as basically referring to their own situations. Some examples follow:

Most of the people I call on tell me that automatic tellers are revolutionizing the banking industry. Do you find this to be true?

Consumer Reports *has rated this product as the best available for its price range.*

Would you say that most people would be willing to pay this amount for a sport-utility vehicle?

A lot of people feel that a formal dining room is not that important to a home, Mrs. Johnson. What do you think?

Third-party questions are especially important in initiating the recognition process for a particular type of buyer. An especially vexing problem for salespeople is presented by prospects who do not open up readily. Third-party questions represent a valuable tool in getting such clients to talk.

Some other techniques for asking sensitive questions are:[15]

Casual Approach: *"By the way, do you just happen to be in the market for a new fax machine?"*

Everybody Approach: *"As you know, many small businesses are using temporary help these days. Are you planning to do so similarly?"*

Every agency (media department, account, ad director, brand manager, etc.) *works differently* (has its/his or her own special needs, own priorities, preferences, etc.). *Tell me* (help me understand) *what criteria will be used here in this agency* (department, company, etc.) *to select online media for your new campaign.*

No two planners view (set priorities, decide, work with their clients) *A's website the same way. Where do you rank our site on your plan?* (What are your priorities?)

Blame Someone Else for the Question: *A good many of your customers say your firm is very conservative, perhaps too conservative. How would you respond to them?*

Imply That the Question Is Playful: *I'd like to play devil's advocate for the moment. What if you . . . ?*

I could be out of line here, but let me ask you, Why would you use websites A, B, and C and miss the . . . on our site? (If the buyer feels you are out of line and says so, the easy reply is a simple "Sorry" or a humorous answer, depending on your personal style. If the buyer does not give an answer, he or she will certainly appreciate your courtesy, which can only help the overall relationship.)

Preface the Question with Praise: *Your company has long been recognized as a leader in the office equipment business, but recently several industry analysts suggest there are product problems with your new Itanium-based PC . . .*

You know the situation (the client, the budgets, the marketing strategy) *best. What could knock us off the list?* (Will you be spending at the same levels you did last year? Are there opportunistic funds for sponsorships?)

9-6b Continuing and Redirecting the Flow of Information

Like most other people, prospects often lose track of their train of thought, wander off the subject, or stop talking before the listener has time to appreciate fully what they are trying to say. Because effective selling requires a complete and accurate understanding of prospect need, techniques are available for encouraging prospects to continue talking.

Continuing questions ask for a more detailed explanation of a prospect's statement. They encourage prospects to pursue their course of a thought in more detail. Inviting elaboration is perhaps the easiest of all the techniques. To do this, all you have to do is ask for more details. Then, watch out! People love to talk, especially about themselves and their concerns. By asking for more information, you open the floodgates and learn more about their problems. Although they sound like closed questions, continuing questions are in fact open. Some examples are:

Could you tell me more about that?

Could you give me an example of what you mean?

continuing questions
Questions that call for more detailed explanations of a buyer response.

Is that the extent of your view on the subject?

Let's get back to the cost-effectiveness issue. Can we make sure that I understand your point?

Besides using continuing questions, the salesperson can encourage the flow of information through two other techniques: the pause and the statement of interest. The pause—a complete verbal silence on the part of the salesperson—not only encourages prospects to continue but also provides salespeople with some time to think and formulate a response. Watch an interview on television: When the interviewee stops talking and the reporter remains silent, inevitably, the interviewee will begin talking again. It also tends to relax the pace of the information exchange, lessening any fears the prospect may have of being pressured. Finally, the pause is valuable to salespeople because it forces them to talk less and listen more.

Statements of interest may be as brief as a simple "Uh-huh." Other interest statements are "Great," "Sure," "That's interesting," and "No kidding." A statement of interest does not even have to be verbalized. It may be a nonverbal demonstration of interest. A nodding of the head, a smile, or leaning forward shows interest and encourages the prospect to continue.

If the customer has strayed or when the salesperson wishes to concentrate on a different feature and benefit, **redirecting questions** can be asked. Examples of such questions follow:

Is _____ also important to you?

Do you have difficulties with _____?

Is this of any interest to you?

How do you feel about _____?

Listening for Key Words and Exploring

In getting prospects to continue to talk and reveal their problems, the salesperson should look for specific key words and explore or "drill down" with further questions. For example, once the prospect starts talking, write their key words on a notepad. What are key words? Look at the following sentence:[16]

Our copier is always broken. Do you have something more reliable?

Next, start with your first key word and focus your questions. As you do this, keep listening for additional key words. For example:

Salesperson: What do you mean by your copier is always broken?

Prospect: It continues to feed two pages at a time, and the quality is poor. (*Note:* "Poor quality" is another key phrase that needs to be explained, so write it down.)

Salesperson: Are you doing a specific job that is causing it to feed two at a time?

Prospect: When we make our catalogs, we use heavier paper than our vendor says the feeder can handle, and they can't fix it. They recommend an expensive upgrade.

Salesperson: Tell more about the heavier paper you are running, and the other jobs you do.

Prospect: Well, we do . . .

Salesperson: When your feeder pulls in two pages, what happens to your business?

Prospect: We can't do anything until they come and fix it.

---

redirecting questions
Questions that can be asked if the customer has strayed or when the salesperson wishes to concentrate on a different feature and benefit.

Salesperson: How long does that take?

Prospect: Three days.

Salesperson: How much does this cost you?

Prospect: It costs us $5,000 to have an outside printer make our catalogs. And that doesn't count the loss of business.

At this point, you may ask them more about the manuals or more about their outside costs. The point is, by focusing or tapering down the key words "always broken," you have narrowed down specifically what they mean by always broken. In addition, you have uncovered the consequences and costs of being "always broken."

Of great use in exploring is *reflection,* which means considering the implications of what the customer just said. An example is when the customer says he was on vacation last week, and you say:[17]

That must mean your desk was piled up when you came in this morning.

Another example is when the person you are talking to says his computer hard drive crashed, losing all the important files. The ineffective listener will immediately begin to relive the last time he or she had this happen and tell how awful it was, totally stealing the conversation from the other person. The sales rep's goal as a listener is to keep kicking the conversation back to the other party. In this situation, a better response, and one demonstrating this technique, would be any of the following:

That must have ruined your morning.

Was there backup somewhere? You might want to check with IT.

Such responses reflect your interest and concern.

One notch up from reflecting on the implication is responding to the feeling. Responding to the feeling is better known as *empathizing* with another person. It means putting yourself in their shoes and really feeling how they must feel. To respond to the feeling, all you have to do is put some version of the word *feel* in your response. That includes all the forms of *found* and *felt.* Examples of this technique, in response to a customer who tells you about being denied purchasing approval by a buying committee, are:

You must feel frustrated having to deal with this situation.

We at XXXXX feel frustrated as well.

Listening between the Lines of Conversation

In asking for continuation, it is important to listen for the implicit as well as the explicit (i.e., to "listen between the lines"). Each line of conversation conveys several messages simultaneously. One of these messages is communicated through the meaning of the words. This is the explicit message. Other messages are transmitted by implication, or implicit messages. The individual's implicit messages often are more important, expressing his or her real feelings or things the person really wants at the moment; you have to listen between the lines and deal with her intentions.

Why do we need two channels of communication—explicit and implicit? The answer is because living in a society requires abiding by a complex set of rules—legal and moral laws, family and community customs, and etiquette. These rules are man-made; we are not born with natures that inherently fit these rules. This means we must continually make compromises between what our natures want and what the rules require. This results in implicit messages and really comes down to five interpersonal operations: (1) building up one's self; (2) attacking others; (3) making demands; (4) controlling; and (5) expressing love.

1. *Building up the self.* Lack of self-confidence is very common. Many voices are saying implicitly, *Look at me! See how clever, handsome, brave, strong, and funny I am! See how much I have and how much I know!* This all reflects a need for reassurance by the buyer. To make buyers more comfortable and more receptive to your ideas, tell them their actions confirm the presence of their desired characteristic.

2. *Attacking.* Words can be used as destructive weapons. Most of us are affected by what others think of us. Often the explicit message—the words themselves—may sound like objective criticism while the attack is implicit. These implicit verbal attacks take four forms: (a) unfavorable comparisons, (b) minimizing (including faint praise and pointed remarks), (c) teasing (including ridicule and sarcasm), and (d) gossip.

3. *Making demands.* The explicit demand is made by directly asking for something. The implicit demand stops short of this. It merely implies what one wants and then relies on the other person's desire to please.

   When a buyer gets up from his or her chair, this is an indication that the interview is over as far as the buyer is concerned. The rising is an implicit demand that the salesperson leave. Another way of making the same demand is to ask, "Is there anything else you'd like to talk about?" The implication of the question is that, if not, then the sales call is over. Interrupting another person in a conversation reflects the implicit demand that he or she stop talking and listen to you.

   When making demands, it is better to be explicit. People generally prefer to be asked for something directly. Implicit demands may actually stimulate more resistance.

4. *Controlling others.* A common way of controlling others is by exploiting their need for others' esteem. The control seeker promises approval for compliance and threatens disapproval for resistance. For example, to an unsure person, an influencer trying to sell an idea might say, "It seems to me that this would be the smart thing to do now." To someone anxious about being considered kind, the influencer might say, "It seems to me that this would be the considerate thing to do at this point." In effect, the influencer is implying that by performing the suggested acts, the self-doubter will demonstrate intelligence.

5. *Expressing friendship.* You may express friendship when you listen to someone's troubles and try to make them more comfortable; when you compliment a person for pleasure and not advantage; when you give advice to be helpful and not to control; when you accept another's anger without attacking, because you want the person to feel comfortable releasing his or her emotions; and when you provide information to be helpful, not necessarily expecting something in return.[18]

9-6c Checking for Understanding

Because communication is imperfect at best, feedback is a critical part of the process. Salespeople may not always understand the intent of the prospect's words, so they must check to make sure. In the course of checking for understanding, the salesperson also helps prospects to comprehend what they have said themselves. The act of answering the salesperson's query aids the prospect's own clarification and comprehension.

The basic mode for checking understanding is the closed question (although continuing questions may be appropriate for deeper understanding), phrased in such a manner as to imply that the response is assumed to be known. That is, the salesperson assumes the customer will answer in the affirmative. For example, a uniform salesperson might ask, "Is the ability of the garment to withstand repeated laundering more important to you than its initial cost?" An automobile salesperson might inquire, "It appears that interior space rather than fuel economy is the critical matter. Is that correct?" Both questions convey the impression that the salesperson anticipates a "yes" response, but is not certain.

Questions that check for understanding have the potential value of intensifying prospect needs, although this is not their primary purpose. The repetition intrinsic in the salesperson's checking and the prospect's responding helps to underline the urgency of need resolution. When, in response to open questions, a home buyer expresses concern about neighborhood schools, and when the salesperson subsequently asks for verification that schools are a critical concern in the decision, the buyer cannot help but firmly recognize and be motivated by this factor. This makes it that much more likely that the prospect will react favorably when the salesperson shows a home that fits this need.

In effect, the salesperson is reflecting here.[19] Rephrasing is just what it sounds like—repeating to the other person, in your own words, what you heard them say. This may sound like a waste of time; after all, if they just said it, why repeat it? Yet, rephrasing is one of the most powerful listening techniques available to you, and it is one of the easiest to learn. Simply think carefully about what you just heard, put it in your own words, and say it back to them in the form of a question. For example, when someone indicates to you they are concerned about getting new service to their facilities under construction, your rephrase and their response might sound like the following:

I can certainly appreciate why having service ready when you are has to be important to you!

Yeah, we've got several buildings under construction now. It costs us a lot of money to wait for you! What can you do to help us?

Rephrasing shows the other person that their situation sunk in with you and you really understand it. It also gives the person a chance to reiterate and expand upon their concern, which makes them feel better about it and gives you the chance to identify something you can do to make a difference. Keep in mind that rephrasing must be sincere. Artificiality does more damage than good. Some good ways to begin rephrase questions are the following:

As I understand it . . .

Do you mean . . .

By properly using checking questions, the salesperson can probe the underlying needs and problems of the prospect. For example, suppose a sales rep is questioning a purchasing agent about a recent proposal:

Salesperson: How did we do on the proposal?

Purchasing Agent: Not bad, really.

Salesperson: Great. When will we know what you're doing?

Purchasing Agent: We think we'll have it resolved soon.

Although superficially this sounds good and the sales rep may leave expecting to hear soon, it's not sufficient. Now notice what happens if the salesperson had responded differently after the purchasing agent's initial reply:

Salesperson: Does that mean you are seriously considering our proposal?

Purchasing Agent: No. There are a number of other things we're considering.

Salesperson: What are some of these?

Purchasing Agent: Well, obviously, we're concerned about the reputation of the supplier, and the ability to meet our specifications and deadlines.

Salesperson: And, how do you feel about our proposal based on those issues?

Purchasing Agent: We are a little concerned about your capability of meeting deadlines.

Notice in the second conversation that the salesperson has penetrated to a deeper level of prospect concerns with open continuing questions and is now prepared to deal with the prospect at a level that will have a real impact. Basically, the sales rep needs to ask questions of the "Oh?" and "Why?" variety.

Some examples are:

Why are you considering that?

What do you hope to gain by the upgrade?

What problems are you trying to solve?

When, exactly, do you expect to begin and finish this project?

Do you have a budget figure in mind?

9-6d An Illustrative Dialogue

At this point, we have discussed several techniques for facilitating the prospect's recognition process. But to speak of them individually and in the abstract does not really demonstrate how they may be used by the salesperson to assist prospects in their recognition process. To depict this fully, let's look at a sample dialogue between Ron Friendly (the surgical uniform sales representative) and a hospital purchasing agent:

Ron: Ms. Smith, I'm calling on you today to see if your hospital might profit from our new blended surgical uniforms. (statement of purpose)

Smith: Fine.

Ron: I wonder if I might ask you a few questions about your current uniform requirements? (permissive question)

Smith: Sure, go ahead.

Ron: Are you currently using all-cotton uniforms in the operating rooms? (a closed question to begin the flow of information by gathering facts about the prospect's current situation)

Smith: Yes, we are.

Ron: How do your people feel about cotton uniforms? (an open question to reveal sources of dissatisfaction)

Smith: Now that you mention it, there have been some derogatory comments. Only yesterday the laundry manager was commenting about the operating room uniforms.

Ron: Could you be more specific about what the laundry manager said? (an open question to continue the flow of information)

Smith: Well, it seems to me that he mentioned something about how quickly the uniforms seem to wear out, and also their high labor cost.

Ron: That's interesting. (statement of interest)

Smith: Yes, it seems the uniforms must be ironed, which, of course, increases labor costs. It seems to me also that the nurses and doctors have complained about the looks of the uniforms.

Ron: (nods his head and leans forward)

Smith: The operating room doctors and nurses say that the appearance of the uniforms is lacking.

Ron: They don't like how they look in the uniforms when they're outside the operating rooms? (a closed question to check understanding)

Smith: Yes, that's right.

Ron: Are you concerned about price in ordering new uniforms? (a closed question to redirect the dialogue to a new topic)

Smith: It depends. Price is only one factor.

Ron: Then other factors, such as quality, cost of use, and service, may be just as important as price, depending on the department in which the uniforms will be used? (a closed question to check understanding)

Smith: Certainly.

Ron: Let me see if I can summarize what you're saying. Your current cotton uniforms are a source of dissatisfaction for some of your people. The laundry manager dislikes their short life and high labor overhead, and the surgical personnel object to the garments' appearance. At the same time, you, as purchasing agent, are concerned about the price of uniforms, but it's not an overriding issue. Would you say that's a fair statement of the way things stand? (In this statement, the sales representative has established the problem and is ready to begin the presentation.)

Smith: Yes, it is. Have you got something new in mind?

Ron: Yes, I do . . . (Now he begins his presentation of features and benefits.)

9-6e Confirming the Problem

The preceding dialogue illustrates how the salesperson can facilitate the prospect's recognition process through skillful use of questioning and other associated techniques. The dialogue ends with a summation of the problem by the salesperson and confirmation by the prospect, the **problem confirmation**. Once this confirmation of the problem is received, the salesperson is prepared to embark on the next step of the discussion process—the presentation.

Probably the biggest source of failure in selling is prematurely presenting features and benefits before the problem has been clearly established. Often the salesperson begins a presentation without the client's clearly recognizing that a problem exists. Although questioning helps the recognition process, it is still necessary to follow up with a confirmation of the problem. This requires a formal statement—either verbal or written—of the problem and agreement by the prospect. At this point the reader might ask, "What happens if the prospect doesn't agree with the salesperson's summation of the problem?" The answer is simply, "try, try again." The salesperson may have to make a number of attempts before confirmation is secured, but once it is, the correct information upon which to base a decision is clearly at hand.

There are two parts to formulate a summation statement, which the prospect may confirm. The first part of the statement may be prefaced with key phrases. For example:

Let me see if I understand . . .

If I may, I will attempt to summarize . . .

I hear you saying that . . .

problem confirmation
A summation statement of the problem to the buyer at the completion of sales rep questioning.

The second part of the statement should end with a question posed to the effect:

Is that a fair statement?

Have I interpreted this properly?

Did I hear you correctly?

A question phrased in this manner will not appear condescending or pressure the prospect because the salesperson is asking for confirmation. Merely telling prospects what their problems are without giving them a chance to answer is too presumptuous.

As much as possible, problem confirmation should include:

- The current situation
- What the prospect wants
- The obstacles

These three parts review the current situation to make sure you've got your facts straight; they outline the objectives (where the prospect wants to be), demonstrating your understanding; and they recall the obstacles, indicating you understand the task that lies ahead. Notice all three elements in the following problem confirmation:

Let me see if I can sum up what we've just been talking about. At present, you're producing about 100 pieces per hour, but that's not sufficient. You need to be making at least 140 per hour or you can't keep your production profitable. The problem is that at that speed you get a slight curl to the edges during the stamping process. That means another production step to remove the curl. You've spent a lot of money on some new dies, but the situation hasn't really improved. Is that pretty much the way you see it?

Confirming the problem sounds a great deal like checking for understanding, and in a larger sense it is. The difference is that in seeking problem confirmation, the salesperson summarizes in one concise statement the entirety of the prospect's problem. Checking for understanding is more limited and occurs in preparation for final confirmation of the problem.

It is important that salespeople not seek problem confirmation prematurely. Successful salespeople, in order to make sure that prospects appreciate the full magnitude of their problems, first ask them about the consequences of the unresolved problems (e.g., "What does this lack of performance cost you?" or "How much employee turnover has this caused?"). The more severely the prospect perceives the problem to be, the greater the prospect's receptivity to the salesperson's presentation and eventual close. Moreover, once the presentation is concluded, the salesperson can confidently close the order, knowing that the product features and benefits will solve the customer's problems. Many salespeople fail to close because they feel somehow they are selling something unneeded. Solidly confirming customer problems, however, should eliminate this feeling.

As problem recognition proceeds, the salesperson should be trying to create an "internal paraphrase" of what the prospect is saying. Think of it as a running mental outline, which the salesperson periodically recaps to himself or herself throughout the conversation. The rep might even want to jot down the principal points. Having such a paraphrase in mind will be invaluable when it comes time for problem confirmation. As the conversation proceeds, close in gaps in your internal paraphrasing with checking and continuing questions. Not only does this lead to an accurate problem confirmation, but it also builds trust because it demonstrates active empathic listening.

Moreover, when several meetings are necessary before a sale is consummated (and most do), repeating the problem confirmation at the beginning of the next

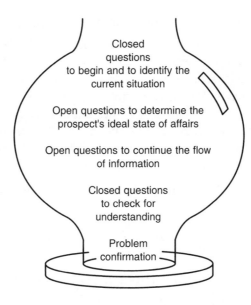

Figure 9-2
The Lantern Principle

meeting facilitates matters and avoids wasting valuable time. It also flatters the prospect, because the sales rep has obviously taken his or her business (and the buyer) seriously enough to ponder what was said in the previous meeting. The buyer is likely used to indifference on the part of most salespeople; summarizing a previous meeting will impress him or her with the rep's professionalism and build the relationship.

9-6f The Lantern Principle

An easy way to understand the questioning process is to visualize a **lantern.** The narrow portions of the lantern shape suggest the need for closed questions, while the wider central section suggests open questions. As illustrated in Figure 9-2, the salesperson begins with narrow, closed questions to gather facts and relax the prospect. Then broader, open questions come into play, as the salesperson seeks to identify the feelings and goals of the prospect. Open, continuing questions are also appropriate in the central part of the lantern, when the object is to get buyers to expand at length so that problems become clearer. Once the salesperson begins to get a grasp of underlying needs and problems, closed questions again are called for, this time to check for understanding and finally to confirm the problem in its entirety.

lantern principle
The narrow portions of the lantern shape suggest the need for closed questions.

9-7 Further Guidelines for Questioning

We have examined the use of questioning and other related techniques in assisting the recognition process. Selling is an art rather than a science, and so only the general form of the question can be indicated. Its specific nature or form will vary widely with the specific product or service being sold. Accordingly, it is up to individual salespeople to formulate their own questions. Here are some further guidelines that should facilitate this process. Salespeople should:

1. Keep the questions simple.
2. Retain the burden of responsibility.
3. Space out the questions.
4. Ask about benefits, not features.
5. Avoid biased questions.

9-7a Keep the Questions Simple

Each question should not contain more than one idea. Too many ideas embedded in one question makes it too difficult for the prospect to answer. For example, the sales representative might ask, "What are your views concerning the low monthly payments, increased mileage, and front-wheel drive of our new Focus automobile?" A buyer facing such a question would be overwhelmed because three separate ideas are contained in this one inquiry. The prospect may not remember all three issues and might simply respond, "They're all fine," to avoid the difficulty of answering. The salesperson should have phrased three separate and distinct questions.

> *How do you feel about our low monthly payments?*
>
> *Is the improved mileage attractive to you?*
>
> *What are your views regarding front-wheel drive?*

9-7b Retain the Burden of Responsibility

In the questioning process, the burden of responsibility should be retained by the sales representative.[20] A question such as "Do you understand?" is likely to offend prospects because it puts the burden of responsibility on them. If they answer anything other than yes, they are admitting to stupidity on their part. The salesperson is better off phrasing the question, "Have I adequately explained this point?" Who bears the responsibility with this question? How differently are prospects likely to respond?

Questions prefaced with *why* are especially likely to violate the principle of burden. They are threatening to the prospect, especially if expressed with a harsh tone of voice. "Why do you feel that way?" can be interpreted by the buyer to mean "I don't approve of your feelings." "Why did you do that?" can be perceived as "I don't approve of what you did." These two "why" questions can be rephrased so as not to offend the client. The first may be reformulated into "How did you come to have these feelings?" and the second into "What was the basis for your decision?"

9-7c Space Out the Questions

Questions that follow one another too closely will threaten buyers. They may feel like a witness being interrogated on the stand. Rapid-fire "Who does the buying around here?" "How many suppliers do you maintain?" and "What are your responsibilities?" are guaranteed to offend even the most thick-skinned prospect. It is much better to space out questions, providing time for the client to think over each answer in a relaxed manner.

What we are recommending here is a principle we call **creative silence**.[21] All creative silence means, as Figure 9-3 indicates, is that the seller needs to pause for

creative silence
A pause for approximately three to four seconds at two different points in the questioning process.

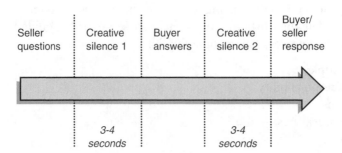

Figure 9-3
Creative Silence

approximately three to four seconds at two different points in the questioning process: after asking the question and after the buyer responds. These two pauses—creative silence 1 and creative silence 2—will dramatically improve the quality and quantity of information the buyer is transmitting. The explanation of efficacy is simple for creative silence 1. The three to four seconds the buyer has to consider and mull over his or her answer is likely to make the information better than if only half the time had been allowed. By practicing creative silence 2 and waiting three or four seconds, you are giving the buyer a better chance to understand what he or she has told you than if, again, only half as much time had been spent in silence. The result of the two portions of creative silence is more leisurely, more thoughtful, and ultimately a more productive flow of information than could be engendered any other way. Moreover, the buyer is not paralyzed with "question shock," the consequence of facing a barrage of questions fired off in rapid sequential order. By waiting to reply, the salesperson implies that the buyer's ideas are important and they deserve consideration, something that will help the buyer be more receptive to the salesperson's coming presentation. If the salesperson is uncomfortable just sitting there, he or she can nod, lean forward, knit his or her brow, or establish eye contact. If after the allotted three to four seconds there is no response, chances are good that the question has been misunderstood and it is time to rephrase another one. An effective technique at this juncture is to say, "My intention in asking that question was to . . ." and then explain what you are trying to find out more clearly.

9-7d Ask about Benefits, Not Features

Earlier we stated that features are physical characteristics of the product, while benefits relate to what the buyer would get from the product (i.e., how the characteristics would fulfill a need). When salespeople ask prospects about their need for specific features, about which prospects may know little, prospects might respond as if they did, not wanting to admit ignorance. As a result, salespeople may think they have made a superb presentation, only to walk out the door without an order. An automobile salesperson, for example, might ask for a buyer's impression of fuel injection, receive a favorable response, and go on to another point, assuming that the prospect already knows the benefits of fuel injection. The salesperson would have been better off asking, "Would you like to escape the expenses of periodic carburetor tune-ups?" Shelf-stable milk not requiring refrigeration is a staple in Europe, but it's clearly an anomaly in the United States, where milk and refrigeration are synonymous. Pitching the product just as shelf-stable got one salesperson nowhere, until he began asking, "How would you like to be able to take milk on camping, fishing, and hiking trips?"[22] Even when the prospect asks about specific features, the salesperson is better off speaking in terms of benefits because the buyer may not know about other features that would serve just as well.

9-7e Biased Questions

If you are not careful and conscious of it, your questions may carry bias. Bias is when the wording or tone of your questions indicates what the correct answer should be. "You do want an energy efficient system, don't you?" and "You'd have to agree our equipment is easier to operate, wouldn't you?" are two questions that carry bias.

Bias diminishes your credibility and makes customers feel they are being manipulated. Depending on how they are asked, questions such as these can be terribly insulting, especially if the customer does not share your opinion.

Raise your awareness to biased-sounding questions and don't let them creep into your discussions with customers. Here are some additional questions that you should not ask:[23]

- *You wouldn't expect our competitor to recommend us, would you?*
- *You do care about the environment, don't you?*
- *You wouldn't put something unsafe in your home, would you?*
- *Saving money is important to you, isn't it?*

9-8 The SPIN Sequence

Neil Rackham, in his book *SPIN Selling,* shows how classic sales techniques such as closing and objection-handling can actually reduce your chance of selling, especially in big business-to-business sales situations, where buyers are savvy to the classic tricks; better to concentrate on questioning, particularly a series of sequenced questions: situation, problem, implication, and need payoff. The first letter of each type of question is the source of the acronym *SPIN.*

Overall, his method, like many other approaches, is a "distress and rescue" approach. The salesperson finds the buyer's problem by a series of well-formulated questions and "distresses" them by exposing the awful things that might happen. The salesperson can then "rescue" the buyer with the product.

The four question types are as follows:[24]

1. *Situation questions.* These are data-gathering questions, such as "How long have you had your current equipment?" or "Could you tell me about your company's growth plans?" Situation questions should not be overused because they can bore or even offend the buyer. He or she thinks about such matters every day. Situation questions can relate to the buyer personally (e.g., "What do you see as your objective here?"); be about the business (e.g., "What is your annual sales volume?"); or concern operations ("What equipment are you using at present?"). The common factor in all these questions is that they collect information on the current situation.

2. *Problem questions.* These explore problems, difficulties, and dissatisfactions (e.g., "Is this operation difficult to perform?" or "Are you worried about the quality you get from your old machine?"). If no problems can be uncovered, there is no basis for a sale (or a relationship). If you are selling tractors, ask about maintenance costs, breakdowns, and so on. If you are selling life insurance, ask how many dependents the person has. A trap here is to dive straight into presenting the benefits of what you are selling. You may know the problem, but they do not! Going straight to the sales pitch will just get you objections.

3. *Implication questions.* These questions ask about the consequences or effects of a customer's problems (e.g., "How does this problem affect your future profitability?" or "What effect does this reject rate have on customer satisfaction?"). Implication questions take problems and explore their effects or consequences. They help customers understand their problem's seriousness or urgency. They take problems buyers perceive to be small and build them up in customers' perceptions, until they believe the problem demands action. For example, the person selling tractors might ask about implications of unplowed fields; the life insurance salesperson could carefully ask what would happen to the children if the target person died or

became very ill. Other examples of implication questions are "What effect does this have on output? Proposed expansion?" If a customer problem, for example, is that the existing machine is hard to use, it should lead the salesperson to ask implication questions, such as "Does this increase training costs for operators?" "Are operators dissatisfied?" "Is turnover a resulting problem?" "Are there problems in recruiting trained personnel at higher salaries?" "Is there a lot of overtime?" "Are there quality problems?" or "Do you have many rejects?"

4. *Need-payoff questions.* These questions achieve two things: They focus customers' attention on solutions rather than problems, and they get customers telling sales reps the benefits. Need-payoff questions create a positive atmosphere by focusing on solutions, not problems, and in response to them, buyers gain their own insight into benefits, rather than being told. For example, a question like "How would a faster machine help you?" might prompt the reply, "It certainly would take away the production bottleneck and it would also make better use of skilled operator time." For example, the tractor salesperson can ask how much better the tractor was when it was new, or whether any of the farmer's neighbors have solved problems of old and problematic tractors. The insurance salesperson could ask questions that build pictures of the target person's children being safe and secure despite whatever "curveballs" the world might throw at the family.

   A rather simplified distinction between implication and need-payoff questions is that the latter are "happy questions"; implication questions, in contrast, are sad. Implication questions are problem-centered (they are designed to make the problem more serious in the buyer's eyes) and hence, sad. Need-payoff questions, in contrast, are solution-oriented and consequently, happy. Need-payoff questions are strongly linked to success in the large sale. They increase the acceptability of the sales rep's solution, and they are especially effective with influencers who will present their case to the real decision makers. That is, need-payoff questions create inside salespeople for reps.

Need-payoff questions can be effective because if you can get the customer to tell you the ways in which your solution will help, then you don't invite objections. Nobody likes being told what's good, especially by an outsider. Customers react more positively if they are treated as experts. Buyers can't be expected to learn about a salesperson's product in enough depth to explain it convincingly to others in their company, but they can be expected to have an understanding of their own problems and needs; they understand these best. After all, it's their business, and they'll know best how it would be helped by the solution the rep is proposing. Moreover, when buyers talk to others in the account, it's with respect to needs, not product features. It's much better to get the buyer actively describing benefits to the salesperson for inside selling to others. Also, they take ownership, feeling their ideas are part of the solution.

The fundamental problem that causes an objection is that the seller offered a solution before building up the need. The buyer doesn't feel that the problem has enough value to merit such an expensive solution. Objection prevention is best handled via the use of implication and need-payoff questions. They are more effective because they attack the causes of objections. As a result, objections don't even arise; this is more effective, regardless of the objection-handling abilities of the salesperson. Forestalling, in other words, is the best means of resolving objections.[25]

Chapter Summary

This chapter began by pointing out how the traditional "telling" approach to the sales presentation falls short in a number of respects. First, the telling method treats the buyer as an object to be manipulated and coerced. Under these circumstances, it is understandable that buyers become defensive and even angry. Second, with the telling method there is no guarantee that the prospect understands that a problem exists to justify product purchase. Telling does not allow prospects to recognize the problem themselves, since problem recognition must come from within. As such, the task of the salesperson becomes one of assisting prospects in reaching the conclusion themselves; this requires skillful questioning and listening.

Two different types of questions are used in fostering problem recognition: closed and open questions. Closed questions solicit specific responses. Answers to closed questions are typically limited—"yes," "no," and the like. In contrast, open questions are phrased to encourage as much prospect response as possible. Usually, open questions begin with *what, how, why, when,* and *where*.

Questions may be used for three basic purposes: (1) beginning the flow of information, (2) continuing and redirecting the flow of information, and (3) checking for understanding. The salesperson should start the questioning process with closed questions designed to discover facts about the prospect's current situation and should follow up with open questions that encourage lengthier responses about that ideal situation where the prospect would like to be. In other words, the idea is to identify the existence of customer problems.

In encouraging the exchange of information, the salesperson makes use of continuing questions, pauses, and statements of interest. A continuing question would be something like, "Could you tell me more about that?"—a question intended to have the prospect pursue a train of thought. The pause—a complete silence on the part of the salesperson—is intended to accomplish the same thing: to encourage the prospect to continue. Statements of interest such as "uh-huh," "great," and "sure" are also helpful in this regard. At this stage, the salesperson may also redirect the flow of information by asking closed questions, such as "Is _____ also of importance?" or "Do you have difficulties with . . . ?"

The basic mode of checking for understanding is the closed question, typically phrased in a manner that assumes an affirmative response (e.g., "Is it fair to say that versatility is the most important factor?").

Once salespeople are sure the problem is recognized and understood, they seek its confirmation. The sales representative summarizes the problem as he or she perceives it, and prospects can then confirm the diagnosis as they see fit. From this point, the salesperson may progress into the sales presentation itself.

A convenient way to remember the proper sequence of questioning is to imagine a lantern. At the narrow top of the lantern, salespeople should begin with closed questions. Progressing to the broader part of the lantern, they should use open questions to reveal prospect hopes and to continue the flow of information. Then they should begin to narrow in again with checking questions and finally confirm the problem.

Additional techniques for asking questions are as follows:

1. Keep questions simple and directed to only one idea.
2. Place the burden of responsibility on the salesperson, not the prospect.
3. Space out questions.
4. Ask about benefits, not features.
5. Avoid biased questions.

The chapter ended with a description of the SPIN cycle of questioning: *Situation, Problem, Implication* and *Need-payoff* questions.

Discussion Questions

1. Why is the traditional method of "telling" ineffective as a means of making the sales presentation?

2. What is a "canned" presentation?

3. What is the place of recognition in the total selling process?

4. Why is problem recognition necessary?

5. What is a need? What is a problem?

6. What is the role of the salesperson in problem recognition?

7. How does the salesperson handle the transition from the approach stage to the problem-recognition stage?

8. What are the two primary techniques for questioning? How do their uses differ?

9. How are closed and open questions used to begin the flow of information? Why is the salesperson advised to start with closed questions?

10. What are the "Three Golden Questions"?

11. How are open questions valuable in revealing the personality style of the prospect?

12. What are third-party questions? Why are they necessary?

13. How can the salesperson encourage the prospect to continue to talk? Redirect the conversation?

14. Explain the salesperson's basic technique for checking for understanding. Are there additional benefits to checking for understanding?

15. What is problem confirmation? Why is it necessary? How does it differ from mere checking for understanding?

16. Explain the lantern principle.

17. What is the concept of burden of responsibility?

18. What are some ways that the salesperson might ask sensitive questions?

19. What is "creative silence"?

20. Interview a salesperson and find out his or her feelings about the importance of questioning and listening.

21. Split into groups of three in your class. Have one student play the part of a salesperson, the second the part of a buyer, and the third the part of an observer who will rate the salesperson's efforts. The salesperson will question the buyer regarding that individual's needs and problems associated with the purchase of one or more of the following products: automobile, skis, DVD player, apartment, shoes, HDTV. The observer should rate the salesperson as

to the quality of the questions asked and as to whether needs were sufficiently identified. Each of the three people should have an opportunity to be the salesperson.

22. Explain the difference between direct and indirect questions.

23. Identify the form of the following questions. What is each question designed to do?
    - Does that check with your experience?
    - How long have you had your dishwasher?
    - Is price more important to you than economy?
    - What factors are important to you in deciding to give shelf space to a new product?
    - What do you see ahead for yourself in the next 10 years?
    - How do you feel about using an employment agency to fill your openings? What kind of billing schedule would best fit your needs?
    - Would you say that most companies in the paper business are cutting back these days?
    - Could you tell me a little bit more about your advertising objectives?
    - Then, as I interpret what you're saying, you plan to acquire new companies, but only if they rank number one or two in their business.
    - What problems have you experienced in packaging your product?

Chapter Quiz

1. By indicating discrepancies between actual situations and ideal states that prospects could experience, salespeople create
   a. a need.
   b. a problem.
   c. a motive.
   d. a solution.

2. Activities that would occur during the recognition stage of the selling process include
   a. getting the interview and relating.
   b. questioning and listening.
   c. questioning and offering solutions.
   d. offering solutions and resolving doubts.

3. In relationship selling, _____ is the most important part of the selling process.
   a. approach
   b. problem recognition
   c. presentation
   d. handling

4. In initiating the recognition process, the salesperson must first make a transition from the approach stage of the selling process to the discussion stage. If possible, the first step by a salesperson should be a
   a. statement of purpose.
   b. permissive question.
   c. dissonance-reducing statement.
   d. relationship-building question.

5. "Do you currently invest in a mutual fund?" is an example of
   a. an open question.
   b. a closed question.
   c. a dissonance question.
   d. the lantern approach.

6. Closed questions serve all of the following purposes *except*
   a. beginning the flow of information.
   b. continuing and redirecting the flow of information.
   c. checking for understanding.
   d. determining the who, what, why response.

7. All of the following would be examples of indirect questions *except*
   a. Is the equipment energy efficient?
   b. What do you feel will be most important in the decision?
   c. Where would you normally go for help with this type of project?
   d. How is your office's heating and cooling system performing now?

8. Based on the lantern principle, all of the following statements are true *except*
   a. the narrow portions of the lantern shape suggest closed questions.
   b. the salesperson begins with closed questions.
   c. the salesperson uses open questions to gather facts and help the prospect relax.
   d. the salesperson uses closed questions to confirm the problem and close the sale.

9. All of the following are good guidelines for asking questions *except*
   a. keep the questions simple.
   b. space out questions.
   c. ask about features, not benefits.
   d. avoid biased questions.

10. Based on the SPIN sequence, an example of a _____ question would be "Are you worried about the quality you get from your old machine?"
   a. situation
   b. problem
   c. implication
   d. need-payoff

Profile

Role-Playing Exercise

For the products and services described in Chapter 6, and the appropriate customers depicted in Chapter 8, formulate open and closed questions that will (1) begin the flow of information, (2) continue and redirect the flow of information, and (3) check for understanding. Remember that your overall goal is to identify and confirm prospect problems that will allow you to focus on the remaining tasks of the selling process.

Web Exercise

The American Automobile Association (AAA) offers services ranging from driving classes to roadside assistance to travel agents. Explore the AAA site at www.aaa.com and study their offerings. Then, prepare questions to help find out the needs AAA can fill for:

- Jenny, an 18-year-old college student living in a new city. Jenny thinks she wants roadside assistance services, but isn't sure exactly what she needs.

- Ursula, a 55-year-old independent traveler. Ursula just bought a vintage convertible and is thinking about taking a road tip from Colorado to California.

- Jack and Simone, a couple near retirement. Jack and Simone are interested in international cruises, but don't know where to start looking.

- The Bellwether family: Janet, Brad, and their three children, ages 2–8. The Bellwethers are looking for good family vacations within driving distance.

Notes

1. Camille P. Schuster and Jeffrey E. Danes, "Asking Questions: Some Characteristics of Successful Sales Encounters," *Journal of Personal Selling and Sales Management,* Winter 1996, pp. 17–27.

2. Neil Rackham, *SPIN Selling,* New York: McGraw-Hill, 1996, p. 161.

3. A. H. Maslow, "A Theory of Human Motivation," *Psychological Review,* July 1943, pp. 370–396.

4. Leon Festinger, *A Theory of Cognitive Dissonance,* Evanston, IL: Row, Peterson, 1957.

5. Mark Haering, "Diagnose before You Prescribe," *Sales & Marketing Management,* April 2004.

6. Leslie Scism, "Many Life Insurance Agents Don't Know Enough about Their Clients," *Wall Street Journal,* May 9, 1995, p. A6.

7. Brian Tracy, "Stop Talking and Start Asking Questions," *Sales & Marketing Management,* February 1995, pp. 79–87.

8. V. R. Buzzotta, R. E. Lefton, and Manuel Sherberg, *Effective Selling through Psychology,* Psychological Associates, 1991.

9. "Closed Questions," *Training, Professional Sales,* http://demo.apogee.net/ccit/train/tpmen.htm, 2004.

10. James Lorenzen, "How to Overpower New Competitors and Their Lines," *Agency Sales Magazine,* March 1997.

11. Kerry L. Johnson, *Mastering the Game,* Tustin, CA: Louis and Ford, 2002.

12. Anthony J. Alessandra, Rick Barrera, and Phillip S. Wexler, *Nonmanipulative Selling,* 2nd Edition, Fireside: 1992.

13. "Direct versus Indirect," *Training, Professional Sales,* http://demo.apogee.net/ccit/train/tpmen.htm, 2004.

14. Carl McDaniel and Roger Gates, *Marketing Research Essentials,* 4th Edition, Indianapolis, IN: Wiley, 2004.

15. Anne Miller, "Asking the Tough Questions," *The Power to Sell,* www.annemiller.com/articles.asp, December 14, 2000.

16. Eric Slife, "Learning to Ask Questions to Uncover Problems," *SalesVault,* June 28, 2004.

17. "Reflect," *Training, Professional Sales,* http://demo.apogee.net/ccit/train/tpmen.htm, 2004.

18. Jesse S. Nirenberg, *Getting Through to People: Techniques of Persuasion-How to Break Through Mental and Emotional Barriers in Person to Person Communication,* Englewood Cliffs, NJ: Prentice Hall, 1989, pp. 88–79.

19. "Rephrase," *Training, Professional Sales,* http://demo.apogee.net/ccit/train/tpmen.htm, 2004.

20. Joseph W. Thompson, *Selling: A Managerial and Behavioral Science Analysis,* 2nd Edition, New York: McGraw-Hill, 1973, p. 438.

21. Robert B. Miller and Stephen E. Heiman, *The New Conceptual Selling® : The Most Effective and Proven Method for Face-to-Face Sales Planning,* Berkeley, CA: Warner Books, 1999, p. 110.

22. "Biased Questions," *Training, Professional Sales,* http://demo.apogee.net/ccit/train/tpmen.htm, 2004.

23. Ibid.

24. Neil Rackham, *SPIN Selling,* McGraw Hill, 1996.

25. Ibid.

Case 9-1

Analyze the following dialogue and indicate what techniques the salesperson is using to encourage the prospect's problem recognition. If you were the salesperson, would you have done anything differently?

Salesperson: Mr. Mayer, I'm Susan Bennet with the Heilman Company. I'm calling on you today to talk about Sauco, our new secret sauce for hamburgers.

Mr. Mayer (supermarket manager): Okay.

Salesperson: I wonder if I might ask you a few questions about your store traffic.

Mr. Mayer: Sure, go ahead.

Salesperson: Have you noticed any decline in store traffic these days because of competition from fast-food restaurants?

Mr. Mayer: You bet I have. With all the women working these days, I lose quite a bit of business.

Salesperson: Have you done anything to draw the traffic back?

Mr. Mayer: Oh, we've really done little, but we do have some plans.

Salesperson: Could you be a little more specific about those plans?

Mr. Mayer: We plan to put in a delicatessen.

Salesperson: Have you thought about carrying more convenience foods?

Mr. Mayer: Yes, but you can only go so far, and it's difficult to compete directly with McDonald's and Hardee's.

Salesperson: Then, as I understand you, if you had a product that would compete more directly with McDonald's and other hamburger franchises, you'd carry it in the store?

Mr. Mayer: Well, maybe.

Salesperson: Let me tell you about Sauco, our new secret sauce for hamburgers.

Case 9-2

Jim Mohr works for Ace Hardware in Oneonta, New York. On June 21, Dan Brown enters the store and the following conversation ensues:

Jim: I notice you're looking at our lawn mowers there. Are you interested in a particular model?

Dan: Well, I've just bought my first home. I'd always lived in an apartment, and I guess I better buy a lawn mower to cut the grass. What about this one here? It looks pretty good. (pause, as Dan looks over the mower) How much is it?

Jim: That one is priced at $199.99. It's on sale, and it's really a good buy.

Dan: On sale, eh?

Jim: Yes, but the sale ends tomorrow.

Dan: Tell me a little bit about the mower.

Jim: Well, it has solid-state ignition, meaning that you'll never have to tune it up. That's really a nice feature. Have you ever tried to tune up your car?

Dan: No, but I imagine it isn't much fun.

Jim: It sure isn't.

Dan: Does it come with a warranty?

Jim: Yes, it certainly does. Ninety days on parts and labor.

Dan: Well, I guess I better buy it if it's on sale.

Jim: Fine, I'll write up a ticket.

(A few months later, Dan returns to the store and sees Jim.)

Dan: You know that mower you sold me just doesn't do the job. I'd like to exchange it.

Jim: I'm sorry. It's a little late for that. What's the problem?

Dan: It takes too long to cut the yard. I've got almost an acre and then I have to rake it and . . .

Questions

1. Who was at fault for what happened?
2. If you had been in Jim's position, what questions would you have asked to encourage problem recognition?

The Presentation

Key Terms

advantage
benefit
cycle selling
demonstration
dramatization

motive
multimedia
neurolinguistic
  programming (NLP)

payback period
return on investment (ROI)

Learning Objectives

After studying Chapter 10, you will understand:

- The deficiencies of the typical sales presentation
- The differences among features, advantages, and benefits
- Ways of making the effective product demonstration
- The importance of audiovisual aids
- How to dramatize product benefits through recommendations, showing

- return on investment, comparison, warranties, free trial periods, and showmanship
- Methods of making yourself more clearly understood during the sales presentation
- How to fit the sales presentation to the personality of the buyer

The importance of making a good presentation cannot be overestimated. Theodore Levitt of Harvard once conducted an experiment in which he compared four selling situations:

1. A good presentation made by a salesperson from a well-known company
2. A good presentation made by a salesperson from a little-known company
3. A poor presentation made by a salesperson from a well-known company
4. A poor presentation made by a salesperson from a little-known company

As expected, the highest ratings were received by the salesperson from a well-known company who made a good presentation. But more important, Levitt found that the salesperson from the little-known company who made a good presentation outsold the representative from the well-known company whose presentation was weak. As Levitt puts it, "A good sales presentation has greater durability than a good company reputation."[1]

However, even though the term *presentation* is used as the chapter title, it is an unfortunate term. Most salespeople are accustomed to "telling and selling" instead of "involving and asking." So far, we have tried to emphasize that people learn a lot more from what they experience and actually do than from what they simply hear. The same is true about your product or service presentation. In fact, it would be better to use the term *application* rather than *presentation*. The former means a mutual discovery or learning experience as your product or service is unfolded to your prospect; the latter term refers to a dull monologue related to your product or service's features and, hopefully, benefits. Always remember that people are far more likely to believe what they experience, do, feel, touch, smell, think, or immerse themselves in than what they simply hear from you![2]

A Typical Sales Presentation

Let's imagine that somehow we have managed to secure a tape of the average sales presentation. In terms of Levitt's analysis, listen and decide if this salesperson from a smaller competitor could outscore a representative from a large, well-known company:

As you see, Mr. Buyer, this particular model is gray, but you can get the XYM 112J in almost any color—brilliant red, seascape blue, elm green, and sand beige. The control buttons, of course, will always be pure white. You'll notice that this model has the R211 antenna on the right side, but you can get it on the left side with a special order, or by ordering the C423 option. The XYM 112J operates in hexadecimal and can process up to 1,500 bits of binaries, given the average application. But if you desire more speed, then I would suggest the UT3460 . . .

This type of presentation, all too prevalent, is a "data dump." Have you ever been close to a dump truck when it's full of sand or the dirt is slowly being raised? At first, the material starts to trickle out, but then the pace accelerates to an avalanche and everything slides at once. This is similar to sales reps who try to discharge everything they know about their product or service in seconds. As a result, prospects are turned off, bored, and begin to build feelings of resistance.[3] Unfortunately, this is typical of many salespeople. They do little more than provide a description of product features, and that may not even be a clear description. Usually it is left up to prospects to determine on their own how the product will solve their problems and satisfy their needs. The fact of the matter is that people do not buy products or services; they buy solutions to their problems. The salesperson who is able to translate product features into "people benefits" will find customers buying faster and returning again and again.

This subject reminds one of the old story about the three blind men and the elephant. The first one feels its side and says, "This animal is very much like a wall." The second, touching its leg, says, "It's more like a tree." The third, feeling its trunk, says, "No, it's like a snake." Each of them forms a totally different impression based on the distinguishing features that he's able to identify, and none of these three impressions is really on target.

But what if you were being asked to sell the elephant? Conventional sales training says to memorize all possible features, all possible impressions, and then spew them out, one by one, until you hit a hot button. That's the product-dump style. It's also selling blind, because until you discuss with the individual what (if anything) he wants in an elephant, you have no idea if any of the animal's features will be relevant. In our approach, you begin by finding out what the customer wants to accomplish, and then you point to the part of the elephant that can help. In addition to being more honest, this method is more efficient. If you understand up front what the customer is looking for, you won't waste time pitching something he doesn't want.[4]

10-1 The Customer's Unstated Questions

Before the salesperson ever begins the presentation, he or she must recognize that the prospect has in mind a number of questions, which may or may not be explicitly spoken, but must be answered nonetheless. If not, the sale is likely to be lost. The professional salesperson prepares his or her presentation to respond to these unstated, but critical questions.[5]

The Six Unstated Questions

Why should I listen to you?

What is it?

What's in it for me?

So what?

Who says so?

Who else has done it?

"Why Should I Listen to You?"

If the salesperson fails to spark an interest, the odds are that the prospect's attention will be absent and this will be the last call. Some of this problem should be handled with an effective approach (e.g., referral, product, curiosity, etc.), but the salesperson must follow up with material and dramatizations that continue to hold prospect interest.

"What Is It?"

This question must be answered with benefits, not features. If you're selling an Itanium IV processor in a PC, you had better be prepared to explain the benefits (i.e., faster payroll processing, accounts receivable, and lower inventory).

"What's in It for Me?"

As we mentioned in Chapter 9, "Problem Recognition," people buy to satisfy their own needs and problems, not the salesperson's. The salesperson should wait to begin the presentation until the prospect has agreed to a problem confirmation statement. If the prospect needs 64-bit processor speed to hasten reordering and decrease inventory, then that's what the salesperson should concentrate on, not a tangential matter, and certainly not the megahertz speed of the PC.

"So What?"

Your company has been in business 75 years. "So what?" Your products are used by the largest companies in the industry. "So what?" You have an online service center. "So what?" Again, it's the benefit of each of these that must be explained—and in terms of specific customer need. Every fact or piece of information you provide must be tied to a personal benefit of some kind for the prospect.

"Who Says So?"

Other than the salesperson, who of repute says that your product or service is as good as you say it is? That is, where's the proof? Otherwise, there will exist an impenetrable wall of skepticism between the prospect and your presentation.

"Who Else Has Done It?"

There's a lot of risk in being the first. In the computer business, vendors call it the "leading edge"; prospects call it the "the bleeding edge." The prospect wants to know, "Who else has done it, besides me?" Especially where a great deal of purchase risk is present and when prospect knowledge and experience are limited, having names of numerous satisfied customers is reassuring.

In other words, preparation is essential to the presentation. It assures the customer that you're familiar with, and sympathetic to, their point of view, and it will make you appear more knowledgeable about your subject. Make sure to:[6]

> *Do your homework.* Find out all you can about the prospect in advance—what business is he in, who are his customers, what types of problems does he typically face? Why is your audience present? What is the location of the meeting? What amenities does the location have (e.g., computers, an LCD projector, and so forth)? What is your exit strategy after you make your presentation?
>
> *Find out who the decision makers are.* Is the person to whom you're delivering the presentation the decision maker? If you're delivering a sales presentation

to a group of people, who is the decision maker and who are the buying influences in that group? What are their backgrounds (e.g., educational level, experience, gender, cultural influences, and age)? What is the audience's consensus attitude toward your subject?

Do they know your product or service? The starting point for your presentation may depend on how familiar the audience is with your products or services. Don't dwell on what they already know.

What is the prospect's prime interest? Your presentation is likely to vary depending on whether the prospect is concerned mainly with the overall benefits of your product or with the details of how it works. CEOs usually prefer the broad picture; plant managers, a nuts-and-bolts approach. *Tip:* If you sense people are not comfortable with high-tech talk, switch to simpler words.

As an example of the value of homework before the presentation, take Daniel Katsin, president of Katsin/Loeb Advertising, Inc. With a $10 million deal on the line, few salespeople would take a risk in a final presentation, but Katsin knew that if he didn't, his sales pitch would be lost amongst the others just like it. He began by doing extensive research on the prospective client, Nexstar Financial Corporation. However, he took that research one step further—he essentially wrote a thesis on how Nexstar should launch its company. He distributed his work a week before his presentation to the four executives he was scheduled to meet, with a note attached that said, "Looking forward to meeting you. Please be prepared to discuss this document next week." How did Nexstar react to being given what amounted to a homework assignment? The CEO showed up with his document marked and highlighted. "The board chairman had written all over it—they all came with questions and the meeting lasted four hours," Katsin says. "I was really nervous when I sent the book over." Through his research, which entailed calling friends in the industry who knew of Nexstar, reading about it on the web, and gathering press clippings, Katsin produced a document that analyzed the client's business. Although you don't need to write a thesis and send it to the client prior to the presentation, the point is made: Do your homework! It will show.[7]

10-2 The Product-Analysis Worksheet

Making a successful benefit-oriented presentation begins before the sales interview. This may sound strange, since we emphasized in Chapter 9, "Problem Recognition," that prospects must first recognize their needs and problems. It is still true—a successful presentation must be directed to the specific problems that the salesperson and prospect agree on at the conclusion of the recognition process. But the salesperson can be prepared beforehand to discuss the agreed-upon problems. By preparing an analysis of product features and benefits, the salesperson is ready to concentrate on those specific prospect problems identified in the recognition process. In other words, by first preparing a fairly complete inventory of product features and benefits, the sales representative is in a position to select the appropriate ones and to individualize them for a particular buyer.

A useful tool in planning the sales presentation is the product-analysis worksheet, as depicted in Table 10-1. The worksheet consists of five elements: the product feature, the advantage, the benefit, the motive satisfied, and the means of dramatization.

A *feature* is any quality inherent in the product or service. It is any fact about it that will be true whether or not the product or service is ever bought or used. A feature may be a tangible part of the product's physical makeup. Important tangible features of an automobile, for example, may include color, air-conditioning, and

T a b l e **10-1** **Product-Analysis Worksheet**

Product Feature	Advantage	Benefit	Motive Satisfied	Means of Dramatization
Polyester-cotton blend	Lasts longer	Buyer doesn't have to reorder as often as with an all-cotton garment	Cost and profit	Show garment that has gone through multiple washings
	Looks better	Surgical personnel don't have to be ashamed of wearing the garment	Self-esteem	Let surgical staff try on uniform and see how good it looks on them
	Needs no ironing	Saves laundering costs	Cost	Give sample garment to laundry manager to verify
Stainless-steel thread interwoven	Grounds static electricity	Minimizes danger of igniting anesthetic in operating room	Safety	Testimonial of independent testing laboratory
Delivery	Delivery will be within two weeks of ordering	Hospital doesn't have to maintain as great an inventory of uniforms	Cost	Recommendation from satisfied users
Ron Friendly, sales rep	Expertise and availability	Knowledgeable advice readily at hand in case of problems	Trust	Recommendation of customers

advantage
Explains what the feature does—its purpose or function.

benefit
The value or worth that the user derives from a product or service

type of interior. The tangible features of Superior Hospital Uniform Company's new surgical uniform include its polyester-cotton blend and its interwoven stainless-steel thread.

Features may also be intangible. Company policies such as service, delivery, and price, for example, are significant product aspects. Another critical intangible feature might be the availability and knowledge of the salesperson, such as Ron Friendly of Superior Hospital Uniform Company.

An **advantage** explains what the feature does. It describes the purpose or function of the feature. Power steering allows easier turning of a car's steering wheel. A coated aspirin tablet is easier to swallow. An automobile air bag inflates when the car is in an accident. A feature describes the product itself; an advantage describes what the feature will do.

A **benefit** is the value or worth that the user derives from a product or service. It tells the customer "what's in it for me." Although a feature is part of the product and an advantage explains what the feature does, a benefit relates all this to the buyer.

Benefits tell buyers what they want. In Chapter 4, "Buyer Behavior," a problem was defined as the difference between the existing situation and the situation desired. A benefit tells about the situation desired: either the acquisition of satisfaction or the avoidance of an unsatisfactory set of circumstances. Unless features and advantages have been related to user needs, no benefit has been demonstrated. This is the critical area in which many salespeople fail. Your prospective clients don't want office equipment. What they want are more profits, which they hope to attain by reducing indirect labor costs as a result of making their office personnel more productive. Likewise, they don't want software. What they want are increased revenues, which they expect to produce by providing their customers the ability to place orders online. Similarly, a primary benefit of Superior Hospital Uniform Company's new surgical uniform is that it needs no ironing, which saves on labor costs in the hospital laundry. A critical factor in the turnaround of one company was its switch from selling features to selling benefits. Ceridian, a Minneapolis-based provider of outsourced human resources services to companies of all sizes, underwent a complete transformation in its sales and marketing forces. "We were almost a sales catalog company, only pushing products," says Pat Goepel, the company's chief revenue officer. "We needed radical change if we were going to become the solution-sell company that I was striving for. The solution was to equip the salespeople with a short elevator speech about how we can help our customers, not just with one or two products, but with a whole suite of services," he says. "Our quick, 15-second speech is that our services free up our customers' executives to focus on their core business. It's a simple but powerful selling point."[8]

Perhaps the best example of the differences between features and benefits is in the computer industry, where technical advances of questionable value have outdistanced the needs of the customer. As one weary customer commented, "Do I really care if my computer uses USB 1.1 or USB 2.0 technology?" One is faster than the other, but the difference must be tangible. Because USB 2 is up to 40 times faster, backing up a PC can be done in minutes, not hours, especially critical if an individual must stay there should problems develop. The computer industry has forgotten that for every new technological advance, there must be a real benefit gained for customers who will be buying these machines.

When determining the benefits of a product, salespeople should ask themselves two questions, one before writing down the benefit and the other after. Prior to determining a benefit, the salesperson may wish to ask, "Does the buyer want the product or the 'product of the product'?" For example, 2 million quarter-inch drill bits were sold in the United States last year. Why? Did the buyers want the quarter-inch bits, or did they really want quarter-inch holes? The answer is that the buyers wanted the holes, which are the end result, the product of the product. After the benefit is determined, salespeople should put themselves in the buyer's position and ask, "So what?" The "so what" test will prevent the salesperson from presenting only features and advantages. For example, let's suppose a vacuum cleaner salesperson exclaims, "This model is a real honey. It has a dual-speed power plant, a crystallator, and a rug renovator." If the salesperson were to ask at this point, "So what?" (as the prospective buyer would), then more-meaningful benefits could be added to the presentation and more sales would be closed.

Although the entries in Table 10-1, "Product-Analysis Worksheet," tend to be brief regarding features and benefits, in actual practice the salesperson would flesh out the material by adding more words, especially transitional phrases. For example, once a problem has been established, a sales representative from Superior Hospital Uniform Company would take the facts in Table 10-1 and say something like:

> *Mr. Prospect, this new surgical uniform consists of a blend of 64 percent Dacron,*
> *34 percent cotton, and 2 percent stainless-steel thread. The combination of polyester and*
> *cotton is important to you because it eliminates the need for ironing, which allows you to*
> *save on labor costs in the hospital laundry.*

Ron has added more words to make his presentation smoother. He has also placed a transitional phrase—"is important to you because"—between the feature and the advantage and benefit. Transitional phrases may be used either between features and advantages or between advantages and benefits. Here is a list of phrases that assist in smoothing out a presentation:

> *This is important because . . .*
>
> *You'll really like this since . . .*
>
> *This means that . . .*

Others have found this valuable because of this feature (advantage) . . .

The important thing here is . . .

However, constant talking can also remove you from the buyer's consideration for both this sale and additional opportunities. When you verbally overpower the client, you risk losing him or her permanently. In fact, your likelihood of getting the sale moves in direct proportion to the amount of airtime you give your prospect during the discussion. The more time your prospect is speaking, the greater the chances that you'll get the business. So how do you use this to your advantage in your selling? Here's an example: Let's say you sell a service that employs digital technology. You could say, "Of course our service is completely digital, and that means you can be sure your information is completely secure." Or, you could say, "How important is it for your own peace of mind to know that the information you're sending is seen only by you and your intended recipient?" If your prospect responds that security is critically important, you can go into greater detail, providing some peace of mind on that particular issue. If, on the other hand, you get a noncommittal nod in response, you know you can move on to other benefits.[9] So, don't just tell, ask whenever possible and make the sale.

In Table 10-1, **motive** refers to the need to which the feature appeals. Identifying the motive helps the salesperson determine the benefit. By knowing something about the general motives that influence buyers, the salesperson can determine specific benefits that apply in the case of individual prospects. Knowing that cost is a strong industrial buying motive aids Ron Friendly in identifying one of the new uniform's important benefits to a hospital: saving on laundering costs. In a similar manner, Ron could go down a list of other buying motives and determine specific benefits that correspond to these general motives. Recognizing that self-esteem is important would assist Ron in developing a portion of his presentation around the improved appearance of the garments, which is surely important to surgical staff.

The final element in Table 10-1 is **dramatization.** Here dramatization is used in the larger sense of the word to mean "a bringing home strikingly; an effective emphasis." Dramatization gets attention and interest, increases understanding, is more convincing, and leaves a lasting impression. Dramatization, of course, includes the traditional idea of showmanship, but it also includes means of dramatization such as demonstrations, audiovisual aids, recommendations, arithmetic comparisons, warranties, and free trial periods. These methods are needed, because merely relating features, advantages, and benefits may not be convincing enough. An example will help illustrate this. Let's compare the presentations of two salespeople:

> *Mr. Prospect, you can forget about damage to your merchandise when you ship in our supercushion corrugated cartons. The cartons are unique in the business, and only top-grade cardboard is used in their construction.*

versus

> *Mr. Prospect, you can forget about damage to your merchandise when you ship in our cartons. Watch this. (Salesperson slams a sealed carton to the floor several times. Upon opening the carton, the sales representative exclaims:) Glass, as delicate a piece of merchandise as you'll ever ship, Mr. Prospect, is still in perfect condition. Here, let's take a look. (After prospect examines glass, salesperson continues:) This protection is provided by the specially designed, double-corrugated walls that give the utmost protection.*

---

motive
Refers to the need to which the feature appeals

dramatization   "Bringing home strikingly" in the presentation by using demonstrations, audiovisual aids, or recommendations.

Yet another example: After setting a new company quarterly sales record, the president of Bill's company called him to congratulate him and asked him what he felt was the secret of his success.[10] Bill replied that he had recently made a minor change to his sales presentation that was making a major difference in his results. During his presentation, he was now using a hammer to strike the safety glass several times to demonstrate its strength and durability. Several months after Bill demonstrated his hammer technique to the rest of the sales force, the company shattered all of its previous records for safety glass sales. The president was extremely pleased with the company-wide results, but noticed Bill's sales had also increased dramatically and that he continued to maintain his lead over the rest of the sales force. Intrigued, he asked Bill if he had discovered any new techniques. Bill replied that he had recently made a subtle change in his presentation. "I still use the hammer technique," Bill said, "except now when I get to the part in my presentation where I demonstrate the strength of the safety glass, I hand the hammer to my customer and let them hit the glass!"

10-3 The Demonstration

In the first example of the corrugated box, the salesperson initially relied solely on the spoken word to convince the buyer. But in the second approach, the sales representative took to heart the old adage "seeing is believing." Demonstrating the strength of the corrugated box represents a vast improvement over just talking about its strength. The best-selling tool is the product itself. With the product at hand, prospects are able to convince themselves because benefits become more evident when they have been witnessed. If you were considering a new multifunction printer for your office, which would you think would be more effective: (1) a brochure detailing pages printed per minute, color capabilities, and networking abilities or (2) actually printing out a document in 256 colors and immediately faxing the document to a customer?

If done correctly, there is nothing more effective than a **demonstration**, but a mishandled demonstration is guaranteed to ruin a sale. In making the demonstration, the smart salesperson follows several rules:

demonstration
Showing the product or service in use to the prospective buyer.

1. The conscientious sales representative plans the demonstration beforehand. The equipment is checked out prior to the demonstration to prevent any embarrassing situations from developing. The sequence of features and benefits is established, with first priority going to those that are most important to the prospect or that have a competitive advantage. The demonstration should be practiced. Fumbling about in front of prospects will raise doubts in their minds about the product, not to mention the salesperson.

2. The environment of the demonstration is an important consideration. Care should be taken to ensure that a neat, clean, and quiet facility is available for the demonstration. A messy environment with equipment strewn everywhere and lots of traffic is unlikely to have a favorable effect on the client.

3. During the course of the demonstration, checking questions should be asked to make sure the prospect has grasped the significance of each feature and benefit (e.g., "Does this look as if it will meet your needs?" "How do you see this fitting your situation?" "Does this make sense for your business?").

4. At every step, the prospect's participation in the demonstration should be encouraged. During the demonstration, if you are not having people push the buttons, make the copies, type on the keyboard, smell the air freshener, open and close the doors, you're not selling—you're showing. You must have

them participate in the performance to make them feel involved. If you market an intangible product or service, be sure to have brochures, graphs, and other items that you can hand to the decision makers. Give them a calculator to prove the figures you're quoting are correct. Show testimonial letters from other happy clients. This creates both physical and emotional involvement.[11] Participation helps attract and hold attention and, especially for more technical products, helps to convince the prospect that the equipment is not that difficult to work with after all. A senior sales representative, training a new rep, had the trainee demonstrate the virtues of a new billing machine. The trainee was well indoctrinated, and his performance on the machine was flawless. Nevertheless, the prospective customers were a little leery of buying until the senior rep asked the clerical employee who would be using the machine to give it a try. Nervous at first, she tentatively began working, and soon her fingers were fairly flying over the keys of the new billing machine. The customer commented later, "If that senior salesman hadn't stepped in, we never would have bought the machine. Seeing the company-trained rep operate the unit effortlessly and efficiently only half convinced us. When we saw our own people doing it, we were sure it was the right machine for us."

5. The demonstration should be made as specific as possible to the needs of each prospect. This helps clients see the true benefits of the product—"what's really in it" for them. If possible, it may be a good idea to interject realism into the demonstration by taking the prospect on a tour of another customer's facility where the product is employed in a manner similar to how the prospect would use it. This adds to believability because such a visit shows the product in a different light from that in a demonstration at the seller's offices. The salesperson should exercise care, however, in selecting a user's site. It should be about the same size as the prospect's operation. If taken to a larger factory, for example, the prospect might be prompted to think, "This is okay for a big corporation with lots of money, but not for me."

10-4 Audiovisual Aids

How important is the visual component of a presentation? The 3M Corp. and the Management Information Systems Research Center at the University of Minnesota[12] found that some 55 percent of the impact of a presentation comes from the visual element (including how *you* look); 38 percent of the impact comes from the sound, including the way in which the message is spoken; and only 7 percent of the impact comes from the *content* of the message or what is actually being said. Presentations that use visual support are 43 percent more persuasive than those that don't, and a spoken message with attractive supporting visuals has more impact than one that's only spoken or one that's primarily visuals. As the old adage goes, "Telling isn't selling."

In the absence of being able to bring the product itself along for a demo, or as additional dramatization, the salesperson may rely upon audiovisual aids. "A-V" includes a great many alternatives:

- Charts and graphics
- Photographs and videos
- Models or mock-ups of products
- Slides and CDs
- Sales manuals and catalogs

- Flipboards and posters
- Advertisements
- Multimedia computer presentations (e.g., PowerPoint)

The last of these deserves definition. **Multimedia** refers to computer-generated presentations that include some mix of sophisticated graphics, animation, digital photographs, full-motion video, and stereo sound.[13]

Following is a list of common audiovisual supports and recommendations on their proper use.[14]

Flipcharts. Use flipcharts for brainstorming sessions, discussions, and presentations with high audience participation, but only with small audiences only because flipcharts are not visible from a distance. Position flipcharts as high as possible. Use wet markers with flipcharts to increase visibility. Use the colors black and blue for the easiest reading.

Slides. Use slides to portray vivid, high-resolution, colorful, and professional images. Show your best or most memorable slide more than once to reinforce the message.

Handouts. Use handouts to provide additional or follow-up information that was not covered in your presentation and distribute them at the end of your presentation to prevent "defections" and audience inattentiveness.

Overhead transparencies. Use overhead transparencies as a less expensive option to slides. Use overhead transparencies when you need to change, write on, or customize material for the audience. Make sure the projector glass and lens are clean before you use them. Use color-in transparencies to maximize attention.

Models. Use models to demonstrate how something works, looks, sounds, or feels for items that are too small or too large to be seen by the audience.

Computer-generated audiovisual supports. A laptop or notebook computer, a lightweight projector (or projector panel), and the right software are the basic tools necessary. In fact, in industries where leading companies are making sales calls featuring presentation technology, competing companies face the danger of being left behind. In competent hands, the automated sales presentation is bound to seem more professional, more dramatic, and more persuasive than nonautomated presentations.[15]

Electronic presentations offer a number of advantages over traditional presentation formats: They are easily transported by disk or laptop; computer-based presentations can be quickly created, altered, or customized, often without technical help; they can be designed to let the viewer or presenter choose the desired path; they can be easily copied; and they can be shown through a variety of display options.

A variety of presentation software packages are available to the sales professional that will help to create high-impact graphics for presentations. Some will lead you through the process of preparing and organizing your presentation. The leading package available is by far Microsoft's PowerPoint. Some of its useful features are:

- *Presentation templates.* These are preformatted presentation outlines for a variety of presentation types and audiences. They can greatly reduce the time it takes to prepare a sales presentation.
- *Animation.* This feature will allow your graphics to move to illustrate graphs showing cost-effectiveness or time saved.

multimedia
Refers to computer-generated presentations that include some mix of sophisticated graphics, animation, digital photographs, full-motion video, and stereo sound.

- *Video.* Video can be presented in either the traditional format or by streaming, if it is saved to the Internet.
- *Narration.* You can narrate your presentation, making it a self-running program you can email to clients as an attachment or you can save it to the web for the clients to access. Be judicious with the use of sound narration, if you are there in person.

Although PowerPoint and other presentation software packages have advantages, they can be incorrectly implemented to the point of numbing rather than energizing clients. No matter how many flying bullets, builds, or fades you can produce with your computer, if buyers are confused or bored by what they are seeing, you will have struck a bad visual chord with them. Don't go overboard with the technology. Keep it simple. You're there to make a sale, not to win an Oscar for special effects.

Some mistakes commonly made by sales reps that degrade their presentation follow.[16]

Using Full Sentences Instead of Bullet Points

A full sentence should only be used when quoting someone. Use bullet points to provide key ideas and fill in the rest with what you say. If you use full sentences, the customer will read the slides instead of paying attention to your message. Instead of using text-heavy visuals, use bullet points, with a maximum of five to six per page; use a maximum of five to six words per line; and separate entries with white space. Compare the following:

Text-heavy visual

- We have 23 million unique users per month, which makes us No. 1 in our category.
- Another advantage is that we offer an unduplicated audience for your advertising.

Non–text-heavy visual

- 23MM unique users per month
- Unduplicated audience

Not Taking Advantage of Graphics

Text is necessary in a PowerPoint presentation, but the solution you are offering to their key problem is enhanced with visuals. Use product photos to show how the product will solve their problem; use graphs to show measurable results from using your product; and use diagrams to explain the process that is used to ensure success. Pick up a copy of your favorite business publication, whether it's *Fortune, Business Week,* or the *Wall Street Journal,* and look at the business-to-business advertising. The majority of ads show a picture with the text because the eye picks up and remembers pictures far better than it does words.

Use the following guidelines to liven up your message.

Explaining trends?	Use line graphs.
Describing a series of steps?	Use a diagram.
Comparing capabilities?	Use a table.
Showing comparisons?	Use a pie chart or bar graph.
Explaining how your site works?	Show the site.

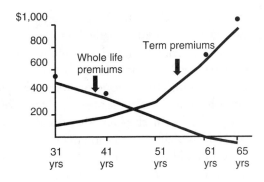

Figure 10-1
How Audiovisuals Can Assist
the Insurance Salesperson

Text Is Too Small

Don't try to jam too much text onto one slide. The text gets so small that no one can read anything, and they get annoyed trying to figure out what the slides say. Use at least 28-point, preferably 32-point type.

Slide Changes Should Never Be Set to an Automatic Time

Doing so does not provide for clients to learn at their own pace or allow you, the salesperson, to adjust to the varying needs of your clients. Audiovisual aids are especially valuable to the salesperson who sells an intangible product. Here the visual serves as a substitute for the real thing. The life insurance salesperson can talk endlessly about how life insurance will provide income for a widow without the prospect's actually grasping the concept. But when the representative shows the buyer a chart or graph of future proceeds, the idea may become more alive and tangible.

Figure 10-1 demonstrates how a graph can make a complex subject like insurance more understandable. The graph shows how premiums (payments) for a whole life policy differ from those for a term policy over the course of a lifetime for a man beginning the policy at age 31. The salesperson could merely cite the different payment amounts, but would this have as much impact on the prospect's understanding as the graph? Figure 10-1 dramatizes the differences. One can really see the existence of a crossover point, when relative costs for the two policies change.

Multimedia is not only helpful for salespeople selling intangibles, but its interactive features also help in explaining complex technical equipment. Bill Burg used Ingersoll-Rand's computer-based presentation for a $100,000 air compressor. Explaining the compressor to the powerhouse chief and the chief engineer, as Burg clicked through the presentation, the chief engineer asked him to change the engineering data, running different scenarios of operating and power costs. In minutes, Burg was squeezed aside as the two customers entered and changed their own numbers. The original 20 minutes for which the sales call had been scheduled expanded to two hours.[17] They also asked Burg to make a copy of the software and leave it with them, illustrating another significant advantage of multimedia—it can sell without the salesperson being there.

10-5 Recommendations

A demonstration represents the most powerful means of dramatization, but it is not always possible. For a recommendation story, the salesperson can create a comparable effect by telling the story of a satisfied customer who was in a similar situation before the purchase. In this manner, prospects can imagine themselves trying out the product without actually doing so.

Recommendation stories are interesting. Even the dullest subjects take on interest when people are included as subjects. An abstract discussion of product features gains life and drama if the same points are emphasized in a story about people solving problems similar to those of the prospect. Stories of people facing similar situations remind prospects of themselves, and they can draw parallels from what happened.

In formulating a recommendation story, there are several things the salesperson can do to add drama and excitement. The basis of all drama is conflict: individual against individual, individual against the elements, or individual against his or her problems. The last represents the dramatic conflict that should be portrayed in the sales story: a hero or heroine who has a problem similar to the prospect's overcomes the problem and lives happily ever after by purchasing the salesperson's product. In the course of relating this tale, the salesperson can enliven matters by describing customers and their problems in some detail while including some dialogue. Repeating what customers actually said makes the story even more persuasive than if there is only an impersonal description of what occurred.[18] Perhaps the best way of demonstrating the value of a recommendation story and illustrating some of the principles for putting one together is by offering an example. What follows is a recommendation story by Ann Fisk (a trade salesperson), who is calling on a supermarket manager:

> *Mr. Prospect, you've told me a number of times that you really want to build traffic and increase inventory turnover in your condiments sections. You know that sounds similar to what other managers are saying and, in fact, it sounds very much like the problem that Jerry Harris over at the Super Saver store on Ninth Street had until just recently. You know Jerry, don't you? He's that tall, rather heavy-set guy who's always wearing an apron and looks like he just stepped out of the meat section. Anyway, Jerry told me last month, "Ann, I'd sure like to do more out of my condiments section. There just doesn't seem to be a nickel's worth of traffic and volume in that aisle. I wish I could think of something."*
>
> *Well, I explained to Jerry that our new product, "Dijo"—our combination mayonnaise-Dijon mustard sauce for hamburgers, would go a long way toward solving his problems, especially if he made room for us to put in our special end-of-the-aisle display. Well, you know Jerry let us put in a big display of Dijo, and his sales from the condiments aisle increased fourfold. That display of Dijo really brought in the traffic.*
>
> *And you know what Jerry said to me just last week? He said, "If you ever need a testimonial, Ann, have them call me. I've got the figures."*

Here you can see the elements of a good recommendation story: a hero faces a problem and overcomes it. The story has lots of dialogue mixed in. Giving the hero or heroine's name, firm, city, state, and phone number adds to the credibility of the technique.

The effectiveness of the recommendation story has a firm basis in social science research. People frequently use beliefs, attitudes, and actions of others—particularly similar others—as a standard of comparison against which to evaluate the correctness of their own beliefs, attitudes, and actions.[19] Thus, it is common for individuals to decide on appropriate behaviors for themselves in a given situation by searching for information as to how similar people have behaved or are behaving.[20]

One sales rep, Barry J. Farber, has a unique way of increasing the credibility of the recommendation story; he tapes the client. He doesn't put words in the customer's mouth; he wants a natural unrehearsed response. Even background noise—

ringing phones, the hum of conversation—works toward realism. Bringing the taped remarks to a sales call with a prospect along with a testimonial letter written on the customer's letterhead is real dramatization.[21]

10-6 Showing Return on Investment

For dramatizing a presentation, showing return on investment is not as powerful as a demonstration or a recommendation story, but when combined with these two methods, it becomes effective. The **return on investment (ROI)** is simply the net profit or savings expected from a given investment, expressed as a percentage of the investment.

$$ROI = Net\ Profits \div Investment$$

Let's show how a business-equipment sales representative would justify the investment in a personal digital assistant (PDA). On the basis of a survey of the customer's current system, the salesperson might find that an hour a day of a clerk's labor could be saved with the purchase of the PDA. If this clerk was paid $20,000 per year, then that hour's time would translate into $10 saved every day and $2,500 over the course of a year. The sales representative could then proceed to show that the cost of the PDA, $295, could be recovered in 30 days ($295 ÷ $10); this is often called the **payback period** or the amount of time it takes to recover your investment. The ROI for one year would be $2,500/$295 or almost 700 percent. Over the course of a year, the prospect would be $2,205 ahead ($2,500 − $295); if the PDA was expected to last nine years, then the total return would be (9 × $2,500) − $295 for a total of $22,205. Alternatively, because some customers are motivated more by thinking in terms of losses, the salesperson could say, "By not acting on this special offer immediately, you and your company stand to lose $208 per month or almost $7 per day."

Frequently, after the prospect has had a chance to see a demonstration and hear a recommendation, questions arise about the economic value of the purchase. The demonstration and recommendation provide evidence that the product will work, but doubt remains as to whether the money expended is worthwhile. This doubt disappears when the salesperson can show that the dollar investment is fully justified by the benefits to be reaped from the purchase. In a large sense, this involves showing that the return (or profit) is well worth the investment.

There are two general ways that an industrial sales representative can present a promise of profit improvement: (1) by showing that operating costs can be decreased and (2) by showing how the customer can increase the revenues earned from operations affected by the salesperson's equipment.

10-7 Comparison and Imagery

Most people use examples to help illustrate their points. However, the most skilled consciously use distinctive and meaningful metaphors, analogies, and comparisons (imagery) to really drive those points home.[22] When Bill Gates was called before the Justice Department to remove his browser from Windows, he didn't just say that Justice was being unfair and ridiculous. To make his point, he couched his statement in a comparison that he knew anyone listening could immediately relate to. He said that telling Microsoft to remove the browser from Windows was as ridiculous as telling automotive companies to remove radios from their cars, because it might put radio manufacturers out of business!

return on investment (ROI)
The net profit or savings expected from a given investment, expressed as a percentage of the investment.

payback period
The amount of time it takes to recover your investment.

Imagine the impact of the following facts without the added imagery.

1. A gigabyte can store a billion characters, roughly the equivalent of 1,000 average-sized novels.
2. A billion dollars is enough to operate every school in America for five hours.

Do you "tell" or "sell" the number of unique visitors to your site? Example: (Talking to a buyer who is a football fan:) "We reach 1,000,000 people. That's 10 Super Bowls of potential buyers for your product!"

One of the oldest and most effective methods of teaching is through the use of comparison and contrast. The idea is to start with something the student (or prospect) is familiar with and compare it to something new and unfamiliar. By comparing similarities and differences, the student is able to understand the new object or concept. If you were to attempt to explain baseball to an English person, you might start with the game of cricket. Similarly, a sales representative trying to sell a digital camera might start by comparing it to an old Polaroid.

There are several ways for salespeople to sell by comparison. They can sell by analogy, that is, by drawing comparisons between essentially dissimilar objects. A life insurance salesperson, for example, might compare investing in life insurance to putting money in a bank until it is needed. The computer salesperson might explain that a disk resembles a phonograph record and that it holds information like a file cabinet: a floppy disk is like a 2-drawer cabinet and a hard disk is like a 20-drawer cabinet. When I considered having my older home improved with steel siding and then balked at the price ($11,000), the enterprising sales representative responded, "If you spent the same amount on a car, would you get a 40-year warranty, and an investment that actually gains in value over the years?"

One computer salesperson, Chet Anderson of Pocatello, Idaho, often makes car analogies. When someone is confused by price differences and the capabilities of the various computer models, he says, "You can get a Ford or you can get a Mercedes. They're both going to get you there; you just get a lot more options with a Mercedes." When customers are surprised about all the extra costs they incur after buying the basic unit, he is ready: "A computer's no different from a car. After you buy a car, you have to pay for repairs and keep gas in it, don't you?"

Salespeople can also use comparison through sales metaphors. Abe Lincoln, Ronald Reagan, and other politicians have long recognized the power of metaphors. The idea is to build a powerful mental picture in the mind of the prospect. People tend to be less critical when listening to stories than when sitting through a fact-packed formal presentation. Your prospect's mood shifts toward receptivity—not unlike when attending a play or seeing a film. Defenses drop. Information and suggestions slip in unnoticed by the conscious mind, yet they have a powerful impact on subconscious buying behavior. Plus there's the metaphor's entertainment and attention value. One top insurance rep, selling to a young prospect who was considering a policy from a smaller, less-known insurance company, countered with this metaphor: "It's like taking you and your family on a long voyage across the Atlantic Ocean; you want to get from here to England; and you have a choice of either going on a sailboat or on the *Queen Elizabeth II*. Which one would you feel safer on?"

10-8 Warranties and Free Trial Periods

Much like a demonstration, warranties and free trial periods are meant to assure the prospect that the product will work and that satisfaction is guaranteed. Backing up a claim with a warranty is a powerful way of dramatizing a company's confidence in its product and ensuring forthcoming prospect satisfaction. In a similar manner, an offer of a free trial period ensures satisfaction. This resembles a sort of "if it doesn't work, send it back and you won't owe a thing" form of proof. Although the free trial is effective, the salesperson must learn not to rely too heavily on it. It is easy for a customer to put off the salesperson by asking for a free trial. By readily providing a free trial, the sales representative may have lost an immediate sale if matters had been pressed. Sales managers have been known to throw up their hands in exasperation when all models in a branch office were found to be loaned out on trial. Some have told their salespeople to bring in the "loaners" or else be prepared to pay for them.

If available, a seal of approval or report from an independent testing agency represents excellent proof of performance. A satisfactory review from organizations such as Underwriters Laboratories or Consumers Union is a powerful testimony to a product's ability to perform. The sales representative should not fail to mention such reports.

10-9 Showmanship

Showmanship is another element of dramatization, but it differs from other methods because it is oriented toward the actions of salespeople themselves rather than toward dramatizing the product. Showmanship also has entertainment value over and above its ability to grab the prospect's attention, further differentiating it from other means of dramatization.

Although showmanship can assist in maintaining attention during the presentation, the salesperson must be judicious in its use. Sales representatives who arrive for the interview in a yellow and blue suit, red shirt, and a carnation in their lapel will probably gain the client's attention, but their credibility is another question. Such actions are likely to awaken a picture of that old salesman stereotype. Suspicion and mistrust are sure to follow. A feeling that "this guy's out to sell me something I don't need" would be a common reaction.

Yet showmanship in moderation can be very effective in securing prospect attention and providing some entertainment. The latter ingredient in sales success is not to be underestimated. The visit of the sales representative provides a break in the normal everyday routine, and the entertaining salesperson may gain a competitive advantage. Paul Stephens remembers his frustration when he first started selling Ben and Jerry's ice cream. Paul would load the trunk of his car with ice cream and dry ice and prospect for customers in Vermont. Paul's prospect strategy was simple: look for and call on "mom-and-pop" stores. He'd talk, leave some samples and a price sheet, and return weeks later, only to find that sample was still in the refrigerator unopened and untried. Paul decided on a different strategy. He headed to the nearest hardware store and purchased a big soupspoon. Calling on the next mom-and-pop store, he scooped some ice cream from a fresh sample and said, "Have a bite." The store owner dug into his first taste of Ben and Jerry's ice cream. "It was pretty smooth sailing from there," explains Stephens, now a regional sales manager for the $132 million company. "It wasn't fancy," Stephens admits, "but it was the only thing that would work."[23] The lesson for beginning and experienced salespeople alike: Never underestimate the value of showmanship.

What are the elements of showmanship? Sales reps may borrow from theories of psychology, the elements of nonverbal behavior, movement, novelty, contrast, and intensity and size to add showmanship to their presentations.

10-9a Nonverbal Behavior

People put out visual signals based on their body language. Often we are not even aware of doing so. These signals include posture, eye contact, gestures, facial expression, and other factors. An effective salesperson needs to know how to master the subtle cues of body language before he or she can be successful. Visual signals can make you appear not to be in control and will detract from your overall presentation . . . and the sale. Accordingly, salespeople should take care that their nonverbal behavior communicates the proper message—in most instances, confidence, caring, and enthusiasm.[24] Table 10-2 defines the nonverbal elements of communicating these three critical attitudes.

It is especially interesting to recognize the leaders personifying these three traits—confidence, caring, and enthusiasm. Margaret Thatcher, former Prime Minister of Great Britain, was renowned for her confidence; she was, in fact, often called the "Iron Lady." Ronald Reagan managed always to convey caring and empathy with his smile, his personalized examples, metaphors, open gestures, and conversational tone. And, of course, John Kennedy always seemed to exude confidence with his upbeat message, smile, sparkling eyes, expansive gestures, and rapid pace.

Posture

An effective salesperson keeps his head up and hands open.[25] Holding your chin raised gives you the aura of being in control. Stand up straight and face your audience head-on. Keep your posture open with arms relaxed and hanging down at your sides. If your hands are clasped firmly in front of you, your feet are crossed, and your body is tight, you are not exactly exuding confidence. Other "don'ts" include hands on hips (you look too condescending or parental); crossed arms (you are not conveying a look that says, "Let's talk"); hands crossed in front of you (otherwise known as the "fig leaf" stance, which makes you look weak and timid); hands joined behind your back (also known as the "parade rest," which makes you seem like you have no energy); leaning back in a chair, if seated (you look like you're ready to pass judgment); and putting your hands in your pockets (this makes you seem nervous and can result in jingling any coins or keys that might be there).

T a b l e **10-2** Communicating the Appropriate Nonverbal Message

	Caring	Enthusiasm	Confidence
Look	Smile, friendly facial expressions Gestures: Extend arms, palms up, touch when greeting Clothing: Warm, low-contrast colors	Smile, sparkling eyes, animated face, big gestures, touch when greeting	Head and eyes up 90 percent of the time, sustained eye contact Gestures: Palms down, steepling Posture: Upright but relaxed, head perpendicular, shoulders parallel
Tone	Conversational, sincere, real voice, warm	Fast pace, punch out key words, expressive, crisp enunciation	Appropriate volume, inflection drops at the ends of phrases, fast pace, crisp enunciation, punch key words, rich pitch
Voice	Use of names, show of appreciation, personalized examples, make the theoretical relevant, listen to audience with ear and eye, recognition of others	Sharing the "dream," show of appreciation, upbeat, positive words, expressing feelings, giving credit to others	Articulating "vision," requesting what you want, short statements, action verbs, no qualifiers or fillers, knowledgeable, facts, statistics, quotes from authorities

Gestures

Gestures are an important part of your visual picture. They are reinforcements of the words and ideas you are trying to convey. Gestures include hand, arm, and head movements.

Gestures are particularly important to a credible presentation. Gesturing can make you more relaxed, reinforce your message, and make the presentation more interesting to watch. Rarely do you hear a dynamic speaker who sounds boring, and conversely, rarely do you see a dynamic speaker who stands motionless. Don't overdo it, while remembering these points:

1. Keep gestures above the waistline. Low gestures are hard to see and imply low demeanor.
2. Open up your arms to the size of the audience. Embrace the audience. Keep your arms between your waist and shoulders.
3. When not using your arms, drop them to the side. Fingertips at thighs are where your arms should be.
4 Avoid quick and jerky motions. They imply nervousness and nothing is worse for credibility. Hold gestures longer than normal for regular conversation to help counter nervousness.
5. Vary gestures. Switch hands, use both hands, or, at times, no hands.
6. Use gestures to reinforce messages. If making three points, for example, hold up three fingers.
7. Keep hands open and fingers together. Avoid pointed fingers and fists that threaten.[26]
8. Two gestures to avoid are using a pointed finger (this makes you look accusatory, even if that wasn't your intent) and fist raising (this is hostile or threatening).

Eye Contact

Even if it's one-on-one, don't be afraid to make eye contact. When you make eye contact, you are relating to your audience, which will help get your message across and possibly close the sale.

If you make eye contact with someone who quickly looks away, try not to directly look into that person's eyes again. In some cultures, direct eye contact is inappropriate, and some people just feel uncomfortable. If you are giving a presentation to a group of people, the eye contact should be done in an irregular and unpredictable "Z" formation—looking at one person for three to five seconds and then moving on to the next face.

The possible problems with eye contact are overdoing it and staring. In conjunction with making eye contact, you can nod your head occasionally. This also helps connect with your listener.

Facial Expressions

Be aware of any artificial, unfriendly, or deadpan expressions you may be making. Do you squint, frown, or make strange faces? Once you are aware of any expressions you may make, it will be easier to eliminate them. Practice smiling and looking pleasant. That's how you want to look when meeting clients or prospects. Some facial expression "don'ts" include arching eyebrows (this makes you seem surprised or questioning); frowning (your moodiness will be the only thing the other person remembers); and grimacing (your prospect will wonder where it hurts).

Salespeople can learn to practice their gestures, posture, eye contact, and facial expressions. Doing so can only help improve your sales performance. The bottom line is that it doesn't matter how exciting or innovating your sales pitch is, because your body language speaks louder than words.

10-9b Movement

Our eyes are attracted to movement. Recognizing this fact, many salespeople turn pages in a flipchart, point to a pertinent fact, hand the prospect a model, take an item from their pocket, or remove an item from their briefcase. The use of something as innocuous as a pencil may provide sufficient movement to maintain attention. Life insurance salespeople are encouraged to use the pencil in determining premiums and the amount of protection needed. Industrial representatives also make heavy use of the pencil in their presentations, drawing plans or designs of particular equipment, for example.

10-9c Novelty

Novelty refers to something new, different, fresh, or unusual. A sales representative wishing to dramatize the return on investment from buying a new electronic calculator might ask the prospect to pull a dollar bill out of his or her wallet and give it to the salesperson. The sales representative might then give the client $2.50 and say, "For each dollar you invest in the Number-cruncher Model 7, you'll get back a $2.50 return during just the first year."

A classic story illustrating the use of novelty is about a sales representative selling advertising for a women's magazine. When a shoe manufacturer canceled advertising in his publication because of little editorial attention paid to shoe styles, the enterprising sales representative decided to use a novel and dramatic tactic. He had the advertising manager of the magazine cut out every article on shoe styles that had appeared since the manufacturer had begun advertising and mount them side by side on an accordion-folder strip, some 25 feet long when pulled out. Armed with this evidence, the sales representative called on the manufacturer, and, upon entering his office, asked the customer to hang onto one end of the portfolio while he began walking out of the office, unfolding the portfolio as he went. Advertising was reinstated.[27]

10-9d Contrast

Contrast represents a change in a stimulus to which the prospect has adapted. The idea is that change itself captures attention. If the salesperson has been doing most of the talking, then asking a question represents a change—and a means of capturing attention through contrast. Introducing the use of visual aids, altering the pitch of one's voice, or pausing in the midst of speaking are ways of introducing contrast into the sales presentation.

10-9e Intensity and Size

When multiple stimuli compete for attention, the bigger, louder, and brighter ones receive the attention. This does not mean, however, as some sales managers seem to believe, that all their salespeople should be over 6 feet tall. And it does not mean that red vests should always be worn. But sales representatives may wish to raise their voices when making an important point, make the print larger when using an especially lengthy visual, or use bright colors in a posterboard presentation.[28]

10-10 Making Yourself Understood

Earlier we identified how communication between sender and receiver can easily go awry. In fact, one might say that misunderstanding rather than understanding is the natural result of communication. It is unlikely that the receiver will comprehend the message exactly as the speaker intended it. Complete accuracy is close to impossible, but during presentations, communicators (especially salespeople) should keep in mind several guidelines. First, structure and organize the presentation. Second, space out your ideas. Third, repetition aids learning. Fourth, words have emotional impact. Fifth, use concrete rather than abstract words.

10-10a Structure the Presentation

An unstructured presentation will lose a prospect before the salesperson gets a chance to make his or her point. Therefore, the professional sales rep makes an outline of the presentation beforehand and works from there. The divisions of the presentation should be as follows:

Introduction. The beginning sets the tone for the rest of what is to follow. Let's start with the very beginning of a presentation, often the most awkward moment in a sales call. In the two examples that follow, the first has no transition; the second does. Notice the difference in effectiveness. Buyers will.[29]

(Weak) You: "OK, enough about the weather. Uh, let me tell you about our new cholesterol drug."
Buyers think: "Oh, no! Not another clueless rep!"

Transition phrases like those in the next example get the presenter, the presentation, and the buyer into the same mind-set right away. Simply begin by stating the physician's objectives and business situation.

(Stronger) You: "The purpose of our meeting today is to help your patients lower their cholesterol with fewer side effects than older drugs on the market" or "What I wanted to talk to you about today was an idea to help you . . ."
"As you told me, you're facing . . ." (fill in the background facts of your doctor's situation) or "Last time we spoke, you said . . ." (background facts) or "As we both know . . ." (background facts). (A confirming question is a good idea here. For example, "Is that right?")
Buyers think: "This rep actually knows something about me and my practice! I think I'm going to like this."

In general, consider the theme of what you are trying to communicate and the one or two major points you want to firmly entrench in the prospect's mind. That constitutes the introduction: "I'm going to talk about _____, how it affects _____, and how my product can solve the problem." That's your intro.

Another good idea: Develop a strong, brief opening using a human-interest story about a satisfied customer. Former president Ronald Reagan, known as the "Great Communicator," rarely made a speech without a human-interest story referencing a brave young soldier, dedicated student, or kindly senior citizen. Because people respond to people, short illustrative stories can help you develop an immediate connection with your audience. Be sure to choose a story that is relevant to your message and your audience.[30]

Motivation. Win the customer's attention by describing the specific need or problem that he or she has. Go back to the problem confirmation that the prospect agreed to. Be sure to tell your prospects why they should listen to you. What are the benefits? What's in it for them? What is it? Who says so?

Agenda. Outline what is to come; this provides organization. "I'll start with _____ and then move on to _____ solutions. I've got a multimedia presentation and some charts and overheads to show you. We'll conclude with questions and answers." Prospects (and all audiences) are more comfortable when they know where they are going and can see that they are making progress toward a definable end.

Content. State the whole idea in overview without specifics. Then break it down into segments. This is where you can enumerate three or four points (audiovisuals are useful here). Spell out clearly the outcomes the decision maker seeks. What positive results will come from meeting the need or solving the problem? What are the possible consequences of inaction? Recommend specifically what you think the decision maker and his or her organization should do. Link your recommendation back to the client's needs and desired outcomes. For substantiation, discuss technical details, cost details, management plans, schedules, risks, logistics, training, documentation, delivery schedules, future implications, conformance to specifications and requirements—whatever. Link the details of your solution to the client's needs and constantly return to the key persuasive point: how the solution components will contribute to maximum return.

Recap. Review each segment before continuing. This captures the inattentive and slow listener as well as those who have misunderstood.

Transition. As you progress from one point to another, note the fact: "Now let's turn to . . ." or "This leads us to the next step . . ." It is very easy for buyers to become bored, lost, or both—especially with PowerPoint screens. To minimize that risk, use connecting phrases like these to move from point to point within each block of information.[31]

You: "In addition . . ." "Moreover . . ." "Another benefit is . . ."

Buyers feel: Buyers feel a growing sense of excitement and the appeal of your message. To double the momentum, couple the transitions within blocks of information with transitions between blocks of information.

You: "So, again, XYZ cholesterol-lowering drug is the fastest growing in its category. And the story gets even better when you look at the increased patient satisfaction with fewer side effects like joint ache . . ." (Click. You're onto this next block of information.)

or

"So, you've seen how popular XYZ is and how responsive patients are. Now, what special promotional opportunities will you have?" (Click. You're onto this next block of information.)

Buyers see: Buyers see cumulative benefits and are increasingly caught up in the possibilities of your drug's story and what it means to them.

Summary. After completing all your points, wrap up by restating the whole idea, touching on the major points, restating your argument, backed up by the data you have just presented.[32] Summaries are always easy when you use a simple client-centered lead-in transition like either of these:[33]

You: "In summary, you want to (treat patients better with fewer side effects)" or "We started by saying you want to . . ."

Buyers: (silently agree) Then, restate your recommendation. Add a final linking transition.

You: "As a result, we will help you treat patients better and increase their satisfaction."

Buyers think: "Yep, that's what I want. What's next?"

10-10b Space Out Your Ideas

Salespeople are often so eager to tell their story that a veritable flood of words and facts is hurled at the poor prospect. One idea flows into another, and prospects get lost in the wilderness of words and ideas. Little time is available for them to absorb the last idea before the next one is upon them. And then salespeople wonder why they leave without an order after making what they believe to have been a great presentation. Successful sales representatives space out their presentation of features, benefits, or whatever else is important, one point at a time. Audiovisual aids can be valuable here. As the salesperson advances from one point to the next, the pages of a flipchart can be turned. A transparency, slide, or posterboard can serve just as well.

After each idea and its supporting material are explained, it is critical that the sales representative check for understanding. The worst possible thing is to assume that the prospect understands and then proceed. Checking questions such as the ones explained in Chapter 9, "Problem Recognition," should be liberally used. After making a point, for example, the salesperson might inquire, "Have I adequately explained the reason for having stainless-steel thread interwoven throughout the uniform, Ms. Prospect?" (Notice also the concept of burden of responsibility in the way the question is phrased.)

10-10c Repetition Aids Learning

Repetition helps in most learning situations. This is not to say, however, that the salesperson should repeat the idea again and again. Too much repetition may antagonize the prospect. But key ideas should be repeated, especially if they are complex.

One way to avoid monotony is by using different examples to illustrate the same basic idea. Advertisers learned this long ago. Brewers make the same point each time (e.g., "Tastes great, less filling"), but use a different cast of sports or entertainment personalities each time with a slightly varied script. There are other methods of making repetition less objectionable. The salesperson may substitute synonyms for key words. Or the sales representative may enlarge upon an idea by adding new bits of information each time the concept is mentioned.

10-10d Words Have Emotional Impact

Words are one reason that communication can be distorted so easily. Words represent things and are symbols for actual things. But the same symbols have different meanings to different people. When a word is used, each of us creates a different image in our minds. For example, if we were to walk up to two children and tell them, "There's a dog behind you kids," one might turn around smiling, and the other might take off running as fast as possible. This illustrates how different experiences can alter the meaning of a word, especially its emotional loading.

Salespeople have to be careful of the emotional impact of words. The retail salesperson should never tell a customer that she looks "skinny in a dress"; "slim" or "slender" would be preferable. One saleswoman found she sold more cosmetic cream when she stopped telling prospects it would "restore" their complexion and began saying it would "preserve" their complexion. The real estate salesperson should speak of the merits of a "home," not a "house." Although the words are synonyms, their emotional loading is far different.

10-10e Use Concrete Rather Than Abstract Words

Buyer understanding is facilitated by the use of specific or concrete words rather than abstract ones. It is much clearer, for example, if the salesperson says, "This unit copies 100 documents per minute" instead of, "This unit copies fast." Words and phrases such as "costs less," "saves money," and "efficient" mean little because they do not tell the customer enough. The prospect needs to know how much less the product costs, how much money it will save, and exactly how much more efficient it is. Note this description of a tax consulting firm (taken, sadly, from an actual presentation):[34]

> *We help identify opportunities for increasing revenues, decreasing costs, and for SR and ED tax credits eligibility.*

Why does this description fail? It is too dull and too abstract. No one can "see" opportunities for increasing revenue. No one gets involved emotionally with the vague phrase "decreasing costs." But people would respond to, "We take the pain out of tax work while lifting your bottom line by as much as 50 percent."

The salesperson should also help the prospect visualize during the presentation. Words are translated into images as the listener hears them. What do you see when "ice cream," "apple," and "MTV" are mentioned? Before making a purchase, buyers imagine a picture of themselves enjoying the product. If you were buying a car, which description would you find more persuasive: "foreign sports car" or "a red Porsche two-seater with a white convertible top." The more the sales representative can paint the prospect into the picture, the more likely the sale.

10-10f Use Action Words

Action words speak loudly and clearly. Which of these statements has greater impact? "You don't build any cash value with term insurance" or "You're burning up money every year with term insurance." Similarly, a salesperson selling replacement windows might say to a prospect, "With your current windows, it's as if each winter you had one window wide open," rather than, "You're wasting energy with your existing windows."

10-10g Avoid Negative Words

Many salespeople use negative words in their presentations, when rephrasing what they say in a positive manner would have a much more favorable impact. They should leave the word *but* and its synonyms at home. For example, which of the following sounds better?

> *It's a good machine, but very expensive.*

or

> *It's an excellent machine and worth every penny.*

Similarly, how should the retail salesperson respond to a customer's request for a certain shirt that is out of stock?

> *It's a nice shirt, but it will take 10 days to get it.*

or

It's a nice shirt and I can get it in your size. It will only take 10 days.

Similarly, if you were forced to choose between a deal that has an 80 percent chance of success and an equivalent deal that has a 20 percent risk of failure, which would you choose? Most people choose the first, even though the options are identical, because people respond more favorably to choices that are framed positively—that is, in terms of success rather than failure.

10-11 Multiple Calls

On the average, from the first meeting of prospect and salesperson, it takes five calls for an order to be closed. This raises the obvious question of planning the objective and narrative of each call. In some instances, it is easy: The approach and problem recognition are handled in the first call, presentation in the second, handling objections in the third, closing in the fourth, etc. Typically, however, the salesperson must plan and vary the presentation for at least several visits. Summarizing what has transpired on earlier calls is an effective beginning for later ones: "Let me summarize what we discussed on the 25th . . ."

Beyond this, the salesperson should make sure there are reasons for subsequent calls, focal points around which to build each presentation. After all, if you're selling cars you don't take customers on their second visit for another test drive. You talk about financing or options or trading up. You might bring a new idea, ask some different questions, make a survey, and ask about new developments that have changed the prospect's situation. New literature, an application by another customer, test results, price changes, coming shortages , new products, new processes—all offer a reason for making new calls. For each call, setting multiple objectives has much to recommend, especially for relationship selling, where many calls may be required before a sale and additional calls may be needed to firmly establish the relationship. Such goals might include setting a date for the next meeting, getting to know the prospect better, continuing to discover prospect needs and problems, and scheduling a demonstration. In addition to focusing the sales rep's presentation, having multiple objectives diminishes the fear of failure by the salesperson. For salespeople with a wide line of products or services, there is **cycle selling.** On the first call, the sales rep stresses the most popular lines plus one or two secondary products. On the next call, he or she again stresses the primary line and two other secondary products. Soon, the whole line has been detailed.[35]

Where multiple calls are required, especially for relationship selling, multiple "closes" are necessary before the final sale is made and the relationship firmly established. After the first call, for example, the sales rep may decide that other buying influences must be consulted, a demo arranged, a plant tour scheduled, etc. To facilitate this sequence of requisite steps, the salesperson may use an advance. One of the most common perceptual problems occurs when the salesperson and prospect misunderstand one another on the next course of action, particularly what decision will be reached by whom and when. Oftentimes, the salesperson leaves thinking he or she will be hearing a decision shortly, while the prospect perceives no particular hurry. This leads to frustration on the part of both parties; hence, the advance. The salesperson tells the prospect what he or she would like to cover in the presentation and agrees on the nature of the next step:[36]

cycle selling
On the first call to a prospect, the sales rep stresses the most popular line and one or two secondary ones; on the next call, the most popular again and another secondary line, etc.

Ms. Smith, I'd like to cover several areas today. I have questions for you, and I'm sure you have several for me. After we go over everything, we need to make a decision about what to do next. If you think my product meets your needs, then we can process the order. If we need to meet with others, we can schedule further meetings. Is this a logical sequence of events?

10-12 Presentation Psychology

Successful salespeople adjust their presentations to the customers they face. This means recognizing buyer personality style—Driver, Amiable, Analytical, or Expressive. This significantly affects the different tactics and benefit statements to be used with each. Salespeople should also adjust their presentations to the characteristic ways that prospects process new information—an emerging field of scientific study with the jaw-breaking title of neurolinguistic programming. Take the assessment in Box 10-1, "Your Neurolinguistic Style," to determine your own approaches. The section with the highest score indicates your preferred style.

10-12a Neurolinguistic Programming

neurolinguistic programming (NLP)
How humans characteristically respond to communication: visually, auditorially, or kinesthetically.

Neurolinguistic programming (NLP) was developed by John Grinder, a professor of linguistics, and Richard Bandler, a therapist, both of the University of California. Grinder and Bandler claim that humans respond to new communication in one of three basic modes: visual, auditory, or kinesthetic (seeing it, hearing it, or touching it).[37] Further, their studies demonstrate that people consistently favor one mode over the other two and that you can communicate more easily with them by using their favored mode. How do you recognize which mode is predominant? According to Grinder and Bandler, it will be evident in eye movement. Someone who processes information visually will look up and off to one side, as if they were imagining what something looks like; auditory, eyes horizontal and to one side, as though imagining what something sounds like; and kinesthetic, eyes down and off to one side. (See Figure 10-2.) Clues also can be found in the characteristic language of each type. Visual people use visual language: "That's not clear to me," "Can you shed a little more light on that subject," or "Hey, that's a bright idea." Auditory types might be heard to say, "Hey, that rings a bell," "I hear you . . . ," or "That really strikes a chord." Kinesthetic types might say, "That feels right," "I have a hunch that . . . ," or "I sense that . . ."

By taking note of prospects' characteristic eye movements and language, salespeople can formulate their presentations accordingly. To sell to the visual customer, paint word pictures of a product: how beautiful something will be, as in, "Can you see the reaction of everyone when they see a new iMac personal computer sitting in your office?" Use visual words, such as *see, look, clear, bright, show, eye-catching*,

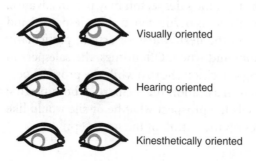

Figure 10-2
Eye Movements Reveal
One's Neurolinguistic Style

Visually oriented

Hearing oriented

Kinesthetically oriented

Your Neurolinguistic Style

The information checklist that follows is designed to help you discover your preferred way of relating to the world. Notice the 20 items in each of the three communication channels. Put a check next to each item that is basically true for you. The scale with the most checks identifies your preferred style.

Information Preference Checklists
Visual Orientation

1. On an evening when I don't have anything else to do, I like to watch TV.
2. I use visual images to remember names.
3. I like to read books and magazines.
4. I prefer to get written rather than oral instructions from my boss.
5. I write lists to myself of things I have to do.
6. I follow recipes closely when I am cooking.
7. I can easily put together models and toys if I have written instructions.
8. When it comes to playing games, I prefer word games like Scrabble and Password.
9. I am very concerned about the way I look.
10. I like to go to art exhibits and museum displays.
11. I keep a diary or a written record of what I have been doing.
12. I often admire the photographs and artwork used in advertisements.
13. I review for a test by writing down a summary of all pertinent points.
14. I can find my way around a new city easily if I have a map.
15. I like to keep my house very neat looking.
16. I see two or more films each month.
17. I think less highly of a person if he or she does not dress nicely.
18. I like to watch people.
19. I always get scratches and dents repaired quickly on my car.
20. I think fresh flowers really brighten up a home or office.

Total Score for Visual Orientation

Auditory Orientation

1. On an evening when I don't have anything else to do, I like to listen to music.
2. To remember someone's name, I will repeat it to myself over and over again.
3. I enjoy long conversations.
4. I prefer having my boss explain something to me orally rather than in a memo.
5. I like talk shows and interview shows on radio and television.
6. I use rhyming words to help me remember things.
7. I am a good listener.
8. I prefer to keep up with the news by listening to the radio rather than by reading.
9. I talk to myself a lot.
10. I prefer to listen to a CD of some material rather than to read it.
11. I feel bad when my car sounds funny (has knocks, pings, etc.).
12. I can tell a lot about a person by the sound of his or her voice.
13. I buy a lot of albums and prerecorded CDs.
14. I review for a test by reading my notes aloud or by talking with other people.
15. I would rather give a talk than write a paper on the same topic.
16. I enjoy going to concerts and other musical events.
17. People sometimes accuse me of talking too much.
18. When I am in a strange city, I like to stop at a gas station to get directions.
19. I talk to my dog or cat.
20. I talk aloud to myself when I'm solving a math problem.

Total Score for Auditory Orientation

Feeling-Movement-Touch Orientation

1. I like to exercise.
2. When I am blindfolded I can distinguish items by touch.
3. When there is music on, I can't help but tap my feet.
4. I am an outdoors person.
5. I am well coordinated.
6. I have a tendency to gain weight.
7. I buy some clothes because 1 like the way the material feels.
8. I like to pet animals.
9. I touch people when I am talking with them.
10. When I was learning to type, I learned the touch system easily.
11. I was held and touched a lot when I was a child.
12. I enjoy playing sports more than watching them.
13. I like taking a hot bath at the end of a day.
14. I really enjoy getting massages.
15. I am a good dancer.
16. I belong to a gym or health spa.
17. I like to get up and stretch frequently.
18. I can tell a lot about a person by the way he or she shakes hands.
19. If I've had a bad day, my body gets very tense.
20. I enjoy crafts, handwork, and/or building things.

Total Score for Feeling-Movement-Touch Orientation: _____

Source: Donald J. Moine and John H. Herd, *Modern Persuasion Strategies: The Hidden Advantage in Selling,* Englewood Cliffs, NJ: Prentice Hall, 1984, pp. 49–51.

shine, and others. To sell to the sound-oriented customer, use sound-based words and phrases, such as *sounds, hear, bells, ring, harmony, bang, I hear that,* and *to tell the truth.* Include testimonials. They are the positive words that other customers say about you and your product. This may not sell the visual customer, but it is effective with the auditory one. The kinesthetic customer constantly monitors his or her feelings. Even highly intelligent customers check out their hunches and gut-level reactions. Salespeople should avoid looking down on this type of customer. To sell to him or her, speak the proper language. "Does that feel OK to you?" "Are we in step?" "Can you grasp the impact of this concept?" And be sure to provide them with a "hands-on" demonstration.

For almost any product, salespeople can adjust their presentations to suit the neurolinguistic style of their buyers. Let's say you are trying to sell someone a sailboat. If you know the prospect is visually oriented, you might describe white sails against the blue sky; auditory, the hiss of the sea and the snap of the sails as the wind fills them; kinesthetic, the tangy feel of the spray in your face.[38] A real estate salesperson might sell a home in a similar manner. Visually oriented buyers would find appealing "the long, tree-filled street" where a house sits; auditory buyers might find the "quietness" of the neighborhood the most important factor; and kinesthetic, "how it feels to sit in front of the fireplace on those long winter evenings."

10-12b Personality Styles

Sales representative Bill Evans could hardly wait to call on ABC buyer John Gorman. Bill had closely analyzed ABC's operations and was certain his product could save the company thousands of dollars. Not only that, he had heard through the grapevine that Gorman was dissatisfied with his current supplier. Yet, following a personal call on Gorman, Bill found himself back on the street without an order and with no appointment to call back.

"I can't understand it," Bill told his sales manager. "I walked in, introduced myself, and started presenting the features and benefits of our product, but Gorman kept interrupting me, asking me where I had gone to school; whether I wanted any coffee; whether I had any girlfriends. I kept trying to get back on our products, but he just seemed indifferent. When I tried to close, he ushered me out the door. I just don't understand what went wrong. I know our products are best for ABC."

The problem is that Bill was not sensitive to the type of buyer with whom he was dealing. In terms of the personality profiles outlined in Chapter 4, "Buyer Behavior," John Gorman is an Amiable. Bill tried to stick to the facts, but Amiables want a personal relationship to be established first. Accordingly, the sales representative should concentrate on making the Amiable a friend first and then doing an informal presentation that is liberally sprinkled with personal assurances. These people value feelings and relationships. They need to feel that what you are presenting is helpful, easy to implement, and safe. They decide by consensus, so you would be smart to present your ideas to them and the other decision makers in a group setting. Think of Oprah's television personality. When you present, use language that appeals to them: feel . . . positive . . . loyalty . . . relationship trust . . . together as a team/group/family . . . consensus . . . proven . . . easy . . . fail-safe . . . low-risk . . . helpful to others . . . upbeat . . . fun . . . positive . . . . Tell success stories, especially of friends.[39]

Never pressure Amiables for an immediate decision. Salespeople should emphasize how the purchase will affect workers. "How will my supervisors react?" "Will I have too many employees?" and "Will I need to have people retrained?" are the sorts of concerns Amiables might have. Especially important to Amiables are relationships with suppliers; the company that provides the best service and commits itself to solving Amiable problems is preferred. They desire a company that marries itself to its customers. Salespeople should stress personalized service, frequent follow-up calls, online availability, and the presence of 800 numbers. Relating the tradition of the salesperson's company, its commitment to quality, and its longevity in the industry helps to assure Amiables that this company will be there when needed. Do not push or rush Amiables, but be assumptive and leading with them when it comes to making decisions, because they need that gentle friendly push, especially from someone they really trust. Suggestions for dealing with Amiables, as well as other personality types, are provided in Figure 10-3.

With the Driver (that personality type characterized by assertiveness and task-orientation), the salesperson should concentrate on the facts and keep the relationship businesslike rather than personal. These people care about results. They care about getting things done in the shortest amount of time . . . solving problems . . . reaching goals . . . winning. This is your Type A personality. Think Donald Trump. Think the general personality of many sales managers! When you present, the language they like to hear is *bottom line . . . net-net . . . the key point is . . . can be done quickly . . . done deal. . . .* They like executive summaries and short presentations with brief bullet points. Keep your diagrams and charts simple. In general, Drivers prefer to deal with sales representatives like themselves, people who waste no time but get straight to the facts. Drivers are bottom-line oriented. They are interested in how new plant equipment will lead to greater profits. "Pays-for-itself" appeals are very effective, so salespeople should show how their wares will decrease material costs, eliminate unneeded labor, streamline production for optimal efficiency, or increase revenue. Because Drivers want to exercise personal control over matters,

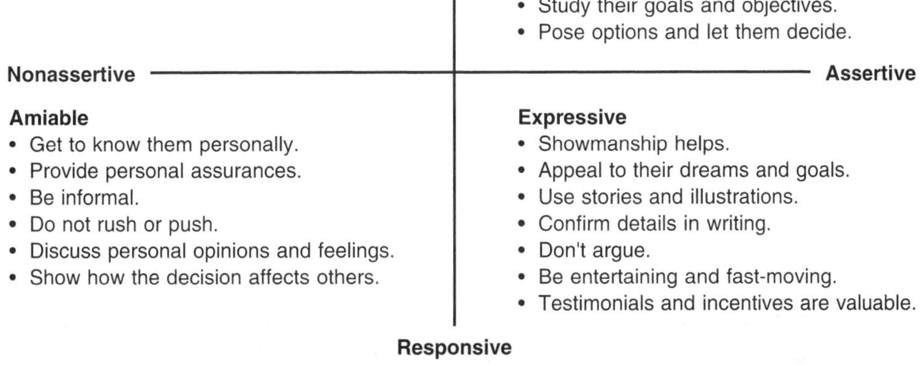

Nonresponsive

Analytical
- Propose logical solutions.
- Do not hurry the decision.
- Provide evidence.
- Emphasize technical information.
- Keep things in writing.
- List both positives and negatives.

Driver
- Get to the point quickly.
- Emphasize the bottom line.
- Be businesslike.
- Define consequences and rewards of the decision.
- Be precise.
- Study their goals and objectives.
- Pose options and let them decide.

Nonassertive ———————————————————————— **Assertive**

Amiable
- Get to know them personally.
- Provide personal assurances.
- Be informal.
- Do not rush or push.
- Discuss personal opinions and feelings.
- Show how the decision affects others.

Expressive
- Showmanship helps.
- Appeal to their dreams and goals.
- Use stories and illustrations.
- Confirm details in writing.
- Don't argue.
- Be entertaining and fast-moving.
- Testimonials and incentives are valuable.

Responsive

Figure 10-3
Dealing with Personality Style in the Presentation

they are interested in products that provide increased discretion over the use of time, data, materials, personnel, space usage, and deadlines. They are ambitious, and new products that help them show a track record of financial success will attract their interest.

Drivers like quick, concise analyses of their needs and your solutions. You should offer options with supporting evidence and leave the final decision to them. "The way I see it, you can go with option A (explain the pros and cons), option B (tell pros and cons), or option C (more pros and cons)." Drivers are very big on autonomy, so let them make the decision.

When dealing with the Analytical, the salesperson must once again deal in facts but also be prepared to prove them. These people value information, logic, and order. They need to feel that whatever you are presenting makes sense, has all loose ends tied together, is rational, objective and organized. Think Sgt. Joe Friday from the old television show *Dragnet*: "Just the facts, ma'am." When you present, the language that appeals to them includes *control . . . systematic . . . monitor . . . check . . . solid, research-based . . . evidence shows . . . proven track record . . . air-tight . . .* and use factored-in components stories. Always bring more information than you think you'll need. Have charts and graphs and sources clearly marked on visuals. Pace yourself to their tempo, which is frequently slower than yours. Guarantees and reports from independent agencies will carry much weight with Analyticals. Listing the advantages and disadvantages in a product proposal is another good tactic because Analyticals pride themselves on their ability to make an objective decision. If you do not bring up the obvious disadvantages in your product or plan, the Analytical will find them and will then believe you are hiding things, thus ending the sales relationship. They are engineering- and detail-oriented. Analyticals expect and relish nitty-gritty details: capacities, tolerances, maintenance and safety features, and setup and downtime data. Their focus is long-range because they will be working directly with the equipment. In contrast to Drivers, they are concerned more with process than with outcome. How the equipment works is more important than results. Quality is as important as or more important than price, and they demand tangible proof: certified testing, warranties, and the testimony of authorities in a field. They like to be identified with equipment that commands technical respect for itself and its buyer. Analyticals prefer written proposals or at least agreements that firmly solidify as many details as possible.

Try not to rush the decision-making process with Analyticals, because they need time to verify your words and your actions. They like presentations that are less dramatic, but more purposeful. In other words, give your presentation using a direct, straightforward, organized, logical delivery with slow, deliberate gestures. They do not appreciate an overenthusiastic, "rah-rah" presentation that is wrought with hyperbole and exaggeration.

The Expressive is characterized by lots of enthusiasm. The enthusiastic salesperson will be well received, and an entertaining delivery will go a long way. These people like to see how your presentation fits in with the big picture, in the long term. They like synergies, challenges; they like to revolutionize and transform the status quo. When you present to them, use their language: *long-term . . . innovative . . . synergy . . . integrated . . . context . . . provocative . . . .* Present your boldest, most creative ideas in the boldest, most creative way possible. Paint a picture for them that is big, exciting, unique, and new. Recommendations, especially those from the well-known, are important. If you were selling real estate to an Expressive, for example, mentioning that a bank president lived on one side and a surgeon on the other might have a strong impact. With Expressives, it is important to solidify details following the completion of a sale. Salespeople should settle matters such as delivery dates, installation requirements, price discounts, and so on, because Expressives tend to be weak on details. Unlike their opposites—Analyticals—Expressives appreciate equipment as a means to an end rather than for its technical sophistication; and that end is gaining status and recognition for themselves in the eyes of company management. Accordingly, appeals that emphasize prospects being "first to lead" or "first to innovate" are effective. As seekers of approval for themselves, their departments, and their companies, they like equipment that shows they have "made it," "arrived," or are "real comers" in their field.[40]

Keep in mind that Expressives want to enjoy life and be entertained. They like presentations that are lively, stimulating, and fun. They like stories of triumph and disaster and prefer visuals and surprises. They like new ideas and thoughts and like to know creative, inventive solutions. They prefer to learn through examples and like to see the big picture and not get bogged down in details. Make sure that you illustrate your ideas and concepts and point out the future prospects of any solution you propose. Their decisions are positively influenced by incentives and testimonials.

Differences in the personalities of buyers present one of the more vexing problems for the salesperson. Salespeople must be able to sell not only to prospects like themselves but also to those considerably different. Many experienced salespeople sell only to their close acquaintances; they avoid buyers with whom they have difficulty dealing. But truly professional sales representatives realize that they owe it to their company and themselves to call on all legitimate prospects. If not, they are forgoing personal rewards—both financial gain and the rewards of meeting and helping people.

Chapter Summary

This chapter describes the sales presentation and ways of improving its effectiveness. First, the salesperson must plan ways of responding to the prospects unstated questions. Then the salesperson should identify product features, advantages, and benefits. A feature is any quality inherent in the product or service, tangible or intangible. An advantage explains what a feature does. A benefit is the value or worth that the buyer receives from a product or service. It tells the customer "what's in it for me."

One of the most important elements in the presentation is dramatization, which represents methods for emphasizing product benefits. A demonstration is the most effective means of dramatization, especially if the sales representative makes the demonstration specific to the prospects' needs and has them participate in it. Other effective methods of dramatization are audiovisual aids, recommendations, showing return on investment, comparison, free trials and warranties, and showmanship. Among elements of the latter are appropriate nonverbal behavior, movement, novelty, contrast, and intensity and size.

A difficult task for salespeople during the presentation is making themselves understood. Among the ways of improving the clarity of the presentation are proper structuring, spacing out ideas, repeating key concepts, watching for the emotional impact of words, restricting oneself to concrete rather than abstract words, and avoiding negative statements.

Suggestions were made for the multiple calls usually required to close the sales and establish the relationship. The advantage of having several objectives for each call was discussed, as were the "advance" and setting the agenda for the next call.

Salespeople must adjust their presentations according to the personal characteristics of the buyers they face. Some buyers tend to process new information visually, while others use auditory or kinesthetic modes. As has been emphasized throughout the text, buyers will react in fundamentally different ways, depending on whether they are a Driver, Analytical, Amiable, or Expressive.

Discussion Questions

1. How do many salespeople go astray when making their sales presentations?

2. What is the rationale for planning the sales presentation? How far should one go in its planning?

3. Enumerate the prospect's unstated questions prior to the presentation.

4. Explain what a product feature is. Define an advantage. What is a benefit?

5. Why is dramatization necessary in the presentation? How might salespeople add dramatization to their presentations?

6. What sorts of activities contribute to the successful sales demonstration?

7. What functions do audiovisual aids fulfill?

8. Define multimedia. What are its advantages?

9. How are recommendation stories effective? What are the elements of a successful one?

9. Explain ways of showing investment to prospects.

10. What is comparison? What does it add to dramatization?

11. Indicate ways of introducing showmanship to the presentation.

12. Sales representative Steven Sorensen learns that prospects are having trouble understanding his presentation. What might he do to improve their understanding?

13. How does the buyer's personality affect the basic strategy of the sales presentation?

14. Why is it important to use action words?

15. Why should the salesperson avoid negative words?

16. How should the salesperson recover from an interrupted sales presentation?

17. What are topics for multiple sales calls? Cycle calls? The "advance"?

18. What is neurolinguistic programming? How is it important to selling?

19. Compose a product-analysis worksheet for one or more of the following products: an office copier for an accounting manager, a DVD recorder for a typical family, an overcoat for a junior executive, stocks for a young married couple, radial tires for a traveling salesperson, a sewing machine for a family with three children, home insulation for a family of four, or a fax for a small business.

20. Put an "F" before each of the following statements that is a feature of an automobile. Put a "B" before the statements that represent a benefit of those features:
    a. _____ Has snow tires
       _____ Will not skid on icy roads
    b. _____ Is easy to park
       _____ Has power steering
    c. _____ Is comfortable to sit in
       _____ Has padded seats
    d. _____ Has a transverse mounted engine
       _____ Has plenty of interior passenger space
    e. _____ Has a GPS system
       _____ Allows you to know where you are at any moment

21. For each of the following products, a feature and benefit are given. Put an "F" before the feature and a "B" before the benefit.
    a. Frying pan
       _____ Has plastic handle
       _____ Won't burn your hand when you pick it up
    b. Pencil
       _____ Has eraser
       _____ You can change mistakes
    c. Boots
       _____ You will not get your feet wet
       _____ Made of rubber
    d. Credit card
       _____ You do not have to carry cash around
       _____ Available from your bank
    e. LCD panel
       _____ Mounted on wheels
       _____ Can be moved easily
    f. Eyeglasses
       _____ Fold up
       _____ Can be carried in your pocket
    g. Fax machine
       _____ Will transmit at 56,000 bps
       _____ Will process stock transactions more rapidly
    h. DVD recorder
       _____ Has 6 gigabtyes of storage
       _____ Will record a TV show remotely at a preset time

22. How should the sales rep adjust to the differing personality styles of buyers? Drivers? Analyticals? Amiables? Expressives?

Chapter Quiz

1. In the product-analysis worksheet, a(n) _____ is the value or worth that the user derives from a product or service.
   a. feature
   b. advantage
   c. benefit
   d. motive satisfied

2. The best-selling means of dramatization is
   a. a demonstration of the product itself.
   b. an audiovisual aid.
   c. recommendations from others.
   d. showing return on investment.

3. A demonstration represents a powerful means of dramatization, but it is not always possible. By means of a recommendation story, the salesperson can
   a. illustrate the impact of the product's benefits.
   b. create a comparable effect by telling the story of a satisfied customer who was in a similar situation before the purchase.
   c. show the return on investment and the financial impact of the product.
   d. provide comparisons and through imagery demonstrate the impact of the product.

4. The return on investment (ROI) is simply the return expected from a given investment, expressed as
   a. Investment ÷ Net Profits.
   b. Investment ÷ Gross Profits.
   c. Revenue ÷ Investment.
   d. Net Profits ÷ Investment.

5. There are several ways for salespeople to sell by comparison. They can sell by _____, which is drawing comparisons between essentially dissimilar objects.
   a. analogy
   b. metaphors
   c. imagery
   d. hyperboles

6. In terms of communicating appropriate nonverbal messages, confidence would be conveyed by
   a. smiling, friendly facial expressions.
   b. smiling, sparkling eyes, animated face.
   c. head and eyes up 90 percent of the time, sustained eye contact.
   d. conversational, sincere, real voice, warm tone.

7. In terms of voice, sharing the "dream," showing of appreciation, upbeat, positive words, expressing feelings, and giving credit to others demonstrates
   a. caring.
   b. confidence.
   c. understanding.
   d. enthusiasm.

8. During presentations, communicators (especially salespeople) should keep in mind all of the following guidelines *except*
   a. structure and organize the presentation.
   b. space out your ideas.
   c. repetition aids learning.
   d. use abstract words rather than concrete words.

9. On the average, from the first meeting of prospect and salesperson, it takes _____ calls for an order to be closed.
   a. two
   b. four
   c. five
   d. seven

10. In terms of personality styles, _____ want to enjoy life and be entertained. They like presentations that are lively, stimulating, and fun. They like stories of triumph and disaster and prefer visuals and surprises.
    a. Expressives
    b. Analyticals
    c. Drivers
    d. Amiables

Profile

Role-Playing Exercise

For the products and services described in Chapter 6, "Beginning the Relationship Selling Process," construct a product-analysis worksheet that will prepare you to make a sales presentation to the appropriate customers depicted in Chapter 8, "The Approach." Take special care with the dramatization part of the worksheet. You may exercise some amount of poetic license in formulating testimonials, comparisons, and other means of dramatization.

Web Exercise

Testimonials and user reviews often help a salesperson place products with buyers. For the salespeople who trade on the online auction site eBay, customer recommendations and feedback are especially important in establishing a reputation as an honest dealer. Go to www.eBay.com and click on "eBay Stores." Select any eBay store that interests you, and look at the feedback for the dealer running the store. What kind of testimonials would encourage you to buy from that individual? What kind of testimonials are less convincing?

Notes

1. Theodore Levitt, *Industrial Purchasing Behavior*, Cambridge, MA: Division of Research, Graduate School of Business Administration, Harvard University, 1965.

2. Bill Brooks, "How to Present Your Product with No Resistance," *SalesVault.com*, 2004.

3. Art Sobczak, "How to Avoid Doing a Data Dump," *SalesDoctors.com*, July 6, 1998.

4. Diane Sanchez, "Think Like Your Customer," *Sales & Marketing Management*, December 1998.

5. Brian Tracy, "Stop Talking and Start Asking Questions," *Sales & Marketing Management*, February 1995, pp. 79–87.

6. William Keenan, "Creating Effective Sales Presentations," Sales Marketing Network at infonow.com, 2004.

7. "Now Presenting Some Homework, *Sales & Marketing Management*, September 2000.

8. "But to Rafferty, Well, Let's Just Say This Site," *Sales & Marketing Management*, July 1, 2003.

9. John Carroll, "Heads Up!" *EyeonSales.com*, January 24, 2003.

10. John Boe, "Show and Tell," *EyeonSales.com*, June 29, 2003.

11. Tom Hopkins, "Award-Winning Presentations," *EyeonSales.com*, February 21, 2003.

12. William Keenan, "Creating Effective Sales Presentations," Sales Marketing Network at infonow.com, 2004.

13. George W. Colomby, "Power to the Salespeople," *Selling*, May 1995, pp. 34–37.

14. Randall P. Whatley, "Final Preparations." *SalesVantage.com*, August 25, 2004.

15. William Keenan, "Creating Effective Sales Presentations," Sales Marketing Network at infonow.com, 2004.

16. Dave Paradi, "How to Avoid the 6 + 1 Mistakes Salespeople Make Using PowerPoint," *SalesVault.com*, April 4, 2004; Anne Miller, "Death by PowerPoint," *The Power to Sell*, www.annemiller.com, November 9, 2000.

17. Ginger Trumfio, "The Future Is Now," *Sales & Marketing Management*, November 1994, pp. 74–80.

18. Larry Wilson, *Counselor Selling*, Eden Prairie, MN: Wilson Learning Corporation, 1972, pp. 24–27.

19. Leon Festinger, "A Theory of Social Comparison Processes," *Human Relations*, 2, 1954, pp. 117–140.

20. S. Schacter and J. E. Singer, "Cognitive, Social, and Physiological Determinants of Emotional States," *Psychological Review*, 69, pp. 379–399.

21. Nancy Arnott, "Testimonials on Tape," *Sales & Marketing Management*, January 1994.

22. Anne Miller, "Make That Selling Point Stick," *Power to Sell*, www.annemiller.com/articles.asp, December 20, 1999.

23. Paul Katzef, "Small Moments of Greatness," *Selling*, January/February 1994, pp. 49–53.

24. Marjorie Brody, "Does Your Body Language Stop a Sales Presentation before It Starts?" www.brodycommunications.com, 2004.

25. Marjorie Brody, "Use Gestures to Improve Your Presentations," *Personal Selling Power*, July/August 1994.

26. C. W. McPherson, "Put Your Customers into the Act," *Salesmanship*, July 27, 1981, p. 1.

27. Joseph W. Thompson, *Selling: A Managerial and Behavioral Science Analysis*, New York: McGraw-Hill, 1973, pp. 458–462.

28. Anne Miller, "Presentations That Move Right to the Sale," *Power to Sell*, www.annemiller.com/articles.asp, October 12, 2000.

29. Jerry Weissman, *Presenting to Win: The Art of Telling Your Story*, Financial Times, Prentice Hall, 2003.

30. Anne Miller, "Presentations That Move Right to the Sale," *Power to Sell*, www.annemiller.com/articles.asp, October 12, 2000.

31. Sondra Brewer, "How to Present So Prospects Listen," *Personal Selling Power*, April 1994, p. 75.

32. Anne Miller, "Presentations That Move Right to the Sale," *Power to Sell*, www.annemiller.com/articles.asp, October 12, 2000.

33. Anne Miller, "Cheers, Not Jeers!" *EyesonSales.com*, June 8, 2004.

34. "How to Use the Cycle-Selling Strategy," *Master Salesmanship*, February 8, 1993.

35. Lloyd Corder, "See It My Way," *Personal Selling Power*, September 1994, pp. 40–41.

36. Donald Moine and Kenneth Lloyd, "Neuro-Linguistic Sales Programming: The Unfair Advantage," *Personal Selling Power*, 3, July–August 1983, pp. 6–7.

37. Tom Pickens, "Much That Is Said Is Unspoken." *Creative Living*, January 1982, p. 14.

38. Anne Miller, "Your Presentation 'Style': Power or Pitfall?" *EyesonSales.com*, January 8, 2003.

39. Hugh J. Ingrasci, "How to Reach Buyers in Their Psychological Comfort Zones," *Industrial Marketing*, July 1991, pp. 60–64.

40. Anne Miller, "Your Presentation 'Style,' " ibid.

Case 10-1

Given the following product and prospect profiles, prepare a product-analysis worksheet, including features, advantages, benefits, motives satisfied, and means of dramatization for the new Focus.

Prospect Profile

- Amy Schraeder, a fifth-grade teacher, lives in Lexington, Massachusetts, and works in Boston, 20 miles away.
- Amy has a daughter, Patty, who loves sports, including softball, basketball, and skiing.
- Amy's 1999 Neon is beginning to show signs of an impending breakdown. The brakes are going, the exhaust system needs replacement, the valves need to be reground, and a new transmission is needed.

Product Description

- The engine is mounted sideways for added passenger compartment space in a small automobile. Also, with the back seat folded down in the hatch-back model, there is more cargo space available.
- The car has front-wheel drive. This means that the engine pulls rather than pushes the car. With 65 percent of the car's weight over the front driving wheels, there is impressive traction on any kind of surface.
- With the standard 4-cylinder engine and 4-speed transmission, EPA mileage estimates are 38 on the open highway and 24 in the city.
- The sticker price is as low as $12,000 excluding dealer preparation, tax, license, and destination charges.

Case 10-2

Tom Mayer works at Timms Hardware in Highland Park, a suburb of Chicago. Joe Duwe has just entered the store and is looking over lawn mowers as Tom approaches.

Tom: I see you're looking over our new line of mowers.

Joe: Yes, I am.

Tom: Have you got a large lawn?

Joe: About medium.

Tom: (showing a demonstrator on the floor) Well, let me show you something about this model. It has electronic ignition and a 4-cycle engine and . . .

Joe: That's nice. What about service?

Tom: Timms has an excellent reputation for service. We have a large staff of well-trained service people, and we maintain a large parts inventory.

Joe: How long have you worked here?

Tom: I've worked at Timms the last two summers in between my semesters at college. It's a great place to work.

Joe: I can see you really like it. It sounds like a real friendly place to work from the way you talk.

Tom: Well, let me tell you a little more about the mower. It's a mulching mower, which, of course, cuts down on the amount of time you have to invest in the lawn.

Joe: Yes, I'm sure. Is it heavy? My wife and children will probably use it at one time or another.

Tom: No problem. This mower is easily pushed around. It's very lightweight. If your wife and kids will be using it, you might be interested in knowing that this mower also has several built-in safety features and an electric starter.

Joe: What about price?

Tom: The price is $549.95, which admittedly seems high, but look at all the features you get on the mower.

Joe: Yes, I can see. Well, I'll think it over and get back to you.

Questions

1. What sort of selling job did Tom do? Did he present benefits? Did he use adequate means of dramatization?
2. How would you describe Joe? Did Tom's presentation take into account Joe's personality?

Handling Objections

Key Terms

boomerang method
compensation method
echo technique
"feel, felt, found" method

forestalling
head-on
indirect denial

mini-max strategy
objection
"polite why"

Learning Objectives

Learning Objectives

After studying Chapter 11, you will understand:

- How to view objections as a necessary and beneficial part of selling
- How to clarify an objection
- How to handle objections through the head-on method, the indirect denial, the compensation method, the continuous-yes method, the "feel, felt, found" method, the boomerang method, and forestalling
- Specific techniques for handling the price objection: breaking price down

into small units, stressing exclusive features or differences, using comparison, converting to a lower-price item, postponing the objection, discussing both initial and ultimate costs, and quantifying differences

- How to handle the procrastinating buyer, the skeptical buyer, the indifferent buyer, the buyer who needs to talk it over with someone else, and the overstocked buyer

objections
Buyer concerns that product or service does not fully meet and resolve buyer problems.

Objections are simply buyer concerns that some part of your product or service offering does not fully meet and resolve buyer problems. The objection may be over price, delivery, timing, skepticism, authority, and myriad other possibilities. Objections may be seen as "road maps" that point you in the right direction toward the successful completion of the sale.[1] Yet, it is surprising how many salespeople struggle to prevent prospect objections. Although objections superficially appear to voice opposition to buying, in fact, they should be treated as signposts to the final sale. As long as selling involves an exchange of feeling and thoughts between human beings, objections are going to arise. They are a normal part of any sale. Objections are necessary for the salesperson to understand what the prospect is thinking. Experienced salespeople will tell you that the most difficult sale is to prospects who are quiet and uncommunicative. Be optimistic when faced with an objection or tough question. Objections are indicators moving you to successful completion of the sale or losing the sale and giving you more time to spend with customers who will buy. In either case, you know where you are and what you need to do in order to move ahead, course correct, or break off the relationship. When a prospect voices his or her concern over a certain aspect of your product or service, price for example, a chance has arisen for you to redirect your points. If the prospect objects to high initial costs, point out how over the course of time, ultimate costs are actually lower, as with a laser printer versus an inkjet model. With explicit objections, you have the chance to move away from things that the prospect sees as undesirable in favor of moving toward those things that the prospect wants from you, your organization, or your product or service.

Experienced salespeople will also tell you that the prospect who speaks up and raises objections is showing genuine interest in the product. So the proper attitude toward objections is to welcome them. If there are no objections, there may be no sale. Figure 11-1 certainly confirms this; in a study by Learning International, note that when customer objections are present, 64 percent of the time the outcome is successful, in contrast to 54 percent when objections are absent.

Most people work hard for their money and, before parting with it, want to make sure they are spending it intelligently. That is why when we are in a store we tell the salesperson, "No, thank you, I'm just looking," even if we see an item we know we intend to buy. We are delaying the moment when we actually have to let go of our hard-earned money. Salespeople may encounter prospect resistance be-

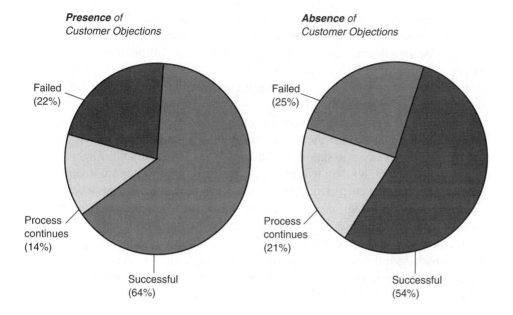

Presence of Customer Objections

Failed (22%)

Process continues (14%)

Successful (64%)

Absence of Customer Objections

Failed (25%)

Process continues (21%)

Successful (54%)

Figure 11-1
Source: Adapted from *Success Factors in Selling*, Learning International, Stamford, CT.

cause of something they haven't made clear. Resistance may be just the prospect's safe way of postponing a decision. "No" is safer than "yes." Salespeople should realize that a "no" might mean "Maybe, but tell me more," or "I don't understand." Real selling pros know that the sale really begins when the customer says "no."

11-1 Preparation

The basic task of sales representatives is to prepare to answer objections before they arise. By anticipating objections, salespeople can ready their answers. This preparation provides salespeople with the confidence of knowing that they can handle almost any situation that arises. Although it is impossible to anticipate every objection, salespeople within two to three months will hear 80 percent of all the objections they will ever face. If the objections are written down, along with the best ways of handling them, salespeople will be prepared for practically any eventuality.[2]

One salesperson keeps what he calls his "Objections Notebook," a loose-leaf binder containing all the objections he has run into, along with appropriate responses. As new ideas for handling objections occur to him, he writes them down, and as new products are introduced or modifications are made in existing ones, he enters the new objections that arise. By studying his objections notebook periodically and glancing at his prospect file, in which the results of each customer visit are recorded along with pertinent customer facts, this salesperson can anticipate the objections each individual customer is likely to raise and can prepare effective answers.

11-2 Ignoring the Objection

In our society, consumers like to think of themselves as shrewd, discriminating buyers who aren't easily convinced or sold. In other words, buyers often put up resistance merely to avoid thinking of themselves as pushovers. The stated objection is groundless; the customer has raised it just as a token objection, one they really don't believe. Fifty percent of the time, it's not an objection at all; it's just a random thought on their part. Moreover, there's often a show-off element in many so-called prospect objections, and the smart salesperson can profit from this tendency. If he or she recognizes that the questioner already knows the answer and/or is trying to score points, the sales rep can appeal to their attempt to demonstrate their cleverness by praising them: "That's an excellent question" or "You raise an interesting point." They'll be so busy congratulating themselves that they'll never notice the sales rep has moved on to something else.

Another pitfall is when the customer makes an erroneous statement because of ignorance of the true facts. If the wrong statement will have little effect on the outcome of the sale, it's best to ignore it. Replying "that's interesting" and continuing the presentation is better than telling him or her outright that they are wrong. If the misstatement must be corrected, then the "yes, but" technique is appropriate. Other effective statements for ignoring the objection include: "Ms. Jones, I appreciate the position you're in. And just to make sure we have the problem in proper perspective, let me recap what benefits you would have . . ." Notice that the salesperson has first acknowledged the objection and then ignored it. This is so as not to offend the prospect's ego. Here are other possibilities for prefacing the focus on benefits: "That's an excellent question," "You raise a very important point," or "I can see how you feel that way."

But what if the objection is real? If the prospect brings up the objection again, then the salesperson can proceed to handle it.

11-3 Clarifying the Objection

Often, the objections that prospects express do not really represent their underlying doubts. In some instances, the prospects themselves are unclear about the nature of their objections, or perhaps they simply have not been able to verbalize doubts well enough for the salesperson to understand. It is also possible that prospects are afraid to state an objection for fear of embarrassment; hence, they alter what they say. On occasion, it even happens that prospects fail to express what they really feel for fear of hurting the salesperson. Social amenities often induce this sort of behavior in everyday life. In social situations, there is a mutual expectation that we will treat one another politely and be considerate of each other's feelings. This isn't lying; when prospects fail to understand the benefits of buying, they are often too embarrassed to tell the truth. This isn't lying, however, as the old adage among veteran salespeople, "Buyers are liars," would have it. Instead of taking the time to listen to the salesperson's presentation, they seek an immediate shortcut by fabricating a small falsehood.[3] Salespeople must be as certain as possible that the objection they answer is in fact the objection the prospect feels. Otherwise, sales representatives' answers will fall on deaf ears, and the opportunity to learn what really is bothering the prospect is lost. Also, the prospect is likely to become annoyed, because his or her doubts are not really being addressed.

An example can illustrate why objections must first be clarified. If prospects raise the objection, "Your price is too high," the salesperson might want to clarify these points:

1. Are prospects referring to list price, discounted price, or even operating and installation costs?
2. Are buyers stating that they cannot afford the price or that it is higher than competitors' prices?
3. What do they consider a fair price?
4. Has the prospect misunderstood or misinterpreted what the salesperson has said?

5. Perhaps the customers really believe that the price is too high, and they're not aware of the total value received in terms of quality, service, back-up support, etc.

6. The customers may be using high price as a cover-up to conceal another objection they don't care to reveal, such as they really don't have the power to make the decision; someone higher up the corporate hierarchy does.

7. Prospects may be hiding yet other doubts. They may not see a real need for the product, or perhaps they have doubts about the delivery and dependability record of the salesperson's company.

Certain objections can be easily voiced by prospects, when they actually have reservations about something entirely different. Price is certainly one example, while others that fall into this category include "I need to talk it over with someone else," "We already have a supplier," "I'll think it over," "I tried a similar product before and it didn't work," "I have no budget for it," and "We'll need to bring this to a committee."[4] For the budget issue, the salesperson needs to clarify: *What is their budget? What financial criteria do they utilize when making a decision? Do they have the ability to pay for the product or service? Do they have the ability to obtain credit? When will their budget allow them to authorize a purchase?* As to the prospect's experience with similar products, the salesperson needs to address: *What was their previous experience? What was the exact product they used? Was the experience positive or negative? What did they like about the product? What didn't they like about it?* Regarding who makes the ultimate buying decision, the following need to be addressed: *Is the buying decision made by an individual or committee? Are there people who can influence the decision makers? Who are they? What is the decision-making process and how long does it take?*

So, how does the salesperson go about clarifying an objection? If the sales representative feels the objection needs elaboration, such as a price objection, the salesperson might use the echo technique or a "polite why" question.

The **echo technique** allows drawing out the prospect's opinions with a question. For example:

echo technique
Clarifying an objection by repeating the last few words of a prospective buyer in the form of a question.

> **Prospect:** I had your goods in my store once before, and they didn't sell!
>
> **Salesperson:** Didn't sell? (echo technique)
>
> **Prospect:** Yes, the price was too high.
>
> **Salesperson:** Too high? (echo technique)
>
> **Prospect:** Yes, your competitors had more aggressive couponing. They ran ads in the local newspaper offering 10 cents off on each bottle.

In each instance, the sales representative was neither negative nor positive but phrased questions to draw out the buyer's opinions and learn more about his or her thinking. Note also that the echo technique is not a closed question; that is, the prospect's response is not limited to a simple yes or no answer. The echo technique has a number of advantages. In the first instance, it checks that you understand what he or she really wants to say. Many "objections" arise from genuine misunderstandings by the prospect, and their repeating their comment (in more logical form) will often lead to them to answering it themselves. Even more objections result from the sales rep's misunderstanding an innocent comment on the part of the prospect, and a restatement on their part should clarify this. Second, the restatement, allows the sales rep to slow down the pace, stopping their reacting too quickly and providing time to think. Third, it shows that the rep has not only noted but also taken the comment seriously.

"polite why"
Politely asking the prospective buyer for an accurate explanation of an objection.

A **"polite why"** question also is useful in getting prospects to open up about their doubts. For instance:

Prospect: I really don't feel that your company stands behind its products.

Salesperson: I would appreciate hearing your viewpoint on that, Ms. Prospect. Could you comment further about what you mean?

By phrasing a question in such a polite manner, a salesperson makes it difficult for prospects to refuse to elaborate. The sales representative might have simply asked "Why?" but most prospects would find this offensive; they would probably feel that the sales representative was critical and was looking down on them. Questions alone can sometimes seem arrogant and harsh, so it is a good idea to lead off with a "softening statement," such as:

Good question.

I'm glad you asked me that.

That's a good point.

That seems to be an important question to you.

If you speak quietly and use softening statements, you will calm the prospect, and your questions will be inoffensive.

If someone objects to the fact that you are asking Block Watchers to wear a reflective vest while out walking the neighborhood, don't say, "What's wrong with it?" Instead, gently ask, "Wearing the vest makes you uncomfortable?" If it does, he'll tell you why. Maybe he's shy. If so, you have to build his confidence in the respect the uniform generates and in the authority it lends to him as a participant.[5]

Once salespeople are fairly certain they understand the objection, they can ask a closed question to check their understanding. This might occur after an echoing question, or a "polite why," or even sooner. Earlier in the sales process, closed questions were used to help identify buyer problems. Here they are used to confirm the source of an objection. A dialogue illustrating the use of the closed question in clarifying objections follows:

Prospect: Your price is too high.

Salesperson: Too high? (echo technique)

Prospect: Right, your product costs $200–$300 more than the competition for basically the same thing.

Salesperson: So, what you're asking, Ms. Prospect, is, What is there in our product that justifies the higher price? (closed question)

Prospect: Yes, that's right.

By phrasing the closed question in such a manner, the salesperson is able to confirm that the objection is as just stated. If the prospect answers "no," however, then the salesperson can simply ask, "Well, what would you say is the question?"

11-4 Tactics for Handling Objections

After salespeople are reasonably sure that the objection has been clarified, they are in a position to answer it with some special tactics. Using their knowledge of product, company, and competition, sales representatives should be well prepared to answer any objection that arises.

11-4a Head-On Method

When using the **head-on technique,** salespeople tell customers directly that they are mistaken. Of course, because few of us enjoy being told that we are wrong, salespeople must be careful here, demonstrating as much tact as possible. If the objection arises from incorrect information about a product, then use of the head-on method can be both effective and tactful. Consider the following dialogue:

> **Customer:** I don't see any reason why we should pay that much for advertising in your magazine. We only market in the Midwest and don't need national exposure.
>
> **Salesperson:** Then, you're saying you only need to advertise in the Midwest?
>
> **Customer:** Yes.
>
> **Salesperson:** Well, *Contemporary Issues* publishes three regional issues. An advertiser can buy space in all three or just one. Here, let me show you an example. Notice many of the ads in this regional edition are from midwestern companies such as yours.

Here the salesperson first asks a closed checking question and then points out that the customer has incorrect information. The closed question serves to lessen the impact of the head-on technique; it demonstrates empathy, showing that the salesperson has been listening carefully to the prospect. In lieu of a checking question, the salesperson may preface the denial with softening statements such as: "Good question," "I'm glad you asked me that," or "That seems to be important to you."

It is also a good idea to offer proof with the head-on method—testimonials, independent tests, or warranties. For example:

> **Customer:** These colors will fade when we wash them.
>
> **Salesperson:** You're concerned about the harshness of the hospital laundering process on the color of the garments?
>
> **Customer:** Yes.
>
> **Salesperson:** No, the colors won't fade. Let me show you a uniform that's been used for a year at Mercy Medical. Notice the almost total absence of any fading or discoloration.

It is important to watch the tone of voice for the head-on method. Because the idea is to give reassurance to the doubting prospect, the tone of voice must be appropriate.

11-4b Indirect Denial

In both the head-on method and the **indirect denial**, the salesperson denies the validity of the objection, but with the latter, the answer is handled more obliquely. The salesperson may first reflect the prospect's objection and then follow it with a "refined" no. For instance:

> **Prospect:** You overcharged us last time!
>
> **Salesperson:** Mr. Prospect, I can understand how you might think that. Since prices vary so much because of trade and cash discounts, transportation charges, and promotional allowances, things get complicated. However, I can assure you that no customer in my territory with the same set of circumstances as your firm receives a better price.

head-on technique
Directly telling prospects why they are wrong in their objections.

indirect denial
A response to an objection that denies the validity of the objection in a refined and oblique manner that is unlikely to upset the prospective buyer.

With the indirect denial, the salesperson never tells prospects directly that they are wrong. Instead, the salesperson sympathizes with the prospect's views, does not get defensive, and still manages to correct the invalid objection. Indirect denial is especially effective for Amiables and Analyticals because they dislike assertive salespeople.

compensation method
The salesperson admits the validity of an objection, but then counterbalances it with more compensating benefits.

11-4c Compensation Method

When the prospect raises an objection that is partially true, but to which the salesperson may point out a compensating factor, the **compensation method** is advantageous. Because the phrase "yes, but" is used so commonly with the compensation technique, it is often called the "yes, but" method. Whatever it is called, the fundamental idea is for the salesperson to convince prospects that the compensating factor is what is really important. A trade salesperson might use the compensation method as follows:

Prospect: Your company doesn't advertise enough.

Salesperson: Yes, but our research indicates that in-store promotion is more critical to sales, so we have the most attractive packaging and eye-catching display of anyone else in our field.

Ideally, with this technique, it is best to compensate with the product's strongest benefit. This method is even better if the benefit is exclusive (something that the competitive product does not have). For example, an organ salesperson might respond, "It is quite true that the *X* organ has more trick sound stops like the calliope and banjo, but you will quickly find that these novelties are seldom used when you're playing music. And our organ is guaranteed to never get out of tune. That's an exclusive feature that saves you a lot of money and avoids the terrible sound of slightly off-key music."

Of course, citing compensating factors is difficult if the salesperson does not know what they are. The prospect might say something vague like, "It looks good, but I'm not sure . . ." or "It has its merits, but I don't know . . ." or similar phraseology.

In other words, the prospect has positive feelings about the offering but something is stopping them from buying now. The sales rep can help them rebuild a sense of urgency and renew their desire for the product/service by having them restate the critical benefits as they see them. After acknowledging the concern, the salesperson might say something like: "Which parts of the proposal do you like best?" (Then ask, "Why?") or "How do you see yourself benefiting from our product/service?" or "Which benefits do you feel are most important to you?" Then the salesperson can use these compensating benefits to make up for the concerns.[6]

The compensation method is effective in a number of respects. First, it avoids a direct argument, which could disturb prospects' feelings of importance and question their ability to give a sound reason for not buying. In contrast, the "yes, but" technique permits the salesperson to first agree with the prospect and then tactfully introduce a logical reason for buying, perhaps one the prospect had not considered. Second, initially agreeing with prospects disarms them and allows the sales representative to shift around and examine the rest of the picture, presenting it positively and sensibly in order to help prospects switch rather than fight. For both these reasons, some recommend that it is even more effective to substitute "and" for "but." Last, the compensation technique is effective because buyers recognize that seldom does a product exactly fulfill all their needs; if it did, it would probably be too expensive anyway. Buyers know that they must counterbalance needs met against those unmet; and they know they can do this logically with the help of the salesperson. As might be expected, the compensation technique is more effective with logical Analyticals and Drivers, who also are predisposed toward rational arguments.

11-4d "Feel, Felt, Found"

The **"feel, felt, found" method** of handling objections is excellent for responding to anxious, worried, fearful clients. Once salespeople have listened to prospects and given them time to air their feelings, they can respond with the "feel, felt, found" method. In some respects, this method resembles a recommendation story because the salesperson indicates how others have found the product or service to be the solution to their needs. Returning to the example of Ron Friendly, the hospital uniform sales rep, the "feel, felt, found" technique could be used to handle the objections of prospects worried about making mistakes and diminishing their self-image by spending too much. For example:

> **Prospect:** You know, these uniforms of yours are pretty expensive. I really wouldn't want to ruin my budget by spending too much. I'd hate to make a mistake that I would have to explain later at a board meeting.

> **Salesperson:** I can understand how you might feel that way. The fact is that many of our customers have felt the same way, but once they purchased the uniforms, they found that their laundering costs dropped dramatically and that the uniforms lasted longer, cutting the costs of frequent repurchasing. Their hospital boards were quite pleased, in fact.

Notice that Ron has agreed with the prospect in the first part of the statement, in effect saying, "It's perfectly natural for you to feel as you do. Others have, so you're not being stupid or unduly worried." Then Ron proceeds to imply that it's perfectly okay to change one's mind given this new information. Salespeople are not telling prospects what to do. Instead, they are simply relating information. The salesperson is not being critical or looking down on the prospect in any way.

"Feel, felt, found" sounds fine to Amiables and Expressives, as these two types tend to care about what other people think and are doing. Hence, the salesperson may say, "I *understand* your thinking. Others have *thought* the same thing at first. However, it has been *found . . .*"

Besides handling emotional objections, the "feel, felt, found" technique is valuable for handling objections when the prospect fails to perceive the value of a particular feature and benefit. For example, a salesperson selling radio advertising might respond to a prospect's objection as follows:

> **Prospect:** I don't see the need for radio advertising. Our store seems to get sufficient traffic with just newspaper ads.

> **Salesperson:** I can understand why you feel as you do. Other hardware store owners like yourself have felt the same way, but they have found that radio ads allow them to reach their specific target market a lot more cheaply than newspaper advertising. After all, with newspapers you're paying for mass circulation to a lot of subscribers you'll never see. Also, radio ads reach people better on the weekends when they do most of their buying. Carl Stapel, over at Kitz and Pfeil Hardware in Lomira, found that advertising three times a day on a Saturday on our station increased his store traffic by 15 percent.

Notice that the salesperson used the name of a customer in a situation similar to that of the prospect. Citing such satisfied buyers, especially if they are acquaintances of the prospect, magnifies the impact of the "feel, felt, found" technique.

VIDEO

"feel, felt, found" method
Method of handling an objection in which the salesperson points to others who have felt the same way, but discovered that purchase of the product or service resolved the problem.

Moreover, the approval implied in the "feel, felt, found" approach appeals to the prospect's ego and shows respect for his or her feelings.

boomerang method
The salesperson's taking an objection and turning it into a reason to buy.

11-4e Boomerang Method

In the **boomerang method,** the salesperson takes the prospect's objection and turns it into a reason for buying. This method also takes away the objection's power, making it difficult to bring up again. Like the compensation method, it is also used for objections that are partially true:

> **Prospect:** The quality of copy on your machine is not as high as that of your competitor.
>
> **Salesperson:** We engineer it that way on purpose. The overwhelming majority of copies made in a business don't need to be of a high quality. This way, each copy on our machine only costs you four cents, versus the seven to nine cents of our competition.

The boomerang method may present a problem for the sales representative, however. It can sound glib and manipulative, or, in other words, like what a stereotypical, self-serving salesperson might say. Therefore, salespeople must take great care with their nonverbal delivery when using the boomerang method. There must be no hint of condescension. The boomerang works best with Drivers, because it gets their attention and challenges them, when that normally might be difficult.

forestalling
Including the answer to a common objection in the presentation itself so that the objection isn't raised.

11-4f Forestalling

Technically, **forestalling** is not a means of handling objections at all because its intention is to prevent (or forestall) the objection from ever being raised. When salespeople hear an objection arising again and again, they may decide to include an answer to it within the context of their presentation. In this manner, the objection never is voiced by the prospect; it's already answered. Some argue that forestalling handles an objection better, because once an objection is actually voiced, no answer to it will ever be satisfactory, as the prospect will always retain some doubt. For example, after hearing numerous objections about the comfort of a polyester-cotton-blended surgical uniform, Ron Friendly, our Superior Hospital Uniform Company sales representative, might incorporate the following statements into the fabric of his presentation:

> **Ron:** . . . and the new Superior uniform stays cool in the operating room. The 35 percent cotton in the garment allows plenty of room for the uniform to breathe. We've had absolutely no complaints about the uniform being too hot under operating conditions. I'll be only too glad to provide you with the names of some hospitals that will attest to that fact.

An embellishment of forestalling is for the sales person to provide a menu of common objections prior to the presentation. That way, they can be addressed then, while minimizing prospect antagonism. Here's an example of what the sales rep might say:

> When I talk about our products and services with potential customers, some of them naturally have concerns and apprehensions. It may not be the case here, but some customers:
>
> . . . *see all suppliers as being essentially the same.*
>
> . . . *hate the agonizing process of selecting among alternative models.*

. . . had a bad experience with our company in the past.

. . . are not sure which direction or application will be best for them.

Which, if any of these, is an issue for you?

There are a number of advantages to forestalling objections. First, prospects often will not voice an objection, and the salesperson never realizes why the sale was lost. With experience, however, salespeople may incorporate answers to such unexpressed objections in the text of their presentations and thus handle the problem. Second, no matter how tactful the salesperson, when prospects raise objections, they have to be proven inaccurate—and none of us likes that. From the latter standpoint, to build the relationship, it may be best to minimize objections. Hence, it is suggested by some sales theorists that it is critical to firmly identify and confirm the problem and follow up with explicit benefits targeted at this problem. By doing so, they claim that objections can be cut in half and sales improved commensurately.[7] Finally, forestalling has considerable merit from a timing standpoint. A typical scenario is one in which the salesperson, following a smooth presentation, moves confidently toward closing the sale, only to have the prospect suddenly begin to bombard the sales representative with objections. Caught off guard, the salesperson responds awkwardly, losing the prospect's confidence. Rather than lose momentum at this critical juncture of the sale, it might be better for the salesperson to forestall the objections in the first place.

Should they desire to do so, salespeople could forestall almost any objection. The problem, of course, is carrying it too far. Forestalling every objection might result in a sales presentation that is far too long. Obviously, only the most common objections are candidates for forestalling.

11-5 Strategies for Handling Objections

What we have outlined so far are tactics for handling objections of all sorts; that is, general techniques that may be adapted to a wide variety of situations (see Table 11-1). If one wished to make an analogy, one could say the techniques are like guns—without ammunition, they have little value. For example, the compensation technique is well suited to counterbalance price objections, but what specific response does one use against a higher price? We have attempted to respond to some of the major sources of customer objections. Obviously, it would be difficult to get too specific. All conceivable objections likely to be encountered in the sale of every good and service cannot be covered, but general strategies for handling broad categories of objections can be discussed.

11-5a Handling the Price Situation

Inevitably, all salespeople have to face objections about the price of their product or service. No sales representative can always have the lowest price, and when he or she does, it usually is for one or a few items in the line, not all. Sooner or later the price objection will come up, and it is not easy to handle. In fact, many salespeople say the price situation is the hardest of all objections to handle. But it does not have to be so. Although a few buyers purchase on the basis of price alone, a good many know that trade-offs between price and quality have to be made. They realize that the old saying "you get what you pay for" holds a large degree of truth. It has long been recognized that buying cheap carries with it a measure of risk. The English writer John Ruskin once wrote: "It is unwise to pay too much, but it is worse to pay too little. When you pay too much, you lose a little money, that is all. When you pay

T a b l e **11-1** A Summary of Objection-Handling Techniques

Method	When to Use	How to Use
Head-on	With objections arising from incorrect information	Salespeople directly, but politely, deny the truth of the objection. To avoid alienating prospects, it is helpful to offer proof.
Indirect denial	With objections arising from incorrect information	Salespeople never tell prospects directly that they are wrong, but still manage to correct the mistaken impression
Compensation	With valid objections but where compensating factors are present	Salespeople agree with prospects initially, but then point out the factors that outweigh or compensate for the objection. For this reason, it is also often called the "yes, but" technique.
"Feel, felt, found"	With emotional objections, and when the prospect fails to see the value of a particular benefit or feature	Salespeople express their understanding for how prospects feel and indicate that these feelings are OK because others have also felt that way; however, others have found these fears to be without substance.
Boomerang	When the objection can be turned into a positive factor	Salespeople take the objection and turn it into a reason for buying.
Forestalling	With any type of objection	From prior experience, salespeople anticipate an objection and incorporate an answer into the presentation itself, hoping to keep the objection from ever coming up.

too little, you sometimes lose everything, because the thing you bought was incapable of doing the thing you bought it to do."[8]

Salespeople with the higher-priced product should not be apologetic about their wares. Other product features are at least of equal importance to most buyers: quality, workmanship, guarantees, and service all receive consideration. The salesperson's job, then, becomes one of justifying the higher price. Salespeople must explain the additional benefits that their product, their company, and they themselves will provide the prospect over and above comparable or lower-priced competition. With the price situation, the sales representative makes the difference. If price were the only feature, the company might just as well send a catalog; salespeople would have nothing to do.

The following strategies are specifically designed for handling price objections. The salesperson may:

1. Break price down into small increments.
2. Stress exclusive features or differences.
3. Use comparison.
4. Convert to a lower-priced item.
5. Postpone the price objection.
6. Talk about both initial and ultimate costs.
7. Quantify differences as much as possible.
8. Sell return on investment.
9. Fire the customer.

Breaking Price Down

The basic idea with this method of handling the price objection is to take the price of the product and break it into small amounts spread over its useful life. For example, Ron Friendly of Superior Hospital Uniform Company might employ this technique in selling his higher-priced surgical uniform:

Ron: Yes, you're right, Mr. Prospect. The Superior uniform is $25 higher than our competitor's garment, but since our uniform will last twice as long, this amounts to very little. When you consider that the Superior uniform will last a minimum of two years, this amounts to only $12.50 per year, or $1.46 per month for all of the added features of the Superior uniform.

In this response, Ron used the compensation technique and then followed it by breaking the price into small increments. The concept that must be placed in the prospect's mind is the difference between initial price and the eventual cost, the cost of the product over the life of its service.

Stressing Exclusive Features or Differences

The price objection is often not so much the absolute value of the price itself as it is the balance of value of the product or service against the price. One way to visualize cost is to use a formula that compares price and value:

$$\text{Value} = \frac{\text{Price}}{\text{Cost}}$$

Value is the buyer's total benefit—the solution to their problem. Because the price is constant, the only thing you can change is the perception of value. Hence, you must build up the value to lower the cost.

Because few products are built exactly alike, the salesperson should determine the unique features of the product. Buyers focused on price deemphasize or entirely ignore factors such as the following:[9, 10]

- *Quality.* Is your product demonstrably better? Will it work better or last longer than the competition's? Murray Weintraub, a Rhode Island tool sales representative, thought so. When faced with cheaper competitive hand tools, Weintraub asked the buyer, a longtime customer, if he could borrow them for analysis. He took them to his company's lab, where they were subjected to stress and other tests. The results of the tests, which Weintraub presented to the customer, showed the competitive tools were half as safe, were likely to last half as long, and were half as reliable. So much for the competition. Quite often, cheaper products are built down to a price rather than up to a standard. The salesperson should write down the names of prospects who have regretted buying such bargains. Their unhappy stories can open up the minds of prospects attracted by a cheaper price. Similarly, if inferior components, like ball-bearings, paint, or struts used in automobile manufacturing, are going to bring the production line to a halt, what good are cheaper prices for relatively cheap component parts? One customer of a business forms company bought cheaper labels, but when they failed to adhere to packages and the customer had to repurchase labels that did and redo the whole process, where were the true savings?
- *Delivery.* Can your company provide swift delivery of product or parts when the customer is in a bind? This is an especially important aspect of relationship selling these days with JIT inventory control systems. The vendor that can consistently deliver right before the subassembly enters the production line is often the chosen supplier, even if their price is not the lowest. Business forms manufacturer Wallace-Moore can deliver forms to customers linked to Wallace's computer system within 48 hours, saving the costs of inventory-handling and warehousing, and can offer one summary bill

at the end of the month, saving costly repetitive bill-processing each time an order is placed, especially from additional forms vendors.

- *Service.* Supplier postsales support capabilities are critical. One sales rep figured out that his competitor's service and support resources were stretched very thin. A few subtle and well-planned comments to the prospect suggesting they look more deeply into certain "areas" pointed them in the right direction. As a result of a bit of probing, the prospect found that the sales rep's competitor couldn't appropriately support them postsale. "If they can't bring people to the party now when they are selling to us, it'll only get worse if we become their customer," the prospect told the sales rep.

  Does the salesperson's company provide superior repair and maintenance service? Are service personnel knowledgeable and readily available? Is there a toll-free 800 HELP number or website the buyer can access when his or her new computer has troubles? If so, the computer salesperson can argue confidently that even a $500 dollar price differential is minimal: "If business activity is stalled because the computer breaks down even once, Mr. Prospect, and it takes you days to get it serviced, it could cost you far more than $500." With consistent delivery and service, there often lies the foundation for establishing a long-term relationship with a partnering buyer.

- *Company reputation.* Is your company financially strong? Does it have a record of standing behind its commitments? Again, companies do not care to establish relationships with companies of doubtful financial stability and integrity. What is the satisfaction level of competitors' customer base? Use references here, both your own and those of dissatisfied competitive clients (be careful here in how you name them). What is the financial position of competitors? If they are publicly held, look at their P&L, balance sheet, and cash flow statement for both the most recent quarter and their history. If they are privately held, get your CFO to create a pro forma set of financial statements that might "represent" what that competitor's financial position might be.

  Look at their corporate culture. What do they value? Integrity? Quality? Are they doing the right things for building a long, profitable future or are they highly opportunistic, with little regard to what will happen tomorrow? Can they sustain?

- *Expertise.* Does your company's engineering, scientific, computer, and other technical personnel represent an advantage over the competition? What do you know about the quality of competitive personnel? Look into staff and executive attrition rates, quantity and quality of SMEs (subject matter experts), levels of staffing, support hours—anything that will point toward discount-caused reduced margins impacting operating effectiveness.

- *Facilities.* Does your company's labs, computer centers, or transportation department give you an advantage? W. H. Brady Company, a maker of labels and other identification materials, has a reputation of being higher priced, but their laboratories, which can analyze customer samples to develop higher-quality adhesives and longer-lasting labels, give them an edge on the competition.

- *Promotion.* For companies that sell to retailers, their price may be higher, but their advertising, point-of-purchase displays, couponing, and other promotional tools can exceed the competition's. How does it help your customer increase volume or selling price and margins?

- *You (the sales rep).* What about your knowledge and expertise? Can you be relied on for regular visits, both sales and service related? What about competitive salespeople?

As an illustration of how to use some of these factors, suppose Ellen Brown, an automobile salesperson, has just received a price objection from a customer:

Ellen: Yes, Mr. Prospect, the Pontiac G6 does cost $1,400 more than the competition, but no other car has its unique features. First, the G6 has front-wheel drive, which gives traction in all kinds of weather, and in Minnesota we have all kinds. No other comparably priced domestic car has this feature. Second, because it's made in this country, parts are readily available if something should go wrong. Third, the Pontiac G6 carries a 5-year warranty on the drive train and one year on the rest of the car. No other car, absolutely none, carries such a guarantee. Now, add up all these features and consider that the extra $1,400, when spread over seven years, adds up to only $200 per year for all these unique features!

In answering this price objection, Ellen has employed three methods: the compensation method, stressing unique features, and breaking price down into small increments.

In the computer industry, Dell is the low-cost competitor, but Hewlett-Packard (H-P) competes by making a broader offer that includes product support and long-term relationships. H-P offers a bigger product line (e.g., printers, cameras, scanners) and generous financing terms via its credit arm; its consulting unit advises customers on how to save money on their technology applications. Recently, H-P was able to get an order for 500 desktop and 165 laptop PCs from Getty Images of Seattle even with a price higher than Dell, with free advice for improving Getty's disaster-recovery plan and creating a digital archive of more than 70,000 film clips. At Starbucks Corp., Walt Disney, and elsewhere, H-P lured new customers with technology "partnerships." The Starbucks marketing plan, partially funded by H-P, lets coffee drinkers make fast wireless connections from their laptops, which has attracted more businesspeople to Starbucks. To cement an alliance with Disney, H-P agreed to buy ads on Disney websites and at theme parks.[11]

When discussing exclusive features or differences, it is often a good tactic to hold off citing the price until the end, by which time, "Price is the good news!" Think back to the time somebody told you about something you really wanted. The more you listened, the more you wanted the product and the higher you thought the cost would be. When you finally heard the price, you were relieved. It seemed too good to be true—much lower than you thought.

"You get these 24 up-to-the minute reference books," winds up the encyclopedia salesperson, "plus the handsome mahogany bookcase, plus this unabridged dictionary, plus the answers to 50 questions from our research department for just . . ."

"Let's review, for a moment, what I'm offering you," says a printing company sales rep before quoting a price. "Here is a completely revamped catalog in which the type has been restyled for eye appeal, readability, and balance; the stock has been upgraded to bespeak quality; the cover has been transformed from run-of-the-mill to exciting; and the layout is guaranteed to rivet attention." By the time price is quoted, it seems eminently reasonable. In other words, preface your price quotation with exclusive features and benefits and make "price the good news."

Using Comparison

Today, the prices of almost all goods and services have increased. When a customer objects to the price of a product, it is a good strategy for salespeople to point out other products whose prices have also risen. Faced with a price objection, you might respond as follows:

> *I appreciate your desire to get the most value for your money. Let me ask you this. Is price always the most important concern? Does the lowest price always equate with value? In automobiles, the Yugo was the lowest-price new car on the market for a while. Or how about a new home? The lowest bidder doesn't always provide the best value in building a new home. And I'm sure you wouldn't want to pick a heart surgeon solely on the lowest price.*

Faced with a patient who objected to restorative surgery and who asked instead to have her teeth pulled and replaced with dentures, a dentist imaginatively replied, "Look, if you knew you were going to lose a leg and be disabled for life but surgery could save the leg and prevent you from becoming handicapped, could you afford the surgery?" When the patient replied that represented a totally different situation, the dentist continued, "No, it's not. If you lose your teeth and have to wear dentures, you'll be a dental cripple the rest of your life." Hearing this, the patient agreed to restorative work. The dentist's success was due not to comparing the price to another alternative so much as comparing it to the discomfort of the cheaper alternative. This, too, represents a way to handle the price objection with comparison.

Converting to a Lower-Priced Item

Sometimes the customer really cannot afford the higher price of a product. In this case, the salesperson may still be able to get an order but for a lower-priced model. This is not always that easy to do, however, especially if the sales representative has already stressed the outstanding features of the higher-priced model. If this is the case, then the salesperson must do some gymnastics in order to sell a lower-priced model without these features. Part of the answer may rest in doing a competent job of qualifying before the interview begins or in clarifying the price objection once the question has arisen. Even so, salespeople may still find themselves in the position of having to convert the prospect to a lower-priced model. Basically, the salesperson should show prospects high-priced models and low-priced alternatives in such a way that, should the customer decide not to buy the higher-priced model, he or she is still free to buy the lower-priced one without feeling it is inferior. This implies that the salesperson should avoid directly comparing the two models unless specifically requested. Rather, the salesperson should present good features and benefits for both models. For example, a retail salesperson selling typewriters might say:

Salesperson: This is our Compact model. It has some outstanding features: antijunk fax function, distinctive ringing, and 50-number automatic dialing. It costs $250 for all this quality.

Prospect: That's a little more than I can afford.

Salesperson: Well, then, it sounds like the Signet, our largest-selling model, is for you. It costs $175 and has such features as an electronic telephone directory and 20-sheet automatic document feeder. The Signet can also be purchased with either thermal or regular paper, whatever you desire. And the fax has an outstanding reputation for service-free operation.

In the dialogue, two points stand out: (1) the salesperson did not downgrade the lower-priced Signet model; both models were sold on their features; and (2) the sales representative did not directly compare the two models.

This bring ups, of course, the issue of how high a price to quote first.[12] When you board an aircraft, you walk through first class; through business class; and, finally, into economy class. You look at the wide first-class and business-class seats, the crisp newspaper, and the personal movie screens. As you squeeze into your tiny economy seat, you watch a crewmember pull the curtain that shields your view of first class. You wish you were in business or first class as you hear champagne glasses; you smell the first-class meal; and you're thirsty. Then, the heavy guy seated right next to you doesn't give you enough room to rest your arm on the armrest. What if you'd gotten into economy via a different door? You wouldn't have seen the wide seats and the fancy trappings, and you wouldn't have heard the champagne glasses clinking. The odds are you wouldn't feel quite as bad as you do now, sitting in economy. If you didn't know any different, you'd accept economy class as an adequate way to travel, and first class wouldn't bother you so much.

Like most businesses and salespeople, you believe in starting with the cheapest price (and product line). Psychologically, you're on your way to losing the battle. Your customers are just like you. They want to fly first class. You can't show them economy class first. First class is always expensive. So your top-of-the-product-line price is going to frighten your prospects. They'll say your product or service is too expensive. Then you show them your "business class" package, which is not as expensive, but still high. Then you show them your "economy class" alternative. If you start with the most inexpensive product line first and then move up, the sticker shock may frighten them. Most buyers aspire for first class, and a lot of clients will buy the top-priced product. Note this routine with salespeople selling TVs in a retail store. They start with the 42-inch $4,000 plasma model and then move to the $139 13-inch model. Most clients settle for somewhere in between. Almost no one makes the $200 choice.

Postponing the Price Objection

When the price objection arises early, it may be a good idea to postpone it until later. Never prematurely present your price until you are in a position to justify how it's perceived value exceeds your asking price. If you prematurely or incorrectly present your price, you will never be able to justify it to your customer.[13] If the sales representative has not had a chance to talk about features and benefits, answering the price objection may only serve to establish a barrier in the prospect's mind that can never be lowered. The suspicion will remain that the product is just too high-priced and that the salesperson is trying to put something over on the poor buyer. As an example, one woman was recently shopping for a gold pen. She pointed to one in the display case of a store and asked the clerk the price. "Five hundred dollars," the clerk quoted. "Five hundred dollars! That's way too much!" she growled and stormed out of the store. The sales clerk remarked to a coworker, "Gosh, I should have told her it comes with a Rolex watch." The customer must first know exactly what they're getting. If, however, you give the impression you're stalling on price, the prospect may assume too high a price and the effect is the same. So the salesperson may wish to say something such as, "I can't really answer the price question, yet, Mr. Prospect, until I know more about your particular situation, your needs, and the features of most benefit to you." If there are several choices, the salesperson might add, "It all depends on which model is best for you."

Postponing may also be employed with other objections besides price if the objection is better answered later in the interview. In such a situation, the salesperson might respond, "That's an important question, Mr. Prospect. However, I believe we can answer it better in a few minutes once I've determined your needs, if that's all right with you."

Discussing Both Initial and Ultimate Costs

If the buyer is perceived to be price conscious, the salesperson should take care to explain that price must often be seen in a lengthier time frame.[14] For instance, "If my competitor's product needs servicing four times a year and my product requires servicing only once a year, the fact that my competitor has a lower price is only part of the equation. At the end of a year, my competitor's product will have a higher cost because of the three additional service calls required."

Ink-jet printers are less expensive, but can cost more per printed page because of expensive inks. A laser printer is quick and easy to set up (costing customers less), it is basically maintenance free, and the consumables (i.e., toner and drum units) are inexpensive, in contrast to ink-jet cartridges. A laser printer makes the most sense, if the prospect mainly prints text (and lots of it) and wants fast, permanent printing. Lasers cost more up front, but less in the long run due to cheaper supplies. Longer-lasting laser printers can also be repaired more easily and less expensively.

Salespeople have to know the buyer. Some buyers want initial costs controlled and are less concerned with the long run. A home buyer who is planning on being in the house for only four or five years is not likely to be swayed by an argument that vinyl siding will last for 30 years. A Mercedes salesperson once said that his customers did not care at all about fuel economy but were persuaded that the styling of the car was unlikely to change radically over the years, thus protecting their original investment.

Quantifying Differences As Much As Possible

It is important to explain price differences objectively and quantifiably. The real estate salesperson must point out explicitly why one house costs $5,000 more than another: at least $2,000 for the central air-conditioning and the rest in the convenient downstairs full bathroom. A copier sales rep asks prospects, "How far off on price are we?" He then asks, "What do you like best about the copier?" If they say "faster feeder time," he subtracts that much off the difference and replies, "Now, we're only $X off." He then asks what further features they like and proceeds to do the same. A salesperson who defines differences in terms of explicit features and associated dollars enables the objector to make comparisons in a realistic way.

Sell Return on Investment

Here the idea is to show the prospect that the product or service more than compensates for its cost by paying for itself or returning the cost of the original investment:

> *The savings from this personal computer will pay for it in 13 weeks. After that, you get a 100 percent return on your investment every 13 weeks. A lot better than most investments today, don't you agree?*

> *With our copier you can turn out 3,000 more copies a day. How much would this be worth to you in labor savings?*

> *Because our guarantee is twice as long as our competitor's, this means twice the performance at an extra cost of only 5 percent. Isn't that 5 percent a good investment?*

"Fire" the Customer

If the salesperson has the power to negotiate somewhat on price, it is critical to not give in too easily and to explain carefully any concessions given. When a price concession is given too quickly and with no strings attached, the customer will always expect to pay no more than 92 cents whenever the salesperson quotes a dollar.

The salesperson should take care to quote prices with authority. Contrast the hardware salesperson who quotes "about $100 for a door" with the one who quotes from a "book" complete with pictures of hinges and doorknobs or the sales rep who totals a column of figures manually versus the one who uses a calculator or laptop computer. The sales representative often can tame the price objection by having the invoice fall in the next price period or by taking an order for future delivery.

If the prospect continues to demand price concessions to the extent that the salesperson would not be making any profit whatsoever for his or her company, the rep can "fire" the account.[15] The rep should explain the realities of the situation, demonstrating the small amount of profit being made and the excellent service he or she has provided in the past. Then, the rep can tell the buyer that his or her time is valuable and, although they enjoy working with the account, lack of profit will force severing the relationship. Finally, the rep can ask which competitor the account would prefer to do business with and offer to share all information on the account to prevent any interruption in service. Sitting back and remaining silent, the sales rep can frequently expect no further resistance and often an increase in business. A summary of techniques for handling the price objection is provided in Table 11-2.

11-5b Handling Procrastination

A common and exasperating objection for the sales representative is the procrastination or stalling objection. This may be expressed by the prospect in a number of ways—typically with a statement such as this:

I have to think it over.

Call me back in 30 days.

Leave your card and I'll call you back.

T a b l e **11-2** Methods for Handling the Price Objection

Method	Strategy
Breaking price down into smaller units	Salespeople take the price of the product and spread it out over its useful life—years, months, etc. When the product is compared to its competition, the same can be done with the difference in prices.
Stressing exclusive features or differences	Salespeople compensate for a higher price by indicating features and benefits absent in competing products.
Converting to a lower-priced item	Salespeople counter the price objection by showing prospects a lower-priced model. The trick is not to downgrade the lower-priced model in comparison with a higher-priced one.
Postponing	To avoid answering the objection early in the interview and losing the sale, salespeople postpone the price question until later.
Talking about ultimate costs	Salespeople should be careful to explain both initial and ultimate costs.
Quantifying differences	It is critical to quantify price difference explicitly as much as possible.
Showing return on investment	Show that the product more than returns its cost.
Firing the customer	Calls their bluff.

Such objections are particularly difficult to handle because they are neither a clear yes nor no. Prospects simply cannot make up their minds; they resist changing habits, they fear the product will not work, the supplier is not servicing it properly, or there is some other element of risk. Yet, if the salesperson leaves without an order—letting the prospect "think it over"—nothing may ever happen; worse, a competitor might walk off with the business after the sales representative has laid most of the groundwork.

There are several strategies for handling the procrastination objection. The first step in handling procrastination should be to clarify. Sales psychologists suggest that the harder you push, the more you may increase prospect resistance. Instead, ask such questions as:[16]

What are some of the issues you want to think over?

I see that this is a difficult decision for you. Would you be able to share some of the reasons for and against buying at this time?

May I ask what concerns you still have?

May I ask what's causing you to hesitate?

May I ask what questions I've left unanswered?

May I ask what your final decision will be based on?

If clarifying fails, it may call for facing up to the issue, regardless. If the product or service saves costs or increases profits, the salesperson can point out that the delay means lost money. An insulation salesperson might say, "If you wait another year, that means $X lost each month in needless heating expenses." A trade salesperson might respond, "As you wait, customers will go elsewhere, and that means lost profits to you." Inducements of various sorts can be effective—free trials, free installation, special discounts, free accessories, special financing, free deliveries, and so on. Sometimes the source of customer procrastination is having to make a choice among several models and wanting to make the right one. In this instance, the salesperson can make a suggestion, given the prospect's own unique situation and needs, and this might close the sale.

If the buying decision has both pros and cons and the latter involve some amount of risk, the sales representative might employ a **mini-max strategy.** The idea here is to minimize the potential impact of risks while maximizing the potential benefits to the prospect. A salesperson selling skis, for example, might explain to a procrastinating customer, "The worst that can happen is, in a few years, you'll want better skis when you really get into the sport. If so, our store is always ready to take a trade-in. In the meantime, you haven't spent that much, and you'll already have boots and poles if you decide to upgrade skis."

Another example of the mini-max strategy comes from real estate sales. An agent might say to prospects, "The worst that can happen is that you buy the property and then decide you don't want it. Due to rising land values, however, you can resell the property for a profit. In the meantime, you will have had the enjoyment of owning the home anyway."

When the prospect indicates a need to think it over, the salesperson may also respond, "I can understand why you want to think things over carefully. Let me briefly summarize some of the major points you'll want to consider." This serves two purposes. First, the prospect will have a clear idea of the major buying criteria before the salesperson departs. Second, the summarization may precipitate a decision to buy, when the prospect has a chance to review the entire matter. Once the list is completed, a variation on this technique is to ask the prospect, "Which objection is ac-

mini-max strategy
Way of handling the procrastination objection by which the salesperson maximizes the potential benefits and minimizes the downside risk.

tually the one that's keeping you from going ahead?" If the prospect has a number of objections, the presentation has not been completed, and the salesperson must begin anew.

Often, procrastination stems from simple inertia. All of us have a tendency to hesitate when making a purchase of consequence. If this is the case, the salesperson can ask: "Whenever I have someone postpone the decision, I get the feeling I haven't done a good job of explaining the product. Where did I slip up . . . what else do you need to know?" Most prospects are likely to react positively to such a diplomatically worded request. After all, the salesperson has placed the burden on himself or herself. "No I'm quite convinced that what you've shown me will do the job" would not be an unusual answer, in which case the salesperson should close the order right then and there.

If there is still resistance, the salesperson might add, "John, successful people usually make important decisions when all the facts are fresh in their minds. And even the most intelligent of them can't retain 100 percent of the information they hear for even a few hours. The law of diminishing returns sets in. By the following day, they might retain 75 percent of what they hear. And by the next day, they might retain only 50 percent, and so on. So, the very best time to make a decision is now. If you need more information, this is the best time to get it—while I'm still here to answer more of your questions."

If your prospect gives you no additional information, say something to the effect, "I don't want you to buy anything you don't need. By the same token, I don't want you to miss an opportunity to buy something that will benefit you. I understand why you want to think about it. When do you think you would be able to say yes or no on the proposal?" Let the prospect pick a date and tell him or her, "If you make up your mind before then, give me a call. I'm going to leave you alone to think about it between now and then. Would you mind if I gave you a call the day after that date if I haven't heard from you by then?"

11-5c Handling Skepticism

With these sorts of objections, prospects indicate their disbelief that a product can deliver a promised benefit. The basic strategy of the salesperson is to offer proof. Some sources of proof are technical brochures, warranties, data from research studies, demonstrations, articles from professional journals, testimonial letters, and third-party references:

> *I can understand your concern about programs living up to their promises. I've brought along the names and phone numbers of customers currently using our program. They've reported a real impact on the objective we just outlined. I encourage you to call them and get some insight from customers already experiencing significant change in sales and turnover.*

If possible, a trial period (at no or very low cost) is an excellent way of demonstrating proof. It may be enough to convince the skeptical prospect that his or her concerns are unfounded. At the very least, it shows that the salesperson and his or her company are willing to go the extra mile.

11-5d Handling Indifference

When prospects are indifferent to the salesperson's presentation, it is because they are satisfied with their current product or supplier or perceive no need for new product benefits. An excellent way of handling this situation is to ask directive questions that

is there any reason why you wouldn't make a decision today?" Because they know that if they don't remove the resort to higher authority up front, then there's a danger that under the pressure of asking for a decision, the other person will invent a higher authority as a delaying tactic. So before presenting your proposal to the buyer, casually say, "Let me be sure I understand. If this proposal meets all of your needs, is there any reason why you wouldn't give me a decision today?" It's harmless for the prospect to agree because they are thinking, "If it meets all of my needs? No problem, there's loads of room to negotiate here." Look at what you've accomplished now: You've eliminated their right to tell you that they want to think it over. If they say that, you say, "Well, let me go over it one more time. There must be something I didn't cover clearly enough because you did indicate to me earlier that you were willing to make a decision today." However, what if you're not able to eliminate their resort to higher authority? Try appealing to their self-image. With a smile on your face you say, "But they always follow your recommendations, don't they?" With some personality styles, a Driver, for example, that will be enough of an appeal that they'll say, "Well, I guess you're right. If I like it, then you can count on it." If this does not work, or you are dealing with another personality style, get their commitment that they'll take it to the committee with a positive recommendation. So you say, "But you will recommend it to them—won't you?" There are only two things that can happen at this point. Either they will say "Yes, they will recommend it to them," or they will say "no they won't." Either way you're successful. Hopefully, you'll get a response similar to, "Yes, it looks good to me. I'll go to bat for you with them." If that doesn't happen and instead they tell you that they won't recommend it, you have an opportunity to draw out the real objection and you're still ahead.[17]

If the salesperson is still faced with this objection, it is better by far to meet with the additional party to the buying decision. There is no guarantee that the original prospect will do a credible job of presenting the product to the next buying influence. The salesperson could ask something along the lines of, "Would you want me to go along to answer any of the technical questions that come up?" This question is effective because the salesperson indicates that he or she expects to accompany, not skirt, the prospect and will provide expert technical assistance, something the prospect might welcome when talking with a superior.

If the salesperson cannot accompany the original prospect, the strategy should be to equip him or her to do an effective job of selling to additional decision makers. The sales representative can provide an outline of product features and benefits, even a sample. One innovative salesperson was known to have tagged the sample, explaining important features. The sales representative might ask what benefits would interest the next decision maker and then summarize the associated product features to the original prospect. Another good idea is to get permission to mail literature to additional decision makers. This further ensures that these people will receive the proper information.

11-5f Handling the Overstocked Customer

Trade salespeople in particular meet this sort of objection from retailers. Quite often, the sales representative can check inventory and prove to buyers that they are not overstocked. Then the salesperson can follow up by asking, "Can you afford to lose business when customers come into the store and can't find our merchandise?" If inventory is truly heavy, then the salesperson can offer promotional assistance in the form of cooperative advertising assistance, in-store displays, couponing, and the like. Another good strategy is to find out if there are slow-moving competitors' products that are holding up orders. If so, the salesperson can demonstrate how moving them off the shelves and allowing additional space for the product can improve profits. If the prospect objects to stocking another size or model of the product, then the salesperson can respond, "Each size (line extension) has a distinct target market, a specific type of user, the same as other categories where you carry multiple sizes (and extensions)."

Chapter Summary

The sales representative must learn to accept objections as an expected and normal part of selling. It is when there are no objections that the salesperson should become concerned. Objections show that the prospect is interested.

Oftentimes, objections are raised by prospects just because they don't want to be "pushovers" or want to demonstrate their expertise. In these instances, the salesperson may simply ignore the objection after first acknowledging it. Many times prospects fail to express their underlying doubts accurately. Accordingly, sales representatives must first clarify objections before handling them. This may be accomplished with the echo technique, the "polite why" question, and the closed question to check understanding.

After the objection has been clarified and the salesperson is sure that it is as it appears, it can be handled with some special tactics. These include the head-on method, the indirect denial, the compensation method, the "feel, felt, found" technique, the boomerang method, and forestalling. When handling the price situation, the sales representative may break price down into small units, stress exclusive features or differences, use comparison, convert to a lower-priced item, postpone the objection, discuss both initial and ultimate costs, and quantify differences. The chapter ended with a discussion on how to handle the procrastinating buyer, the indifferent buyer, the skeptical buyer, the overstocked buyer, and the buyer who needs the approval of others.

Discussion Questions

1. "Objections are to be avoided by the sales representative." Discuss.

2. Explain how the salesperson may prepare to answer prospect objections.

3. When the prospect raises emotional objections, what can the sales representative do?

4. When is it proper to ignore an objection and how should the salesperson do it properly?

5. Why is clarifying the objection necessary?

6. What is the echo technique?

7. What is a "polite why" question?

8. Explain how a closed question may be used to clarify an objection.

9. When is the head-on method appropriate for handling objections? What are some ways of lessening the impact of this technique?

10. Explain the method of indirect denial. With which personality styles is it most appropriate?

11. Explain the compensation method of handling objections. Why is it effective?

12. What is the "feel, felt, found" method? When should it be used?

13. What is the boomerang method? Are there occasions when it is appropriate?

14. What is forestalling? Is it always a good idea?

15. How can the price objection be handled?

16. Outline some typical sources for developing exclusive features or differences.

17. What does it mean to "make price the good news"?

18. How does one use comparison to deflate the price issue?

19. How should the salesperson properly convert the prospect into buying a lower-priced model?

20. Why is postponing the objection sometimes necessary?

21. How can a salesperson deal with procrastination?

22. How does the salesperson handle objections arising from skepticism?

23. How can sales representatives handle prospects' objections arising from indifference toward their product? Toward their company as a supplier?

24. What techniques can the salesperson use to respond to overstocked customers?

25. The following are some common objections to the purchase of products. List your response to each of these objections:

Automobile: "I need to talk it over with my wife."

Software: "I don't need a spreadsheet software."

Life insurance: "I feel perfectly healthy."

Vacuum cleaner: "This model costs more than your competitor's."

Lawn mower: "This electric start option seems like an unneeded expense to me."

Personal computer: "I've heard you have some problems with your machines."

Copier: "Your machine doesn't have the ability to reduce copy."

Microwave oven: "I don't see the advantage of cooking faster."

Radio advertising: "I don't see any advantage over advertising in the newspaper."

Listing a home: "Why should I pay a real estate agent a commission, when I can sell it myself?"

Steel-belted radial tires: "These tires cost a lot."

Home insulation: "I hear your company doesn't stand behind its work."

Drugstore buyer: "I'm already overstocked with nonaspirin pain killers."

26. When responding to a price objection, how does the salesperson talk about ultimate costs?

27. How does the sales representative quantify price differences as much as possible?

28. At what price level should the salesperson begin?

Chapter Quiz

1. Objections are simply buyer concerns that some part of your product or service offering does not fully meet and resolve buyer problems. In a study by Learning International, when customer objections are present
   a. 75 percent of the time, the sale is put off until the next visit.
   b. customers tend to be quiet and uncommunicative.
   c. 64 percent of the time the outcome is successful, in contrast to 54 percent when objections are absent.
   d. 36 percent of the time the outcome is successful, in contrast to 64 percent when objections are absent.

2. In terms of handling objections, a basic task of sales representatives is to
   a. keep a log of all objections and prepare written material that can then be given to prospects each time an objection arises.
   b. prepare to answer objections before they arise.
   c. develop an in-depth knowledge of product features that will eliminate objections.
   d. handle all objections in a separate meeting so the current sales presentation will not be sidetracked.

3. When the customer makes an erroneous statement because of ignorance of the true facts, all of the following are acceptable strategies to handle this type of situation *except*
   a. firmly correct the customer so he or she will not go through the entire presentation with an erroneous idea.
   b. the salesperson can use the "yes, but" approach where the statement is acknowledged, but then ignored as the salesperson continues the presentation.
   c. the salesperson can ignore the erroneous statement and just continue with the presentation.
   d. the salesperson can respond the statement is "interesting" but then continue with the presentation.

4. The echo technique allows drawing out the prospect's opinions with a question. For example, if the prospect says, "I had your goods in my store once before, and they didn't sell," an echo response question would be:
   a. Why did you quit stocking the goods?
   b. I would appreciate hearing your opinion. Can you explain what happened?
   c. Didn't sell?
   d. How long ago was that?

5. After a salesperson is reasonably sure that the objection has been clarified, he or she is in a position to answer it. In using the _____ method, the salesperson would respond with a statement such as "I can understand how you might think that. Because prices vary so much because of trade and cash discounts, transportation charges, and promotional allowances, things get complicated. However, I can assure you that no customer in my territory with the same set of circumstances as your firm receives a better price."
   a. head-on
   c. boomerang
   b. indirect denial
   d. compensation

6. After a salesperson is reasonably sure that the objection has been clarified, he or she is in a position to answer it. In using the _____ method, the salesperson would respond with a statement such as "I can understand how you might feel that way. The fact is that many of our customers have felt the same way, but once they purchased the uniforms, they found that their laundering costs dropped dramatically and that the uniforms lasted longer, cutting the costs of frequent repurchasing. Their hospital boards were quite pleased, in fact."
   a. indirect
   c. boomerang
   b. forestalling
   d. "feel, felt, found"

7. In handling objections, the best time to use the boomerang method is
   a. when the objection can be turned into a positive factor.
   b. with objections arising from incorrect information.
   c. with valid objections but where compensating factors are present.
   d. with any type of objection.

8. "The Superior uniform is $25 higher than our competitor's garment, but because our uniform will last twice as long, this amounts to very little. When you consider that the Superior uniform will last a minimum of two years, this amounts to only $12.50 per year, or $1.46 per month for all of the added features of the Superior uniform." Which method of handling price objections is illustrated by this salesperson?
   a. comparison
   b. stressing exclusive features or differences
   c. breaking the price down into small increments
   d. converting to a lower-priced item

9. _____ objections are particularly difficult to handle because they are neither a clear yes nor no. Prospects simply cannot make up their minds; they resist changing habits, they fear the product will not work, the supplier is not servicing it properly, or there is some other element of risk.
   a. Indifference
   c. Skepticism
   b. Overstocked
   d. Procrastination

10. When prospects are indifferent to the salesperson's presentation, it is because they
   a. believe the price is too high and feel the salesperson will not negotiate price.
   b. are satisfied with their current product or supplier or perceive no need for the new product benefit.
   c. do not have the authority to make a decision.
   d. are skeptical of the product's benefits.

Profile

Role-Playing Exercise

For the products and services described at the end of Chapter 6 and the customers characterized at the end of Chapter 8, prepare responses to objections you are likely to encounter.

Take special care with price objections, procrastination, skepticism, and overstocking.

Web Exercise

Visit one of the following websites and find information about both higher- and lower-priced lines of products and services. What kinds of objection-handling techniques are being used even through the website to counter potential resistance? Prepare a chart showing the techniques in use and how they are applied.

www.lawnboy.com

www.mrcoffee.com

www.timewarnercable.com

www.toyota.com

www.apple.com/ipod

Notes

1. Bill Brooks, "Are Objections Really That Bad?" www.brooksgroup.com, 2004.
2. Paul S. Goldner, "Overcoming Price Objection," *Agency Sales,* 30, February 2000, pp. 61–63.
3. Gerhard Gschwandtner, "Lies and Deceptions in Selling," *Personal Selling Power,* 1995, pp. 62–66.
4. Timothy F. Bednarz, "Avoiding Very Common Stalls," *SalesVantage.com,* 2004.
5. Tom Hopkins, *Selling for Dummies,* 2nd Edition, Hoboken, NJ: Wiley Publishing, Inc., 2001.
6. Brian Jeffrey, "I Want to Think about It," *SalesVault.com,* February 11, 2004.
7. Neil Rackham, *SPIN Selling,* New York: McGraw Hill, 1988, p. 131.
8. Roy Chitwood, "Guide Your Client through Buying Decisions," *SalesVault.com,* June 18, 2004.
9. Dave Stein, "How to Outsell a Competitor Who Slashes Their Price to Win," *SalesVault.com,* May 31, 2004.
10. Jack Malcolm, "Moving Beyond Price," *SalesVantage.com,* 2004.
11. David Bank and Gary McWilliams, "Picking a Fight with Dell, H-P Cuts PC Profits Razor-Thin," *Wall Street Journal,* May 12, 2004, p. A1.
12. Sean D'Souza, "The Secret of Sequence in Selling," *MarketingProfs.com,* September 14, 2004.
13. Bill Brooks, "When Your Prospect Says Your Price Is Too High What Do You Say?" www.brooksgroup.com, 2004.
14. Ibid.
15. Steve Donovan, "Last Chance," *Personal Selling Power,* November/December, 1994, p. 78.
16. Gerhard Gschwandtner, "How to Handle Procrastinators," *Personal Selling Power,* May/June 1993, p. 43.
17. Roger Dawson, "How to Negotiate When the Other Person Tells You They Don't Have the Authority to Decide," *SalesVault.com,* December 16, 2003.

Case 11-1

Analyze how the following salesperson handles prospect objections to buying a new full-function financial calculator. Identify the techniques being used and explain what you might have done differently, including the use of alternative methods.

Prospect: Your price is too high.

Salesperson: Too high?

Prospect: Yes, your price is almost $75 higher than the competition's.

Salesperson: That's the very reason that you should buy our product. We have so much more quality in our product. Everyone knows you get what you pay for. And no one else has our exclusive time feature. All you have to do is push this one button, and you have the time and date.

Prospect: That's great, but I'm interested in a calculator for my secretary to work on payroll, taxes, and other business applications.

Salesperson: Then you're saying all you need is a basic calculator that handles just minimal functions?

Prospect: That's right and at the lowest possible price, which you don't have.

Salesperson: I understand what you're saying, but I think you would agree that quality is also an important consideration, and our calculators are guaranteed to last five years without service. That's two years more than competitive models. It breaks down to only $2 per month, or 50 cents a week.

Prospect: Well, you might be right there, but I need to think it over.

Salesperson: Ms. Prospect, how much do you pay your secretary?

Prospect: About $10 per hour.

Salesperson: Well, earlier we figured that with our calculator, you'll save two hours of work time and that adds up to $20 per day, $100 a week, and $400 per month. That represents money out of your pocket, a real loss, if you delay in making a decision.

Prospect: I guess maybe you're right, but I really don't trust your company.

Salesperson: You're wrong there, Ms. Prospect. Our company has the highest reputation in the business. No one has ever questioned our integrity!

Prospect: Well, I know Tom Henson down the street who bought a calculator from you and never did get it to work right, and your company didn't make any restitution whatsoever.

Salesperson: I find that hard to believe. Our company simply doesn't treat customers that way. You must have heard about this secondhand.

Prospect: Well, wherever I heard it, I'm not interested in doing business with your company at this time. Now I've got some work that needs to be done, so I would appreciate it if you could let me get to it.

Case 11-2

With the following dialogues, identify the objections-handling technique being used, tell what factors might have led to its use, and indicate whether you might have used a different technique.

Salesperson calling on an office manager, who is a prospect for CAD computer assisted design software:

Prospect: Well, I really need to talk it over with some other people.

Salesperson: Some other people?

Sales representative calling on a purchasing agent for a large chemical company:

Prospect: You know, I used to do business with your company, but they burned me on a couple of orders. I couldn't get delivery in time and ran a danger of having to shut down the line for a while. If it hadn't been for a local supplier, I'd have really been in trouble!

Salesperson: I can understand how you might feel that way. Any buyer would. Unfortunately, all companies occasionally have troubles with deliveries, and ours is no different. I think that if you talk with some of our current customers, however, you'll hear that they've found our service to be prompt, with a minimum of back orders.

Salesperson calling on a food broker:

Prospect: I hear you give better deals to some brokers than others.

Salesperson: That's totally untrue. Our company is known throughout the food industry for its integrity. We offer identical prices to all of our customers.

Real estate agent to a home buyer:

Prospect: It seems to me that this house has a smaller dining room and yet has a higher price.

Salesperson: Yes, that's true, but you're in a nicer neighborhood here. Your kids will be in a good school district and you won't have to worry about who they're playing with.

Insurance agent to a prospect:

Prospect: We can't afford this policy.

Salesperson: That's the very reason you should buy this policy! You say you can't afford it. Let me ask what would happen to your family if something happened to you?

Hardware salesperson to a prospect for a lawn mower:

Prospect: I don't know if those extra features are worth $40.

Salesperson: Look at it this way. The mower is guaranteed for two years, and it should last you at least five years without trouble. That works out to $8 per year for the mulcher and self-starter options. Now just think how much raking time the mulcher will save you and how much easier it'll be to start the mower without pulling that cord every time.

Salesperson to a car buyer:

Salesperson: Yes, the price of the new Focus seems high, especially if you haven't bought a new car for awhile. But think of what you'll be giving up if you don't buy: improved gas mileage, up to 40 mpg on the highway; the traction of front-wheel drive for our Iowa winters; and freedom from those repair bills you've been paying on your old car.

Salesperson to a prospect for a washer and dryer:

Salesperson: Well, Ms. Jones, I would quote you a price right now, but by the time I explained all the different features and options you can get, I might be quite a bit off from my original quotation. So, if you don't mind, I'd prefer to wait until I know more about your needs and can indicate the features I believe you'll want to consider, before I give you a price.

Sales Negotiation: Building Win–Win Relationships

Key Terms

auctioning
BATNA
bring them to their senses
budget bogey
deadline
don't reject, reframe
escalation
go to the balcony
good-guy/bad-guy

have them take ownership
I-message
I need to get this approved tactic
information claim
interest
option
position
principled negotiation

rock-bottom price
stepping to their side
sticks and stones
take it or leave it
threat
veiled threat
warning

Learning Objectives

After studying Chapter 12, you will understand:

- That negotiating for the long term requires an agreement that is satisfactory to both parties
- The axioms of "principled negotiation"
- Tactics

- How to negotiate if prospects play by different rules
- How to turn an opponent to principled negotiation
- How to counter win–lose tactics

Until this point, we have assumed that selling transpires in an atmosphere of routine exchange—that is, there exist established prices and distribution procedures from which there is no deviation. In a negotiated exchange, price and other terms—including time of contract completion, quality of goods or services, volume of goods sold, financing risk taking, promotion, and safety standards—are set by bargaining. At least two parties are typically involved, and there is conflict on one or more issues. Negotiation usually involves the presentation of demands or proposals by one party and the evaluation of these by the other, followed by concessions and counterproposals. The activity of negotiations is thus sequential rather than simultaneous.[1] Usually, negotiation, rather than a routine exchange, occurs when many factors bear not only on price but also on quality and service; when a long period of time is required to produce items purchased; and when production is interrupted frequently because of numerous change orders.[2]

Traditionally, negotiation is viewed as the art of getting what you want without regard to the cost to the other side. The success of an agreement is often measured in terms of gains made by your side and concessions forced on the other. Unfortunately, these "win–lose" agreements have a tendency to ultimately become "lose–lose" agreements. In contrast to a prevailing attitude that negotiation resembles war and one side must win at the expense of the other, this text takes the view that negotiation should be such as to ensure a long-term relationship between buyer and seller. In a "win–lose" situation, which is usually the way negotiation is viewed, long-running relationships are unlikely. As one purchasing agent put it, "Unless our suppliers also think they have a reasonable deal, we may come up short. The other side could lose interest in our order. They could fail to ship parts on time, thus causing assembly lines to shut down." You don't get high performance from people who feel beaten or abused. If you need a low price for something, ask for the other side's help in lowering costs or see what you can do for them in return. What would it cost to try to enforce the agreement or to replace it? Courts may refuse to enforce an agreement found to be "unconscionable." To prosper in the long run, salespeople should look for relationship management, not just immediate gains. As one put it metaphorically, "Instead of dividing up the apples, we both shake the tree to get more apples." Positional bargaining is a negotiation strategy that involves holding onto a fixed idea, or position, of what you want and arguing for it and it alone, regardless of any underlying interests. The prevailing view is that there can only be one winner and one loser in negotiations.

The classic example of positional bargaining is the haggling that takes place between proprietor and customer over the price of an item. The customer has a maximum amount she will pay and the proprietor will only sell something over a certain minimum amount. Each side starts with an extreme position and proceeds from there to negotiate and make concessions. Eventually, a compromise may be reached. For example, a man offers a vendor at the flea market $10 for a rug he has for sale. The vendor asks for $30, so the customer offers $15. The merchant then says he will accept $25, but the customer says the highest he will go is $20. The vendor agrees that $20 is acceptable and the sale is made at $20. The customer pays $10 more than he originally wanted and the vendor receives $10 less. Positional bargaining tends to be the first strategy people adopt when entering a negotiation. This is often problematic, because as the negotiation advances, the negotiators become more and more committed to their positions, continually restating and defending them. A strong commitment to defending a position usually leads to a lack of attention to both parties' underlying interests. Therefore, any agreement that is reached will "probably reflect a mechanical splitting of the difference between final positions rather than a solution carefully crafted to meet the legitimate interests of the parties."[3]

12-1 Principled Negotiation

Interactive selling accepts the views of **principled negotiation,** as outlined by Fisher and Ury.[4] They view the typical conceptualization of negotiation with one side winning at the expense of the other as unacceptable: It lengthens negotiations, and ongoing business relationships are unlikely. When parties engage in positional bargaining, invariably positions harden. The more committed one party becomes to a position and tries to get the other side to accept it, the more committed to that position they become. Much the same occurs with the other party to the negotiation. With so much invested in saving face, any agreement, if concluded at all, may reflect a mechanical splitting of the difference of the final positions, rather than a solution carefully fashioned to meet the interests of both parties. When such a mechanical agreement is finally concluded, it is only after a lengthy investment of time. Moreover, both parties are likely to be alienated from one another; further dealings, if they occur at all, are likely to be equally as fractious, and any long-term relationship where both parties come out ahead—expanding their total profits or lowering their total costs—are unlikely.

Bargaining over positions stimulates impediments to settlements. The parties start with extreme positions and make only enough small concessions to keep negotiations going, while strongly holding onto their initial positions as long as possible. In contrast, principled negotiation, according to Fisher and Ury, demands (1) separating the people from the problem, (2) focusing on interests, not positions, (3) inventing options for mutual gain, and (4) insisting that the result be based on some objective standard.[5] The differences between positional and principled negotiating are shown in Figure 12-1.

12-1a Separate People and Problems

No one is free of emotion. We all have egos, and it is easy for them to become a stake in the negotiation. Egos and emotions easily become entangled with the objective criteria of the negotiation process. Taking positions makes things worse because egos easily become identified with positions, further lessening the chances of a friendly settlement. In principled negotiation, the parties must see themselves as attacking a problem for mutual benefit instead of each other.

principled negotiation
In contrast to maintaining positions, the parties separate people from problems, focus on interests not positions, invent options for mutual gain, and measure the agreement with objective standards.

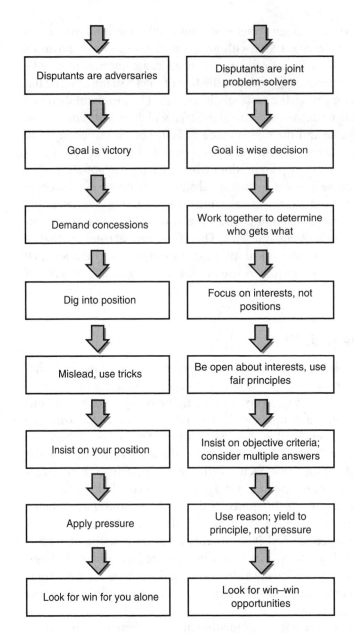

Figure 12-1
Differences between
Positional and Principled
Negotiating

Source: Spangler, Brad "Integrative
or Interest-Based Bargaining" in
Beyond Intractability: The
Intractable Conflict Knowledge
Base, Heidi Burgess and Guy Burgess,
editors. Available online at http://
www.beyondintractability.org/m/
interest-based_bargaining.jsp.
Reprinted by permission of Heidi
and Guy Burgess and the Conflict
Research Consoritium."

People problems often require more attention than substantive ones. The human
tendency for defensive and reactive behavior is a major reason (perhaps *the* major reason) why so many negotiations fail when they make the best sense for both parties.
The more seriously you disagree with someone, the more important it is that you deal
well with that disagreement. A good working relationship is one that can deal with
such major disagreements. We need not like each other (although it certainly helps),
but as long as we find ourselves negotiating, we would like to use a process that enables
us to handle our differences agreeably, making it easier to negotiate the next time.[6]

The most common negotiation error is to lump together the people and the
problem. We all tend to confuse matters of relationship (i.e., how we deal with disagreement, hurt feelings, or anger) with those of substance (i.e., numbers, dates,
terms, and conditions). Failure to separate the two—substance and relationship—
may lead us to fix relationship problems by making uncalled-for substantive concessions. Experience suggests that appeasement does not often work. You might

think that doing so implies that it is their turn to concede next time; they might instead believe that if they are stubborn enough, you will give in again.[7]

You cannot cure hurt feelings with substantive concessions, any more than you can make up for a significant loss of money with a simple apology. Moreover, you should not try; it is likely to make matters even worse. If you allow the relationship to be held hostage by substantive matters (and concessions), you are in trouble. Rather, substantive issues need to be separated from relationship and process issues. The content of a possible agreement needs to be separated from questions of how you talk about it and how you deal with the other side. Each set of issues needs to be negotiated on its own merits. The following lists enumerate the distinction:[8]

Substantive Issues
- Terms
- Conditions
- Prices
- Dates
- Numbers
- Liabilities

Relationship Issues
- Balance of emotion and reason
- Ease of communication
- Degree of trust and reliability
- Attitude of acceptance (or rejection)
- Emphasis on persuasion or force
- Degree of mutual understanding

Of course, it helps to adjust your style to the personality style of your counterpart. Is your counterpart a Driver, Analytical, Amiable, or Expressive?[9]

Amiables want you to like them. They concentrate directly on you during the negotiation. Their major concern is stability—the stability of personal associations. Atmosphere and style will be most important in relating with this person. They hate to feel used or slighted. If you don't say hello, if you cut them off, if you become pushy, you will lose in negotiations with Amiables. To interact effectively with Amiables, be open, honest, and start with small talk. Get to know them as people. Don't rush to the substance of the negotiation. Amiables often don't reveal what they are really thinking. Because they don't like conflict, they hide strong disagreements or key points. They will often end the conversation with a "We'll get back to you," and you will never hear from them again. They will harbor a grudge if they feel you have belittled them or treated them discourteously.

Drivers are direct, to the point, goal-oriented, and in a hurry. They enjoy the "game" of negotiating because it excites their intellect. You do not need to yield to succeed with Drivers. They are typically not out to humble you, but they want a good deal. They will not take the first deal offered. If you offer them your best deal and refuse to budge, you disappoint them, because you don't let them use their skill. So offer a good deal, but be prepared to make small concessions.

Expressives desire fun, excitement, and applause. They like to win arguments. They like the big picture, and they are usually not good at details. They will be congenial and friendly and might well spend most of the negotiation in small talk. They will negotiate by instinct, and their positions will be based largely on how they feel about you. If you force them to focus on too many details, they will shut down. To interact effectively with Expressives, show them how this negotiation will benefit them and their company. This appeals to their need for recognition. Expressives like to close the deal on the spot. Because they are not usually good at details, they are not your best contact people once the negotiation is done. Be sure to get everything in writing immediately, as Expressives often change their mind and/or forget what they just agreed to.

Analyticals desire accuracy and want the details first; then, they want the big picture. Their greatest concern is accuracy, and they want to make sure they have all the facts before they make a decision. Broad, sweeping statements annoy them. Give them the facts—and make sure they add up. Whatever you hand them will be read closely, either immediately or after you leave. Analyticals do not like to finalize a negotiation on the spot. They like to mull the decision over and give you an answer by email, letter, or phone. If you try to intimidate an Analytical during negotiations, you will lose. Remember, accuracy is vitally important to this person. Analyticals will often focus on what could go wrong, even if it's unlikely. They may seem to make a mountain out of a molehill. Actually, they are just trying to be accurate. Appreciate that desire for accuracy; show why the risk is worthwhile, or demonstrate why it's worth taking.

If, in spite of your best efforts, relationship problems interfere with substantive negotiations, negotiate the relationship also. Raise your concerns about the other side's behavior and discuss it with them as with any substantive matter. Avoid making harsh judgments and attacking their motives. Instead, describe your perceptions and feelings and ask them about theirs. Propose external standards or fair principles to guide dealing with one another and resist giving in to pressure tactics.

Of particular assistance in separating people from the problem is creative use of the **"I-message,"** which softens the blow while making your point known and leaves the field free to solve the problem. Here are a few examples:

> *I would appreciate it if . . .*
>
> *I'd like to . . .*
>
> *It would be helpful to me . . .*
>
> *I would certainly appreciate . . .*
>
> *When I'm interrupted, I don't get to finish what I am saying and I feel that what I have to say is considered unimportant.*
>
> *I would appreciate receiving the agenda for the meeting in advance, so I can bring the necessary information.*

I-messages can elicit help from those with whom one is negotiating rather than make them take a defensive posture. No one need feel angry or bad, and most people are more than happy to help someone else if they have nothing to lose in the process and everything to gain. I-messages help negotiating parties deal with the issues and leave personalities aside.[10] Box 12-1 shows a questionnaire that you can use to determine your conflict style.

12-1b Focus on Interests

The second criterion for principled negotiation is to focus on interests, not positions. A **position** is a stance; an **interest** is what occasioned the position. For example, a bargaining position may be that a contract must include a stiff penalty for late shipment; the interest behind the position is desiring to maintain an unbroken flow of raw materials. So many negotiations fail because the salesperson doesn't ask,

I-message
A nonthreatening request that can elicit help from negotiating partners rather than making them take a defensive posture (e.g., "I would appreciate it if . . .").

position
In negotiations, a stance.

interest
In negotiations, what occasioned a position.

Box 12-1

How Do You Deal with Conflict?

All of us deal with conflict in different ways. Some of us try to avoid or minimize conflict at all costs; others may thrive on conflict and may be very difficult people with whom to negotiate. A third group may see conflict as a necessary evil and try to make the best of such situations. The following questionnaire is designed to determine your conflict style. Simply place a "T" next to the items with which you agree and an "F" next to those with which you disagree.

Conflict Style Scale

1. When there is a conflict among groups, I like to be right in the middle of it.

2. I find conflicts among people or groups very uncomfortable.

3. When I'm involved in a conflict, I don't let it linger but get to work to try to resolve it.

4. Sometimes I try to produce a conflict in a group on purpose just for the excitement of it.

5. I enjoy helping people or groups resolve their conflicts.

6. Whenever I have a conflict with someone, I tend to withdraw into my own shell and ignore that person.

7. I usually try to get my own way in most situations.

8. I hold grudges for long periods of time.

9. I avoid criticizing people for their mistakes and try to help them avoid mistakes in the future.

10. I tend to let others have their way just to minimize conflicts.

11. I often find myself involved in resolving conflicts between friends.

12. I tend to keep my feelings to myself if I think they might produce some conflict.

If you have marked "true" for items 2, 6, 10, and 12, you have an *avoidant style* of dealing with conflict—you try to avoid it if at all possible. If you answered "true" for items 1, 4, 7, and 8, you are a *conflict seeker*. You tend to enjoy conflicts and may even try to generate them. If you answered "true" for items 3, 5, 9, and 11, you take a *problem-solving* approach to conflict. You try to find ways to help people and groups deal with conflicts.

Source: Robert A. Baron and Paul B. Paulus, *Understanding Human Relations,* Boston: Allyn and Bacon, 1991, pp. 326–527.

"Why?" For example, your buyer might demand: "I want reports weekly." You should ask, "Why is that important to you?" The interest might be, "I'm afraid I'll lose control of my ad effectiveness."[11] The basic needs of life are the most important. These include security, economic well-being, a sense of belonging, recognition, and control over one's life. Although these needs seem obvious, they are often easy to overlook. Often we believe that the only thing that matters in negotiation is money. Yet even when the matter being discussed does involve money, often there is a more fundamental need behind it. When a homeowner wants to set the price of his home too high, it could be because he wants recognition for the superiority of his house over others, or because he wants to retain control over his life.[12]

According to Fisher and Ury, the parties to a negotiation should concentrate on their interests rather than on positional bargaining. They illustrate this with a story of two children arguing over an orange. One wants the peel to bake a cake; the other wants the orange to make orange juice. Each insists on a fixed position: "Hey, I get the orange!" Eventually, following much acrimony, they split the difference, dividing the orange in half. Unfortunately, with their differing interests they could have both come out ahead if one had gotten the peel and the other gotten the fruit.

Here's a *bad* way to phrase positions for buying a car. "My interest as a buyer: getting the cheapest deal. "The salesperson's position:" selling a car for as much as possible to get the highest commission." This positioning is bad for two reasons. First, the buyer's basic interest is not simply having a cheap car. Even at the most superficial level, the buyer wants a reliable car, not simply a cheap one. Second, both the salesperson and buyer share an interest in being able to look each other in the eye afterwards. Certainly the buyer wants to be able to take the car back to the dealership if necessary and get it serviced readily, and the salesperson would like the buyer to come back for service or for other, future car purchases and provide word-of-mouth references.[13]

Reconciling interests rather than positions works better because for every interest, there usually exist several possible positions that could satisfy the interest. A good start to reconciling different interests is to look for items that are of low cost to you and high benefit to them, and vice versa. Each side should try to make proposals that are appealing to the other side and that the other side would find easy to agree to. If buyer and seller, for example, talk only about their positions on the charges for transporting goods, they are unlikely to consider a number of other options, such as varying schedule; finding possible loads of their own or even others to ship back in order to save making an empty trip home; or sharing maintenance responsibilities. Also, opposing positions may hide shared and compatible interests (for example, a salesperson wants the predictability of a steady flow of orders, while the customer wants the security of an unbroken flow of raw materials). Reconciling interests rather than compromising positions also works because behind conflicting positions lie many more shared and compatible interests than differing ones.

We tend to assume that because the other side's positions are opposed to ours, so too must be their interests. If we have an interest in defending ourselves, then they must want to attack us. If we have an interest in maximizing price, then their interest must be to minimize it. In many negotiations, however, close examination of the underlying interests often reveals the existence of many more interests that are shared or compatible than ones that are opposed.

Let us stick with the example of pricing. There are usually many more criteria of importance than price in the negotiation between buyer and seller. The seller is interested in a fair price but not one so high as to motivate the buyer to look to competitors. The seller may be willing to take a lower price in return for continual blanket purchase orders in which the buyer contracts with the supplier to accept delivery of a specified quantity at a specified price over a specified period of time. The buyer may find a blanket purchase order acceptable because it minimizes paperwork and the administrative overhead (e.g., numerous purchasing agents) involved in dealing with a number of suppliers, each with individual purchase requirements, quantity discounts, and delivery schedules. The seller here may be willing to accept a lower price in order to be able to schedule long cost-minimizing production runs, or the seller might accept a lower price in return for an annual purchase agreement that calls for providing parts at a specified discount schedule over the contract period. The seller is protected from the inroads of competitors; the buyer can gain additional price discounts by buying more over the period of the contract. The buyer may be willing to accept a higher price in return for better shipping terms (e.g., F.O.B. destination instead of F.O.B. factory) or better promotional terms, such as sharing half of the costs of advertising with the seller. To ensure a steady, uninterrupted supply of materials, the buyer may be willing to pay a premium; the seller may agree to pay a penalty if he or she fails in this effort, just so he or she can get the business in the first place and hold onto it. The same may be true of quality: The buyer will pay more for guaranteed quality; the seller may agree to penalties for failing to meet quality standards to win the sale and begin a continuing relationship. In return for a higher trade-in allowance, the buyer may be willing to pay a higher price. Much the same may be true of financing terms. For a larger cash discount, the buyer may be willing to pay a higher price. For a greater trade discount, a wholesaler may agree to inventory the goods of a manufacturer. For a larger-sized order, the seller may discount the price; the seller might ask the buyer to omit a specification that adds to the cost but not the quality of the item in return for a lower price; the seller can request the buyer add items to the purchase (e.g., "If you agree to take the service contract for two years, I can reduce the price 3 percent"); extend the contract (e.g., "If we can have your floor maintenance contract for two years, I can give you an extra month of service free"); consider lower-cost packaging that can lead to a lower price offering; and have the buyer absorb some costs (e.g., "If you paint the door after installation, I can reduce the price by $100"). The possibilities of negotiation are virtually endless.

Agreement is often made possible precisely because interests differ. Without differing forecasts for the value of a stock, there would be no stock market; no one would be willing to buy a share for more than the seller thought it was worth. Without differing team loyalties, sporting events would be a bore. In a negotiation, anything that you value highly and the other party does not represents an opportunity for trade-off. Consider the following common sources of difference:[14]

Risk. Some people hate it; others love it. Often, large institutions are better prepared to handle risk than smaller organizations or individuals. Look for differences in risk aversion between negotiators; these represent foundations for a final agreement.

Timing. Look for the possibility that what is impossible this month is easy next month, or what is unaffordable in next year's budget can be freed from discretionary funds this year.

Perceptions. To some, the opinion of others is critical; to others, it might matter little, if at all. Look for ways the former can have a public victory if needed, while the other satisfies interests of greater personal value.

Marginal value. When people have several of something, the value of the last one is worth less than the preceding ones. This is the old economic law of *diminishing marginal utility.* To illustrate this principle, if I already have three bananas, I probably value a fourth one less than an orange, of which I now have one. You, on the other hand, might have five oranges and no bananas, and we could both be better off with a trade. Differences in the marginal value to each party of negotiated goods, services, and terms create opportunities to draft the final agreement.

How does a salesperson identify interests? One way is to exercise empathy. The salesperson puts himself or herself in the customer's position and asks why he or she is taking a certain position. Coming right out and asking a customer's interests is perfectly legitimate: "What is your basic concern in not wanting to sign an agreement on prices for more than one year at a time?" Ask other similar questions, such as, "For what purpose?" "What would be wrong with that?" or "Please help me understand your major concerns." Another useful idea is to ask what interests of theirs stand in the way of what the salesperson is asking. If the salesperson wants the other side to appreciate his or her interests, they should tell them what those interests are. The salesperson should demonstrate that he or she understands what their counterparts' interests are: "As I understand it, your interests are. . . ."

T a b l e **12-1** Customer's Currently Perceived Choice

Question: Shall I make Solutions, Inc., our exclusive supplier for computers?

Consequences If I Do	*Consequences If I Don't*
Con: I won't have the option of calling on several companies for service.	*Pro:* I can call on two or three suppliers to support my machines.
Con: Solutions may increase the price on me after it gets the exclusive.	*Pro:* I can keep competitive pressure on prices.
Con: Solutions might go bankrupt; all my eggs are in one basket.	*Pro:* I diversify my risk by spreading my purchases among several suppliers.
Con: If something goes wrong with our deal, my boss will blame me.	*Pro:* I can always defend myself by saying I diversified the risk.
Con: I might not be able to get as large a discount.	*Pro:* Solutions might give me a volume discount.
	Pro: I keep my options open.

Suppose you are an important customer of mine, and I want to convince you to make my company, Solutions, Inc., your exclusive supplier of computers. To understand your position better, I work out a chart such as the one shown in Table 12-1. If it represents a good approximation of your thinking, then I will be able to better understand your reasoning.[15]

Having produced this chart, I will understand that to improve my chances of being selected as your sole supplier, I must change the way you see your choice. Perhaps I can offer to contract service to a larger company, guarantee prices below a certain benchmark, diversify risk by subcontracting with other companies, or improve your position in your company by helping you prepare a presentation demonstrating how much money this contract would save. Upon reflection, I might conclude that I should change my goal and only seek to be your lead supplier.

An example of a creative way to use interests in negotiation is offered by Benjamin Franklin, a renowned negotiator. Franklin always spoke about his proposal in terms of what it offered for his opposite across the negotiating table. Obviously, his basic interests were for his own benefit, but by arguing in terms of his opposite's interests, agreement was much more likely. When he negotiated for French participation in the American War for Independence in terms of French gains from a British defeat and not what the colonists themselves stood to gain, Franklin demonstrated creative negotiating skills.

option
In negotiations, possible agreements or pieces of a possible agreement.

12-1c Invent Options for Mutual Gain

The third precept for principled negotiation is to invent options for mutual gain. By **option,** we mean possible agreements or pieces of a possible agreement. Good agreements focus on the parties' interests, rather than their positions. As Fisher and Ury explain, "Your position is something you have decided upon. Your interests are what caused you to so decide."[16] Defining a problem in terms of positions means that at least one party will "lose" the dispute. When a problem is defined in terms of the parties' underlying interests, it is often possible to find a solution that satisfies both parties' interests.

For example, the buyer's interests may be revenue, quality, and reliability. Possible options could be paying a premium price for premium quality, paying a bonus for on-time delivery, or granting an exclusive contract (i.e., establishing a relationship or partnering). Negotiators often quarrel over interests that are important to both. This reflects the common belief that if we both value something, guide the prospect into realizing the value of promised benefits. For instance, a sales representative selling security systems using TV monitors might proceed as follows:

Prospect: We've already got a security system composed of guards who walk through our plant day and night.

Salesperson: How many guards do you use on each shift?

Prospect: As large as our plant and warehouse are, we need five or six.

Salesperson: How much could you save by having just one guard per shift watching TV monitors that cover your entire operation?

Salespeople have had success with a low-pressure approach that even places the prospect on the salesperson's side in proving that the product or service might be useful. "Ms. Prospect, I honestly don't know if this product could help your current procedure or not, but you would want to be sure, either way, wouldn't you? Could we make a quick survey to find out?" Curiosity tends to win out for the salesperson who presents the survey opportunity.

If prospects indicate satisfaction with their current supplier, there are several strategies salespeople might employ:

1. The salesperson can ask an open question, such as, "Could you outline the reasons why you are satisfied with XYZ Company?" The idea is to get prospects talking and perhaps to reveal some sources of dissatisfaction. Upon reflection, they might discover that they are not all that satisfied.

2. The salesperson can point out to prospects the dangers of "putting all their eggs in one basket." "With just one supplier, possible dangers include shortages, strikes, delivery problems, and the like. Just as an insurance policy, I'd like to show you how our products compare with what you're using now."

3. The salesperson can discuss the healthful effects of competition. A sole supplier can get overconfident and not deliver the best services, but with competition, the incentive to deliver is greater.

4. The salesperson can cite examples of other customers who changed over to them because of superior quality, delivery, warranty, service, facilities, and the like. "Several of my customers used to buy from them. If you will allow me to do an item-by-item comparison, I'll show you why they decided to switch to us."

5. The salesperson can seek to make inroads with small orders of goods not handled by the competition. With this foot-in-the-door strategy, the salesperson seeks gradual expansion with increasing customer satisfaction.

11-5e Handling Buyers Who Need Others' Approval

One of the most vexing problems for salespeople is dealing with multiple buying influences. One way of handling the problem is to get to the primary decision maker as soon as possible. On the initial call the sales representative should first ask, "Does your company buy this product?" and then, "Is it bought through this office?" These questions can save a considerable amount of frustration later.

When the prospective buyer remarks, "I need to talk it over with Mr./Ms. . . ," the salesperson is in a real quandary as to what action to take. The first attempt should be to eliminate the prospect's resort to higher authority before the negotiations even start. Get them to admit that they could make an immediate decision if the proposal was attractive. Real estate agents say to buyers before showing a house, "Let me be sure I understand, if we find exactly the right property for you, the only thing left to do is to divide it between us, in an adversarial, zero-sum manner: More for me means less for you. Participants can avoid falling into a win–lose mentality by focusing on shared interests. When the parties' interests differ, they should seek options in which those differences can be made compatible or even complementary. The key to reconciling different interests is to "look for items that are of low cost to you and high benefit to them, and vice versa."[17] Instead, the parties to the negotiation should look for ways to increase the size of the total pie rather than split it. The key idea is to suspend criticism and decision making from inventing. It is important to look for ways of leaving the other side satisfied as well. If a customer feels cheated in a purchase, the store owner has also failed; he or she may lose a customer, and reputation may suffer. Look for dovetailing differing interests. A satisfactory agreement often depends on each side wanting differing things. What makes for a stock trade is when one buyer believes the market for a particular stock will rise, while another believes exactly the opposite. Find out how customers feel by creative trial ballooning. Offer them several options.

Think beyond just price; this is bound to be an area of controversy. Focus on variables where the customer's interests and your own have more in common: a longer contract, a bigger order, more add-on items, an introduction to another key decision maker in the company, access to their mailing list or client database, or payment terms.[18] You can negotiate for products and services that the other person or company offers, such as consulting, office equipment, computers, furniture, or business services. Instead of the manufacturer taking the stance that the retailer must have ads of a certain height and width displaying the manufacturer's product to receive a cooperative advertising allowance of $.25 per case, the retailer insisting on $.50, and both parties settling grudgingly on $.375 after acrimonious debate, they might agree that their mutual interest is to maximize the overall impact of all promotional dollars, optimizing profit for both. This opens up other alternatives. The manufacturer might be willing to bargain the size of the ad in return for more prominent shelf position. The retailer might be willing to increase the size of the advertised product in return for coupons sent directly through the mail by the manufacturer. If the product is a food item, both would stand to profit by free samples being prepared and handed out by a manufacturer's representative. The retailer might agree to a more prominent advertising position for the product in return for a truckload sale by the manufacturer, whose lower prices typically bring increased overall traffic into the store. If both will only put aside niggling over an imagined fixed pie and begin inventing options to increase the size of the overall pie, they both might come out ahead. A negotiation often appears to be a "fixed-sum" game; $100 more for you on the price of car, for example, means $100 less for me. In this way of thinking, I can only satisfy you at my expense, but creative brainstorming might create a larger pie from which both of us may come out ahead.

Here are a few ways you can effectively state these requests.

If I could do that price for you, would you be willing to extend the length of the contract for an additional three months?

If I could work that out, would you be prepared to give me advertising space?

The only way I could give you that is if you add one more line of products.

Let's put that aside for the time being. Would you be able to give a similar amount of . . . in exchange for that concession?

Another effective approach is to make the concession but take something away from the initial offer. For example, you could say, "I can do that. However, I will have to charge you for . . ." or "I can do that. Do you want free delivery or after-hours service taken out of the contract?"

Most people will expect you to keep all the conditions "as is," but they will want the lower price. By demonstrating how much the concession is worth, you can reduce the effectiveness of their request.

Fisher and Ury also suggest techniques for overcoming these obstacles and generating creative options. Initially, it is important to separate the invention process from the evaluation stage. The parties should come together in an informal atmosphere and brainstorm for all possible solutions to the problem. Wild and creative proposals are encouraged. Consider the seller who demanded all cash for the sale of her office building. She explained that the cash would be used to send her sons to college, and that if she didn't have the cash, she wouldn't be able to send them at all. Because both sides generated a number of options, the owner learned how the down payment could be invested in zero coupon bonds to provide for the first year of school and to amend the annual payments on the owner-carried financing to better conform to the cash flow needs of the student. The sale of this office building might never have been closed if the parties had not sought to solve each others' problem.[19]

Brainstorming sessions can be made more creative and productive by encouraging the parties to shift between four types of thinking: stating the problem, analyzing the problem, considering general approaches, and considering specific actions. Parties may suggest partial solutions to the problem. Only after a variety of proposals have been made should the group turn to evaluating the ideas. Evaluation should start with the most promising proposals. The parties may also refine and improve proposals at this point.

12-1d Negotiate Objective Criteria

After separating people from problems, focusing on interests, and inventing options for mutual gains, the fourth point of principled negotiation is insisting on negotiation of objective criteria. That is, instead of arguing over position, a good strategy is to insist that the agreement reflect some fair, objective standard independent of the position of either side. This will help reach solutions on principle, not pressure. By discussing objective criteria instead of stubbornly held positions, neither party is giving in to the other; both are yielding to a fair solution. Such objective criteria for a negotiated price might be market value, replacement cost, depreciated book value, competitive price, or wholesale price index. Whatever they are, these objective standards should be independent of the will of either side. In reaching an agreement on the price of a house, for example, the two sides should jointly search for objective criteria, such as the cost of the house adjusted for depreciation and inflation, recent selling prices of similar houses in the neighborhood, and independent appraisal. The trick here is to never submit to pressure, only to principle. Ask the other side to explain their reasoning on why the standard they support is fair.

Take a moment to ask yourself if you would assist a buyer who says, "I'm looking for a good, secure investment with lots of potential." You probably wouldn't, even if he were an astute and experienced investor with more than $100,000 in ready cash. You wouldn't assist him because the specifications he listed are not specific. The words he used—*good, secure, potential*—are all fluff words and are not measurable criteria. Insist on developing specific criteria.[20] If you have buyers who say they want to see only 2-storey homes, they may really be looking for a 4-bedroom home, privacy, or an image of success.

Occasionally, however, it is difficult to identify objective standards to help reach an agreement. Often, even with objective criteria to define the boundaries of an agreement, a way is still needed to progress toward a final agreement on specifics. In such situations, it pays to invest time in considering "fair" procedures for closure.

Think of ways of deciding (as opposed to actual decisions) that appeal to both sides because of their fairness (i.e., furnish neither side with an unfair advantage). Those childhood stratagems—"I cut, you choose," or "flipping a coin"—have their analogues in business. Agreeing to go to a trusted impartial third party, for example, may resolve late stalemates.

12-2 What If the Clients Are More Powerful?

Of what use is talking about interests, options, and objectives if the other side is more powerful? No method can guarantee success if all the leverage lies with the other side. If a salesperson represents a small company, how can he or she expect to withstand the demands of a General Motors or IBM buyer? If there are several alternatives to the salesperson's product or the warehouse is piled high with inventory, how can he or she negotiate forcefully? In any negotiation there exist realities that are hard to change. In response to power, the most any method of negotiation can accomplish is to meet two objectives: (1) to protect the salesperson from making an agreement he or she should reject and (2) to help the salesperson make the most of their assets so that any agreement reached will satisfy his or her interests as well as possible.

When trying to catch a flight on time, one's goal may seem paramount, but looking back on it, one realizes the next flight could have served just as well without major schedule disruptions. Negotiation will often present a similar situation. A salesperson begins to worry if he or she has not reached agreement in an important business deal in which much time and effort have been invested. In these circumstances, the salesperson stands in real danger of being too accommodating to the views of the other side and may end up with a deal that he or she should have rejected.

The theory behind negotiating is to produce better results than what would have been obtained without negotiating. What are those results? What is that alternative? What is the **BATNA**—the best alternative to a negotiated agreement? After all, what is the point in negotiating to increase the trade-in value of a car from $200 to $300, when its junk value is $500? That is the standard against which any proposed agreement should be measured. A BATNA is the standard of comparison that can protect a salesperson from accepting terms too unfavorable or from rejecting terms that would be in his or her interest to accept. It is a natural tendency to approach a negotiation, thinking, "Let's negotiate first and see what happens. If things don't work out, then I'll figure out what to do." But this might make the salesperson agree to terms he or she would be better off leaving; the salesperson tends to see the results of a breakdown in negotiations as being much worse than they actually are.

Recognizing his BATNA saved John West, founder and CEO of Cimlinc, a small software company, millions of dollars in sales to Boeing, the huge Seattle aircraft manufacturer. Cimlinc had a software package that enabled factory workers to receive routing orders, blueprints, and even video demonstrations from various systems on their individual computers—an electronic version of the greasy see-through envelope of paperwork that usually accompanies parts through a shop. Although Boeing's engineers wanted the software, their negotiators stalled until March 31, which they knew was the end of Cimlinc's fiscal year. That afternoon,

BATNA
The best alternative to a negotiated agreement; BATNA helps the negotiator not to settle for less in the negotiation.

Boeing's negotiators declared that they might buy only a few hundred thousand dollars of Cimlinc's product. West, despite the temptation to get his foot in the door of a big account, insisted a deal only made sense if it totaled in the millions of dollars. West arranged a call to company headquarters in Chicago to get preliminary financial figures. Because Boeing people might overhear the conversation, he told his financial people to answer, "This is Nancy," if Cimlinc could afford to forego the Boeing deal. The code "Nancy" referred to Nancy Sinatra, who sang "These Boots Are Made for Walkin.'" Receiving the message—that Cimlinc could get by without closing a deal—caused West and his negotiating team to get up to leave after the initial Boeing offer. Suddenly, with the valuable software about to slip away, Boeing responded with a bigger number. Shortly before midnight, Boeing agreed to a $6.8 million sale. The lesson: Always know your BATNA![21]

Protecting oneself from a bad agreement is one thing. Making the most of one's assets in order to produce a good agreement is another. How is this done? Once again, the answer lies in a BATNA.

Negotiating power generally is thought of as a function of financial resources, political connections, friends, or military might. In fact, the relative negotiating power of two parties primarily depends on how attractive the option of not reaching agreement is to each party. Even if the salesperson represents a small firm and is negotiating with a General Motors or IBM, if he or she has another prospect close by, he or she is in a position to negotiate a better agreement.

Vigorous exploration of other options if agreement cannot be reached can greatly strengthen a salesperson's hand, but he or she has to go out and develop alternatives. Generally, this requires three steps: (1) inventing a list of acceptable options if no agreement can be reached, (2) improving some of the better ideas and converting them into practical options, and (3) selecting the best option.[22] In sales situations, this usually means prospecting for other equally good prospects, but it could mean developing a joint venture with a well-connected larger concern, marketing overseas, borrowing funds, or many other alternatives.

The result of this is that the salesperson now has a BATNA against which every offer should be judged. The more attractive the BATNA, the greater the salesperson's confidence and the greater the likelihood of negotiating better terms. It is much easier for a salesperson to break off negotiations if he or she has an alternative; thus, interests can be presented more forcefully.

The advisability of a salesperson's disclosing his or her BATNA to the other side depends on assessment of their thinking. If a salesperson's BATNA is very attractive—if he or she has another customer in the next room—then by all means the other party should be informed. If a salesperson believes they think his or her BATNA is less attractive than it really is, then he or she should again apprise them differently. If their BATNA is worse, however, than they might think, then it is smart to keep quiet. By the same token, if the other party's BATNA is so good they don't see any need to negotiate on merit, the salesperson should consider what he or she can do to reduce it in their eyes.

12-3 Some Tactical Considerations

The theory and standards of principled negotiation present broad guidelines or strategies for the conduct of negotiations. There are, however, some important specific questions or tactics that are important (e.g., Who should make the first offer? How high should I start?).[23]

Who Should Make the First Offer?

It is not always a good idea to be the first to place an offer on the table. Without first discussing interests, options, and objectives, the other side may view a first offer as "railroading" them. Once the sides have a chance to outline the problem, then an offer is appropriate.

How High Should I Start?

Unfortunately, many (perhaps most) measure the success of a negotiation by how far the other side has budged. Even if the first figure is a wholly arbitrary "sticker" or "list" price, and not even in touch with the real market value, many buyers receive satisfaction from paying less than the first asking price.

Accordingly, the sales rep should start with the highest figure that can be reasonably justified without embarrassment. One way of thinking about it is to begin with the highest figure an impartial third party would view as logical. Such a figure need not be advanced as a firm proposition. In fact, the more firm you are at the beginning, the more you damage your credibility with concessions later on. It is safer to start with something like, "Well, one factor would be what others are paying for comparable work. In Chicago, for instance, they pay $20 an hour. How does that sound?" With such a statement, you have put out a standard and a figure without firmly committing yourself to it. If you could drop your price by 10 percent, start out with 2 percent or 4 percent. Leave yourself more room to negotiate. Who knows—you may get it for a 2 percent reduction. You might have to go all the way to 10 percent, but often you won't.

Get Something in Return for Your Added Value

What if you discover that the buyer wants to be able to track his expenditures in a way that is more detailed and complex than standard for your industry? What if your account-tracking system is set up in a way that you can provide that information at essentially no cost to you? Often the salesperson's first impulse is to jump in and say, "Oh, we can do that. That's no problem." However, it is better to think about your options. You could throw it in as part of the package and try to build goodwill. Or you could take a deep breath and try something like, "That's a difficult problem that will require some effort on our part, but it's doable." In the second instance, you've told the buyer you definitely could do it, but you have not yet agreed to do it. You may not be able to get him to pay extra for it, but you may be able use it as a bargaining chip in resisting price concessions. Which way you choose to go will depend on who your customer is and on the situation. However, you do have options.[24]

Strategy Follows Preparation

Strategy is a function of preparation. If you are well prepared, a strategy will logically suggest itself. If you have prepared and prioritized your interests, it will be obvious which ones to discuss and which ones the other party should initiate. If you have identified objective standards, you will know which to bring up and which to hold back. Of critical importance, if you know your BATNA, you will know when it's time to walk.

Think about Agreement from the Beginning

As you prepare to negotiate, it makes sense to imagine the outline of a successful agreement. This will assist in determining what issues need to be dealt with and what it might take to resolve them. Think of requirements for implementing the agreement. Then, work backwards. Ask yourself how the other side can justify an agreement to their constituents. Ask yourself the same question. In your own negotiations, how do you feel about explaining the result by saying, "Well, I started by asking for 100, but they offered 20. After a lot of haggling, we settled on 60." You probably cringe at the thought of a critic asking, "Why didn't you start at 150? Why weren't you tougher?" Remember, you both need to be able to sell the agreement to your constituents, or there is likely to be no agreement. You need to consider if their people will "buy it."[25]

Consider Constructing a Framework Agreement

In negotiations that will end with a written agreement, it is typically a good idea to sketch in the outlines of an agreement as you progress. Such a framework agreement is an agreement document, but with blank spaces for each term to be resolved. A standard purchase requisition may serve. In other instances, merely a list of headings will serve as well. Working on a framework agreement will ensure that all important issues are discussed and will serve as an agenda, keep discussions focused, provide a sense of progress, and keep a record of past discussions, reducing the chances of later misunderstanding.

Move toward Commitment Gradually

Negotiations seldom proceed linearly. It's seldom a good idea to lock in a particular point, as it may be a candidate for compromise in conjunction with another issue. If settlement can't be reached on one point, narrow the range of options if possible or move on. Be prepared to move through the issues several times, looking at them in light of an overall agreement. Offer options and ask for criticism: "What would you think of an agreement along the lines of this draft?" Pushing hard will usually have the opposite effect, causing intransigence on the part of the other party and minimizing the chances of developing the relationship.

12-4 What If the Clients Play by Different Rules?

To negotiate with an opponent who is not playing by the rules of principled negotiation, one needs to follow five basic steps to break the impasse. The essence of this 5-step strategy is indirect action. Instead of meeting resistance head-on, the idea is to go around it. It is the art of letting the other person have it your way.[26]

12-4a Go to the Balcony

go to the balcony
Imagine you are negotiating on a stage and that you detach yourself by imagining that you climb onto the balcony overlooking the stage.

Go to the balcony is a metaphor for a mental attitude of detachment. Imagine you are negotiating on a stage and then imagine yourself climbing onto a balcony overlooking the stage. From the balcony, you can calmly evaluate the conflict, as if you were a detached third party. Don't react to provocations. Step away from the scene, calm down, and carefully plan your response. Do not respond automatically, because most automatic responses are negative and further escalate the situation.[27]

The trick in going to the balcony is to forestall an immediate reaction and to avoid instinctively launching a counterattack. Instead, you should buy time to think. For example, suppose you have just concluded a sale and you are going over the contract with the customer, when he or she says, "I think we have a terrific package here and I'd be willing to go ahead if you will throw in the service contract for free. What do you say? Can we call it a deal?" If you respond immediately to the trick and say yes or no, it will probably be a mistake. Instead, gain time to think. Look the customer in the eye and say, "Hold on, Tom, I'm not sure I'm following you. Let's back up for a minute and review how we got here. We started discussing this deal three months ago, back in July, right? At the start, I thought you said you wanted to negotiate the service contract separately from the purchase. Tom, correct me if I'm wrong, but didn't you and I reach final agreement on all terms the day before yesterday?" However Tom answers now, you are on the balcony and not responding to his last-minute demand. You have not fallen for the trick. In fact, you have made him shift from the offensive to the defensive. Other similar questions or statements that allow you to "go to the balcony" are "Let me just make sure I understand what you are saying," "You've given me too much information to digest so quickly; let's back up," or "I need you to tell me again how the different parts of your plan fit together. I missed the connections between a couple of them."

Use the time you have gained to once again determine your ultimate interests and your BATNA; then, decide if you should continue negotiating. Your walkaway alternative to the negotiation may be the best route to travel. Focus on the ultimate prize. Don't get mad or get even—concentrate on what you want. In short, "go to the balcony."

12-4b Step to Their Side

The next step is to disarm the opponent by **stepping to their side.** The goal is to reassure the opposite side and help them regain their own mental balance. Listen actively to them by asking clarifying questions and paraphrasing their statements. Acknowledge their points and feelings. Apologize, if appropriate, or at least express sympathy for their problem. Focus on areas of agreement. Ury stresses the importance of saying and eliciting the word "yes" to reduce tensions and foster an atmosphere of agreement. In expressing your own views, adopt a both/and approach. Say "Yes, and . . ." instead of "But. . . ." Make I-statements rather than accusative you-statements. "Whatever language you use, the key is to preset your views as an addition to, rather than a direct contradiction of, your opponent's point of view."

Although people often do not negotiate rationally, it is worth trying it yourself. Dealing rationally with the irrational often forces them to reciprocate sensibly. Second, it is quite possible that your perception of their "irrationality" is mistaken; they may be disagreeing for what they perceive are perfectly rational reasons. People who have an "irrational" fear of flying, after all, do have a point that the plane can actually crash! In fact, at a deep level they actually believe it *will* crash. If you believed similarly, you wouldn't fly either. It is their perception that is skewed, not their reaction to that perception. Citing statistical studies about the safety of flying and telling them they are irrational is unlikely to work, but taking their fears seriously, exercising empathy, and inquiring sympathetically just might.[28] Before you can engage in principled negotiation, you must create a favorable climate. You need to defuse your opponent's anger and fears. They expect you to attack or resist. Instead, do the opposite. Listen to them, agreeing whenever you can. Also acknowledge their authority and competence. Disarm them by stepping to their side. You're selling something, and the other person says, "Your price is way too high." If you argue with him, he has a personal stake in proving you wrong and himself right. Instead, you say, "I understand exactly how you feel about that. Many other people have felt exactly the same way as you do when they first hear the price. When they take a closer look at what we offer, however, they have always found that we offer the best value in the marketplace."[29] You might recognize this as the "feel, felt, found" method for handling objections, and it is especially appropriate here. In general, begin by letting them know you are listening. Maintain eye contact, nod, and interject with

stepping to their side
To difuse anger, one negotiator agrees with his or her opponet without contradiction.

"Uh-huh" or "I see." Reflect back what you hear and acknowledge their point, saying, "You have a point there" or "I understand what you are saying" or "I know exactly what you mean." Even if you disagree with 99 percent of what they have said and agree with only 1 percent, concentrate on that 1 percent, saying, "Yes, I agree with you. . . ." To acknowledge that you respect them and are not attacking them, you may further preface your remarks with a statement such as, "You're the boss" or "I respect your authority." Then respond, "Yes, and . . .," presenting your views. For example, you might say, "Yes, you're absolutely correct that our price is higher. And what that buys you is higher quality, greater reliability, and better service." Whatever language you use, the key is to present your views as an addition to, rather than a direct contradiction of, your opponent's point of view.

As you express your views, you are less likely to provoke your counterpart if you speak about yourself, rather than about them. I-messages are also valuable here. Instead of the accusatory, "You only care . . ." or "You never think . . .," describe the impact of the problem on you, saying, "I feel that . . .," "I get upset when . . .," "I'm not comfortable with . . .," or "The way I see it. . . ."

12-4c Don't Reject, Reframe

The next step is to focus on each side's interests. Instead of rejecting your opponent's position, which usually only reinforces their determination to stick with it, direct their attention to the problem of satisfying each side's interests. Take whatever they say and reframe it as an attempt to deal with the problem, that is, **don't reject, reframe.**

Ask problem-solving questions, such as, "Why is it that you want that?" "What are your concerns?" or "What if we were to . . .?" If asking why doesn't work, then ask why not: "Why not do it this way?" or "What would be wrong with this approach?" People reluctant to disclose their own concerns are usually happy to criticize yours.

To introduce a host of possible solutions without provoking your opponent, ask, "What if?" "What if we were to move the goods off the shelves faster with coop advertising?" "What if we were to stretch out the payments over 48 months?" "What if we were to downsize the project to fit your budget limitations?" or "What if we can help you show your boss how the benefits to your company justify asking for a budget increase?" An especially good tactic is to ask them, "What would you do if you were in my shoes?" This educates them to your interests and provides insight into your constraints.

If your opponent's position strikes you as unreasonable, use it as a starting point for a discussion of fairness. Tell them, "You must have good reasons for thinking that's a fair solution. I'd like to hear them." Suppose that a potentially profitable prospect asks you to throw in free service for the price of the product. You may feel you can't say no without offending the client. Yet, if you say yes, it will be expensive. So, ask them: "What's your thinking about what makes that fair? Does our competition throw in service for free?"

Whatever the precise language, make sure to phrase your questions as open-ended rather than closed. Your opponent will find it difficult to answer "no" to questions such as, "What is the purpose of this policy?" instead of "Are there any exceptions to this policy?" Preface questions with "how," "why," or "who." "Who has the authority to grant an exception?" or "How would you advise me to proceed?"

Although problem-solving questions enable you to reframe your opponent's position in terms of interests, options, and standards, you also need to reframe

don't reject, reframe
Instead of rejecting an opponent's position outright, reframe it as an attempt to deal with the problem.

their tactics and games. For tips on how to accomplish this aim, see Section 12-5, "Win–Lose Maneuvers."

12-4d Have Them Take Ownership

Essentially, **have them take ownership** means constructing an agreement that your opponent can call a victory. This is accomplished by first involving them in crafting the agreement. Second, it means satisfying more than just their monetary needs— it also includes their intangible personal needs, such as recognition and autonomy. Third, it means helping your opponent back away from their initial position without losing face and finding them a way to present the proposal to their constituents as a victory. Last, it means going slowly rather than abruptly to make the whole agreement acceptable. Slow, point-by-point assent to the agreement may be more palatable to them, whereas agreeing all at once may not.

People see things differently when they become involved and accept ownership of an idea. Your opponent is likely to make allowances they would not otherwise make. They may become favorable to ideas earlier rejected. As they add their ideas into the proposal, they make it their own. Ask for and build on your opponent's ideas. Ask, "Building on your idea, what if we . . ." or "As a follow-up to our discussion yesterday, it occurs to me that . . ." or "I got this idea from something you said at the meeting the other day. . . ."

As ideas are developed, keep your opponent involved by inviting their criticism. Ask problem-solving questions such as, "Which interests of yours does this approach fail to satisfy?" "In what respect is this not fair?" "How would you improve on this proposal?" "Is there any way we can make it better for your side without making things worse for mine?" If such questions fail, offer choices: "We can resolve the difference between your asking price and my offer by comparing sale prices of similar goods, or I can pay the difference with assets besides cash, or I can spread out the payments over time. Which approach would you prefer?" Once they select an alternative, it becomes their idea.

Don't assume there's a fixed pie. It is not necessarily true that by satisfying your opponent's needs you are automatically sacrificing your own. Look for ways to expand the total pie. Seek low-cost, high-benefit trades. Identify items you can give your opponent that are a high benefit to them but a low cost to you. In return, seek the same from them.

Help your opponent save face. Often, they have a constituency that must be satisfied, such as a purchasing agent's boss. Demonstrate that conditions have changed. Explain why originally they may have been right, but circumstances have changed: "Your no-changes policy has always been the right one for a regulated marketplace, but now the government has deregulated this business and we're all facing intense competition." If possible, look for a third-party mediator—an independent expert, a mutual friend, CPA, and so on. A proposal unacceptable from you can become acceptable if it comes from a third party. Look further for a standard of fair comparison. For example, check out the marketplace for trade-in values of similar equipment.

Above all, go slow. An agreement reached slowly, step by step, may be acceptable whereas seeking agreement on an entire proposal all at once is unacceptable. If too much has to be decided immediately, it may fail abruptly. It is a good idea to reassure an opponent that they do not need to make a final commitment until the very end, when they know exactly what they will get in return.

If your opponent accepts the agreement, great. If not, you need to make it as hard as possible for them to say no. This is the next step.

have them take ownership
Crafting an agreement that one's negotiating partner can also call a victory, especially to his or her constituents.

12-5e Bring Them to Their Senses

bring them to their senses
Letting one's negotiating partner know the consequences of not reaching agreement by asking questions that prompt them to think through those consequences.

The common reaction at this point is to resort to power tactics and try to force your opponents to agree. This is counterproductive. Ury says, "Instead of using power to bring your opponents to their knees, use it to **bring them to their senses.**"[30] The goal is to educate the other party to realize that an agreement is in their best interest. Ask them reality-testing questions about what will happen if no agreement is reached. Alert them (without threatening) to your BATNA. If they still resist agreement, you may need to deploy your BATNA. Ury offers this rule for any exercise of power in negotiations: "The more power you use, the more you need to defuse your opponents resistance." Couple power tactics with conciliatory moves. Seek to neutralize your opponent's attacks, rather than responding with counterattacks. Seek allies from the larger community. Third parties can inhibit threats or attacks and can pressure both sides to resume negotiations. Remind your opponent of the attractiveness of the proposed agreement and reassure them that your aim is mutual satisfaction. Because imposed settlements are unstable, it may be better to negotiate an agreement even in cases where you have a decisive advantage. If your opponent still resists and thinks they can win without negotiation, you must educate them to the contrary. You must make it hard for them to say "no." You might use threats and force, but in all likelihood this will only make them more intransigent. Ask reality-testing questions, warn rather than threaten, and demonstrate your BATNA. Yet, at the same time, exercise restraint and reassure them that mutual satisfaction, not your victory, is the final goal. In short, use power to "bring them to their senses, not their knees."

Let your opponent know the consequences of not reaching agreement by asking questions that prompt them to think through those consequences. Ask, "What do you think will happen if we don't agree?" "What do you think I will do?" With the latter, you inform your opponent about your BATNA. Let them know you have satisfactory alternatives. "Do you realize how many other prospects I have for my goods?" Ask, "What will you do?" "How much will it cost you?" "How will that satisfy your interests?" Let them know that their BATNA may not be that satisfactory. "If you don't sign an annual purchase agreement with us, will you have other guaranteed alternative sources of supply? Is it possible you may not be able to negotiate delivery on short notice from our competitors and you will have to shut down your production line?"

threat
What you will do to your opponent if he or she does not agree.

warning
What will happen if agreement is not reached.

Be careful to warn and not threaten. A threat appears subjective and confrontational; a warning sounds objective and respectful. A **threat** is *what you will do* to your opponent if they do not agree. A **warning** is *what will happen* if agreement is not reached. It is easier to agree to an objective reality than back down to a threat. Let them know that the previously formulated agreement always offers an acceptable resolution.

12-5 Win–Lose Maneuvers

In Section 12-4, "What If the Clients Play by Different Rules," we discussed the strategies of handling those who choose not to follow the rules of principled negotiation. Problem-solving questions enable you to reframe your opponent's position in terms of interests, options, and standards. But you also need to deal with their tactics, those "win–lose" maneuvers designed to back you into a corner and meekly fold into submission. Generally, there are three steps in dealing with win–lose maneuvers or "dirty tricks": recognize the tactic, raise the issue explicitly, and question the tactic's legitimacy and desirability (i.e., negotiate over it).[31]

You need to recognize a tactic before you can adjust to it. Learn to spot the ploys; often just recognizing a tactic will neutralize it. After recognition, point it out to the other side, "Doug, I'm not always right, but it seems as if you and Stan here are using the 'good-guy/bad-guy' ploy. If there are real differences between you, however, we can recess for you two to straighten them out." If they care about the negotiation at all, they are likely to cease. Moreover, bringing up the tactic gives you an opportunity to negotiate about the rules of the game. Insist that the goal of the negotiation is to effect an agreement satisfactory to all—not to damage the interests of one partner to the profit of the other.

Besides these general tactics, there are also special tactics specific to each dirty trick. Descriptions of these win–lose ploys along with specific recommendations for dealing with them are shown here.

12-5a "I Need to Get This Approved"

When the sales representative believes he or she has worked out an agreement, the buyer claims, "I have to take this plan to the company controller for approval." The idea is to give the buyer's organization another chance for getting concessions from the sales representative—to give them a "second bite at the apple," so to speak. The buyer usually uses this tactic with sales reps who have the power to give concessions. Perhaps the best defense against the **I need to get this approved tactic** is to establish first how much negotiating power the other party has. Before you present your proposal to the other person, before you even get it out of your briefcase, you should casually say, "Let me be sure I understand. If this proposal meets all of your needs (That's as broad as any statement can be, isn't it?), is there any reason why you wouldn't give me a decision today?"[32] If he or she indicates some ambiguity, the salesperson may ask, "I would like to talk directly to the individual from whom final approval is required." Failing this, the salesperson may respond to the last-minute demand, "Are you suggesting that we reopen the negotiation?" If he or she says "no," you can say, "Well, then, I think we should just stick with the agreement we've already reached." If, however, he or she says "yes," you can respond, "We'll treat it as a joint draft to which neither side is committed. You check with your boss, and I'll check with mine, and let's meet tomorrow to discuss possible changes." If he or she wants something extra, you should get something in return.

I need to get this approved tactic
When the sales representative believes he or she has worked out an agreement, the buyer claims, "I have to take this plan to my boss for approval."

12-5b "What's Your Rock-Bottom Price?"

Rock-bottom price usually works this way: The buyer claims, "I don't have much time. What is the least you will take for this property?" The salesperson must avoid giving too quick a response with no room for negotiation. "How many do you need?" is a good response. Responding with a negotiable figure is appropriate: "Well, I think that $75,000 is a fair price. Do you agree?" Both sales rep and buyer know this represents a starting point.

rock-bottom price
A win–lose negotiation tactic in which the buyer initially approaches the seller with the question, "What's the lowest price you will accept?"

If a client asks for a 20 percent discount and you immediately say yes, they walk away feeling two things:[33]

1. The price must have been inflated to start with, and
2. I should have asked for bigger discount. Next time, I will!

Neither of these outcomes is good for you. The next time your prospect asks for a reduction in price, instead of just giving in, try responding with one of the following instead:

How many will you need?

I can appreciate that you're looking for the best deal, but I can tell you that we've already given you our best price.

You're smart to be looking for the best deal, but our pricing is always competitive, and I just can't go any lower.

A discount? (in a surprised tone)

12-5c The Information Claim

The aim for this buyer is to keep the sales rep blind to his or her needs and interests. Sometimes called the *red herring*, with the **information claim,** the buyer makes a phony demand that he will subsequently withdraw, but only in exchange for a concession from the salesperson. If the red herring distracts the sales rep, it will deceive him or her into thinking that it's of major concern to the other side when it may not be. The buyer might, for example, demand that a new multifunction unit absolutely have the ability to fax, in addition to copy, scan, and print. However, the real intention is to gain price or other concessions for a model without faxing abilities. In fact, at the office, they have an inexpensive older fax that is quite functional. After the salesperson finally tires of trying to include a fax, the prospect might say, "Okay, if you can't include it, I guess I can get one separately, but I need a $100 discount for the model without it."[34]

Often, the buyer tries to throw the salesperson off by first appearing to have an interest in something else rather than the product or service eventually purchased. If the prospect has a real desire to own the deluxe model A business copier, she might first encourage the salesperson to make a proposal on the lesser model B. With the sale of model B getting nowhere, the prospect says, "Well, I don't know. What kind of deal would you give me on model A?" Having invested the time and now apparently losing the sale, the salesperson is expected to come up with a better proposition on model A than would have been the case if he or she had originally started with model A. The best thing for the salesperson to do is to qualify the prospect before the call or within the first few minutes of the visit. The salesperson skilled in asking questions has the advantage.

12-5d The Veiled Threat

With the **veiled threat,** the buyer lets the salesperson subtly know how much power he or she possesses: "Last year, we had to drop a supplier after we found out that one of our competitors was getting an additional 5 percent discount from them. Of course, I know the reputation your company has in this business." Threats are one of the most abused tactics in negotiation. A threat is easy to make, easier than a legitimate offer. All it takes is a few words, and if it works, you don't have to carry it out. However, threats can lead to counterthreats in an escalating spiral that can unhinge a negotiation and even destroy a relationship.

When pitted against such a buyer, the salesperson is best advised to play to these feelings of superiority. To the threatening buyer, acting subservient toward them increases their feelings of superiority: "I certainly respect your position, Mr. Sterling, and I only ask that we be given a fair chance to show you that we can do a good job for you at a reasonable price." Depending on the salesperson's BATNA, he or she can also reply, "I only negotiate on the merits. My reputation is built on not responding to threats."

12-5e Sticks and Stones

Some buyers take delight in poking fun at salespeople or making disparaging remarks to them: "Hey, Tom, you don't look well. Aren't you selling anything these days?" or "Come on, that's the most ridiculous proposal I've heard from a salesper-

---

information claim
After expressing great interest in model A, the buyer asks about model B, hoping for favorable terms after the sale rep has invested time and effort in selling the first model.

veiled threat
A win–lose negotiating maneuver in which the buyer lets the sales rep know how much power he or she possesses.

son this week." **Sticks and stones** assumes that browbeating will make the salesperson feel inferior and acquiesce to their demands.

The humiliation such buyers seek to wreak upon buyers may be nonverbal. Buyers can let salespeople know their status by making them sit in their office for long periods before meeting, letting others interrupt their presentation, making telephone calls, or continuing to read or work while the salesperson talks. They can imply that the sales rep is ignorant. They can refuse to listen and ask the rep to continually repeat himself or herself.

The sales rep can respond with two tactics. He or she can reframe the personal attack as an attack on the problem: "You may have a point there. How would you improve the proposal to make it fly?" Failing this, the salesperson may remain professional while still acknowledging the tactic, "Ms. Stevens, I've apparently called you at a bad time. I have some important information you should know, so can we set another time when it would be more convenient for you? How about Thursday at 10?"

sticks and stones
A win–lose negotiating tactic in which the buyer disparages salespeople, hoping to bully them into concessions.

12-5f Budget Bogey

In the **budget bogey,** The buyer states a fixed dollar amount beyond which he or she cannot go. A seller who accepts this budget constraint feels compelled to reduce the price. Therefore, a seller should never accept the budget figure as fixed without testing for other sources of funding. Most budgets are more flexible than they look. Large amounts can often be shifted from account to account by a clever accountant if the seller refuses to accept a budget figure as nonnegotiable. The amazing part of the budget maneuver is that sellers often bring the problem on themselves. A buyer or engineer asks the seller for some approximation of the cost months before the final design and quantity are fixed. The seller, eager to please, states a figure and thereafter is boxed in because the buyer incorporates the premature figure into plans. Such early price quotes are often "words without thoughts."

To gather more information to help the prospect solve the no-money problem, continue the discussion by asking the following questions:[35]

How have you funded this type of project in the past?

We encounter this quite often. Let me suggest how other organizations have found ways to handle it.

What are some other budget areas that support this endeavor? Let's examine ways we could work with them to help fund this activity.

How much money have you set aside that may not be used? Are there ways we could access those funds to start this project?

budget bogey
A win–lose negotiating maneuver in which the buyer details a budget limit he or she cannot exceed.

12-5g Escalation

Escalation is a tricky maneuver. After two parties have come to an agreement regarding a point of the negotiation, one side raises its demand, the object being to wear down the resolve of the other. Alternatively, they might raise an issue you thought had already been settled. The tendency is for the other party to settle quickly from then on—before the perpetrator has a chance to escalate. Occasionally, a seller decides to raise the proposal price immediately before the negotiation. The other party may fight desperately to get back the original figure rather than some lower target. A wise negotiator will recognize the tactic, point it out to the perpetrator, and refuse to go along. He or she might also call for a break while they

escalation
A win–lose negotiation tactic; after the parties believe they have come to an agreement, one side then raises its demands, hoping to wear down the other's resolve.

consider whether or not they want to continue the negotiation. This prevents an impulsive reaction, while indicating the gravity of their conduct. Be sure to insist on negotiating on the basis of principle.

Try these strategies:[36]

- *Protecting yourself with higher authority.* Tell them that their suggestion does not offend you, but that your board of directors will never renegotiate a deal once it has been made and they will force you to walk away. Then position for easy acceptance by telling them that although you cannot budge on the price, you might be able to offer them something of value in another area.
- *Escalating your demands in return.* Tell them that you are glad that they want to reopen the negotiations because your side has been having second thoughts also. Of course, you would never renege on a deal, but because they have chosen to negate the original proposal, your price has now gone up also.

It is better to avoid escalation than to have to deal with it. Avoid it by using these techniques:

- *Tying up all the details up front.* Don't leave anything to "we can work that out later." Unresolved issues invite escalation.
- *Building personal relationships with the other parties.* This technique makes it harder for them to be ruthless.
- *Getting large deposits.* With a large deposit, it's harder for them to back out.
- *Building win–win negotiations.* With win–win negotiations, they won't want to back out.

12-5h Deadline

deadline
A win–lose negotiation ploy in which the buyer sets a phony deadline to gain concessions prior to the fake deadline.

Deadline is a powerful maneuver because many agreements are reached at the last minute. Interestingly, people often accept the other party's deadline as their own despite the fact that often the deadline favors one party more than the other. Never accept an opponent's deadline unquestioned.

You can sometimes turn your opponent's deadline to your own advantage. If he or she has given you an inflexible deadline, for example, you can say, "I'd like to be able to convene my management to make you a more generous offer, but in view of the time problem, this is the best I can do under short circumstance" or "To meet the deadline, we'll need your help. Can you take care of pickup and delivery?"

12-5i The Good-Guy/Bad-Guy Routine

good-guy/bad-guy
A win–lose negotiating tactic in which two buyers will stage a quarrel, one being harsh and the other easy on the salesperson, hoping to get concessions from him or her.

You've seen the **good-guy/bad-guy** routine tactic in old police movies and cop shows.[37] Officers bring a suspect into the police station for questioning, and the first detective to interrogate him is a rough, tough, mean-looking guy. He threatens the suspect with all kinds of things that they're going to do to him. Then the detective is mysteriously called away to take a phone call, and the second detective, who's brought in to look after the prisoner while the first detective is away, is the warmest, nicest guy in the entire world. He sits down and makes friends with the suspect. He gives him a cigarette and says, "Listen kid, it's really not as bad as all that. I've taken a liking to you. I know the ropes around here. Why don't you let me see what I can do for you?" It's a real temptation to think that the Good Guy's on your side when, of course, he really isn't.

Then the Good Guy would go ahead and close on what salespeople would recognize as a minor point close. "All I think the detectives really need to know," he tells the suspect, "is where did you buy the gun?" What he really wants to know is, "Where did you hide the body?"

Similarly, in negotiations, two people on the same side will stage a quarrel. One will take a tough stand: "We won't pay one cent more than $25 per case, and that's too much as it is." Her partner chimes in, "Franny, be reasonable, these goods are almost brand new, and I think $26 per case is perfectly reasonable." Turning to the sales rep, she asks, "Could you sell at $26?" The concession isn't large, but it seems that way given the first partner's stubborn behavior. Sometimes the "hardhearted" partner is absent, with the one present claiming: "I think your price is absolutely reasonable, but my partner will never settle for that figure." There are two ways of dealing with this ruse. The smart negotiator may insist on knowing the objective reasons behind the price request: "I appreciate that you are trying to be reasonable, but I want to know why $30 per case is unreasonable. What's your rationale for a lower price, when we're in the ballpark with our initial price?" Another tactic is to let them know you recognize their tactic: "I wasn't born yesterday. I know the game you are playing. Your tactic isn't going to work" or "There seems to be some disagreement between you. Perhaps the two of you need a few minutes to sort out your objectives here today. Why don't we break for 15 minutes while you work it out?"[38]

Or the salesperson might respond laughingly, "You guys are terrific! That is the best good-guy/bad-guy routine I've seen in years. Did you plan it or was it just coincidence? Seriously now, let's see if we can establish a fair price for the goods." By showing admiration for the partners' skill and making light of the tactic, the salesperson helps them save face. A tactic acknowledged is a tactic disarmed.

12-5j "Take It or Leave It"

This refers to **take-it-or-leave-it** tactics. The buyer exclaims: "I won't pay more than $12,500 for this car. That's my last offer. Take it or leave it." Test the buyer's seriousness by ignoring the tactic. Keep talking about the problem as if you didn't hear what the buyer said, or change the subject altogether. If he or she is serious, the message will be repeated. If so, then let them know what they have to lose if no agreement is reached and look for a face-saving way, such as a change in circumstances, for them to get out of the situation. After the buyer has announced his or her "final" offer, the sales rep can respond, "A $12.50 per case price was your final offer before we discussed our cooperative advertising program."

take it or leave it
One negotiator demands his position be met or he will walk away.

12-5k Auctioning

Auctioning has the buyer negotiating with two or three suppliers simultaneously, each of whom he or she makes sure knows of the others' presence. The only countermeasure for this tactic is for the seller to study the buyer closely and determine his or her true desires. The seller who feels confident enough of his or her edge should stick to the offer and test the buyer as if the other sellers weren't present. The idea is to make the buyer reveal his or her bias and thereby provide a signal on how to proceed. If your opponent sees that his or her abusive tactics do not work, often he or she will stop. Take the buyer who liked to keep his competitive vendors waiting outside his office in order to unsettle them and make them more pliable to the terms he sought. One shrewd vendor decided to ignore the tactic, and he brought along a novel to read. When the buyer finally ushered him in, the vendor made a show of reluctantly closing the book, as if he had not been inconvenienced in the slightest. When the buyer took a long phone call in the middle of the meeting, out came the novel. After two or three such meetings, the buyer realized the tactic wasn't working and stopped using it.

auctioning
A win–lose negotiating maneuver in which the buyer negotiates with many potential buyers, letting each know of the others' presence.

The tactic is to know more about your competition than they'll ever learn:[39]

Homeowner: I want to check with some other people before I make my final decision.

You: I absolutely agree with you.

Salespeople should always agree initially and then work to turn it around. "I absolutely agree with you. You should check with other companies before you make a decision. But look, let me save you some time. Have you talked to Ted Smith over at ABC Construction? He uses XYZ cabinets that have this feature, this feature, and this feature; but they don't have this. Then, if you talk to the national department store company down at the mall, the salesperson who'll come out will be Fred Harrison, and he'll tell you about model number such and such. . . ."

By the time you've let her know how much you know about the competition, she's going to think, "Why on Earth do I need to waste my time talking to all these other people, when this person knows more than I'll ever learn."

Chapter Summary

The chapter began with a description of how negotiation differs from more typical types of selling environments. Whereas much of what we have discussed to this point has been associated with routine exchange (e.g., set established prices, promotional terms, delivery, and so on) in negotiation, these terms are set by bargaining between buyer and seller. We then established that the proper manner of negotiation is principled negotiation, or win–win negotiating, as it is sometimes called. Here, both sides work together to set an agreement from which both profit. This contrasts with a great deal of literature that advocates win–lose negotiating, where one side, through smart use of various negotiating tactics, profits at the expense of the other. Principled negotiation demands (1) separating people from the problem, (2) focusing on interests, not positions, (3) inventing options for mutual gain, and (4) insisting that the result be based on some objective standard.

A significant problem is presented when the other side is more powerful. The key to responding to this situation is to develop one's BATNA—best alternative to a negotiated agreement. A BATNA will prevent a salesperson from accepting a settlement that should be rejected and will help the salesperson to make the most of his or her assets to produce a good agreement.

To negotiate with an opponent who is not playing by the rules of principled negotiation, use these five basic steps to resolve the impasse: (1) going to the balcony; (2) stepping to the side; (3) not rejecting, but reframing; (4) having them take ownership; and (5) bringing them to their senses, not their knees.

Despite the benefits of principled negotiation, there is the possibility of meeting a negotiator who uses win–lose maneuvers. Some practical suggestions were offered for countering the following tactics: "I need to get this approved," "What is your rock-bottom price?" the information claim, the veiled threat, sticks and stones, budget bogey, escalation, deadline, the good-guy/bad-guy routine, take it or leave it, and auctioning.

Discussion Questions

1. Explain what negotiation means in a selling context.

2. What is principled negotiation, and how does it differ from win–lose negotiation?

3. How does the principled negotiator "separate people from the problem"?

4. What are "I-messages"?

5. What does it mean to "focus on interests, not positions"?

6. What is meant by shared and compatible interests?

7. Why is it true that agreement is often made possible precisely because interests differ?

8. How do principled negotiators identify interests?

9. What does it mean to be "hard on the problem and soft on the people"?

10. How was Benjamin Franklin successful in negotiations?

11. How does the principled negotiator invent options for mutual gain?

12. What does it mean to negotiate on objective criteria instead of positions?

13. What if the other party to the negotiation seems determined not to negotiate on principle?

14. What should the negotiator do when the other side is more powerful?

15. What does it mean to "go to the balcony"?

16. What does "stepping to their side" mean?

17. To what does "don't reject, reframe" refer?

18. What does it mean to "have them take ownership"?

19. How does the principled negotiator bring the other party in the negotiation "to their senses, not their knees"?

20. How does one counter the "I need to get this approved" tactic?

21. How should the negotiator respond to, "What's your rock-bottom price?"

22. What is the information claim tactic?

23. How can one respond to the veiled threat?

24. How can the salesperson respond to the sticks and stones tactic?

25. Explain the budget bogey tactic.

26. What is escalation, and how does one counter it?

27. Why should deadlines be questioned?

28. What is the good-guy/bad-guy routine?

29. Explain the auctioning maneuver.

Chapter Quiz

1. Principled negotiation, according to Fisher and Ury, demand all of the following *except*
   a. inventing positions for personal gain.
   b. focusing on interests, not positions.
   c. separating the people from the problem.
   d. insisting that the result be based on some objective standard.

2. Substantive issues need to be separated from relationship and process issues. An example of a substantive issue would be
   a. price of the product.
   b. ease of communication.
   c. degree of mutual understanding.
   d. attitude of acceptance or rejection.

3. In negotiating with a customer, he or she begins with the statement, "I am limited to spending no more than $500 for this new PC." This is known as the _____ maneuver.
   a. sticks and stones
   b. escalation
   c. reunion
   d. budget bogey

4. BATNA is the standard of comparison that can protect a salesperson from accepting terms that are too unfavorable or from rejecting terms it would be in his or her interest to accept. BATNA stands for
   a. the best approach to a negotiated agreement.
   b. the best approach to a negotiated alternative.
   c. the best alternative to a negotiated approach.
   d. the best alternative to a negotiated agreement.

5. To negotiate with a customer who is not playing by the rules of principled negotiation, one needs to follow five basic steps to break the impasse. The first step is to go to the balcony, which is
   a. a technique for disarming the opponent by stepping to their side.
   b. taking whatever the customer says and reframing it as an attempt to deal with the problem.
   c. a metaphor for a mental attitude of detachment.
   d. constructing an agreement that your opponent can call a victory.

6. When negotiating an agreement with a customer who plays by different rules, it is important to construct an agreement that the customer can call a victory. This is accomplished by all of the following strategies *except*
   a. involve the customer in crafting the agreement.
   b. go quickly rather than slowly to prevent the customer from raising objections.
   c. help the customer to back away from his or her initial position without losing face.
   d. satisfy more than just the customer's monetary needs—it also includes intangible personal needs, such as recognition and autonomy.

7. All of the following are win–lose maneuvers designed to back the salesperson into a corner and meekly fold into submission *except*
   a. "I need to get this approved."
   b. sticks and stones.
   c. budget bogey.
   d. the balcony.

8. In win–lose maneuvers, sometimes the sales representative believes he or she has worked out an agreement and then the buyer claims, "I have to take this plan to the company controller for approval." The idea behind making this statement is to
   a. find a reason not to make the purchase.
   b. stall the negotiations so the buyer can obtain bids from competing suppliers.
   c. obtain the controller's approval so the sale can be culminated.
   d. give the buyer's organization another chance for getting concessions from the sales representative; this is known as escalation.

9. "Hey, Tom, you don't look well. Aren't you selling anything these days?" or "Come on, that's the most ridiculous proposal I've heard from a salesperson this week" represents the _____ win–lose maneuvering method on the part of the buyer.
   a. sticks and stone
   b. budget bogey
   c. information claim
   d. escalation

10. Escalation is a tricky win–lose maneuver because, after the two parties have come to an agreement regarding a point of the negotiation, one side raises its demand. The object of this maneuver is to
    a. force the seller to offer his or her rock-bottom price.
    b. bring the negotiation process to an end.
    c. wear down the resolve of the other party in order to obtain a better deal.
    d. get out of the negotiations without losing face.

Web Exercise

Go to www.justsell.com/content/printnroute/tools/gst0013a.htm. This site provides a printable checklist for sales negotiation. Prepare a role-play with a classmate in which each of you takes a turn as the seller and buyer. Using the checklist, go through a negotiation scenario. Which elements on the list are the most useful? Which require additional preparation or practice?

Notes

1. Philip Kotler, *Marketing Management,* Englewood Cliffs, NJ: Prentice Hall, 2004, p. 705.
2. Ibid.
3. Roger Fisher and William Ury, *Getting to Yes: Negotiating Agreement without Giving In,* 2nd Edition, Boston: Houghton Mifflin, 1992, p. 57.
4. Ibid.
5. Ibid.
6. Ibid.
7. Roger Fisher and Danny Ertel, *Getting Ready to Negotiate,* London: The Penguin Group, 1995, pp. 86–88.
8. Ibid.
9. Anne Warfield, "How to Leave with More Than What You Wanted," *SalesVantage.com,* August 6, 2004.
10. Lynn Kirby, Education 388/588, "I-Messages," *Interpersonal Relations,* 2004.
11. Anne Miller, "Negotiating: Don't Get Stung," *SalesVantage.com,* 2004.
12. David E. Benson, "The Art of Principled Negotiation," *Real Estate Business,* Fall 1997, pp. 22–24.
13. Stephen Chilton, "Introduction to Principled Negotiation," www.d.umn.edu/~schilton/3221/LectureNotes/3221.F&U._Introduction.2003.Spring.html, May 10, 2003.
14. Roger Fisher and Danny Ertel, *Getting Ready to Negotiate,* London: The Penguin Group, 1995, pp. 86–88.
15. Roger Fisher and William Ury, *Getting to Yes: Negotiating Agreement without Giving In,* 2nd Edition, Boston: Houghton Mifflin, 1992, p. 57.
16. Ibid.
17. Ibid.
18. Kelley Robertson, "Focus on a Trade, Not a Discount," *EyeonSales.com,* May 12, 2004.
19. David Benson, "The Art of Principled Negotiation," *Real Estate Business,* Fall 1997, p. 22–24.
20. Ibid.
21. Thomas Petzinger, Jr., "Once the Foot Is in the Door, Be Sure to Leave It Open," *Wall Street Journal,* July 21, 1995, p. B1.
22. Roger Fisher, William Ury, and Bruce Patton, *Getting to Yes: Negotiating Agreement without Giving In,* Boston: Houghton Mifflin, 1991.
23. Herb Cohen, *You Can Negotiate Anything,* Toronto: Bantam Books, 1990, p. 121.
24. Michael Schatzki, "Managing the Sales Negotiation Process," *EyeonSales.com,* July 11, 2003.
25. Roger Fisher and William Ury, *Getting to Yes: Negotiating Agreement without Giving In,* 2nd Edition, Boston: Houghton Mifflin, 1992, p. 57.

26. William Ury, *Getting Past No: Negotiating with Difficult People,* New York: Bantam Books, 1991.

27. William Ury, "William Ury—Overcoming Barriers to Principled Negotiation," Conflict Research Consortium, 1998.

28. William Ury, *Getting Past No: Negotiating with Difficult People,* New York: Bantam Books, 1991.

29. Roger Dawson, "Setting the Climate for a Nonconfrontational Negotiation," *SalesVault.com,* March 2, 2004.

30. William Ury, *Getting Past No: Negotiating with Difficult People,* New York: Bantam Books, 1991.

31. Herb Cohen, *You Can Negotiate Anything,* Toronto: Bantam Books, 1990, p. 121.

32. Roger Dawson, "How to Negotiate When the Other Person Tells You They Don't Have the Authority to Decide," *SalesVault.com,* December 16, 2003.

33. Colleen Francis, "Five Steps to Negotiating Like an Expert," *SalesVantage.com,* June 12, 2004.

34. Roger Dawson, "Unethical Negotiating Gambits," *EyeonSales.com,* March 22, 2004.

35. Bill Brooks, "No Money, No Problem," www.brooksgroup.com, 2004.

36. Roger Dawson, "Unethical Negotiating Gambits," *EyeonSales.com,* March 22, 2004.

37. Roger Dawson, "Good Guy–Bad Guy," *EyeonSales.com,* June 7, 2004.

38. Hilka Klinkenberg, "The Niceties of Negotiating," *SalesVantage.com,* September 18, 2004.

39. Roger Dawson, "Unethical Negotiating Gambits," *EyesonSales.com,* March 22, 2004.

Case 12-1

The following are statements by purchasing agents interacting with salespeople on a business basis. Identify the particular negotiating tactic they are using, and identify how you would react to it.

1. "Ms. Jones, I believe we have worked out some things regarding a possible arrangement between our companies. However, I have to take our agreement to be approved by my boss, Jim Johnson, corporate vice president of purchasing."

2. "I don't believe in hemming and hawing around the point. Let's get right down to business. What's the lowest price you can offer me?"

3. "I don't know. That's a lot of money to spend. What kind of deal can you give me on model C? I really don't think we need the ability to copy on both sides of the document."

4. "We discovered one of our suppliers offered blanket contracts to some of our competitors but not to us. We cut them off cold. Your company doesn't engage in such activities, does it?"

5. "What's going on, Tom? You look like you're coming in with your tail tucked between your legs. Aren't you having a good week?"

6. "I have been authorized to spend no more than $10,000 for a material requirements planning system on our personal computer. What can you do for me?"

7. "I know you thought we had an agreement, but my boss refuses to pay any more than $10 per case. Can you come down from the price we agreed on earlier? I'm sorry, but what can I do?"

8. "I need to have a blanket contract agreed to and signed by a week from Tuesday. Sorry, but that's what my boss is pressuring me for."

9. "I know your price is reasonable, but my partner is difficult to work with. How about $30 per case? Can you settle on that? It's still better than the $28 figure he demanded."

10. "I'm willing to pay no more than $10 per hundredweight. Take it or leave it!"

11. "We're dealing with and receiving quotes from IBM, Burroughs, Sperry, NCR, and Univac. What can you do for me?"

12. "I must tell you that I absolutely refuse to pay more than $250 per boxcar load. I don't think any more than that is called for, and I can't go any higher without seeking approval of upper management. Time isn't of any consequence to me, either. I can wait all winter if necessary. So make up your mind!"

13. "I guess you're right. Five dollars per dozen is fair. The $4 figure is too low, given your F.O.B. factory terms. Now, what are you going to do for me in return for my acquiescence to your figure?"

Case 12-2

Ron Hansen, salesperson for Hansen Tire Company, is negotiating with Bo Ansfield, purchasing agent for one of the three major automobile manufacturers, for a contract to deliver tires for new cars coming off the production line.

Bo: My position is that we're prepared to pay no more than $45 per tire—steel belted, warrantied for 40,000 miles. What are you willing to offer?

Ron: We're prepared to deliver such tires to you at $55 per tire. That's as low as we can go. We're barely making any money at all at that price.

Bo: Come on. What kind of fool do you take me for? You guys have a reputation in this business for sticking it to your customers. I know your costs can't be any more than $18 for those tires. We'll probably be ordering some 800,000 sets of tires for our new model this year. Let's skip the preliminaries and get down to the lowest price you guys can give me. You know we have other vendors we're talking to, and they are all willing to come down in price for this much business.

Ron: Our price is $55. Given the quality of our product, we feel we don't have to negotiate a price. The product sells itself.

Bo: What you mean is that you really want to stick it to your large original equipment manufacturers. Even with the volume we're talking about, you are too greedy. If you really wanted our business, you'd try to do business with us. This take-it-or-leave-it attitude of yours is going to backfire on you one of these days.

Ron: Fine. The company doesn't allow us salespeople any leeway in setting price.

Bo: You mean you can't come down, even with the volume we're talking about here?

Ron: That's right. We have the best steel-belted radials in the market, and we can afford not to negotiate on price.

Bo: All right. You're missing an opportunity here for some big business, but if that's the way you do business, then you're never going to be able to sell to us.

Questions

1. Is this a good illustration of how negotiation should take place?

2. How should Ron have handled the negotiation?

The Art of Closing

Key Terms

assumptive close
balance-sheet close
close
closing on a question
(contingent decision close)
continuous-yes close
demonstration close

direct close
"does-it-all" close
door-in-the-face close
minor-point close
"pave-the-way" question
probability close
qualifying close

standing-room-only close
suggestion close
summarization close
tentative-confirmation close
trial-order close

Learning Objectives

Learning Objectives

After studying Chapter 13, you will understand:

- How the many myths about closing err
- Why it is difficult for many salespeople to close
- When it is appropriate to close
- The purpose of the trial close

- How to handle the close itself
- How to handle "no"
- Future call strategy
- Proper techniques for departure and follow-up

Imagine an automobile salesperson talking to a prospect just after presenting features and benefits and taking the prospect for a demonstration ride. The prospect might ask, "When can I get a car like this?" The salesperson might reply with one of the following statements: "It depends on what we have on the lot" or "It depends on the options you want" or "In a week maybe." But the salesperson should not be surprised if none of these statements prompts a sale. A response on the order of "When do you want it?" or "We'll have it ready for you on Tuesday" is needed to close. The other responses are not closes; they merely provide additional information. To them, customers can easily answer, "Fine, I'll think it over," but to "When do you want it?" they must commit themselves. Either they decide they want the car, or they must reveal their remaining doubts and objections to the salesperson.

What then, is the definition of a close? A **close** is a question, declaration, or action by a salesperson designed to secure from the prospect an affirmative decision to buy.[1]

close
A question, declaration, or action by a salesperson designed to secure from the prospect an affirmative decision to buy.

13-1 Myths about Closing

Probably no other part of the selling process is subject to more myths and half-truths than the close. Many sales executives view a successful close as something akin to a combat victory. Salespeople stalk prospects, meeting each of their delays and objections with a telling counter. One sales manager commented about the close, "That's when you zero in. You've found out where your prospect's soft spots are, and you come in for the kill."[2]

This picture of the close as a wrestling match is reinforced in the popular literature. Books and articles portray the customer as a relatively passive creature just waiting to be manipulated by the aggressive salesperson. The salesperson is admonished to be more aggressive—to try just one more time and eventually maul the prospect into submission.

Experienced salespeople will recognize this picture as totally inaccurate. Things just do not happen this way. Seldom does the sales representative leave a wounded purchasing agent in the office. In relationship selling, the close is viewed as the culmination of the problem-solving process. The close is seen as an integral part of the two-way communication process. No close can handle a sale that was mishandled earlier. The salesperson earns the right to close by establishing a counseling relationship with the prospect, discovering the prospect's needs and problems, establishing an agreement as to the nature of the problem, and demonstrating in a convincing manner how the product or service will resolve this problem.

If salespeople look upon their job as one of helping people (the real principle behind relationship selling), they are likely to be successful. Although the stereotype of salespeople is one of aggressiveness and manipulation, these people are the exception, not the rule. Their longevity in the selling profession is limited.

13-2 The Need for the Close

Although the salesperson should learn to view the close as an opportunity to help rather than do battle, this does not diminish the need for closing. A sales representative is doomed to disappointment if he or she depends on the prospect to take the initiative and sign the order. After a good presentation, many salespeople feel the prospect should take the initiative and buy without being asked. Sometimes that happens, but not often. No matter how badly the prospect wants the product, negative thoughts may interfere. Thoughts of possible loss (spending money on something that does not work) or fear of disapproval from one's associates can become powerful enough to halt the purchase. At this point, it is likely that prospects begin to think of other competing wants—that new tennis racquet or set of golf clubs—that they will have to postpone buying. Whatever the specific reason, when the time for commitment arrives, prospects may develop "buyer's crisis."[3] Think back to the last time you bought a DVD player, car, or some other major item. You know you wanted it badly, but you just could not quite come around to that final decision to buy. At this point, many buyers (probably most) require the salesperson's help. The salesperson must do something to induce commitment by the prospect. Otherwise the prospect is never going to enjoy the benefits and satisfactions of buying. The sales representative must close the order and halt the "yes or no" battle going on in the prospect's mind.

Despite the need for closing, it is astounding how many salespeople never attempt a close. According to one estimate—and as shown in Figure 13-1, in 20 percent of all contacts, the customer takes the initiative and closes the sale; in about 20 percent of the cases, the salesperson tries to close the sale; and in 60 percent of all customer–salesperson contacts, the salesperson makes no effort to close, and the sale is never made.[4]

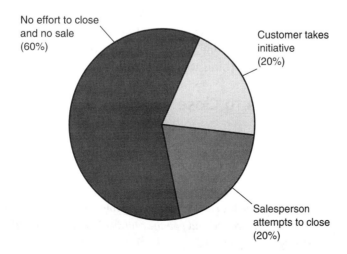

Figure 13-1
Attempts at Closing

13-3 Why Salespeople Don't Close

If the need for closing is so evident, why is it that salespeople do not ask for the order? The answer is simply fear; they fear rejection. Hearing "No!" is a blow to one's pride and self-esteem. It is no wonder then that many salespeople put off asking for the order. They know that if they don't ask, they won't be rejected.

Failing to close is like the baseball player who stands with his bat on his shoulder, never swinging at a pitch. Babe Ruth is not remembered for his record number of strikeouts. He is remembered for his home runs.

The most the batter who never swings can hope for is a walk. The salesperson who never attempts a close can only hope for mediocrity. As one successful salesperson put it, "I figured out the worst that could happen was the prospect would say no and I'd lose the sale. Since I'd lose if I didn't ask for the order, things could only be better if I gave it a try . . . and they were."

Salespeople need to recognize that buyers are not rejecting them as individuals; it is their product or service about which the prospect has doubts. What sales representatives need to do is separate "I failed" from "I'm a failure" in their minds. "I failed" means that "it didn't work" or "this time, I didn't get the order." "I'm a failure" says "I'm not much as a person." From "I failed," the salesperson can learn and try again. But from "I'm a failure," only more failure will come, and this can destroy self-esteem. Few people can take "no" personally day after day without suffering.

Failure to close is also symptomatic of another problem. Despite all the features and benefits present in the product, many salespeople still feel they are selling people things they do not need and are putting something over on them. They seem to feel as if they are somehow begging for money instead of solving prospect problems. This becomes evident in their failure to use proper closing techniques. They use statements such as, "You wouldn't want to buy this, would you?" and indicate nonverbally that they don't feel comfortable or confident about asking prospects to buy.

Salespeople should honestly view the close as an opportunity to help prospects. If salespeople know from the recognition process that their product is best for the buyer, then they should close with the idea in mind that failure represents a loss for both buyer and seller. One loses the satisfaction of helping someone else solve a problem and the other loses the satisfaction of ownership.

A critical skill that diminishes the chances of a rejection is asking for feedback throughout the call, for example, after you have delivered your presentation, responded to an objection, or answered a question. Illustrations of checking questions are, "How does that sound?" "How would that work?" "What do you think about. . . ?" By asking for feedback on what you have said, you gain critical information and you increase your confidence to close. If you don't check for feedback throughout the meeting, asking at the end of the call becomes an all-or-nothing situation with everything at stake; hence, many salespeople are reluctant to ask.[5]

13-4 When to Close

Although the salesperson must accept the necessity of closing, this does not deny its difficulty. The close requires some tactical gymnastics by the sales representative. As one sales manager commented:

> You've built up this nice friendly thing; you're interested in him, in his problems, in his accomplishments. He likes you. Everything's warm and beautiful. Then suddenly you have to turn around and pop the contract in front of him. It's like your mother suddenly asking you to pay rent.[6]

One way of easing this difficult transition into the close is by knowing when to close. If the buyer has signified some interest in the product, then the transition will not be nearly as abrupt and fraught with anxiety.

The basic idea is to close only when the buyer appears interested. The salesperson, despite admonitions to be a "tiger," should avoid closing attempts when clients seem disinterested, confused, or otherwise not ready to act. Closing at the wrong time can antagonize a buyer, even an interested one. For example, if a buyer has shown interest in the presentation to this point but suddenly states, "I don't understand how that feature works," attempts to close are likely to prove fatal. A close here would make the salesperson appear to be pushing too hard. The probable reaction of the prospect would be to push back—a no-win confrontation for both parties.

So when should the salesperson seek to close? The answer is any time during the course of the interview when the opportunity arises. In contrast to past theories, no longer is there thought to be just one magic moment at which the sales representative should close.[7] The typical sales conversation includes many points at which it is perfectly logical for the salesperson to seek a favorable decision:

1. *When the prospect agrees with the value of a benefit just described by the sales representative.* For example, if Ron Friendly from Superior Hospital Uniform Company were to say, "Experience has shown that laundry costs will drop by 10 to 15 percent with our new garments" and the prospect replies, "That sounds great!" then Ron should close. There is no reason to go on without at least an attempt. Continuing allows time for more objections to arise or, even worse, for "buyer's crisis" to develop.

2. *When the prospect agrees with the salesperson's response to an objection.*[8] Again, with Ron Friendly, a dialogue like the following might develop:

    Prospect: Your costs are $50 greater than the competition.

    Ron: Yes, but when you consider that our uniform last two years longer, that works out to be a little over $2 a month, or 50 cents a week.

    Prospect: Yeah, I guess you're right.

    Here, too, an attempt to close is appropriate.

3. *When there is a propitious silence.*[9] The salesperson has ceased talking, and the prospect has asked all the questions that have occurred to him or her. Both sit there like a couple of chess players figuring out their next move. Close!

4. *When buyers give some verbal indication that they are sold on the product.* This might include questions or statements such as:[10]

    It sounds pretty good to me.

    Will you have a project leader assigned to this?

    Shipment must be complete in 15 months.

    You say your people will help train us to use it?

    How would I have to pay for it?

    What would happen if I changed my mind?

    Is delivery included in the price?

    Does it come in light blue?

    How soon can you deliver it?

    Can you refresh my memory about how the service contract works?

5. *After the buyer has given some nonverbal indication of interest.* Reading nonverbal signals is imperfect at best, but the following actions do indicate that a prospect may be ready to buy:[11]
   a. Reexamining the product
   b. Picking up a pencil and starting to figure
   c. Leaving the room to talk with someone else about the presentation
   d. If the call is being made at home, suggesting a move from the living room to the more relaxed atmosphere of the kitchen or dining room
   e. Subtle indications of interest such as nodding one's head up and down, rubbing and holding one's chin, leaning forward with a friendly facial expression and gesture, relaxed body posture, and a normal even-modulated voice

6. *The customer has been fairly quiet and then suddenly begins asking a lot of questions or the pace of the conversation picks up or slows down significantly.*[12] Salespeople must continually look for closing signals; otherwise, there is always the danger of passing up an opportunity to close and ultimately losing the sale. Too many salespeople are more adept at talking than listening and end up talking their way out of a sale. If the customer is ready to buy, the salesperson should stop talking immediately and close. This is especially true for big-ticket times, if the buyer is very sophisticated (e.g., a professional purchasing agent), and if there is the intention of establishing a continuing long-term relationship. In such situations, closing is still necessary, but the salesperson should avoid too much pressure. Put simply, the psychological effect of pressure seems to be that with small decisions, it's easier for the buyer to say "yes" than to have an argument; hence, pressure is positive here. However, this isn't evidently the case with big decisions. The bigger the decision, the more negatively buyers react to pressure. Therefore, the salesperson should still attempt to close, but with fewer attempts and with less pressure.[13] Figure 13-2 summarizes the ways to tell when the time is right to close a sale.

13-5 The Trial Close

In addition to closing opportunities that arise spontaneously, the sales representative may create opportunities for closing by using a trial close. In contrast to full-fledged closing methods, the trial close is a question designed to elicit prospects' reactions without forcing them to make a firm yes-or-no buying decision.[14] It will reveal either further objections or an unmistakable opportunity to close.

A trial close might be phrased in the form of an open question. For example, the salesperson might ask: "Do you have any other questions?" A negative reply would suggest the prospect is close to making a decision. Or the open question might take the form: "Where shall we go from here?" "How should we proceed on this?" or "What's your overall opinion on this?" If the prospect were to respond, "You've given me all the information I need" or "I think you've made a good presentation," then the salesperson can close the order."

A trial close might be a **"pave-the-way" question.**[15] Such a question is not a close itself but tells the salesperson how to close. For example, an automobile salesperson might ask, "Is there any reason, besides money, that would prevent you from buying?" The real estate salesperson might ask, "Is there anything besides financing

"pave-the-way" question
A question that tells the salesperson how to close. The salesperson might ask, "Is there anything besides financing that would keep you from buying?

Here are four ways to tell when the time is right to close the sale:

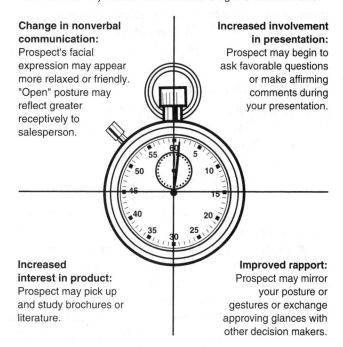

Change in nonverbal communication: Prospect's facial expression may appear more relaxed or friendly. "Open" posture may reflect greater receptivity to salesperson.

Increased involvement in presentation: Prospect may begin to ask favorable questions or make affirming comments during your presentation.

Increased interest in product: Prospect may pick up and study brochures or literature.

Improved rapport: Prospect may mirror your posture or gestures or exchange approving glances with other decision makers.

Figure 13-2
When to Close

that would keep you from putting in an offer on this home?" If the answer is "yes," then the sales representative can spend time handling the objection. As one top sales rep explains, "People often won't want to share the real reason why they're not buying, so you have to be a little sneaky," she says. "I like to ask, 'Other than that, is there anything else that's bothering you?' When you ask if there's anything else, they'll get to what they're really thinking. I use that all the time."[16] If the answer is "no," then money is the problem, and alternative means for financing can be introduced. Though it may resemble a definite attempt to close, the trial close is used only to probe and reveal how far along prospects are in their decision making. The advantage of the trial close is that it avoids a confrontation with prospects. Because it requires no conclusive yes or no answers from prospects, the salesperson can determine what they are thinking without running a risk of hardening their positions. This is especially true early in the interview. A full-fledged close requiring a yes or no may force prospects into an intractable position, one from which they will never deviate. So the trial close is a subtle way of testing prospects' temperaments. The salesperson may hope to close but doesn't really expect to. If prospects answer affirmatively, however, the sales representative may move on to asking directly for the order. If not, the salesperson can seek clarification and handle objections without putting prospects on the defensive.

13-6 The Close Itself

Closes come in literally hundreds of forms. However, they basically represent variations on comparatively few techniques, and it is these we will discuss. Few attempts or more, persistence is based on being able to effectively use and blend different closing methods each time. If not, it is extremely difficult to make a second and third closing attempt with the same technique. Moreover, some techniques are more appropriate at certain times than others. Since it may appear to be confrontational, many sales reps reserve the direct close until the very last, figuring if all the prior indirect methods have failed, why not try it? Even if only one out of 20 prospects then decide to buy, that is 5 percent better than walking out the door with nothing.

13-6a The Direct Close

Here the salesperson asks directly for the order: "Can I get your signature on this contract?" or "Why don't you write out a check and we'll get this purchase order processed." This close is simplicity itself, yet it may be quite effective in certain circumstances. When the prospect has raised straightforward business objections to which the salesperson has responded satisfactorily, the **direct close** is appropriate.

direct close
The salesperson directly asks the prospect for a yes or no answer.

The big disadvantage to the direct close is that if it fails, you've probably lost the sale. Unlike lower-pressure closes, such as the assumptive or summarization, to which the prospect is likely to respond, "I haven't decided yet," the direct close does not allow the opportunity of continuing the sale. You've more or less demanded that the customers commit themselves, and if they give you a "no," it's hard to get a second chance. You have put them in a position where, in order to buy, they must reverse themselves. Nobody likes to be caught equivocating, and in a sales situation, it's especially distasteful, because it suggests a lack of sales resistance. Experienced salespeople may attempt to recover by asking politely, "Could you explain why you can't buy at this time?" and after receiving a response, "How can we resolve that?"

The suitability of a closing technique varies by the four personality types: Driver, Analytical, Amiable, and Expressive. The direct close is especially valuable in closing with Drivers. Because such buyers appreciate directness and forthrightness from salespeople, asking for the order is a good tactic, provided that the merits of the product or service have been persuasively presented. In contrast, the direct close is likely to be ineffective with Amiables (and Analyticals), who find it difficult to make a decision.

summarization close
The salesperson takes the major benefits and presents them in summary form.

13-6b The Summarization Close

In the **summarization close,** the sales representative takes major benefits in which the prospect has indicated interest and presents these benefits in summary form. This repetition is especially advantageous if several calls have preceded the close and many important points were covered. In using the summarization close, Ron Friendly of Superior Hospital Uniform Company might say:

> *Of course, Mr. Prospect, this is an important decision, so to make the best possible choice, you may want to go over some of the major concepts we've discussed. I believe we more or less agreed that Superior's new surgical uniform will provide some definite advantages. First, it will lower your hospital laundry costs; second, the uniforms will last longer, saving you money; and third, your surgical people will be happier because they'll look better in our uniforms.*

In the summarization close, the salesperson does not explicitly ask the prospect to reply, but the silence following the summary carries that unspoken imperative to answer. If no answer is forthcoming, however, it is appropriate to follow with another type of close.

The summarization close is valuable in reminding prospects of benefits mentioned in previous sales calls or earlier during a current call. It is also helpful in reminding buyers of objections they had raised previously but that the salesperson handled satisfactorily.

In ordering the points in a summarization close, many salespeople begin with those to which prospects have demonstrated the most agreement and end with one to which they have shown some resistance. The underlying philosophy of this strategy is to build momentum toward a favorable decision. Each time the prospect mentally agrees with a point, disagreement is that much less likely on the following one. A series of positive mental responses establishes an immovable predisposition to buy.

The summarization technique is a good closing technique for the Driver and the Analytical. Both of these personality types like to make their own decisions on the basis of the objective facts. Closes that are anything but straightforward are likely to backfire with them.

13-6c The Balance-Sheet Close

With the **balance-sheet close,** the sales representative takes out a sheet of paper and draws a large "T" across it. For this reason, it is sometimes called the *T-account close.* The salesperson lists reasons for buying on one side of the T and on the other side reasons for not buying. A balance sheet for selling a new PC might look like this:

balance-sheet close
The salesperson draws a large "T" on a sheet of paper, listing the reasons to buy on one side and not to buy on the other.

Reasons for Acting	Reasons for Not Acting
1. It will cut your inventory costs.	1. Price is $500 higher than the NRC396.
2. It will run Windows XP.	2. It will require some initial up-front investment in new software.
3. It will handle your payroll faster and with fewer errors.	
4. It requires only a minimum of operator training.	
5. It can be expanded easily to accommodate a laser printer, disc drives, and DVD so that the Cybertron should suffice for many years to come.	
6. A substantial trade-in allowance is offered on your old 1.5-gigahertz processor PC.	

Notice that the reasons for acting are stated with respect to the prospect's major alternative, an NRC396. If there had been a different alternative, the balance sheet would have to be restructured. Also, notice that the criteria include the prospect's major buying motives—cutting inventory, processing payroll faster, and easy expansion. Once the balance sheet is drawn up, the sales representative must request the order or ask an open question such as, "How do you feel about this?"

The sales representative may wish to elaborate on this closing method by arranging pros and cons in order of priority because some points will always be more important than others. Prospects can then make a decision by comparing the total priority points associated with reasons to buy with those associated with reasons not to buy. Some sales representatives have augmented the balance-sheet close by listing advantages themselves and then turning the sheet over to prospects to fill in the disadvantages, the idea being to increase the salesperson's credibility in the process.

Whatever the exact form, the balance-sheet close is useful with Drivers and Analyticals because it appeals to their rationality and logic. For Analyticals, the balance-sheet close is especially advantageous. Because Analyticals have a tendency to extend the decision-making process, the salesperson may hasten action by clearly spelling out the problem in the balance sheet and letting the Analytical demonstrate his or her problem-solving ability.

The balance-sheet close is further valuable for situations in which prospects have raised relatively inconsequential, but nevertheless valid, objections. If so, the salesperson can still close the order, pointing out, "Mr./Ms. Buyer, are you willing to give up all these benefits for these minor inconveniences?"

VIDEO

13-6d The Continuous-Yes Close

This close uses the principle that saying "yes" gets to be a habit. The salesperson asks a number of sequential summary questions, each formulated so that the prospect answers "yes." The final question asks for the order. For example:

Salesperson: Do you feel that a good education is important to your children?

Prospect: Yes.

Salesperson: Do you think that a child who does his or her homework well will get a better education?

Prospect: Yes, I believe so.

Salesperson: Don't you agree that doing research and homework is easier for children with a PC at home?

Prospect: Yes.

Salesperson: Then it sounds to me as if you are ready to buy this PC.

The continuous-yes technique has a firm theoretical base in psychology. First, personal consistency is highly valued by members of society, whereas inconsistency is negatively valued. Second, generally consistent conduct provides a reasonable orientation to the world. Usually, we will be better off if our approach to the world is consistent. Otherwise our lives would be difficult, erratic, and disjointed. Finally, personal consistency provides a valuable shortcut through the disorder of modern life. Once we have made up our minds about an issue or have decided how to act in a given situation, we no longer have to process all of the relevant information when subsequently confronted with the same (or a similar) issue or situation. We only need to recall the earlier decision and respond consistently with it.[17]

The salesperson has a variety of yes sets from which to choose: "Will you agree with me?" "Do you ever encounter?" "Does this sound like something you've heard before?" Ending a statement with "OK" or "all right" represents yet another alternative.

It is also helpful to make the client comfortable by presenting undeniably true statements that are easy to agree with. The more people agree, the more likely they are to continue agreeing. It can be as simple as, "You're interested in saving on your taxes, aren't you?"

When prospects say "no," the salesperson can replay their response and substitute a yes response. "Then price is the most important factor to you, is that right?"

The **continuous-yes close** is most appropriate for Amiables, who may have trouble making decisions. With Drivers, who like making their own decisions quickly and decisively, other closes may be more effective. When employing the continuous-yes close, salespeople must take great care. They should be careful to pace prospect body language, tempo, loudness, and pitch. They should avoid giving any messages of condescension. Certainly, they should avoid sounding like a hawker at a carnival: "You say you want performance, tell you what I am going to do." Seeking "yeses" in rapid-fire order also should be avoided.

continuous-yes close
The salesperson asks a series of questions, each designed to elicit a "yes" from the prospect, the last one of which is the request to buy.

13-6e The Assumptive Close

In the **assumptive close,** the salesperson assumes that agreement has already been reached. For instance, a salesperson might tell a purchasing agent, "I'll help your assistant write up the order." The assumptive close is effective because it makes prospect inertia work for salespeople rather than against them. Most closes require positive action by prospects, but many prospects resist taking action. However, with the assumptive close, prospects have to take action to stop the salesperson. If they sit there passively, the sale is made. Moreover, should there still remain latent resistance, it is likely to come out now because prospects must respond overtly to say "no". Few, if any, negative consequences result from the assumptive close, but there are two positive ones: either the sale is closed or prospect objections are quickly identified. Moreover, the assumptive close can be used in conjunction with almost any other close and at most any time during the call after the problem has been satisfied.

The assumptive close is useful when commitment and decision making are difficult for prospects (Amiables and Analyticals, but to a lesser degree). It is also more effective with existing customers than with new ones. When there is a long-term relationship between buyer and seller, the buyer is more likely to accept the seller's recommendation without question.

In using the assumptive close, the salesperson frequently leaps right over the basic buying decision to a subordinate or subsequent question. This might include:

1. *A "which" choice.* "Should we deliver on Monday or Tuesday?" "Should we order the executive or standard model?"
2. *An "implicit" choice.* These questions also assume that the customer has already made the basic decision to buy, but the choice is not as explicitly spelled out as earlier; rather, a subordinate choice is implied, such as "How soon do you need it?" "How many do you need?" or "Do you want to take it with you?"
3. *Action closes.* Here a physical action by the sales representative may work just as well as an assumptive question. When the salesperson starts the presentation, he or she pulls out a blank "agreement" form. It's a good idea to get the agreement or order form in front of the prospect as soon as possible, so when it comes time to begin filling it out, the prospect won't be startled by its sudden appearance. As he or she discusses the customer's wants, they fill in the blanks. When everything is specified, the salesperson asks the customer to "verify" it. That is, hand over the agreement after you've finished writing up the sale. Ask the buyer to double-check the facts and figures, while running through the selling points one more time for verification. Notice here that asking for verification is less offensive than asking the prospect to "sign here." For the same reason, it is good to leave out the word *order.* Similarly, an *agreement* is better than a *contract.* Should the prospect protest when the salesperson fills out the agreement during the course of the presentation, the salesperson replies, "Don't be concerned. It's simply a worksheet for me to make sure I consider all your needs." Another example of an assumptive close would be for a salesperson to say: "What you need is our model A unit. May I use your phone to see if we have one in stock?" If the prospects say you can use the phone, they, in effect, are saying they will take the model. Some salespeople just pull out their laptop computer, saying, "Let me take a minute to confirm what we've talked about. . . ."[18] Assumptive closes are especially useful for trade salespeople who frequently must confront buyers in a hurry. In these situations, the trade representative can proceed: "After taking your current inventory and considering your last two years' orders, I believe two cases should handle you through October. Is that about right?"[19]

VIDEO

assumptive close
The salesperson assumes that the buyer wishes to buy and it is time to make a subordinate decision. The assumptive close can ask for a "which" choice, an implicit choice, or involve an action.

13-6f The Minor-Point Close

A variation of the assumptive close (but one so common that it merits separate mention) is the **minor-point close,** which seeks agreement on relatively minor issues associated with the full order. Instead of asking the prospect to buy, the salesperson asks whether the prospect would prefer *cash or charge, red or green, with or without a bag.* The basic premise of the minor-point close is that small decisions are easier than major ones. It is easier for a car buyer to decide on color, white sidewall tires, or cruise control than it is to decide whether to buy the car. The salesperson often uses a number of minor points and builds momentum toward the final decision. As the final step, the salesperson might request that the prospect "verify" the agreement: "Is this quantity satisfactory?" Other possibilities suffice (e.g., "Will this be cash or charge?") as does, "Would you prefer to accept delivery today or would next week fit your schedule better?" The minor-point close is particularly useful with people who have difficulty making decisions and are cooperative. They feel more comfortable with little decisions than with big ones, especially if much money is involved. Accordingly, like the assumptive close, the minor-point close is advisable for Amiables (and Analyticals), not Drivers. The minor-point close works for Analyticals, because they like to follow a step-by-step approach. They are the prospects who speak in terms of "First, we need . . ., second, we have to . . ., and third, we'll have to. . . ."

13-6g The Qualifying Close

With the **qualifying close,** salespeople seek to close by disproving a prospect's objection. In fact, this close if often known as *closing on an objection.* When prospects object to a certain point, sales representatives seek a commitment to buy if they can show the objection to be without substance. For example, the following dialogue might occur in the sale of a vacuum cleaner:

> **Prospect:** But your machine isn't that good with drapes, is it?
> **Salesperson:** If I can show you that it will clean drapes, you'll want to buy it now, won't you?

After getting commitment, the salesperson would then proceed to demonstrate the ability of the machine to vacuum drapes. After agreeing to buy upon demonstration, the prospect can recant only with some loss of integrity.

Although the qualifying close sounds similar to a pave-the-way question, there is a subtle but important difference. In a pave-the-way question, the salesperson raises the issue, "Is there anything besides financing that stands in our way?" In a qualifying close, it is the prospect who raises an objection.

Because Expressives enjoy an exciting, fast-moving, and challenging environment, the qualifying close can be an effective tactic with them. If it appears transparently manipulative, however—as if the salesperson is trying to put something over on the buyer—the qualifying close can backfire. Hence, it is important to watch nonverbal behavior and convey an image of sincerity when using the qualifying close.

13-6h The Standing-Room-Only Close

With a **standing-room-only close,** the salesperson tries to get the prospect to act now to take advantage of an impending event or an opportunity soon to end. An industrial sales representative, for example, might say to a prospect, "We're looking at an across-the-board price increase in the next two weeks, so my advice is to buy now." A retail salesperson might tell a customer, "We only have one more dress available in your size in that style. The way it's been selling, I don't think it will be here if you wait until Saturday." Or a real estate salesperson might say, "If you're interested in this house, then I would recommend putting in an offer on it immediately since there are a lot of people looking at it." Other sources for putting together a standing-room-only (SRO) close are extended credit terms, advertising allowances, seasonal packaging, and cash discounts.

A special form of the SRO close is appropriately enough named the *special inducement close.* The salesperson offers a special onetime deal to get the prospect to buy. For example, a business equipment salesperson might say, "If you buy today, we'll include free installation and a 2-hour training course for your people for nothing."

The standing-room-only close and the special inducement work because of the human desire to avoid a loss. If your neighbor knocked at your door at 3 A.M. to tell you how to make $100, you would think him crazy and kick him out. But if he came to your house to tell you someone was stealing the $75 tires off your car, you would bolt down the stairs in an effort to halt the theft.

The SRO close is firmly based in social science research.[20] As opportunities and the items they contain become more scarce, they are perceived as more valuable. Precious stones and metals, for example, are precious precisely because of their scarcity. There is a direct relationship between limited supply and assigned worth; in fact, an item's availability is often taken to indicate it's worth. In one study, wholesale beef buyers who were told of an impending beef shortage purchased significantly more than those who were not informed. Moreover, it has been found that scarcity is more effective when it is produced by social demand. This finding supports the importance of competition in the pursuit of limited resources. We want a scarce item even more when in competition for it.

Still, SRO and special inducements are not universally effective. They work best with excitable and enthusiastic Expressives, but even here it is important to exercise care. The SRO close can appear manipulative and high-pressured, causing prospects to resist rather than buy. It is good idea to deliver the SRO in a matter-of-fact tone, hoping to leave the impression that the salesperson is merely stating the fact and not trying to maneuver the prospect into an unfortunate buying decision.

13-6i The Demonstration Close

Because of multiple buying influences, closing represents an especially difficult task for the industrial salesperson. One way of handling this problem is by bringing together all the participants in a buying decision at a demonstration of the product; this is known as the **demonstration close.** Among this group, the sales representative should arrange to have one or more preferably influential persons who are convinced of the product's merits. They can be used as "inside salespeople" with the other buying influences. After showing the machine in operation, the sales representative can seek agreement from the inside salespeople, hoping that their enthusiasm will convince the skeptics.[21]

This close is strictly low-pressure because the prospects are totally in control of the situation. By seeing the equipment in operation, skeptical buyers like Analyticals may be convinced. This will be particularly true if pressure is put on them from other members of the group.

13-6j The Tentative-Confirmation Close

When a prospect has trouble making a decision, it frequently pays to confirm the sale by using the **tentative-confirmation close.** This technique can be very effective because it tends simultaneously to build momentum toward firm confirmation and

demonstration close
The salesperson brings all the multiple buying influences together at a demonstration, hoping those favorable to the purchase will influence those unfavorable.

tentative-confirmation close
Seeking a conditional "yes" from a prospect contingent on such matters as financing or delivery.

to end the prospect's shopping process. For example, when a prospective customer's finances must be checked out and this process requires a week or more, the salesperson can say, "Our finance department typically requires a week to approve customer credit. Why don't we go ahead and place your order? Next week, by the time your credit has been approved, if you decide differently, you can always cancel the order. There's no charge."

Some industries require long delivery dates because of manufacturing, production, or some other lag time. If the salesperson works in such an industry, the tentative confirmation is a useful close. An example of what can be said to an uncertain prospect is, "It's going to be six weeks before it leaves the warehouse anyway. Why don't we go ahead and order one? I'll give you a call at the end of the fifth week to confirm that you still want it. If you change your mind, fine. I'll use it for another client."

Another possibility is the "subject to" close. The "subject to" close is the same one that your life insurance agent uses on you when he or she says, "Quite frankly, I don't know if we can get this much insurance on someone your age. It would be 'subject to' you passing the physical anyway, so why don't we just write up the paper work subject to your passing the physical?" The life insurance agent knows that if you can fog a mirror during that physical, he or she can get you that insurance. But it doesn't sound as though you're making as important a decision as you really are. The qualified "subject to" close in this instance would be, "Let's just write up the paperwork subject to the right of your specifications committee to reject the proposal within a 24-hour period for any specifications reason." Or, "Let's just write up the paperwork subject to the right of your legal department to reject the proposal within a 24-hour period for any legal reason." Notice that you're not saying subject to their acceptance. You're saying subject to their right to decline it for a specific reason. If they were going to refer it to an attorney, it would be a legal reason. If they were going to refer it to their CPA, it would be a tax reason, and so on. But try to get it nailed down to a specific reason.[22]

The advantage of the tentative confirmation is that it begins the commitment, and sometimes prospects (e.g., Amiables and Analyticals, to a lesser extent) need a little impetus to do what is in their best interest. Granted, it might not be the strongest commitment, but it still represents a commitment. Moreover, people tend to stop shopping around once they have given a commitment. Psychologically, once they've made some form of commitment, no matter how tentative, they feel the decision is made and they don't bother to keep shopping.

13-6k The Trial-Order Close

trial-order close
Order of less than typical size to use a product for free for a specified time.

Another method of closing is the **trial-order close,** in which the salesperson attempts to convince the prospect to place a trial order. This may include orders of less than the typical size so that the prospect may try out the product. Sometimes it involves placing a piece of equipment (a copier, for example), which the prospect may use at no charge. The idea in both instances is for prospects to convince themselves of the merits of the product. Some experts call the trial order the "puppy-dog" close. After taking the puppy home from the pet store and having it a week, who can take the puppy dog back? Initially, 3M's Post-it® notes were not well received. When the idea was presented to office supply distributors, they took market surveys that showed a negative response. It wasn't until the little notepads were sent to secretaries of CEOs at *Fortune* 500 companies that the idea caught on. They couldn't do without the puppy dog.

Usually, the trial order is used only as a last resort. Processing orders in less than minimum quantities is an expensive proposition. Putting demonstrators in prospects' offices is also expensive and prevents the equipment from being used in selling to other prospects. This is why to close the sale many sales reps should first mention the money-back guarantee, if the prospect is not completely satisfied. This doesn't require delivering the product to the prospect's site of business. Nonetheless, the trial order may be effective in convincing skeptical clients (Analyticals, for example).

13-6l The Suggestion Close

Of all the closing techniques, this is the most low-pressured. The objective of the **suggestion close** is to have prospects accept the salesperson's recommendation without a great deal of thought. This sounds as if the salesperson is trying to manipulate the buyer into doing something unintentional, something to the seller's benefit and not the buyer's. Appearance to the contrary, the suggestion close is completely acceptable in the proper set of circumstances. Imagine an executive buying a small business computer for the first time. Faced with a seemingly endless series of choices regarding hardware and software, and with little experience on which to base a decision, the executive might easily back away rather than make a wrong choice. Here the salesperson might suggest: "Many hardware dealers like yourself have opted to buy only PCs with Windows XP."

Expressives will react favorably to suggestion closes, especially when testimonials are used. Amiables are also candidates for this type of close because it speaks to what *others* are doing. It may require follow-up by an assumptive close, however.

The suggestion close works because it is low pressure, and we all feel less risk if we know we are buying what the majority of people are purchasing. This is especially true when our technical knowledge of the new product or service is limited.

suggestion close
The salesperson's objective is to get the prospect to accept the salesperson's recommendation without much thought. Often, it involves telling what other buyers in the same situation have done.

13-6m Closing on a Question (Contingent Decision Close)

When customers ask the salesperson a question such as, "Can I get it in red?" instead of simply answering "Yes," the salesperson can respond, "Do you want it in red?" When they respond in the affirmative, the sale is closed. Another example might be: "Can I get it delivered by the first of the month?" The salesperson can reply, "Do you want it the first?" Of course, there is the question of what to do if the prospect answers "No!" The response is that the salesperson can then take a different tack or approach in the presentation.

> **Prospect:** Will this policy feature a cash value?
>
> **Salesperson:** Is cash value important to you?
>
> **Prospect:** Definitely not! I don't want to be paying extra for cash value.
>
> **Salesperson:** I'm happy to hear you say that. Let me show you how our 10-year term policy works. . . .

It should be pointed out how **closing on a question** differs from a qualifying close, because they sound similar. The difference is that in the qualifying close, the sales rep closes on an objection; here, the sales rep closes on a question. Because the salesperson puts the issue squarely back in the prospect's lap, closing on a question is sometimes called a "porcupine" close. If someone tossed you a porcupine, what would you do? You'd toss it right back.

This close is best for Drivers and Expressives, who are competitive, fast acting risk-takers. For these reasons, it is less useful for Amiables and Analyticals.

**closing on a question
(contingent decision close)**
When prospects ask a question, sales reps respond with a question that closes the sale.

13-6n The Probability Close

When the prospect indicates, "I want to think it over" or some variation of that objection, the salesperson may respond, "Mr./Ms. Prospect, that would be perfectly fine. I understand your desire to want to think it over, but let me ask you this. When I call back next week, what is the probability, in percentage terms out of a total of 100, that you and I will be doing business?" This technique is called the **probability close.**

The prospect's response can generally be divided into three possible categories:

1. *More than 50 percent but less than 85 percent.* Prospects who respond in this range typically still have some remaining objection. The salesperson should ask what the remaining percentage is against and remain silent, putting pressure on them to reveal their hidden objections. Once these are identified, the salesperson can proceed, answering the objection and moving to the close.

2. *Above 85 percent but not 100 percent.* In this range, the salesperson should respond, "As it is almost certain that we are going to do business together, why wait another week? Let's go ahead right now and get a running start on the project. If you decide in the next couple of days to change your mind, I'll gladly tear up the order."

3. *Less than 50 percent.* Something is amiss. The prospect has many objections and doubts remaining. The salesperson must begin the selling process anew, starting with open questions.

Because it objectively lays out the chances of buying, the probability close fits best for Drivers and Analyticals.

13-6o The "Does-It-All" Close

The **"does-it-all" close** is used when it appears that the prospect wants to shop around even if there is no need to do so. The salesperson should describe (point by point, if necessary) how the product or service fulfills every requirement of the prospect and that the price is reasonable, eliminating the need to spend valuable time looking at other choices. "Why spend a couple of days and $20 worth of gas shopping around, when the XYZ does everything you need and at a reasonable price?" the salesperson might ask. If the prospect admits the salesperson is correct, the sale is closed. A variation that one salesperson uses is to ask, "When you buy things, like a car or DVD, there are three decisions you make. One, can I afford it? Two, do I like it? Third, do I need it? If you answer yes to all of these, what do you do? You buy it, right? Well, we've answered yes to all three of these questions here, so why don't we move on this today?"

Because it seeks a fast decision, the does-it-all close is best for competitive, fast acting, take-charge Drivers and Expressives. It is not good for slower-acting Amiables and Analyticals.

13-6p The Door-in-the-Face Close

The **door-in-the-face close** works as follows. Suppose you are selling life insurance, for example, and you know a person who is likely to be a very difficult prospect, one likely to buy only after a number of attempts. The strategy is to give in by intentionally requesting something we know will be refused initially. Perhaps we suggest that he or she should buy a $1 million whole life policy. When the suggestion is refused (as expected), we engage in a bit of conciliation, making sure that the prospect recognizes that our next request indeed represents a concession. The second request, then, might be something like: "Well I see you're not interested in a whole life

probability close
The salesperson asks the prospect what is the probability of buying in percentage terms out of a possible 100 percent.

"does-it-all" close
The salesperson should describe (point by point, if necessary) how the product or service fulfills every requirement of the prospect and that the price is reasonable, eliminating the need to spend valuable time looking at other choices.

door-in-the-face close
The salesperson makes a large initial request that he or she expects to be rejected to get an acceptance of a smaller follow-up request.

policy; perhaps a term life arrangement, requiring considerably less cash, but sacrificing no protection, would suit your needs better."[23]

This door-in-the-face close works because of the principle of social reciprocity. This is why it is mandatory that the second request of the salesperson be recognized firmly as a concession. Transitional comments on the part of the salesperson should indicate acceptance of the initial refusal, and the second request must be significantly smaller (as perceived by the prospect) than the first. Otherwise the close might not work.

Scientific evidence to support the door-in-face close is available.[24] In a series of experiments, researchers determined that target persons who perceive that a requester has made concessions to them are more likely to comply with a second, moderated request than are those persons who are asked to yield only to the second request. For example, one group was asked to serve as counselors to juvenile delinquents for a period of two years and, having refused, were then asked to chaperone these delinquents on a 2-hour trip to the zoo. An equivalent group of people received only the chaperoning request. Whereas only 17 percent of the latter group complied, 50 percent of the first (door-in-the-face) group yielded to the chaperoning request.

The door-in-the-face close works best for Amiables, who are cooperative, "go along" individuals. It is less useful for other personality styles. Table 13-1 gives a summary of the methods that salespeople can use to close a sale.

13-7 Handling "No"

No matter how eloquent the presentation or well structured the close, sooner or later every salesperson is going to be turned down. The poor ones never get this far because they do not ask for the order; the mediocre ones meekly pack up their briefcases and leave; good sales representatives diplomatically, yet determinedly, try to find out why. Quite often, if the hidden objection can be found and satisfactorily responded to, the sale can still be closed.

If salespeople have some suspicion about the source of the resistance, they can probe to find it out. Closed questions can help here:

Do you feel our delivery schedule is adequate?

Have you found other prices more competitive?

Have you experienced trouble with our company in the past?

If the hidden objection is revealed in response to closed questions, the salesperson may respond, using any of the objections-handling techniques outlined in Chapter 11, "Handling Objections."

If, however, the salesperson has little idea about the source of resistance, an open question is called for. A salesperson might ask, "Apparently, somewhere or another, I've inadequately explained the merits of our product. For some reason, you still have grave doubts. Could you tell me what they are?" Only the most hardened of buyers could respond negatively to such a tactfully worded request. Quite often, the response will reveal—to the prospect as well as to the salesperson—that the resistance is not justified; the prospect reacted hastily or automatically without really thinking matters through objectively.

Still, there will be those occasions when there is no rescuing the sale. The salesperson must recognize failure. The trick is to exit gracefully, leaving an opening for future sales. One successful salesperson adopts this strategy: "I thank the fellow who

Table **13-1** A Summary of Closing Methods

Close	Examples	Useful With
Direct	"Shall we sign the order and schedule delivery for next week?"	Drivers
Summarization	"Mr. Jones, we have agreed (review all major points and benefits)."	Drivers and Analyticals
Balance sheet (T-account)	"On this side of the T, Ms. Prospect, we'll list all those reasons for acting, and on the other side we'll list some reasons for not acting."	Drivers and Analyticals
Continuous yes	"Don't you agree that this is the cheapest policy?" "Don't you agree that it provides you with the best coverage?" "Don't you think that the premiums are the finest in the industry?" "Shouldn't we sign the policy, then?"	Amiables (but use this method carefully)
Assumptive	"Then we'll be shipping in four weeks, correct?" "How many would you like to start with?" "Do you want to take it with you?"	Amiables (and Analyticals, to a lesser extent)
Minor point	"Which color is best for your office?" "Is this cash or charge?" "Would you like automatic fine tuning?"	Amiables and Analyticals
Qualifying	"If I can get you an extra $300 trade-in for your car, then you'll buy today, right?"	Expressives
Standing-room-only (SRO)	"Orders for the new line are coming in faster than our factory can turn them out. To protect your delivery needs, we need to get your order in by tomorrow afternoon." "If you order by Friday, you can get the special advertising allowance; after that, it's back to the list price."	Expressives
Special inducement	"If you buy this tent today, I'll throw in the backpack for free."	Expressives
Demonstration	The salesperson brings together all buying influences for a demonstration and lets an inside salesperson do the convincing.	Multiple Buying Influences and Analyticals
Tentative confirmation	"Why don't you go ahead and place the order? It'll take a week for the credit check and if you change your mind, it's no big deal."	Amiables (and Analyticals, to a lesser extent)
Trial order	The salesperson gets the prospect to place a limited trial order to try out the product or service.	Analyticals
Suggestion	The salesperson subtly suggests that a prospect buy, employing a testimonial, warranty, or competitive contrast. The idea is to get acquiescence without a great deal of thought.	Expressives and Amiables
Closing on a question	In response to the question, "Can I get it tomorrow?" the salesperson responds, "Do you want it tomorrow?"	Drivers and Expressives
Probability	The salesperson asks, "What is the probability in percentage terms of us doing business together?"	Drivers and Analyticals
Does-it-all	"What can you gain by shopping around except wasted time, tired feet, and worn nerves? You agree it fits your needs and our price is competitive. And when you buy from a reputable company like ours, our policy states that you can always bring it back if it isn't right."	Drivers and Expressives
Door-in-the-face	Make a large initial request that you expect to be rejected to get acceptance of a smaller second request.	Amiables

turns me down more than I do one who gives me an order. I want to show no hard feelings. I am there to service him any time he needs service. With so much discourtesy around, it's bound to make an impression."

13-8 Future Calls

A recent study of industrial salespeople found that:[25]

- 2 percent close the sale on the first call.
- 3 percent close on the second call.
- 4 percent close on the third call.
- 10 percent close on the fourth call.
- 81 percent close the sale on the fifth call.

Still, this persistence must be tempered. Studies of relationship selling demonstrate that closing attempts should be limited to one or two per sales call.[26] Accordingly, salespeople must be sure not to make a nuisance of themselves or to appear overly aggressive on subsequent sales calls, or they will ruin the chances of establishing a long-term relationship. It's hard to keep saying "no" to someone if they're likable and helpful. The more times the salesperson calls on prospects and shows a genuine, friendly interest in their problems, the harder it is for prospects to refuse them.

The best way to represent a product or service is simply to explain that since the salesperson made the previous offer to the prospect, he or she has acquired additional knowledge about it. Because so much forgetting between calls is likely, the salesperson can typically repeat benefits and features stressed on earlier calls without annoying the client with the repetition. Moreover, the price may have changed in the interval between calls; a lower price always demands a follow-up call. Since the last visit, the salesperson also may have received several orders from other clients; this allows the sales representative to quote the compliments given by the clients and recite the benefits they have received from the product or service. In other words, it is possible to maintain contact in nonconfrontational ways. Subsequent calls don't even have to be made in person; periodic letters, phone calls, and faxes are often as effective and less confrontational.

13-9 Departure and Follow-Up

After successfully closing the sale, the sales representative still has two tasks remaining: the departure and follow-up. These two activities are frequently ignored by many salespeople, but they are critical to the development of future sales.

The Departure

The foundation for making future sales begins with the departure. On successfully completing the sale, the salesperson should be sure to thank the prospect for the order. This should be done sincerely and without hints of patronization or condescension. The sales representative should let the prospect know that the order is appreciated and the prospect will always be treated with consideration.

One difficult question presents itself with the departure: how soon to exit the prospect's office. After getting the order, many experienced salespeople recommend leaving as soon as possible. Waiting longer, they argue, opens up opportunities for further prospect doubts and questions to arise. The worst that could happen, of course, is that the order could be canceled. Although there is some logic to this recommendation, the salesperson should take care not to leave too soon. Details concerning delivery, installation, and operator training must be settled. If the prospect shows inclination to talk further, especially about unrelated matters, the sales representative should be courteous enough to stay and listen. This tendency to socialize probably will be most frequent in smaller accounts because purchasing agents at large companies are likely to have more pressing matters.

The Follow-Up

Following up the sale with subsequent calls is important to the development of repeat sales. Imagine how you would feel if you never saw the salesperson again following your buying decision. A follow-up thank-you note is a good idea. Recently, we received such a note from our broker after a stock purchase. We couldn't help but be impressed by his thoughtfulness. Though it might appear transparently self-serving, it still had a favorable effect; if nothing else, it's so rare that it stands out. The underlying purpose of the follow-up is to ensure that the buyer is as satisfied as possible. There is a tendency for many buyers to develop cognitive dissonance following a purchase. Many automobile buyers experience anxiety after deciding to buy one make of car over several other attractive alternatives. They begin to wonder whether one of the rejected models might have been a better choice. The smart automobile salesperson calls back to make sure that the buyer is satisfied. Callbacks to minimize cognitive dissonance are important for most other large-dollar purchases as well as for automobiles.

Besides demonstrating care, there are some objective matters that may require handling. Among these are:

1. *Checking on the order.* There may be problems because the item is not readily available in inventory so delivery will be delayed. If so, the buyer must be immediately informed. Take the initiative to make sure the order is fulfilled correctly and on time. If any delays occur, make sure to let the customers know what's going on. Once they take delivery, call to confirm that all went according to plan and to determine if there is anything else you can do.[27]

2. *Adjusting the size of the order.* Buyers may have decided that they need to increase their order. The salesperson should check on this possibility.

3. *Installation.* Proper installation is important to satisfaction. In the computer industry, this is a time when cognitive dissonance is likely to occur, because computer installation is an involved process and time is needed to eliminate bugs. Without fail, the sales representative should be on hand to answer buyer questions.

4. *Training.* The salesperson may have to assist in the training of customer personnel who will be operating the equipment.

5. *Billing and paperwork.* Have you ever been billed incorrectly? You know what your immediate reaction was. To avoid these maddening situations with customers, first make sure all your paperwork for the order is correct, including model/product code, pricing, discounts, percentage rates, trade-ins, and tax, if applicable. Be sure a special price hasn't expired or that the customer's tax exemption is on file. Double-check math. Make sure your handwriting is neat and legible. For billing, find out who in the customer's office should receive the bill. Make sure this information is clearly spelled out in the "bill to" section of the order. If invoices arrive incorrectly, it is important to respond promptly. Take action before late-payment notices start to arrive.

6. *Keeping in contact.* Small gestures can do wonders for helping you stand out in customers' minds. Send a thank-you note for every order. Remember birthdays and special occasions. Always write a personal note in longhand. When you see an article or hear news that might affect your customers, let them know. Call even when you don't have anything specific to discuss, just to say, "Hi," and make sure everything's going smoothly.[28]

7. *Punctuality counts.* You can talk about making customers your number one priority all you want, but it won't make any difference if you don't return their calls promptly. If you need time to find the answer to a customer's question, call to say so. Then give a specific time when you will call back with the answer.[29]

During follow-up calls, salespeople should take the opportunity to cement their relationship with buyers. Don't wait for customers to let you know about changes affecting their business. Make it a point to look forward and anticipate changing needs. Think about changes in the industry, the economy, and technology, and proactively go to your customers to predict how you can help them respond to shifting tides. The sales representative may provide customers with word of new business opportunities, ideas for increasing profit, and recommendations for filling positions in customer organizations. Sometimes the salesperson may even keep the prospect informed of positions in other companies, although care must be exercised here. One experienced hospital salesperson I knew helped many purchasing people he called on find their jobs. Think of the advantageous position in which this put him. In the highly competitive business world of today, relationship selling is what separates profitable companies from all the rest.

Chapter Summary

This chapter explained the close: a question or action by a salesperson designed to secure a prospect's affirmative decision to buy. Of all the parts of the selling process, probably no other element is more misunderstood than the close. Much writing about the close (especially in popular literature) urges salespeople to be extra aggressive in closing, to "wrestle" the prospect into submission. To a considerable extent, this view explains why many salespeople are reluctant to close; they reject suddenly, turning into closing "tigers."

Although myths are replete about the close, there is no denying its importance. Making that final commitment to buy, no matter how desirable the product, is difficult for buyers. Fears of possible loss and thoughts of forgoing competing desires give the prospect "buyer's crisis," a sort of paralysis that impedes final commitment. The salesperson must do something to induce the client to go ahead and make the final decision.

Much of the success in closing comes from knowing when to close. Many opportunities for closing present themselves throughout the course of the interview. Among them are:

1. When the prospect agrees with the value of a benefit the salesperson has just explained

2. After the prospect has accepted the salesperson's answer to an objection

3. When there is a propitious silence

4. Following a verbal indication of interest

5. After a nonverbal sign of interest

In addition, salespeople may create some opportunities on their own for closing. These include asking an open question and using a "pave-the-way" question. Of course, establishing a long-term relationship typically calls for fewer and nonconfrontational closing attempts.

Although closes come in many varieties, they basically represent variations of a lesser number of methods. The direct close is the simplest of closes; the sales representative merely asks for the order. In the summarization close, the salesperson repeats the major benefits as perceived by the prospect and presents them in summary form. With the balance-sheet close, the sales representative draws a large "T" on a sheet of paper and proceeds to present reasons for buying on one side of the T and reasons for not buying on the other side. With the continuous-yes close, the salesperson asks a number of sequential summary questions, each structured so the prospect will answer "yes." In the assumptive close, the salesperson assumes that agreement has already been reached and seeks affirmation of some subordinate and subsequent decisions. In the minor-point close, the sales representative seeks agreement on relatively minor aspects of the total decision, the idea being that small decisions are easier to make than major ones. In the standing-room-only close, the salesperson tries to get the prospect to act immediately in order to take advantage of some impending event. The qualifying close features the salesperson trying to close by disproving a prospect's objections. In the tentative-confirmation close, the salesperson uses the gap between placing the order and shipment, asking, "Why don't we go ahead and place an order? Shipment takes six weeks and you can cancel at no penalty later." The demonstration close is used when multiple buying influences are present, as for industrial sales. It involves assembling all the buying influences for a demonstration of the product. The trial-order method (which is usually a last resort) may include an order of less than typical size to allow the prospect to try out the product. In a suggestion close, the salesperson indirectly recommends that the prospect buy. Typically, suggestion closes are stated in the form of a testimonial, declaration of warranty, or competitive comparison. In closing on a question, in response to a question such as "Can I get it in red?" the salesperson responds, "Do you want it in red?" In the does-it-all close, the salesperson alludes to the fact that the product satisfied all buying criteria and there is little to be gained from shopping around. With the probability close, the salesperson asks, "What is the probability in percentage terms of us do-ing business together?" In the door-in-the-face technique, the sales rep initially makes a large request, which he or she expects to be rejected, and then makes a second smaller request, which he or she expects to be accepted.

The chapter ended with a discussion of the departure and follow-up. Departures from both successful and unsuccessful interviews should pave the way for a return visit. Suggestions for follow-up activities include checking on the order, adjusting its size or installation, and training. During follow-up calls, the salesperson is advised to be aware of buyer's cognitive dissonance, or postdecision doubt, which often arises with major purchases.

Discussion Questions

1. Which of the closing methods would be most effective with you? Why?

2. If you were a salesperson, which closing method would appeal to you most?

3. "There is no need for closing." Discuss.

4. Why are so many salespeople reluctant to close?

5. How does the salesperson know when to close?

6. Are there techniques for creating opportunities to close?

7. What is the trial close? When should it be used? What are some examples?

8. Describe each of the following closing methods and indicate when they are most appropriate:
   a. the direct close
   b. the summarization close
   c. the balance-sheet close
   d. the continuous-yes close
   e. the assumptive close
   f. the minor-point close
   g. the qualifying close
   h. the standing-room-only close
   i. the tentative-confirmation close
   j. the demonstration close
   k. the trial order
   l. the suggestion close
   m. closing on a question
   n. the probability close
   o. the does-it-all close
   p. the door-in-the-face close

9. How should salespeople conduct themselves following the successful close of a sale? After an unsuccessful close?

10. Why are follow-up calls important?

11. Which of the following prospect statements and actions represent closing signals?
    a. "Plastic doesn't look to be as durable as metal."
    b. "That sounds great!"
    c. "It looks pretty heavy to push around."
    d. "You say a service contract is available?"
    e. "And copy time is only half a second?" (with rising voice inflection)
    f. "These gas-permeable contact lenses will last how long?"
    g. "You've really answered my biggest concern."
    h. "Well, I would also like to be able to do something about my labor costs, but I really don't have any ideas about how to do it."
    i. "My wife would love it."
    j. Purchasing agent suddenly lifts up the phone and calls in an engineer from research and development
    k. "What about the trade-in allowance?"
    l. A retail buyer picks up a dress and looks at it every way
    m. A purchasing agent sits in a chair with arms and legs crossed
    n. "What sort of warranty do you offer?"
    o. "Can I get back to you on it?"
    p. "A critical factor is the ability to expand as growth demands it. Can we add to the model you described or would we need to buy a new one?"

12. Identify the following closing techniques:

a. "With your approval, I'm reserving a full-page ad in our March issue—or would you prefer to start with the April issue?"

b. "Can I write up the order for you?"

c. "We can have a model exactly like what you want here on Saturday."

d. "These tires have been selling fast. I can't guarantee we'll have them in stock if you wait."

e. "Would you like to put it on layaway?"

f. "Which would you prefer: the built-in or portable model?"

g. Pointing to a sheet of paper, a salesperson says, "Mr. Buyer, are you willing to give up all of these advantages because of this relatively minor disadvantage?"

h. "I'll be glad to come in when the merchandise arrives and build your end-of-aisle display for you."

i. "Are there any other problems facing you?"

j. "You can see how this plan will make your job easier, can't you?"

k. **Salesperson:** Then smooth riding and safety on long trips are of prime importance to you?

Prospect: (nods head)
Salesperson: And do you agree that this model offers great fuel economy?
Prospect: Yes, I can see that.
Salesperson: And as you indicated, your wife will like the styling and interior?
Prospect: No doubt about that.
Salesperson: How would you prefer to finance it?

l. "Do you want to start with 40 or 50 cases?"

m. "If I can get you a model with elite type, then you'll buy it. Is that correct?"

n. "Then as I see it, we've got the automatic buttonhole-maker, electric foot button, and embroidery stitch options that you desire."

o. "Would you like white sidewall tires?"

p. "Do you want it in blue?"

q. "Why wait? Our product does everything you want."

r. "What is the probability that we'll be doing business together?"

s. **Salesperson:** Would you be willing to invest $1,000,000 in a whole life policy?
Prospect: That's too much money!
Salesperson: Perhaps, you are right. What about a $100,000 term policy?

Chapter Quiz

1. In relationship selling, the close is viewed as
a. a success if the buyer places an order.
b. an opportunity to begin a relationship with the buyer.
c. the culmination of the problem-solving process.
d. the end of a persistent effort to answer all of the buyer's objections.

2. In terms of closing the sale, according to one estimate in 60 percent of all customer–salesperson contacts, the
a. customer takes the initiative and closes the sale.
b. customer breaks off the sales closing.
c. salesperson makes no effort to close, and the sale is never made.
d. salesperson successfully closes the sale.

3. All of the following nonverbal actions indicate that a prospect may be ready to buy *except*
a. sitting silently throughout the presentation and having no questions.
b. reexamining the product.
c. picking up a pencil and starting to figure.
d. leaving the room to talk with someone else about the presentation.

4. The direct close is especially valuable in closing with
a. Analyticals.
b. Drivers.
c. Amiables.
d. Expressives.

5. With the _____, the sales representative takes out a sheet of paper and draws a large "T" across it. The salesperson lists reasons for buying on one side of the T and on the other side reasons for not buying.
a. summarization close
b. tentative close
c. assumptive close
d. balance-sheet close

6. The _____ is effective because it makes prospect inertia work for salespeople rather than against them. Most closes require positive action by prospects, but many prospects resist taking action. However, with this close, prospects have to take action to stop the salesperson. If they sit there passively, the sale is made.
a. continuous-yes close
b. assumptive close
c. standing-room-only close
d. does-it-all close

7. The following statement by a salesperson represents the _____ close. "It's going to be six weeks before it leaves the warehouse anyway. Why don't we go ahead and order one? I'll give you a call at the end of the fifth week to confirm that you still want it. If you change your mind, fine. I'll use it for another client."

a. tentative-confirmation

b. trial-order

c. probability

d. suggestion

8. Of all closing techniques, the _____ is the most low-pressured. The objective is to have prospects accept the salesperson's recommendation without a great deal of thought.

a. demonstration close

b. suggestion close

c. summarization close

d. probability close

9. When a salesperson receives a "no" answer in response to their closing and if the salesperson has little idea about the source of resistance, the salesperson should

a. use an open-ended question to explore the cause of the resistance.

b. switch to a door-in-the-face close.

c. reexplain the benefits of the products.

d. ask for another visit to explain further the benefits of the product.

10. The foundation for making future sales begins with the

a. presentation.

b. follow-up.

c. closing.

d. departure.

Profile

Role-Playing Exercise

Prepare closes for the products described at the end of Chapter 6, "Beginning the Relationship Selling Process," and the customers depicted at the end of Chapter 8, "The Approach."

Make sure that the closes you plan are appropriate to the personality style of the customer.

Web Exercise

How well can you close a deal? Take this quiz on closing, offered by Monster.com, to see how you'd do: http://sales.monsterindia.com/quizzes/closing. After you've taken the quiz, think about the kinds of questions it asks. Were there questions you wish you could have answered by using other options presented in this chapter?

Notes

1. J. Porter Henry, "The Ingredients and Timing of the Perfect Close," *Sales Management,* 1991.
2. Jane Templeton, "The Psychology of the Close," *Sales Management,* June 1, 1991, pp. 11–16.
3. Larry Wilson, *Stop Selling, Start Partnering: The New Thinking about Finding and Keeping Customers,* Indianapolis, IN: Wiley, 1996.
4. Jacques Werth, "You Can Close More Sales—Without Stress and Anxiety. Learn to Work Smarter—Not Harder," www.highprobsell.com/html/closing_sales.html, 2004.
5. Linda Richardson, "Be a Closer," *SalesVantage.com,* 2004.
6. J. Porter Henry, ibid.
7. Ibid.
8. Ibid.
9. Alan N. Schoonmaker and Douglas S. Lind, "One Custom-Made Close Coming Up," *Sales & Marketing Management,* 1997.
10. "When Prospects Beg for a Close," *SellingPower.com,* 2004.
11. J. Porter Henry, ibid.
12. Renee Houston Zemanski, "Buying Signs Give Us Clues to Close," *SellingPower.com,* 2004.
13. Neil Rackham, *Spin Selling,* Hampshire, UK: Gower Publishing Limited, 1995.
14. J. Porter Henry, ibid.
15. Ibid.
16. Malcolm Fleschner, "Close Lines," *SellingPower.com,* 2004.
17. Robert B. Cialdini, "Principles of Automatic Influence," in *Personal Selling: Theory, Research, and Practice,* edited by Jacob Jacoby and C. Samuel Craig, Lexington, MA: Lexington Books, 1984, p. 10.
18. Gerhard Gschwandtner, "Six Ideas to Close More Sales," *SellingPower.com,* 2004.
19. J. Porter Henry, ibid.

20. Robert B. Cialdini, "Principles of Automatic Influence," in *Personal Selling: Theory, Research, and Practice,* edited by Jacob Jacoby and C. Samuel Craig, Lexington, MA: Lexington Books, 1984, p. 10.

21. W. J. Crissy and R. M. Kaplan, "Tactics and Strategies of the Close," *Sales & Marketing Management,* 1991.

22. Roger Dawson, "How to Negotiate When the Other Person Tells You They Don't Have the Authority to Decide," *SalesVault.com,* December 16, 2003.

23. J. L. Freedman and S. C. Fraser, "Compliance without Pressure: The Foot-in-the-Door Technique," *Journal of Personality and Social Psychology* 4, 1986, pp. 195–202.

24. Jerome B. Kernan and Peter H. Reinge, "Behavioral Influence Applied to Retail Selling Situations: When Actions Speak Louder Than Words," in *Personal Selling: Theory, Research, and Practice,* edited by Jacob Jacoby and C. Samuel Craig, Lexington, MA: Lexington, Books, 1984, pp. 65–68.

25. Jacques Werth, "You Can Close More Sales—Without Stress and Anxiety. Learn to Work Smarter—Not Harder," www.highprobsell.com/html/closing_sales.html, 2004.

26. Neil Rackham, *Spin Selling,* Hampshire, UK: Gower Publishing Limited, 1995.

27. "After the Close—What's Next?" *SellingPower.com,* 2004.

28. Ibid.

29. Ibid.

Case 13-1

Read closely and analyze the following dialogue between salesperson and prospect:

Salesperson: This Murphy bicycle should handle your need to commute to and from work at the university each day.

Prospect: Well, it sounds like it.

Salesperson: What do you think of this bike?

Prospect: It seems okay.

Salesperson: What color would you like?

Prospect: I think yellow is a nice color.

Salesperson: Well, let's go over to the cash register and you can ride home.

Prospect: I'm not sure.

Salesperson: Well, this bike is on sale only until tomorrow, after which the price goes up by $15, so I would advise buying now.

Prospect: Well, it seems like a nice bike, but it's a little expensive.

Salesperson: That's right and that's why you should buy it. You get what you pay for.

Prospect: I suppose.

Salesperson: I'll tell you what. Let's look at this systematically. Let's draw a "T" on this sheet of paper and write down some reasons for buying on one side of it, and some reasons for not buying this Murphy on the other side. Now doesn't it sound like you should buy?

Prospect: I don't know. I think I'm going to think it over. I'll be back in touch with you later. (exits store)

Questions

1. What closing techniques were used by the salesperson?
2. Were the closing techniques appropriate? What would you have done differently?

Case 13-2

Several examples of closes follow. Identify each closing method and indicate what factors (including the characteristics of the buyer) may have influenced their choice.

1. Salesperson calling on hospital purchasing agent:
   Salesperson: Shall I put you down for 12 uniforms for your nurses?

2. Real estate agent to home buyers:
   Agent: Then as I see it, your primary interests with this home are (a) its formal dining room that allows you to do the entertaining you desire, (b) its family room, where you can put the TV and the kids can play, (c) the full basement, giving you space for a washer and dryer and eventually a game room, and (d) the three bedrooms, including a 14 x 16 master bedroom for yourselves.

3. Salesperson to owner of small business:
   Salesperson: Let me draw a "T" on this sheet of paper and indicate some reasons for buying the new Neon on one side and some reasons for not buying it on the other.

Reasons for Acting	Reasons for Not Acting
Four-wheel drive provides traction in all types of weather.	$26,000 sticker price
Transverse mounted engine provides increased passenger space.	$700 lower trade-in offered than with competitive import.
The economical 4-cylinder engine gets 39 mpg on the highway and 24 mpg in the city.	
Parts are readily available because the car is domestically produced.	
The design allows more cargo space for hauling sales samples, POP displays, etc.	
With inflation, the price of the car is likely to go higher.	

4. Salesperson to prospect for home videocassette recorder:

   Salesperson: Then you agree that the Boss DVD/VCR player will allow you to tape those programs you aren't now able to see?

   Prospect: Yes.

   Salesperson: Don't you feel that the Boss will give you a chance to play premium quality digital movies?

   Prospect: Yes.

   Salesperson: Wouldn't you say that the price is reasonable for everything you get?

   Prospect: Yes.

   Salesperson: Then, shouldn't we order one today?

5. Salesperson calling on supermarket manager:

   Prospect: Yes, it sounds like an excellent idea.

   Salesperson: How many cases do you need?

6. Salesperson to prospect for some new shirts:

   Salesperson: Cash or charge?

   Prospect: Charge.

   Salesperson: Then, if I can get your signature on the charge slip, we'll have you all ready to go.

7. Salesperson talking to a prospect looking for a new multifunction printer:

   Prospect: You know, on thinking it over, I believe I really need the model with fax capabilities.

   Salesperson: If I can get you one with fax, are you ready to buy?

8. Copier salesperson to prospect:

   Salesperson: I'll tell you what. I'll let you use it in your office for a week.

Retail Selling—
A Special Type of Selling

Key Terms

greeting approach	service approach	verbal contract
merchandise approach	suggestion selling	

Learning Objectives

After studying Chapter 14, you will understand:

- The importance of prospecting to retail selling
- Proper methods for approaching retail customers
- How to handle the three categories of retail shoppers
- The merchandise knowledge required of retail salespeople
- Successful methods for demonstrating retail merchandise

- Effective means of closing the retail sale
- How to increase total sales through suggestion selling
- The influence of technology
- Methods of handling substitutions
- How to deal with exchanges and returns

Retail selling represents a special kind of selling. Although consumers often enter a store with a need or purchase already in mind, retail salespeople must be careful not to let the order slip away. They must be sure to close the sale while the customer is still in the store, because there may not be a second chance. Salespeople must conduct themselves with such courtesy and tact that the customer returns again and again. In other words, retail salespeople must be experts at both closing and human relations.

Retail selling is changing because of the influence of the Internet. In the consumer electronics business, for example, after seeing its largest competitor, 47th Street Photo, go out of business, J&R Electronics decided to adjust its retailing strategy and build a web presence. This is especially difficult to do in electronics because many of the products are now commodities that could be bought anywhere. An iPod is an iPod, whether you buy it at J&R or Best Buy. An important part of their strategy was to partner with Amazon.com as an affiliated merchant. When a customer is viewing an electronics item on Amazon's website, the "Add to Cart" option lists J&R among several other sites where the same purchase can be made. Amazon handles all of the back-end payment and shipping arrangements. Another part of J&R's strategy evolved from customer surveys that showed that as many as half of the respondents search for goods online and end up buying them off-line. Hence, J&R believes that exploring the links between the online and off-line worlds is the "next frontier" of growth. Search engines such as Google are developing technologies to help customers search for items in their own town instead of the entire world, and smart retailers are increasing their ability to bring the two worlds together. This can be accomplished by allowing customers to order and pay online and then pick up the order in-store.[1] In apparel, even high-end retailers such as Neiman Marcus and Bergdorf are building a web presence to attract a younger clientele and expand their market. Commented the CEO of Neiman Marcus Direct, "Over half our business on neimanmarcus.com comes from places we don't have a store."[2]

14-1 Uniqueness of Retail Selling

Study after study has demonstrated the importance of personal selling to the image of many retail stores. In an investigation of specialty women's clothing store customers, it was found that the "knowledgeability and friendliness" of salespeople were critical factors in determining store choice.[3] Yet, frankly, retail selling has a bad image. It would be nice to say that the reputation is undeserved, but the truth is that in too many instances it is warranted.

In defense of retail salespeople, it must be said that their function is not the same in all retail stores. The duties of salespeople at a discount store, for example, are considerably different from those working at a specialty store catering to an exclusive clientele. In the first instance, salespeople are expected to complete the transaction in what is essentially a self-service operation; in the second, they are expected to perform more of the classic functions of selling, from prospecting to closing. Yet, even with discount stores, retail consultants maintain that a prime reason why Wal-Mart has the edge over rival Kmart is Wal-Mart's customer service. At a Wal-Mart store in Madison, Wisconsin, an aggressively friendly grandfather guards the entrance, smiling at babies and striking up conversations with shoppers, while another employee follows customers to their cars to pet a puppy. At the nearby Kmart, a young woman working as a greeter stands stoically and waits for people to ask questions. You might not think so, but this makes a difference. Many consumers in focus groups praise Wal-Mart for making them "feel more welcome," for taking "time out to treat you like they're glad you're doing business with them, or for smiling and saying, 'How are you doing today?'"[4]

Much anecdotal information points to ineffective retail selling. One letter in an East Coast paper said, "Inattentive, discourteous, even rude sales clerks fail to understand the importance of satisfied customers, and retail mechanization has made it difficult to buy even necessary items . . . ." Another on the West Coast wrote, "You can talk about merchandising, management strategy, and image till the cows come home. But what about the customer's needs? [That store] is no longer the place to be . . . . Forget the service. There is either no one to ask, or if you are lucky to find a stray salesperson, they don't have any idea what's where."

Explained one recent shopper of her experience:

"It's a great feeling when you give yourself permission to spend money—It's time I go shopping and spend a little on me!" My journey began at the counter of my favorite cosmetics retailer. They were having a gift-with-purchase offer, and I can be talked into anything during this time, so I circled around the counter a few times trying to decide what to buy.

I was approached with, "Can I help you find something?"

"Yes, do you have a shimmering type of blush—something good for summer?"

"Oh, we don't carry any of that!" was her reply, before directing me to another counter.

"Okay," I said still circling, my eyes madly searching for something I didn't currently own.

"How about eye shadow?"

"Over here," was all she said.

I followed her lead. I looked them over silently, saying to myself . . . anything she says, I will buy, I will cave in, I will surrender! Silence.

"Okay, thanks." I left.

I made my way to another store, a well-known chain of lingerie stores. The manager, her back to me, was telling her two sales associates that if they sold six pairs of nylons, they would get lunch "on her." After she walked away, I said to them, "I'm not buying any nylons but I do want to try these on," holding up a couple of halter tops. After exiting the dressing room, I walked, merchandise in hand, trying to decide if I should get them. The two sales associates walked by me a couple of times. So I left.

I made my way into the jewelry department of a large department store. I noticed a necklace I had seen in a magazine. I grabbed two—one for me, one as a gift. I turned around and there was a smiling associate ready to help. After complimenting my selection, she immediately began to sell me on the benefits of opening a charge account when she discovered I was paying cash. "No thanks," I said. But I appreciated the offer. I had done it! I had purchased something![5]

And all of this is happening when high technology supposedly is revolutionizing retailing with bar coding to speed up the transaction process, rapidly noting best sellers, providing immediate figures for reordering, keeping fashion merchandise current, highlighting distress goods for immediate markdown, decreasing inventory life, and allowing customers to order from terminals for in-store pickup.[6] The irony of all this high-tech gadgetry is that customers are more than willing to subscribe to all of this convenience, but when they do interact with humans, they expect even more from those encounters—more humanity, more accuracy, more pleasantry, and more personal recognition. The buying public has made a pact with retailers: Give us machines to make our lives easier and your costs less, but when we meet up with a human, it had better be good.

Not all the responsibility for these weaknesses rests solely with the salespeople. Their management must bear a substantial portion of the responsibility, if not the major part. Management may tend to be shortsighted when it comes to pay and training. It may look only at the cost side and ignore the benefits from higher pay and improved training for salespeople. It may rely too heavily on advertising to presell the merchandise. Although this strategy is effective with many convenience items, it is not universally applicable. In their sporting goods, household furnishings, watches, jewelry, and appliance departments, even discount stores generally offer many personal selling services. Merchandise in these categories is seldom completely presold to the point where customers enter the store and take the goods off the shelves without being told about models, styles, and features.

Then there is the question of staffing. The quality and quantity of customer service can have dramatic impacts on closing ratios and thereby sales. In most stores, fluctuations in the ratio of shoppers to staff are huge. It is not uncommon to see ratios of the number of customers entering a store during an hour to the number of staff present to be as high as 50:1. No matter how good they are, it is impossible for salespeople to acknowledge 50 shoppers per hour and still sell.[7]

14-2 Steps in Retail Selling

There is a great deal of similarity between retail selling and other types of selling. The main distinctions tend to be ones of emphasis rather than substance. Any of the material discussed up to this point applies to the retail situation, but there are certain situations unique to retailing that have occasioned specific adaptations of technique. The best way of describing these adaptations—and similarities—is by going through the steps of the selling process.

14-2a Prospecting

Prospecting is generally ignored by retail salespeople. The assumption is that prospects are readily supplied by advertising or store traffic. Although these represent the largest source of prospects, retail salespeople (especially those for big-ticket items) can dramatically improve their sales through prospecting. There are many slack periods during the day when traffic is sparse; salespeople can productively use this time for prospecting. Salespeople in the appliance department can check through back records and send out mail to customers with appliances more than five years old. They might also glance at invoices of more-recent sales, looking for an opportunity to sell a related item—a dishwasher when someone has recently bought a washer and dryer or perhaps a trash compactor. The clothing salesperson can telephone customers when new items have arrived in the store, saying, "Our new winter coats have just come in, and I think you might be interested in seeing them." It is also possible to make use of off-work time for prospecting. Furniture salespeople can drive through subdivisions, looking for new houses that have been sold. On spotting one, they can find the name of the buyer through courthouse records. The carpet salesperson can do the same.

Tony Ferguson is a successful salesperson for a large department store in South Carolina. Recently a major tire manufacturer offered a free set of tires to the salesperson who sold the most tires in a 30-day promotional period. Setting out to win the prize, Tony had a print shop emboss the following on small cards:

> Hello–
>
> My name is Tony Ferguson. While passing your car, I noticed that some of your tires are dangerously worn. I represent a famous tire manufacturer, and we have quality tires on sale right now! My phone number is 233-2165 and you can call me from 8 A.M. to 5:30 P.M., Monday through Saturday. Thank you.

Keeping a supply of the cards in his shirt pocket, Tony kept his eyes peeled for cars with worn tires. When he spotted one, he placed one of the cards under the windshield wiper. Tony sold twice as many tires as the next salesperson and won the free tires. Whatever the individual product, most retail salespeople could do a better job if they were to prospect. The whole area is open to creativity. Increased sales and recognition await the retail salesperson with initiative.

14-2b The Approach

Although the approach is important in most fields of selling, it is critical in retail selling. First impressions of the salesperson and store are likely to prejudice the buyer for a long time to come. Waiting too long or being greeted discourteously is guaranteed to alienate or drive away even customers with the firmest intentions of buying.

It is essential to greet the customer as soon as possible. Some stores say to do it within 10 seconds. If you wait longer, the customer is likely to feel ignored. It is a feeling similar to one you might have if you were invited to a party and ignored. How would you feel if you accepted an invitation, arrived, and found the door open, only to be neglected by the host or hostess who failed to greet you. You need not read a book on etiquette to know this is inexcusable behavior. Similarly, the retail store advertises and invites people to come in—and the doors are usually open. So how is the customer expected to feel if ignored?

Greeting More Than One Customer

As a salesperson, you often are required to assist more than one customer at a time. Most salespeople simply tell the first customer they will be right back when they leave to approach the second customer. Some customers take this differently than others. Some don't mind at all (they might even feel less pressured being left alone). Others may feel it is rude. After all, you were waiting on them first, it may take forever for them to determine what they want, and they may choose to leave the store

verbal contract
The salesperson asks the current customer for permission to greet a waiting customer.

now. Making a **verbal contract** with the customer in the beginning will avoid any potential problems.

The following illustrates a verbal contract, which means the salesperson asks the first customer for permission to greet the waiting customer.

> **Salesperson:** Could you excuse me for a moment? I'd just like to let this customer know someone will be with her shortly. Would that be all right?
>
> **Customer:** Sure. (Rarely, if ever, will the customer say "no.")
>
> **Salesperson:** Thanks, I really appreciate it.

When you ask for customers' permission and get no objections, they will wait patiently for as long as necessary. They made an agreement or contract with you to do so. The same type of verbal contract should be made with waiting customers as well. Now they also will wait patiently—and respect you for at least acknowledging their presence in the store. Then you can give your full attention back to the first customer.

The retail salesperson may choose among three basic approaches to greeting customers: (1) the service approach, (2) the greeting approach, and (3) the merchandise approach.

The Service Approach

service approach
The salesperson greets the customer with "How may I help you?"

The **service approach** is the weakest approach. How often are customers greeted with the overused, "May I help you?" Worse, what is the reply nine times out of ten? The customer is almost forced to answer, "No, thank you. I'm just looking." "May I help you?" forces buyers to take a position on their readiness to buy even though most buyers want to see the merchandise before buying. Moreover, the "No, I'm just looking" response leaves salespeople in an awkward position. Because their services have been refused, they have little choice but to leave customers alone. Hovering too closely will drive customers away, and leaving may lose the sale when customers do not find what they want.

The service approach is so weak that, in evaluating its retail salespeople, one retail chain subtracts five points from their score whenever they greet a customer with "May I help you?" Points also are subtracted for these greetings:

> *Have you been waited on?*
>
> *Do you wish to be served?*
>
> *Is there something that interests you?*

An improvement is this: "What can I help you with?" "May I help you?" asks for a yes or no answer; "What can I help you with?" is more likely to encourage a merchandise-specific response from the prospect. However, if the customer is already looking at some merchandise, then the merchandise approach is still preferable.

The Greeting Approach

greeting approach
The salesperson greets the customer with a sincere "Good morning" and then continues the conversation with topics of interest to the customer.

In the **greeting approach**, the salesperson simply greets the customer with a sincere "Good morning" or "Good afternoon." Better yet, if the customer's name is known, the greeting may be extended to, "Good morning, Mr. Jones" or "Good morning, Ed." In the latter instance, the customer should be a long-term acquaintance of the salesperson.

After the greeting, it is important for the retail salesperson to continue the conversation—to take it a little further.

> **Salesperson:** Hi there! How are you today?
>
> **Customer:** Fine, thank you.

Salesperson: That parking lot is a mess today. Did you have a lot of trouble finding a parking place?

Customer: Oh yes. It makes me want to just give up and go home.

Salesperson: I know what you mean. The next time you come, try going around to the east side of the shopping center. No one seems to know that there's more parking over there.

Customer: No kidding? That's great to know. Don't tell anyone else!

Salesperson: No problem. It'll be our secret!

This salesperson succeeded in getting the customer to talk more and will have a better chance of gaining the customer's cooperation when the time comes to talk about what it is the customer wants. Even a follow-up conversation about the weather is useful following the greeting, "Is it still cold outside?" Here are some other useful greeting topics:

- *Children.* Any time a customer comes in with a child, you have been given an obvious topic of conversation. All parents love to talk about their children. Don't just remark how cute the child is. Find out how old he or she is, if the child is always good-natured, if the baby sleeps through the night, and so forth. You could also comment on how well the child speaks for someone that age or talk about the design of the child's stroller.

- *Personalized clothing.* Whenever someone comes in wearing a college or professional sports-team shirt, you have an obvious topic for conversation. Did they go to that school? What's the campus like (you heard it was quite large)? Did they watch the game yesterday? What do they think of the team this year?

- *Current events.* If there are exciting things happening in the world that most people are familiar with, you may wish to use this information for your opening lines. Possible topics can come from the newspaper: an election, an important sporting event, weather disasters, and so forth. Whatever current event you choose, make sure it isn't too controversial.

In the greeting approach, the nonverbal behavior of the salesperson is critical. The manner in which the customer is greeted is as important as what is said. "Good morning" should be expressed with a smile and a rising inflection to the voice. When shopping, how do you feel when greeted by salespeople with scowls on their faces and voices that indicate indifference or even annoyance at your presence? Do you feel like coming back or recommending the store to your friends?

The Merchandise Approach

If the customer is already looking at some merchandise, the **merchandise approach** is probably the best. After saying "Good morning," the salesperson may make reference to the merchandise with a statement like one of these:

Customers tell us those shirts are very comfortable.

This car gets almost 30 miles per gallon.

That fan is on sale right now. We also have some that turn so they cool the whole room.

That's been a popular color this fall.

That's on sale this week only.

merchandise approach
The salesperson greets the customer by mentioning something about the merchandise.

That handbag has perfectly matched skins and was made in Europe expressly for us.

Did you notice the wrinkle-resistant fabric in this dress?

By directing attention immediately to the merchandise, the salesperson is likely to forestall the reply, "No, thank you, I'm just looking," because the customer really is too busy looking! Moreover, because the merchandise approach is in the form of a statement, not a question, it limits the customer's tendency to respond "No." In formulating a merchandise approach, salespeople should stick to factual statements and avoid expressions that reflect their own taste; the customer might not agree. A sale could be spoiled without its ever having a chance.

14-2c Problem Recognition

When shoppers first enter the retail store, they may be classified into three categories with regard to the extent of their problem recognition: (1) those who know exactly what they want, (2) those who have only a general idea of what they want, and (3) those who are "lookers." For each group, the salesperson must employ different tactics.

Buyers with Firm Intentions

For the customer who enters the store and asks to see a gray, pinstripe suit, the salesperson must bring out the item immediately unless, of course, it is unavailable. If there is more than one style of such a suit, then the salesperson should bring them out and let the buyer decide which gray suit is desired. The only real problem arises when the salesperson knows that the item requested will not fulfill the buyer's needs.

Whenever such a situation arises, the best strategy for the salesperson is to bring out both the requested item and an alternative the salesperson believes will more nearly fulfill the buyer's needs. When the customer examines and tries on the initial item, the salesperson may ask questions such as:

Do you have trouble with . . .?

Have you ever noticed . . .?

Is it comfortable enough?

After these questions have raised some doubts in the buyer's mind, the salesperson can then offer the second item as an alternative.

Buyers with a General Idea of Need

Many buyers enter the retail store with only a general idea of their needs in mind. They may know they want a shirt, a suit, a living-room pattern, or a gift item—but little more than that. In these situations, the salesperson must get a clearer picture of the buyer's needs. The best way of doing this is to ask questions. All of the questioning techniques discussed in Chapter 9, "Problem Recognition," apply here. Open, closed, checking, and continuing questions are all applicable to the retail situation. For the buyer interested in a shirt, the salesperson might start with questions such as:

Is the shirt for sport or dress?

Did you have any particular colors or styles in mind?

What size do you need?

For the furniture buyer, the salesperson might ask:

How much use will the furniture get?

What is the color pattern of the room?

How large is the room?

For the gift buyer, the salesperson might ask:

For whom are you buying?

How much do you want to spend?

In asking the latter question, the salesperson must be extremely careful because the buyer can easily take offense. The salesperson might be able to make some assumptions from the general appearance of the customer, but these are not always accurate. Sometimes the appropriate price range cannot be determined until the presentation of the merchandise itself.

Although salespeople will find questioning valuable, a hazard exists in asking too many questions. Salespeople may ask such specific questions regarding price, style, and other features that finally they are forced to admit, "I'm sorry, I don't have exactly what you want." On most occasions, it is better to delineate the problem just enough so that the buyer may be shown merchandise from which to make a final choice.

Lookers

Even with the best approach, the salesperson will often be told, "No, I'm just looking." Here are some ideas for handling this issue:[8]

1. Not only should you never refuse a customer's right to browse, but you should also make them feel instantly comfortable in your store. When a customer says they are "just looking," respond immediately with energy and excitement. Tell them, "That's terrific! We're delighted to have you here today!"
2. At this moment, keep the customer engaged, but without pressuring him or her in any way. The best question to ask is usually, "Have you shopped with us before?" If the answer is yes, say, "Great. Let me tell you quickly what's new (or on sale, etc.)." If the answer is no, then give the customer a quick overview of who you are and what you sell.
3. Now, ask the customer one more question: "What can I do to get you started?" It is at this point that many of the customers who initially tried to push you away will respond by saying, "As a matter of fact, can you show me where I can find . . . ?"

Even at that, it may be perfectly clear from their nonverbal behavior that some customers clearly want to be left alone. As soon as they see the salesperson approaching, they begin looking for a way out. To overcome this and leave room for an approach later, the "80-degree pass-by" is very effective.[9] It simply involves walking past the customer, offering a casual "hello," and then making a turn and approaching the customer later. By not stopping, it appears as if the salesperson is busy doing something else. It's also important not to walk directly toward them, as they feel they own the space in front of them. If the customer does not directly ask for assistance, the salesperson may have to watch for nonverbal indications of interest. If the customer has been looking for several minutes at a particular piece of merchandise, then the salesperson may try again with a merchandise approach.

14-2d The Retail Presentation

As with most other steps in the selling process, there is much similarity between the retail sales presentation and the presentation in other fields of selling. As with the other steps, however, there is a difference in emphasis. For one thing, the retail presentation typically occurs sooner than it does in the other types of selling. It has been said that retail buying is all in the eye, so it is usually a good idea to get the merchandise in the hands of the buyer as soon as possible. Of course, this presumes some amount of merchandise knowledge, at least to the extent of knowing where the merchandise is.

Merchandise Knowledge

Retail salespeople have been roundly criticized for not knowing their merchandise. Have you ever gone shopping and had a conversation like this?

> **Buyer:** I'd like to see those shirts advertised for $19.95.
>
> **Salesperson:** I didn't know that we had any advertised at that price.

There have been instances in which buyers have asked for certain items, only to have salespeople say they do not carry them. Later the buyers discover that the item was in fact not only in stock but also carried in a display or, as one shopper recently wrote, "Over the weekend, I went shopping for a clock radio with big numbers so I don't have to put my glasses on to see the clock. I also wanted to buy a user-friendly cordless phone for an elderly relative. So I went to a large electronics retailer. There were a lot of clock radios on display, but very few boxes were underneath. Half of the clocks on display were not in stock, but the display models were still there. So, I went over to the cordless phone department. Instantly I saw one that would be perfect. On the receiver was a tag that read: *This is not a working model. Display only.* No working models in boxes were anywhere to be found. I tried to get someone's attention to ask about this, but all the blue-coats running around the store seemed to have their own agendas: Look busy. Don't talk to customers. I saw one clerk coming down the aisle wearing his nametag. As he walked by without looking at me, I stepped out right in front of him. It was great. I almost knocked him down. I sure got his attention. I found out that he was the department manager. When I asked him how I could buy the phone I was interested in, it was like I had asked him to take a pay cut. He mumbled under his breath, grabbed an inventory control number, went to a computer, and five minutes later, told me there were four on order. He didn't know when they'd be in. I asked him, 'Why is it on display if there are none in stock?' He said he could give me four or five reasons: Stock was lean, trucks weren't coming in, there was snow on the roads, and it was two months after the holidays. I guess I could take the one I liked the best. I left a few other things I had intended to buy on the floor and walked out."[10]

Because customers seldom possess all the facts, it is the salesperson's responsibility to supply them. Although it would be impossible to relate all the kinds of merchandise information retail salespeople should possess, some general categories of product knowledge can be provided:

1. Familiarity with the features and benefits of specific items in the store's advertising and displays.
2. Knowledge of the merchandise stock and its location.
3. A sufficient knowledge of product facts (both advantages and limitations) to enable the salesperson to prove value, answer questions, and overcome objections.
4. A knowledge of product performance, use, and care. Many returns are caused by salespeople providing erroneous instructions in the first place.

Features versus Benefits

What is true about selling in general is true of retail selling. Sell benefits! Don't say, "This men's polo shirt is made of combed cotton." Instead say, "Natural fabrics breathe better, so when you wear them on hot days you'll stay cooler and more comfortable."[11]

Showing the Goods

In retail selling, it is particularly important to have customers participate in the demonstration. Salespeople should have customers try on the merchandise or get them to touch, operate, or hold it in some manner. In this way, customers are given an opportunity to imagine how it would be to have the merchandise. They should be more eager to own it and be convinced that the product is the one they really want. If they do buy, it is less likely that they will return the item.

In showing merchandise, it is a good idea to limit the choice of alternatives. If a buyer asks to see shirts, the salesperson should bring out no more than three or four to be examined. With more, the customer may become confused and have trouble making a decision. With one or two, it can easily become a "something or nothing" decision. Three to four allows comparison and shows the merchandise to advantage. Should the customer reject some of the items and still not make a final selection, the salesperson should replace the rejected items, still limiting the number of choices to three or four.

When determining the alternatives to show, a problem arises when the price range desired by the customer is unknown. If the prospect has indicated the range, then there is no problem. The salesperson might ask, but this runs a danger of offending the customer. Guessing by the customer's appearance alone may not always be correct. Earlier in the book, we recommended starting at the top. In retail selling, however, a high-end retailer like Neiman Marcus recommends bringing out one model in the high range but not the highest; a medium-priced model; and a model in the low range but not the lowest; and beginning the presentation with the medium. In this manner, transition to a higher- or lower-priced model will be easier than if the salesperson began at one of the extremes.

Showmanship is important to the retail presentation. The salesperson should feel and show excitement. Desirability can be increased by the manner in which the item is shown. Merchandise can be belittled, regardless of the cost, when it is carelessly handled and sloppily displayed. A dress can just be held in front of the buyer or it can be twirled around and placed before the customer with its bottom touching the floor to show the soft draping ability of the fabric. Similarly, salespeople can talk about the lightness of a vacuum cleaner, or they can pick it up and hand it to the prospect to illustrate the feature better.

14-2e Handling Objections and Closing

When it comes to handling objections and closing, few differences exist between retail selling and other types of selling. All of the methods for handling objections discussed earlier are applicable. The same is true of closing, along with a couple of additional variations. Assumptive closes and minor-point closes such as the following are especially valuable in retail selling:

Would you like to charge this or pay cash?

How many pairs would you like?

Is there any other information I can give you before I write this up?

I'll have this wrapped for you in just a minute.

One of our attractive bags will make carrying your packages easy.

Would you like the blue or gray suit?

Would you like this gift-wrapped?

14-2f Suggestion Selling

suggestion selling
Promoting an ancillary sale, suggesting a larger quantity, or trading up to higher quality.

After the sale is closed but before it has been rung up, there is usually a chance for the salesperson to use **suggestion selling**. With this technique, the salesperson suggests merchandise related to the item already chosen. This may be effective because it reaches buyers when they are already in a positive frame of mind. Unfortunately, suggestion selling is often mishandled by retail salespeople. It is not suggestion selling for the salesperson merely to ask, "Will there be anything else?"

Suggestion selling may occur in three situations: (1) promoting two sales instead of one, (2) suggesting a greater quantity or larger container, and (3) suggesting better quality, often called *trading up.*

Promoting Two Sales Instead of One

When suggesting additional sales, the salesperson may offer a related item. The salesperson might suggest:

I have the perfect shirt and tie to go with this suit, Mr. Jones.

We have a new line of pocketbooks that would be stunning with that coat, Mrs. Finn.

May I suggest some pillowcases to complement your new sheets?

Will you need some film for your new camera?

In suggestion selling, it is important that the salesperson not ask something like, "Is there anything else?" or "Will that be all?" Nothing will happen. Rather, suggest specific items and, even better, show them.

Another technique to promote multiple sales is a technique called *subtract-off selling,* which includes the following

- Filling a counter, table, cart, or basket with all the possible items a customer may want or need
- Explaining the reason for the product selections
- Providing selected features and benefits
- Explaining benefits to getting the entire package
- Instructing the customer to remove (or "subtract") any unwanted items

For example, one computer/electronics retailer encourages their salespeople to load a shopping cart with everything the customer needs to actually operate the PC (printer, cables, battery pack, optical mouse, etc.) Then, after explaining the purpose/need for each item in the cart, the salespeople instruct the customer to remove (subtract) anything they feel they can do without. And it works! Eventually, they are going to need all this ancillary gear.[12]

Suggesting Greater Quantity

In promoting additional sales, the salesperson may also suggest a greater quantity or a larger container. For example:

Here is a special value. Will just one be enough?

This is something you can always use. Would you like several?

A pair of these (lamps, chairs, art objects, etc.) *would be lovely and effective.*

This is an advertised special.

Trading Up

When trading up, the salesperson seeks to sell better quality. When the customer requests an item at a particular price, it is shown first. The professional salesperson may then show a related model with a higher price, explaining why the higher price is justified. However, salespeople should restrict themselves to describing the additional features and benefits of the higher-priced model without disparaging the lower-priced one. That is, don't sell away from anything. It is natural to attempt to sell the better quality or attractive design by comparing it too favorably with the lower-level product. Salespeople should curb the urge to do so; what they say against the lower-priced model will be remembered more than what they say about the higher-priced one. It is possible that the buyer has already decided in favor of the lower-priced model, only to walk out of the store with nothing because the seller criticized it.

Be sure to sell each item on its own merit; never compare. Let's assume that model A costs $75 and model B costs $50. If you begin to compare the two by saying, "A is better than B. . . .," what happens when the customer decides she is only willing or able to spend the $50? Will she buy B? Not after it fared so badly in the comparison. If you do find yourself in a demonstration showing two similar, but differently priced, models sell each on its own merit. This can be done by saying, "A is good because. . . ." and "B is good because . . . ." This way, if the customer decides his budget can only handle B, and not the more expensive A, there is no problem. Alternatively, the salesperson should be able to close the sale of the lower-priced item by emphasizing its bargain value: "You get everything in this model except the _____ and it's $20 less." If the customer does ask you why there is a difference in price, simply explain that the features found in the higher-priced item are more expensive to produce and, therefore, the finished product is more costly. Workmanship, materials used, details, and even brand names are all features that affect price. With this viewpoint, many customers will choose quality over price.

Another good idea is to ask checking questions during the presentation to help aim one's presentation at the correct model level:

Isn't this a helpful feature?

Would you want to get this level of performance out of the product?

Are there times when this larger capacity would be important to you?

Technology and Suggestion Selling

Too frequently, this scenario occurs:[13] A customer enters a store and proceeds to the electronics department. After searching for several minutes, she finds her desired selection of products and begins reading price tag information. Five minutes later, a sales associate arrives and inquires whether he can be of assistance. The customer requests information and the associate answers a few of her questions, leaves briefly to consult a large product catalog, and returns to provide the customer with some additional information. The customer then makes a selection, leaving the electronics department satisfied—her shopping cart holding the same quantity and quality of products she had intended to buy from the beginning, but the scenario could have been far different if the customer had immediate access to useful product information at the moment she entered the electronics department via continuously updated information displays. If so, she might have chosen a higher-priced item or bought some peripheral products related to her primary purchase. Retailers can increase their sales by providing customers and/or employees with relevant, real-time information at precisely the right moment. Today, advances in information, systems, and personnel management technologies are enabling retailers to transform their sales process. Retailers that can identify what their customers need and want can then successfully up-sell customers as well as encourage them to purchase items that complement their primary purchase. This process of up-selling and cross-selling requires correlations between market basket data—information on what a customer has in his/her shopping basket at checkout; customer purchase history; and product relationships. These correlations can be used to define *business rules* designed to optimize cross-selling and up-selling processes. For example, as depicted in Figure 14-1, business rules can enable retailers to move customers from lower- to higher-margin items, increasing the features and functionality customers receive, as well as encouraging them to purchase additional products.

In apparel, technology could help customers imagine a greater set of ensembles than just the handful on display. Systems could also link to records of customers' previous purchases and enable them to match ties to shirts they already have at home. In home improvement, sales associates and customers could use simulation technology to design their ideal kitchen or bathroom. They could then leverage

Figure 14-1
An Example of Rules-Based Cross-Selling and Up-Selling: The Camera Purchase

Customer and product/analytics

Business rules

Market basket data

Customer purchases history

Correlations

Product relationship strength

Business rules are created on product relationships to maximize the propensity to purchase

Rule 1 dictates that there is a high likelihood to move from camera A to higher-profit-margin product: digital camera B.

Rule 2 then dictates the relative likelihood that a customer will purchase complementary products related to camera B.

The up-sell

The cross-sell

Camera B

Camera A

Memory card

Case

Spare battery

Source: From "Retail Selling Optimization," from IBM Retail Store Operations. Copyright © 2004 International Business Machines. Reprinted courtesy of International Business Machines.

technology-enabled room planning and decorating tools to carry out the project. Grocers and discount retailers are already equipping shopping carts with "cart companions"—wireless devices that offer customers layouts, recipes, promotions, coupons, and frequent shopper loyalty programs.

14-2g Substitutions

When a customer enters a store requesting a specific item not carried in stock, the salesperson should not automatically assume that a sale cannot be made. The salesperson should not stop with, "I'm sorry, but we don't stock that item," and send the customer to another store. Neither should the salesperson try making a substitution by exclaiming, "We quit stocking that item because we had so much trouble with it" or "They've just about quit making them." In both instances, customers will not be favorably disposed to make a substitution. The salesperson has questioned the customer's ability to make a rational choice. Instead, the salesperson should indicate that although the requested item is not available, a similar and perhaps preferable alternative is carried. For example, consider the following dialogue with a customer looking for a particular kind of hat:

Prospect: I've been looking everywhere for a plain felt hat, the kind I've worn all my life. It has a large brim and is pinched in the front.

Salesperson: Yes, sir, I know the kind of hat you're talking about. Unfortunately, we don't carry that style any longer. I have a thought, however. (returns with a hat) This is a velour felt with a nice-sized brim. When I pinch the front like this, it should be close to what you want.

Notice that the salesperson has indicated that the desired item is not in stock, but a similar alternative is available. The salesperson has not given up the possibility of making a sale but is still trying to fill the customer's needs.

If a similar item is unavailable, the retail salesperson can adroitly question the prospect about the need that occasioned the original request and recommend something that would serve as well. For example, analyze the following dialogue:

Prospect: Do you have a gray, room-sized rug?

Salesperson: Come to think of it, I haven't seen a gray rug in that size for quite a while. I really don't know why; gray is such a relaxing color and it goes with almost anything. For which room had you planned the rug?

Prospect: The family room.

Salesperson: What kind of furniture and what colors do you have in the room?

The salesperson then proceeded to show some rug samples, which, although not gray, still complemented the existing decor of the prospect's family room, and a sale resulted. The customer left this store happy, unlike her leave-taking from competitors' stores, where the salespeople had said, "Sorry, we don't have it."

14-2h Exchanges and Returns

Although the salesperson might think otherwise, exchanges and returns represent selling opportunities. When handling the return, well-trained salespeople—familiar with the merchandise—can offer suggestions to help customers and sometimes save a sale:

Let me show you—this is the way it works (or fits).

What you need is another type, and we have it right here.

I know you really don't need two toasters. What about this blender?

Well, it does look like a defect. Let me open another one for you and we'll check it.

It comes in four colors, so maybe peach would look better.

Chapter Summary

Retail selling is a special kind of selling. Some elements, such as prospecting, are less important here than in industrial selling, but in other respects retail selling is even more demanding. Relating to people is especially important. When shopping, people are easily turned off by aggressiveness and condescension, so retail salespeople must be experts in human relations. They must be good at closing; customers who leave the store without buying may never return, especially if the salesperson does not have the initiative to contact them again. Unfortunately, it must be admitted that much retail selling is characterized by low standards of selling expertise.

Of critical importance to the successful completion of a retail sale is the approach. It is essential that customers be greeted promptly. Some authorities recommend greeting them within 10 seconds. There are three basic ways of approaching retail customers: (1) the service approach, (2) the greeting approach, and (3) the merchandise approach. Of these, the service approach is the weakest. Greeting customers with the hackneyed "May I help you?" may prompt the reply, "No, thank you, I'm just looking." The greeting approach represents an improvement because at least the salesperson is not compelled to leave immediately. Here, the salesperson greets the customer with a "Good morning," or perhaps "Isn't it a nice day?" Of even greater effect is the merchandise approach. Here, the salesperson makes reference to goods the customer is examining. For example, a clothing salesperson might approach and remark to a customer, "Those shirts have been popular this fall."

When shoppers first enter the retail store, they may be classified into three categories: (1) those who know exactly what they want, (2) those who have only a general idea of what they want, and (3) those just interested in looking. Each category requires different tactics on the part of the retail salesperson.

In making the retail sales presentation, it is especially important to have customers participate. Encouraging customers to try on the goods or touch, operate, or hold them are all good ideas. When doing so, it is important to limit the number of alternatives, usually to no more than three or four. Otherwise the customer may have trouble making a choice and leave without being able to make any decision.

Handling objections and closing in retail selling are similar to those in other types of selling. Assumptive and minor-point closes are especially valuable because they are unlikely to offend. Closing a sale presents an opportunity for suggestion selling through such methods as promoting two sales instead of one, suggesting a greater quantity or larger container, or recommending better quality ("trading up").

If a customer requests an item that is out of stock, the salesperson should suggest the substitution of a similar alternative without disparaging the customer's original request. Exchanges and returns also present opportunities to substitute a new item.

Discussion Questions

1. What are some common weaknesses in retail selling?

2. Explain the differences between retail selling and other types of selling efforts.

3. "Prospecting is of limited value for retail salespeople." Discuss.

4. Why is it important to greet retail customers promptly?

5. While the retail salesperson is waiting on one customer, how should he or she greet new customers who have entered the department?

6. What are the three basic retail approaches? Which is the best? Which is the least desirable?

7. When it comes to problem recognition, what three categories of retail buyers may be identified? How does category affect the actions of the salesperson?

8. What sorts of merchandise knowledge should retail salespeople possess?

9. How should retail merchandise be shown?

10. What is suggestion selling? Explain some ways for promoting additional sales.

11. How can substitutions be handled in retail selling?

12. What is the proper attitude of a retail salesperson toward exchanges and returns?

13. A woman in a retail-clothing store has just tried on a pair of slacks that are too small for her. What would you tell her?

14. A man walks into a clothing store and asks if you carry Hart, Shaffner, and Marx suits. If you do not, what will you say?

15. A college student enters a bicycle shop and asks to see a bike for commuting back and forth to school. After showing him a 3-speed bike, you notice disappointment in his facial expression. How would you go about the process of trading up?

16. Identify opportunities for suggestion selling with the following products: skis, sport coat, jogging shoes, tennis racquet, dress, couch, golf clubs, desk, lawn mower, shoes, hunting rifle, car battery, frying pan, compact disc player, perfume.

17. Critique the following statements overheard in a retail store:

You wouldn't want to buy this fur coat, would you?

I would suggest you take the fiberglass model with the electric foot button.

Customers seem to like those options.

What do you need?

How much can you afford?

Which one of these five compact disc players looks best to you?

Well, do you want it or not?

Will that be all?

You don't want that $24.95 battery. They just advertise it to bring customers in.

Sorry, we're out of those.

Would you like this gift-wrapped?

Everything we have is out on the tables. Why don't you look over there?

Isn't that a sharp-looking blouse? They're on sale, you know.

We don't have that brand. Let me show you something cheaper.

It doesn't work, huh? We haven't had any other complaints.

You look great!

18. Explain the influence of technology on retail selling.

Chapter Quiz

1. In terms of retail selling, study after study has demonstrated the importance of personal selling to the _____ of many retail stores.
   a. friendliness
   b. success
   c. image
   d. attractiveness

2. The step in the retail selling process that is almost always ignored by retail salespeople is
   a. the approach.
   b. prospecting.
   c. problem recognition.
   d. suggestive selling.

3. Salespeople in the appliance department can check through back records and send out mail to customers with appliances more than five years old. They might also glance at invoices of more recent sales, looking for an opportunity to sell a related item—a dishwasher when someone has recently bought a washer and dryer or perhaps a trash compactor. This is an example of
   a. the retail presentation.
   b. problem recognition.
   c. the approach.
   d. prospecting.

4. Of the following approaches to retail customers, the weakest approach is the
   a. service approach.
   b. greeting approach.
   c. merchandise approach.
   d. problem approach.

5. When shoppers first enter the retail store, they may be classified into one of three categories with regard to the extent of their problem recognition. Possible categories include all of the following *except*
   a. those who know exactly what they want.
   b. those who have only a general idea of what they want.
   c. those who are substituting or exchanging.
   d. those who have no idea what they want.

6. In showing retail merchandise, it is a good idea to limit the choice of alternatives. If a buyer asks to see shirts, the salesperson should
   a. bring out only two to be examined.
   b. bring out no more than three or four to be examined.
   c. bring out at least four, preferably five to eight, to be examined.
   d. first ask how many different kinds the customer would like to see.

7. The two most valuable types of closing in retail selling are
   a.   suggestion and summarization.
   b.   qualifying and tentative.
   c.   assumptive and minor-point.
   d.   direct and demonstration.

8. Suggestion selling may occur in all of the following situations *except*
   a.   promoting two sales instead of one.
   b.   suggesting a greater quantity or larger container.
   c.   suggesting an alternative product that better fits the customer's needs.
   d.   suggesting better quality, often called "trading up."

9. In terms of using technology to enhance suggestion selling, the process of up-selling and cross-selling requires correlations between all of the following *except*
   a.   consumer promotions available at the time of purchase.
   b.   market basket data (i.e., information on what a customer has in his/her shopping basket at checkout).
   c.   customer purchase history.
   d.   product relationships.

10. When a customer enters a store requesting a specific item not carried in stock, the salesperson should
   a.   assume a sale cannot be made.
   b.   say "I'm sorry, but we don't stock that item any longer."
   c.   say "We quit stocking that item because we had so much trouble with it."
   d.   indicate that although the requested item is not available, a similar and perhaps preferable alternative is carried.

Web Exercise

Sales techniques work through online retailers, too. Go to www.amazon.com. How does the interface of the website work to encourage purchases? After looking at a few items, what kinds of recommendations are you given? What kinds of related products does the site suggest?

Notes

1. Andrew Blackman, "A Strong Net Game," *Wall Street Journal*, October 25, 2004, p. C6.
2. Cheryl Lu-Lien Tan and Sally Beatty, "Surfing for Jimmy Cho: Luxury Hits the Web," *Wall Street Journal*, October 21, 2004, p. D1.
3. Ronald B. Marks, "Operationalizing the Concept of Store Image," *Journal of Retailing*, 52, Fall 1976, p. 37.
4. Francine Schwadel, "Little Touches Spur Wal-Mart's Rise," *Wall Street Journal*, September 22, 1999, p. B 1.
5. Andrea Waltz, "Help Your Customers Buy," *Accelerated Performance Training*, 2004.
6. Ralph Shaffer, "High-Tech Gadgetry Can't Replace the Human Touch," *Wall Street Journal*, December 27, 1996.
7. Keith Bagley, "Converting Browsers to Buyers More Important Than Ever," *Retailernews.com*, 2004.
8. Richard Fenton, "Responding Positively to Just Looking," *Retailernews.com*, 2004.
9. Lois J. Moseson, "Who Killed the Sale?" *Sales & Marketing Management*, July 10, 1998, pp. 46–48.
10. Bob Popyk, "Trying to Sell What You Don't Have," *Retailernews.com*, 2004.
11. Richard Fenton, "Prove It—Presenting Product with Passion, Pictures, and Proof," *Retailernews.com*, 2004.
12. Richard Fenton, "'Subtract-Off' Selling: Wave of the Future," *Accelerated Performance Training*, 2004.
13. "Retail Selling Optimization," *IBM Retail Store Operations*, IBM Co., 2004.

Case 14-1

Read and analyze the following dialogue between a customer and salesperson in a men's clothing store. As the conversation begins, the customer, Tim Witt, has just entered the store and is looking at some shirts. The nearest salesperson is already waiting on another customer.

Tim: (after looking at some shirts for a minute or so) Are these shirts on sale?

Salesperson: Yes, they are. (Tim turns away to look at the shirts again. The salesperson completes a transaction with the previous customer and again approaches Tim.)

Salesperson: May I help you?

Tim: Well, I'm not really sure what I need. Maybe I should look a little more.

Salesperson: Fine. (walks away)

Tim: (turning in the direction of the salesperson) I think I'm ready now.

Salesperson: Good. What price range are you interested in?

Tim: I'm not really sure. I've got a party to go to tomorrow night, and I think maybe I should get a new shirt for it. It's my daughter and son-in-law's first get-together since they've been married.

Salesperson: That's nice. Why don't you look at these shirts here. They look like your size and they're on sale.

Tim: Okay. (after looking for awhile) These all seem to be for leisure.

Salesperson: That's right. They're all famous-maker labels and really attractive shirts. What size do you take, by the way?

Tim: 16–32.

Salesperson: (looking through rack) This one should be just right for your party.

Tim: (trying on shirt) Could this shirt be worn for dress also? I hate to buy a shirt I can't wear to the office, too.

Salesperson: It looks great on you.

Tim: Yes, it does. (looks at himself in the mirror admiringly for awhile) Well, I don't know. I guess I need to think it over. I'm just not that sure.

Salesperson: Fine. Here's my card. When you return, please ask for me.

Questions

1. Analyze the conversation and determine what the salesperson did correctly. What was done incorrectly?
2. Rewrite the dialogue as you think the salesperson should have handled matters.

Case 14-2

Read and analyze the following dialogue. Joyce DuBord, a senior at the University of Missouri, has just entered Seifert's, a women's clothing store in Columbia, Missouri.

Salesperson: Good morning. Is there anything I can help you with?

Joyce: I'm graduating this spring and I need a new outfit for job interviews.

Salesperson: That's great. Did you have something specific in mind?

Joyce: A nice skirt, maybe. I doubt if a pair of pants will impress interviewers.

Salesperson: I suppose not. Were you thinking about a wool skirt?

Joyce: Probably. Do you have any in navy blue?

Salesperson: Yes, over here. (picking out one skirt to show) How about this one? It looks like it'll do.

Joyce: (looking at the skirt and examining it) I think I'd like to try it on. I'm not sure, but maybe I'll know when I do.

Salesperson: Fine.

Joyce: (looking in mirror) I believe it needs to be a little shorter.

Salesperson: It sure looks good on you, and shortening it is no problem. We can have it ready by next week at the latest.

Joyce: That sounds good, but let me look at some other skirts. (looking through the rack and pulling out four more) These look good, too. (pausing and thinking about money) I believe I'll try this one on.

Salesperson: Okay.

Joyce: (looking at herself in the mirror) This looks good, too. But, then, so did the first one. And these others are attractive. I don't know which to choose.

Salesperson: You're right. All five are attractive.

Joyce: (after looking at the skirts and pondering for awhile) This one should suffice.

Salesperson: Fine. Will there be anything else?

Joyce: No, that's all.

Salesperson: All right. It'll take just a minute to wrap it up.

Questions

1. Did the salesperson do a good job? What would you have done differently?
2. Rewrite the dialogue the way you think matters should have been handled.

Self-Management

Key Terms

advance
circular routing
cloverleaf routing
email

Internet
leapfrog routing
list generation software
skip-stop routing

straight-line routing
to-do list

Learning Objectives

Learning Objectives

After studying Chapter 15, you will understand:

- The importance of planning to selling success
- How too much time can be expended on unprofitable accounts
- How to conduct an activity analysis
- The importance of planning strategy before each call
- Ways of recognizing additional buying influences

- Methods of maximizing time spent with customers
- Ways of limiting travel time through effective routing
- Uses for the cellular telephone, electronic mail, and fax machines
- The critical nature of postcall analysis
- The use of personal computers in self-management

Thomas Carlyle, the English historian and essayist once said, "People who would never think of committing suicide or ending their lives would think nothing of dribbling their lives away in useless minutes and hours every day." Certainly, truer words cannot be spoken about selling.

Earlier we explained that an important aspect of selling, independence, represents both an advantage and a disadvantage. Independence provides the salesperson with a great deal of discretion in deciding what to do, but it also presents a temptation for misuse. No one is around to prevent salespeople from waiting until 9:30 A.M. to make their first call or quitting at 4:00 P.M. to beat the traffic home. Nor is there anyone around to stop their picking up a few odds and ends between sales calls or taking off at 1:00 P.M. on Friday; after all, what buyers are interested in seeing a sales representative at that time?

Even salespeople with the most brilliant sales skills will ultimately fail if they do not demonstrate sufficient self-discipline. Many salespeople of average ability are successful because they channel themselves into productive activities; they know how to manage themselves. They plan their activities and work at 100 percent efficiency year in and year out. They call from Monday morning until 5:00 P.M. Friday, and they never waste time running errands.

Many line sales executives feel the problems that plague them most about their subordinates are poor utilization of time and the planned sales effort. Perhaps if someone presented salespeople with a bill for time wasted during a week, they would take more care. Yet, in truth, they are paying such bills in sales they might have made and commissions they might have earned.

15-1 Time Management

The real crux of self-management is learning how to manage time. Other resources can be stockpiled in inventory, but time can never be recovered or stored for future use. Once wasted, it is gone forever. The salesperson and sales manager must carefully plan and make use of the time available. Each evening a complete plan of the coming day's work should be written out in an activity planner. That way, salespeople will not have to stop work several times a day to decide what to do next. All that is necessary is to pull out the activity planner and get started.

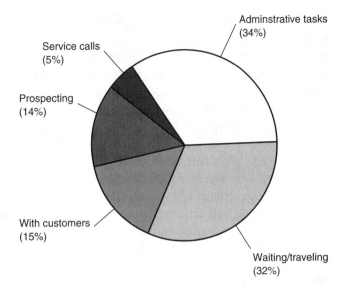

Adminstrative tasks
(34%)

Service calls
(5%)

Prospecting
(14%)

With customers
(15%)

Waiting/traveling
(32%)

Figure 15-1
How Salespeople Spend
Their Time
Source: From "How Salespeople
Spend Their Time" from Fenemore
Group, *Sales and Marketing
Management,* March 1996.
Reprinted by permission of The
Fenemore Group.

Planning is especially important because so much of the salesperson's time is taken up in nonselling activities. Figure 15-1 shows the results of a survey on the use of the salesperson's time. Note that the average salesperson spends just 15 percent of their time directly in front of customers.

Success in selling is a result of what salespeople do, as well as how they do it. No matter how skillful a salesperson is, output is bound to suffer if too much time is spent unproductively on travel, waiting, and paperwork. Salespeople must plan to make use of each precious minute of customer contact. This means carefully analyzing each account, scheduling calls to contact them, and assessing performance after each call to improve matters the next time around. Otherwise, as Laurence J. Peter, author of *The Peter Principle,* warned, "If you don't know where you are going, you will end up somewhere else."

15-1a Account Analysis

The first step in planning is to determine who should be called on, how often, and for what duration. On a yearly basis, this logically leads to monthly, weekly, and daily plans. At the beginning of the year, salespeople must sit down and determine objectives for the ensuing 365 days. Time used wisely at this point will bring more than proportionate returns later on.

15-1b The Value of Time

In choosing which accounts to contact, salespeople should realize that their time is worth something. Not all accounts generate sufficient business to justify an expenditure of time. To illustrate, let's suppose that a salesperson is making $50,000 per year. With weekends, vacations, and holidays, let's further suppose the salesperson works about 240 days per year. Assuming the salesperson works eight hours per day, 1,920 hours are available for selling, 40 percent of which (768 hours) are actually spent in front of customers. This works out that each hour of the salesperson's time is worth approximately $65. Any account that generates less than this amount per call should be eliminated. This goes for prospects, too; calling too many times without results is also a waste.

15-1c The Important Few and the Unimportant Many

In analyzing their accounts, salespeople should keep in mind a principle that is true for almost every sales territory: A relatively small number of customers usually account for a disproportionate share of sales. As depicted in Figure 15-2, assume that 15 percent of a salesperson's customers (let's call them A accounts) generate 65 percent of sales for a total volume of $325,000. The next 20 percent of customer B accounts provide 20 percent of volume, a total of $100,000, and the final 65 percent of accounts generate only 15 percent, or $75,000, of the salesperson's total sales.

This principle—that a relatively few customers account for a majority of sales—holds true whether they are ranked by volume, profits, or units. Different bases of classification might slightly alter the absolute numbers, but the percentages remain about the same. Now let's see what this means to salespeople when allocating their time. Two mistakes are frequently made by those who fail to plan their efforts carefully; either mistake will result in lost sales dollars.

Mistake Number One

The first mistake is to spend too much time with smaller accounts. Let's assume that the salesperson makes 1,000 calls a year (excluding stocking and goodwill calls). Let's further suppose that the salesperson calls on each customer with equal frequency: 1,000 calls divided by 200 customers, or five calls apiece. If these calls are allocated by customer type, then 150 calls per year are made on A accounts, 200 on B accounts, and 650 on C accounts. Dividing these calls by the appropriate sales volume results in sales per call estimates of $2,167, $500, and $115 for A, B, and C accounts, respectively. (See Figure 15-3.)

Calling on customers with equal frequency means that each call is worth $2,167 for large accounts, but only $115 for small accounts. At this point, the salesperson should question the necessity of calling as often on small, less profitable accounts. Calls could be profitably reallocated from smaller to larger accounts. Such a strat-

Customers Ranked by Volume

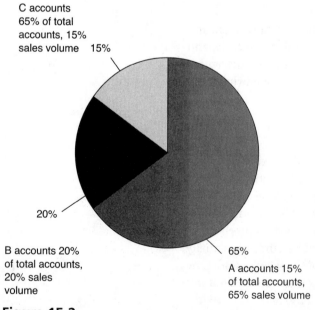

Customers Ranked by Number and per Unit Volume

130 C accounts
$75,000/accounts

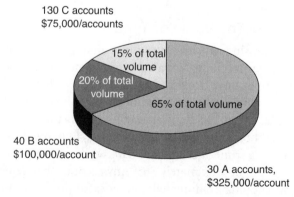

40 B accounts
$100,000/account

30 A accounts,
$325,000/account

Figure 15-2
Sales Volume in Percent by Sales Volume and Percent of Total Accounts

Customer Type	Number of Customers	Number of Calls	Sales Volume	Sales Volume Per Call
A	30	150	$325,000	$2,167
B	40	200	$100,000	$500
C	130	650	$75,000	$115
Total	200	1,000	$500,000	X

Figure 15-3
Customers by Number and per Unit Volume

egy would make even more sense if it developed that the salesperson did not have enough time available to make all the calls planned.

A customer's annual sales (or potential sales) divided by the volume the salesperson must make on each call gives the approximate number of calls he or she can afford on each class of customer. For example, if the salesperson determines that he or she must average $50 in sales per call to make his or her quota, and class A customers buy an average of $3,000 per year, then the salesperson could call on class A customers as often as once a week. However, if class C customers average only $750 a year, the sales rep can't afford to call on them more than once a month.

Mistake Number Two

As indicated in Table 15-1, because they spend too much time with smaller accounts, salespeople may over-budget their time without realizing it. For example, let's suppose that a salesperson has budgeted 15 calls per year on A accounts, 10 calls per year on B accounts, and 5 calls per year on C accounts, for a total of 1,500 calls. The question now becomes how many calls the salesperson can make in a year.

Suppose the salesperson averages five calls per day for 240 working days, for a total of 1,200 calls per year. But that leaves 300 planned calls that cannot be made! This does not include calls on new prospects, and it ignores the fact that the salesperson should probably spend more interview time with each large account. Once again, the salesperson should carefully analyze the smaller accounts and determine if they can get by with fewer calls. It is also possible that some can be dealt with on the telephone, without personal visits.

15-1d Analyzing Prospects

For the salesperson involved in new-business selling, a different problem is presented. Because prospects are new, it is difficult to plan calls on the basis of volume. However, it remains important that the sales representative classify prospects as to the time that should be allocated to each. Nine or 10 calls expended on a prospect without getting an order is a waste of time. It is also a waste of time if only nominal orders are obtained.

T a b l e **15-1** Overbudgeting

Calls Planned	Calls Actually Completed
15 calls per year × 30 A accounts = 450 calls	25 per week × 48 working weeks = 1,200 sales calls
10 calls per year × 40 B accounts = 400 calls	Neglected calls = 1,500 − 1,200 = 300 sales calls
5 calls per year × 130 A accounts = 650 calls	
Total budgeted calls = 1,500 calls	

It is a good idea for the salesperson to rate each prospect on the probability of obtaining an order. The evaluation form in Figure 15-4 represents one manner of completing this evaluation. The salesperson rates the prospect on a number of important criteria and on that basis makes an overall determination of the likelihood of obtaining the business. More and more companies are questioning the advisability of putting as much effort in calls on new accounts as is commonly the case. In a survey of 192 companies and 10,000 salespeople on sales-force productivity undertaken by *Sales & Marketing Management,* survey respondents reported that it took an average of seven calls to close a first sale, compared with only three calls to close a sale on an existing account. By multiplying the difference of four sales calls by the average cost of a sales call approximately ($250), we can see that it's more than twice as expensive to land a new account as it is to penetrate an existing account. Specifically, the cost of a sale to a new account comes to $1,750 versus $750 for an existing one, a whopping 235 percent premium on the cost of a new sale over one to an existing account. Moreover, survey participants reported an average of only 17 percent of their companies' sales volume coming from sales to new accounts. That figure isn't surprising when one considers that managers at most firms indicate that the margins accepted to get a foot in the door are often lower than those for subsequent sales, making new-account business the least profitable as well as the most expensive.[1]

PRODUCT FIT (how well our products fill the prospect's need)
The product/services we offer are pretty much what this company needs:

Good fit		Some difficulty in meeting needs		Many difficulties in meeting needs
5	4	3	2	1

TIME INVESTED
The amount of time that would have to be invested to get this account would be:

Not time-consuming		Moderately time-consuming		Very time-consuming
5	4	3	2	1

COMPETITION (all aspects of the competition, including product, service, and sales representatives)
Competition for this account's business is:

Low		Moderate		High
5	4	3	2	1

QUICKNESS
We can obtain this business:

Immediately		In the not too distant future		In the distant future
5	4	3	2	1

GROWTH
Over the past five years the growth in sales to this account has been:

High		Moderate		Low
5	4	3	2	1

PROFIT (revenue less expenses of handling the account)
The profit from this account is likely to be:

High		Moderate		Low
5	4	3	2	1

PROBABILITY
Overall, the likelihood of getting this business is:

High		Moderate		Low
5	4	3	2	1

Figure 15-4
Sample Evaluation Form

Sales reps need to "move them forward or move them out" when referring to prospects. This means if the prospect isn't moving closer to purchasing each time you speak, they're taking your valuable time. If "no" is ultimately what you're going to hear, fine, hear it today, find out why, and you've been successful. Here's a way to figure out if they really are a prospect and worth following up.[2]

1. *First, determine if they truly are interested.* "I see. Let's talk about that. So you're saying that you are interested in doing business together, but there's something that makes now a bad time?" If they affirm that they are interested, proceed with the next steps. However, they might confess that there really isn't much potential to working together. If so, at least find out why.
2. *Find out when the timing will be right.* Get them to tell you when you should reestablish communication. "OK, when do you want me to call back so we can resume our conversation?"
3. *Confirm that they'll buy.* Get commitment they will buy at the time they provide you. "So in three months when I call back you'll be in a position to move forward, right?"
4. *Find out why that's a better time.* There must be a reason that the future will be a more opportune time. Find out. "What's going to happen between now and then that will make the third quarter a better time?"

By following this process, you narrow down the pool of prospects you're pursuing long-term and save time.

15-2 Scheduling Activities

After determining the accounts that should be called upon and how often they should be contacted, the salesperson must plan activities on a yearly, monthly, weekly, and daily basis. To begin the process, the salesperson needs to calculate goals as illustrated in Figure 15-5. This so-called funnel process determines daily sales calls, assuming a targeted earnings goal and various ratios of closes per prospect and prospects per call. Once completed, a salesperson can tentatively schedule calls on a monthly basis. By

Figure 15-5
Conversion Ratios through the Funnel

plotting accounts and their call intervals for a year, the salesperson is prepared to schedule calls on a weekly and daily basis. Of course, this implies even more detailed planning. For example, daily planning requires that appointment times be firmly established. Failure to do so wastes considerable time and production.

15-2a Activity Analysis

Once sales representatives begin to work their plan, they often discover that they are unable to meet their goals, even though they are working a 9-hour day. In other words, there has been a breakdown between the plan and its implementation. It then becomes a question of revising either the plan or the means of implementing it. Because the former may require lowering sales and profit goals, it is a good idea to examine implementation first. Basically, this involves analyzing how time has been spent. One way of determining this is to perform an activity analysis.

In the activity analysis, salespeople should analyze their activities by marking off 30-minute intervals on a sheet of paper. This can be done for a week or for a random sample of 5 to 10 days. Then the salesperson can mark off, as in Figure 15-6, how much time was spent in actual customer contact and in waiting, travel, service activities, and administration.

The salesperson in the exhibit has sampled work for one day, but let's assume for discussion purposes that the summary figures also represent a week's averages. Over the course of this period, the salesperson averaged 175 minutes per day in travel, 50 minutes in waiting, 185 minutes in contact, 105 minutes in service, and 30 minutes in administrative activities. If these figures are unsatisfactory, then the sales representative is faced with answering two questions:

1. Is time being properly allocated among activities?
2. How can time be used more efficiently with each activity?

Answers to these two questions follow.

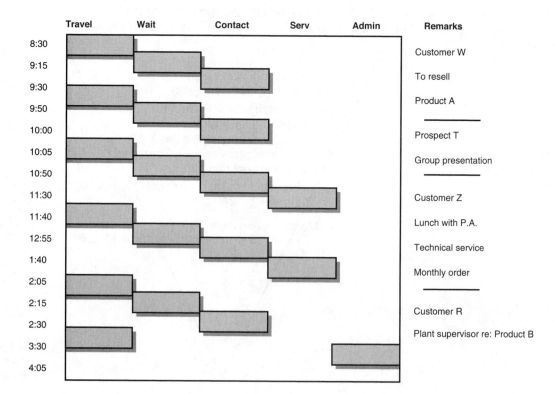

Figure 15-6
Activity Analysis

15-2b Allocating Time

There is no universal answer to the question of whether salespeople have allocated their time optimally among activities. No two sales jobs are exactly alike regarding the activities required and the time that should be spent on each. However, salespeople should have some idea of the priority of each activity.

Biggest Time-Wasters

Before beginning a discussion of what to do, it makes sense to begin with a list of the biggest time-wasters on the part of salespeople:[3]

1. *Spending time on the trivial.* Salespeople love to be busy and active. A customer calls with a back-order problem, so, we drop everything and spend two hours expediting the back order. In retrospect, couldn't someone in purchasing or customer service have done that? Didn't something urgent but trivial delay making some sales calls? Aren't sales calls a much better use of time? Or, another customer mails a very involved request for a quote. We become immediately involved with this task, working on this project half a day, complete with specifications, calculated prices, and compiled literature. Couldn't we have just communicated the guidelines to a customer service rep and then reviewed the finished proposal?

2. *The comfort of the status quo.* Many salespeople have evolved to the point where they have a comfortable routine. They make enough money with established routines and habits that are comfortable. They really don't want to expend the energy it takes to do things in a better way, or to become more effective. They could still be writing phone messages down on little slips of paper when entering them into a contact manager would be more effective. The same could be asked about other activities.

3. *Lack of trust in other people in the organization.* Salespeople have a natural tendency to work alone. We spend most of the day by ourselves, we decide where to go by ourselves, we decide what to do by ourselves, and we are pretty much on our own all day long. It's no wonder that we want to do everything by ourselves. The point is that many of these tasks can be done better or cheaper by someone else in the organization. The salespeople don't release the tasks to them because they, the salespeople, don't trust others to do them.

4. *Lack of tough-minded planning.* Ultimately, time management begins with attention to detail. Good time management is a result of thinking about it before you do it. Good time managers invest sufficiently in this process. They set aside time each year to create annual goals; they invest planning time every quarter and every month to create plans for those times; and they plan every week and every sales call. Poor time managers don't dedicate sufficient time to the planning phase of the job. Not only do good time managers invest a sufficient quantity of time, but they also are disciplined and tough-minded about how they think. They ask themselves good questions and answer them with as much objectivity as they can muster. "What do I really want to accomplish in this account?" "Why aren't they buying from me?" "Who is the key decision maker in this account?" "Am I spending too much time in this account, or not enough in that one?" "How can I change what I am doing in order to become more effective?"

Sales representatives must fight the tendency to think that all things are equally important. Priorities must be established for the performance of each task. Each night, salespeople should prepare a **to-do list** of prioritized activities for the following

to-do list
List of daily activities arranged in priority order.

day. Generally, contact time will have the highest priority. After all, without it, nothing would be sold. It is also important to arrange sales calls in order of priority. Some are obviously more important than others, so salespeople should phone for appointments in order of call importance. After arranging appointments, they may wish to set aside some part of the day for prospecting, whether cold-calling or phoning. Next, salespeople should schedule service calls, including goodwill calls and those necessary to check inventory, train customer personnel, erect displays, and make technical adjustments. After scheduling service calls, it is a good idea to make provisions for handling administrative duties such as completing sales reports. Remember to allow enough travel time to reach the day's assorted appointments.

Contact

It is vital that salespeople make maximum use of time spent in each activity. To profit most from time spent with customers, sales representatives should plan each call, thinking through their strategy and establishing clear objectives. If salespeople are going around to visit customers to see what develops, they are just well-paid tourists. Knowing where you are going definitely increases the likelihood of getting there. However, in major relationship-type sales, relatively few calls (less than 10 percent) actually result in sales or refusals. Hence, in these larger sales, it is difficult to judge when a call has been successful. Merely an agreement to meet again is not sufficient. Between a commitment to buy and a refusal is an **advance,** any event that takes place, either in the call or after it, that moves the sale toward a decision.[4] Typical advances can include:

advance
Any event that takes place, either in the call or after it, that moves the sale toward a decision.

- A customer's agreement to attend an off-site demonstration
- A clearance that will get the salesperson to a higher-level decision maker
- An agreement to run a trial or test of the rep's product or service
- Access to departments in the account, previously inaccessible

Completing a form like the one in Figure 15-7 is a valuable exercise for call planning. Note that the salesperson will plan SPIN questions to progress to the advances necessary to establish a long-term relationship.

Notice that the salesperson not only indicates questions to ask, important aspects of the presentation, answers to likely objections, and possible closes, but he or she also identifies the major source of influence in the buying decision. It is estimated that fully 60 percent of all sales calls are made on the wrong individual, even though it is vital that salespeople not waste their efforts. Some techniques for identifying decision makers follow:

1. *Get in there early.*[5] The best insurance against your losing control of timing at the end of the sale is to build relationships with key buyers and future decision makers. Get involved in "new task buys" or "modified rebuys." If another company already has the account set up as a "straight rebuy," better to spend your time elsewhere. Target the companies you are going to invest time in selling to. Meet the key executives. Provide value. Understand their business. Establish yourself as a knowledgeable and trusted resource. Later on when they are buying, you'll be connected to the people who have the authority to shorten the buying process. Early in the process, negotiate with people in your prospect's companies to whom the users and purchasing agents report. At the beginning of an evaluation cycle, you can negotiate skipping (or at least expediting) some steps later: "Ms. Prospect, I'm going to

ACCOUNT _____ LOCATION _____

1. Who must I see to take action? (In what order should they be contacted?)

        NAME   JOB RESPONSIBILITY

_____   _____

_____   _____

_____   _____

2. What are his/her specific wants and problems? (If you are not completely sure, you must find this out during the call.) _____

3. What <u>S</u>ituation, <u>P</u>roblem, <u>I</u>mplication, and <u>N</u>eed-Payoff questions do I need to ask?

_____

4. Based on his/her wants and problems, list the features, advantages, and benefits that are relevant.

    FEATURES   ADVANTAGES   BENEFITS

_____   _____   _____

_____   _____   _____

_____   _____   _____

5. What evidence can I present that will substantiate what I am saying? _____

6. What objections are likely to be raised? _____

7. What closing techniques will I use if the opportunity arises? _____

_____

8. Based on this information, what results should I achieve today? _____

_____
_____
_____
_____

Figure 15-7
Sales Call Strategy

pull out all the stops to provide you with what you need to evaluate my offering. If, at the end of your evaluation, you decide that my company is in the best position to provide you with a solution, can I count upon you to work alongside me to expedite the process through purchasing and legal?" Uncover or create urgency on their part. Find out who the people are who are financially responsible for that project, operation, or initiative. The pressure is on for them to perform strategically, operationally, and financially. Get them to help you drive the process forward.

2. *In a large, complex sale, if the first call cannot be made on the economic buyer, then calls should be made at many levels throughout the organization.* Questioning individuals at each level will provide insight into the decision-making process. If the initial call is made on the purchasing agent, the salesperson should offer assistance in disseminating information to other departments.

3. *The salesperson can learn much about the decision-making process by examining purchase requisition forms.* If a certain department specifies the supplier, then this group should receive more attention from the sales representative.

4. *It is critical to call on user buyers.* Even if they are not the ones who make the final decision, they probably will know who does. It is also true that they often have great influence on this decision.[6]

5. *If the prime decision maker cannot be identified or is unapproachable, the salesperson may supply lower-echelon contacts with information for making a presentation to their boss themselves.* The salesperson might sit down and outline a presentation step by step with the prospects, leaving the outline with them to discuss with their boss.

Planning each call is important. Making use of all the time available for selling is also crucial in maximizing customer contact. Many salespeople avoid making calls on Monday morning or Friday afternoon. The usual excuse is that prospects are too busy or unreceptive during these times to see a salesperson. The fact of the matter is that many serious prospects are eager to see salespeople at these times. Their willingness to see sales representatives at unusual hours indicates how much interest they have in the product or service. Salespeople also lose valuable contact time by refusing to deviate from the standard 8:00–12:00, 1:00–5:00 schedule. A great deal of business can be accomplished over the business lunch. The salesperson has a chance to get prospects out of the office, where they can relax and really think about their needs and the sales representative's proposal. The same is true of a breakfast or dinner meeting, perhaps even more so. The sales representative might even consider seeing prospects on a Saturday morning. Many executives work at this time and the salesperson is likely to gain their undivided attention with so few others around.

If a buyer is unavailable, trade salespeople often take a stock check and work up a suggested order, leaving it with a subordinate. Later, they can contact the buyer on the phone and confirm the order. In any type of selling where substantial repeat orders are characteristic, salespeople can do the same thing.

When salespeople are with customers, they should make sure that they have attempted to close the sale. Persistence is critical, although in relationship selling, closing attempts should be limited to no more than two per call. A study by Haley Marketing, a management consultant firm, explains why appropriate persistence is required: Recent studies indicate that 50 percent of salespeople stop trying after the first call. That percentage increases to 65 percent after the second call and to 80 percent after the third call. A whopping 90 percent of all salespeople throw in the towel after four calls.[7] Salespeople who persist are the ones who finally close the order.

To maximize the effectiveness of your contact time with prospects, it is important to know your circadian rhythm, which refers to the ebb and flow of your energy during the course of the day. Some of us are morning people; others are "night owls." Most of us have some idea of the regularity of our ups and downs. It is important for you to determine when you're at your best so that you can organize your calls to coincide with your peaks and take advantage of that energy. When you are not effective, when your circadian rhythm is on the downswing, use that time to plan, do paperwork, service clients, write letters, or call for appointments.

Waiting

All salespeople spend time waiting; there is no getting around the fact. The average salesperson is kept waiting 12 1/2 minutes by the average prospect, and that adds up to a lot of minutes in a year. Successful sales representatives reduce waiting time to its absolute minimum. They know what days and times are best for their customers, and they try to schedule appointments during these periods. Successful salespeople also confirm appointments before coming. This way, time will not be wasted if customers cannot keep the appointment or if they are going to be delayed. If the appointment is canceled, it is also a good idea to reschedule another time immediately. Many a sale has been lost in the time it takes to set up another appointment.

While waiting, sales representatives can make use of their time in a number of ways. They can review preapproach information and sales call strategy. They can use the phone to call for further appointments or confirm existing ones. They might use the time to do some of the paperwork that is a part of all sales positions. There is always that sales report that is waiting to be written, that order that needs to be completed, or the correspondence with the customer service or credit department that needs to be handled. Waiting time can also be constructively employed to sound out other salespeople about prospects; they are probably looking for a way to occupy themselves, too. There may even be some reading the salesperson can do to catch up on new-product releases, competitive analyses, or trade publications.

Of course, there is the difficult question of deciding on how long to wait to see the prospect. Many salespeople insist on waiting no longer than 20 to 30 minutes. Waiting longer, they insist, puts them in a bad frame of mind for the presentation to follow. They claim it also gives the prospect the idea the salesperson has nothing else to do and no other prospects as important. If the rep decides not to wait, he or she should tell the receptionist that they have to leave for another commitment; they should then make another appointment or leave word that they will phone the prospect back. Some sales reps claim prospects tend to be apologetic about missing an appointment and are more willing to give a fair hearing on the next call.

Service

Servicing accounts (whether checking inventory, building displays, stocking shelves, or training dealer personnel) is an important part of the selling job. To eliminate wasted service activity requires both anticipation and thoroughness. If inventory needs to be checked every 30 days, the salesperson should schedule this activity on the monthly calendar. If dealer sales personnel need to be trained, the date should be firmly established with the dealer, and the sales representative should arrive for the task fully prepared, with charts, visuals, and handouts intact. Furthermore, the salesperson should realize that service half-done is no service at all. Tasks not thoroughly completed will require callbacks and additional servicing. The best advice is to do the job correctly the first time.

Administration

The task many salespeople enjoy least is paperwork. Reports must be completed, correspondence must be written, and calls must be planned. Some of these jobs can be done while waiting for interviews, but it is usually necessary to schedule paperwork on a regular basis in other than prime time. At the end of each day, take time to organize paperwork. Fill in the blanks while your memory is still fresh. File customer information in folders, cards, or on the computer so you can find it when you need it. Most salespeople don't like paperwork, but keeping up with it makes good sense. Letting it go usually leads to frantic attempts to finish it in response to a sales manager's demand (hopefully, a polite one). Handling paperwork on a crisis basis is wasteful; it can infringe on time better suited for customer calls.

A must is making out a to-do list the evening before or early in the morning. Here, the salesperson makes out a list of the activities that must be completed that day, along with their priorities. Without priorities, the tendency is to get as many jobs done as possible regardless of each one's importance. In fact, the tendency is to complete the easy ones first. Another common error is to start at the top of the list, taking the jobs in order without regard to importance. There are various systems of setting priorities, but a simple one is the A-B-C method. A for top priority jobs, B for important, and C for least important. These can be further broken down by A-1, A-2, and so forth. The procedure is to start working with the As; once they are completed, move on to the Bs, and finally the Cs. In setting priorities, use the three "Ds" to help set the schedule. Take a look at a task and ask yourself, can I *delete* it? If it isn't essential, forget it. If the task requires completion, ask can I *delay* it? If you can't delay it, try to *delegate* it. Can you get somebody else (e.g., secretary or customer service rep) to do it? Once prioritized, it's not necessary that you get through the list by the end of the day. Today's B can become tomorrow's A. Most sales software has a to-do list feature built into the package; some programs will even beep and display a pop-up reminder on the screen when a task's time has come. It is important to prepare a realistic list for the day. Plan activities that will require only 50 percent of your available time. Experts agree that this is the best way to accommodate unexpected changes or urgent activities that inevitably arise during a typical workday. Planning a minute-by-minute agenda will limit flexibility in adjusting to the changes and demands of your day, causing frustration and stress from an unrealistic schedule. With 50 percent of your day planned, you will have the ability to handle interruptions and the unplanned emergencies.[8]

New developments in technology—cellular phones, PDAs, pocket PCs, and **email**—have also eased administrative chores for salespeople.

email
Messages sent electronically from computer to computer.

Cell Phones, PDAs, and Pocket PCs

Let's follow a salesperson around during the course of a morning and afternoon to assess the advantages of a cellular phone.[9] John Technophone, who sells mainframe computers, has three calls to make between 9 A.M. and 2 P.M. He heads out in his car at 8 A.M. and runs into a traffic jam on the interstate. There is no public phone in sight, but it's no problem. John merely phones his customer on his cellular phone and tells the secretary he might be late. When John does arrive for his appointment, he picks up the phone again and dials a brief code on the touch-tone pad. While he's inside selling, any calls that might come to his car phone are automatically routed to his sales office, where sales support personnel take messages. Finished with his first call, John phones in and learns that his second appointment is sick and has canceled his appointment. John could use the time to make a phone call to an unscheduled prospect in the vicinity, seeking an impromptu meeting. In this instance, however, John receives a call from the third prospect, who says she has an urgent meeting coming up and can't meet at the time scheduled. His time freed, John asks, "How about if I come an hour early? I just had an opening."

"Sounds good. Say, I just remembered a question I wanted to ask your boss. Is he available?" John dials his boss at the office and, through his 3-way-calling feature, puts his boss in touch with the prospect over the cellular phone. Her question answered satisfactorily, John's prospect is well prepared for the call. Unfortunately, John finds he is not. He has forgotten his proposal, but this presents no problem with his cellular phone. He retrieves his proposal online from the company computer with his phone and modem. He prints out the proposal on his portable computer terminal in the front seat of his car. In the same way, if he had not forgotten his proposal, John could have phoned into the computer's data bank to access information about his next prospect or to pull up the latest price and technical information on a new product line he might detail in the next call.

Of course, new technology has incorporated cell phones with personal digital assistants and even pocket PCs, allowing even greater flexibility. The personal digital assistant can store the salesperson's customer files, a schedule planner, a notepad, a calculator, address book, reminder list, travel itinerary, Rolodex, notes, to-do lists, and calendar. They can even swap data with a desktop PC. They have fax and email capabilities and pen-based devices with a message-pad screen. They allow you to write notes and drawings on-screen, and then they read your scribbles and translate them into neatly typed text. If Don King, owner of Express Personnel Services, a staffing firm based in Atlanta, wants to contact his sales staff coast to coast, he hits the "alert" button and contacts them directly on his Nextel i95CL. That's because King is contacting them via radio, on his Nextel phone. The $10-a-month service connects the company's reps from Georgia to California. A continuous connection to the Internet means emails sent to King's account in his office are uploaded onto his phone throughout the day. However, the device's real advantage, King insists, is quick communication with clients. Most of the company's customers have similar devices, so they can radio King or one of his reps in seconds with a personal request. The phones also alert King to business changes that can affect the outcome of sales calls. Just before a recent presentation to Wal-Mart, in LaGrange, Georgia, King's office tipped him off via radio that Wal-Mart's vice president of operations would be attending the presentation. "Sitting in the parking lot, we adjusted our presentation on our laptop. The original presentation would have been too general," he adds. Because the vice president was a decision maker on the deal, this was an opportunity for King to close a deal worth about $1 million a year in revenue rather than simply make a presentation.

Ron Romanchik, vice president of global sales for Ai-Logix, Inc., a telecommunications company based in Somerset, New Jersey, closed a $1 million-a-year deal while lounging on the beach by conducting business through his BlackBerry 6750. The popular handheld lets Romanchik receive calls and emails simultaneously. While negotiating contract specifications and pricing changes with the e-learning company Envision, Romanchik could talk on his BlackBerry to the four Ai-Logix employees involved in the deal at the same time that he was opening Microsoft Word attachments on the device. "If I'm on a call on my BlackBerry, I can hide the phone call and go right to an email that I've received, open up the attachment on the BlackBerry, and view it as I'm talking," Romanchik says. Without his BlackBerry, Romanchik would have had only one phone line to use at his beach house. "I'd have had to dial into a server on my laptop to retrieve information about the deal," he says. "Then I'd have to hang up, call back my reps, and make conference calls to close the deal, which would have been impossible. I probably would have been on the phone for countless hours trying to get everything coordinated." Instead, about an hour on his BlackBerry was all Romanchik needed for Ai-Logix to seal the deal.

Email

Electronic mail will never replace face-to-face meetings or the telephone, but it is fast becoming the next generation of relationship-building communication. It is being used in a number of ways by sales organizations.[10] Email provides an easy link between salespeople and headquarters, and allows continual contact between sales personnel and customers, improving the relationship because the rep is never more than a computer keyboard away. For example, the sales rep can immediately dispatch customer service personnel from headquarters to handle customer problems. Email allows sales reps to enter orders while meeting with clients or immediately thereafter, reducing shipment time to customers and inventory for both buyer and seller. As opposed to phone orders or orders placed verbally with the salesperson, there are fewer discrepancies with email because orders are written clearly and concisely on standardized forms. Email provides salespeople with complete information—booking and backlog reports, shipping and billing reports—on all clients, and this information is waiting in the rep's email every morning. That leverage of knowledge naturally provides a competitive edge. In today's relationship selling, the salesperson frequently needs input from many sources in his or her company. When the salesperson needs approvals or suggestions on proposals from several internal sources (e.g., upper management, financial personnel, or production people), they can email messages to everyone simultaneously with the proposal attached. The recipients can then send back suggestions immediately. With email, salespeople are not bound by normal work hours. They can make calls all day and then pick up their email messages when they come home in the evening. They start the next day, then, updated on important matters. Salespeople can send information relevant to their clients' company or personal situation. Simply put, email facilitates keeping customers up to date and informed. Acting as a resource to customers is a critical part of relationship selling. Email can speed the dissemination of important information like price changes and new-product announcements to accounts. Response to client messages is also faster because the rep can receive a message immediately and react just as quickly without waiting to catch up with the client by phone first.

Travel

Approximately one-fourth of a salesperson's time is spent traveling, which is largely unproductive time. Any steps to reduce travel are steps in the right direction. The sales representative must do everything possible to maximize face-to-face selling time.

A critical step is a routing-pattern analysis. Accounts should be spotted on a map with pins, preferably different colored pins to represent A, B, and C accounts. With an appointment already scheduled at a target account, one rep looks at the map and, time permitting, immediately spots other accounts in close proximity. This makes it possible to make profitable unscheduled calls. He then calls on his cellular phone, "I'm in the area talking to one of your neighbors and wondered if you could see me for a few minutes." Next, the accounts should be connected in a manner that will minimize travel time.[11] Figure 15-8 illustrates one possible such strategy.

Several routing patterns (while still clustering accounts) have proved helpful in this regard, including the straight-line, circular, cloverleaf, leapfrog, and skip-stop approaches.

Straight-Line Routing

Starting from their offices, salespeople make calls in one continuous direction to the end of their territories. They then make calls on a straight line in another direction.[12] Eventually, they return to the base point, again in a straight line, a process that is depicted in Figure 15-9. This is known as **straight-line routing.**

The straight-line approach works best if there are clusters of accounts at the terminus of each straight line. The salesperson then makes a straight line to each cluster, calls on the accounts in the cluster, and makes a straight line to the next cluster.

Circular Routing

Beginning from their office, sales representatives make calls in a series of concentric circles or a spiral through their accounts; this is called **circular routing.** Or they may begin at the terminus of the outermost circle and work their way back to the office. This circular approach is best when the accounts are distributed uniformly throughout the territory, and the call frequency is similar among accounts. This pattern is shown in Figure 15-10.

Cloverleaf Routing

Similar to the circular approach, **cloverleaf routing** has the salesperson circle just part of the territory instead of the entire area. The next trip is an adjacent circle, and so on, until the entire territory is covered. If considerable distances are involved, the salesperson may choose a hub point at the terminus of each leaf and make calls

straight-line routing
Starting from their offices, sales reps make calls in one continuous direction to the end of their territories, then call in another straight direction, and so forth.

circular routing
Starting from their offices, sales reps make calls in a series of concentric circles.

cloverleaf routing
The salesperson circles just part of his or her territory, then an adjacent circle, and so forth.

Cluster B accounts and A prospects around at least one solid A account each day (or week). Use the measurement of travel and selling time to decide the number of calls to be covered in each day or week.

Divide territory into four quads. Work one quad at a time. Base each day (or week) around A accounts, A projects, nearby B accounts, and uncoded prospects. Also, a number of service accounts should be called each week.

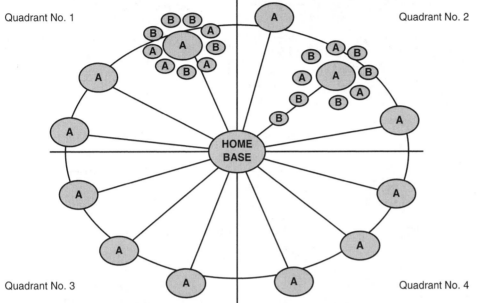

Quadrant No. 1

Quadrant No. 2

Quadrant No. 3

Quadrant No. 4

In this example, we assumed that you saw every A customer once a month and therefore covered your entire territory every month. If you cover your territory in more time, or less time, it's easy to adjust this method. Suppose, for example, you see all your A customers every week. Then you'd probably divide your territory into five parts, one for each day.

If you cover your territory every two weeks, you might use four quadrants, spending two or three days in each quadrant. If it takes you two months to cover your territory, you can split it into four quadrants and work two weeks in each quadrant or break into eight pieces and spend one week in each piece.

Figure 15-8
Cluster Quadrant Rating
System Form

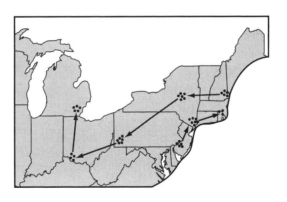

Figure 15-9
Straight-Line Routing

from that hub, returning home at a later date. This approach is valuable when there are concentrations of accounts in specific parts of the territory. Accounts that need less frequent calls can be alternated on each loop. Figure 15-11 depicts the clover-leaf pattern.

Leapfrog Routing

Starting at a distant point from the office, sales representatives work their way back, making calls as they return. A salesperson might fly out to the farthest point in the territory and then drive back, for example. On the next trip, he or she goes

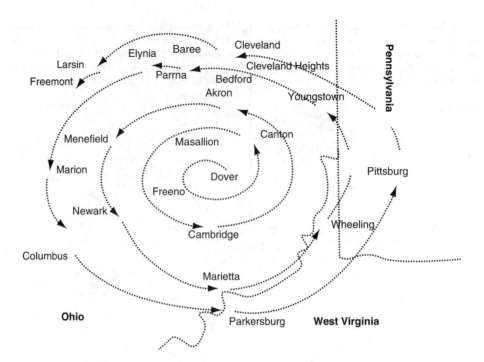

Figure 15-10
Circular Routing

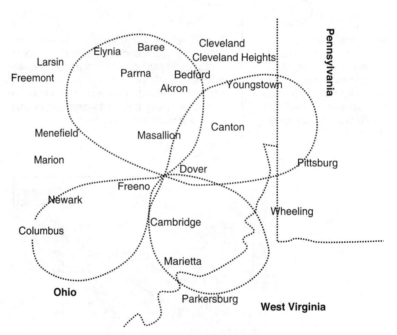

Figure 15-11
Cloverleaf Routing

leapfrog routing
Starting from their offices, sales reps work their way back, making calls as they return.

in the opposite direction. Though the salesperson might appear to be jumping randomly without plan, he or she has, in fact, determined the best route home, one that will provide chances to make all the calls needed. This allows the salesperson to skip some customers along the route and call on only those demanding attention that day. Figure 15-12 illustrates this routing pattern, which is known as **leapfrog routing.**

Whatever specific methods of routing they use, salespeople should plan first to visit existing A accounts. Nearby B accounts and A prospects should next receive attention. Going out of one's way for C accounts when more profitable customers or prospects are close by makes little sense.

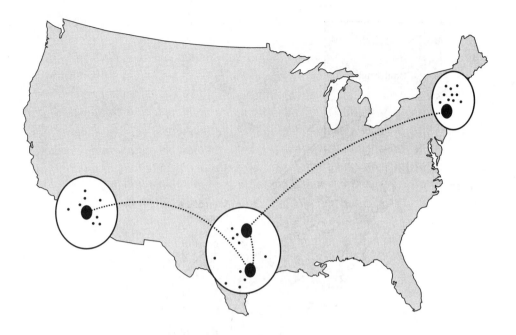

Figure 15-12
Leapfrog Routing

Skip-Stop Routing

A *call cycle,* also known as **skip-stop routing,** is a round of calls in which all A accounts are called on at least once and a portion of B and C accounts are covered in one swing through the territory, or a portion thereof. In a simplified example as depicted in Figure 15-13, a call cycle in a territory might cover two weeks and provide the following coverage: on the first trip (the solid lines), all the accounts are visited; on the second trip through the territory (the dotted lines), all the A accounts are again visited, but only a portion of the B and C accounts. Depending on the details of the full territory coverage plan, the salesperson might contact some of the missed accounts by telephone. This plan is called the *skip-stop* method because the salesperson skips some customers and stops at others according to a prearranged system.

skip-stop routing
Method of routing in which the salesperson skips some customers and stops at others according to a prearranged plan.

15-3 Postcall Analysis

A unique aspect of selling is its freedom and independence. However, this also makes it extremely difficult to assess performance. After all, no manager is present, and the only other party to the interview is the customer, hardly an objective observer. Sales representatives must act as their own judges, which is not an easy task but a necessary one. Improvement demands that salespeople take a hard look at their efforts and determine what needs to be done. There is no other way to grow in the job. Unfortunately, if improperly handled, self-analysis can lead to destructive self-criticism and, in turn, to poor morale and a decline in self-confidence. The trick is to be able to analyze one's efforts objectively without indulging in either self-belittlement or self-glorification. A form like the one shown in Figure 15-14 can be invaluable in encouraging such an attitude, while still maintaining objectivity. One innovative rep takes along a small tape cassette recorder that has a voice activation switch. He suggests wearing it on at least five calls (hanging it from a belt, shoulder, or placing in a briefcase). After recording the sales calls, the salesperson should listen to them at night and take notes on what he or she did right, did wrong, and to

Figure 15-13
Skip-Stop Routing

ACCOUNT _____ LOCATION _____

Did I contact whom I set out to contact? If not, why not? Is this the person I should be seeing? _____

_____

Did I get the results I set out to get (order received, feature and benefit explained, service work completed, etc.)? If
not, why not? _____

_____

Was my approach effective? _____
Did I adequately determine the prospect's needs and problems? If not, what further information do I need to do so?

_____

Was my presentation effective? Did I explain benefits and advantages instead of just features? Did I provide sufficient dramatization and proof? _____

_____

Did I listen effectively? Did I talk too fast or too slow? Did I watch for significant nonverbal behavior? _____

_____

Were there any objections raised that I could not answer? _____ If there were, what can I do to prepare
myself for them next time? _____

_____

Did I close at the right time? Was my close effective? If not, why not? _____

_____

Considering the results of this call, what should I do next time to achieve the sales objective I desire? _____

_____

Figure 15-14
Postcall Analysis

what the prospect responded favorably and negatively. This analysis should lead to improvements in subsequent calls.[13]

Analyzing each sales call qualitatively is important. It is equally important to assess quantitative efforts over a longer expanse of time. A form such as the one in Figure 15-15 helps in the process. As shown, salespeople can compare the plan with what actually transpired. A deviation of significant magnitude calls for further review. For example, failing to meet a goal for the number of calls per day should trig-

Criteria		Planned	Achieved
Time	Number of days worked	_____	_____
	Number of hours worked	_____	_____
	Average length of call	_____	_____
Calls	Number of calls per day	_____	_____
	Number of demonstrations	_____	_____
	Number of prospects generated	_____	_____
	Number of calls per sale	_____	_____
Sales	Sales volume (for relevant time period)	_____	_____
	Increase in sales (dollars, percentage, etc.)	_____	_____
	Average order size	_____	_____
	Percent of quota achieved	_____	_____
	New accounts sold	_____	_____
	Profit (gross margin, net margin, etc.)	_____	_____
Service	Number of displays	_____	_____
	Number of goodwill calls	_____	_____
	Number of inventories checked	_____	_____
	Number of dealer personnel trained	_____	_____

Figure 15-15
Standards of Performance

ger an activity analysis. Cutting travel time, reducing time spent waiting, and phoning ahead for appointments all represent means for improving the picture. Similarly, not meeting sales volume goals would call for account analysis (dropping some accounts and increasing efforts with others) or reexamining selling skills, all the way from prospecting to closing. The important point is that salespeople evaluate their own performance and make adjustments for the better. Who is in a better position to do so?

15-4 The Use of Personal Computers in Self-Management

Sales automation is revolutionizing the sales process by using technology to serve customers better and increase sales productivity. For example, today's systems make it possible to:[14]

- Automate an entire sales process, from generating a lead to closing the sale
- Manage customer relationships more effectively by providing easy access to customer and contact information
- Improve customer communications by automating letter-writing, faxing, emailing, and even dialing the telephone in telemarketing operations
- Rapidly generate many reports, including lead sources, close ratios, geographic trends, and industry sales trends
- Easily plan sales trips geographically
- Make it easy for salespeople to share information and ideas among team members or with other departments on a real-time basis
- Mail or fax customized personal letters in bulk to specific customer groups
- Improve close ratios by focusing sales efforts on the people most likely to buy, thus shortening the selling cycle
- Keep track of customer needs and buying schedules
- Serve customers better by giving them easy access to the information they need from your company to make quicker, more informed decisions

Of the hundreds of sales automation software packages available today, most fall into two main groups: contact management and enterprise-wide solutions. *Contact management software* allows salespeople to keep and use information about their customers and prospects. With it, salespeople can store basic information about a customer (company name, address, phone number) plus additional facts, such as hobbies or a spouse's name. Salespeople can also print letters instantly and track each time they meet or speak with a client.

With contact managers, as this type of software is often called, customer information is not only at the user's fingertips, but it can also be manipulated in many useful ways. For example, the software could search for all clients in Dallas or sort contacts based on company size. In addition, the system can prevent important prospects from falling through the cracks by reminding salespeople of the next step to be taken with each account and indicating when they need to provide more information or follow up with a phone call, letter, or fax.

Contact management software is essential for individual salespeople, and it may be all that's required for small sales forces or for organizations that just want to get their feet wet before embarking on an enterprise-wide sales automation effort. With an enterprise-wide system, all departments work from one centralized database. Thus, when a salesperson changes a contact's information, not only will everyone in sales have access to the new information, but everyone in marketing, accounting, and any other department using the system will also have the new information.

Contact management software usually includes several modules:

15-4a Lead Tracking/Contact Management

This module allows keeping track of potential and current customers, including purchase histories. With this module, the sales rep can store detailed information on each prospect, and then retrieve and display prospect records by identifying appropriate criteria (e.g., size, location, or SIC code). Figure 15-16 contains a typical prospect record from ACT!, one of the leading contact management programs.

15-4b Word Processing/Mail Merge

Because the letter is one of the most common and cost-effective formats for a direct mail campaign, a strong word-processing program is mandatory. A mail merge component enables you to personalize the letter to specific prospects in your database. Word-processing software can also increase salesperson productivity by easing the preparation of sales proposals. A prospect-specific proposal can be prepared in less than 10 minutes instead of hours. By standardizing proposals for the various product lines handled, all the salesperson needs to do is insert the individual customer's name, quantity desired, and price to have a tailored proposal ready for presentation. If the rep uses standard-sized labels, this desktop software module will meet the need, printing personalized labels for the envelopes containing the direct mail piece.

15-4c List Generation

The best contact managers will help the salesperson build, revise, refine, and generate highly targeted mailing or telemarketing prospect lists. Either using the rep's own database or in combination with a purchased database (typically on a CD-ROM), lists can be developed using geography (e.g., ZIP code, county, metropolitan area, or state); size, usually by number of employees; and type of business, typically using the federal government's Standard Industrial Classification Code, or SIC code, as it's most commonly known. Dun and Bradstreet offers desktop publishing software, containing most of the modules explained here, plus a CD-ROM with information on over 10 million U.S. businesses. **List generation software**

list generation software
Software that helps the salesperson build, revise, refine, and generate highly targeted mailing, email, or telemarketing prospecting lists.

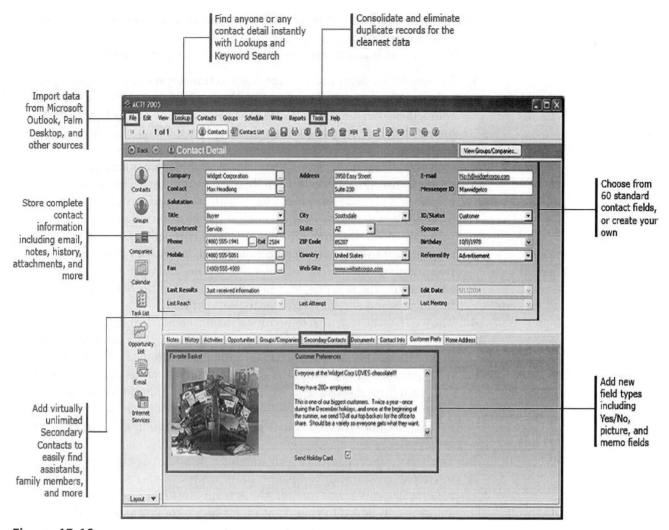

Find anyone or any contact detail instantly with Lookups and Keyword Search

Consolidate and eliminate duplicate records for the cleanest data

Import data from Microsoft Outlook, Palm Desktop, and other sources

Store complete contact information including email, notes, history, attachments, and more

Choose from 60 standard contact fields, or create your own

Add new field types including Yes/No, picture, and memo fields

Add virtually unlimited Secondary Contacts to easily find assistants, family members, and more

Figure 15-16
Prospect Record Items

Source: "Sales Prospect Record" from ACT website, www.act.com. © 2005 Best Software SB, Inc. All rights reserved. ACT! is a registered trademark of Best Software SB, Inc. Reprinted by permission.

allows any company, even small ones, to perform sophisticated desktop marketing, importing lists and sending out prospecting letters.

The rep can also build *tickler files*, which indicate the date of the next contact to be made with a prospect or customer. The most sophisticated contact managers will even beep and flash a message on the PC when it comes time to make a phone call.

15-4d The Internet

The **Internet** is a physical network, a social network, and a rapidly developing business network, too. The Internet is the world's largest computer network. Actually, it's a global network of networks—hence, Internet.

The web is a way of organizing the Internet's information resources in such a way that you see on-screen images and hear sounds. Even better, web resources are linked so that you can click on words or pictures to go to related web resources. Using the web is called *browsing* because it's so easy and inviting to wander from resource to resource. Increasingly, the Internet is becoming a business network; more than half of all Internet domains—registered computer addresses—are

Internet
The backbone of the information superhighway, it allows easy and cheap communication between computers.

commercial (.com), and there are now more dot-com domains than there are educational (.edu) ones.

How can the Internet be of assistance in marketing and sales?[15]

1. Companies are using online technology to transform one of selling's basic tasks, the presentation. There are two obvious advantages. First, scheduling conflicts can be minimized because the client can choose the time to go online and observe a presentation that employs the kind of multimedia techniques once reserved for elaborate "dog-and-pony" shows.

2. One of the biggest challenges that field salespeople face is accessing up-to-date information, especially when they're responding to a customer's questions. Thus, salespeople can immediately access information ranging from product descriptions and technical specifications to price quotes, reference sheets, and even information about competitors.

3. One of the most dramatic applications of web technology promises to be in sales training. The interactivity that the Internet and corporate intranets allow means that salespeople can be trained while in the field, a convenience for the reps and a money-saver for the company.

4. The web has the potential to become a major medium for reaching people when they're in a buying mode. People use online services when they need information. This gives marketers the potential to provide information and to reach people in need.[16] Marketers have the ability to target people precisely and reach them day or night, 365 days a year. With traditional media, organizations have to pay to reach thousands of people who have no interest in their product or service. That's great for brand-building, but bad for day-to-day sales.

5. The web provides a low-cost way to build a database of people specifically interested in what your company sells. When your website works, people voluntarily provide information about themselves in a format that's automatically added to your database for future communication. These are the people you really want to know: prospects or customers keenly interested in your company's products or services. You can then target them with email, for example.

6. The web gives salespeople an exceptional ability to communicate regularly with customers and prospects at a fraction of the cost of traditional direct mail or print and broadcast advertising. Once your website is up, the cost of distributing information decreases rapidly.

7. Thanks to the emergence of websites that allow customers to serve themselves, the Internet has great potential for improving customer service. Web-based customer service not only saves money but, by involving the customer in the process, it also often leads to greater customer satisfaction.

As an example, J. P. McHale Pest Management's web goal was to generate leads for metropolitan New York–area business via a website. To make sure it attracted only those concerned about pests, the company created a pest-control information service and called it www.nopests.com. It hired editors and writers to create useful, authoritative articles on such topics as major pests in the region, how to combat them, and the use of integrated pest management. Currently, a viewer enables people to see 4-color pictures of common household pests. The site includes an ask-the-expert section, a seasonal pest update, and details about free home inspection. J. P. McHale mentions the site in its advertising and brochures and has registered it on major search engines. By following up on people who "asked the expert" or who requested a free inspection, the company made enough sales in four months to recover the costs of developing the site. Leads continue to come in at hardly any additional cost.

Chapter Summary

This chapter began with a discussion of the importance of time management. Even those sales representatives with the most brilliant persuasive skills are doomed to failure unless they can manage their time. The reality of selling is that much time is spent on unproductive activities such as waiting, travel, and paperwork. Salespeople must learn to minimize these time-wasters and maximize their contact time with profitable customers.

One of the first steps in effective self-management is to recognize that not all accounts deserve the same amount of effort. Typically, a relatively small number of customers account for a disproportionate share of the salesperson's volume. This fact may occasion two mistakes commonly made by salespeople. First, they may spend too much time with their smaller accounts when they could profitably reallocate time to the larger ones that generate more sales dollars. Second, because salespeople may spend too much time with unprofitable accounts, they may overbudget their time, finding themselves unable to make all the calls they had planned. If a salesperson depends heavily on prospecting for success, he or she needs to rate prospects by some criteria to ensure that only those most likely to buy are visited.

After determining what accounts should receive attention and how often these accounts should be called upon, salespeople should establish an appropriate schedule; however, they may still find their time being used inefficiently. One way of determining this is to conduct an activity analysis for a period of time, a week to 10 days. Sales representatives can keep track of their time by marking off 30-minute intervals on a sheet of paper. They then can determine how many of these intervals were spent in customer contact, waiting, travel, service, and administration. If it turns out that too much time is spent in unproductive activities, salespeople can begin to take some remedial steps.

First, they can ensure that time spent in front of customers is used optimally. They can ask questions to identify the relevant decision makers, because calls on the wrong people are much too common of a time-waster for salespeople. Also, they can plan their calls beforehand. A certain amount of spontaneity is valuable in a sales call, but it is necessary for salespeople to keep in mind objectives and have a strategy before each call. A second major time-waster is waiting to see customers. Successful salespeople can minimize waiting by scheduling calls on days best suited for their customers, calling ahead for appointments, and confirming these appointments just before arriving for the interview. Salespeople can also use waiting time to do some of the paperwork required of all sales representatives. For paperwork that cannot be completed while waiting, salespeople should schedule regular periods for finishing their sales reports and other required correspondence. A third major time-waster is travel. To minimize travel, salespeople can route themselves by a number of methods that have proved helpful: straight-line routing, circular routing, cloverleaf routing, leapfrog routing, and skip-stop routing.

A cellular telephone, PDA, or pocket PC in the salesperson's car can save significant amounts of time. Appointments can be set up or confirmed, order status checked, and communication with one's sales manager speeded up.

A final step in self-management is for salespeople to analyze their performance after each call. With managers absent, salespeople must determine for themselves what went right or wrong.

The chapter ended with a discussion of the ways in which personal computers can ease the salesperson's task of self-management. PCs allow the salesperson to virtually conduct an entire marketing campaign via his or her PC. Typical software modules of contact management software were discussed, and the vast marketing capabilities of the Internet were described.

Discussion Questions

1. Why is time so critical to selling success?

2. How should the salesperson go about deciding which accounts to visit?

3. What are the two major errors made by salespeople in their call patterns?

4. "Each of my customers deserves equal treatment. I give no preferred treatment." Discuss this statement.

5. What is an activity analysis? Why is it necessary?

6. How might salespeople go about the task of establishing priorities for the day's activities?

7. "There's no point in planning a sales call because who knows what's likely to happen." Discuss.

8. Explain some ways to minimize waiting time.

9. When should salespeople do their paperwork?

10. Describe the following methods of routing: the straight-line method, the circular pattern, the cloverleaf pattern, the leapfrog approach, and the skip-stop method. What conditions influence the choice of one pattern over another?

11. A student's finding time to study is similar to a salesperson's maximizing customer contact time. Plan your efforts for the next week to maximize study time. Do an activity analysis of your time at the end of the week. Did you meet your plan? Did you spend your time effectively? If not, why?

12. Plan a sales call for trying to sell one of the following to a friend: portable DVD player, car, tennis racquet, suit or dress, speed-reading course, calculator, moving into an apartment, joining a social or professional fraternity, and enrolling in a selling course.

13. Interview a salesperson about time use. Better yet, travel with one. Would you say that the salesperson makes optimal use of time? If not, why? What would you do differently?

14. Explain how personal computers can assist salespeople in self-management.

15. How can cellular telephones be valuable to the salesperson?

16. What is contact management software?

17. How can the Internet assist salespeople?

Chapter Quiz

1. On the average, salespeople spend just _____ percent of their time directly in front of customers.
   a. 15
   b. 25
   c. 35
   d. 50

2. The first step in planning is to
   a. divide the customer database into various groups based on each customer's cost.
   b. determine who should be called on, how often, and for what duration.
   c. conduct a time analysis of the job.
   d. analyze the prospects in terms of future sales potential.

3. In analyzing their accounts, salespeople should keep in mind a principle that
   a. 90 percent of sales comes from approximately 50 percent of the customers.
   b. the best customers should consume no more than 25 percent of the salesperson's time.
   c. average customers can become good customers by spending more time calling on them.
   d. a relatively small number of customers usually account for a disproportionate share of sales.

4. In a survey of 192 companies and 10,000 salespeople on sales-force productivity undertaken by *Sales & Marketing Management,* survey respondents reported that it took an average of _____ calls to close a first sale, compared with only 3 calls to close a sale on an existing account.
   a. 5
   b. 7
   c. 10
   d. 12

5. In terms of allocating time properly, salespeople should first look at time-wasters. All of the following tend to be big time-wasters for salespeople *except*
   a. spending time on large accounts.
   b. being comfortable with the status quo.
   c. planning how to answer likely objections.
   d. lack of trust of other people in the organization.

6. Sales representatives must establish priorities for the performance of the various selling tasks. The task that should receive the highest priority is
   a. prospecting for new customers.
   b. service calls with customers.
   c. contact time with customers.
   d. sales call planning.

7. It is important to build relationships with key buyers and future decision makers before they are in buying mode. If another company already has the account set up as a "straight rebuy," it is
   a. important to make frequent sales calls.
   b. important to contact the economic buyer.
   c. better to use email or the telephone to make contact rather than in person.
   d. better to spend your time elsewhere.

8. A critical step in planning is a routing-pattern analysis. In using the _____ routing method, salespeople start at a distant point from the office and work their way back, making calls as they return.
   a. leapfrog
   b. cloverleaf
   c. circular
   d. skip-stop

9. Contact management software usually includes several modules. The _____ module allows salespeople to keep track of potential and current customers, including purchase histories.
   a. lead tracking/contact management
   b. word-processing
   c. mail merge
   d. list generation

10. The list generation module of contact management software allows sales reps to build tickler files, which
   a. list a customers hobbies, interests, and other personal facts that can be used during the sales call.
   b. includes all of a customer's past purchase history.
   c. are prospects that are the most likely to make purchases.
   d. indicate the date of the next contact to be made with a prospect or customer.

Web Exercise

What tools will you need as you plan routes and make calls? How can the web help you do this? Check out www.mapquest.com, www.act.com, and www.microsoft.com for software commonly used by sales professionals. What other services and products can you find to help organize your time and make you an efficient sales representative?

Notes

1. William A. O'Connell and William Keenan, Jr., "The Shape of Things to Come," *Sales & Marketing Management,* January 1990, pp. 36–41.
2. Art Sobczak, "Quit Wasting Time with Worthless Follow-Ups," *EyesonSales.com,* 2003.
3. Dave Kahle, "Biggest Time Wasters," *SalesVault.com,* 2004.
4. Neil Rackham, *SPIN Selling,* New York: McGraw-Hill, 1996.
5. Dave Stein, "Timing Is Money," *EyeonSales.com,* May 23, 2003.
6. Robert B. Miller, Stephen E. Heiman, and Tad Tuleja, *Strategic Selling,* New York: Warner Books, 1985, pp. 55–56, 72–87.
7. Anita Sirianni, "Balancing the Time Management Tight Wire," *EyeonSales.com,* April 8, 2003.
8. Betsy Cummings, "Tools of the Trade," *Sales & Marketing Management,* October 2003.
9. Ginger Trumfio, "The Case for Email," *Sales & Marketing Management,* July 1994.
10. William J. Tobin, "80–20 or Perish," *Sales & Marketing Management,* August 13, 1984.
11. "Tape It," *Personal Selling Power,* January/February 1994.
12. George Colombo and Leanne Benfield, "Sales Automation," Sales Marketing Network at info-now.com, 2004.
13. Marshal M. Rosenthal, "Increasing Sales Productivity via Internet and Intranet," Sales Marketing Network at info-now.com, 2004.
14. Bruce Bolger, "An Internet Primer," Sales Marketing Network at info-now.com, 2004.
15. Marshal M. Rosenthal, "Using the Internet to Improve Customer Service," Sales Marketing Network at info-now.com, 2004.
16. Philip Holmes, "Relationship Marketing via the Internet," Sales Marketing Network at info-now.com, 2004.

Case 15-1

Analyze the day's activities for Mary MacDonald, salesperson for Standard Office Supplies Company. Make suggestions for ways of improving Mary's use of time.

9:00–10:10. Called on Lusinski Candles. Waited in the lobby until 9:40 to see the purchasing agent, Mr. Thomas. Discussed office supplies ordering procedures. Found out that certain standard forms are ordered through Mr. Thomas's office, but others are left up to the individual department heads.

11:00–11:30. Cold-called Leach Truck. Was able to see Mr. Smith, the purchasing agent, after 25 minutes. He was interested in Standard's line of office supplies but was in a hurry to go to an executive meeting. Requested that I call for an appointment next time.

11:45–12:00. Called on Tom's Hardware to make sure that office forms previously ordered had been delivered. Only half the order ($100) had arrived. Tom was not upset at all.

12:05–12:55. Took Tom to lunch at Hermann's Bar and Grill.

1:00–1:30. Called on Mercury Marine. On last month's call, I determined that a redesigned order form was needed for the new order-entry system. Discovered that they have just ordered $10,000 worth of forms from Greer Register but are still open to competitive bids in the future.

1:45–2:30. Called on Harwell Insurance. Received order for $50 worth of typing paper.

3:30–4:00. Called on Garden City Community College. Learned that orders for office supplies are placed in Jefferson City, the state capital. To receive bid requests, Jones must meet certain standard requirements for all authorized vendors.

4:15–4:25. Called on Thill Corporation to see the purchasing agent. She had been called out of town, however.

4:30. Returned to the office to fill out my call report and other required correspondence.

Case 15-2

Ron Friendly, sales representative for Superior Hospital Uniform Company, has the following accounts in his territory in Wisconsin. Plan Ron's day for a Tuesday; Ron will be working out of Milwaukee. A map of Ron's territory should help the scheduling, so visit www.johnnyroadtrip.com/cities/greenbay/maps/map_wisconsin.htm before you begin this exercise. Indicate how you would improve his routing.

Mercy Hospital, Green Bay. Annual sales volume, $10,000: 5 percent of Ron's yearly sales. Reorders are sent in regularly by mail, but Ron can usually stimulate larger orders with a personal call. On his two previous calls, Ron talked to the purchasing agent about Superior's new operating room uniforms. On this next call, Ron must contact the operating room administrator and the laundry manager.

Scharp Uniforms, Chilton. Annual volume to Ron, $1,500. Scharp is patronized by local nurses who buy their own uniforms. Ron typically checks the stock for Mary Hennessey, the owner, before reorders are placed.

St. Mary's Hospital, Fond du Lac. A 100-bed hospital, St. Mary's has provided orders sporadically in the past, primarily because of the purchasing agent. The head of the operating room, however, is noted as being progressive and innovative. St. Mary's is located on the east side of Fond du Lac.

Riverside Linen, Appleton. Riverside is a typical industrial launderer; they rent out and clean uniforms for a number of businesses and hospitals. Price is the critical factor to them, with delivery a close second. Superior has received orders in the past from Riverside but not in the same volume as Angelica, Superior's largest competitor. Angelica has been able to underprice Superior in the past, especially on the sort of stock items that a company such as Riverside orders. However, Angelica's biggest plant in St. Louis is on strike and shipments must come from the West Coast.

St. Theresa's Hospital, Appleton. One of Ron's largest accounts, St. Theresa's annual sales volume is $20,000. Ron has no special plans at the hospital, but reorders generally follow Ron's visits. Ted Jones, the purchasing agent, has been a loyal Superior customer for years.

Belton Hospital, Green Bay. Belton is a loyal customer of Ron though only a moderate-size one ($7,000 annual volume). There is much potential for increased business because, at 500 beds, Belton is one of the largest hospitals in the Fox Valley.

Baptist Hospital, Manitowoc. Annual sales volume to Ron is $8,000. Baptist, a 250-bed hospital, has been a steady customer of Ron's in the past. However, Angelica has been making some inroads here.

Winnebago State Hospital, Oshkosh. One of the main state hospitals in Wisconsin, Winnebago places orders on a bid basis. Superior has just received a bid request for approximately $25,000 worth of cotton patient gowns. In the past, Superior has failed to receive many bids because of price considerations, but quality is becoming more important to Winnebago, as reflected in the bid specifications. Because Superior's uniforms vary somewhat from these specifications, a personal call by Ron is necessary.

Sales-Force Management

Key Terms

Behavioral Event Interview
bonus
call reports
career path

combination plans
knockout factors
management by objective
perquisites

sales quotas
straight commission
straight salary

Learning Objectives

Learning Objectives

After studying Chapter 16, you will understand:

- How a knowledge of sales management will aid the beginning salesperson
- The critical importance of recruitment and selection to successful sales management
- Methods for determining the number of salespeople to be hired
- How to develop qualitative hiring standards through conducting a job analysis, writing a job description, and specifying selection criteria
- How to identify sources for recruiting sales applicants
- Methods for making the selection decision
- The critical nature of sales-force motivation and evaluation
- The role of automatic supervisory techniques

- Methods for establishing sales territories
- Ways of setting equitable sales quotas
- The value of call reports
- The advantages and disadvantages of the three major ways of compensating salespeople
- Why compensation is not the sole factor in sales-force motivation
- The use of noncash perquisites (or "perks")
- Principles for structuring an effective sales contest
- The importance of leadership style to sales-force morale
- The role of meetings and conventions
- How management by objective works
- The value of the career path concept
- The problems and methods of sales-force evaluation

This chapter discusses sales management. In the broader sense, sales management can include all of a firm's various marketing activities, such as advertising, distribution, and pricing. However, sales management is restricted here to only those activities directly associated with managing the efforts of field sales personnel.

16-1 Why Study Sales Management?

The student might ask why it is necessary to examine the topic at this time. After all, not too many college students are going to start as sales managers right out of school. There are several answers to this question.

1. Sales management requires different skills from selling and, as such, represents a dramatic adjustment for the promoted salesperson.
2. Not all companies do a creditable job of training field sales managers.
3. An understanding of sales management helps salespeople in dealings with superiors.
4. A career in sales management is a worthy goal for ambitious beginning salespeople.

As depicted in Figure 16-1, sales management requires not only the interpersonal skills acquired in selling, but also administrative and leadership skills. The skills needed change from selling to supervisory, to managerial, to administrative and leadership skills. The latter almost exclusively demand planning, motivating, and directing skills, ones that don't naturally evolve with field sales.

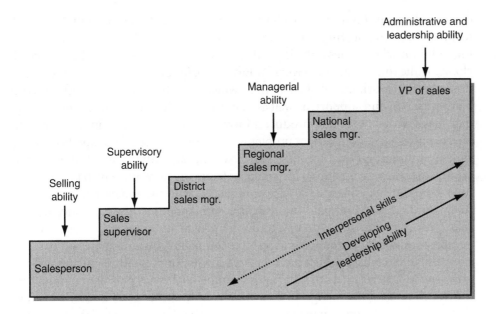

Figure 16-1
Changes in Ability
Requirements As Position
Changes
Source: Rolph E. Anderson,
Joseph H. Hair, Jr. and Alan J. Bush,
Professional Sales Management,
New York: McGraw-Hill, 1992.

Unfortunately, this problem is compounded by the fact that many companies do little, if any, training of sales managers. Preparation for the job is often limited to instruction in how—and how often—to fill out a seemingly endless stream of reports. In one survey, an overwhelming majority of sales managers said that their company's sales management training wasn't up to preparing either them or their subordinates for management duties. Commented one sales manager about his training, "When I was promoted, I was just kind of dropped off the end of the pier. If you swam, you made it."[1] The result is that many sales managers differ from salespeople in title only, and they continue to spend their time helping out in the field. Oftentimes, the company compounds this problem by requiring the new manager to keep key accounts while learning to manage others.[2] After all, it is a lot more comfortable and familiar. The sad thing is that this often leads to arrested development in the sales force. Why learn to close if "Old Harry," the boss, is the best closer around? It is a lot easier just to bring him along; he is probably dying to come anyway.

Knowledge of sales management is valuable to students from another standpoint. Acquaintance with sales management helps if you are promoted into such a position; it also helps in getting the promotion in the first place. Familiarity with management issues provides salespeople with insight into the activities of their superiors, facilitating communication with them. When a position in management becomes available, the individual who already appears to know something about the subject will have the jump on the competition.

A sales manager's job is worthy of a student's ambition. The typical sales manager is well paid. Though figures vary somewhat, depending on the type of selling and the number of people supervised, the median total compensation is approximately $122,899.[3] From a monetary standpoint, then, the sales manager's job is worth having. For the ambitious, hardworking, beginning salesperson, it is also within reach.

A final reason to be cognizant of sales management is that it is changing dramatically with technology. Several business trends have coincided to reduce the number of sales managers with some companies or, at least, increase their span of control. New communications technology, sales-force automation, empowerment, team selling, reengineering, quality management, customer focus, relationship selling, solution selling, telemarketing, integrated marketing—each of these trends is changing the role of sales managers. At Edward D. Jones, the financial services firm, new reps now work out of their homes, which have become virtual offices. Sales administration and support, as well as sales training, is all electronic. The reps update files and download new product information by a computer linked to the corporate offices in St. Louis; client problems, questions, and special requests are taken care of by phone; product training, sales coaching, and other general advice is covered by the company's nationwide videoconferencing network, which is also linked to St. Louis. At such financial services companies, where reps have always been virtually on their own and paid by straight commission, the disappearance of sales managers isn't surprising with new technology. With automation and restructuring at more traditional production and services companies, the primary effect has been on the span of control, which has increased at GE Supply, with 17 to 40 sales reps now reporting to a single sales manager. Comments the vice president of sales, "We haven't eliminated the manger; we've broadened and changed his role." Although there will always be sales managers, obviously, the sales manager of the future will be different. The traditional sales manager—the exhorting, demanding, numbers-oriented field general—is vanishing. In his or her place, the new manager will become more attentive to developing the personal skills of salespeople and creating an environment of learning. For new sales managers, the future promises to be exciting and offer opportunity for managerial creativity.[4]

Two areas will receive primary emphasis in our discussion of sales management: (1) building the sales force and (2) motivating and evaluating salespeople. Directing the efforts of field sales personnel could involve a number of additional topics, but these two are perceived to be the most critical to beginning managers. The first of these tasks, building the sales force, basically requires two activities: recruiting and selecting salespeople.

16-2 Recruitment and Selection

Probably the most important of all the sales manager's tasks are the recruitment and selection of competent sales representatives. No matter how refined a manager's other skills, it is difficult to compensate for hiring poorly qualified salespeople on whom training, compensation, and motivation techniques will all have negligible impact. If the beginning sales manager has a choice of skills at which to become proficient, recruitment and selection are the ones to choose.

16-2a Determining the Number of Sales Personnel Needed

The initial step in recruitment and selection is determining the number of sales representatives needed. If few needs exist for additional people, there is no need to begin an extensive recruitment program. However, with long-term expansion in the economy and the turnover that characterizes many sales forces, it is unusual for a company not to need significant numbers of new recruits.

If little or no time were required to recruit, select, and train salespeople, then the problem would not be so great. However, it takes time to attract sufficient applicants for the job, it requires some investment of time and effort to select competent people, and it takes time to train them. In this light, the smart sales manager plans well ahead. Half-measures are destined to failure.

The general approach to determining quantitative requirements is the formula:

Salespeople Needed − Salespeople Available = Additional Salespeople Required

Calculating the first part of the equation—workers needed—makes use of the company sales forecast. For discussion purposes, let's assume that a company now employs 800 salespeople with sales volume of $100 million per year. On average, this means that each salesperson's volume is $125,000 annually. If sales are forecasted to be $125 million in two years, then 1,000 salespeople will be needed, which we determine by dividing forecasted total sales ($125 million) by average volume per salesperson ($125,000). The number of current personnel that should still be available is determined by subtracting the expected turnover from the current number of sales personnel. (Expected turnover is calculated by multiplying the current number of salespeople times the annual turnover rate times the number of years.) If the company averages 10 percent turnover per year, then 640 current employees will still be available at the end of two years, since $[800 − (800 \times .1 \times 2)] = (800 − 160) = 640$. In total, this means that if the company will require 1,000 salespeople two years hence, then 360 additional sales representatives must be hired ($1,000 − 640 = 360$).

16-2b Determining Qualitative Requirements

Determining the number of sales personnel needed is only the first step in recruiting and selection. Knowing how many salespeople to hire is of limited value if there is no determination of what kind are needed. Of course, developing qualitative requirements is not that easy. If it were, the rate of sales-force turnover would not be so high. No factors contribute more to poor selection by sales managers than not knowing what qualities make a successful salesperson and not making any systematic attempt to determine what they are.

Developing qualitative standards is a 3-step process:

1. Conducting a job analysis
2. Writing a job description
3. Specifying selection criteria

Job Analysis

The job analysis, if done correctly, represents a critical inquiry into the nature of the sales job. Much like a time-and-motion study, the job analysis seeks to break the sales job down into its component parts. Generally, the job analysis should include careful examination by management of the job's environmental factors and its performance factors. Environmental factors refer to characteristics such as the nature of the competition, industry structure and practices, and the typical channels of distribution used. Performance factors refer to how the company's sales force spends its time (traveling, waiting, selling, and so forth). It is necessary to examine time use, especially selling time, in minute detail. For example, is the salesperson expected to prospect for new customers or deal with existing ones? Is closing part of the selling job, or does the job consist exclusively of detail work? Is support work involved, such as stocking shelves, setting up displays, and training distributor personnel? Is the nature of the job changing? All of these and similar factors should be studied.

Consider facsimile (fax) machines. Original models did little more than transmit a document over phone lines. This technology required salespeople who could sell machines. Today, fax machines are sophisticated pieces of technology that are able to reproduce photographs and blueprints; simultaneously send multiple pages to locations around the globe; print error reports; are often integrated into PCs; and even make copies. The marketplace is now flooded with a variety of sophisticated models and manufacturers. The salesperson for the product has to be a consultant who is able to identify and analyze the needs of an organization before suggesting the appropriate model. The salesperson must not only understand the technology, but the applications and the competition, as well.[5] Clearly, all this will have an impact on hiring criteria.

Job Description

The culmination of the job analysis is a written job description. Notice the use of the word *written*. To be effective, the job description must be committed to paper. Verbal descriptions are easily misinterpreted, leading to misunderstandings and mistakes. Job descriptions that are not written down are often worse than no job description at all. At a minimum, the job description should include:[6]

1. Job title
2. Title of the immediate supervisor
3. Job summary (general responsibilities)
4. Major job duties
5. Minor job duties
6. Unusual responsibilities (regardless of frequency)
7. The job's relation to other positions
8. Organizational reporting relationships

The job description should present a complete and accurate profile of the duties to be performed by salespeople. Indeed, research has demonstrated that inconsistency between job expectations and actual job activities increases turnover.[7] If the job description specifies "merchandising store promotions" when, in fact, it requires little more than stocking shelves and taking inventory, a newly hired salesperson is likely to be disappointed. The three functions of sales personnel must be explicitly stated: servicing, counseling, and selling.

The job description, as outlined in Box 16-1, should strike a happy medium with regard to the extent of its detail. As far as possible, the salesperson's duties should be described in measurable terms, such as number of calls per day, dollars or units sold, number of displays set up, and number of new accounts opened. However, the job description also should avoid too much detail, which would make it difficult or impossible for the sales manager to use.

Selection Criteria

No matter how careful the job analysis or how accurate the job description, it is all for naught without the sales manager's knowledge of the qualifications needed for success in the job. Often sales managers rely on intuition alone, and the results are disastrous. The problem is compounded by the fact that no universally applicable characteristics have been discovered that preordain sales success. As one researcher concluded:

> Progress to date has clearly established that sales occupations should not be presumed to be homogeneous. Rather research has indicated the need to recognize differences in various types of selling and to treat major product classifications separately if more accurate performance indices are to be developed. In fact, it may well be that predictors for one type of personal selling work may simply be of little value in a different personal selling setting.[8]

Box 16-1

Sample Job Description for College Textbook Publisher

Sales Account Managers

We are looking for regional account managers to manage our territories throughout the United States. We will provide extensive training at our company headquarters.

During the training period, the new account manager will spend approximately two weeks at the company headquarters becoming familiar with our product and sales tools. As part of the training process, the new account managers will also attend sales calls and presentations and work with product development.

Upon successful completion of the training period, the new account managers will return to their territories to assume responsibility for all sales activities. The contact base focuses on college and university professors in the given territory.

The account management position requires some overnight travel (25%–35%) within the territory during the key selling months of January to June and September to December. The sales process includes a combination of face-to-face, email follow-up, and telephone selling.

Candidate Requirements

Minimum of 2–3 years of experience in the higher education market, preferably in sales and/or marketing. Ability to work in a start-up environment. Extremely professional and team-focused. Bright, creative, hardworking, flexible, and dedicated. Strong presentation and sales skills, including the ability to build relationships via regular telephone and email contact with customers. Ability to handle the travel required with the position. BA/BS required.

In the absence of universal characteristics, sales managers must take steps to establish criteria for their individual sales positions. At a minimum, an examination of the job description should provide clues to needed qualifications. For example, the job description for textbook salespeople indicates that applicants should possess an understanding of universities and should have an ability to express themselves—obviously vital traits for selling texts. Similarly, a sales representative's job description at Lily's Tulip Division (which makes plastic cups) establishes that intelligence and perseverance are required for job success. These qualifications evolve from the fact that salespeople are expected to sell to many types of industries—hotels, hospitals, fast-food chains, and vending locations—which calls for an ability to learn and adjust quickly. Because each of these accounts needs frequent calls, perseverance is a further requirement.

Another approach to determining job qualifications besides the job description is the "retrospective" approach. In this method, past and present salespeople are classified into categories of performance—"successful" versus "unsuccessful," for example. These groups are then compared regarding their characteristics at the time of hiring (i.e., education, experience, family responsibilities, habits, employers). Customers are surveyed to determine the characteristics they consider most important in the salespeople who call on them. Studies indicate that customers are much better judges of performance criteria than either managers or salespeople.[9] If statistically significant differences manifest themselves between "successful" and "unsuccessful" sales reps, management then has a profile of the kind of applicant who will make the best sales representative. With statistically significant differences among groups, management has a profile of the kind of individual having the highest probability of success.

16-2c Recruiting

Once quantitative and qualitative requirements are developed, the sales manager must determine where to find recruits. Fruitful sources of sales recruits are within the company itself, other companies, educational institutions, employment agencies, and advertising.

Company Sources

The sales manager should never ignore the possibility of securing recruits from the company's own production or office personnel. Some clear advantages come with these recruits:

1. They are familiar with company products and policies.
2. Their work habits and potential are already known.
3. Overall company morale is improved with the possibility of promotion into sales.

Survey results also confirm the success of hiring from within, as one-third of top-performing salespeople surveyed earlier held nonsales positions within the same firm.[10]

Other Companies

Salespeople who are currently working for other firms may be available. These people may be recruited from distributors, customers, and competitors. Recruits hired from distributors and customers may already have product knowledge, and something may be known about their work history. However, to solicit them actively can sour relations with their employers and cause serious damage to the company. Much the same is true of hiring competitors' salespeople. Although they possess product knowledge and are already acquainted with many of the company's customers, soliciting them can destroy competitive relations. Retribution from competitors can come in the form of slurring the hiring company's products. It is also true that "bidding" for competitors' salespeople can inflate salaries beyond a realistic range. Under these circumstances, sales representatives may spend more time collecting offers than working. Big hiring bonuses for new salespeople can also shatter morale among current employees. When current salespeople see newly hired recruits being paid more, and those new recruits produce no more than the current salespeople themselves, morale is bound to suffer. Also, sales reps from rival companies may find it difficult to adjust their selling style and attitudes to fit a new company. For these reasons, many companies make it a rule not to seek out competitors' salespeople unless the salespeople approach them first.[11]

Educational Institutions

Colleges, universities, and 2-year institutions represent rich sources for sales recruits. If a technical background of some sort is required or if potential managers are desired, then this source is especially good. Recent college graduates are likely to be enthusiastic, able to manage their time, and have the ability to learn. Disadvantages are that they likely lack sales experience and once hired, expect rapid promotion.

Rather than taking the approach of interviewing through the placement office, which limits interaction to 20 brief minutes with students, sales managers can make contacts with faculty members and seek permission to speak before their classes. Inevitably, the brightest and most aggressive students will come forward to ask questions, and these are the ones who will be hired for summer internship programs. Later, after these students have developed into mature young salespeople, they can be sent back to campus to repeat the routine again.

Employment Agencies

If sales managers do not have enough time for recruiting, they might consider using a professional employment agency. Certainly agencies can perform a valuable screening function, weeding out applicants who are clearly unqualified for the job. However, the manager should be careful in selecting an employment agency. Many do not possess good reputations as sources for salespeople. They show no real concern for either the client's or the job seeker's needs in referring qualified people to appropriate firms.

Classified Advertisements and Online Advertising

Advertisements in trade publications, newspapers, or on the web are frequently used to attract sales recruits. If a technically qualified or experienced individual is needed, an ad in a trade magazine or industry-related website is appropriate. Such advertising will reach a wide audience, attracting many applicants, but this may be its biggest disadvantage if many underqualified candidates are attracted.

Referrals

Another excellent source of recruits is suggestions from current employees, especially salespeople and sales managers, who will have many contacts through networking with customers and fellow salespeople. Statistics prove referrals are among the top source of recruiting effective salespeople.[12]

Organizing the Recruiting Effort

Whatever sources turn out to be most fruitful for the sales manager, it is critical that the recruiting effort be organized. This means that recruiting must be continuous and that an applicant file must be established.

Too often a sales manager starts recruiting only when a vacancy occurs. The tendency is to see too few applicants and then make a hurried choice. One way of avoiding this danger is to recruit continuously (even if there are no current openings), placing information about recruits in a file. When a vacancy occurs, the manager will have a list of prescreened applicants available.

16-2d Selection

Once recruits are attracted to apply for the position, it is necessary to select those to be hired. Among the tools that aid the manager in this task are:

- Application blanks
- Interviews
- Reference checks
- Tests

Typically, these methods are used sequentially. At each step, unqualified applicants are eliminated. However, before using any selection tool, sales managers should be aware of the legal aspects of hiring.

Legal Aspects of Selection

In the selection process, the manager must be aware of recent rulings that restrict the use of certain preemployment information. If discrimination occurs, the firm may have its hiring practices investigated by the Equal Employment Opportunity Commission (EEOC).

Though it is difficult to make a definitive statement about the law, it is generally true that if the firm's hiring practices show a high rate of rejection of women and minorities, the company's selection procedure may be reviewed. Any criteria used in the process must be demonstrated to have validity. For example, it is legal for a firm to hire more men than women for a job if it can be proven that men possess more of some trait or ability that will enable them to do the job better. That is, the company must show that men do, in fact, perform better. On the other hand, if there is not a disproportionate rejection of minorities, then there is no validation requirement.[13]

Application Forms

Typically, the job seeker is asked to fill out an application form prior to the interview. The application form serves two purposes. First, it collects important information. Second, it aids the interview.

In the first instance, the application form identifies basic qualifications such as the individual's education and experience. In doing so, the sales manager should have in mind characteristics that have proved critical to the success of past sales representatives. Additionally, the manager should look for overall patterns of achievement in education, jobs, and personal life. In this respect, the application form offers an advantage over the interview. Although a sales manager can be impressed in the interview by the applicant's appearance and personality, the application form contains facts, not impressions. Seldom do people change their patterns dramatically. A person's past record is a good indicator of future behavior. The smart sales manager recognizes this and examines the application form closely.

knockout factors
Characteristics that tend to reduce the probability of job success.

Besides looking at qualifications, many companies advise their sales managers to look for **knockout factors.** These factors represent disqualifying information—characteristics that tend to reduce the probability of job success. Each company should determine its own, just as it sets its own job qualifications. Some common examples of knockout factors follow:

1. *Job-hopping tendencies.* Too many jobs (three or more in the past five years) is a danger signal.
2. *Excessive personal indebtedness.* Debt (excluding a home mortgage) is generally considered excessive when it cannot be met within two years from earnings on the new job.
3. *Recent business failure.* If applicants have failed in their own businesses within the past two years, they may constitute a risk.
4. *Too high a previous salary.* Although some applicants are searching for advancement opportunities, accepting markedly lower earnings may call for too dramatic an adjustment in lifestyle. The person might see the current job opening only as a means of earning some quick money while seeking a better job.
5. *Unexplained gaps in employment.* Gaps of six months or longer should be investigated.
6. *Overqualification for the job.* Someone who is overqualified for the job will seldom stick around for long.[14]

The application form is also an effective aid in interviewing. The completed form should be reviewed by the sales manager to formulate hypotheses prior to the interview. For example, if the applicant has listed the reason for leaving a previous job as "personal," the manager may check to see if the applicant is hiding having been fired. Or if several questions on the form have been neglected, the sales manager may hypothesize that the applicant is careless about details. Several jobs within a few years should raise a red flag for the interviewer. The interviewer may be able to identify such "job-hoppers," who are unlikely to stay with the company very long. One study conducted by a pharmaceutical firm found that typical application blank information, such as job history and sales experience, was able to predict candidates most likely to remain on the job.[15]

Interviews

Interviews are an important aspect of hiring salespeople. Interviews profile applicants' characteristics that are difficult to assess with other selection techniques. Intelligence, the ability to converse articulately, appearance, personality, motivation, and poise become evident in the interview.

Unfortunately, sales managers are not always the best interviewers. They have a tendency to talk too much. This is all right when explaining the job, but when determining an applicant's qualifications, it is the applicant who should be talking. Sales managers also tend to feed desired answers to applicants. A conversation like the following is not unusual:

> **Sales Manager:** Our job requires a lot of travel. How do you feel about travel?
>
> **Applicant:** I like it just fine. The more the better, with me.
>
> **Sales Manager:** You have to do a lot of prospecting in our job. Do you like to prospect?
>
> **Applicant:** I enjoy prospecting, especially cold-calling.
>
> **Sales Manager:** You know, you sound just like the person we need.

To encourage the applicant to talk, the manager should ask open-ended questions, such as "Why did you leave this position?" or "How do you feel about selling as a career?" Good questions to ask of all applicants are: "What is the single most important thing that has happened to you so far in your life?" "Are there any others that come close in significance?" Because most sales positions demand that salespeople set goals and meet them, it is especially important to ask, "What goals did you set in your last job? Walk me through, in detail, the steps you took to achieve those goals." Answers to such questions will indicate a great deal about the basic motivation of the applicant. The manager can then decide if the applicant has enough of the attributes required for success in the job.

During the course of questioning, it is important for the manager to listen closely, especially for signs of resistance and defensiveness. It is critical to avoid jumping to conclusions. Because the applicant looks good or speaks well, many sales managers reach an immediate decision to hire without listening carefully to what the applicant has to say. For this reason, many companies insist that job seekers be interviewed by more than one executive. When more than one interviewer is used, it becomes essential to have some consistency in interviewing to allow common comparisons. A universal form with standard questions is a great help when it is completed by each interviewer. The ratings can then be totaled for each common category, and a decision can be made.

David McClleland, Harvard psychologist and motivation expert, has developed the **Behavioral Event Interview** (BEI).[16] As the critical component in this technique,

Behavioral Event Interview
Asking the applicant three incidents in which he or she did particularly well and three in which they did poorly.

McClelland recommends asking the applicant three incidents in which he or she did particularly well and three in which they did poorly. For each scenario, the interviewer should ask:

What were the events that led to the incident?

Who was involved?

What did you think about, feel, and want to accomplish?

What exactly did you do and say?

What was the outcome?

In the applicants' answers, the interviewer should look for the ability to influence others; a high level of achievement motivation; initiative; strong interpersonal skills; and customer orientation.

Reference Checks

Character and credit references offer important evaluative information. No matter how promising a candidate appears on the application blank and in the interview, some things will go unnoticed. Many of these facts will appear in reference checks. One study by a Michigan State University researcher, in fact, found that reference checks were twice as reliable as prehiring interviews, which are still far and away the most used selection tool.[17]

One good source of information about an applicant is a former manager. Superiors will have knowledge of applicants' on-the-job performance, their promptness, their ability to get along with others, their tenacity, and their other strengths and weaknesses. Probably the key question to ask a former manager is, "Would you hire this individual again?"

Former customers are another good reference source. In fact, some experts say that customer references are more reliable than former employers, who may be afraid of lawsuits. During interviews, ask candidates to list four important customers and explain the results they achieved with them.[18]

More and more employers these days are using credit reports to help screen applicants, the theory being that knowing how an applicant handles bills, loans, and other financial obligations tells much about their motivation, reliability, and sense of responsibility. Managers should be advised, however, that when rejecting someone "either wholly or partly because of information contained" in a credit report, the law demands that the manager let the applicant know this, and also identify the agency supplying the report.[19]

In general, the best way to check references is in person. However, this may be difficult to arrange. If such is the case, then a phone check is preferable to a written reference request. People are usually reluctant to say anything bad in writing.

Tests

An extensive discussion of tests is beyond the scope of this text. A thorough coverage of the subject requires a whole text in itself. Briefly, the idea behind tests is to build a series of paper-and-pencil questions that will provide a representative sample of a person's likely behavior on the job.

Tests used for assessing selling ability come in several varieties. Probably the most widely used are intelligence tests. These are helpful in determining whether an applicant has sufficient mental ability to handle the job.

Sales aptitude tests are designed to measure what an applicant already knows about selling. They pose a number of hypothetical selling problems that people with selling ability should know how to solve.

Personality tests are designed to measure the degree to which an individual possesses various personality traits. Although there is considerable intuitive appeal in personality tests, their results in selecting salespeople have been mixed, depending on the type of selling and organization.

Interest tests seek to determine if applicants have interests in common with working salespeople. The idea is that those with similar interests will be able to develop into successful salespeople. Again, interest tests have had mixed results.

Two factors should be pointed out about the use of tests. First, because no universal traits have been discovered that automatically lead to sales success, tests should be developed individually for each company and each type of position. Second, if tests tend to reject a high proportion of women and minorities, the government may ask for validation, which is not always easy for a company to demonstrate.

Nonetheless, if done correctly and developed and validated for the individual company, tests are a greater predictor of success than alternative methods. Table 16-1 provides a brief summary of research.

The table shows that ability testing is far and away the best predictor of future job performance, with biographic data (the application) also scoring high marks. Most surprising is the placement of the interview, which is probably the most widely used method, near the bottom in predictiveness.

16-3 Motivating and Evaluating the Sales Force

Consider the unique aspects of the salesperson's job:

1. The salesperson has only limited personal contact with management.
2. Many sales positions are characterized by extended periods of travel, much of it associated with loneliness and inconvenience.
3. The salesperson typically experiences wide emotional swings between the elation of getting an order and the frustration of losing one.
4. The salesperson has strong status and recognition needs, which stem from the stereotype of salespeople.

All of these factors create a strong need for motivation, but the physical separation of salespeople and their sales managers makes it a difficult task at best. A sales representative may work a territory in the Midwest, while his or her manager resides in New York. Their only contact for months (even years) may be over the phone or through the mail. Motivating the sales force in this environment calls for creating a climate in which salespeople can motivate themselves with the incentives provided by management.

16-3a Automatic Supervisory Techniques

First, let's take a look at some automatic supervisory techniques, such as territories, quotas, compensation plans, and call reports. Once established, these mechanisms motivate the salesperson to perform without close supervision in ways desired by management.

Territories

By establishing geographic territories, management directs salespeople where to call. In the absence of firm geographic boundaries, sales representatives would be jumping all around, costing the company money and getting into disputes with one

Table **16-1**
Predictors of Sales Performance

Predictor	Validity
Ability composite (tests)	.53
Job tryout	.44
Biographics (application)	.37
Reference check	.26
Experience	.18
Training and experience ratings	.13
Academic achievement	.11
Education	.10
Interest	.10
Age	−.01

Source: Adapted from John Hunter, "Validation: What the Numbers Show," *Sales & Marketing Management,* 1988; John E. Hunter and R. F. Hunter, "Validity and Utility of Alternative Predictors of Job Performance," *Psychologcal Bulletin,* 96, 1984, pp. 72–98; Douglas Dalrymple, William L. Cron, and Thomas DeCarlo, *Sales Management,* New York: John Wiley & Sons, Inc., 2001, p. 339.

another. But with the provision of a designated territory, salespeople know exactly which customers they are responsible for. Not only that, the establishment of territories builds a proprietary attitude. Salespeople treat their territory as if they actually owned it, as if it were their own business. If they are successful, they are the ones responsible, and they can take great pride in their accomplishment. If their sales are unsatisfactory, they will be motivated to work harder and improve the picture. Moreover, research on territory alignment suggests that there are three reasons at a minimum for properly aligning sales territories within a proper workload and potential range:[20]

- Increased sales
- Cost savings
- Higher morale

Whether the territory is organized by geographic area, type of product, or customer, classification will further direct the efforts of salespeople. If organized just by geography, salespeople will sell all products in their company's line. If organized by product, salespeople reap the rewards of specialization of efforts. Individual salespeople can develop expertise with the technical attributes, uses, and the most effective selling methods associated with a limited number of products. Accordingly, if management wishes to devote more effort to a product, it can simply assign more salespeople to that product. The costs of product organization will be higher than the simpler geographic organization. Sales territories may also be organized by type of customer. In an effort to convert their sales force "from order-takers to business advisers," IBM reorganized them into 14 separate specialties, including such areas as banking, retail, travel, and insurance.[21] Here, too, the costs are higher than the simpler geographic organization, but salespeople become experts in the applications of their customers, facilitating communication and selling to them.

Territories can be created by sales potential or by workload. When using potential to establish territories, management assesses the sales potential that exists in a geographic region—a county, for example—and puts together enough regions to constitute a territory of adequate potential for one salesperson. In the workload approach, management looks at the number of customers in an area, how often they require calls, and the duration of each call. By knowing how much time is available to the average sales representative, management can establish a territory with sufficient workload to occupy the salesperson's time. An optimum division of territories would feature territories of equal potential and equal workload. However, with wide variance in the number of customers, geographic size, and amount of traveling required, the optimum is never attained.

Creating territories logically allows management to establish fairer compensation plans. By knowing the workload and sales potential in a territory, management can adjust compensation to correct for territorial differences. For example, a territory of great size but limited sales potential might prompt management to give the salesperson a higher base salary to compensate for decreased commission opportunities. Knowledge of a territory will also allow management to do a better job of evaluating performance. By knowing the workload and potential of a territory, management will be in a position to judge accurately the efforts of salespeople. Otherwise, they will have to rely on sales volume alone, which is not always the truest reflection of job performance.

sales quotas
Goals for the salesperson's performance in the coming year, typically in the form of dollar volume.

Sales Quotas

All of us work harder and with more purpose when we have a goal in mind. This is the basic idea behind a **sales quota.** Salespeople will work longer days, make more calls, and close more orders if they know their end-year evaluation depends on meeting their quota. This will be truer still if earnings are tied to the quota. Besides motivation, quotas help direct salespeople in putting forth effort. When companies assign quotas for each product in their line, this communicates to sales reps where they should concentrate. Frequent communication of results compared to quota assists with both motivation and direction. GE Fanuc, a manufacturer of factory automation products, recently installed a new web-based quota system that allows salespeople to track their quota numbers, as well as customer-buying patterns in real time.[22] Quotas, if properly established, also provide standards for performance evaluation.

The most common quotas are those based on dollar sales volume alone. However, this is not always the best idea because salespeople may concentrate on easy-to-sell, high-volume items while ignoring profitability. For this reason, many companies fix their quotas by product line. Each product line has a certain quota, based on its profitability. Some companies also establish quotas on the basis of gross margin rather than sales volume, which further ensures that salespeople will direct their efforts toward the most profitable items. For salespeople primarily involved in missionary and trade selling, quotas often consist of points awarded for building displays, securing cooperative ads, and training dealer personnel.

Quotas can be a powerful means of motivating sales personnel, but they can be counterproductive if handled incorrectly. Quotas set far beyond the reach of salespeople are likely to result in poor morale, low sales, and higher turnover. Quotas should be established fairly and within the reach of salespeople. Of course, deciding on the exact amount of the quota is not an easy task. Many companies merely multiply last year's sales by an arbitrary amount to establish the quota. Unfortunately, this may hide both productive and unproductive performance. For example, a sales representative who has done only a mediocre job in the past may easily be able to reach a new quota because great potential still remains in the territory. In contrast, salespeople who have done an outstanding job may be penalized because it is nearly impossible to increase sales further; they have achieved the market share they could be expected to get in their territory, and it is unrealistic to expect more. Unfortunately, they may be punished for their efficiency in the past because of the arbitrary way in which the quota is set.

To do a proper job of setting quotas, a company should have some idea of the sales potential in a territory and set a quota accordingly. Such information is available from a number of sources, including government documents like census data. Another excellent source is *Sales & Marketing Management* magazine's annual "Survey of Buying Power" (which provides information on consumer sales).

Call Reports

Completing sales **call reports** like the one illustrated in Figure 16-2 serves two purposes. First, knowing that the reports will be reviewed by management motivates salespeople to make the appropriate number of calls, minimize their travel time, and do their best to close each order. In the absence of call reports, some salespeople might take it easy, waiting until 10:00 A.M. to make their first call and quitting at 4:00 P.M. Having to catalog and explain their activities on the call report tends to limit such unproductive behavior.

Second, the sales call report provides management with much useful information. It gives data regarding sales representatives' efforts, including call frequency, hours worked, success ratio, and routing efficiency. Without such information, it is difficult, if not impossible, to evaluate performance. Only sales volume figures would be available, and evaluation on the basis of these alone is chancy at best. Call

call reports
Reports of each day's activities by the salesperson indicating accounts called on, results, comments, and so forth.

Person making call	Ron Friendly	Office	Kansas City	Date of call	4/9/06	Personal ☑ Phone ☐

Company	St. Joseph Hospital		Distribution

Address (where call made)	10458 Wornall	Phone	816-555-6029	

City Kansas City	State Mo.	ZIP 64114	

Discussed with | Mailing list code

1 Dale Molander   Purchasing Agent

2 Jim Gueths   Laundry Manager

3 Dorthy Wentort   Operating Room Head

Project Scrub Dress Model 8022-A   **Location**

Comments
Purchasing agent objects to high price. OR head likes looks of scrubs dresses. Laundry manager washing samples. Will contact again in one week.

Figure 16-2
Sales Call Report

reports also help provide a better picture of what is happening in the field. A commonality of response by salespeople may indicate increased competitive activity, a decline in a product's appeal, or certain trends in industry practices.

A logical step with call reports is filing by computer. Often, sales reps' results are transmitted while traveling to the next customer's plant or that evening from their homes. The next morning, the company's sales manager knows exactly what has been accomplished in the field by the sales force and what remains to be done.

Compensation Plans

Any discussion with sales executives would bring forth a consensus that compensation is the most important element in motivating the sales force. As we will discuss, it is not the whole story in motivation, but it is undoubtedly the most important and sometimes the most complex.

A properly designed and implemented compensation plan must be geared to both the needs of the company and the products and services the company sells. At the same time, it must attract good salespeople and keep them motivated to produce at increasing rates.

Recent studies reveal a distinct relationship between pay levels and sales-force turnover. They show that the higher the firm's average total cash compensation for sales reps, the lower their likely turnover. In the lowest quartile of pay plans, sales-force turnover was 37 percent, versus 24 percent in the highest quartile. The same survey showed that the more a firm pays the rep, the more he or she will produce for it.[23]

Sales managers can choose among three basic methods of compensating the sales force:

1. Straight salary
2. Straight commission
3. Combination plans

Table 16-2 shows the use of the various plans and their combinations.

T a b l e **16-2** Use of Compensation Plans

Compensation	Percentage of Companies Using
Straight salary	18
Straight commission	19
Salary plus bonus	24
Salary plus commission	20
Salary plus bonus plus commission	18
Commission plus bonus	1

Source: Adapted from "Dartnell's 30th Sales Force Compensation Survey," 1999.

Straight Salary

With **straight salary,** salespeople receive pay at a fixed rate, regardless of their performance. In the long run, salary can be adjusted to reflect productivity, but in the short run there is no direct relationship between sales volume and compensation. Accordingly, salespeople receiving straight salary are typically involved in nonselling activities (building displays, checking stock, offering promotional assistance), team selling, or positions where a lengthy period of negotiation is required before the sale.

Straight salary presents advantages for both sales representatives and their companies because:

1. It provides the security of a regular income.
2. It develops company loyalty.
3. It ensures management control over the performance of nonselling activities.
4. It tends to reduce the rate of turnover.
5. It eases the problems of recruiting new hires.

However, the straight salary plan does have disadvantages:

1. It provides limited financial incentive.
2. It tends to restrict the weeding out of unproductive salespeople.
3. It increases the fixed costs of selling because straight salary does not vary directly with sales.
4. It may encourage an unbalanced sales mix because sales representatives concentrate on easy-to-sell items.

Straight Commission

With **straight commission,** salespeople are paid in direct proportion to their sales volume. If they do not make any sales, they do not get paid. Often, commission includes some level of guaranteed draw. That way, if commissions do not come up to a set amount, the sales representative still receives a check for the draw amount anyway. At some future date, however, commissions must equal or exceed the amount of the draw, or the salesperson will probably be looking for another job.

The advantages of the straight commission plan are:

1. It provides a maximum amount of incentive.
2. Selling costs vary directly with the level of sales.
3. The system is easy to understand and administer.
4. The company's selling investment is reduced. (This is particularly valuable for small or new companies with limited financial resources.)
5. Salespeople who remain with the company tend to be the most productive.

straight salary
Salespeople receive pay at a fixed rate.

straight commission
Salespeople are paid a percentage of sales volume or gross margin.

The disadvantages of this plan are:

1. Turnover in the sales force tends to be high.
2. Control over salespeople is weaker, especially for nonselling activities.
3. Emphasis may be on volume rather than profits. Because the profit margin for some items is low and because selling costs vary by account (i.e., some are too small or too far away), selling more can actually decrease total profits.
4. Typically, there is little company loyalty among the sales force.
5. There may be a tendency to skim the territory, concentrating on easy-to-sell accounts and ignoring long-term development work.
6. Overstocking and thereby alienating customers are distinct possibilities.

Combination Plans

combination plans
Include all variations of salary plus some monetary incentive. These combinations can include salary plus commission, salary plus bonus, and salary plus commission and bonus.

bonus
In contrast to commission, a bonus is less directly tied to sales, typically being paid quarterly, semiannually, or annually for exceeding quota.

Combination plans include all variations of salary plus some monetary incentive. These combinations can include salary plus commission, salary plus **bonus,** and salary plus commission and bonus.

Bonuses are a common ingredient in combination plans. In contrast to a commission, a bonus is tied less directly to sales. Whereas a commission is paid immediately upon the sale (or a short time after), a bonus is paid quarterly, biannually, or even annually. Usually, but not always, a bonus is given for meeting or exceeding a quota. Sometimes the award of bonuses is left to the discretion of individual sales managers. Other common bases for bonuses include increases in territorial sales, market share, product mix, unit sales, and sales to new accounts.

Bonus payments should be structured to begin at the 70 percent- to 75 percent-of-goal level to provide suitable motivation. Payment for reaching a lower percentage works against incentive; waiting until the 100 percent goal is reached discourages many salespeople along the way. Although payment rates may be uniform both under and over the 100 percent mark, increasing the rate over the 100 percent goal provides additional incentive.

To maximize incentive, it is a good idea for bonuses to be paid on a quarterly or biannual basis. However, full payment should wait until the end of the year. Withholding a small percentage each quarter until the end of the year avoids overpayment for the total year's bonus. Otherwise, it is conceivable that a salesperson could earn a bonus by exceeding some quarterly targets and yet be under the total year's target. A proper adjustment can then be made with the final quarter's payment.

Among the advantages of the combination plan are:

1. It offers both the security of straight salary and the incentive of commission.
2. It compensates salespeople for all activities, including nonselling efforts.
3. It allows compensation to be structured to include a wide variety of goals.
4. It makes possible a favorable ratio of selling expense to sales. At higher levels of sales, straight commission may cost the company a lot. At low levels, straight salary may be too expensive. Combination plans allow a happy medium.

Disadvantages to plans are:

1. It may be complex and difficult to understand.
2. It may be costly to administer.
3. It may include too many objectives, some of which are ignored by sales representatives.

Additional Incentives

As many sales managers have discovered, compensation (and other automatic supervisory techniques) is not the whole story in motivating the sales force. Two unique aspects of the selling job are (1) the wide swings in morale that characterize selling and (2) the status and recognition needs of salespeople. In the first instance, maintaining the morale of the sales force is critical because salespeople must face rejection in the marketplace. Granted, making a sale leads to elation and enthusiasm, but rejection is also a reality. Accordingly, an important part of the sales manager's job is to cushion dejection, making sure that it doesn't get too deep and lead to permanent morale problems. In the second instance, sales managers must deal with the needs of salespeople for status and recognition. To one degree or another, all employees have these needs, but salespeople are especially vulnerable because of the stereotype problem.

To counter swings in morale and provide for the status and recognition needs of the sales force, several management techniques have been developed. These motivators may be financial or nonfinancial.

Financial Motivators

Additional financial motivation is offered through noncash perquisites (better known as *perks*) and sales contests. Although both incentives are financial, perks and contests do not always involve direct monetary payment.

Perks

Noncash **perquisites** have been part of executive compensation for a long time. Increasingly, many companies also are making them available to top sales performers. An advantage of most perks is that they are an ideal form of recognition as well as incentive compensation. Frequently, they are used in combination with career paths. The following represents a fairly complete, though not exhaustive, list of perks:

perquisites
Extra sources of compensation for salespeople such as trips, use of a company car, or club memberships.

1. Extra paid vacation
2. Club memberships—tennis, golf, etc.—not directly related to business and available to salesperson's family
3. Use of company resort facilities
4. Paid trips for spouses and families to specific resort areas
5. Tuition reimbursement
6. Interest-free or low-interest loans, particularly for dependents' education
7. Personal use of a company car with no charge to the salesperson
8. Reimbursement for expenses over and above those covered by the company's regular group medical and dental plans
9. Optional supplemental life insurance on a contributory basis
10. Stock purchase opportunities
11. Legal and financial counseling services
12. Sabbatical leaves for civic services, teaching, and so forth

Sales Contests

Sales contests are a well-developed technique for stimulating salespeople. Many companies use sales contests, the only exception being companies selling big-ticket items to industrial accounts. With these types of sales, a long period of negotiation precedes the order, making contests inappropriate.

Contests usually run for one or two months, but those as short as a week can produce results. Contest rewards can take the form of cash, merchandise, or travel. Whatever the specific form of reward, every member of the sales force should have an opportunity for winning. Contests with just a few winners fail to motivate the majority, so most companies offer rewards for exceeding quota during a specified period. Assuming properly set quotas, this works well. In addition to the rewards themselves, sales contests motivate because they offer recognition to the salesperson. Those who win prizes stand out as competent, hardworking professionals. The importance of this is not to be underestimated. The smart company will reinforce the recognition value of contests by awarding plaques or publishing winner's names and pictures in the company newspaper.

It is also true that contests are effective because of the excitement they provide. A sales contest adds spice to the ordinary performance of the job; it introduces a game element, and all of us like to play. A contest is a challenge to which salespeople will respond. It provides excitement, counters bad morale, and helps to overcome the routine in selling. To generate interest, contests should be launched with a flourish. Follow-up promotion and performance are also required to maintain interest.

Although contests generate excitement and improve sales-force morale, the sponsoring company should have some additional objectives in mind before starting a contest. Besides the typical objectives of increased sales volume, sale calls, and new accounts, contests can be used to build off-season business, increase the number and quality of displays, stimulate cooperation with dealers, revive dead accounts, and reduce costs.

Nonfinancial Motivators

Management practices that are not associated with financial reward also serve to build strong motivation in the sales force. As illustrated in Maslow's hierarchy, once an individual's basic physiological and security needs are satisfied, higher-level needs for social interaction and recognition become active. Monetary rewards satisfy the lower-level needs in the hierarchy; for the higher-level needs, sales management must take additional steps. In one study of salesperson motivation, compensation was found to be only the third most powerful motivator.[24] Commented one marketing director: "Recognition is something that can't be bought; it has to be earned. Money can be spent, but recognition, in the form of jewelry or a plaque, is a constant reminder of a salesperson's accomplishment and the company's recognition." Said another marketing manager, "Our surveys show that our President's Club is the single most important goal they [salespeople] have other than making a living."[25] Obviously, management must take great care with nonfinancial motivators. One important motivator here is an appropriate management style on the part of sales administrators.

Management Style

Two basic elements determine a manager's leadership style:

1. Whether the sales manager communicates with salespeople
2. The nature of the communication

In the first instance, poor morale is likely without communication between manager and subordinate. Imagine how salespeople feel if there is no evaluation of their performance each year. How are they to know where they stand with the organization or whether steps can be taken to improve their performance and aid their chances for advancement? Furthermore, when a promotion occurs and they are passed over, imagine how they feel without an explanation.

It isn't necessary for communication to be frequent or even face-to-face, but some form of communication between salesperson and manager is critical. A study of industrial salespeople indicated that job satisfaction was significantly related to whether salespeople believed their performance was being supervised. Interestingly, however, the frequency of the contact was not significant, suggesting that the existence of the contact and its content were the important considerations.[26]

Nothing will alienate a salesperson faster than being treated with a "holier than thou" attitude by management. The best leadership style avoids an autocratic approach in which the sales manager tells the salesperson what to do, with limited opportunity for response. A fundamental reason for the collapse of a stock brokerage firm was the way salespeople were treated by company management. In one instance, the manager, 10 salespeople, and 3 operations workers walked out of one of the firm's offices to join a competitor. "There was an air of regimentation," commented one of these people. "There was a more programmed approach toward selling. But what got us was the way things were presented. Rather than creating a desire to do it, management told us, 'You must do it.'"

Besides adopting an autocratic approach, management can "demotivate" salespeople by:

1. Being sarcastic about the efforts of salespeople. Always belittling salespeople with no praise will make them feel small.
2. Ignoring suggestions and constructive criticisms from salespeople. Running a one-person show and never allowing salespeople to influence matters is a definite demotivator.
3. Playing favorites.
4. Accepting all credit when things are favorable and blaming others when things go bad.
5. Manipulating salespeople to the exclusive favor of the manager.
6. Boasting or always talking about "How I would have done it.[27]

It is easy enough to speak in general of a proper management style and indicate some "don'ts" of management. Coming up with some positive "do's" is a little more difficult. Still, there are mechanisms that facilitate the motivating process, including the use of meetings and conventions, management by objective, and career paths.

Meetings and Conventions

Local meetings are attended by salespeople in a local office or district and are usually held weekly or monthly. Conventions, which may be held once or twice a year, are national or regional in scope. National conferences assemble salespeople at a central place and feature prominent speakers and top company personnel. Such national gatherings can promote much enthusiasm in the sales force and help to promote company loyalty. Unfortunately, they are also costly, not only with regard to travel and hotel expenses but also in terms of lost sales due to representatives being absent from their territories.

Meetings and conventions should have a specific purpose. There is no value to meeting just for meeting's sake. A meeting without purpose will do nothing but alienate salespeople, who will resent losing valuable selling time. Some good reasons for having meetings and conventions follow:

1. *Product training.* Information can be presented to a maximum number of salespeople at one time.
2. *Recognition.* The performance of outstanding sales representatives can be pointed out.

3. *New sales techniques.* Through panel discussions and role-playing, recent developments in selling can be discussed. This is especially valuable if conducted by outstanding sales representatives. They love the recognition, and the rest of the sales force can learn some of the reasons behind their success.

4. *Feedback from the sales force.* It is vital that the manager be informed about product problems, competitive activity, and industry trends. No one is in a better position to provide this information than those in the field.

5. *Building enthusiasm.* Salespeople work alone; morale may suffer in the isolation. Sales meetings and conventions allow sales reps to see that their problems are not unique and that many other salespeople have similar concerns. Meetings also allow discussion of ways to solve many of these problems. In any regard, merely being with people who understand one's problems is valuable.

6. *Explanation of company policies.* A meeting is a good place to provide information about changes that occur.

7. *Building company loyalty.* It is necessary that salespeople believe in the products or services of their company, its integrity, and its future. Meetings represent an excellent opportunity to make the sales force feel that they are part—an important part—of a vital, ongoing organization.

Management by Objective

management by objective
Management in which salespeople participate in the planning, direction, and control of their jobs.

Management by objective, or MBO, as it is commonly called, is a technique that builds strong motivation in the sales force because participation is an integral part of the program. Because salespeople are directly involved in the planning, direction, and control of their jobs, they are heavily committed. This heavy commitment leads to strong motivation and performance. In essence, MBO develops a framework for participation; most of the decisions that affect the selling job are made jointly by salesperson and manager.[28] Generally, an MBO system involves three steps: setting goals with the salesperson, planning strategies to reach these goals, and appraising performance.

In the first step, the manager and salesperson determine firm, measurable objectives for the conduct of the salesperson's job. Although some negotiation is expected, the final output of the meeting should be a mutually agreed upon, clearly written set of goals for the ensuing year. Generally, these goals will be of two kinds: those related to the job and those related to personal development. Job elements might include firmly specified objectives as to sales volume, gross margin on goods sold, number of calls per day, order-to-call ratio, average order size, expenses and expense ratios, and new accounts. Objectives related to personal development could include setting goals for bettering interpersonal skills, improving technical skills, and preparing for advancement. In each instance, these goals can be met by attending seminars or academic courses and demonstrating improvement to the manager.

Once objectives are specified, the next step is to plan strategies for reaching these objectives. If increased calls are a goal, for example, the salesperson can plan a strategy for improvement. Account analysis and routing efficiency can be valuable here.

The final step in MBO is appraisal. Ideally, this should be an ongoing process, with both manager and salesperson noting progress. A meeting at the end of the year is mandatory; a meeting should also be held when deviations from the plan are significant. MBO adds two major advantages to performance appraisal. First, without an adequate appreciation for each territory's uniqueness, management may tend to set unrealistic goals. This is unlikely to occur when the salesperson participates in the process, as in MBO. Second, because salespeople help establish the standards by which they are evaluated, they are much more likely to work toward achieving them. If they fall short, it is difficult to argue that the problem was in the standards and not in the effort.

MBO is also valuable because of the interaction between manager and salesperson. When asked how he finds time to meet with each member of his sales force, one manager commented, "I can't afford not to spend that time. It allows me to get a feeling for the problems of my salespeople, and it also improves the morale of my salespeople by showing them that someone listens."

Career Paths

Career paths are directly aimed toward the satisfaction of status and recognition needs of salespeople.[29] The underlying rationale for the career path concept is that salary growth alone loses its motivational value for experienced salespeople. Some salespeople can satisfy status and recognition needs by advancing into management, but this path is not open to all. No sales force is composed exclusively of managers.

career path
A separate direction for promotions, while still remaining in sales.

To fulfill the status and recognition needs of salespeople, two basic career paths are offered. In one path, the salesperson can opt for management. In the other, the salesperson can remain in sales but at increasing levels of responsibility. The latter usually involves responsibility for dealing with key accounts or leading sales teams. To make advanced sales positions more attractive, many firms provide those people additional perquisites ("perks") including increased bonuses, more prestigious titles, increased peripheral benefits such as contest rewards, and wider communication with company management. An upgrade of the company car for senior reps should definitely be a part of a career path for top performers. A car is the field office (and status symbol) for a sales rep. For the very highest producers, management might investigate "golden handcuffs," an especially attractive pension and retirement package, a profit-sharing program, the accumulation of special bonuses, and even stock options. Making the top salespeople responsible for mentoring new hires appeals to their need for recognition over and above the financial. Another possibility is establishing a senior sales council where one senior rep from each region attends a quarterly, closed-door, open-ended meeting with the senior sales management or the CEO and is asked to report back to the rest of the sales force.

16-3b Evaluating Salespeople

Many companies, even those noted for otherwise outstanding management, do a poor job of evaluating salespeople. They may use formal appraisal programs for all employees except salespeople because they feel that "selling is an art." Salespeople, they believe, cannot or should not be subjected to administrative practices that are well accepted in other areas of business.

When sales-force evaluation is performed, it often borders on the mystical. Listening to sales managers describe their most successful salespeople, one is apt to hear such descriptions as "a real go-getter," "money hungry," "has the killer instinct," or "a born salesperson."

By now, the reader may wonder whether it is possible to establish an effective evaluation system for salespeople. The answer is yes. It requires a lot of work and analysis, but companies must put forth the effort. Poor evaluation of performance is one of the most important factors contributing to the high rate of turnover experienced by many sales forces.

Why Evaluate

What does a sales manager expect to accomplish through sales-force evaluation? The following list suggests desired outcomes:

1. To determine areas where each salesperson needs improvement
2. To assess the validity of the standards used
3. To identify salespeople who are ready for promotion, salary raise, or reassignment
4. To spot sales representatives who should be fired
5. To check on the effectiveness of the compensation, training, recruitment, and selection programs[30]

Obstacles to Evaluation

There are significant problems in evaluating sales-force performance. When creating and administering an evaluation program, these obstacles will make any plan less than ideal.

Isolation of Salespeople

Most salespeople work beyond the direct observation of their managers. Rarely can a sales manager afford the time to travel with each salesperson more than once a month. This creates two problems for evaluation: judgment by inference and biased direct observation.

Because managers seldom observe salespeople in action, they have to assess performance on the basis of indirect evidence, which does not always lead to correct evaluation. For example, let's assume that a salesperson's quarterly results show sales, gross margin, and new accounts well below quota. The manager might conclude that the salesperson was slackening in effort. However, the results might seem more reasonable knowing that strikes had crippled three of the sales representative's largest customers.

When the manager is able to travel with salespeople, the experience may not be typical. First, salespeople are not going to call on their toughest customers the day their manager accompanies them; they are going to pick the easiest and friendliest ones. Second, a manager's visit might change a customer's behavior in some way. Some customers might not voice objections they ordinarily would share, while others might use the opportunity to vent complaints to a higher authority. Finally, many salespeople, especially the newer ones, will be nervous and self-conscious with a manager present.

Difficulty of Isolating Criteria

When discussing the job description, it is not always easy to identify the performance criteria that really lead to top sales performance. This adds to the difficulty of evaluation.

Lack of Control Over Some Conditions

Salespeople do not always have complete control over all the conditions that contribute to sales. Competitors may cut prices by half. There may be a business recession or a construction strike. In other words, many external facts can affect the sales picture.

Common Measures of Performance

Although many criteria used for evaluation will vary from one sales position to another, some are fairly uniform across jobs. Generally they can be categorized into objective and subjective factors. Among objective factors typically reviewed are dol-

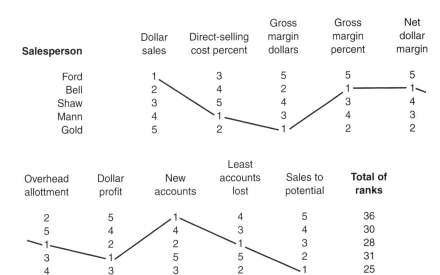

Salesperson	Dollar sales	Direct-selling cost percent	Gross margin dollars	Gross margin percent	Net dollar margin
Ford	1	3	5	5	5
Bell	2	4	2	1	1
Shaw	3	5	4	3	4
Mann	4	1	3	4	3
Gold	5	2	1	2	2

Overhead allottment	Dollar profit	New accounts	Least accounts lost	Sales to potential	**Total of ranks**
2	5	1	4	5	36
5	4	4	3	4	30
1	2	2	1	3	28
3	1	5	5	2	31
4	3	3	2	1	25

Figure 16-3
Ranking on 10 Performance Factors

lar or unit sales volume, market share, number of orders, gross margin, number of calls, completed sales versus potential sales, ratio of orders to calls, and number of new accounts opened. Subjective factors include judgment, emotional stability, self-discipline, product knowledge, and ability to close.

When using these criteria, it is important to use more than one measure. The use of just one measure may lead to an incorrect picture of performance. If sales volume had been the sole criterion used to rate the sales force in Figure 16-3, Ford would have received the highest evaluation. However, by some other standards of performance—sales as a percentage of potential, accounts lost, and gross margin, for example—Ford does not come out as well.

Not only may using one measure of evaluation be deceptive, but it also may promote counterproductive behavior. For example, if a company uses only sales as a measure of performance, salespeople may ignore profitability and concentrate on items that are easy to sell but have a low margin. They may also ignore missionary and nonselling activities, minimize customer service, and fail to control expenses.

Chapter Summary

This chapter began a discussion of sales management. Although few recent college graduates will start out as sales managers, the topic is still of critical importance for several reasons:

1. Promotion into sales management requires a dramatic adjustment from field sales.

2. Not all companies are proficient at training sales managers.

3. An understanding of sales management aids salespeople in their dealings with managers.

4. Sales management positions are well paying and offer a goal for beginning salespeople to direct their efforts.

5. Many dramatic changes are taking place in contemporary sales management.

A complete coverage of sales management topics is beyond the scope of this text. For that reason, the discussion is limited to the two topics of most relevance to new sales managers: (1) building the sales force and (2) motivating and evaluating salespeople.

Building the sales force consists of two basic activities: (1) recruiting and selecting salespeople and (2) training those hired. Of all the tasks of the sales manager, recruitment and selection are probably the most important because even the best training, compensation plan, and motivation techniques will be wasted on poor hires. The first job in recruitment and selection is to determine the number of new sales personnel needed. The general approach to making this decision is given by the formula:

Salespeople Needed − Salespeople Available =
Additional Salespeople Required

Determining qualitative requirements is not as simple. This requires a 3-step process: (1) conducting a job analysis, (2) writing a job description, and (3) specifying selection criteria. Of these, the last step is the most difficult. Some criteria are readily evident in the job description, but a more developed list depends on other sources. Probably the most fruitful means of identifying job criteria is comparing the profiles of successful and unsuccessful sales representatives.

Once criteria for applicants are specified, the task is to attract sufficient numbers of sales recruits. Among sources for recruits are the company itself, other companies, educational institutions, advertisements, referrals, and employment agencies.

After a requisite number of recruits have applied for the job, it is necessary to select those to be hired. Tools that assist in making this decision include application forms, interviews, reference checks, and tests.

Because of the unique nature of selling, salespeople have a strong need for motivation. Yet because of the physical separation of manager and salesperson, it is difficult to supply the motivation directly. Instead, sales management must create a climate in which salespeople can motivate themselves with incentives provided by management.

One way is through the use of automatic supervisory techniques, such as territories, quotas, compensation plans, and call reports. Sales territories motivate salespeople because they designate a specific geographic area for which the salesperson is solely responsible, thus encouraging the development of a proprietary attitude. After all, there is no one else around to take credit for success (or blame, if things go amiss). Sales quotas represent volume goals toward which salespeople can direct their efforts. By requiring salespeople to turn in call reports, management tries to ensure that they will make the appropriate number of calls, minimize travel time, and do their best to close orders. Compensation is probably the most important means of motivating the sales force, though certainly not the only one. Sales managers can choose from among three basic methods of compensating salespeople: straight salary, straight commission, and combination plans that include a blend of salary along with commission or bonus.

Because of two aspects of selling—the wide swings in sales-force morale and the status and recognition needs of salespeople—automatic supervisory techniques are not the complete answer to motivation. To provide this additional motivation, various financial and nonfinancial methods have evolved. One financial motivator is perks, or noncash perquisites, such as club memberships, tuition reimbursement, low-interest loans, and other incentives traditionally restricted to upper-level company management. Sales contests are another example of a financial motivator. They provide a pleasant break from the everyday course of the selling job and add spice and excitement.

Among nonfinancial motivators are an appropriate management style, meetings and conventions, management by objective, and career paths. Two basic elements determine a manager's leadership style: (1) whether the sales manager communicates with salespeople and (2) the nature of this communication. The critical matter is not that communication occurs so much as it is avoiding an autocratic manner and encouraging participation. One means for implementing a more participative style of management is to institute management by objective (MBO). With MBO, manager and salesperson sit down and establish goals for the salesperson for the ensuing year, plan strategies to reach these goals, and appraise performance. Meetings and conventions also can help to motivate the sales force, but only if they have a specific purpose such as product training or recognition. Career paths are intended to satisfy the status and recognition needs of salespeople by offering an alternative to promotion into management. As sales representatives progress through a career path, they qualify themselves for increased bonuses, a more prestigious title, and increased peripheral benefits.

The chapter ends with a discussion of performance evaluation. Although evaluation is necessary, three conditions make it difficult to evaluate salespeople: their isolation, their lack of control over some conditions affecting their job, and the difficulty of separating performance criteria. For these reasons, it is important that more than one measure of performance be used and that both objective and subjective measures be evaluated.

Discussion Questions

1. Why should students study sales management? After all, not many will graduate with positions as sales managers.

2. What are the two primary tasks in building the sales force?

3. A sales manager for a copier machine company is making out a yearly plan. How might he or she determine hiring requirements for the ensuing year?

4. How might this same sales manager determine what sort of salespeople should be hired?

5. What is a job analysis? Define job description. Of what value are job analyses and job descriptions?

6. What is the retrospective approach to determining hiring qualifications?

7. List some common sources for obtaining sales recruits. What are the advantages and disadvantages associated with each source?

8. What selection tools can be used by sales managers? Which are the most useful? What purposes do they serve?

9. Of what legal aspects of hiring should managers be aware?

10. What are "knockout factors"? Indicate some common ones.

11. How would you advise sales managers to interview applicants?

12. Of what value are references? How should the sales manager go about the process of checking references?

13. "Tests should not be used in selecting sales applicants. They are unreliable and an invasion of privacy." Discuss.

14. Which methods of sales training would you advise for someone who has just taken a job selling computers for IBM?

15. A company with 25 salespeople has a sales volume of $10 million. The forecast for the next three years indicates that sales will triple by the end of the third year. In the past, the company has experienced a yearly turnover of 15 percent in the sales force. In general, two to three months are required to hire new sales representatives, and another six months of training are needed before they are proficient enough to send into the field. Advise this company regarding its hiring practices for the next three years.

16. Interview a sales manager about the characteristics desired in a salesperson. Do you agree with the person's answers? Ask about methods of selection. Is a good job of selection being done? Would you do anything differently?

17. Go to the placement office at your school and obtain various companies' brochures describing sales positions. Which contain the best descriptions? Why?

18. From your college placement office, obtain employment application forms, fill them out, and trade them with others in your class. Analyze the forms, formulate questions, and interview another student for a sales position.

19. "There is no difference between being a sales manager and being any other kind of manager." Discuss.

20. Why are territorial divisions necessary for a successfully performing sales force? Can you think of any kinds of selling where clearly defined territories are not needed?

21. What is the value of a sales quota? What are some important rules for setting proper quotas?

22. Explain how call reports motivate salespeople.

23. What is a commission? What is a bonus? Which do you think is preferable to the salesperson? Which is preferable to the firm?

24. Contrast the advantages and disadvantages of straight salary, straight commission, and combination plans. What role can customer satisfaction play?

25. "Good salespeople are motivated only by money, so there is no reason to worry about managing them as long as they are adequately compensated." Discuss.

26. What are "perks"?

27. Of what value are sales contests? What are some considerations when putting together an effective sales contest?

28. Why is the style of management important to sales-force morale? What is an appropriate management style?

29. Why are meetings and conventions valuable?

30. What is management by objective? Explain its value for sales-force management.

31. Many companies have adopted the career path concept for their sales force. How would you explain this?

32. "Evaluating salespeople is easy. All you have to do is look at how much they've sold." Discuss.

33. Why is sales-force evaluation so important?

34. Interview a sales manager about the compensation plan used for his or her sales force. What other motivational tools are used? What is his or her philosophy of management? By what means are salespeople evaluated? What things would you do differently?

35. Recommend a compensation plan for salespeople selling the following products or services:
    a. A sales representative selling or leasing large computer systems to industry
    b. A real estate salesperson
    c. A sales representative selling a nationally advertised soft drink to grocery stores
    d. A salesperson selling life insurance
    e. A sales representative detailing drugs to doctors
    f. A salesperson selling newspaper advertising space
    g. A salesperson selling automobiles

36. Evaluate a salesperson with the following record: sales volume below average, a greater than average number of sales calls, and a sales expense ratio (expense/sales) that is greater than average. Is other information required to make a thorough evaluation?

Chapter Quiz

1. The traditional sales manager—the exhorting, demanding, numbers-oriented field general—is vanishing. In his or her place, the new manager will become
   a. more involved in territory management and training.
   b. more attentive to developing the personal skills of his or her salespeople and creating an environment of learning.
   c. more involved with technology and managing the sales staff through virtual management.
   d. part of the sales team and will be used to close major accounts.

2. Probably the most important of all the sales manager's tasks are
   a. the recruitment and selection of competent sales representatives.
   b. the training and supervision of the sales representatives.
   c. the motivation and rewarding of the sales representatives.
   d. the evaluation and motivation of the sales representatives.

3. In determining the number of salespeople needed in the future, a company will make use of all of the following information *except*
   a. company's current annual sales.
   b. average sales per salesperson.
   c. company sales forecast.
   d. number of competitive salespeople.

4. Statistics prove that among the top sources for recruiting effective salespeople is
   a. other companies.
   b. employment agencies.
   c. referrals.
   d. classified and online advertising.

5. Besides looking at qualifications, many companies advise their sales managers to look for "knockout factors" in selecting sales recruits. Examples include all of the following *except*
   a. job-hopping tendencies.
   b. promotions.
   c. recent business failure.
   d. overqualification for the job.

6. Which of the following methods has the most success in selecting salespeople?
   a. validated tests
   b. interviews
   c. references
   d. age

7. Recent studies show that the higher the firm's average total cash compensation for sales reps,
   a. the higher their turnover.
   b. the more the sales rep will produce.
   c. the lower their turnover.
   d. both b and c.

8. In terms of sales-force motivation, bonus payments should be structured to begin at the _____ percent-of-goal level to provide suitable motivation.
   a. 50
   b. 50 to 70
   c. 70 to 75
   d. 80 to 90

9. Management by objective, or MBO, as it is commonly called, is a technique that builds strong motivation in the sales force because
   a. salespeople set their own goals without input from management.
   b. participation by salespeople is an integral part of the MBO program.
   c. each salesperson has a different MBO, based on their territory characteristics.
   d. bonuses are tied into achieving each objective.

10. Obstacles in evaluating sales-force performance include all of the following *except*
    a. isolation of salespeople.
    b. difficulty of isolating criteria.
    c. EEOC Guidelines.
    d. lack of control over external conditions that may impact results.

Web Exercise

Go to the job-search site www.monster.com and search for sales positions. What do they have in common? In what ways will the employee be evaluated? What kind of responsibilities will the employee have? What companies have the best job descriptions?

Notes

1. Bill Kelley, "From Salesperson to Manager: Transition and Travail," *Sales & Marketing Management*, February 1992, p. 33.

2. Jack Falvey, "Wishful Thinking," *Sales & Marketing Management*, December 1994.

3. "2002 Salary Survey," *Sales & Marketing Management*, May 2002.

4. William Keenan, Jr., "Death of the Sales Manager," *Sales & Marketing Management*, October 1994.

5. Roger W. Rogers, "Make Hiring More of a Science, Less of an Art," *Sales & Marketing Management*, September 1991.

6. Goutam Challagalla and Tasaddug A. Shervani, "Dimensions and Types of Supervisory Control: Effects on Sales Performance and Satisfaction," *Journal of Marketing*, January 1996, pp. 47–60.

7. *How to Select a Sales Force That Sells*, Kettering, OH: 1998.

8. Gilbert A. Churchill, Jr., Neil Ford, Orville C. Walker, Jr., Mark W. Johnston, and John F. Tanner, Jr., *Sales Force Management*, New York: McGraw-Hill, 2000.

9. Arthur Bragg, "Another Case of the Customer Knows Best," *Sales & Marketing Management*, February 1992, pp. 117–118.

10. Tricia Campbell, "Finding Hidden Sales Talent," *Sales & Marketing Management*, March 1999.

11. Julia Chang and Andy Cohen, "Should You Raid Your Rival's Sales Force?" *Sales & Marketing Management*, August 2002.

12. Andy Cohen, "Hire Power," *Sales & Marketing Management*, December 2001, p. 13.

13. Gilbert A. Churchill, Jr., Neil Ford, Orville C. Walker, Jr., Mark W. Johnston, and John F. Tanner, Jr., *Sales Force Management*, New York: McGraw-Hill, 2000.

14. Thomas Rollins, "How to Tell Competent Salespeople from the Other Kind," *Sales & Marketing Management*, September 1990.

15. Myron Gable, Charles Hollon, and Frank Dangello, "Increasing the Utility of the Application Blank: Relationship between Job Application Information and Subsequent Performance and Turnover of Salespeople," *Journal of Personal Selling and Sales Management*, Summer 1992, pp. 39–55.

16. Niklas von Daehne, "Hiring Top Performers, *Success*, May 1994.

17. Arthur Bragg, "Checking References," *Sales & Marketing Management*, November 1990, p. 68.

18. Robert G. Head, "Systematizing Salesperson Selection," *Sales & Marketing Management*, February 1992, p. 68.

19. Gilbert Fuchsberg, "More Employers Check Credit Histories of Job Seekers to Judge Their Character," *Sales & Marketing Management*, May 30, 1990, p. B1.

20. Andris Zoltners, Prabhakant Sinha, and Greggor Zoltners, *Accelerating Sales Force Performance*, New York: ANACOM Books, 2001, pp. 136–140.

21. Bart Ziegler, "IBM Plans to Revamp Sales Structure to Focus on Industries, Not Geography," *Wall Street Journal*, May 6, 1995.

22. Michelle Marchetti, "The Art of Setting Sales Quotas," *Sales & Marketing Management*, April 2000, p. 4.

23. William A. O'Connell and William Keenan, Jr., "The Shape of Things to Come," *Sales & Marketing Management*, January 1990, p. 40.

24. Bill Kelley, "Recognition Reaps Rewards," *Sales & Marketing Management*, June 1986, p. 101.

25. Gilbert A. Churchill, Jr., Neil M. Ford, and Orville Walker, "Organizational Climate and Job Satisfaction in the Sales Force," *Journal of Marketing Research* 13, November 1976, pp. 323–333.

26. Julia Chang, "The Buck Stops Here," *Sales & Marketing Management*, November 2004.

27. Douglas J. Dalrymple, William L. Cron, and Thomas E. DeCarlo, *Sales Management*, Hoboken, NJ: Wiley, 2004, pp. 540–542.

28. Gilbert A. Churchill Jr., Neil Ford, Orville C. Walker, Jr., Mark W. Johnston, and John F. Tanner, Jr., *Sales Force Management*, New York: McGraw-Hill, 2000.

29. Donald W. Jackson, John L. Sclacter, and William G. Wolfe, "Examining the Bases Utilized for Evaluating Salespeople's Performance," *Journal of Personal and Sales Management*, 15(4), Fall 1995, p. 65.

30. Ibid.

Case 16-1

Analyze the following transcript of a conversation between Chuck Lanham, sales manager for Valley Office Machines, and Thomas Bruce, a job applicant.

Chuck: Good morning, Tom. Come into my office and make yourself comfortable. Can I get you some coffee?

Tom: Sounds great.

Chuck: Here you go. (hands Tom a cup of coffee) I see from your application that you played some football.

Tom: Yeah, I played fullback.

Chuck: No kidding. So did I. In fact, I got a scholarship to play for State when I graduated from high school. Played on the bench most of the time, though. Johnny Roland played first string ahead of me. Remember him?

Tom: I sure do. That punt return he made against Missouri was something else.

Chuck: It sure was. It won the conference championship for us.

Tom: I still think Johnny should have made All-American that year.

Chuck: You bet he should have. Nobody deserved it more than Johnny.

Tom: Absolutely.

Chuck: Well, I suppose we should get on with this interview. I'm supposed to be interviewing you for a job instead of talking about football.

Tom: Yeah, I guess so. (laughing)

Chuck: Are you working now?

Tom: Yes, for Johnson Foods. They're a food broker, and I sell for them.

Chuck: Oh, you've got sales experience then?

Tom: Yes. With two jobs. I sold radio time for awhile, too.

Chuck: Great. When will you be available?

Tom: I'm leaving next month.

Chuck: How come?

Tom: I'm getting married and . . .

Chuck: And you need more money, right? I remember when I got married. I sure could have used a little more cash.

Tom: I know what you mean.

Chuck: Well, I tell you what. I'll explain something about our job, because I think the potential is unlimited with us—if you're willing to work hard, that is.

Tom: I am.

Chuck: Good. You know you're going to have to make six to eight calls per day, however. And many of these are going to be cold-calls. You've got to be tough to handle that.

Tom: I think I can do it.

Chuck: Good. You've got to do some traveling, too. Maybe a couple nights a week sometimes. How do you feel about that?

Tom: I don't mind traveling at all. And I know Marsha, my fiancée, won't mind either.

Chuck: Excellent. I tell you what. I've got a sales meeting coming up shortly, and I need to look at some papers. I'll get back in touch with you and let you know about the job. You sound like the sort of guy we need.

Tom: Thanks. I look forward to hearing from you.

Questions

1. What mistakes did Chuck make in interviewing Tom?
2. What further questions might you have asked?

Case 16-2

The following dialogue represents a conversation between the sales manager of a lawn mower manufacturer and a management consultant.

Consultant: Good morning, Ms. Johnson. I'm Jeff Michels with Haden and Company. I hope that we can be of service to you.

Sales Manager: I'm sure you will be. Can I get you some coffee?

Consultant: No, thank you. I'd like to get right to business if that's all right with you, so if you could tell me a little about your situation, I would appreciate it.

Sales Manager: Fine. Basically, we're dissatisfied with how we're paying our salespeople. We feel that we're just not handling things correctly with the current compensation system.

Consultant: Could you tell me something about what tasks you expect your salespeople to perform?

Sales Manager: Well, first of all, we expect them to maintain and build sales volume in their territories . . .

Consultant: Excuse me. Does that mean they have to do a lot of prospecting for new retail accounts?

Sales Manager: No. Prospecting doesn't take up a lot of time, but we do expect our sales representatives to call on new hardware stores as they open.

Consultant: Then, basically, you rely on building sales volume through existing accounts?

Sales Manager: Yes, that's right.

Consultant: How does the sales force help in this process?

Sales Manager: Our line of mowers is heavily advertised on television and in the paper. It's up to our sales force to make sure that dealers know about special promotions that we run. Especially with newspapers, we try to get our dealers to participate in cooperative advertising programs; our salespeople must explain the advantages of these programs.

Consultant: Anything else?

Sales Manager: Yes, when we bring out a new model, we rely on our salespeople to detail it to the dealers and convince them to stock it. Also, we depend on our salespeople to handle any service problems that happen out in the field. We pride ourselves on the relations we have with our dealers. Oh yes, in this same vein, our salespeople are responsible for training retail sales personnel. Our dealers rely heavily on us for that.

Consultant: Then your sales force acts mainly in a service capacity?

Sales Manager: Yes, but it's important to provide some incentive for them to get out and do all that we expect of them.

Questions

1. If you were the consultant, what sort of compensation system would you recommend?
2. What other questions would you have asked if you were the management consultant?

Case 16-3

The following represents a dialogue between a sales manager and a subordinate.

Sales Manager: It's good to talk with you again, JoAnne. It's been a year since we talked last, hasn't it?

Salesperson: Yeah, it sure has.

Sales Manager: I called you in today to evaluate your performance over the past year.

Salesperson: Okay.

Sales Manager: Let me say first that you've turned in a creditable performance. You seem to know the product. Of course, I haven't had a chance to travel with you in awhile, but in our informal discussions around here, you seem to know what you're talking about.

Salesperson: Thank you, sir.

Sales Manager: But we feel that perhaps your sales volume could have been a bit higher. We're a little disappointed there.

Salesperson: I'm sorry to hear that. I feel I did the best that could be expected. Is there something that I can do to improve?

Sales Manager: Well . . . making more calls usually works.

Salesperson: I average six to eight calls per day, and I think that's all that can be expected. More calls don't necessarily translate into more sales in the mainframe computer business. There aren't all that many prospects for large equipment, you know.

Sales Manager: Perhaps your closing needs improvement. Confidence is critical when you get to the close.

Salesperson: You know, I really don't feel that sales alone is a fair measure of performance in this job.

Sales Manager: Maybe not, but it's one that my boss looks at closely.

Salesperson: Yes, but it's a little unfair. In the computer business, you're dealing with an average replacement cycle of five to six years, so you can't expect many repeat sales in the short run. Of course, you've still got to make calls during that time, especially on accounts that have competitive systems already installed. And you need to make service calls on your own accounts and be around when they need add-on equipment. Otherwise, another vendor may get in the door.

Sales Manager: There's truth in what you say, but the bottom line is still sales volume, and that's how we have to evaluate salespeople.

Questions

1. Has this sales manager demonstrated good management practices? What could have been done differently?
2. Should sales volume be the only criterion for evaluation? If not, what else is important?
3. What kind of compensation system would you say is best suited to this type of selling position?

Your First Sales Job— Selling Yourself

Key Terms

behavioral interviewing
chronological resume

Learning Objectives

Learning Objectives

After studying Chapter 17, you will understand:

- How to assess your strengths and weaknesses
- How to prepare a resume that effectively communicates your abilities and job desires

- How to plan a job campaign
- The sources for researching prospective employers
- Tips for successful interviewing

By this time, many of you probably have decided that a career in selling sounds great. It looks like a lot of work, a lot of fun, and some frustration. (Of course, nothing worthwhile comes easily.) But for others of you, selling is not appealing at all. You just cannot imagine yourself prospecting for customers, making sales calls, and closing orders. It does not sound like your cup of tea. There is nothing wrong with that either. Still, your first job out of school will be selling yourself, getting an employer to offer you a job. The discussion that follows will assist both those interested in a selling career and those interested in other positions. In either instance, selling is required.

As a salesperson, you would never dream of selling without systematically studying your product, researching your customers, planning a presentation, and anticipating likely objections and closes. Yet most people—even experienced salespeople—neglect these essentials when selling themselves in the job market. The large majority of applicants go job seeking with more hope than system—about 99 percent hope and 1 percent system. People will spend more time planning for a vacation than mapping out a job campaign.

17-1 Knowing Your Product—You

If you were a salesperson for a manufactured product, you would try to convince your customer that it was well made, that it would perform properly, and that it could be purchased at a competitive price. When you are looking for a job, you are in much the same position, except you are both the salesperson and the product.

Before you can sell any product, you must first learn all you can about its features, its advantages, and its benefits. At the same time, you must realize its limitations, its drawbacks, and disadvantages. When selling yourself, the same is true. You must know all your strengths, the things you can do. And, as with any other marketable product, you must also know your weaknesses, the things you cannot do.

17-1a Taking Stock of Yourself

To make a proper assessment of your strengths and weaknesses, first make a record of what you have in stock—those things you have learned and done in the past. You should amass information about yourself and then reflect on it because what's past is prologue to the future. If you've always felt cooped up sitting in a classroom, imagine being confined to a desk eight hours a day.

To begin, list all of the things that have contributed to your development as a person. This process will be aided if you organize your activities into six areas:[1]

- Interests
- Abilities

- Education
- Experience
- Personality
- Goals

Interests

List all of your favorite activities in order of preference. Do you like working with mechanical things? Do you enjoy physical activities? Does your taste run to music and art? Do you belong to many organizations?

Abilities

Write down all the things you do well. Review all projects, awards, hobbies, and other things that have called upon your skills and abilities within the last three to five years. Have you taken any aptitude tests that showed special abilities and talents? If not, the placement offices at most colleges and universities have a variety of such tests. However, remember to not look upon these tests as providing the final answer. Instead, take them and see if they confirm your own insights into your character. Some tests, like the Strong–Campbell Interest Inventory, match a number of your traits with those of people in various professions. If you share a number of characteristics with computer programmers, for example, the odds are improved that you will "fit in" with this field. Other tests, like the Myers–Briggs Type Indicator, help discover your personality type—whether you tend toward introversion or extraversion, are fact-based or intuitive, logical or emotional, or see the world as a judge rather than as a passive observer. Such information helps you avoid paperwork and analytic-oriented fields and focus on areas where social interaction is essential, such as sales and marketing.

Education

Have you taken courses that prepare you for a particular career? When interviewing for sales positions, you should mention that you have had a selling course. Are there other courses that further delineate a career path? For example, computer programming courses plus this selling course represent an attractive combination for business machines companies.

Experience

List all the full-time and part-time jobs you have ever had, including those you had while you were in school. Write down all the duties and responsibilities involved in each job. Can any be related directly to the professional career you plan to pursue?

Personality

List all your personal traits, both good and bad. Are you usually optimistic? Do you work well under pressure? Do you work well with others? Are you demanding? Are you a fast worker, or more slow and methodical? Do you usually keep your opinions to yourself? Or are you always ready to reveal them? Review how you responded to the personality inventory in Chapter 4, "Buyer Behavior." Are you a Driver, Analytical, Amiable, or Expressive?

Goals

What would you like to be doing five years from now? Ten years from now? What sort of job and industry are most likely to make this true?

Are you career-oriented to the exclusion of other matters? Or do you view your-self as having broader interests—family, civic, parental, and so forth? Some jobs and companies leave less time for the latter.

17-1b Identifying Your Strengths and Weaknesses

The next step is to complete a strengths and weaknesses inventory. Divide a sheet of paper into two columns by ruling it down the center. At the top of one column, write "Strengths." At the head of the other, write "Weaknesses."

With the information you have already organized into the six previously men-tioned categories, write down in the "strengths" column everything you believe to be of value to potential employers. On the other side, write down your limitations.

In the process it is important to be absolutely honest, even if it hurts. There is no purpose in kidding yourself. Listing a strength that you desire but do not have can backfire with disastrous results later. You might get the job, only to lose it be-cause of the deficiency. Having a bad mark on your job record is far worse than hav-ing the sense to avoid the situation in the first place.

Listing strengths and weaknesses will be invaluable when it comes time to make out your resume and begin interviewing. In the strengths and weaknesses inventory, you will find many of the answers to questions prospective employers are likely to ask. The inventory helps to refresh your memory and organize your thinking.

In doing the inventory you may want to ask yourself these questions:

1. Do I prefer to work with people or with data and things?
2. What is my need for structure?
3. Am I motivated?
4. Do I handle stress and rejection well?
5. Can I start a job on my own and follow it through to completion?
6. What is my attitude toward supervision? Do I need supervision to complete the job?
7. Am I easily frustrated? Do I give up easily?

In answering these questions, it is important to be honest, perhaps brutally honest. Mistakes at the beginning of a career can be devastating. In many sales positions, the assignments are ambiguous. You have to determine your strategy and follow through. Can you set your own deadlines? Many sales positions in trade and missionary sales are well structured with well-defined procedures and routines. Others, like new-business sales demand that the salesperson work with a minimum of guidance and structure. What motivates you: money, recognition, independence? Can you motivate yourself on your own? If not, then maybe sales isn't the career for you. Can you handle stress and rejection? If not, then new-business sales may not be for you. Some positions like trade and pharmaceutical sales involve only working with existing customers, and sales reps incur little outright rejections. Every grocery store, for example, carries Procter & Gamble products.[2]

Table 17-1 shows a completed inventory by Lynette Friendly, who is about to graduate from college. Notice that Lynette has been completely candid with herself. She has listed some strong qualifications, but she has also written down some po-tential problem areas. She appears to have a good background for a selling position, but she should avoid jobs requiring her to work with figures and those involving close supervision.

T a b l e **17-1** Strengths/Weaknesses Inventory for Lynette Friendly

Strengths	Weaknesses
Works well without supervision	Impatient
Self-confident	Sometimes overly aggressive
Assertive	Occasionally sarcastic
Dependable	Poor with figures
Self-starter	At times inconsiderate
Drive	Resent close supervision
Ambitious	Sometimes angered easily
Hard worker	Weak on details
Good sense of humor	
Communicate well	
Not easily frustrated	
College degree in marketing	
Completed course in sales and selling management	
Outgoing personality	

17-2 The Resume—Putting Yourself on Paper

The rationale for preparing a resume is simple: almost all employers require one. The resume serves a purpose similar to that of a piece of sales literature for a product. It tells interested employers who you are, what you have accomplished, what you can do, and when you are available. Following are some suggestions for making your resume stand out.

17-2a Neatness

One of the most important things to remember when writing a resume is that physical appearance counts heavily. Imagine the reaction of personnel managers when they see barely legible resumes cross their desks. Why should they even bother with one that is a weak photocopy or printed with a nearly empty ink cartridge? It is understandable that managers assume that sloppy resumes belong to sloppy workers.

There are some simple rules for creating an attractive resume. First of all, the resume should be printed neatly on an $8\frac{1}{2} \times 11$–inch paper. Anything larger will not fit into standard-size filing cabinets and may be thrown away. Because more companies are using optical scanning devices to read resumes directly into computers, use simple black type on white paper. Don't fold or staple pages. It isn't necessary for each copy of the resume be individually typed. Managers are realistic enough to recognize that applicants are looking at a number of companies. However, it is important that high-quality copies be reproduced on good bonded paper. A blurred reproduction on cheap paper will not attract favorable attention and may be rejected by a scanner for those companies using computers.

Be sure to spell-check your resume. Comments one expert recruiter, "Nine out of ten resumes I have seen claiming that the applicant is 'detail oriented' have a typo on them somewhere. Some of these typos are tricky, like extra spaces and missing hyphens. Others, sadly, are not. Don't forget to look over headers and addresses, even your name."[3]

Keep your resume to one page, if possible—certainly no longer than two pages. Layout is just as important as content.[4] Avoid excessive punctuation and allow for plenty of white space in the margins. The argument for keeping resumes one to two pages long is that readers don't have the time to read anymore because of the large number of resumes they receive. However, some experts would argue there is no way any reader can get an idea of what the person is about from just one page. The contrary view maintains that the reader wants to be impressed by accomplishments and to perceive that those accomplishments are relevant to their needs. This may require more than one page. This is not to say that you should needlessly "puff up" your resume, but don't cram and overlook relevant issues that give people a sense of your abilities and applicable accomplishments. Unfortunately, there is no absolute rule; you'll have to do the best job of listing your accomplishments. If this requires more than one page, you should understand that some recruiters may look unfavorably upon it, or even ignore it. However, it is better to err on the side of completeness.

17-2b The Chronological Resume

chronological resume
Resume organized in order of time sequence with the most recent activity first.

The most common form of the resume is the **chronological resume,** which is organized in order of time sequence, with the most recent activity first. For recent graduates, it is the recommended form. It is simple to write, and it tells the story in a quick and orderly fashion.

The specifics of the chronological resume may differ somewhat among applicants. The one shown in Box 17-1 is that of a recent college graduate. The resume of someone with professional work experience would be different, emphasizing experience rather than education.

The first items to be typed on the resume are one's name, address, and phone number, which go in the upper-left corner of the page. The phone number is especially important because a manager may want to call you immediately instead of taking the time to write a letter. To handle this eventuality, it may be a good idea to hire an answering service or use an answering machine if you are frequently away from home.

About five spaces below the name and address, type your professional objective; indicate your career goals. Although great detail is not needed, the objective should be stated succinctly and with little ambiguity. Stating goals only in a general way—a position in management—will make readers wonder about your dedication. After all, you are asking them to invest a good deal of time and money in you; vaguely stated goals fail to specify what you will do in return. If you are unsure of what you want to do after graduation, then it might be a good idea to consult the counseling department at your school; they can suggest some directions for investigation.

After specifying your professional objective, your educational experience should be stated next. Your degree and major field of study should be indicated. Special courses should be pointed out, and any courses related to your objective should be listed. For example, if you are interested in selling advertising for a radio or TV station, mention any advertising courses you have taken. Special college projects should be enumerated. In the sample resume, you will notice that Lynette Friendly won the top sales award her senior year. Next, any special skills and interests should be noted. This section helps to show you as a person, not just as a professional. The intent is to strike a note of interest with a prospective employer.

Following skills and interests, you should describe your work history, with the most recent position coming first. For someone with professional work experience, this section should precede the education section, but a recent college graduate should emphasize education first. With each job listing, be sure to indicate the dates of employment, including both the month and year, and the full name and address of the

Box 17-1

Sample Resume

Lynette Friendly
3847 Pine Street
Appleton, WI. 54911
(414) 555-7511

Professional Objective

To work for a large consumer goods company as a sales representative. Would like to work into a marketing management position.

Education

B.S., May 2006, University of Wisconsin. Marketing major with 18 hours in communication. Special courses include selling, sales management, and advertising.

Special Projects

As a member of the marketing club, I won the top sales award my senior year.

Skills and Interests

Excellent writing and speaking skills. Experience with multimedia presentations. Traveled extensively.

Employment

Summer 2002–2005: Olive Garden Restaurant, Appleton, WI. Waitress and receptionist
Academic year 2002–2006: Younkers, Madison, WI. Sales associate

Background

Born and raised in Appleton. Have worked since high school. Active in high school and college drama club. President of the marketing club.

References

Dr. Mark Vorhies, (414) 555-1427
Dr. Burke Tower, (414) 555-1746
Dr. Gordon Smith, (414) 555-1625

---

company. The job title should also be provided along with a description of duties and responsibilities, but only if the job was of some significance. Be sure to emphasize retail sales experience. It shows you have developed sales and customer-service skills. One student who lacked the stated job requirements for a position had partially paid for college by selling household goods door to door for three years. In the process, he had learned how to handle rejection, gained sales experience, and proved his initiative and enthusiasm. His experience sold him into the next level of interviews.

Use action verbs to describe your abilities and accomplishments. Words such as *created, designed, maintained, organized, arranged, served,* and *supervised* sound positive and indicate that your experience, however brief, has helped you build on your strengths. It's also the most effective way to highlight your accomplishments by describing the results.

Next, a background section should be provided. This section can be used to describe your most significant achievements in high school as well as your family background. As with the skills and interests section, the background portion of the resume will help to portray you as a whole person and not just as an academic being. Remember, extracurricular and personal activities can demonstrate that you're self-disciplined, motivated, willing to work hard, and can bounce back from defeat. Be sure to mention your involvement in clubs, organizations, sports, or social activities, particularly if you held office. All of these show your ability to get along with people and communicate skills requisite for success in selling.

The final section of the resume is the references section. Here, list faculty and previous employers who have knowledge of you. These individuals must be contacted first and their permission must be received prior to your including them on your resume. This eliminates the possibility of receiving a bad reference. Usually, three references are needed, but there is nothing magic about this number. Stating that "references will be provided on request" is not a good idea because potential employers may want to get in touch with your references before contacting you.

17-2c Six Resume Mistakes

In composing a resume, the student can make six fatal mistakes. The first is aiming too high, too soon. For example, let's take Nancy. She is 20 years old, majoring in communications and minoring in journalism. Her work experience includes instruction in aerobics and waitressing, and she has been a receptionist-bookkeeper. However, she lists as her career objective as "seeking a position as public relations director with a large organization." Maybe in 10 or 15 years, she could become a director, but certainly not with her current background and experience.

The second resume mistake is to give all experience equal billing. Important items need to be emphasized; less important ones, the opposite. James has set his career sights on a position in sports promotion. On his resume, however, he has treated his position as sports editor on the college newspaper equally with a summer job in lawn maintenance. Obviously, the former should receive more attention than the latter. In addition to content, important points can be stressed with underlining, bolding, or capitalizing and by moving pertinent information to the left-hand margin.

The third resume mistake is to bury critical information. Psychologists tell us that information presented first or last is more likely to be remembered. Marie, aiming for a career in media sales, has buried her two job-related work experiences in the middle of her resume. Instead, she should move such material to a more prominent position. She could have selected a "half-and-half" style for her resume in which one paragraph is titled "Objectives" and the other "Qualifications." What the applicant is seeking is paired with what she has accomplished and is related to that objective.

Highlighting the irrelevant is a fourth fatal mistake. It is always a good idea to analyze past jobs and highlight specific relevant skills. In a document like the resume, abbreviated by definition, there isn't space to emphasize all previous positions; some must be emphasized, and these should be those related to the job objective.

The fifth fatal resume mistake is to keep the employer in the dark about qualifications. Even though you are young and may not have much work history, you can still find life experiences that demonstrate your ability to get things done, solve problems, and work with others. Perhaps you led a food drive at the fraternity or sorority; maybe you were a leader on a sports team or in a Scout troop; maybe you organized a litter cleanup in a local park. Maybe your achievements are more personal and private: You taught yourself how to draw or paint or maybe you started a diet and exercise regimen and lost 40 pounds.[5] Take Jack, for example, an older-than-average student majoring in biology. Jack's career ambitions are in pharmaceutical sales. His work experience, at first glance, seems totally unrelated to this career goal. Jack's jobs have been as a subpoena server, a wood-stove salesperson, a waiter, a groundskeeper for a lawn service, and a roustabout for an oil rig. However, close analysis shows that his job experiences do have value for the work of a pharmaceutical sales representative. Doctors are pressed for time, well educated, want the best for their patients, and don't suffer fools gladly. Accordingly, pharmaceutical sales reps need to be knowledgeable and confident enough to persuade doctors of their expertise, and they must be able to work on their own, calling doctors for appointments and managing these personal visits with little supervision from sales management. Closer scrutiny of Jack's work experience and academic credentials demonstrates relevance to his career ambitions. His sales experience with wood stoves implies persuasiveness; his work as a subpoena server shows initiative and self-direction; and his college degree in biology illustrates both the intelligence needed to work with doctors and a background in science.

The sixth mistake is to demonstrate poor writing skills in the resume and cover letter. You give employers their first chance to assess your writing skills when you send your cover letter and resume. You could end your on-the-job success with poorly written work-related memos and email, says a report from the College Board's National Commission on Writing for America's Families, Schools, and Colleges. The commission surveyed human resources directors in companies affiliated with Business Roundtable, an association of chief executive officers from U.S. corporations that employ more than 10 million people. Poorly written cover letters and resumes are the kiss of death for a job seeker looking for a professional job, says the report. "You can't move up without writing skills," noted one survey respondent. "Writing ability could be your ticket in . . . or it could be your ticket out" of a job, said another. Each year, employers polled for the *Job Outlook* (www.jobweb.com/joboutlook/default.htm) say that communication skills—written and verbal—are among the top qualities they look for in job applicants.[6]

One final word about the resume. Neatness, education, and background should all say just one thing: "I can do this work for you because I have done well for someone else." At school or work, the idea is to show a record of accomplishment.

17-3 The Job Campaign

Being out of a job can easily lead to panic, and panic leads to disorganized and haphazard action, which inevitably ends in frustration and disappointment. So far, you have done all right. You have completed your strengths and weaknesses inventory and created your resume. Now is not the time to panic; it is time to sit down and plan a systematic and organized job campaign.

17-3a Researching Companies

Researching companies is crucial to a successful job search. Employers perceive researching a company as a critical factor in the evaluation of applicants because it reflects interest and enthusiasm. In the interview, it shows that you understand the purpose of this process and establishes a common base of knowledge from which questions can be asked and to which information can be added. It enables both applicant and interviewer to evaluate the position match more accurately. You will want to do some employer research to:[7]

- See if you are interested in working for that particular company or organization
- Find out about different types of jobs or work that you may be hired to do
- Prepare for an interview

Information to Look For

- History and potential growth for the employer and the industry
- Restructuring, downsizing, reengineering activities
- Products and services
- Locations

- Annual sales in the past year(s) compared to industry trends
- Employer's major competitors
- Ownership of organization; impact of family ownership on possible advancement potential
- Management style, corporate culture
- Number of employees
- Training and development programs

Where to Research Companies

- Company links site
- Career services office
- Internet
- State directories of manufacturing and service companies
- Local newspapers
- Chamber of Commerce
- The company itself: brochures, annual reports, and other literature
- Thomas Register of American Manufacturers
- Business Index, Information Access
- U.S. Industrial Outlook, U.S. Department of Commerce
- Business Periodical Index
- *Hoover's Handbook of American Business*
- *Hoover's Guide to Private Companies*
- *Directory of Foreign Manufacturers* (U.S. Georgia State University Business Press)
- *World Business Directory* (Gale Research, Inc.)
- Business International Index

17-3b Sources of Job Leads

In conducting your job campaign, you have six primary sources for learning about openings:

1. The college placement office
2. Advertisements and web postings
3. Direct mail to prospective employers
4. Friends, relatives, and business associates
5. Employment agencies
6. Cold-calling

The College Placement Office

The logical place to start your job campaign is the college placement office. Beginning there offers several advantages. First, your search efforts and costs are minimized. Second, most companies coming for campus interviews are large and offer extensive training programs, an advantage for recent graduates with little professional experience.

Besides offering low-cost interviewing, the placement office is helpful in other respects. There is usually a great deal of information on hand about interviewing companies. The counselors themselves are important people to get to know. They can offer advice about career opportunities throughout your college years and recommend courses that will make you more marketable to prospective employers. They are also of great assistance in assessing offers because they have knowledge of salary ranges on both local and national levels.

However, it is a mistake to rely solely on the placement office to secure a job. A point frequently overlooked is that only a small number of college graduates are hired as a result of campus interviews. Campus recruiting is expensive for employers, and they recruit actively only for jobs where demand is great. The demand for sales positions is usually high, but openings may not be exactly in the area you want. If this is true, the odds are good that you will have to go off campus to find your job.

Job/Career Fairs

Many types of career and job fairs occur regularly. Companies send employees to these fairs to meet and recruit top prospects. Your goal is to prepare beforehand, identify the key employers in attendance, and then develop a strategy for breaking through the clutter of perhaps thousands of other job seekers. Even if the employer is not in the market for someone with your mix of skills and experience, you can still get your foot in the door.

Answering Advertisements and Online Job Sites

One important source of job leads is the classified section of your daily newspaper. First, look for ads in your field, such as "salesperson, large national company." Then go back and read every ad from A to Z. Possibly, you might see an ad such as "chemical salesperson, local company." Openings are usually listed by alphabetical heading, but there are exceptions, and the exception might be the job you are seeking.

Besides the newspaper, another source of leads is the trade press. Almost every industry has a trade publication associated with it. These publications are read by practically every owner and manager in the industry, and most carry help-wanted advertising.

Numerous generic and career-specific job sites are located on the Internet. There are also geographic-specific job sites, such as TexasJobs.com. Although the Internet can be a great source of leads, the reality is that recruiters receive thousands of resumes for every job posted. After you identify a specific job and company, use personal contacts, direct mail, or email to follow up with the recruiting sales manager but not the human resources department, where your resume can get lost among many.

One of the fastest growing sources of job leads has been the development of online corporate career (human resource) centers. Many companies, large and small, including just about all of the *Fortune* 500 companies, continue to build these corporate career centers, which often include job openings, guidelines for submitting job-search materials, and a wealth of information about the company (such as corporate culture, career paths, benefits, and more).

Direct Mail

A job-search campaign should include some direct mail promotion. Direct mail will probably put your resume on the desk of the appropriate manager. The advantages of this should be self-evident. Whereas you may be interviewing with a recruiter from the personnel department in a campus interview, direct mail generally reaches the desk of the line manager.

This presumes that you have a good mailing list. You will need the names of the people you want to contact, their titles, the names of the firms, and the addresses. This information should be available from the same sources consulted earlier when researching prospective employers. The name of the relevant manager is the most important piece of information to secure. If you only address your letter to the "Sales Manager," you lose much of its effectiveness. Such a letter will probably be opened by

Box 17-2

The Cover Letter

Cover Letter Format

Opening paragraph: Attract attention, state the position you are applying for and mention how you learned about it (mention any contacts you have). Reveal your knowledge about the company. Make the employer want to read on!

Second paragraph: Describe your qualifications. Outline the qualifications that you possess that match the requirements of the position. Indicate when and from where you will be graduating. State why you are interested in working for the company and specify your reasons for desiring this type of work.

Third paragraph: Make reference to your enclosed resume, but do not restate the information it contains. Point out college or work experience that might be of particular interest or contribute to the company.

Closing paragraph: Show appreciation and ask for action (i.e., request an interview and state when you would be available). Indicate when you will follow up instead of leaving it up to the employer to contact you. Briefly thank the prospective employer for their consideration.

Source: "Career Library," *UW Oshkosh Career Services,* 2004.

a receptionist and then routed through channels to the personnel department. Because of the numbers involved, these letters may receive little more than a cursory glance.

When forwarding your resume as part of a direct mail campaign and in response to advertisements, it is necessary to include a letter of transmittal. Your objectives with the letter of transmittal are to introduce yourself, briefly call attention to your special capabilities and experiences outlined in the resume, and request consideration for a job. Box 17-2 gives some suggestions for composing your transmittal letter.

Personal Contacts

Many jobs never appear in want ads, employment agencies, or college placement offices. Nearly 64 percent of the nation's jobs were obtained through "who-you-know" systems, only 13 percent through advertisements, and 12 percent through employment agencies.[8] Many times, knowledge of the opening never leaves the department where it originates. An informal network of communication puts the word out without the personnel department ever becoming involved.

To learn about these openings, be sure that all of your acquaintances—friends, relatives, professors, and business contacts—know of your availability. Begin with alumni. They are by far the easiest to contact. As a graduate, you have something in common with them. Don't forget your roommate's mother, a professor's brother, anyone who is off campus and in the real world. With friends and relatives, nothing is required beyond simply telling them about your job desires. With professors and business contacts, it is a good idea to drop off a resume. Otherwise, they may have difficulty reaching you when an opening arises. For business contacts especially, it is a good idea to arrange an interview to make an impression, even if there is no opening. Hopefully, the contact will be impressed enough to provide names of other people along with a recommendation. This will lead to a pyramiding effect, with one interview leading to others, and ultimately a job offer.

Every career field has at least one professional organization. Whether it's at the annual conference or an on-going process, most trade organizations offer some sort of job posting/resume exchange program. Find the process for getting the latest job postings and respond as soon as you get them. Of course, professional organizations are also great places to network. If you're not currently a member of any organization, how can you find one for your trade or profession? Go to "General Professional Organizations and Associations" at www.quintcareers.com/professional_organizations.html.

Most campuses do have affiliate student chapters of professional organizations. For example, Pi Sigma Epsilon is the student affiliate to Sales & Marketing Executives International. Don't just attend meetings and listen, however. Volunteer to help solicit and arrange for the speakers the club brings to campus. That way you make personal contacts with the outsiders before, during, and after meetings (with your thank-you notes).

Employment Agencies

Many people contact an employment agency only as a last resort after all other sources have been exhausted. Unfortunately, by this time they have been unemployed for an extended period, making them less attractive to employers. If you plan to use an agency, the best advice is to start the process early in the job campaign.

A good employment agency can assist the job search in several ways:

1. The agency acts in a brokerage capacity, bringing applicants and employers together. In this way, the costs of search are reduced for both parties. By contacting an agency, the applicant may learn of more jobs in one moment than in weeks or months of searching through other channels.
2. Agencies often have exclusive job listings. Many companies deal only with employment agencies, and there is no other way of learning about their openings.
3. The service is free if there is no opening. If you appear promising, an employment agency will conduct an extensive job-hunting campaign on your behalf without charging a cent until a job is found. Accepting a job may cost quite a bit, usually a percentage of salary, but often the hiring company pays the fee.
4. A good agency will perform a valuable screening function. It will screen the job orders it has in its files to find the ones that fit your qualifications and objectives. Unfortunately, many agencies take an expedient approach; their idea is to run you past a number of employers, many of whom you will not be interested in, hoping an offer will develop merely by the laws of chance. The best advice, then, is to deal with a reputable agency. The only way of determining an agency's quality is by checking with knowledgeable sources such as the Better Business Bureau, teachers, and business contacts.

Cold-Calling

An unconventional strategy, one not for the faint of heart, is to cold-call prospective employers. In selling, this represents an especially good approach because sales managers are looking for exactly the characteristics the applicant is demonstrating: initiative, self-discipline, an ego that can withstand rejection, and assertiveness.

17-4 Sweaty Palms Time—The Interview

You have checked the placement office, sent out resumes, and talked with friends and acquaintances. You have had some luck, and now you have an interview scheduled, but you are uneasy. This is your first interview, and you do not know what to say or do. Well, don't feel bad; you are in the majority. Almost everybody is nervous before an interview, even those who have done it dozens of times. But as you sit there, with palms sweating and hands trembling, remember that there is plenty you can do before the interview. It is amazing how many intelligent, well-educated, and qualified individuals walk into an interview and destroy their chances for the job. Why? Because they fail to prepare, and preparation is the key element in making a good impression.

17-4a Preparing for the Interview

A sales representative would never call on a prospect without first preparing, but the same individual might do little before an important job interview, trusting it to fate and luck. The typical interviewee might spend hours and hours getting an interview; but, once scheduled, he or she may figure the interview will take care of itself and require little special preparation beyond getting up in the morning and spending a little more time than usual dressing.

One of the biggest mistakes candidates make during interviews is spending too much time focusing on WIIFM—"what's in it for me"—before they have sold the interviewer on why they are right for the job. It is important to come prepared with questions, but don't ask about compensation, vacation time, or benefits. Those topics are irrelevant until the interviewer has interest in your skills. For example, asking, "What characteristics best describe individuals who are successful in this position?" is better than asking, "How much vacation time will I get?" Don't get ahead of yourself. Stay focused on the task at hand, which is convincing the interviewer that you are the ideal person for the job. Once he is sold on you, he will begin to sell you on the opportunity. He may even bring up the fact that the company offers excellent compensation and benefits. At the very least, those issues will be discussed during the offer stage.[9]

So what can the interviewee do? One answer is to put extra effort into the research process you started at the beginning of the job campaign. Now is the time to learn even more. Some interviewees conclude erroneously that the interviewer will control the interview; this is not necessarily the case at all. By knowing about a company—its products, growth, financial strength, and so on—you can do much to control the tempo of the interview and its outcome. The way you accomplish this is through the questions you ask. Judgment about the suitability of a candidate is often made on the basis of the questions he or she asked. What are the questions that most favorably impress recruiters?

In a survey conducted by the Endicott Placement Center at Northwestern University, more than half the recruiters chose as the most important question, "What is the time frame for advancement?" Asking this question demonstrates that the candidate possesses serious ambition and is interested in a long-term commitment. Questions about the financial stability and future growth plans of the company were listed as the next most important. Because specific job duties should be of concern, recruiters expect candidates to ask, "What are typical first-year assignments?" Other key questions concern the uniqueness of the organization itself. "How does your firm differ from competitors?" "What are its strengths and weaknesses?" "What is its corporate personality?" "Why do you enjoy working for your company?"[10] For a complete list of questions that favorably impress recruiters, see Box 17-3.

Interviewers are going to be favorably impressed by interviewees who ask penetrating questions about their company. If an interviewer has to explain basic

Box 17-3

Interviewee Questions

Interviewee questions expected and recommended by company recruiters include:

1. What are the opportunities for personal growth?

2. Identify typical career paths based on past records. What is the realistic time frame for advancement?

3. How is an employee evaluated and promoted?

4. What is the retention rate of people in the position for which I am interviewing?

5. Describe typical first-year assignments.

6. Tell me about your initial and future job training programs.

7. What are the challenging facets of the job?

8. What are the company's plans for future growth?

9. Is the company stable and financially sound?

10. What is the company's record of employment stability?

11. What industry trends will occur in this company?

12. How has this company fared during the recent recession?

13. What makes your firm different from its competitors?

14. What are the company's strengths and weaknesses?

15. How would you describe your corporation's personality and management style?

16. Is it company policy to promote from within? Tell me the work history of your top management.

17. What kinds of career opportunities are currently available for my degree and skills?

18. What are your expectations for new hires?

19. Describe the work environment.

20. How can you use my skills?

21. What is the overall structure of the department where the position is located?

22. Why do you enjoy working for your firm?

23. What qualities are you looking for in your new hires?

24. Why should I want to work for your organization?

25. What characteristics does a successful person at your company have?

Source: Adapted from "Northwestern Lindquist-Endicott Report," The Placement Center, Northwestern University, Evanston, Illinois, 1991.

facts to an applicant who has failed to prepare, the impression is guaranteed to be unfavorable. An applicant who has shown limited talent for industry and planning is not likely to receive an offer. Candidates who have done their homework earlier will find themselves at an advantage.

Another important element in preparing for the interview is to anticipate likely interviewer questions. Box 17-4 contains some common on-campus interview questions. Most can be answered from researching the company and reviewing your strengths and weaknesses inventory. For other questions, it may be a good idea to compose and write down possible answers. However, you should not commit them to memory for playback to an interviewer like a tape recording. This will not make much of an impression. Rather, keep general responses in mind and formulate specific answers during the course of the interview.

One especially vexing question for interviewees is, "What is your major weakness?" After all, who likes admitting weaknesses, not to mention one that could eliminate an applicant from consideration? One way of resolving this

Box 17-4

Fifty Questions Asked by Employers during the Interview with College Seniors

1. What are your long-range and short-range goals and objectives; when and why did you establish these goals; and how are you preparing yourself to achieve them?

2. What specific goals, other than those related to your occupation, have you established for yourself for the next 10 years?

3. What do you see yourself doing five years from now?

4. What do you really want to do in life?

5. What are you long-range career objectives?

6. How do you plan to achieve your career goals?

7. What are the most important rewards you expect in your business career?

8. What do you expect to be earning in five years?

9. Why did you choose the career for which you are preparing?

10. Which is more important to you, the money or the type of job?

11. What do you consider to be your greatest strengths and weaknesses?

12. How would you describe yourself?

13. How do you think a friend or professor who knows you well would describe you?

14. What motivates you to put forth your greatest effort?

15. How has your college experience prepared you for a business career?

16. Why should I hire you?

17. What qualifications do you have that make you think that you will be successful in business?

18. How do you determine or evaluate success?

19. What do you think it takes to be successful in a company like ours?

20. In what ways do you think you can make a contribution to our company?

21. What qualities should a successful manager possess?

22. Describe the relationship that should exist between a supervisor and those reporting to him or her.

23. What two or three accomplishments have given you the most satisfaction? Why?

24. Describe the relationship that should exist between a supervisor and those reporting to him or her.

25. If you were hiring a graduate for this position, what qualities would you look for?

26. Why did you select your college or university?

27. What led you to choose your field of major study?

28. What college subjects did you like best? Why?

29. What college subjects did you like least? Why?

30. If you could do so, how would you plan your academic study differently? Why?

31. What changes would you make in your college or university? Why?

32. Do you have plans for continued study? An advanced degree?

33. Do you think that your grades are a good indication of your academic achievement?

34. What have you learned from participation in extracurricular activities?

35. In what kind of a work environment are you most comfortable?

36. How do you work under pressure?

37. In what part-time or summer jobs have you been most interested? Why?

38. How would you describe the ideal job for you following graduation?

39. Why did you decide to seek a position with this company?

40. What do you know about our company?

41. What two or three things are most important to you in your job?

42. Are you seeking employment in a company of a certain size? Why?

43. What criteria are you using to evaluate the company for which you hope to work?

44. Do you have a geographical preference? Why?

45. Will you relocate? Does relocation bother you?

46. Are you willing to travel?

47. Are you willing to spend at least six months as a trainee?

48. Why do you think you might like to live in the community in which our company is located?

49. What major problem have you encountered and how did you deal with it?

50. What have you learned from your mistakes?

Source: "Getting Chosen—The Job Interview and Before," Career Center, University of Minnesota–Morris, 2003.

problem, though admittedly awkward to carry through, is to cite a "weakness" that is actually a possible strength in the desired job. For example, you could say, "I'm not the most organized of individuals, so I always answer my emails and phone calls right away. I'm aware of the problem and I have strategies to deal with it."[11]

Other so-called weaknesses: "I have a tendency to take on too much, so I'm trying to learn how to delegate more" or "I've realized I'm a workaholic, but I'm doing my best to remedy this by taking a course in time management." Some difficult questions arise for recent college graduates because potential employers have little to rely on, other than school performance; hence, they concentrate on questions that reveal how willing you are to learn and get the job done; how manageable you are; and your maturity. For example, they might ask, "Why did you decide to go to this particular school?" The school choice isn't as important as the reasons, and these should be your reasons. Emphasize that it was your choice and not your parents' choice. Focus on the practical: "I chose Northeast Missouri State because I wanted a school that would give me a good business education and prepare me for the real world. I knew that Northeast Missouri had a good internship program, and I wanted to be prepared for my future career in the business world." Another problematic question is, "How did you rank in college?" If your grades were good, then obviously play this up. If not, then you may want to emphasize your need to work to finance your education. You might also wish to answer something along the lines of, "Of course, an employer should take everything into consideration. Along with grades, they should evaluate your willingness to work hard, your manageability, and, of course, your actual work experience." A critical question to answer is, "What are your future vocational plans?" Too many recent grads make the conventional mistake of answering, "In management," because they believe this shows drive and ambition. This trite answer, however, usually generates a string of questions that most recent graduates find awkward to answer: "What is your definition of *management?* What is a manager's prime responsibility? A manger in what area?" A safer answer identifies you with the profession you desire, "I want to learn all I can about technical selling in the computer area first with your company, and then I can make a decision about my future vocational plans. I definitely want to get ahead, but I will decide after further experience, whether it be in sales management or marketing management." Finally, in response to why you changed majors, you might admit outright that it took awhile to find your direction. After all, how many know from the start that they want to be accountants or city planners? Tell how your previous studies also contribute to the job and company you are interviewing.[12]

When interviewing, make sure you talk with the person who would be your first boss. Who you work for and with is the single most important factor in a first job. Don't accept a position for assignment to someone, somewhere, at a later date. Personal chemistry is critical for initial success.

Behavioral Interviewing

As discussed in the previous chapter, **Behavioral interviewing** is a technique used by employers in which the questions asked assist the employer in making predictions about a potential employee's future success based on actual past behaviors, instead of based on responses to hypothetical questions. In behavior-based interviews, you are asked to give specific examples of when you demonstrated particular behaviors or skills. General answers about behavior are not what the employer is seeking. You must describe a particular event, project, or experience in detail; explain how you dealt with the situation; and tell what the outcome was.[13] The behavioral interviewer works from a profile of desired behaviors needed for success on the job. Because behavior patterns are likely to be repeated, you will be asked to share situations in which you may or may not have exhibited these behaviors. Box 17-5 provides samples of behavioral questions.

behavioral interviewing
Technique in which the questions asked assist the employer in making predictions about a potential employee's future success based on actual past behaviors, instead of based on responses to hypothetical questions.

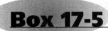

Box 17-5

Sample Behavioral Questions

1. Tell me about a time when you showed initiative.

2. Describe how you keep up with recent developments in your field.

3. Can you recall a mistake you made? What did you learn from that mistake?

4. Describe a major problem you have faced and how you dealt with it.

5. Tell me about a time when you helped a coworker learn a new task or procedure.

6. Describe a time when you had lots of projects to complete and very little time in which to complete them.

7. Tell me about the last time a new idea of yours helped an organization or group work better.

8. Give me an example of when you had to handle a difficult situation.

9. Give me an example of a time when you had to resolve a conflict.

Source: Beth Heuer, "Are You Ready for a Behavioral Interview?" *UW Oshkosh Alumni Association Newsletter,* Summer 1998.

17-4b The Small Things That Make a Difference

More often than not, it is the small things in the interview that make the difference between getting and not getting a job. All the things you say and do help to build an impression in the interviewer's mind. It is purely a subjective feeling, so your close attention to the little things is essential.

Be Punctual

If you are late for an interview, you go in with two strikes against you. No matter how valid your excuse or how legitimate the circumstances, your lateness marks you as being unreliable. Write down the time of the interview and try to arrive early. If you plan on arriving 15 minutes before the appointment, you will have a cushion against unforeseen delays, such as getting caught in traffic. Being early also provides a favorable initial impression of your reliability and interest.

Make Your First 10 Words Count

The most effective way to begin an interview is to send a "thanks" message:

Thank you for taking the time to meet with me this morning, Ms. Smith.

It's a pleasure to finally meet you in person, Mr. Jones.

Note the use of the interviewer's name. Most of us tune in when we hear our names.[14]

Bring a Pen and Notebook

The notebook should fit easily into your pocket or purse, and you should have a pen with you. This serves two purposes. First, when interviewers give you some information to write down, you will not have to ask for writing material. This will save time and impress them with your preparation. Second, immediately following the interview, jot down your impressions. This will help later on when it comes time to make a decision about the job.

Remember the Interviewer's Name

Few sounds are sweeter than the sound of one's own name. If you do not know the interviewer's name prior to the interview, concentrate on the name when you are first introduced. Repeat the name to yourself, and try to form a mental association with it. One important rule: Never call the interviewer by his or her first name unless invited to do so. Calling someone you have just met by first name without invitation may offend.

Watch Your Dress and Appearance

Go to Chapter 5, "Effective Communication," and review the material on dress. You should dress conservatively—dark suits for men and 2-piece suits for women. Especially if you are a young graduate, choose conservative colors such as gray and blue. Avoid loud ties. Shine your shoes. Make sure your hair is cut and well groomed. An unkempt appearance is a guarantee of failure in an interview.

Make an Effective Approach

It is difficult to define the approach, beyond its consisting of physical yet intangible impressions that come through at the outset of the interview. But there is no denying its critical nature. A proper approach will do much to spark a positive feeling with an interviewer.

Enter the room confidently. When you meet your interviewer for the first time, hold your head up, put on a smile, and be sure you look like you are enthusiastic about the opportunity. Interviews are not fun, but if you go into them anticipating torture, your body language will reflect this attitude.[15]

Never initiate a handshake; let interviewers offer theirs first. Many interviewers are extremely formal and prefer not to shake hands until a later date.

When you get the chance to shake hands, do it right. Avoid the limp handshake; also avoid crushing the interviewer's hand. Most important, avoid shaking with sweaty hands. A clammy hand will leave a negative impression every time. Of course, the obvious question is how to prevent it. If you are nervous, your hands are bound to sweat. One method is to sit with your palms exposed while you wait for the interview. Allowing air to get at them tends to minimize the problem. It might look a little awkward at the time, but the interviewer is not going to see you sitting that way, and that is the important thing. The only legitimate form of touch in an interview is the handshake. Unless you've established close rapport with someone, a pat, nudge, or touch on the arm can be perceived as being too friendly.[16]

Never sit down until you are invited to do so by the interviewer. It is a matter of common courtesy to wait until a chair is offered. Just because the interviewer is seated is no excuse to head immediately for a chair and plop yourself down without invitation. When you do sit down, sit up straight. Slouching or throwing an arm over the chair makes a bad impression. It looks as if you are waiting to be entertained.

The manner in which you answer questions is as important as what you actually say. It is critical to speak clearly, enunciate your words, and answer all questions in a straightforward manner. Take time to answer questions (this makes you appear more thoughtful), and make sure that interviewers understand your answer. Questions that remain in their mind are not likely to work in your favor.

Don't swing your legs, tap your feet, twirl your hair, wring your hands, or bite your fingernails. All of these actions demonstrate lack of confidence and fear and can be extremely distracting. You want to make sure your interviewer concentrates on your great answers, not your fidgety behavior. Pay attention to your posture. Sitting up straight and having good posture will tell your interviewer that you are confident and have a strong personality; slouching will paint you as lazy and weak. As uncomfortable as you might be in that business suit, sit up straight and keep your head up. Don't cross your arms in front of your body. Sitting with your arms crossed in front of you indicates defensiveness, resistance, aggressiveness, or a closed mind. Use your hands to be expressive when you are talking. When the interviewer is speaking, keep your hands folded in your lap, rested on the arms of your chair, or in another position that is lower than your elbows. Make and keep eye contact. Failing to make eye contact with your interviewer will keep you from truly connecting with him or her and might make you seem shy or even evasive. Yes, making eye contact can be uncomfortable, but it is an important tactic. Similarly, try to utilize other body expressions that demonstrate interest, such as nodding, tilting your head, or raising your eyebrows when the other person is making a point. Don't change positions often. Constant shifting is distracting and can make a candidate seem untrustworthy. If you do opt to cross your legs, make sure they are crossed all the way. Resting your ankle on your knee will come across as too casual and even overconfident.[17]

Watch Your Language

Most of us are products of our environment—for better or worse. In many instances, the words we use and the way in which we use them are based on what our parents and peers say. Sometimes, this is unfortunate. I was 30 years old before I learned there is no such word as *anyways*. There are many such words, many of them regional colloquialisms. In Northeastern Wisconsin, one can *borrow from* or *borrow to!* Imagine the interviewer's reaction to the latter.

Using sloppy words will also lessen the impression you make. Some examples are *yeah* rather than *yes, you guys* rather than *you,* and *okey dokey* rather than *all right.* Many of these too are regional colloquialisms. In Northeastern Wisconsin, for example, it's common to hear *youse* or *youse guys.*

Just like your physical motions, your tone of voice says a lot about you. Be sure to answer questions in a strong, consistent tone. Avoid wavering or talking too softly, mumbling or speaking too quickly. A good thing to remember before answering a question is to take a deep breath, think for a second, and then begin to answer. This will help calm your nerves and will give you the opportunity to "look before you leap" when it comes to your important answers.

Be Kind to Former Employers

Be sure not to "knock" a former manager, company, or professor. You may have worked for or been a student of the worst incompetent around, but saying so can brand you as a malcontent. When looking for a new job, try to leave the impression that you are not too unhappy with your current position, but that you are looking for a better opportunity.[18]

17-4c Be Yourself

Earlier we suggested that it is important to first question prospects about their needs to avoid making a presentation about the wrong features and benefits. The same is true of interviewing. Before talking about your qualifications and experience, it is important to find out what the job requires and what sort of individual the interviewer is seeking. In other words, never start talking about yourself until you know something about the situation. Then stress those qualities that qualify you for the position.

But there is no need to go overboard. It is important to be yourself. There is a great temptation to become what the interviewer wants, even if it is not really you. You might play a role so well that you get the job, only to find yourself unhappy once you start work. It is likely your employer will not be happy either, and you will be worse off than if you had never gotten the job.

17-4d How to Handle Nervousness

More often than not, people with confidence are the ones who get the job. Those who do not get frightened and who act the most at ease do the best job of interviewing. If you can get yourself to relax and can tell yourself how well you are doing, you will do well. Those who know how not to panic do better than those who become nervous wrecks.

Of course, admonitions to relax come easily. The irony is that trying too hard to relax is doomed to failure. You are likely to become self-conscious and panic at the first signs of nervousness. It might sound so obvious as to be absurd, but the key to relaxing is in the mind. The proper attitude goes a long way toward relaxing, and that attitude should come easier with the following in mind:

1. *The subject of the interview is you.* One source of nervousness is fear of the unknown, but this should not be the case in an interview. You know more about the subject of the interview—you—than the interviewer does. All he or she knows about you is what is in your resume.
2. *You have nothing to lose.* Nervousness is often caused by fear of losing. But what have you got to lose? Before you walked into the interview, you did not have a job. The worst that can happen is that you still will not have one when you walk out. So why worry?
3. *You are interviewing the interviewers, too.* While they are evaluating you, you should be doing the same with them. In other words, go into the interview with the intention of finding out enough about the interviewer's company to make a job decision. This impresses the interviewer with your seriousness, and it reduces nervousness.[19]

If you are not fired with enthusiasm, you will be fired with enthusiasm.

—Vince Lombardi

17-4e Enthusiasm

"Nothing great was ever achieved without enthusiasm," said Ralph Waldo Emerson, and nothing impresses the interviewer more than the enthusiasm of the interviewee. Enthusiasm is the exhibition of fervent interest. Enthusiasm comes through in what you say, even more in how you say it and in all your nonverbal behavior. Be enthusiastic with interviewers, and demonstrate interest in them, the job, and the company.

Even if you find out things that you do not like during the interview, maintain your enthusiasm. You might change your mind later. Besides, enthusiasm is infectious. Even if you fail to meet the qualifications for the opening, it is possible that the interviewer will give you such a good recommendation that you will be called for a future opening more in line with your capabilities.

17-4f The Question of Salary

No subject causes more concern among interviewees than the subject of salary, and several aspects of the problem represent legitimate sources of concern. When should the subject be raised? How much should you ask? Should you be willing to settle for less?

The answer to the first question is simple. Never bring up the question of salary yourself. Interviewers will not want to discuss salary until they have formed a favorable image of you. For one thing, if you broach the subject too soon, you may turn them off permanently. The interviewee's goal should be to create a positive feeling with interviewers; putting them on the spot too early may halt the formation of that feeling. Most jobs are established with an acceptable salary range rather than with a fixed figure. Until interviewers know more about your background and experience, they will not want to quote a specific dollar amount from the higher or lower end of that range. So when the interviewer asks for your desired salary, the best approach is to get the employer to toss out the salary figure first by responding with this question, "What's the range that this job pays?" This practice preserves the most negotiating power when you're offered the job.[20]

Once you are quoted the range and you have an idea of your competitiveness and the interviewer's feeling about you, quote a figure within the range. Never sound apologetic about what you are asking. State your figure and stop, without adding any "if's" and "but's." Never say something like, "I want a salary of $35,000, but I am willing to start for less for an opportunity." Once you state a figure, stick with it. Backing off makes you sound less confident about yourself and your abilities. How can you expect an interviewer to feel any differently?

There is another reason for sticking firm. Because salary is typically negotiable within some range, you might prematurely settle for a lower figure when the company was actually prepared to pay more. They would be getting a bargain and you would take a loss.

17-4g Closing

Over the past 5 to 10 years, companies have had an increasingly difficult time finding salespeople who can close a sale. Sales managers recognize this problem and intensely look for salespeople with closing abilities. So, at the end of the interview, ask yourself, is this the type of company and type of job I am looking for? If all the pluses are there, then go for it! Close on the interviewer just as you would for a product or service; after all, you're selling a great product, you!

Here is how to handle the close. Thank the employer for the time he or she granted you for the interview. Express your pleasure at being there. Tell him or her that you are impressed with him, the company, and the job. Then continue, "Ms. Smith, if I understand you correctly, you are looking for someone who can. . . ." At this juncture, name the four most important aspects of the job, such as knowing the product or service, closing ability, handling rejection, and so forth. Then assure him or her that you can handle all this, work hard, and be a success. Look the employer straight in the eye and ask, "Can I come to work with you?" Then shut up.[21]

17-4h The Follow-Up Letter

The interview has gone better than expected, and you feel enthusiastic about the job. You left the interview with assurance from the interviewer that he or she

Box 17-6

Thank-You Letter

1108 Cleveland
Norman, Oklahoma 23465
January 30, 2006

Mr. Kurt Roller

Sales Manager

Wallace Computer Products, Inc.

1220 Warwick Ave.

Tulsa, Oklahoma 23607

Dear Mr. Roller:

I wish to thank you very much for interviewing me yesterday for the position of sales associate with Wallace. I enjoyed meeting with you and learning more about opportunities in sales with your company.

My enthusiasm for the position and my interest in working for Wallace were strengthened as a result of the interview. I think my education and my experience in retail sales offer a good fit for the sales associate position.

I want to reiterate my strong interest in this position and in working with you and your staff. You provide the sort of challenging opportunity I seek. Please feel free to call me at 804-555-5554 if I can provide you with any further information. Otherwise, I look forward to your call this coming Thursday.

Let's hope between now and then we have a "Sooner" victory to celebrate. As we discussed, we might see each other at the game Saturday.

Again, thanks for the interview and your consideration.

Sincerely,

Cindy Ryan

would call you on Thursday to let you know if another interview was required. All you need to do, then, is to sit back and confidently await the call. Right? Wrong. By Wednesday this busy executive, in addition to his or her usual heavy workload, has seen five additional applicants, dealt with a number of crises, and had about 40 telephone conversations. If he or she remembers your interview, let alone your name, you should feel lucky. This is why it is critical to write a follow-up letter. Career consultants estimate that only 5 percent of applicants send follow-up letters. This is curious because to the busy executive, out of sight is out of mind. The follow-up letter, as depicted in Box 17-6, if nothing more, will make you stand out. It should include:

1. Thanks to the person for valuable time expended in interviewing you
2. An expression of enthusiasm about the job
3. If possible, a reference to some part of the personal conversation (e.g., the outcome of Sunday's football game)
4. A summary of talents that make you especially suited for the position
5. Reference to the next step in the hiring process: "I look forward to your call on Thursday. . . ."[22]

17-4i Be Persistent

Sometimes the "least-qualified" applicant on paper gets the job and well deserves it.[23] What distinguished their efforts, when thousands of other candidates' records languished in the files?

Most of the job hunters—the unsuccessful ones—focused on their resumes. However, a resume and just one or two phone calls or messages often get lost in the shuffle at a busy company. Those candidates who got the offers realized their biggest challenge was to get and keep their resumes in front of the manger doing the hiring. They weren't afraid to use the telephone again and again, even though they had to cold-call managers with whom they had no previous relationship. By continuing to make those calls, these candidates located jobs that weren't advertised to the general public; in several instances, they created the jobs themselves with their persistence. Few job hunters extended this sort of effort, but it paid off.

Bill Staab, Steve Covington's new manager at Silicon Graphics, commented, "While Steve's resume was the least qualified on paper, he wanted the job more than anyone else." Despite living two states away, he offered to drive to Bill's office. He provided several dates when he would be in town and told Bill meeting him was his most important agenda item for the next month. Bill sensed Steve's dedication and made an effort to accommodate him. Steve was able to keep Bill's attention for months following an interview, despite being rejected by Bill's boss and the vice president of sales. As Bill said, "It came down to motivation and desire. He was more motivated and had more desire than anyone else."[24]

As indicated, it is critical to persist even after an initial objection. Successful candidates don't take "No" for an answer, even when they hear there are no openings. They ask about time frames and future hiring plans and if they can keep in touch on a regular basis. They also ask for the names of additional managers in other departments or even other companies. They network for additional leads and ask if they can use the original manager's name as an introductory reference. In other words, in selling themselves, they act like they would in selling a product or service.

17-5 How to Handle Failure

You have spent much time and effort in putting together a resume, writing transmittal letters, and interviewing. You have been as careful as possible to put your best foot forward, and you have done the best you can. But still you get that letter turning you down. What can you do?

First, review your notes and impressions from the interview. What went wrong? Box 17-7 shows negative factors that most often contribute to rejection.[25] Did you commit any of these errors? If so, then make sure it does not happen the next time. Do you have some problems that tend to reduce your attractiveness to interviewers? Is there anything you can do about them? Sometimes the problems can simply be attributed to lack of interviewing experience. If this is the case, practice interviewing with a friend; if facilities are available at your school, practice taping yourself with a video camera.

Above all, don't panic. Of all who interviewed for the job, only one was hired. Unless you were the only other applicant, you are still in the majority. You can't get discouraged or you'll be dooming yourself to further failure. There will be more interviews. Confidence and enthusiasm are the keys to making a favorable impression, so stay calm; it isn't the end of the world.

Box 17-7

Negative Factors That Most Often Lead to Rejection As Listed by 186 Companies (Factors listed by 10 or more companies and number of companies listing factor in parentheses.)

1. Poor scholastic record; low grades without reasonable explanation; low level of accomplishment (99)

2. Inadequate personality; poor attitude; lack of poise; lack of self-confidence; timid, hesitant approach; too introverted (89)

3. Lack of goals/objectives; poorly motivated; does not know his interests; indecision; poor planning (80)

4. Lack of enthusiasm; lack of drive; not sufficiently aggressive; little evidence of initiative (50)

5. Lack of interest in our type of business; lack of interest in our company; not interested in the type of job we have to offer (48)

6. Inability to express himself; poor speech; inability to sell himself (45)

7. Unrealistic salary demands; more interested in salary than in opportunity; unrealistic expectation; overemphasis on management positions; unwilling to start at the bottom (39)

8. Poor personal appearance; lack of neatness; careless dress (35)

9. Lack of maturity; no evidence of leadership potential (35)

10. Lack of extracurricular activities; inadequate reasons for not participating in activities (22)

11. Failure to get information about our company; lack of preparation for the interview; did not read the literature (22)

12. Objects to travel; geographical preference; unwilling to relocate (20)

13. Excessive interest in security and benefits; "What can you do for me?" (15)

14. Inadequate preparation for type of work; inappropriate background (10)

Source: "Getting Chosen—The Job Interview and Before," Career Center, University of Minnesota–Morris, 2003.

Chapter Summary

This chapter discusses one of the more important events in your life—getting your first full-time job. It might not be readily apparent, but this requires great selling skill, even from those with few aspirations for a career in sales. Yet many people, experienced salespeople among them, ignore some of the basic principles of selling when it comes to looking for a job. Experienced salespeople would never dream of making calls without first studying their product, but most job seekers begin their search without really knowing what they have to offer. They did not sit down and systematically analyze what they bring to their employer, their interests, their skills, their strengths, and their weaknesses. The first step in getting a job is taking stock of yourself.

An important element in knowing oneself is to review past activities. A useful way of doing this is to organize activities into six categories: interests, abilities, education, experience, personality, and goals. Once you complete your list, you are in a position to complete a strengths and weaknesses inventory. Being completely honest with yourself, use the information contained in your activities analysis to complete the inventory. It will prove valuable as you create a resume and prepare for questions during the interview.

The resume is one of the most important tools in the job search. It tells employers who you are, what you have accomplished, what you can do, and when you are available. An important rule to keep in mind when preparing the resume is that its physical appearance counts heavily. Interviewers are likely to see sloppy resumes as indicative of applicants who do sloppy work. Many versions of the resume exist, but probably the most common is the chronological resume. As the nomenclature indicates, the applicant's activities are arranged in order of time, with the most recent activity first.

With the resume prepared, the applicant is ready to embark upon the job campaign. The place to start is with researching companies for which the applicant might wish to work. Among sources of information are various publications, stockbrokers, professors, and even hangouts near the company headquarters.

In conducting the job campaign, applicants have six main sources for learning about openings:

1. The college placement office

2. Advertising and online job sites

3. Direct mail to prospective employers

4. Friends, relatives, and business associates

5. Employment agencies

6. Cold-calling

There is no one best source. Each has its advantages, disadvantages, and costs.

The most frightening part of the process is the interview, but it need not be that bad. Many applicants wrongly think that it is up to interviewers to control the interview, but applicants can do much to control the tempo themselves through preparation. They should take pains to learn as much as possible about the company: its products, customers, industry, growth pattern, financial strength, training programs, and so on. This puts the applicant in a position of controlling the interview with questions regarding these matters, and it serves to present an image of industry and planning. It is also a good idea to review answers to anticipated interviewer questions.

Once the interview begins, many small things can make a big difference. Among these critical details are being punctual, bringing along a pen and notebook, remembering the interviewer's name, dressing properly, using proper language, and making an effective approach. It's especially important to be kind to former employers. Your boss may have been a gross incompetent, but telling an interviewer so will only serve to brand you as a malcontent.

During the course of the interview, it is important to be yourself. You might play a role, becoming what the interviewer wants, and get the job, only to find yourself unhappy once you start work. It is also important to control one's nervousness in the interview, though this is easier said than done. Enthusiasm is another critical matter in getting an offer. Show interest in the company, the job, and the interviewer. It is important not to broach the subject of salary too soon. Some interviewers will not want to discuss the question until they are convinced you are the one for the job.

It is critical to be persistent, just as though you were already in sales. Often, persistence will override all other factors, even though other candidates are more technically qualified. Finally, job applicants should be prepared for being turned down. After all, only one person can be hired for the job. It helps to sit down and review notes and impressions from the interview because these can provide a clue as to what you could have done better. Above all, it is important not to panic; there will be other interviews.

Good luck!

Discussion Questions

1. Before seeking a job, why is it important to first know yourself?

2. Take stock of yourself. On a sheet of paper, list your interests, abilities, education, experience, personality, and goals.

3. What are your strengths? Weaknesses?

4. How does one prepare an effective resume?

5. Where would you go if you wanted to research a company for which you might wish to work?

6. Why should job seekers visit the college placement office? What are the advantages of advertisements and online job sites, direct mail, personal contacts, and employment agencies?

7. What facts about a company are of interest to job seekers?

8. How would you answer the questions posed in Box 17-4?

9. It has been said that the small things make the difference in the interview. What are these small things?

10. Why is it so important not to malign former employers?

11. How does the job applicant go about combating nervousness?

12. When should the subject of salary be brought up during the interview?

13. What is the value of persistence in the job search?

14. Trade resumes with a roommate or classmate and practice interviewing for a sales position. If possible, videotape and review the interview.

15. After preparing a strengths and weaknesses inventory, go to the college placement office or look in the newspaper and find jobs for which you feel especially well suited. Explain why you feel that way.

16. Go to your placement office and identify a company for which you might want to work. Research the company and decide whether you still want to work there.

17. Write a good prospecting letter.

18. What are six fatal resume mistakes?

19. Why is a follow-up letter a good idea? Write one you can use.

20. What are common reasons for applicant rejection and how do you plan to prevent them?

Chapter Quiz

1. To make a proper assessment of your strengths and weaknesses, first
   a. develop your resume.
   b. take an ability test, such as the Myers–Briggs Type Indicator.
   c. make a record of what you have in stock: those things you have learned and done in the past.
   d. develop a list of all of your strengths and weaknesses, not just those related to selling.

2. It is recommended that at the top of your resume you should place your name and contact information. Immediately below this information, next on your resume, should be
   a. your professional objective.
   b. educational experience.
   c. professional experience.
   d. your special skills and interests.

3. In composing a resume, students can make six fatal mistakes. These include all of the following *except*
   a. aiming too high, too soon.
   b. giving all experience equal billing.
   c. burying critical information.
   d. supplying references with contact information.

4. In terms of your resume, neatness, education, and background should all say just one thing:
   a. "My education and background fit your job requirements."
   b. "My talents and abilities demonstrate I can sell."
   c. "I can do this work for you because I have done well for someone else."
   d. "I have the necessary qualifications for an interview."

5. Nearly 64 percent of the nation's jobs were obtained through
   a. advertisements.
   b. "who-you-know" systems.
   c. employment agencies.
   d. college placement centers.

6. One of the biggest mistakes candidates make during interviews is spending too much time focusing on
   a. why they are right for the job.
   b. WIIFM—"what's in it for me."
   c. what it takes to advance in the corporation.
   d. the skills the company desires in a successful candidate.

7. Behavioral interviewing is a technique used by employers in which the questions asked assist the employer in making predictions about a potential employee's future success based on
   a. projecting the applicant's behaviors from current company situations.
   b. a case or scenario analysis.
   c. a series of hypothetical questions.
   d. actual past behaviors, instead of responses to hypothetical questions.

8. The most effective way to begin a job interview is to
   a. say "thanks for your time" to the interviewer.
   b. inquire about the skills needed for the position.
   c. compliment the interviewer in some way.
   d. tell the interviewer why you applied for the job.

9. No subject causes more concern among interviewees than the subject of salary. When should the subject be raised?
   a. After discussing the qualifications for the position and the interviewee is confident he or she meets the qualifications.
   b. The subject should never be raised by the interviewee.
   c. Only when the interviewer asks if there are any questions the interviewee would like to ask.
   d. The subject should only be brought up at the end of the interview when the interviewer understands the interviewee's qualifications.

10. In closing an interview, the best closing for the interviewee is to
    a. close the interview as they would a sales presentation, asking for the position.
    b. thank the interviewer for the opportunity to interview and ask permission to call them later for a decision.
    c. thank the interviewer for the opportunity to interview and ask when a decision will be made.
    d. wait for the interviewer to close the interview.

Web Exercise

Do you have a resume? It's time to put one together. Make a list of your accomplishments, including work experience and education. Then go to the following sites for some help on making your resume the most polished and professional it can be.

www.10minuteresume.com—Offers a free trial: give it a try!

www.rockportinstitute.com/resumes.html—Good general advice for writing your first resume and making sure it's appropriate for the job you want.

http://resume.monster.com/restips/sales—Monster's tips for sales resumes are great for getting ideas and updating an older resume. You can even look at samples at http://resume.monster.com/archives/samples.

Notes

1. Leonard Corwen, *Job Hunter's Handbook,* 2nd edition, New York: MacMillan Publishing Company, 1980.
2. Jack Chapman, "Have You Considered Sales?" *Marketing News,* Fall 1996, pp. 17–19.
3. Peter Newfield, "Ten Most Common Resume Mistakes," http://careers.msn.com, 2003.
4. Kate Lorenz, "How to Answer: 'Why Should We Hire You?' " *CareerBuilder.com,* 2004.
5. "Writing Is Your Ticket to a Professional Job," *JobWeb.com,* 2004.
6. "Career Library," *UW Oshkosh Career Services,* 2004.
7. Randall S. Hansen, "10 Ways to Develop Job Leads," www.quintcareers.com, 2004.
8. Dan Martin, "From the Recruiter: Questions to Avoid Asking during an Interview," *Sales & Marketing Management,* November 2004.
9. "Northwestern Lindquist–Endicott Report," *The Placement Center,* Evanston, IL: Northwestern University, 1991.
10. Barbara Mulligan, "Interviewers' Favorite Questions . . . and Answers," *JobWeb.com,* 2004.
11. Ron Fry, *101 Great Answers to the Toughest Interview Questions,* Cincinnati: Thomson Learning, 2000.
12. Beth Heuer, "Are You Ready for a Behavioral Interview?" *UW Oshkosh Alumni Association Newsletter,* Summer 1998.
13. Ann Marie Sabath, "Business Etiquette: 101 Ways to Conduct Business with Charm and Savvy," *Career Press Inc.,* 2002.
14. "Actions Speak Louder Than Words: Dos and Don'ts of Interview Body Language," *MSN Careers,* http://careers.msn.com, 2004.
15. Joy Davia, "Shake It Like You Mean It," *Rochester (N.Y.) Democrat and Chronicle,* 2004.
16. "Actions Speak Louder Than Words: Dos and Don'ts of Interview Body Language," *MSN Careers,* http://careers.msn.com, 2004.
17. Ibid.
18. Jennifer Rae Atkins, "9 Things You Should Never Say in an Interview," www.wetfeet.com, 2004.
19. H. Anthony Medley, *Sweaty Palms: The Neglected Art of Being Interviewed,* New York: Warner Business Books, May 19, 2005; Robin Ryan, "Quiz: Ace These Interview Questions," *MSN Careers,* http://careers.msn.com, 2004.
20. Jackie Larson, "To Get a Job, Be a Pest," *Wall Street Journal,* April 17, 1995.
21. Jackie Larson, "To Get a Job, Be a Pest," *Wall Street Journal,* April 17, 1995.
22. Ibid.
23. Ibid.
24. "Career Library," *UW Oshkosh Career Services,* 2004.
25. Ibid.

Case 17-1

Read the following transcript of an interview between a job applicant and an interviewer from General Register, an office forms manufacturer.

Applicant: (stepping into the office, but stopping one foot inside the door) Is it okay to come in?

Interviewer: Sure, come right in here, Mark, and sit down in this chair across from me.

Applicant: Thank you, sir.

Interviewer: (extending hand) I'm Rod Pung, with General Register.

Applicant: Glad to meet you. (extending hand in return) Mark Johnson.

Interviewer: It's a pleasure, Mark. What interests you about our company?

Applicant: Well, Rod, I know it's a large company.

Interviewer: Yes, we are a large company. Three hundred million dollars in sales last year, and we should reach half a billion within the next couple of years. Do you know anything about our products?

Applicant: No, I've been busy with tests here at school and haven't been able to read up about your company.

Interviewer: I understand. Well, basically we manufacture business forms. We make all types of forms for all kinds of businesses, manufacturers, banks, hospitals, whatever.

Applicant: Great!

Interviewer: Have you thought about what sort of position you're most interested in?

Applicant: Well, (pause) I suppose I'd be most interested in a sales position, but I really haven't decided exactly.

Interviewer: Why sales?

Applicant: Well, I majored in marketing, and I guess that's what I'm best suited for.

Interviewer: Let me ask you, Mark, where do you want to be 5 to 10 years from now?

Applicant: I suppose I'd like to work up into management someday. I like money, so I think I'd like to be in some position of authority. By the way, how much do you pay to start?

Interviewer: It all depends on the position and the experience of the applicant. I'm really not in a position to quote you a figure right now.

Applicant: Sorry.

Interviewer: I see from your application that you worked selling encyclopedias for awhile. Did you enjoy it?

Applicant: Yeah, it wasn't bad. But I didn't care for my boss too much.

Interviewer: Is that right?

Applicant: Yeah, he always expected more than you could possibly do.

Interviewer: What sort of extracurricular activities did you engage in at State?

Applicant: Well, I spent most of my time studying and working part-time as a bartender.

Interviewer: How much time did your job require?

Applicant: About 10 hours per week. I guess that doesn't sound like much, but it was enough to interfere with my studying. Otherwise, I think my GPA would have been higher than 2.3.

Interviewer: Well, is there anything else I can tell you about General Register?

Applicant: (pause) No, I don't think so, Rod.

Interviewer: Fine, Mark. Thank you so much for dropping by to see us today. We'll be in touch with you later on.

Applicant: Thank you.

Questions

1. Did this applicant do a good job of interviewing?
2. What could have been done differently?

Case 17-2

Julie Schutz has jotted down the following information about herself. From this information, write a resume that will be attractive to potential employers.

Will graduate in May with a major in marketing from San Jose State University. GPA is 3.5 out of a possible 4.0. My favorite courses were in marketing and drama. Was an active member of the University Drama Club. Appeared in several university theatre productions in both lead and supporting roles. Was a member of a social sorority, in which I held several offices, including treasurer, recording secretary, and rush chairperson. I am 21 years old. I live at 706 Fremont Ave., San Jose, California. Panhellenic representative for my sorority. Single. Was a member of the University Business Club, for which I was in charge of ar-

ranging speakers from area businesses. Part-time employment as retail sales clerk for Seifert's, a clothing store here in town. Employment last three summers: worked for the university calling on potential students, worked in retail sales for Sears, and worked in a bookstore. Born and raised in Los Angeles, California. Member of National Honor Society in high school. Cheerleader and prom queen in high school. My greatest strengths are being able to relate easily to people, organizing them, and motivating them. My greatest weakness is impatience. Upon graduation, I hope to get a job as a marketing manager, although I realize I might have to start in sales. I can use Dr. Stan Abernathy, Dr. Dale Molander, and Dr. Patrick Brown, all university professors, as references.

Glossary

A

advance Any event that takes place, either in the call or after it, that moves the sale toward a decision.

advantage Explains what the feature does—its purpose or function.

advertising A nonpersonal sales presentation paid for by an identified sponsor, usually directed to a large number of potential customers.

after-marketing Applies marketing principles to customers after they've made a purchase.

allowances Similar to discounts in that they are deductions from the list price. For example, advertising allowances are provided by the manufacturer to encourage retailers to promote the manufacturer's goods through local advertising.

amiables Individuals who are high in responsiveness and low in assertiveness. They value highly personal relationships, dislike risk, and are slow to act.

analyticals Technicians who are persistent, systematic, problem solvers. Details of performance are their forte; they gather all the facts and attempt to make decisions free of personal and emotional considerations.

approach The first face-to-face meeting between salesperson and customer, during which the sales rep must gain the potential customer's attention.

assertiveness Refers to the amount of control and forcefulness a person attempts to exercise over other people and situations.

assumptive close The salesperson assumes that the buyer wishes to buy and it is time to make a subordinate decision. The assumptive close can ask for a "which" choice, an implicit choice, or involve an action.

assurance The knowledge and courtesy of employees and their ability to convey trust and confidence.

auctioning A win–lose negotiating maneuver in which the buyer negotiates with many potential buyers, letting each know of the others' presence.

B

balance-sheet close The salesperson draws a large "T" on a sheet of paper, listing the reasons to buy on one side and not to buy on the other.

BATNA The best alternative to a negotiated agreement; BATNA helps the negotiator not to settle for less in the negotiation.

behavioral event interview Asking the applicant three incidents in which he or she did particularly well and three in which they did poorly.

behavioral interviewing Technique in which the questions asked assist the employer in making predictions about a potential employee's future success based on actual past behaviors, instead of based on responses to hypothetical questions.

benefit How the feature helps satisfy a need or problem for the customer; relates a benefit to the user.

bonus In contrast to commission, a bonus is less directly tied to sales, typically being paid quarterly, semiannually, or annually for exceeding quota.

boomerang method The salesperson's taking an objection and turning it into a reason to buy.

bring them to their senses Letting one's negotiating partner know the consequences of not reaching agreement by asking questions that prompt them to think through those consequences.

budget bogey A win–lose negotiating maneuver in which the buyer details a budget limit he or she cannot exceed.

buyclass One of three types of organizational buying situations: new task, modified rebuy, or straight rebuy.

buyers People who actually contact the selling organization and place the order.

C

C.B.D. (cash before delivery) A credit term.

C.O.D. (cash on delivery) Probably the most common credit term.

C.W.O. (cash with order) A credit term.

call reports A report of each day's activities by the salesperson indicating accounts called on, results, comments, and so forth.

candor Your presentations are balanced and fair (e.g., product limitations as well as advantages are discussed).

CAN-SPAM Act Law requiring that "from" lines identify the email message initiator. The act makes it clear that the initiator will almost always be the advertiser or marketer. Under most circumstances, it will not be a party who merely transmits the message, such as an email service provider.

career path A separate direction for promotion, while still remaining in sales.

cash discounts The reductions in price that are provided to buyers for early payment of their bills.

centers of influence People who, because of their position, responsibility, accomplishment, and personality, exercise more than ordinary influence and can direct salespeople to prospects.

chronological resume Resume organized in order of time sequence with the most recent activity first.

circular routing Starting from their offices, sales reps make calls in a series of concentric circles.

close A question, declaration, or action by a salesperson designed to secure from the prospect an affirmative decision to buy.

closed questions Specific questions that seek specific answers.

closing Securing the customer's commitment to buy.

closing on a question (contingent decision close) When prospects ask a question, sales reps respond with a question that closes the sale.

cloverleaf routing The salesperson circles just part of his or her territory, then an adjacent circle, and so forth.

cold-calling Method of prospecting in which the salesperson goes door to door, office to office, or factory to factory searching for potential clients face-to-face.

combination plans Include all variations of salary plus some monetary incentive. These combinations can include salary plus commission, salary plus bonus, and salary plus commission and bonus.

compensation method The salesperson admits the validity of an objection, but then counterbalances it with more compensating benefits.

competence You display technical command of products and applications (i.e., you are accurate, complete, and objective).

contact management software Software that facilitates keeping track of potential and current customers, including their purchase history.

continuing questions Questions that call for more detailed explanations of a buyer response.

continuous-yes close The salesperson asks a series of questions, each designed to elicit a "yes" from the prospect, the last one of which is the request to buy.

creative silence A pause for approximately three to four seconds at two different points in the questioning process.

customer relationship management (CRM) The marketing strategy that combines sales-force automation, marketing, and customer service into a seamless provision of products, service, and customer support, typically using software that creates a customer database.

customer-orientation You understand the buyer's needs and place them on a par with your own (and your organization's).

cycle selling On the first call to a prospect, the sales rep stresses the most popular line and one or two secondary ones; on the next call, the most popular again and another secondary line, etc.

D

deadline A win–lose negotiation ploy in which the buyer sets a phony deadline to gain concessions prior to the fake deadline.

decider (or economic buying influence) Role in buying center with the formal power to select or approve the supplier that receives the contract.

decode To translate a message from source to receiver into words and ideas.

demonstration Showing the product or service in use to the prospective buyer.

demonstration close The salesperson brings all the multiple buying influences together at a demonstration, hoping those favorable to the purchase will influence those unfavorable.

dependability Your actions fulfill your prior (verbal) promises.

developmental selling Characterized by (1) locating and qualifying potential buyers, (2) securing specifications and approval for purchases, and (3) closing sales (that is, actually getting the order).

direct close The salesperson directly asks the prospect for a yes or no answer.

direct questions Questions that go straight to the point and their intent is obvious.

discounts Reductions in list price for paying in cash, for services rendered as a member in the channel of distribution, or buying in quantity.

discrete transaction   Money on one side and and an easily measured commodity on the other. No further interactions between buyer and seller are expected over time.

dissonance   The discomfort people feel on recognizing contradictions in their beliefs.

"does-it-all" close   The salesperson should describe (point by point, if necessary) how the product or service fulfills every requirement of the prospect and that the price is reasonable, eliminating the need to spend valuable time looking at other choices.

don't reject, reframe   Instead of rejecting an opponent's position outright, reframe it as an attempt to deal with the problem.

door-in-the-face close   The salesperson makes a large initial request that he or she expects to be rejected to get an acceptance of a smaller follow-up request.

dramatization   "Bringing home strikingly" in the presentation by using demonstrations, audiovisual aids, or recommendations.

drivers   Individuals who are task- and bottom-line oriented, high in assertiveness, and low in responsiveness.

E

E.O.M. (end of month)   Regardless of the time during the month when the purchase is made, the credit period under E.O.M. terms will not begin until the end of the month.

echo technique   Clarifying an objection by repeating the last few words of a prospective buyer in the form of a question.

email   Messages sent electronically from computer to computer.

emotional intelligence   Has five dimensions: (1) self-motivation skills; (2) self-awareness, (3) the ability to manage one's emotions and impulses; (4) empathy, or the ability to sense how others are feeling; and (5) social skills, or the ability to handle the emotions of other people.

empathy   The provision of caring, individualized attention to customers.

encode   Translating ideas into symbols—words, pictures, and numbers—that represent the ideas to a receiver.

endless chain   A method of prospecting in which the salesperson asks each client the names of other people who might be interested in the product or service.

escalation   A win–lose negotiation tactic; after the parties believe they have come to an agreement, one side then raises its demands, hoping to wear down the other's resolve.

esteem needs   Needs that reflect an individual's desire to feel a sense of respect from others.

ethics   Moral principles and values that govern the actions and decisions of an individual or group.

exclusive dealing   Forbidding a distributor to handle competitive products, usually vulnerable under antitrust laws.

expressives   Individuals who are lively, animated, and intuitive, high in responsiveness, and high in assertiveness.

F

F.O.B. destination   The buyer pays no transportation charges whatsoever; the seller pays for everything.

F.O.B. plant (or **F.O.B. origin**)   The buyer must pay for all the freight charges.

feature   Any fact about a product or service that will be true, whether or not it is ever bought and used; may be tangible or intangible.

feedback   Communication to determine if the receiver understands the message as sent by the source.

"feel, felt, found" method   Method of handling an objection in which the salesperson points to others who have felt the same way, but discovered that purchase of the product or service resolved the problem.

forestalling   Including the answer to a common objection in the presentation itself so that the objection isn't raised.

G

gatekeepers   The role of the gatekeeper in the buying center is to screen out possible suppliers. Their focus is on the product or service itself, and they make recommendations based on how well the product or service meets a variety of objective specifications.

go to the balcony   Imagine you are negotiating on a stage and that you detach yourself by imagining that you climb onto the balcony overlooking the stage.

good-guy/bad-guy   A win–lose negotiating tactic in which two buyers will stage a quarrel, one being harsh and the other easy on the salesperson, hoping to get concessions from him or her.

greeting approach   The retail salesperson greets the customer with a sincere "Good morning" and then continues the conversation with topics of interest to the customer.

H

have them take ownership   Crafting an agreement that one's negotiating partner can also call a victory, especially to his or her constituents.

head-on   Directly telling prospects why they are wrong in their objections.

I

I need to get this approved   When the sales representative believes he or she has worked out an agreement, the buyer claims, "I have to take this plan to my boss for approval."

I-message   A nonthreatening request that can elicit help from negotiating partners rather than making them take a defensive posture (e.g., "I would appreciate it if . . .").

inactive ("orphan") accounts   People who have bought from the vendor before, but currently do not have an assigned salesperson.

inbound telemarketing   The prospect calls the company.

indirect questions   Questions that are softer and more comfortable for customers to answer.

influencers   Individuals in the buying center who influence, while not actually having formal decision-making power.

information claim   After expressing great interest in model A, the buyer asks about model B, hoping for favorable terms after the sale rep has invested time and effort in selling the first model.

instant replay   How the customer makes his or her decisions on a step-by-step basis on the basis of preceding similar buying decisions.

interest   In negotiations, what occasioned a position.

Internet   The backbone of the information superhighway, it allows easy and cheap communication between computers.

J

just-in-time (JIT)   Frequent deliveries with small lot sizes synchronized with manufacturer production schedules.

K

knockout factors   Characteristics that tend to reduce the probability of job success.

L

lantern principle   The narrow portions of the lantern shape suggest the need for closed questions and wide, open.

leapfrog routing   Starting from their offices, sales reps work their way back, making calls as they return.

libel   Unfair and untrue statements in writing communicated to customers.

likability   You and the buyer share and talk about areas of commonality—goals, interests, even comparable business intelligence; this extends to nonbusiness topics.

list generation software   Software that helps the salesperson build, revise, refine, and generate highly targeted mailing, email, or telemarketing prospecting lists.

list price   Rate usually cited to customers before discounts and allowances.

M

maintenance selling   Typically involves (1) servicing existing accounts, (2) securing promotional cooperation, whether in the form of media advertising or point-of-purchase displays, (3) counting inventory and taking replenishment orders, (4) developing and perpetuating personal relationships with potential decision makers, and (5) delivering the product.

management by objective   Management in which salespeople participate in the planning, direction, and control of their jobs.

marketing concept   The belief that management decision making should concentrate on satisfying consumer needs and wants.

marketing mix   The marketing variables the manager can structure to satisfy the needs of the target market.

merchandise approach   The retail salesperson greets the customer by mentioning something about the merchandise.

message   Communication, both verbal and nonverbal, that is transmitted from source to receiver.

mini-max strategy   Way of handling the procrastination objection by which the salesperson maximizes the potential benefits and minimizes the downside risk.

minor-point close   The assumption is that it is easier to say yes to a minor point than the overall yes–no decision.

misrepresentation and breach of warranty   When a salesperson begins to make statements of fact regarding product capabilities, the law treats these as statements of actuality and warranty. When a customer relies on a salesperson's statements, purchases the product or service, and then finds that it fails to perform as promised, the customer can sue.

missionary selling   The primary responsibility of missionary selling is to provide the firm's direct customers (wholesalers and retailers) with personal selling assistance. This is done by providing product information to indirect customers and persuading them to buy from the firm's direct customers.

modified rebuy   Buying that seeks to make modifications in product specifications, delivery schedules, prices, or suppliers.

monopsony   Similar to a monopoly, but where a large buyer (not seller) controls a large proportion of the market and drives the prices down. Sometimes referred to as *buyer's monopoly.*

motives   Drives, urges, wishes, or desires that initiate the sequence of events known as behavior.

multimedia Refers to computer-generated presentations that include some mix of sophisticated graphics, animation, digital photographs, full-motion video, and stereo sound.

N

National Do-Not-Call Registry The registry is nationwide in scope and commercial telemarketers are not allowed to call consumers if their number is on the registry.

need A feeling, which, if left unsatisfied, produces anxiety or tension . . . yet if satisfied, imparts a sensation of well-being.

neurolinguistic programming How humans characteristically respond to communication: visually, auditorially, or kinesthetically.

new task A buying circumstances never before considered by buyers, which accordingly demands much learning and deliberation on their part.

new-business selling The primary responsibility of new-business selling is to seek and persuade new customers to buy from the firm for the first time.

noise Any unneeded factor that interferes with transmission and reception of a message.

nonverbal communication Actions, gestures, facial expressions, and other nonspoken forms of expression that reveal underlying thoughts and emotions.

O

objection Concern or question raised by the buyer.

open questions Questions designed to get customers to respond at length.

option In negotiations, possible agreements or pieces of a possible agreement.

outbound telemarketing The company calls the prospect.

P

pacing Aligning oneself as closely as possible with another in mood, attitude, and verbal and nonverbal behavior.

"pave-the-way" question A trial close that tells the salesperson how to close. The real estate salesperson might ask, "Is there anything besides financing that would keep you from putting in an offer on this home?"

payback period The amount of time it takes to recover your investment.

permanence Telling oneself that a bad sales experience will last indefinitely when it will not.

permissive question Before questioning the buyer, the sales rep asks for permission to ask questions.

perquisites Extra sources of compensation for salespeople such as trips, use of a company car, or club memberships.

personal selling A seller's presentation conducted on a face-to-face basis with a buyer.

personality An individual's characteristic way of reacting to a situation.

personalization Blaming yourself for a bad sales experience, rather than externalizing the problem.

pervasiveness Universalizing one bad experience.

physiological needs Group of needs that includes basic necessities such as shelter, clothing, food, water, sex, and sleep.

"polite why" Politely asking the prospective buyer for an accurate explanation of an objection.

position In negotiation, a stance (e.g., "I will not pay more than $2000 for this PC").

preapproach All those activities that precede actual personal contact and that provide additional personal and business information about the prospect.

price discrimination Prices charged different purchasers of goods of "like grade and quality" that may tend to "injure, destroy, or prevent competition."

principled negotiation In contrast to maintaining positions, the parties separate people from problems, focus on interests not positions, invent options for mutual gain, and measure the agreement with objective standards.

probability close The salesperson asks the prospect what is the probability of buying in percentage terms out of a possible 100 percent.

problem Difference between an ideal state of affairs and the current state.

problem confirmation A summation statement of the problem to the buyer at the completion of sales rep questioning.

product disparagement False or deceptive comparisons or distorted claims concerning a competitor's product, services, or property.

prospecting The identification of potential new customers and their qualifications (i.e., need, ability, and authority).

proxemics The distances at which people interact.

Q

qualifying close The salesperson seeks to close on an objection.

quantity discounts Reductions granted for purchasing in large amounts; may be either noncumulative or cumulative. Noncumulative quantity discounts are one-time discounts offered for buying in volume. Cumulative quantity discounts are reductions offered over a longer period of time.

R

reciprocity   Firms arranging to buy goods or services from one another to the exclusion of competitors.

redirecting questions   Questions that can be asked if the customer has strayed or when the salesperson wishes to concentrate on a different feature and benefit.

refusal to deal   The right of businesspeople to select customers. Generally, they can cut off business or refuse to deal with someone, *provided they have a good business reason for doing so that can be proven.*

relationship marketing   The marketing principle that stresses that the selling firm should concentrate on the relationship with buyers throughout the life of the product or service with the emphasis on service and value-added activities.

reliability   The ability to perform promised service dependably and accurately.

requirements contracts   Contracts in which purchasers are required to buy or lease a specified percentage of their requirements for a product from a vendor, typically within a specified lapse of time.

responsiveness   Readiness with which a person outwardly shows emotions or feelings and develops relationships.

retail selling   The characteristic that distinguishes retail selling from other types is that the customer comes to the salesperson.

return on investment   The net profit or savings expected from a given investment, expressed as a percentage of the investment.

rock-bottom price   A win–lose negotiation tactic in which the buyer initially approaches the seller with the question, "What's the lowest price you will accept?"

S

safety needs   Needs associated with the desire to avoid physical harm, the need for economic safety and security, and a preference for the familiar rather than the unexpected.

sales puff   Opinions, not fact (e.g., "it's the best around" or "our service can't be beat").

sales quotas   Goals for the salesperson's performance in the coming year, typically in the form of dollar volume.

screener   Individual in the buying center assigned to ensuring that only important contacts are placed through immediately to the executive on the telephone.

self-actualization needs   Needs that represent the desire to grow, to fulfill one's capabilities, to become everything that one is capable of becoming.

service approach   The retail salesperson greets the customer with "How may I help you?"

skip-stop routing   Method of routing in which the salesperson skips some customers and stops at others according to a prearranged plan.

slander   When an unfair or untrue oral statement is made about a competitor to a third party (e.g., a customer) and can be construed as damaging that competitor's business reputation or the personal reputation of an individual with that company.

small talk   A discussion between sales rep and customer on such topics as hobbies or sports that are unrelated to the sale itself.

social needs   At this stage of the hierarchy, individuals begin to experience their need for love, affection, and belonging.

source   The initiator of communication who has certain thoughts and ideas in mind to communicate.

standing-room-only close   The salesperson seeks to elicit a "yes" from a prospect by mentioning an impending event or an opportunity soon to end.

statement of purpose   Before questioning the buyer, the salesperson first states his or her rationale for the sales call.

sticks and stones   A win–lose negotiating tactic in which the buyer disparages salespeople, hoping to bully them into concessions.

straight commission   Salespeople are paid a percentage of sales volume or gross margin.

straight rebuy   Perfunctory purchase of a standard item from the same supplier on a routine basis.

straight-line routing   Starting from their offices, sales reps make calls in one continuous direction to the end of their territories, then call in another straight direction, and so forth.

suggestion close   The salesperson's objective is to get the prospect to accept the salesperson's recommendation without much thought. Often, it involves telling what other buyers in the same situation have done.

suggestion selling   Promoting an ancillary retail sale, suggesting a larger quantity, or trading up to higher quality.

summarization close   The salesperson takes the major benefits and presents them in summary form.

T

tangibles   Regarding service quality, the appearance of physical facilities, equipment, personnel, and communication materials.

target market   A group of consumers with homogeneous needs to which the manager aims the marketing mix.

technical selling   The primary responsibility of technical selling is to increase the company's volume of sales to existing customers by providing them with technical advice and assistance.

telephone track The steps of a telephone conversation in which a sales rep seeks to obtain an appointment to see a prospect in person.

teleselling Salespeople who work in making telephone contact, inbound and outbound, with customers and prospects.

tentative-confirmation close Seeking a conditional "yes" from a prospect contingent on such matters as financing or delivery.

third-party questions Indirect questions asking prospects to relate their opinions in terms of others' reactions (i.e., third parties).

threat What you will do to your opponent if he or she does not agree.

tickler file File maintained by week or month in which the sales rep can place the name of the prospect for follow-up activities.

to-do list List of daily activities arranged in priority order.

trade discounts Deductions from list price offered to members of the channel of distribution.

trade selling The primary task of trade selling is to build sales volume through promotional assistance.

trial-order close Order of less than typical size to use a product for free for a specified time.

tying arrangement Requirement that in order to receive a desired product in a manufacturer's line, the distributor must buy a substantial or even full line of offerings.

U

unfair competition Statements made by the salesperson that reflect upon his or her own product and misrepresent its characteristics or qualities.

user buying influences In the buying center, buyers make judgments about the potential impact of the product or service on their job performance.

V

veiled threat A win–lose negotiating maneuver in which the buyer lets the sales rep know how much power he or she possesses.

verbal contract The salesperson asks the current customer for permission to greet a waiting customer.

W

warning What will happen if an agreement is not reached.

Index